Notes on Epistles of St. Paul

I —II Thessalonians, I Corinthians 1-7,
Romans 1-7, Ephesians 1:1-14

J. B. Lightfoot
Edited by J. R. Harmer

BAKER BOOK HOUSE
Grand Rapids, Michigan

Reprinted 1980 by
Baker Book House Company
from the edition published by
Macmillan and Co.

First published in 1895

ISBN: 0-8010-5602-0

PHOTOLITHOPRINTED BY CUSHING - MALLOY, INC.
ANN ARBOR, MICHIGAN, UNITED STATES OF AMERICA

INTRODUCTORY NOTE

THE present work represents the fulfilment of the under-
taking announced in the preface to 'Biblical Essays' a
year and a half ago. As that volume consisted of introductory essays upon New Testament subjects, so this comprises
such of Dr Lightfoot's notes on the text as in the opinion of
the Trustees of the Lightfoot Fund are sufficiently complete
to justify publication. However, unlike 'Biblical Essays,'
of which a considerable part had already been given to the
world, this volume, as its title-page indicates, consists entirely
of unpublished matter. It aims at reproducing, wherever
possible, the courses of lectures delivered at Cambridge by
Dr Lightfoot upon those Pauline Epistles which he did not
live to edit in the form of complete commentaries. His
method of trusting to his memory in framing sentences in
the lecture room has been alluded to already in the preface
to the previous volume. But here again the Editor's difficulty
has been considerably lessened by the kindness of friends
who were present at the lectures and have placed their note-
books at the disposal of the Trustees. As on the previous
occasion, the thanks of the Trustees are especially due to
W. P. Turnbull, Esq., formerly Fellow of Trinity College,
Cambridge, and now one of Her Majesty's Inspectors of
Schools, and to the Rev. H. F. Gore-Booth, Rector of Sacred
Trinity, Salford ; and the notes lent for the present work by
the Right Reverend F. Wallis, D.D., Senior Fellow of Gonville

and Caius College and Lord Bishop of Wellington, New Zealand, and by the Rev. A. Lukyn Williams, Chaplain and Head of the London Mission of the Jews' Society, have been of great service. Those who attended Dr Lightfoot's lectures will recollect that he was accustomed to deliver them slowly, thus rendering it possible for a fast writer to take them down almost word for word. The materials thus rendered available have been carefully compared with the original draft. The Editor feels confident that the result may be accepted as representing with fair accuracy the Bishop's actual words.

The above explanation applies to the notes on the Two Epistles to the Thessalonians, and on the first seven chapters (for no more is here published) of the First Epistle to the Corinthians and of the Epistle to the Romans. In the case of the fragment of the Epistle to the Ephesians (Eph. i. 1—14) no qualification is necessary; for in this case the Bishop's manuscript is written out fully, just as he intended it for publication in his contemplated edition of that Epistle. It thus represents his final judgment on these verses.

In a few places, quotations, carefully specified, have been inserted from Dr Lightfoot's book 'On a Fresh Revision of the English New Testament' (3rd Edition with an additional appendix, 1891), a work which, though published with a special purpose, yet contains a great amount of New Testament exegesis of permanent value.

The Trustees gladly take the opportunity of again expressing their thanks to the officers and workmen of the University Press for their intelligent criticism and their unfailing courtesy.

J. R. H.

CORPUS CHRISTI COLLEGE, CAMBRIDGE,
Feast of the Conversion of St Paul, 1895.

EXTRACT FROM THE LAST WILL AND TESTAMENT OF THE
LATE JOSEPH BARBER LIGHTFOOT, LORD BISHOP OF
DURHAM.

"I bequeath all my personal Estate not hereinbefore other-
"wise disposed of unto [my Executors] upon trust to pay and
"transfer the same unto the Trustees appointed by me under
"and by virtue of a certain Indenture of Settlement creating
"a Trust to be known by the name of 'The Lightfoot Fund
"for the Diocese of Durham' and bearing even date herewith
"but executed by me immediately before this my Will to be
"administered and dealt with by them upon the trusts for the
"purposes and in the manner prescribed by such Indenture
"of Settlement."

EXTRACT FROM THE INDENTURE OF SETTLEMENT OF 'THE
LIGHTFOOT FUND FOR THE DIOCESE OF DURHAM.'

"WHEREAS the Bishop is the Author of and is absolutely
"entitled to the Copyright in the several Works mentioned in
"the Schedule hereto, and for the purposes of these presents
"he has assigned or intends forthwith to assign the Copyright
"in all the said Works to the Trustees. Now the Bishop
"doth hereby declare and it is hereby agreed as follows:—
"The Trustees (which term shall hereinafter be taken to
"include the Trustees for the time being of these presents)

"shall stand possessed of the said Works and of the Copy-
"right therein respectively upon the trusts following (that is
"to say) upon trust to receive all moneys to arise from sales
"or otherwise from the said Works, and at their discretion
"from time to time to bring out new editions of the same
"Works or any of them, or to sell the copyright in the same or
"any of them, or otherwise to deal with the same respectively,
"it being the intention of these presents that the Trustees
"shall have and may exercise all such rights and powers
"in respect of the said Works and the copyright therein
"respectively, as they could or might have or exercise in
"relation thereto if they were the absolute beneficial owners
"thereof....

"The Trustees shall from time to time, at such discretion
"as aforesaid, pay and apply the income of the Trust funds
"for or towards the erecting, rebuilding, repairing, purchas-
"ing, endowing, supporting, or providing for any Churches,
"Chapels, Schools, Parsonages, and Stipends for Clergy, and
"other Spiritual Agents in connection with the Church of
"England and within the Diocese of Durham, and also for
"or towards such other purposes in connection with the said
"Church of England, and within the said Diocese, as the
"Trustees may in their absolute discretion think fit, provided
"always that any payment for erecting any building, or in
"relation to any other works in connection with real estate,
"shall be exercised with due regard to the Law of Mortmain ;
"it being declared that nothing herein shall be construed as
"intended to authorise any act contrary to any Statute or
"other Law....

"In case the Bishop shall at any time assign to the
"Trustees any Works hereafter to be written or published by
"him, or any Copyrights, or any other property, such transfer

" shall be held to be made for the purposes of this Trust, and
" all the provisions of this Deed shall apply to such property,
" subject nevertheless to any direction concerning the same
" which the Bishop may make in writing at the time of such
" transfer ; and in case the Bishop shall at any time pay any
" money, or transfer any security, stock, or other like property
" to the Trustees, the same shall in like manner be held for
" the purposes of this Trust, subject to any such contempo-
" raneous direction as aforesaid, and any security, stock or
" property so transferred, being of a nature which can lawfully
" be held by the Trustees for the purposes of these presents,
" may be retained by the Trustees, although the same may
" not be one of the securities hereinafter authorised.

" The Bishop of Durham and the Archdeacons of Durham
" and Auckland for the time being shall be *ex-officio* Trustees,
" and accordingly the Bishop and Archdeacons, parties hereto,
" and the succeeding Bishops and Archdeacons, shall cease to
" be Trustees on ceasing to hold their respective offices, and
" the number of the other Trustees may be increased, and the
" power of appointing Trustees in the place of Trustees other
" than Official Trustees, and of appointing extra Trustees,
" shall be exercised by Deed by the Trustees for the time
" being, provided always that the number shall not at any
" time be less than five.

" The Trust premises shall be known by the name of
" ' The Lightfoot Fund for the Diocese of Durham.' "

TABLE OF CONTENTS

THE EPISTLES OF ST PAUL

I

THE SECOND APOSTOLIC JOURNEY

I

FIRST EPISTLE TO THE THESSALONIANS

Surely I come quickly.

Surely He cometh, and a thousand voices
  Shout to the saints and to the deaf are dumb;
Surely He cometh, and the earth rejoices,
  Glad in His coming, Who hath sworn, I come.

Ad hoc regnum me vocare,
Juste Judex, tu dignare,
Quem expecto, quem requiro,
Ad quem avidus suspiro.

ANALYSIS

I. SALUTATION. i. 1.

II. NARRATIVE PORTION. i. 2—iii. 13.

    i.   The Apostle gratefully records their conversion to the Gospel and progress in the faith. i. 2—10.

    ii.   He reminds them how pure and blameless his life and ministry among them had been. ii. 1—12.

    iii.   He repeats his thanksgiving for their conversion, dwelling especially on the persecutions which they had endured. ii. 13—16.

    iv.   He describes his own suspense and anxiety, the consequent mission of Timothy to Thessalonica, and the encouraging report which he brought back. ii. 17—iii. 10.

    v.   The Apostle's prayer for the Thessalonians. iii. 11—13.

III. HORTATORY PORTION. iv. 1—v. 24.

    i.   Warning against impurity. iv. 1—8.

    ii.   Exhortation to brotherly love and sobriety of conduct. iv. 9—12.

    iii.   Touching the Advent of the Lord. iv. 13—v. 11.

        (*a*)   The dead shall have their place in the resurrection. iv. 13—18.

        (*b*)   The time however is uncertain. v. 1—3.

        (*c*)   Therefore all must be watchful. v. 4—11.

    iv.   Exhortation to orderly living and the due performance of social duties. v. 12—15.

    v.   Injunctions relating to prayer and spiritual matters generally. v. 16—22.

    vi.   The Apostle's prayer for the Thessalonians. v. 23, 24.

IV. PERSONAL INJUNCTIONS AND BENEDICTION. v. 25—28.

CHAPTER I

I. SALUTATION, i. I.

THE prefatory salutations in all the acknowledged Epistles of St Paul are the same in their broad features, though exhibiting minor variations often very significant. These variations may most frequently be traced to the peculiar relations existing between the Apostle and those whom he addresses. Even in other instances where the motives which have influenced the choice of the particular expression are too subtle to be apprehended, the differences of expression are still significant from a chronological point of view, as denoting a particular epoch in the Apostle's life. We have examples of both kinds in the salutation to the Epistle ; of the former in the omission of any allusion to his Apostleship, of the latter in the expression τῇ ἐκκλησίᾳ.

In this salutation the Apostle attaches the names of Silvanus and Timotheus to his own. They were staying with him at Corinth at the time when the letter was written (see Acts xviii. 5, 2 Cor. i. 19), and as they were joint founders of the Thessalonian Church (see Acts xvi. 1—3, xvii. 4, 10, 14), are naturally named in conjunction with him. The degree of participation in the contents of the letter on the part of those, whose names are thus attached, will vary according to the circumstances of the case. Here, for instance, the connexion is close ; for Silvanus and Timotheus (the former especially) stood very much in the same position as St Paul himself with respect to the claim which they had on the obedience of their Thessalonian converts : and thus the Apostle throughout uses the plural 'we beseech,' 'we would not have you ignorant' (iv. 1, 13). On the other hand, in the First Epistle to the Corinthians, the name of Sosthenes appears with that of St Paul in the introductory salutation simply as a Corinthian brother who was with St Paul at the time. Accordingly, as he did not stand in any position of authority, he has no special connexion with the contents of the Epistle, and does not reappear again directly or indirectly, but the Apostle at once returns to the singular, 'I thank my God' (1 Cor. i. 4).

The name of Silvanus is placed before that of Timotheus, not only because he held a superior position in the Church generally—he was a leading man among the brethren ἀνὴρ ἡγούμενος ἐν τοῖς ἀδελφοῖς (Acts xv. 22), while Timotheus was only a young disciple (Acts xvi. 1 sq.)—but also because he took a more prominent part in founding these very churches of Macedonia (Acts xvi. 19, 25, 29, xvii. 4, 10).

1. Παῦλος] On the omission of the official title ἀπόστολος in both Epistles to the Thessalonians, as well as in those to the Philippians and to Philemon, see the note on Phil. i. 1.

Σιλουανός] So called wherever he is mentioned by St Paul (e.g. 2 Thess. i. 1, 2 Cor. i. 19), is to be identified with Silas of the Acts. This appears from the identity of situation ascribed to the two in the historical narrative and the allusions in the Epistle. Later tradition distinguishes Silas from Silvanus, making the former Bishop of Corinth, the latter of Thessalonica. The multiplication of persons is not un-common in ecclesiastical legends, where it was necessary to make up a list of bishops—though in the parallel instance of Epaphras and Epaphroditus there is better ground for the distinction of persons.

The name Silas is contracted from Σιλουανός, as Λουκᾶς from Λουκανός, Παρμενᾶς from Παρμενίδης, Δημᾶς from Δήμαρχος or Δημήτριος, this con-traction applying equally to Greek and Latin names and without respect to their termination.   See the note on Νυμφᾶς (*Colossians*, p. 242), where instances are given from inscriptions.   Similar con-tractions are found in classical writers also, Ἀλεξᾶς for Ἀλέξανδρος, Κτῆσις for Κτησίας, Νῖκις for Νικίας, Σίβυρτις for Σιβύρτιος (see the examples given in Schoemann on Isaeus p. 274 quoted by Koch p. 50). Waddington (*Voyage en Asie-Mineure*, 1853, p. 32) instances the form Ἀρτᾶς (Thuc. vii. 33, Boeckh, *C. I. G.* III. no. 3960 *b*) as a further contraction of Ἀρτεμᾶς, itself contracted from Ἀρτεμίδωρος.   Letronne (*Recueil des Inscriptions Grecques et Latines*, 1848, II. p. 54) gives among other examples Μηνᾶς for Μηνόδωρος, Κλεοπᾶς for Κλεόπατρος, Ζηνᾶς for Ζηνόδωρος, and a number of words in -ᾶς contracted from -έας, Πρωτᾶς, Φιλωτᾶς, Ἀριστᾶς, Σωτᾶς, Σαυρᾶς etc., with genitives in -ᾶτος. On the other hand Jerome (*de nom. Hebr.* s. v.) considers Silas to be the original Hebrew name שׁילח equivalent to 'apostolus'; comp. his commentary on Gal. i. 1 (*Op.* VII. p. 374). It appears as a Jewish name in Josephus (*Ant.* xiv. 3. 2, xviii. 6. 7. 1), and in inscriptions, e.g. Boeckh, *C. I. G.* III. no. 4511 Σαμσιγέραμος ὁ καὶ Σείλας (Emesa). The name Silvanus also is not uncommon in inscriptions ; it occurs e.g. Orelli no. 2566 and in an inscription found at Ancyra (Boeckh III. no. 4071).

Silas first appears in the narrative of the Acts in the account of the Apostolic Congress (xv. 22), on which occasion he is employed with Judas, as bearer of the letter to the Gentile Christians at Antioch. He subsequently accompanies St Paul, as it would appear, during the whole of his second missionary journey, only parting from him in order to maintain his intercourse with the Macedonian Churches (see *Biblical Essays*, p. 245 sq.). He is not mentioned as accompanying St Paul, when the Apostle left Corinth at the close of this second missionary journey, nor is his name found subsequently in St Luke's narrative. He was obviously a Jewish Christian (Acts xvi. 20), but, like St Paul, a Roman citizen (Acts xvi. 37, 38). Hence his Roman name Silvanus. The Silvanus mentioned as the bearer of St Peter's first Epistle (1 Pet. v. 12) is probably the same person, but the name is too common to allow of the identity being pressed. See on this point Bleek, *Hebr.* I. B, p. 408, and on Silas generally Cellarius, *dissert. de Sila viro apost.* 1773, referred to by Koch *ad loc.*, Cureton, *Syriac Gospels*, p. viii, Zimmer, *Jahrb. f. Prot. Theol.* 1881, p. 721, Jülicher, *ib.* 1882, p. 538, Seufert, *Zeitschr. f. Wiss. Theol.* XXVIII. 1885, p. 350, and Klöpper, *Theol. Stud. u. Skizz.* 1889, p. 73 sq.

Τιμόθεος] Timotheus appears prominently in ten out of the thirteen Epistles of St Paul, the exceptions being Galatians, Colossians and Titus. Having joined St Paul about a year before this, his earliest Epistle, was written, he remained with him with occasional interruptions to the end of his life.

τῇ ἐκκλησίᾳ Θ.] This form of address is peculiar to the five earliest of St Paul's Epistles, 1, 2 Thessalonians, 1, 2 Corinthians, and Galatians. His later letters to Christian communities are addressed τοῖς ἁγίοις or τοῖς ἀδελφοῖς, or in some similar way. Until a satisfactory explanation is given of this variation, we must be content with its significance as a chronological mark. Dr Jowett accounts for the omission in the later Epistles as follows, 'perhaps because to the Apostle, in his later years, the Church on earth seemed already passing into the heavens' (*The Epistles of St Paul*, I. p. 43, 2nd ed.).

Θεσσαλονικέων] The history of Thessalonica and of the establishment of Christianity there is treated fully in *Biblical Essays*, pp. 235 sq., 251 sq.

ἐν Θεῷ πατρί...Χριστῷ] It is doubtful whether these words should be taken (1) with τῇ ἐκκλησίᾳ Θ., as denoting the sphere in which the Church moved; or (2) separately, as applying to the word understood in the ellipsis, whether χαίρειν or γράφουσι. The clause ἀπὸ Θεοῦ πατρὸς κ.τ.λ. is probably not genuine : otherwise it would decide in favour of the first construction by which a meaningless tautology would be avoided. On the other hand the absence of the article τῇ before ἐν Θεῷ κ.τ.λ. is by no means decisive against the first construction, for the New Testament usage is far from uniform in this respect; see ii. 14, iv. 16, 2 Thess. iii. 14, and the note on Gal. i. 13 (ἀναστροφήν ποτε). On the whole probably we should connect with τῇ ἐκκλησίᾳ ; for *first* it is more in accordance with St Paul's manner, in designating those whom he addresses, to add some words expressive of their calling in God and Christ, as a comparison with the salutation in his other Epistles will show ; and *secondly* the words τῇ ἐκκλησίᾳ can scarcely have been stamped with so definite a Christian meaning in the minds of these recent and early converts to the Gospel, as to render the addition of the words ἐν Θεῷ πατρὶ κ.τ.λ. superfluous. As St Chrysostom says, who adopts the construction here preferred in his comment on the passage, it was necessary to distinguish it from πολλαὶ ἐκκλησίαι καὶ Ἰουδαϊκαὶ καὶ Ἑλληνικαί. See e.g. 1 Thess. ii. 14, and the note there on the word ἐκκλησία.

χάρις ὑμῖν καὶ εἰρήνη] This peculiarly Christian greeting is generally regarded as a blending together of the heathen form of salutation χαίρειν, and the Jewish שׁלוֹם. But χάρις has only the very slenderest connexion with χαίρειν in respect to meaning, though derived from a common root. Χάρις is the source of all real blessings, εἰρήνη their end and issue.

This is the form of greeting adopted in all St Paul's Epistles (with the exception of those to Timothy), and in the Epistles of St Peter. In the two Pastoral Epistles above, and in 2 Joh. 3, the form is χάρις, ἔλεος, εἰρήνη. Perhaps it is no idle fancy to trace in the additional touch of tenderness communicated by ἔλεος in these later Epistles a sense of the growing evils which threatened the Church. Clement of Rome begins his genuine epistle with the salutation χάρις ὑμῖν καὶ εἰρήνη ἀπὸ παντοκράτορος Θεοῦ διὰ Ἰησοῦ Χριστοῦ πληθυνθείη, probably following the First Epistle of Peter, which he quotes frequently. On the other hand, in the Ignatian Epistles the regular expression is πλεῖστα χαίρειν.

2. NARRATIVE PORTION, i. 2—iii. 13.

i. *Grateful record of their conversion and progress* (i. 2—10).

2. In almost all the Epistles of St Paul the salutation is followed immediately by a thanksgiving, generally in the form εὐχαριστῶ, εὐχαριστοῦμεν τῷ Θεῷ (in 2 Thess. εὐχαριστεῖν ὀφείλομεν), but twice (2 Cor. and Ephesians) εὐλογητὸς ὁ Θεός. This was always St Paul's first thought (πρῶτον μὲν εὐχαριστῶ, Rom. i. 8), and how lofty a view he took of the duty of thanksgiving appears from 2 Cor. iv. 15, ix. 11, 12, and below v. 16, where see note. This thanksgiving is omitted only in the Pastoral Epistles (with the exception of 2 Timothy, where it is found in a modified form) and Galatians. In the Epistle last mentioned its place is occupied by a rebuke Θαυμάζω ὅτι οὕτω ταχέως κ.τ.λ. In this, as in other cases (see e.g. above on ver. 1), the expressions in our Epistle most resemble those in the Philippian letter in the strength of language and the earnest reiteration of the sentiment : see *Philippians*, pp. 66, 82. Pelagius well remarks : 'In indesinenti oratione, memoriae quantitas et dilectionis ostenditur, quam eorum merita postulabant.'

Dr Jowett points to this passage (i. 2— 10) as thoroughly characteristic of St Paul's style. He remarks admirably : 'A classical or modern writer distinguishes his several propositions, assigning to each its exact relation to what goes before and follows, that he may give meaning and articulation to the whole. The manner of St Paul is the reverse of this. He overlays one proposition with another, the second just emerging beyond the first, and arising out of association with it, but not always standing in a clear relation to it' (I. p. 45).

εὐχαριστοῦμεν] 'We,' i.e. Paul, Silvanus and Timotheus. On this word it may be remarked, as to (1) *its occurrence*, that it seems to be very rare in authors of the classical period and no instance has been pointed out of it in Attic Greek. It appears in Hippocrates, *Ep.* II. p. 1284, σώζων ἀνθρώπους κεραυνοῖς εὐχαρίστηται, and in inscriptions, especially a very old one Boeckh, *C. I. G.* I. no. 34, and in the decrees (if they be genuine) attached to Demosthenes (e.g. p. 257, 2, the ψήφισμα Χερρονησιτῶν in the *de Corona*, p. 92). Εὐχάριστος however is found in Xen. *Cyrop.* viii. 3. 49 and ἀχαριστεῖν is common. (2) *Its use.* The original meaning of the verb is 'to do a good turn to,' hence 'to return a favour,' 'to be grateful'; but the sense 'to express gratitude' seems to be confined to later writers from the time of Polybius onwards. See Lobeck on Phrynichus, I. p. 18. In Demosth. *de Cor.* 92 οὐκ ἐλλείψει εὐχαριστῶν καὶ ποιῶν ὅ τι ἂν δύνηται ἀγαθόν, it is unnecessary to assign this meaning to the word.

The exact punctuation of these verses is doubtful. If the second ὑμῶν (after μνείαν) were genuine, the first clause would naturally end with περὶ πάντων ὑμῶν. But ὑμῶν is not read by אAB etc. and should be omitted here and in Eph. i. 16. Accordingly the words περὶ πάντων ὑμῶν are better taken with what follows ; because the words μνείαν ποιούμενοι cannot well stand alone, but need some explanation, such as is found e.g. in Plato, *Protag.* 317 E, where they are constructed with the genitive. It is more difficult to determine whether ἀδιαλείπτως is to be taken with what precedes or what follows. A comparison with Rom. i. 9 ὡς ἀδιαλείπτως μνείαν ὑμῶν ποιοῦμαι supports the former view : but in all such cases the requirements of the sentence itself are a safer guide than parallel passages ; and the position of the words seems at first sight to favour the construction with μνημονεύοντες as the Greek commentators appear generally to have done. But on the whole it is more forcible to connect the word with what goes before, and this view is borne out by 2 Tim. i. 3 ὡς ἀδιάλειπτον ἔχω τὴν περὶ σοῦ μνείαν.

μνείαν ποιούμενοι] While μνήμη is 'memory' generally, μνεία is 'remembrance' in a special case, and may be defined to be 'the direction of μνήμη to some particular object.' Thus, while μνήμη may be used for μνεία, it is not true conversely that μνεία can take the place of μνήμη.

Μνείαν ποιεῖσθαι is found in three other passages of St Paul (Rom. i. 9, Eph. i. 16, Philem. 4), and always, as here, in connexion with prayer. In 2 Pet. i. 15 the words are μνήμην ποιεῖσθαι. Bruder indeed mentions a v. l. μνείαν, but it has very little textual support. It is questionable

whether μνείαν ποιεῖσθαι means 'to remember,' or 'to mention.' Either
sense would equally suit the passages where the phrase occurs. In
favour of 'remember' it may be urged (1) that μνήμην ποιεῖσθαι has
certainly this sense in 2 Pet. l.c., and (2) that in a parallel passage in
2 Tim. i. 3 St Paul speaking in the same way of his thanksgiving uses
μνείαν ἔχειν, which can only mean 'to remember.' On the other hand,
Plato (*Protag.* 317 E, *Phaedr.* 254 A) employs μνείαν ποιεῖσθαι for 'to
mention,' and so do other writers (e.g. Æschines and Andocides). It is
safer therefore to give the phrase this meaning in St Paul. Certainly it
makes better sense here, 'making mention incessantly, as we remember.'
It will be seen that this signification of 'mention' is not contained in
μνεία, but is derived from ποιεῖσθαι. For μνήμην ποιεῖσθαι in the sense of
'making mention' comp. *Clem. Hom.* i. 16 παντὰ γὰρ...ἡμῖν ἀντέβαλε
Βαρνάβας, σχεδὸν καθ' ἡμέραν τὴν ἀγαθήν σου ποιούμενος μνήμην.

ἀδιαλείπτως] See the note on v. 17.

3. μνημονεύοντες] '*remembering.*' The word is sometimes translated
'making mention of'; but verbs of 'informing' (according to Winer, § 30,
10, p. 257 ed. Moulton) are never found in the New Testament with a
simple genitive but with περί, and μνημονεύειν is always used by St Paul
in the sense of 'remember' (Gal. ii. 10, Col. iv. 18; comp. Eph. ii. 11,
2 Thess. ii. 5, 2 Tim. ii. 8).

ὑμῶν] is the possessive genitive referring to all three clauses which
follow—τοῦ ἔργ. τ. π., τοῦ κόπ. τῆς ἀγ., τῆς ὑπομ. τῆς ἐλπ.

τοῦ ἔργου τῆς πίστεως κ.τ.λ.] The three genitives πίστεως, ἀγάπης,
ἐλπίδος are best regarded as cases of the same kind describing the
source—'the work which comes of faith, the labour which springs from
love, the patience which is born of hope.' This triad of Christian graces
is distinctly enunciated by St Paul in 1 Cor. xiii. 13 only, but the same
conception underlies the Apostle's language frequently, even where the
words are not directly mentioned. The combination is especially to be
noticed as occurring in this his earliest Epistle. The same order is
found in Col. i. 4, 5 ἀκούσαντες τὴν πίστιν ὑμῶν...καὶ τὴν ἀγάπην...διὰ τὴν
ἐλπίδα and in Gal. v. 5, 6, where see note. On the other hand, in 1 Cor.
xiii. 13 the sequence is different, ἀγάπη being placed last. Each order is
equally natural in its place. Here we have *first* faith, the source of all
Christian virtues, *secondly* love, the sustaining principle of Christian life,
lastly hope, the beacon-star guiding us to the life to come. This
prominence given to hope is in accordance with the pervading tenour of
the Thessalonian Epistles, where the Apostle is ever leading the minds of
his hearers forward to the great day of retribution (see 1 Thess. v. 8,
where again the triad is found). Ἐλπὶς is closely connected with σωτηρία
(1 Thess. v. 8) and with δόξα (Rom. v. 2, Col. i. 27), and indeed is sometimes used as equivalent to ἐλπὶς σωτηρίας 'the hope of glory, of salvation,'
e.g. Acts xxiii. 6 (a speech of St Paul's) περὶ ἐλπίδος καὶ ἀναστάσεως νεκρῶν
ἐγὼ κρίνομαι. In 1 Cor. xiii. 13, on the other hand, the prominent position

is given to ἀγάπη, which alone shall abide when faith is swallowed up in sight and hope is dissolved in fulfilment.

On the fundamental distinction of the two graces in the present passage Severianus (in Cramer's Catena) says well, ἡ μὲν πίστις ἐγείρει πρὸς καμάτους, ἡ δὲ ἀγάπη ἐπιμένειν ποιεῖ τοῖς πόνοις. Compare Ignatius, *Polyc.* 6 ἡ πίστις ὡς περικεφαλαία, ἡ ἀγάπη ὡς δόρυ, ἡ ὑπομονὴ ὡς πανοπλία, and Polycarp's own words (*Phil.* 3) πίστιν, ἥτις ἐστὶν μήτηρ πάντων ἡμῶν, ἐπακολουθούσης τῆς ἐλπίδος, προαγούσης τῆς ἀγάπης, where προαγούσης is used in reference to ἐλπίς, not to πίστις, for πίστις precedes ἀγάπη: see Ign. *Ephes.* 14 ἀρχὴ μὲν πίστις, τέλος δὲ ἀγάπη. In the Epistle of Barnabas the same triad is also found, § I, ὅτι μεγάλη πίστις καὶ ἀγάπη ἐγκατοικεῖ ἐν ὑμῖν ἐλπίδι ζωῆς αὐτοῦ. See the notes on Col. i. 5, Polyc. l. c. and comp. Reuss, *Théol. Chrét.* IV. 20, vol. II. p. 219.

On the order of these results (ἔργον, κόπος, ὑπομονὴ) see Rev. ii. 2 οἶδα τὰ ἔργα σου καὶ τὸν κόπον καὶ τὴν ὑπομονήν σου. The words are distinguishable in meaning, and are arranged in an ascending scale as practical proofs of self-sacrifice. Ἔργον is simply active work ; κόπος is a greater exhibition of earnestness, for it is not work only but fatiguing work ; ὑπομονὴ is higher evidence still, for it involves a notion of indignity offered, of suffering undergone without any present countervailing result. Thus it is βασιλὶς τῶν ἀρετῶν, as Chrysostom says (see Trench, *N. T. Syn.* § liii. p. 197 ed. 9).

On the appropriateness of the results to the graces, notice that ἔργον is elsewhere represented as the practical fruit and evidence of faith, see Gal. v. 6, James ii. 18; κόπος is closely connected with ἀγάπη in Rev. l. c., where in ver. 4 τὴν ἀγάπην σου τὴν πρώτην seems to be a direct reference to τὸν κόπον of ver. 2 (see also a v. l. in Heb. vi. 10, where however the words τοῦ κόπου should probably be omitted). Again ὑπομονὴ 'the patient endurance which bides its time' implies the existence of hope, comp. Rom. viii. 25 ἐλπίζομεν δι' ὑπομονῆς ἀπεκδεχόμεθα and xv. 4 ; and indeed is sometimes found where we should expect ἐλπίς, as in 2 Thess. iii. 5 εἰς τὴν ὑπομονὴν τοῦ Χριστοῦ, and Tit. ii. 2 τῇ πίστει, τῇ ἀγάπῃ, τῇ ὑπομονῇ. See the note on Ign. *Rom.* 10 ἐν ὑπομονῇ 'I. X., and on the distinction between ὑπομονὴ and μακροθυμία the note on Col. i. 11.

τοῦ Κυρίου ἡμῶν 'I. X.] As it would be somewhat harsh to make these words depend on all three words πίστεως, ἀγάπης, ἐλπίδος, we must suppose the parallelism of the three clauses interrupted by the third being lengthened out by means of the explanatory words τοῦ Κυρίου κ.τ.λ., i.e. 'the hope of the coming of our Lord Jesus Christ.'

ἔμπροσθεν τοῦ Θεοῦ καὶ πατρὸς ἡμῶν] Is this clause to be taken (1) with μνημονεύοντες, or (2) with τοῦ ἔργου...Χριστοῦ, or (3) only with τῆς ὑπομονῆς ...Ἰησοῦ Χριστοῦ? In favour of the first view may be urged the fact that in iii. 9 we have ἔμπροσθεν τοῦ Θεοῦ ἡμῶν in a similar connexion. But on the other hand μνημονεύοντες ἔμπροσθεν τοῦ Θεοῦ would be unnecessarily tautological after εὐχαριστοῦμεν τῷ Θεῷ, nor is it easy to see why ἔμπροσθεν τοῦ Θεοῦ should stand so late in the sentence. Again the two other constructions are much more in accordance with the general use of ἔμπροσθεν τοῦ Θεοῦ, ἐνώπιον τοῦ Θεοῦ, appealing to God's witness and judgment of conduct concealed from, or misinterpreted by men. It is thus equivalent to 'your righteous conversation in the sight of God.' It is less easy to choose between (2) and (3). On the whole, if τοῦ Κυρίου ἡμ. Ἰ. Χ. is restricted to τῆς ὑπομονῆς τῆς ἐλπίδος, the same restriction probably applies to ἔμπροσθεν τοῦ Θεοῦ 'the patient endurance of hope which reposes in the coming of Christ and is manifested in the sight of God.' The words ἔμπροσθεν τοῦ Θεοῦ καὶ π. ἡμ. are then complementary to Ἰησοῦ Χριστοῦ, as so frequently in St Paul, e.g. 2 Cor. ii. 17 κατέναντι Θεοῦ ἐν Χριστῷ λαλοῦμεν (so again xii. 19); and the expression closely resembles 1 Thess. iii. 13, ἀμέμπτους ἔμπροσθεν τοῦ Θεοῦ καὶ πατρὸς ἡμῶν ἐν τῇ παρουσίᾳ τοῦ Κυρίου ἡμῶν Ἰησοῦ. The sentence for the sake of the parallelism should have closed with ἐλπίδος; but St Paul runs off, so to speak, on the third clause of the triplet, to introduce the hallowed names in and through and for whom all good things are done.

τοῦ Θεοῦ καὶ πατρὸς ἡμῶν] 'before Him, who is not only our Supreme Ruler, but has also all the tenderness and affection of a father towards us, who watches all our actions with a fatherly solicitude.' See note on Gal. i. 4, where the same phrase occurs, and comp. ver. 4, ἠγαπημένοι ὑπὸ Θεοῦ.

εἰδότες] 'for we know,' giving the reason, whereas the previous participles explain the circumstances, of εὐχαριστοῦμεν.

4. ἠγαπημένοι ὑπὸ Θεοῦ] 'beloved by God,' comp. 2 Thess. ii. 13, ἠγαπημένοι ὑπὸ Κυρίου, where see the note. Both expressions occur in the LXX., ἠγ. ὑπὸ Θεοῦ, Sir. xlv. 1 ; ἠγ. ὑπὸ Κυρίου, Deut. xxxiii. 12, Sir. xlvi. 13. The construction of the E.V. is quite inadmissible, though supported by some respectable commentators ancient and modern.

ἐκλογήν] On this word, which is never used in the New Testament in the sense of election to final salvation, see the note on Col. iii. 12 ἐκλεκτοὶ τοῦ Θεοῦ.

5. ὅτι] is generally translated in this passage with the E.V. 'for.' But the meaning which the phrase εἰδέναι τι ὅτι universally bears in the New Testament, and the idiomatic character of the expression, seem decisive in favour of the interpretation 'knowing the circumstance or manner of your election, how that.' Comp. Acts xvi. 3, Rom. xiii. 11, 1 Cor. xvi. 15, 2 Cor. xii. 3, 4, and below ii. 1. So προγιγνώσκειν ὅτι Acts xxvi. 5 : βλέπειν ὅτι, 1 Cor. i. 26 βλέπετε τὴν κλῆσιν ὑμῶν ὅτι οὐ πολλοὶ σοφοὶ κ.τ.λ., and see the note there.

τὸ εὐαγγέλιον ἡμῶν] 'the gospel we preach'; as in Rom. ii. 16, xvi. 25, 2 Cor. iv. 3, 2 Tim. ii. 8, and see the note on 2 Thess. ii. 14.

εἰς (v. l. πρὸς) ὑμᾶς] Both readings εἰς and πρὸς are supported by parallel passages. For εἰς compare Acts xxi. 17, xxv. 15, xxviii. 6, and especially Gal. iii. 14, from which passages it will appear that γίγνεσθαι εἰς is 'to arrive at,' 'reach.' For πρὸς see 1 Cor. ii. 3, κἀγὼ ἐν ἀσθενείᾳ καὶ ἐν φόβῳ καὶ ἐν τρόμῳ πολλῷ ἐγενόμην πρὸς ὑμᾶς, 'exhibited myself in my dealings with you,' which seems however to suggest taking ἐν λόγῳ with ἐγενήθη here 'exhibited itself not in word only' (compare 2 Cor. iii. 7, 8); πρὸς ὑμᾶς meaning *apud vos*. But γενέσθαι πρὸς ὑμᾶς would be a legitimate construction. However in this passage manuscript evidence is undoubtedly in favour of εἰς. On the fundamental difference between εἰς and πρὸς see the notes on 2 Thess. iii. 9 and Philem. 5 πρὸς τὸν Κύριον Ἰησοῦν καὶ εἰς πάντας τοὺς ἁγίους, and comp. Winer, § 49, p. 494, Meyer on 1 Cor. ii. 3.

ἐν λόγῳ μόνον...πληροφορίᾳ πολλῇ] The preposition should probably be repeated before each substantive, except πληροφορίᾳ, though the MS. authority is not unanimous on this point. Each word is an advance upon the preceding, and the repetition of καὶ ἐν expresses this gradation. Comp. ἀλλὰ in 2 Cor. vii. 11.

The passage may be paraphrased thus: 'Our preaching was not mere declamation, a hollow and heartless rhetoric: in it there was earnestness and power. Yet this is not enough. There may be a power which is not from above, a fearful earnestness which is not inspired by God. Not such was ours, for we preached in the Holy Spirit. Still even the holiest influences may be transitory, the noblest inspirations may waver from lack of faith. Far otherwise was it with us, for we preached in a deep conviction of the truth of our message, in a perfect assurance of the ultimate triumph of our cause.'

λόγῳ] The same opposition of λόγος and δύναμις is found in 1 Cor. ii. 4 καὶ ὁ λόγος μου καὶ τὸ κήρυγμά μου οὐκ ἐν πειθοῖς σοφίας λόγοις, ἀλλ' ἐν ἀποδείξει πνεύματος καὶ δυνάμεως.

δύναμις] has here no direct reference to the working of miracles, which would require the plural δυνάμεσι (cf. 1 Cor. xii. 10, Gal. iii. 5). There are but few allusions in St Paul to his power of working miracles, partly because he assumes the fact as known to his hearers, and partly because doubtless he considered this a very poor and mean gift in comparison with the high spiritual powers with which he was endowed. Compare a similar case, 1 Cor. xiv. 18.

πληροφορίᾳ] Πληροφορία and πληροφορεῖν are found seven times in St Paul and only three times in the rest of the New Testament (Luke i. 1, Hebr. vi. 11, x. 22). The noun, which occurs in Clem. Rom. 42 μετὰ πληροφορίας πνεύματος, is not found in the LXX., but the verb appears once, Eccles. viii. 11 ἐπληροφορήθη καρδία υἱῶν τοῦ ἀνθρώπου ἐν αὐτοῖς τοῦ ποιῆσαι τὸ πονηρόν, where the corresponding Hebrew is מלא לב 'the heart was full to do etc.' πληροφορία may mean either (1) 'fulfilment,' or (2) 'conviction, assurance.' The meaning (1) must be discarded, because St Paul is still speaking of the character of the message, not yet of the acceptance of it. Πληροφορία is therefore 'conviction, confidence' on the part of St Paul and his fellow-preachers. For πληροφορία see the note on

Col. ii. 2; for πληροφορεῖν the note on Col. iv. 12. The words seem to be confined almost exclusively to biblical and ecclesiastical writings.

καθὼς οἴδατε] He appeals to the Thessalonians themselves to bear witness to the character of his preaching; comp. ii. 5. Thus καθὼς οἴδατε must not be regarded as correlative to εἰδότες above. Such a correspondence could only confuse the order of thought in the passage.

ἐγενήθημεν] Not ἦμεν 'we were,' but ἐγενήθημεν 'we became, were made' by the transforming power of Christ. On the distinction of γίγνεσθαι and εἶναι see the notes on Col. i. 18 ἵνα γένηται and 1 Cor. i. 30 ἐγενήθη, with references in both places to Christ.

6. καὶ ὑμεῖς κ.τ.λ.] The fact of their election by God was evinced in two ways; *first* by the divine character of the message imparted to them (ver. 5), and *secondly* by their sincere acceptance of it: in other words, not only by the offer of the Gospel, but by their response to the offer. This last evidence is given in the words καὶ ὑμεῖς κ.τ.λ. which, though logically dependent on εἰδότες τὴν ἐκλογὴν ὅτι, are thrown into the form of an independent sentence as regards their grammatical structure.

καὶ τοῦ Κυρίου] For the spirit in which these words are added to soften and qualify the preceding expression μιμηταὶ ἡμῶν see 1 Cor. xi. 1 μιμηταί μου γίνεσθε, καθὼς κἀγὼ Χριστοῦ.

δεξάμενοι κ.τ.λ.] 'inasmuch as ye received the word,' explaining the feature in which the invitation consisted. They endured tribulation with a holy joy, as Paul had set them the example, who, after the pattern of Christ, rejoiced in his sufferings (Col. i. 24). The degree in which the believer is allowed to participate in the sufferings of his Lord, should be the measure of his joy; see 1 Pet. iv. 13 καθὸ κοινωνεῖτε τοῖς τοῦ Χριστοῦ παθήμασι, χαίρετε. On the privilege of sharing in Christ's sufferings, comp. Phil. i. 29 ὅτι ὑμῖν ἐχαρίσθη τὸ ὑπὲρ Χριστοῦ οὐ μόνον τὸ εἰς αὐτὸν πιστεύειν, ἀλλὰ καὶ τὸ ὑπὲρ αὐτοῦ πάσχειν, where see the note.

θλίψει] The persecutions instigated by the Jews in Thessalonica (Acts xvii. 5 sq.) doubtless continued long after the Apostle had left, for the pertinacity with which they followed St Paul to Berea (Acts xvii. 13) shows their determination; see *Biblical Essays*, p. 262 sq. But though the Jews were the instigators, the heathen population did not stand aloof, as appears from 1 Thess. ii. 14.

Πνεύματος Ἁγίου] 'proceeding from, inspired by the Holy Ghost.'

7. τύπον] 'an ensample of a Christian community.' The singular is more forcible than τύπους, and should be read, though τύπους has strong support. Comp. for the expression and for the singular number Barnabas 19. 7 ὑποταγήσῃ κυρίοις ὡς τύπῳ Θεοῦ ἐν αἰσχύνῃ καὶ φόβῳ.

πᾶσι τοῖς πιστεύουσιν] Used substantively, 'to all believers,' without any special reference of present time.

ἐν τῇ Μακεδονίᾳ καὶ ἐν τῇ Ἀχαΐᾳ] The repetition of the preposition and article is in place here, because St Paul speaks of them as two distinct provinces, 'not only in Macedonia, but also in the neighbouring province

of Achaia': but in the next verse ἐν τῇ is correctly omitted by some of
the best authorities, because there the two are classed together, in
opposition to the rest of the world.

The peninsula of Greece under the Roman dominion included parts
of three provinces—Macedonia, Achaia, and Illyricum.

8. ἀφ' ὑμῶν] i.e. 'spreading from you onward.' Ἀπὸ is simply local
here.

ἐξήχηται] *'has sounded forth,'* like thunder. A strong word and
especially used in this metaphor: Pollux i. 118 ἐξήχησεν βροντή, comp.
Ecclus. xl. 13 ὡς βροντὴ μεγάλη ἐν ὑετῷ ἐξηχήσει, where the goods of the
unjust are said to exhaust their power, to roar themselves out, as thunder
in rain. 'Non verba sed tonitrua' says Jerome of St Paul's writings : he
seems to hear them as he reads them. The verb appears to be a middle
here.

ὁ λόγος τοῦ Κυρίου] This expression occurs again in 2 Thess. iii. 1
(cf. ἐν λόγῳ Κυρίου, 1 Thess. iv. 15 and note there). Comp. also τὸ ῥῆμα
Κυρίου, 1 Pet. i. 25, and ὁ λόγος τοῦ Χριστοῦ, Col. iii. 16 (on the meaning
of which last passage see the note *ad loc.*). Ὁ λόγος τοῦ Θεοῦ is tolerably
frequent in St Paul. Are these genitives then, Θεοῦ, Κυρίου, subjective or
objective? i.e. do the expressions mean 'the word uttered by God, the
message of the Lord,' or 'the tidings which speak of God, of the Lord'?
An answer seems to be supplied to this question by the fact that the
expressions are derived from the Hebrew prophets, e.g. Is. xxxviii. 4,
'Then came the word of the Lord unto Isaiah,' which is equivalent to
'thus saith the Lord' of the following verse, and is rendered in the LXX.
λόγος Κυρίου. This Old Testament usage is decisive in favour of the
subjective use here.

ἀλλ' ἐν παντὶ τόπῳ κ.τ.λ.] The opposition is restricted to ἐν τῇ Μακ. κ.
Ἀχ. and ἐν παντὶ τόπῳ as the position of οὐ μόνον shows. It does not
extend also to ὁ λόγος τοῦ Κ. and ἡ πίστις ἡ πρὸς τὸν Θεόν, as some would
take it.

The sentence, if grammatically regular, would have stopped at ἐν παντὶ
τόπῳ. But the addition of a new subject and predicate (ἡ πίστις...ἐξελήλυθεν)
should create no difficulty in St Paul, whose characteristic earnestness is
often exhibited in thus lengthening out a sentence in order to enforce a
lesson or dwell upon an important fact. See e.g. ver. 3 above.

ἀλλά] The omission of καί, besides being best supported by the MSS.
(e.g. B, which shows the superiority of its reading over the received text by
omitting also ἐν τῇ before Ἀχαίᾳ above), is also internally more probable,
as preparing us for the new form which the sentence is to take. Had
it stopped with ἐν παντὶ τόπῳ, then ἀλλὰ καὶ would have been more
natural.

ἐν παντὶ τόπῳ] The favourable position of Thessalonica situated as it
was on the Via Egnatia, and its mercantile importance, will explain the rapid
spread of the tidings ; see *Biblical Essays,* p. 254 sq. Wieseler (*Chronol.*

p. 42) suggests that St Paul may have learnt from Aquila and Priscilla, who had recently arrived at Corinth from Rome (Acts xviii. 2), that the faith of the Thessalonians was known there. The expression ἐν παντὶ τόπῳ is of course not to be pressed. For a similar hyperbole see Col. i. 6 ἐν παντὶ τῷ κόσμῳ, Rom. i. 8 ἐν ὅλῳ τῷ κόσμῳ, Phil. i. 13 τοῖς λοιποῖς πᾶσιν, and 2 Cor. ii. 14, where the same expression ἐν παντὶ τόπῳ occurs. ἐξελήλυθεν] 'has spread abroad.' Comp. Rom. x. 18, 1 Cor. xiv. 36, where the verb is found in the same sense.

9. αὐτοὶ] 'of themselves.' Their minds are so full of the subject that unasked they proffer us the information.

The substantive to which αὐτοὶ is to be referred is contained implicitly in ἐν παντὶ τόπῳ, i.e. 'strangers from all parts.'

εἴσοδον] 'approach, access.' We are tempted by the recollection of St Paul's favourite metaphor of a door being opened (1 Cor. xvi. 9, 2 Cor. ii. 12, Col. iv. 3, where see the note : comp. Acts xiv. 27 a reference to St Paul's language) to take εἴσοδος here in a metaphorical sense 'access to your hearts': but a comparison of ii. 1 renders the literal meaning more probable.

πρὸς τὸν Θεὸν ἀπὸ τῶν εἰδώλων] showing that the majority at least of the Thessalonian converts were heathen and not Jews: comp. 1 Thess. ii. 14, 16. That this was the case appears likewise from the fact that St Paul refrains from any direct allusions to the Old Testament, which would certainly have occurred had he been addressing Jews chiefly or proselytes. Again, had the mass of the converts been Jews or proselytes the expression would have been not πρὸς τὸν Θεὸν but πρὸς τὸν Κύριον. Contrast Acts ix. 4 τίς εἶ, Κύριε the cry of the proselyte Saul with xv. 19 ἀπὸ τῶν ἐθνῶν ἐπιστρέφουσιν ἐπὶ τὸν Θεόν : and comp. Gal. iv. 8 οὐκ εἰδότες Θεὸν of the Galatian idolaters, Acts xiv. 15 ἀπὸ τούτων τῶν ματαίων ἐπιστρέφειν ἐπὶ Θεὸν ζῶντα in St Paul's speech to the people at Lystra.

Θεῷ ζῶντι καὶ ἀληθινῷ] 'a living and real God': as opposed to the phantom and senseless gods of the heathen. See Acts xiv. 15, already cited. The E.V. here by translating 'the living and true God' has weakened the passage, just as some Greek transcribers in Acts l. c. by writing τὸν Θεὸν τὸν ζῶντα for Θεὸν ζῶντα followed by the Textus Receptus. The word ἀληθινὸς occurs in this passage only in St Paul's writings: it is found as a v.l. in Heb. ix. 14 εἰς τὸ λατρεύειν Θεῷ ζῶντι καὶ ἀληθινῷ, doubtless from a reminiscence of this passage. On the difference between ἀληθὴς and ἀληθινὸς see Trench, N. T. Syn. § 8, p. 26.

10. καὶ ἀναμένειν τὸν υἱὸν αὐτοῦ ἐκ τῶν οὐρανῶν] This appeal well illustrates the doctrinal teaching of this Epistle. It is thus, 'Live a holy life, that you may be prepared to meet your Lord.' In St Paul's later Epistles, his appeal generally assumes a different form, 'Christ died for you : therefore die with Him to sin.' Both the one lesson and the other have their office in the instruction of the Church through all ages, addressing themselves to different minds, and frames of minds—the one

making itself heard where the other would be ineffective. The 'coming of the Lord' is the refrain, as it were, with which St Paul clenches paragraph after paragraph in this Epistle. See *Biblical Essays*, p. 224 sq., where the characteristics of the groups of the Pauline Epistles are treated at length.

οὐρανῶν] The plural οὐρανοὶ is not classical. Neither was the Latin *caeli* which, though occurring once in Lucretius for a special reason (II. 1097 *caelos omnes*, where see Munro's note), is condemned by Julius Cæsar in Aulus Gellius xix. 8. 3—5. On the other hand the Hebrew equivalent has no singular, the plural being always used, with a reference perhaps to successive heavens receding one beyond the other (2 Cor. xii. 2 ἕως τρίτου οὐρανοῦ); see Koch's note here.

ὃν ἤγειρεν ἐκ νεκρῶν] This clause is generally considered to be added as a decisive proof of His Sonship, as in Rom. i. 4. It seems however to be appealed to here rather as an earnest of His coming again in judgment and of the general resurrection, 'He will judge the world in righteousness by that man whom he hath ordained: whereof he hath given assurance unto all men in that he raised him from the dead,' Acts xvii. 31, in St Paul's speech before the Areopagus which was delivered within a few months of the writing of this Epistle. The parallel therefore from this almost contemporaneous speech may fairly be allowed to decide the train of thought here, even if the context were not so strongly in favour of this interpretation.

Ἰησοῦν τὸν ῥυόμενον κ.τ.λ.] i.e. Jesus, Who, as His name betokens, is our deliverer etc., an allusion to the meaning of the name Jesus, 'the Saviour.' In Isai. lix. 20 cited in Rom. xi. 26, ὁ ῥυόμενος is the LXX. translation of גֹאֵל. So also in Gen. xlviii. 16, and ὁ ῥυσάμενος frequently (Isai. xliv. 6, xlvii. 4, xlviii. 17, xlix. 7, 26, liv. 5, 8).

τῆς ὀργῆς] used thus absolutely of the divine wrath, as in ii. 16, Rom. iii. 5, v. 9, ix. 22, xiii. 5. Compare especially Rom. xii. 19, δότε τόπον τῇ ὀργῇ where τῇ ὀργῇ cannot refer to one's adversary, for it is not a question of his wrath, but of his injustice. The difficulty of the phrase has led to explanatory glosses, 1 Thess. ii. 16 τοῦ Θεοῦ, Rom. iii. 5 αὐτοῦ.

τῆς ἐρχομένης] '*which is even now approaching.*' Comp. v. 2 ἡμέρα Κυρίου ὡς κλέπτης ἐν νυκτὶ οὕτως ἔρχεται, Eph. v. 6 ἔρχεται ἡ ὀργὴ τοῦ Θεοῦ ἐπὶ τοὺς υἱοὺς τῆς ἀπειθείας, Col. iii. 6 δι' ἃ ἔρχεται ἡ ὀργὴ τοῦ Θεοῦ. The word may refer either to the present and continuous dispensation or to the future and final judgment. The present ἔρχεσθαι is frequently used to denote the certainty, and possibly the nearness, of a future event, e.g. Matt. xvii. 11, Joh. iv. 21, xiv. 3, whence ὁ ἐρχόμενος is a designation of the Messiah: see Winer § xl. p. 332, and *Biblical Essays*, p. 149.

CHAPTER II

ii. *Character of the Apostle's life and ministry among them* (ii. 1—12).

1. St Paul in the former chapter had alluded to two proofs, which convinced him of the election of the Thessalonians, *first* the conduct of the preachers (ver. 5), and *secondly* the reception of the message by the hearers (vv. 6—10). He now enlarges on the same topics, and in the same order, speaking of the preachers (ii. 1—12), and of the hearers (vv. 13 sq.), but of the latter more briefly, because he had already spoken at some length on this head, while he had dismissed the other topic more summarily.

Αὐτοὶ γάρ] The explanation of γάρ is to be sought rather in the train of thought which was running in the Apostle's mind, than in the actual expressions: 'I speak thus boldly and confidently as to my preaching, *for* I have a witness at hand. You *yourselves* know, etc.' There seems to be no contrast implied in αὐτοὶ to the external testimony alluded to in i. 8, 9. Such a contrast would only interfere with the explanation of γάρ. The emphatic position of αὐτοὶ is quite characteristic of this group of Epistles; comp. iii. 3, v. 2, 2 Thess. iii. 7.

κενή] Not 'fruitless, ineffective' (μάταιος), but 'hollow, empty, wanting in purpose and earnestness.' The context shows that κενὴ must refer to the character of the preaching, not to its results; in fact οὐ κενὴ is equivalent to the οὐκ ἐν λόγῳ μόνον ἀλλὰ καὶ ἐν δυνάμει of i. 5. Κενὸς and μάταιος nowhere occur together in the New Testament, though in 1 Cor. xv. 14, 17 (κενὸν τὸ κήρυγμα—ματαία ἡ πίστις) they appear in close proximity; but they are found in combination in Clem. Rom. 7 ἀπολείπωμεν τὰς κενὰς καὶ ματαίας φροντίδας, where the former epithet points to the quality, the latter to the aim or effect of the action. For instances of the combination in the LXX. and classical Greek see the note on Clem. Rom. l.c.

γέγονεν] '*has proved, has been found,*' not as E.V. 'was.' Does the perfect here glance obliquely at the lasting effects of his preaching, or does it imply that his sojourn in Thessalonica was recent? On the former supposition we may compare 2 Cor. xii. 9 εἴρηκεν, on the latter 2 Cor. ii. 13 ἔσχηκα.

2. **ἀλλὰ προπαθόντες κ.τ.λ.**] 'On the contrary, though we had had a foretaste of what awaited us in the sufferings and indignities which we underwent, as ye know, at Philippi, yet were we nothing daunted but were bold, etc. Our courage under adverse circumstances is a sufficient proof that there was nothing hollow, specious or unreal in our preaching.'

προπαθόντες καὶ ὑβρισθέντες] '*having before been maltreated and that with contumely.*' The force of the preposition προ- in the first participle is carried on to the second, or rather the preposition having been expressed in the first instance, it is unnecessary to repeat it. Comp. probably I Cor. xvi. 16 παντὶ τῷ συνεργοῦντι καὶ κοπιῶντι, where καὶ κοπιῶντι is equivalent to ὥστε καὶ κοπιᾶν. For this classical idiom of an additional feature comp. Demosth. *Conon* p. 1256 ὑβρισθείς, ὦ ἄνδρες δικασταί, καὶ παθὼν ὑπὸ Κόνωνος quoted by Wetstein, and such passages as Soph. *Ant.* 537 καὶ συμμετίσχω καὶ φέρω τῆς αἰτίας where see Blaydes' note.

ὑβρισθέντες] i.e. we experienced not only bodily suffering (παθόντες), but indignity superadded. This word ὑβρισθέντες indicates the same feeling which prompted St Paul, on the occasion especially alluded to, to demand that the magistrates should in person escort himself and Silas from prison, οὐ γάρ· ἀλλὰ ἐλθόντες αὐτοὶ ἡμᾶς ἐξαγαγέτωσαν, Acts xvi. 37. It was the consciousness of an *indignity* offered. St Paul was not above (or, should we not say, below) entertaining a sense of what was due to his personal dignity. His social position had been contemned. It was in the essence of ὕβρις that it could not be done to slaves: Ar. *Rhet.* ii. 24, § 9 (p. 1402) εἴ τις φαίη τὸ τύπτειν τοὺς ἐλευθέρους ὕβριν εἶναι, Demosth. *Nicostr.* p. 1251 ἵν᾽ εἰ καταλαβὼν αὐτὸν ἐγὼ πρὸς ὀργὴν δήσαιμι ἢ πατάξαιμι ὡς δοῦλον ὄντα, γραφήν με γράψαιντο ὕβρεως, with the comment of Meier and Schömann, *Att. Proc.* p. 325. Thus this one word embodies the incident in the Acts. It was the *contumely* which hurt St Paul's feelings arising from the strong sense of his Roman citizenship.

ἐν Φιλίπποις] See Acts xvi. 19—40, Phil. i. 30.

ἐπαρρησιασάμεθα λαλῆσαι] Comp. Eph. vi. 20. On παρρησία (παν-ρησία, so Steph. *Thes.*), the boldness of speech which suppresses nothing, see on Col. ii. 15, and Eph. iii. 12. The verb παρρησιάζεσθαι however is always found in the New Testament in connexion with speaking, and so it is best to translate it here 'were bold of speech' (and so Eph. vi. 20), not simply 'took courage.'

ἐν τῷ Θεῷ ἡμῶν] 'This boldness however was not our own. We were courageous in our God, in spite of our sufferings and yet in some sense by reason of them. For we have this treasure in earthen vessels, that the excellency of the power may be of God, and not of us (2 Cor. iv. 7). For when I am weak, then am I strong (*ib.* xii. 10).'

λαλῆσαι] Not equivalent to ὥστε λαλῆσαι ('we were bold of speech, so that we told'); but simply the objective infinitive, as the run of the sentence points to a closer connexion with ἐπαρρησιασάμεθα, 'we were bold of speech to tell.' Λαλεῖν is stronger than λέγειν, see Trench, *N. T. Syn.* § 76, p. 286.

τὸ εὐαγγέλιον τοῦ Θεοῦ] Is τοῦ Θεοῦ the objective or the subjective genitive? Or is it not idle in many cases, and perhaps in this, to seek to limit the genitive to one sense, when it is in itself comprehensive, and includes several senses, all of which will suit the context? Certainly, whatever may be the case with the corresponding phrase τὸ εὐαγγέλιον τοῦ Χριστοῦ (Gal. i. 7), the subjective genitive seems more natural with τοῦ Θεοῦ.

ἐν πολλῷ ἀγῶνι] '*amidst much conflict,*' i.e. beset by much opposition. The Christian sufferer is an athlete who contends for the victor's chaplet. Sometimes the ἀγὼν takes the form of an outward, as Phil. i. 30; sometimes, as Col. ii. 1, of an internal conflict. The allied words ἀθλεῖν, ἄθλησις occur in this connexion in 2 Tim. ii. 5, Heb. x. 32, and the idea is constantly present to St Paul's mind. The metaphor was speedily taken up: e.g. Clem. Rom. 5 ἔλθωμεν ἐπὶ τοὺς ἔγγιστα γενομένους ἀθλητάς, Ign. *Polyc.* 1, 2, 3 πάντων τὰς νόσους βάσταζε ὡς τέλειος ἀθλητής...νῆφε ὡς Θεοῦ ἀθλητής· τὸ θέμα ἀφθαρσία...μεγάλου ἐστὶν ἀθλητοῦ τὸ δέρεσθαι καὶ νικᾶν, where see the notes and also that on Ign. *Eph.* 3 (ὑπαλειφθῆναι).

3. ἡ γὰρ παράκλησις] 'I said that we were bold in our God, and that it was the Gospel of God we preached, and I said rightly. For our appeal is not to be traced to error or impurity or to any human passions, or human imperfections. It has received the sanction of God, and His commission is upon us.' Παράκλησις may perhaps be translated 'appeal': it is an exercise of the powers of persuasion, either in the way of (1) comfort, or (2) encouragement, or (3) exhortation, according as the reference is to (1) the past, what has happened, (2) the present, what is happening, or (3) the future, what is to happen.

οὐκ ἐκ πλάνης] '*It does not arise from error.*' Πλάνη is used either in an active sense 'deceit,' 'the leading astray,' or in a passive 'error,' 'the being led astray.' But in the New Testament it seems always to have the latter meaning, and this is better suited to the context here. For ἐκ πλάνης will thus be distinguished from ἐν δόλῳ. The preposition ἐκ as opposed to ἐν likewise points to this meaning. False teachers are 'deceived' as well as 'deceivers' (2 Tim. iii. 13 πλανῶντες καὶ πλανώμενοι).

οὐδὲ ἐξ ἀκαθαρσίας] '*nor yet from impurity,*' i.e. from sensuality. This disclaimer, startling as it may seem, was not unneeded amidst the impurities consecrated by the religions of the day. The meaning of the Hebrew or rather Phoenician words קָדֵשׁ fem. קְדֵשָׁה from קָדֵשׁ 'to be holy' (Deut. xxiii. 17), properly 'the consecrated ones,' tells its own terrible tale. St Paul was at this very time living in the midst of the worship of Aphrodite at Corinth, and had but lately witnessed that of the Cabiri at Thessalonica (see *Biblical Essays*, p. 257 sq.). The religion of Rome, again, though in its origin far purer than those of Greece or the East, had been corrupted from extraneous sources: and we need not go farther than the Roman moralists and satirists to learn how much of the vice and impurity which hastened the decline of Rome was due to the introduction of foreign religious systems. How naturally prone the early converts were to sensualize even the religion of Christ may be inferred from many passages in St Paul's Epistles (e.g. 1 Thess. iv. 3 where the 'idea of holiness is regarded as almost equivalent to abstinence from the commission of fornication' : see Jowett I. p. 88), and is seen in the monstrous aberrations of some forms of Gnosticism, i.e. of Simon Magus.

The word ἀκαθαρσία is frequently interpreted in this passage to mean 'covetousness' (comp. the Latin *sordes, sordidus*) ; but no instance is produced to show that ἀκαθαρσία, ἀκάθαρτος are ever used in this sense. In 1 Esdras i. 42 indeed ἀκαθαρσία is used of the spoliation of the temple, but here the word points to the defilement, not to the avarice involved in the act. In Barnab. 19. 4 οὐ μή σου ὁ λόγος τοῦ Θεοῦ ἐξέλθῃ ἐν ἀκαθαρσίᾳ τινῶν the context shows that the language is not a warning against preaching for money, but against ruining the effectiveness of preaching by personal impurity. By the analogy of the figurative language of the O.T. ἀκάθαρτος in the mouth of a Jew might get to mean 'idolatrous, profane,' but scarcely 'sordid, avaricious.' There is as little ground for asserting conversely that πλεονεξία is equivalent to ἀκαθαρσία : see note on Col. iii. 5. For ἀκαθαρσία of the pollution of the temple see Test. xii. Patr. *Levi* 15.

οὐδὲ ἐν δόλῳ] The better supported reading οὐδέ, if not actually required for grammatical reasons (see Hermann, *Opusc.* III. 143), gives a much better sense than οὔτε. Each clause disclaims an entirely distinct motive, and therefore the disjunctive particle οὐδέ is preferable : 'not from error, nor yet from impurity, nor again in guile.' See the note on Gal. i. 12.

4. **ἀλλά**] On the contrary, so far from its being due to human passions and imperfections, it is in accordance with the test which we have satisfied in the sight of God.

δεδοκιμάσμεθα] The word δοκιμάζειν signifies properly to examine an object with a view to its satisfying a certain test, and hence naturally glides into the meaning 'to approve.' In δεδοκιμάσμεθα this latter signification is prominent, in τῷ δοκιμάζοντι it is kept in the background. Still, as Trench remarks (*N. T. Syn.* § 74, p. 278 sq.), there is always the underlying sense not merely of a victorious coming out of trial, but of the implication that the trial is itself made in the expectation that the issue would be favourable—an implication wanting in the word πειράζειν. Thus the word most nearly approaches the classical sense of ἀξιοῦν.

πιστευθῆναι τὸ εὐαγγέλιον] '*to be trusted with the gospel*,' 'to have the gospel committed to us.' For the construction see Rom. iii. 2, 1 Cor. ix. 17, Gal. ii. 7, 1 Tim. i. 11, Tit. i. 3, 2 Thess. i. 10 (v. l.). Not only do verbs which in the active take an accusative of both person and thing retain the latter in the passive, e.g. 2 Thess. ii. 15 παραδόσεις ἃς ἐδιδάχθητε:

but also those which in the active are constructed with a dative of the person and an accusative of the thing, e.g. πιστευθῆναι τὸ εὐαγγέλιον here, and Acts xxviii. 20 τὴν ἄλυσιν ταύτην περίκειμαι, see Winer § xxxii. p. 287. οὕτως] 'accordingly, in accordance therewith,' i.e. with this commission, answering to καθώς. This correspondence of καθώς, καθάπερ, and οὕτως is frequent in the New Testament : comp. e.g. in St Paul, 2 Cor. viii. 6, x. 7, Col. iii. 13. Ὡς has no dependence on οὕτως. For though οὕτως...ὡς 'in such a manner...as' is a frequent combination in St Paul, οὕτως here cannot well refer both to καθὼς and ὡς, inasmuch as it would require to be taken in two different senses. It is better therefore to treat οὐχ ὡς ἀνθρώποις κ.τ.λ. as an independent clause, explanatory of καθὼς...οὕτως. For this use of ὡς comp. especially 2 Cor. vi. 8—10.

ἀνθρώποις ἀρέσκοντες] Compare Gal. i. 10 and the notes on Col. i. 10 (ἀρέσκειαν), iii. 22 (ἀνθρωπάρεσκοι).

τὰς καρδίας ἡμῶν] It has been maintained by some (e.g. Conybeare and Howson II. p. 95 note 1, p. 419 note 3) that St Paul uses 'we' 'according to the idiom of many ancient writers' where a modern writer would use ' I.' Or as it is expressed elsewhere, ' He uses ἐγὼ frequently interchangeably with ἡμεῖς, and when he includes others in the ἡμεῖς he specifies it.' On this point the following facts may be worthy of consideration. (1) The Epistles which are written in St Paul's name alone are the Romans, Galatians, Ephesians, 1, 2 Timothy, and Titus. In all of these the singular is used when the writer is speaking in his own name. The plural is never so used. It is only employed where he speaks of himself as the member of a class, whether embracing either the other preachers of the Gospel (Gal. i. 8, ii. 9), or the persons to whom the letter is addressed, or the whole body of Christians generally. (2) Of the other Epistles, those to Philippians and to Philemon (after the opening salutation) adhere to the singular throughout. The others use the plural. In 1 Corinthians the plural occurs every now and then. It is very common in 2 Corinthians, and in 1, 2 Thessalonians it is very seldom departed from. As a general rule we may say that wherever the communication is more direct and personal, there the singular is used : wherever it is more general, the plural is preferred. (3) In every instance where the plural is used, we find that it will apply to those who are associated with the Apostle, as well as to the Apostle himself. (4) There are passages where it is quite impossible to refer the plural to St Paul alone without making havoc of the sense. The passage in the text is one of these instances. 2 Cor. vii. 3 προείρηκα γὰρ ὅτι ἐν ταῖς καρδίαις ἡμῶν ἐστὲ εἰς τὸ συναποθανεῖν καὶ συνζῆν is another instance. For though no one will deny that a king or a reviewer may employ the plural 'we' with propriety, it may fairly be questioned whether the one would talk of 'our crowns' or the other of 'our pens,' when only one of each class was meant. And thus, though the Apostle might say 'we,' he could not call himself 'Apostles' ὡς Χριστοῦ ἀπόστολοι (1 Thess. ii. 6) or speak of his 'hearts.' (5) In other passages St Paul's own language shows that by the use of the plural he does generally include more than himself, for in particular cases where he refers to himself personally he takes care to substitute the singular for the plural or in some other way to qualify the expression. Thus below ii. 18 διότι ἠθελήσαμεν ἐλθεῖν πρὸς ὑμᾶς, ἐγὼ μὲν Παῦλος καὶ ἅπαξ καὶ δίς, καὶ ἐνέκοψεν ἡμᾶς ὁ Σατανᾶς, St Paul is careful to distinguish himself from the others who are included in the plural—'we were desirous of visiting you (for my own part I have entertained the desire more than once), but Satan hindered us.' We may conclude therefore that a case for an epistolary plural in St Paul's Epistles has not been made out.

5. **ἐν λόγῳ κολακείας ἐγενήθημεν**] '*were we found employed in words*' etc. For the construction γίγνεσθαι ἐν compare 1 Tim. ii. 14, and see the note on i. 5.

κολακείας, πλεονεξίας] are probably subjective genitives, 'the words, which flattery uses, the pretext of which avarice avails itself.' It is objectionable to apply a different sense of the genitive to the two clauses when the same will hold. Κολακεία, a word which occurs here only in the New Testament, is defined both by Theophrastus (*Char.* 2) and Aristotle (*Eth. Nic.* iv. 12) to involve the idea of selfish motives. It is flattery not merely for the sake of giving pleasure to others but for the sake of self-interest. The words of Aristotle are ὁ δὲ ὅπως ὠφέλειά τις αὐτῷ γίγνηται εἰς χρήματα καὶ ὅσα διὰ χρημάτων, κόλαξ. For πλεονεξία see Col. iii. 5.

προφάσει] '*pretext.*' The word πρόφασις (from προφαίνω) signifies generally the ostensible reason for which a thing is done (comp. Joseph. *Ant.* xvi. 6. 5 quoted in Wetstein); sometimes in a good sense (e.g. Thuc. i. 23, vi. 6 ἀληθεστάτη πρόφασις), but generally otherwise, the false or pretended reason as opposed to the true, and so, as here, 'a pretext,' and takes the genitive.

Θεὸς μάρτυς] He had appealed to the Thessalonians themselves (καθὼς οἴδατε) to testify to his outward conduct (ἐν λόγῳ κολακείας). Of his inward motives (προφάσει πλεονεξίας) God alone could bear witness. So Chrysostom and others interpret the passage. Comp. ver. 10, where we have the double appeal ὑμεῖς μάρτυρες καὶ ὁ Θεός.

6. There is a slight difference in the force of the prepositions ἐξ ἀνθρώπων, ἀφ' ὑμῶν, which may be expressed by the paraphrase 'to *extract* (ἐξ) glory from men,' '*deriving it* (ἀπὸ) either from you or, etc.' Ἐκ is the preposition which would naturally be attached to ζητοῦντες: and for an explanation of the adoption of ἀπὸ in the next clause we need not perhaps go farther than the natural desire of a change, though ἀπὸ brings the source (ἐκ) more prominently forward as an agent. Compare John xi. 1 ἀπὸ Βηθανίας, ἐκ τῆς κώμης κ.τ.λ., where Bethany is perhaps the district which would explain the ἀπό. See Winer § xlvii. p. 453 sq. On the other hand, Rom. iii. 30 should not have been classed by Winer among these examples, for there is a marked emphasis in the change of expression from ἐκ πίστεως to διὰ τῆς πίστεως.

δυνάμενοι ἐν βάρει εἶναι κ.τ.λ.] '*though we might have been burdensome,*
oppressive.' What sense are we to attribute to ἐν βάρει εἶναι here? Does
it refer to the levying of pecuniary aid, or to the assumption of authority
and the exaction of respect to one's office? In other words, does it refer
specially to ἐν προφάσει πλεονεξίας, or rather to ζητοῦντες ἐξ ἀνθρώπων
δόξαν? In favour of the former sense is the fact that the kindred phrases
in St Paul are used in this connexion : comp. ver. 9 πρὸς τὸ μὴ ἐπιβαρῆσαί
τινα ὑμῶν repeated again 2 Thess. iii. 8, 2 Cor. xii. 16 κατεβάρησα, xi. 9
ἀβαρῆ ἐμαυτὸν ἐτήρησα. On the other hand the position of δυνάμενοι ἐν
βάρει εἶναι in close connexion with ζητοῦντες δόξαν speaks strongly on
behalf of the other sense, and βάρος, like ὄγκος, can fairly have this meaning. See 2 Cor. iv. 17 βάρος δόξης and comp. Diod. Sic. iv. 61 διὰ τὸ βάρος
τῆς πόλεως, where the writer is speaking of Athens. Perhaps it is safer to
assign to ἐν βάρει εἶναι a comprehensive meaning, including both these
royal prerogatives, so to speak, of the apostleship, the assertion of
authority and the levying of contributions. On the supplies sent to him
from Philippi at this time see the note on Phil. iv. 16.

ὡς Χριστοῦ ἀπόστολοι] '*by virtue of our office as Apostles of Christ.*' So
strongly does St Paul assert the right of the teacher to be provided for
by the taught, that writing to the Corinthians he, with a touch of irony,
expresses his fear lest, by having failed to assert this claim, he might
have led them to question his authority (2 Cor. xi. 7 sq.).

The twofold anxiety displayed here to indicate his own disinterestedness and at the same time not to compromise his rightful claims as an
Apostle, is expressed so entirely in the spirit of St Paul that it is strange
such a proof of the authenticity of the Epistle could be overlooked by
those who have denied the Pauline authorship.

7. νήπιοι] '*children, babes.*' This is by far the best supported reading, being found in אBC*D*FG it. vg. cop. *al.*, nor does it present any
considerable difficulty. The inversion of the metaphor which it introduces,
the Christian teacher being first compared to the child and then to the
mother, is quite in St Paul's manner : e.g. v. 2, 4 where the day of the
Lord is compared to a thief and then the idea is reversed and the unpre-
pared Christians become the thieves (ὡς κλέπτας καταλάβῃ, the true
reading). Compare also the use which is made of the allegory of the
vailed face of Moses (2 Cor. iii. 13—16), where the vail is represented
first as on the law, then as on the hearts of the Jewish nation ; of the
metaphor of second marriage (Rom. vii. 1 sq.) where we should expect not
ὑμεῖς ἐθανατώθητε τῷ νόμῳ (ver. 4) but ὁ νόμος ἐθανατώθη ὑμῖν ; and of the
idea of the triumphal procession in 2 Cor. ii. 14 sq., where the Apostles are
compared, first to the captives led in triumph, then to the odour of the
incense : see for a less striking example Rom. vi. 5, and the notes on Gal.
ii. 20, iv. 19. St Paul's earnestness and rapidity of thought led him to
work his metaphor to the utmost, turning it about and reapplying it, as it
suggested some new analogy. It was of no importance to him, as it

would be to a modern writer, that his image should cut clean. This disregard of rhetorical rules it was which made his 'speech contemptible' (2 Cor. x. 10 ὁ λόγος ἐξουθενημένος, comp. 1 Cor. ii. 1, 4). Rhetorical rules were as nothing to him compared with the object which he had in view. The word νήπιοι was read here by Origen, *Matth.* i. p. 375 ed. Huet (quoted by Bentley, *Crit. Sacr.* p. 61) ὁ ἀπόστολος ἐγένετο νήπιος καὶ παραπλήσιος τροφῷ θαλπούσῃ τὸ ἑαυτῆς παιδίον καὶ λαλούσῃ λόγους ὡς παιδίον διὰ τὸ παιδίον, followed by Pelagius *facti sumus parvuli.* So too Clement of Alexandria (*Paed.* i. 5. 19 p. 108) quotes the passage as given in the text, and explains the distinction between the two words thus : οὐκ ἐπὶ ἀφρόνων τάττεται τὸ νήπιον, νηπύτιος μὲν γὰρ οὗτος, νήπιος δὲ ὁ νεήπιος, ὡς ἤπιος ὁ ἀπαλόφρων, οἷον ἤπιος νεωστὶ καὶ πρᾶος τῷ τρόπῳ γενόμενος : compare also *Paed.* i. 6 p. 117. Compare also Irenæus (iv. 38. 2) speaking of Christ, διὰ τοῦτο συνενηπίαζεν υἱὸς τοῦ Θεοῦ τέλειος ὢν τῷ ἀνθρώπῳ...διὰ τὸ τοῦ ἀνθρώπου νήπιον οὕτω χωρούμενος, ὡς ἄνθρωπος αὐτὸν χωρεῖν ἠδύνατο. The same reading ἤπιοι for νήπιοι occurs in A on Eph. iv. 14, showing the readiness with which the words would be confused.

On the other hand, ἤπιοι makes very excellent sense, as this is a word specially used to express 'fatherly tenderness,' e.g. Hom. *Od.* ii. 47 πατὴρ δ' ὡς ἤπιος ἦεν, comp. *Il.* xxiv. 770. It occurs 2 Tim. ii. 24 δοῦλον Κυρίου οὐ δεῖ μάχεσθαι ἀλλὰ ἤπιον εἶναι, where again the variant νήπιον is found.

ἐν μέσῳ ὑμῶν] not simply ἐν ὑμῖν or παρ' ὑμῖν, but more fully, 'as though I were one of you, mixing freely among you.' The expression here used indirectly hints at the terms of equality on which the Apostle placed himself with his converts : comp. St Luke xxii. 27 of his Master ἐγὼ δὲ ἐν μέσῳ ὑμῶν εἰμὶ ὡς ὁ διακονῶν.

If νήπιοι is the correct reading, a colon should be placed after ἐν μέσῳ ὑμῶν : if ἤπιοι is adopted, perhaps even then it should be so punctuated. It may however be a question in this case, whether ὡς ἐὰν τροφὸς κ.τ.λ. should not be connected with what goes before, though it has an apodosis of its own. For such a construction see Soph. *Ajax* 839.

ὡς ἐὰν θάλπῃ] For ὡς ἂν see Hermann on Soph. *Ajax* 1096, and comp. Winer § xlii. p. 385 ; on ἐὰν for ἂν see Winer § xlii. p. 390.

τὰ ἑαυτῆς τέκνα] Thus by τροφὸς here is meant a mother who suckles and nurses her own children. This use is not unclassical : e.g. Soph. *Ajax* 849 γέροντι πατρὶ τῇ τε δυστήνῳ τροφῷ. Theocr. xxvii. 66 γυνὰ μάτηρ τεκέων τροφὸς (see Steph. *Thes.* s. v.).

8. **ὁμειρόμενοι**] This is the best supported reading and the word occurs also in Job iii. 21 (LXX.), Psalm lxii. 2 (Symmachus), in both passages however with the same variety of reading (ἱμείρεσθαι) as here. Two explanations are given of the form. *First*, that it is derived from ὁμοῦ and εἴρειν, and means 'to be attached to' (so Theophylact and others). To this there are two objections : (1) that the verb would in this case take a dative instead of a genitive. Perhaps the instances of συλλαμβάνεσθαι, ἅπτεσθαι, etc. are not exact enough parallels to meet this

objection. (2) That verbs compounded with ὁμοῦ are always derived from substantives as ὁμοδρομεῖν, ὁμευνετεῖν, ὁμιλεῖν, etc. and there is no substantive to which to refer ὁμείρεσθαι. *Secondly*, as the form μείρεσθαι (=ἱμείρεσθαι) is found in Nicander, *Ther.* 402, it is supposed that ὁμείρεσθαι is a lengthened form from this, as ὀδύρομαι from δύρομαι, ὀκέλλω from κέλλω, etc. Against this it is urged that no instance is adduced of a verb so lengthened by an aspirated vowel. But on the other hand too much stress must not be laid on this in the New Testament, where ἐλπὶς for instance is written ἐλπὶς (see note on Phil. ii. 23 ἀφίδω). In this case the word may have arisen from ἱμείρεσθαι by an imperfect articulation of a very short vowel, as in the case of Κολασσαεῖς for Κολοσσοεῖς ; or lastly the reading may be ὁμειρόμενοι (Lobeck, *Path.* I. 4. I p. 72).

εὐδοκοῦμεν] The imperfect tense. On the omission of the augment see Lobeck, *Phryn.* pp. 140, 456 ; but the best manuscripts of the New Testament are not agreed on this point, and probably ηὐδοκοῦμεν should be preferred here. On the verb εὐδοκεῖν see the note on Col. i. 19. It is not found in the writers of the classical epoch.

καὶ τὰς ἑαυτῶν ψυχάς] '*to give even our own lives.*' The simple verb δοῦναι is to be understood from the compound μεταδοῦναι of the former clause. For the zeugma compare Kühner, II. p. 606, and on the word ψυχὴ see note on I Thess. v. 23.

ἀγαπητοί] The metaphor is still preserved in the term which is specially used of an only or favourite child (see e.g. Hom. *Od.* ii. 365 μοῦνος ἐὼν ἀγαπητὸς κ.τ.λ.) and consecrated in this sense by its application to the Son of God Himself; comp. Matt. iii. 17, and the note on νήπιοι above (ver. 7). On the term ὁ ἀγαπητός, as a complete title in itself, see the note on Col. iv. 14.

9. μνημονεύετε γὰρ] referring to εὐδοκοῦμεν μεταδοῦναι τὰς ἑαυτῶν ψυχάς. 'You will not regard this declaration of our readiness to lay down our lives as a mere idle vaunt, for you have a proof of our self-sacrificing spirit in the recollection of our toils and labours when among you.' Or the γὰρ may refer back to ver. 5.

τὸν κόπον καὶ τὸν μόχθον] '*our toil and our struggling.*' The words occur together also in 2 Thess. iii. 8 and 2 Cor. xi. 27 (so too in Hermas, *Sim.* v. 6. 2), and we must seek for some distinction of meaning between the two expressions.

Κόπος (from κόπτω) is properly a 'blow' or 'bruise,' and hence signifies 'wear and tear,' the fatigue arising from continued labour, and hence the labour which brings on lassitude.

In μόχθος on the other hand the leading notion is that of struggling to overcome difficulties. It is connected with μόγος, μόγις and perhaps μόλις, μῶλος, in all of which words the same idea is prominent. Thus κόπος is passive, μόχθος active, and the distinction may perhaps be represented by the two words 'toil and moil.' See Trench, *Seven Churches*, p. 65.

νυκτὸς καὶ ἡμέρας κ.τ.λ.] This clause is added as an epexegesis of τὸν κόπον ἡμῶν καὶ τὸν μόχθον, and therefore has no connecting particle. Some even of the best MSS. have supplied the apparent deficiency with γάρ. 'Laborem manuum nocte et fatigationem verbi die; caeterum semper operabatur quando docebat' says Pelagius.

The explanation of the order νυκτὸς καὶ ἡμέρας is not to be sought in the fact that the Jews, as did also the Athenians (Plin. *Nat. Hist.* ii. § 79), commenced their reckoning with sunset. For we find the Jewish writers, both in the Old and New Testaments, frequently adopting the reverse order 'day and night' (e.g. Jer. xvi. 13, xxxiii. 25); while the Romans, who reckoned from sunrise, as often as not speak of 'night and day' (e.g. Cic. *de fin.* i. 16. 51, *de orat.* i. 16, 260, Cæsar, *de bell. Gallic.* v. 38. 1). The latter however is the order always observed by St Paul (Lobeck, *Paral.* p. 62 sq.), and by Luke in the expression νύκτα καὶ ἡμέραν (e.g. Luke ii. 37), but not when he uses the genitive (e.g. Luke xviii. 7). St John, who uses the genitive only, always employs the order ἡμέρας καὶ νυκτός, and his style is the most Hebraic of New Testament writers.

ἐργαζόμενοι] St Paul himself doubtless worked while at Thessalonica at his trade of tent-maker, on which we find him employed at Corinth about the time when this Epistle was written (Acts xviii. 3). It was a recognized custom of every Jewish parent, enforced by many maxims of the Rabbins, to teach his son a trade. This fact therefore does not imply any inferiority of social position in the case of St Paul (see the note on 2 Thess. iii. 10, where St Paul reiterates this proof of his disinterestedness). The choice of this particular trade was probably determined by the fact that canvas for tents was largely manufactured from the goat's hair of his native country from which it got its name *cilicium* (Conybeare and Howson, I. p. 58).

St Paul however during his stay at Thessalonica was not entirely supported by the labour of his own hands. He more than once received contributions from Philippi (Phil. iv. 15). In the same way, while at Corinth, he received contributions from Macedonia to make up a sufficient sum to support him, see 2 Cor. xi. 9, where τὸ ὑστέρημά μου means 'what was wanting, after I had plied my trade.' Besides Thessalonica and Corinth (Acts xviii. 3), we find him labouring with his own hands also at Ephesus (Acts xx. 34).

On the bearing of these facts on the question of the length of his stay at Thessalonica, see *Biblical Essays*, p. 259.

10. **ὑμεῖς μάρτυρες καὶ ὁ Θεὸς**] 'You are witnesses of our outward actions, God of our inward thoughts.' See ver. 5.

ὁσίως καὶ δικαίως] '*how holily towards God and how justly towards men.*' The two words often occur together and represent, ὁσίως one's duty towards God, δικαίως one's duty towards men. See Plato, *Gorg.* p. 507 B καὶ μὴν περὶ μὲν ἀνθρώπους τὰ προσήκοντα πράττων δίκαι' ἂν πράττοι, περὶ δὲ θεοὺς ὅσια (comp. *Theæt.* p. 176 B), and so St Paul's contemporary

Philo ὁσιότης μὲν πρὸς Θεὸν δικαιοσύνη δὲ πρὸς ἀνθρώπους θεωρεῖται. Simi-larly Marcus Antoninus says (vii. 66) of Socrates that he was δίκαιος τὰ πρὸς ἀνθρώπους, ὅσιος τὰ πρὸς θεούς. Cf. Luke i. 75, Tit. i. 8, Ephes. iv. 24, where see Wetstein. It is not intended however to be implied that this meaning always attaches to δίκαιος, which in its technical legal sense is used of righteousness before God, i.e. having fulfilled the terms of the compact with Him, but only generally and more especially when distinguished from ὅσιος. See Trench, *N. T. Syn.* § lxxxviii. p. 328. The combination is found in Clem. Rom. 48 κατευθύνοντες τὴν πορείαν αὐτῶν ἐν ὁσιότητι καὶ δικαιοσύνη and [2 Clem.] 5 τὸ ὁσίως καὶ δικαίως ἀναστρέφεσθαι, where see the notes. In the present passage the correspondence is inverted by chiasmus, ὁσίως referring to ὁ Θεός, δικαίως to ὑμεῖς μάρτυρες.

ἀμέμπτως] is more comprehensive, including both ὁσίως and δικαίως contemplated from the negative side. The word is coupled with ὁσίως in Clem. Rom. 44 as descriptive of a blameless Christian ministry.

ὑμῖν τοῖς πιστεύουσιν] If this dative could mean 'in the opinion of,' then all difficulty arising from τοῖς πιστεύουσιν would cease. The sense would then be, 'much as our conduct has been misinterpreted by the unbelievers, at least in the sight of you who believe' etc. But the sense would be sacrificed to get over this one difficulty, for St Paul would then be made to say 'We call you to witness (and God also), how in your opinion we acted holily, etc.,' which is inconceivably flat and unmeaning. The sense 'towards you who believe' is at once a very natural interpretation of the Greek and better suits the context.

τοῖς πιστεύουσιν] Not that his conduct had been otherwise towards unbelievers, but that believers had a special claim upon him. There was here an additional motive for uprightness. Comp. Gal. vi. 10, 'Let us do good unto all men, but especially unto them who are of the household of the faith.' Thus the words are especially connected with ἀμέμπτως. The Apostle's obligations had been loyally fulfilled.

ἐγενήθημεν] For this use of γίγνεσθαι with an adverb 'how holily we conducted ourselves, etc.' see on i. 5. Ἐγενήθημεν is here not a simple copula, but has a fuller meaning, 'we presented ourselves, behaved ourselves': comp. 1 Cor. xvi. 10 ἵνα ἀφόβως γένηται πρὸς ὑμᾶς. See Krüger's *Sprachlehre* § 62. 2, p. 269 (cited by Koch). For this idiomatic use comp. Thucyd. ii. 14 χαλεπῶς αὐτοῖς ἡ ἀνάστασις ἐγεγόνει, and see Matth. *Gr. Gr.* ii. § 309 c.

11.   The construction in the sentence beginning with ὡς ἕνα ἕκαστον κ.τ.λ. is defective from the absence of a finite verb. There are two ways of supplying the ellipsis, either (1) by a verb such as ἐνουθετοῦμεν to govern ἕνα ἕκαστον, or (2) by understanding ἐγενήθημεν with παρακαλοῦντες καὶ παραμυθούμενοι, in which case these participles have a double accusative ἕνα ἕκαστον and ὑμᾶς. This double accusative would present no difficulty; for even if no exact parallel is to be found in St Paul, it is still so entirely after his manner, that it would need no such support. The real difficulty

in this construction consists in the harshness of ἐγενήθημεν παρακαλοῦντες: and probably the correct explanation is to supply some such verb as ἐνουθετοῦμεν suggested above. The sentence is so suspended by the insertion of the participial clause, that the finite verb which ought to close the sentence is lost sight of. On ellipses in St Paul see *Journal of Class. and Sacr. Philol.* iii. p. 85.

ὡς πατὴρ τέκνα] It is remarked by the commentators from St Chrysostom downwards, on ver. 7, that when the Apostle wishes to dwell on his tenderness and affection for his converts he uses the figure of a mother; while here, where he is dwelling on his teaching and advice, he adopts that of a father as more appropriate. 'Parvulos nutrix fovet: proficientes vero pater instituit' says Pelagius.

παρακαλοῦντες καὶ παραμυθούμενοι] Compare 1 Cor. xiv. 3 ὁ δὲ προφητεύων ἀνθρώποις λαλεῖ οἰκοδομὴν καὶ παράκλησιν καὶ παραμυθίαν. Perhaps there is this difference that παρακαλεῖν is 'to exhort to a particular line of conduct,' while παραμυθεῖσθαι is rather 'to encourage to continue in a course.' The sense of 'consolation' which some would here attribute to παραμυθεῖσθαι is not more inherent in this word than in παρακαλεῖν. See above, ii. 3 (with the note), below v. 14 παρακαλοῦμεν δὲ ὑμᾶς...παραμυθεῖσθε τοὺς ὀλιγοψύχους, Col. ii. 2, and the notes on παράκλησις and παραμύθιον (Phil. ii. 1).

μαρτυρόμενοι] This is a better supported reading than μαρτυρούμενοι, and is certainly required by the sense. The distinction between μαρτυρεῖσθαι (the passive of μαρτυρεῖν) 'to be borne witness to,' and μαρτύρεσθαι 'to invoke witnesses' and so 'to appeal to as in the sight of witnesses, to charge, protest,' ought not to require restatement: for it holds equally in classical authors, and in the New Testament without, so far as I am aware, a single exception. Compare e.g. Rom. iii. 21 μαρτυρούμενοι ὑπὸ τοῦ νόμου with Gal. v. 3 μαρτύρομαι δὲ πάλιν παντὶ ἀνθρώπῳ κ.τ.λ. and see note there. Μαρτυρεῖσθαι, the middle, seems to be used for the active in Lucian, *de Sacr.* c. 10 (I. p. 534), but with a sort of middle sense, 'testifies in himself, bears evidence in himself.' Probably at a later period the two words were confused, and hence the various readings in the MSS. here and in Acts xxvi. 22, where however the preponderance of authority is decidedly in favour of μαρτυρόμενος the right reading. Μαρτύρεσθαι bears the same relation to μαρτυρεῖν as ἔρεσθαι to ἐρεῖν.

12. **τοῦ καλοῦντος**] the present participle, as below, v. 24, though the aorist is more frequently used. Either tense may be employed indifferently. Compare Gal. i. 6 ἀπὸ τοῦ καλέσαντος ὑμᾶς with Gal. v. 8 ἐκ τοῦ καλοῦντος ὑμᾶς. The fact that we never find the present of the finite verb in this sense, but always a past tense, as ἐκάλεσεν, κέκληκεν, ἐκλήθητε, suggests as the true explanation of the present participle that it is used substantively, without any idea of time, referring to the person and not the act, 'your caller' like ὁ τίκτων etc. See note on Gal. i. 23 ὁ διώκων ἡμᾶς ποτέ.

τὴν ἑαυτοῦ βασιλείαν] not the future heavenly kingdom of Christ, but the actual spiritual kingdom of which they were present members. Comp. 2 Thess. i. 5 τῆς βασιλείας τοῦ Θεοῦ. It is a state of things which has already begun. Δόξαν on the other hand points to the glorious development of that kingdom in which they hoped to participate hereafter.

iii. *Repetition of thanksgiving at their conversion and patience under persecution* (ii. 13—16).

13. **διὰ τοῦτο**] '*for this reason,*' 'seeing that we have bestowed so much labour and affection upon you, we are the more thankful that we have laboured to some purpose.' This seems better than referring διὰ τοῦτο solely to the dependent clause τοῦ καλοῦντος ὑμᾶς κ.τ.λ. which is not prominent enough to introduce it   A new paragraph may be supposed to begin at ver. 13.

καὶ ἡμεῖς] 'we also, we on our part—as *you* bear witness to our devotion in your service, so *we in return* thank God that you have listened to our teaching.' The words καὶ ἡμεῖς correspond in some sense to αὐτοὶ γὰρ οἴδατε (ii. 1); and fitly introduce the new paragraph, in which St Paul turns away from the teachers to speak of the taught.   The same expression occurs in Col. i. 9, where see the note.

παραλαβόντες ἐδέξασθε] Any attempt to translate these words into the corresponding English, as e.g. παραλαμβάνειν 'to take,' δέχεσθαι 'to accept,' tends to exaggerate the distinction.   Nevertheless it must not be lost sight of. Δέχεσθαι implies a slight degree of acquiescence or appropriation, or at least consciousness, which is absent in παραλαμβάνειν ; or in technical language, while παραλαμβάνειν denotes simply the objective fact, δέχεσθαι presents the subjective aspect of the act of receiving.   Compare Demosth. *F. L.* p. 384 οὐκ ἐδέξαντο οὐδ' ἔλαβον ταῦτα οἱ τῶν Θηβαίων πρέσβεις, 'they did not snap at nor would they even accept the money,' and Xen. *Cyrop.* i. 4. 26 τοὺς μέντοι λαβόντας καὶ δεξαμένους τὰ δῶρα λέγεται Ἀστυαγεῖ ἀπενεγκεῖν, quoted by Koch.   See also the commentators on the parable of the sower, Luke viii. 13 μετὰ χαρᾶς δέχονται τὸν λόγον, and Mark iv. 16 μετὰ χαρᾶς λαμβάνουσιν αὐτόν.   The distinction is significant here : 'when the word of hearing was delivered to you, you took it to yourselves as the word of God.'   See Acts xi. 1, where the word δέξασθαι is coupled with τὸν λόγον, as here, and the note on Col. ii. 6.

λόγον ἀκοῆς] The word ἀκοῆς is not an idle addition here, but derives its force from the accompanying expressions ἐδέξασθε and ὃς καὶ ἐνεργεῖται. 'The word of hearing was delivered to you, but it became something more than the word of hearing to you.   You appropriated it.   It sank into your hearts, and produced fruits in your practice.'   The phrase ὁ λόγος τῆς ἀκοῆς occurs also in Heb. iv. 2 ἀλλ' οὐκ ὠφέλησεν ὁ λόγος τῆς ἀκοῆς ἐκείνους, μὴ συγκεκερασμένους τῇ πίστει τοῖς ἀκούσασιν, where, as here, it

II. 14]   FIRST EPISTLE TO THE THESSALONIANS.   31

stands in contrast to the faithful reception of the Gospel. Compare also
Rom. x. 17 ἄρα ἡ πίστις ἐξ ἀκοῆς, ἡ δὲ ἀκοὴ διὰ ῥήματος Χριστοῦ.

παρ' ἡμῶν] naturally attaches itself to παραλαβόντες, and not to ἀκοῆς,
a harsh construction which however has found favour with many.

τοῦ Θεοῦ] is emphatic by its position, and is intended to deprecate any
false deduction from παρ' ἡμῶν. 'Ye ‚received the word of hearing from
us, albeit it came in fact from God.' Τοῦ Θεοῦ is therefore a subjective
genitive 'proceeding from God, having God for its author,' as its emphatic
position requires; and not 'about God, of which God is the object,' as we
might otherwise be disposed to take it. Œcumenius explains the phrase
rightly παρ' ἡμῶν μὲν παρελάβετε, οὐχ ἡμέτερον δὲ ὄντα, ἀλλὰ τοῦ Θεοῦ. The
Apostle betrays a nervous apprehension that he may be unconsciously
making claims for himself; the awkwardness of the position of the words
τοῦ Θεοῦ is the measure of the emphasis of his disclaimer.

οὐ λόγον ἀνθρώπων] 'Ye received it not as the word of men, but as etc.'
i.e. 'with the respect and obedience due to it, as the word of God. It was
to you in your welcome of it the word of God.' For the omission of ὡς
comp. Kühner II. p. 226, Lambert Bos, *Ellips.* p. 781 ed. Schäfer 1808.
That this is the sense of the passage appears not only from the general
context, but especially from the phrase καθὼς ἀληθῶς ἐστίν, which would
be rendered meaningless if the words were translated, 'ye received not the
word of men, but the word of God,' as it is taken by some.

ὃς καὶ ἐνεργεῖται] This is to be referred not to Θεός, but to λόγος; for,
first, St Paul observing a very significant distinction always uses the
active ἐνεργεῖν of God, and so by contrast of the spirit of evil (Ephes.
ii. 2), and the middle ἐνεργεῖσθαι in other cases (see the note on Gal.
v. 6): and, *secondly*, the natural sequence in the passage is preserved
by taking the verb with λόγος. (1) The word received into the ears,
(2) the word appropriated in the heart, (3) the word fructifying in good
works—these are the stages which the Apostle here expresses.

ἐν ὑμῖν τοῖς πιστεύουσιν] Πίστις and ἀκοή are contrasted in the passages
cited above in the note on λόγος ἀκοῆς. This passage, like Gal. v. 6,
πίστις δι' ἀγάπης ἐνεργουμένη (ἰσχύει), supplies the link which connects the
teaching of St Paul on faith and works with that of St James.

14. ὑμεῖς γὰρ] 'for you showed signs of the active working of the
Gospel, in the persecution which you endured.'

ὑμεῖς γὰρ μιμηταὶ κ.τ.λ.] This passage, implying an affectionate
admiration of the Jewish Churches on the part of St Paul, and thus
fully bearing out the impression produced by the narrative in the Acts,
is entirely subversive of the theory maintained by some and based on a
misconception of Gal. ii. and by the fiction of the Pseudo-Clementines, of
the feud existing between St Paul and the Twelve. The staunchest main-
tainer of this theory by a sort of *petitio principii* uses this passage as a
strong argument against the authenticity of the Epistle (Baur, *Paulus*,
p. 482 sq.).

τῶν ἐκκλησιῶν] The word ἐκκλησία, as most other terms relating to the ministry and organization of the Christian community, e.g. ἐπίσκοπος, λειτουργία, is borrowed from the civil polity of the heathen, their religious terms having been so indelibly stamped with a meaning of their own as to render them unavailable for the purposes of Christianity. Just in the same way, at a later stage, for the most part the basilicas, not the temples, were employed for Christian worship. At the same time however, though this was the original and prominent signification of the ἐκκλησία, it was not unknown as applied to religious assemblies among the Jews, e.g. Acts vii. 38 ἡ ἐκκλησία ἐν τῇ ἐρήμῳ, and is in fact the word used to translate קָהָל, e.g. in Psalm xxii. 22. We must remember however that in the theocracy 'political' and 'religious' were convertible terms. And, though the word συναγωγὴ was used for a meeting in a fixed place for purposes of prayer by the Jews and even by the Jewish Christians (James ii. 2), so that the heretical Ebionite sect clung to the term for some centuries (Epiphan. xxx. 18 συναγωγὴν δὲ οὗτοι καλέουσι τὴν ἑαυτῶν ἐκκλησίαν καὶ οὐχὶ ἐκκλησίαν), still the word ἐκκλησία might fairly apply to a Jewish religious assembly. Hence it was not sufficient to describe the Christian communities in Judæa as αἱ ἐκκλησίαι, or even as αἱ ἐκκλησίαι τοῦ Θεοῦ, for these expressions would apply equally well to the Jews; but it was necessary to specify them as ἐν Χριστῷ Ἰησοῦ 'the Christian Churches in Judæa.' The same fear of misapprehension is observable elsewhere, e.g. Gal. i. 22 ταῖς ἐκκλησίαις τῆς Ἰουδαίας ταῖς ἐν Χριστῷ, where see the note: see above, i. 1; and further in the next note.

ἐν Χριστῷ Ἰησοῦ] Not to be taken with μιμηταὶ ἐγενήθητε, but with τῶν ἐκκλησιῶν οὐσῶν ἐν τῇ Ἰουδαίᾳ. The absence of the article is no objection (see i. 1, iv. 16). The reason why these words are added is given in the last note, and applies equally to the parallel passages, Gal. i. 22, 1 Cor. i. 2, which serve to explain the construction here.

καὶ ὑμεῖς...καὶ αὐτοὶ] The comparison is strengthened by the insertion of καὶ in both clauses. Compare Eph. v. 23 ὡς καὶ ὁ Χριστός (where see Ellicott's note), Rom. i. 13 καὶ ἐν ὑμῖν καθὼς καὶ ἐν τοῖς λοιποῖς ἔθνεσιν. Καὶ αὐτοὶ 'they themselves,' to be understood from τῶν ἐκκλησιῶν κ.τ.λ.

συμφυλετῶν] That the Gentiles are here meant is clear from the marked opposition to ὑπὸ τῶν Ἰουδαίων, further enforced as it is by ἰδίων. Though the Jews appear in the Acts as the chief persecutors of St Paul at Thessalonica, yet we cannot doubt that the course of events was the same there as elsewhere; the opposition to the Gospel instigated by the Jews was taken up by the native population, without whose cooperation the Jews would have been powerless. The words συμφυλετῶν, Ἰουδαίων denote rather national than religious limits. Thus συμφυλετῶν would include such Jews as were free citizens of Thessalonica. See Paley, Horae Paul. ix. 5.

Upon the word the grammarians remark that the earlier writers adopt the simple forms in this and similar cases, e.g. φυλέτης, πολίτης, δημότης

(Arist. *Av.* 367 ὄντε ξυγγενῆ καὶ φυλέτα), and that the compounds συμφυλέτης, συμπολίτης, συνδημότης are of later introduction. This is true as a
general rule, but the word συμφυλέτης is apparently an exception, occurring in Isocr. *Panathen.* 27 (p. 263 A) if the reading be not doubtful.
See Lobeck, *Phryn.* pp. 172, 471, Herodian p. 471, ed. Lobeck, and the
note on Gal. i. 14 συνηλικιώτας.

καθὼς] is equivalent here to ἅπερ, and corresponds to τὰ αὐτὰ above,
'the same...as.' See Lobeck, *Phryn.* p. 426 sq., Kühner ii. p. 571.

15. What account can we give of this digression on the conduct of
the Jews, so unexpected and startling at first sight? What was the
impulse at work in the Apostle's mind? A ready answer to these
questions suggests itself in the circumstances of this period of his life.
At no other time probably did he suffer more from the hostility of the
Jews. They had driven him from Thessalonica, had tracked him out at
Berea, and expelled him thence, and they still continued their persecution
of him at Corinth on the occasion of the visit during which these Epistles
were written. They were to him therefore the embodiment of the
opposition to the Gospel, the very type of Antichrist himself.

τῶν καὶ τὸν Κύριον ἀποκτεινάντων κ.τ.λ.] *'who killed both the Lord Jesus
and the prophets.'* Καὶ before τὸν Κύριον couples it with καὶ τοὺς προφήτας.
The emphatic word from its position in the sentence is not τὸν Κύριον, as
is generally assumed, but Ἰησοῦν, 'they killed the Lord, for they killed
Jesus.' Compare St Peter's words in Acts ii. 36 ὅτι καὶ Κύριον αὐτὸν καὶ
Χριστὸν ἐποίησεν ὁ Θεὸς τοῦτον τὸν Ἰησοῦν ὃν ὑμεῖς ἐσταυρώσατε, where the
emphatic words are placed last; and above i. 10, where a like prominence
is given to the name.

καὶ τοὺς προφήτας] They are the same from first to last. They killed
the Lord Jesus in the end, as they had killed the prophets before Him,
in whose case at least they could not plead the excuse of ignorance
(Matt. xxiii. 29 sq.). Thus the parable of the Unjust Husbandmen
applies to them.

Tertullian (*adv. Marc.* v. 15) accuses Marcion of inserting ἰδίους in the
text before προφήτας ('*suos* adjectio haeretici') with the intent to show
that the prophets belonged not to the Church of Christ, but to the Jews.
Tertullian however is so reckless in his charges against Marcion, that
no stress can be laid upon this as a fact. The authority of the MSS. is
certainly in favour of omitting ἰδίους, and there is a tendency to the
insertion of the word elsewhere, e.g. iv. 11, Ephes. iv. 28 (where possibly
it may stand), v. 24. This is a transcriber's trick for the sake of precision, and is quite innocent of any doctrinal bias. See the note on
Col. iii. 18 τοῖς ἀνδράσιν, where again ἰδίοις is an unwarrantable insertion.

ἐκδιωξάντων] A.V. 'persecuted.' More than this, '*persecuted and
drove us out,*' stated generally, but doubtless with a special reference
(which would be caught up by his readers) to his expulsion from Thessalonica (Acts xvii. 5—10).

πᾶσιν ἀνθρώποις ἐναντίων] This expression at once recals the language of Tacitus (*Hist.* v. 5) speaking of the Jews 'adversus omnes alios hostile odium.' Nor is this a mere resemblance of expression, though the two phrases are not coextensive. The spirit in which Tacitus so describes them may be inferred from the account given by Juvenal (xiv. 103, 104) of this unfriendly race, which denied even the commonest offices of hospitality to strangers—'non monstrare vias eadem nisi sacra tenenti, Quaesitum ad fontem solos deducere verpos.' Comp. Philostr. *Vit. Apoll. Tyan.* v. 33 οἱ Ἰουδαῖοι βίον ἄμικτον εὑρόντες, καὶ οἷς μήτε κοινὴ πρὸς ἀνθρώπους τράπεζα μήτε σπονδαὶ μήτε εὐχαὶ μήτε θυσίαι πλέον ἀφεστᾶσιν ἡμῶν ἢ Σοῦσα κ.τ.λ., Diod. Sic. xxxiv. I τοὺς Ἰουδαίους μόνους ἁπάντων ἐθνῶν ἀκοινωνήτους εἶναι τῆς πρὸς ἄλλο ἔθνος ἐπιμιξίας καὶ πολεμίους ὑπολαμβάνειν πάντας κ.τ.λ. St Paul on the other hand views their hostility to mankind as exemplified in their opposing the extension of the Gospel to the Gentiles (see next note). But both the one and the other characteristic—their exclusiveness in the matter of spiritual privileges, and their selfish narrowness in the common things of life—were due to the same unloving and illiberal spirit, all the more odious in that it was a caricature and an unnatural outgrowth of the isolated purity of their old monotheism.

16.   κωλυόντων] '*in that they hinder us.*' This clause is most naturally taken as explanatory of πᾶσιν ἀνθρώποις ἐναντίων, otherwise it would have been τῶν κωλυόντων or καὶ κωλυόντων. This was the ground of the opposition of the Jews to St Paul as recorded in the Acts, elsewhere (xiii. 48 sq.), and at Thessalonica itself (xvii. 5 ζηλώσαντες δὲ οἱ Ἰουδαῖοι κ.τ.λ.).

λαλῆσαι ἵνα σωθῶσιν] is capable of two interpretations, either (1) 'to speak to them, to the end that they may be saved' or (2) 'to tell them to be saved,' as if the infinitive had been used. The latter, though not a classical usage of ἵνα, is quite legitimate in New Testament (see Winer, § xliv. p. 420 sq.), and in modern Greek its equivalent νὰ has displaced the infinitive in common use. Here however the former sense seems required to give force to the passage, and is borne out by corresponding passages in St Paul: e.g. 1 Cor. x. 33, where the same phrase occurs ; see also the note on v. 4.

ἀναπληρῶσαι] Not exactly equivalent to the simple verb πληρῶσαι, 'to fill the measure'; but 'to fill *up* the measure' of their sin, implying that the process of filling had already begun, drop after drop being poured into the cup of their guilt. Compare the LXX. of Gen. xv. 16, where the word is a translation of שָׁלֵם. On the other hand in Gal. vi. 2 ἀναπληρώσετε τὸν νόμον τοῦ Χριστοῦ the idea of completeness is uppermost ; see the note there.

εἰς τὸ ἀναπληρῶσαι] '*so as to fulfil.*' The preposition εἰς with the infinitive in the New Testament generally, it is true, signifies the purpose 'with a view to,' 'in order to,' but it sometimes expresses nothing more than the consequence 'so that.' Comp. e.g. 2 Cor. viii. 6 εἰς τὸ παρακαλέσαι ἡμᾶς Τίτον κ.τ.λ., and perhaps Hebr. xi. 3. We cannot therefore insist in this passage on the idea of a conscious intention on the part of the Jews, or even of a divine purpose overruling their conduct, though the latter is not an improbable interpretation either grammatically or theologically.

πάντοτε] 'at all times'; by the persecution of the prophets before Christ, by the persecution of Christ Himself, and by the persecution of His disciples after Him. Πάντοτε is condemned by the Atticists; see Lobeck, *Phryn.* p. 103, Moeris, p. 319.

ἔφθασεν δὲ] This verb occurs seven times in the New Testament. In five of these the construction is φθάνειν ἐπὶ or εἰς, the exceptional cases being 1 Thess. iv. 15, 2 Cor. x. 14, and in all seven passages but 1 Thess. iv. 15 φθάνειν means 'to arrive.' The original notion of anticipation or surprise is sometimes weak in the New Testament, as 2 Cor. x. 14, Phil. iii. 16; but here it may well bear that meaning, compare also Matt. xii. 28.

It is doubtful whether ἔφθακεν or ἔφθασεν is the right reading. The perfect is easier of explanation, denoting a judgment which had already arrived but was not yet completed. The aorist however has somewhat the stronger support from the manuscripts, and is usually explained either (1) as a prophetic anticipation, but there is no prophetic colouring in the diction here; or (2) as a reference to the foreordained counsels of God, but there is nothing in the expression itself, or the context, to lead to such an interpretation. If therefore we prefer this reading, it is better to adopt (3) the simple explanation that it denotes merely past time, without any thought of the continuance of the action itself or of its effects (the notion conveyed by the perfect), such continuance however not being negatived, and in fact it must from the circumstances of the case be understood. There may however be a special reference to the act of infatuation on the part of the Jews evidenced by slaying the Saviour. Their conduct towards our Lord may well be regarded by the Apostle as the beginning of the end. In the *Test. xii Patr.* Levi 6 the passage is quoted with the reading ἔφθασεν.

ἡ ὀργή] See the note on i. 10, and compare ἡ ἡμέρα (om. ἐκείνη), 1 Thess. v. 4, Heb. x. 25.

εἰς τέλος] 'to the uttermost.' This meaning of εἰς τέλος is indeed unsupported elsewhere in the New Testament, where apparently it always signifies 'to the last,' 'for ever,' as John xiii. 1; comp. Ignat. *Ephes.* 14 ἐάν τις εὑρεθῇ εἰς τέλος. It is however frequent in the LXX. (e.g. Ps. xii. 1), and elsewhere, e.g. Ep. Barnabas, § 19. 11 εἰς τέλος μισήσεις τὸν πονηρόν, Hermas, *Vis.* 3. 10. 5 ἱλαρὰ εἰς τέλος. The sense 'at last' would be appropriate here, 'at last they were overtaken in the midst of their wickedness'; but the only biblical passage quoted in support of this meaning (Luke xviii. 5) is capable of another interpretation. For the sentiment comp. Wisdom xix. 1 τοῖς δὲ ἀσεβέσι μέχρι τέλους ἀνελεήμων θυμὸς ἐπέστη.

What was this divine judgment, which the Apostle speaks of as

having already fallen on the Jews? We might be tempted to think that
he foretold the final overthrow of the nation and the destruction of their
city and temple. But this is an inadequate explanation. There is no
sign of any kind that the inspiration of the Apostle here assumes a
directly predictive character. There is no prophetic colouring in the
passage. On the contrary, he spoke of some stern reality which was
already working before his eyes : and even to one not gifted with an
Apostle's prophetic insight, yet endowed with average moral sensibilities,
there was enough in the actual condition of this nation to lead him to
regard them as suffering under a blow of divine retribution. There were
the actual physical evils, under which they were groaning. There was
the disorganization of their internal polity. There was their utter disregard of all moral distinctions, to which their own historian Josephus
draws attention. There was above all their infatuated opposition to the
Gospel, than which no more decisive proof of judicial blindness, or it
might be of conscious and headlong precipitation into ruin, could be
conceived by the Christian mind. The maxim 'Quem deus vult perdere,
prius dementat' is not a Christian maxim; but it has a Christian counterpart, in that those who 'like not to retain God in their knowledge, God
gives over to a reprobate mind' (Rom. i. 28). God's wrath then was
no longer suspended; it had already fallen on the once hallowed, but
now accursed, race. We may suppose moreover that the prophecies of
our Lord relating to the destruction of Jerusalem were floating before
St Paul's mind—prophecies dim and vague indeed and, we may fairly
assume, not fully understood even by St Paul—but sufficiently portentous
to arouse fearful anticipations. They would give new meaning and
importance to the actual evils of which he was an eyewitness. The end
was not yet, but the beginning of the end was come. For a similar
anticipation compare i. 10.

iv. *Anxiety of St Paul on their behalf, until reassured by the
report brought by Timothy* (ii. 17—iii. 10).

17. ἡμεῖς δὲ] '*But we.*' To return from this digression about the
Jews (vv. 15, 16) and speak once more of ourselves.

ἀπορφανισθέντες] '*bereft of and separated from*'; as children deprived
of their parents.

The word ὀρφανός (Latin 'orbus'), though most frequently applied to
the bereavement of a child who has lost a parent, is in itself quite general
in meaning, denoting the loss of any friend or relation and including
the bereavement of a parent. Probably however here the best and most
touching sense is to render as above, carrying out the Apostle's metaphor
of νήπιοι ii. 7 and to translate, 'we are like children who have lost their
parents.' See Æsch. *Choeph.* 249, where the word occurs in this sense.
In any case, the aspect of the word here would not be perceptibly influenced by ἀδελφοί; see above ver. 9.

πρὸς καιρὸν ὥρας] '*for the measure of a season*,' i.e. for a brief period. This is a stronger expression than πρὸς καιρὸν and πρὸς ὥραν, both of which phrases are found in St Paul (1 Cor. vii. 5 ; 2 Cor. vii. 8, Gal. ii. 5, Phil. 15). On καιρὸς see the note on v. 1. The word ὥρα is connected with ὅρος, denoting properly 'a limited time.' The signification of an hour is of comparatively late introduction, dating from about the second century B.C.

προσώπῳ οὐ καρδίᾳ] is parenthetical, and qualifies the expression ἀπορφανισθέντες, 'though in one sense we are always with you': comp. 1 Cor. v. 3 ἀπὼν τῷ σώματι, παρὼν δὲ τῷ πνεύματι, and Col. ii. 1, 2, 5 (with the notes).

περισσοτέρως] here, as always in St Paul, is strictly comparative, referring to ἀπορφανισθέντες. 'Separation, so far from weakening our desire to see you, has only increased it. When we could see you day by day, our yearning was not so intense.' On the word itself see Gal. i. 14 (with the note).

18. διότι] '*because*.' This is the best supported reading and is generally translated 'therefore,' as if διό : comp. 1 Pet. ii. 6, where also it is the best supported reading. But it is questionable whether it can bear this meaning, though Fritzsche on Rom. i. 18 (1. p. 57) adopts this view, translating it 'hanc ob rem.' Elsewhere in the New Testament, as always in classical writers, the word has one of three meanings, either (1) '*on what account*,' (2) '*because*,' or (3) '*that*,' but never 'therefore.' This distinction from διό is due to the indefiniteness of ὅτι. If διότι then be the right reading, it must be taken 'because,' i.e. 'in proof whereof,' 'that.' Διότι in the sense of ὅτι 'that' occurs in several spurious documents in Demosthenes, e.g. de Corona pp. 279, 284, 290.

ἐγὼ μὲν Παῦλος κ.τ.λ.] 'I Paul at least desired it more than once, whatever may be the feelings of Silvanus and Timotheus.' The suppressed clause with δὲ might have run οἱ δὲ ἄλλοι περὶ ἑαυτῶν λεγέτωσαν. For this suppression of the second member compare Col. ii. 23 ἅτινά ἐστιν λόγον μὲν ἔχοντα σοφίας (with the note). Thus ἐγώ is not coextensive with ἡμεῖς. The genius of the language will not admit it. The words ἐγὼ μὲν Παῦλος then do not simply give the subject of ἠθελήσαμεν, for then μὲν would be robbed of any meaning, but they explain and qualify the general assertion 'we desired'; and the following words καὶ ἅπαξ καὶ δὶς may be taken, not with ἠθελήσαμεν, but with ἐγὼ μὲν Παῦλος, for the order shows that the μὲν clause includes them. Accordingly the comma in the E. V. after 'Paul' should be omitted. On the whole question of St Paul's supposed use of the epistolary plural, see above, ii. 4.

καὶ ἅπαξ καὶ δὶς] Not necessarily 'twice only,' but '*more than once*,' '*again and again*.' Comp. Phil. iv. 16 (with the note).

ἐνέκοψεν] On this word see the note on Gal. v. 7. The same metaphor is employed below, iii. 11 κατευθύναι τὴν ὁδὸν ἡμῶν.

ὁ Σατανᾶς] with a genitive Σατανᾶ, is the form always found in the New Testament, except possibly 2 Cor. xii. 7, where some manuscripts read Σατᾶν indeclinable. Theophil. ad Aut. ii. 28, 29 has Σατᾶν and Σατανᾶς in two successive chapters. Σατᾶν is the pure Hebrew form שָׂטָן, Σατανᾶς seems to be derived from the Aramaic שָׂטָנָא. The shorter form is found in I Kings xi. 14, the longer form in Ecclus. xxi. 27.

It is idle to enquire what was the nature of this hindrance. The most likely conjecture refers it to the opposition of the Jews. Or it might have been some illness, with which the Apostle was afflicted. Or again many other solutions are conceivable. The 'temptation in the flesh' alluded to elsewhere (Gal. iv. 14) refers to the same period in St Paul's life. We are tempted at once to connect it with the thorn in the flesh which St Paul represents as 'an angel of Satan given to buffet him' (2 Cor. xii. 7): But Satan works in many ways ; and even if we were sure that the hindrance was the same in both cases, we are still far from a result, for the 'thorn in the flesh' is an expression which itself admits of more than one explanation. See the note on St Paul's infirmity in the flesh (*Galatians*, p. 186 sq.).

19. **χαρά, στέφανος**] He uses similar language in addressing the other great Church of Macedonia, which he regarded with even greater affection, Phil. iv. 1 ἀδελφοί μου ἀγαπητοὶ καὶ ἐπιπόθητοι, χαρὰ καὶ στέφανός μου. For the ideas conveyed by the word στέφανος and its distinction from διάδημα, see the note on the passage, and add to the references there given 2 Tim. iv. 7, 8, *Ep. Vienn. et Lugd.* ἐχρῆν γοῦν τοὺς γενναίους ἀθλητὰς…ἀπολαβεῖν τὸν μέγαν τῆς ἀφθαρσίας στέφανον, and a little below of Blandina μέγαν καὶ ἀκαταγώνιστον ἀθλητὴν Χριστὸν ἐνδεδυμένη…καὶ δι' ἀγῶνος τὸν τῆς ἀφθαρσίας στεψαμένη στέφανον (Routh, *R. S.* I. pp. 309, 311).

ἐλπὶς ἢ χαρὰ κ.τ.λ.] St Paul is not speaking here of the prospect of a reward or of any selfish rejoicing or triumph. The Thessalonians are his hope and joy, and the crown of his glory, as a child is of its parent. So Chrysostom : τίς οὐκ ἂν ἐπὶ τοσαύτῃ πολυπαιδίᾳ καὶ εὐπαιδίᾳ ἀγάλλοιτο ;

στέφανος καυχήσεως] A phrase borrowed from the LXX. Ezek. xvi. 12, xxiii. 42, Prov. xvi. 31.

καυχήσεως] 'wherein we boast, the subject of our boasting.'

ἢ οὐχὶ καὶ ὑμεῖς] The E. V. following the vulg. ('nonne') takes ἢ as an interrogative particle ; and this is so far unobjectionable that it fulfils the conditions of ἢ interrogative in that it is preceded by another interrogative. But this interpretation makes no account of the καὶ. Hence it is better to consider ἢ here as a disjunctive particle, 'or (if others are our joy, etc.), are not ye *also*,' in other words, 'if you are not our joy, no one else is.' So Chrysostom : οὐ γὰρ εἶπεν 'ὑμεῖς' ἁπλῶς ἀλλὰ 'καὶ ὑμεῖς,' μετὰ τῶν ἄλλων.

ἔμπροσθεν τοῦ Κυρίου κ.τ.λ.] refers to the whole of the preceding sentence τίς γὰρ…ὑμεῖς, i.e. 'in the presence of the Lord, when all things will appear in their true light.'

ἐν τῇ αὐτοῦ παρουσίᾳ] '*at His advent.*' For παρουσία see the note on 2 Thess. ii. 8.

20. **ὑμεῖς γὰρ**] '*Yes truly, ye are.*' For this use of γὰρ introducing a reply, comp. Acts xvi. 37 οὐ γὰρ ἀλλὰ κ.τ.λ., I Cor. ix. 10, and see Winer, § liii. p. 559.

CHAPTER III

1. Διό] '*On which account*,' i.e. 'on account of this very fervent desire, which I was unable to gratify.'

μηκέτι] The frequent use of μή with a participle in later authors, where in writers of the classical epoch we should have found οὐ, is too marked to escape notice. We are not however justified on this account in saying that later writers are incorrect in their use of the negatives. The distinction of οὐ as the absolute and μή as the relative, dependent or conditional negative, is always observed, at least in the New Testament. Μή for instance is never used in a direct, absolute statement. But in participial clauses it is most frequently possible to state the matter in either way, either absolutely, or in its relation to the action described by the finite verb of the sentence. Here, for instance, οὐκέτι στέγοντες might easily stand, in which case the sense would be, 'we could no longer contain and we thought fit' ; whereas μηκέτι στέγοντες is 'as being able no longer to contain, we thought fit.' This phenomenon of the displacement of οὐ by μή in the later Greek may perhaps be explained by the general tendency in the decline of a language to greater refining and subtlety in contrast to the simplicity of the earlier syntax. In the earlier stages of a language, and in languages whose growth has been for some cause arrested (the Hebrew, for instance, and in a still greater degree the Chinese), as in the talk of children, the sentences consist of a number of absolute, finite statements strung together, with little or no attempt to express their relation or interdependence by any grammatical expedient. As the syntax is developed, it is enabled to express these relations with more or less nicety. In the case before us the earliest form of the sentence would be οὐκέτι ἐστέγομεν καὶ ηὐδοκήσαμεν, which simply states the two facts side by side without expressing any connexion : the next advance is οὐκέτι στέγοντες ηὐδοκήσαμεν, which synchronizes the two facts, yet does not state any other relation but that of time, though it may suggest such. At this stage the language has arrived in the classical period. The third and later form is μηκέτι στέγοντες ηὐδοκήσαμεν, which not only synchronizes the two facts, but also expresses that 'the inability to contain' was a motive which determined the 'determination.' See Winer § lv. p. 593 sq., Madvig, *Syntax* § 207.

στέγοντες] The verb στέγειν 'to cover,' 'to shelter,' means primarily either 'to keep in' or 'to keep out' (compare the expression 'to be water-tight, air-tight'); and, like the Latin 'defendere,' takes an accusative either (1) of the thing protected or (2) of the thing against which the shelter is extended. It thus gets two different meanings, (a) 'to protect, contain,' (b) 'to ward off, keep out.' Thus a tower is said στέγειν πόλιν (Soph. Œd. Col. 15), and also στέγειν δόρυ (Æsch. Sept. c. Theb. 216). In the same way the English word 'leak' has two senses 'to let water in,' and 'to let water out.' To one or other of these leading ideas all the subordinate uses of στέγειν, either with the case or absolutely (i.e. with the accusative suppressed as here), may be referred. In the passage before us στέγοντες can be taken with almost equal propriety in either of these two meanings : (1) 'no longer able to keep our feelings tight in': comp. Plato, Gorg. p. 493 C, where the soul is compared to a sieve unable to hold anything in by reason of its fickle and forgetful nature (οὐ δυναμένην στέγειν δι' ἀπιστίαν τε καὶ λήθην, where see Thompson's note, and comp. Ecclus. viii. 17 of the fool οὐ δυνήσεται λόγον στέξαι); or (2) 'no longer able to bear up against the pressure of this desire.' On the whole however the usage of the word in later Greek seems decidedly in favour of the sense 'to keep off,' 'to bear up under' and so 'to endure,' see Philo in Flacc. § 9 p. 526 (ed. Mangey) μηκέτι στέγειν δυνάμενοι τὰς ἐνδείας : and this agrees with St Paul's use elsewhere, 1 Cor. ix. 12 πάντα στέγομεν, which must, and 1 Cor. xiii. 7 πάντα στέγει which may bear this meaning.

εὐδοκήσαμεν] 'we,' referring to St Paul and Silvanus : see the note above (ii. 4) on St Paul's use of the plural in his letters.

καταλειφθῆναι] 'to be left behind,' more definite than λειφθῆναι. In order to give its proper significance to the compound verb, we must suppose that Timotheus had joined St Paul at Athens, though in the Acts (xvii. 15) we only read of St Paul's expecting him there, not of his actual arrival; and had been despatched thence to Thessalonica. If Timotheus had been sent to Thessalonica from Berea, without seeing the Apostle at all at Athens, the proper word would have been μένειν or at most λειφθῆναι. On the probable movements of the party see the next note.

2. ἐπέμψαμεν] 'we,' i.e. again Paul and Silvanus. So Bengel rightly. In order to reconcile the expressions here with the account in the Acts, the occurrences may be supposed to have happened in the following order. St Paul is waiting at Athens for Silvanus and Timotheus, having left them at Berea, and charged them by message to join him without delay (Acts xvii. 15, 16). They join him at Athens. Paul and Silvanus despatch Timotheus to Thessalonica (1 Thess. iii. 2). Silvanus is despatched on some other mission to Macedonia, perhaps to Berea. St Paul goes forward to Corinth (Acts xviii. 1). After he had been in Corinth some time, Silvanus and Timotheus return to him from Mace-donia (Acts xviii. 4, 5). Thereupon the Apostle writes from Corinth to the Thessalonians, in the joint names of himself, Silvanus and Timotheus.

Though this mission of Timotheus was the joint action of Paul and Silvanus, yet St Paul, as might be expected, was the prime mover and most urgent promoter of it. See ver. 5 κἀγὼ and the note there.

τὸν ἀδελφὸν ἡμῶν] The same phrase is also used of Timotheus, as distinguished from ἀπόστολος, in the salutations of 2 Corinthians, Colossians, and Philemon, and by the author of the Epistle to the Hebrews (xiii. 23). He was not therefore, it would seem, an 'Apostle,' a term which, while applying to others besides St Paul and the Twelve (Acts xiv. 14), would appear to be restricted to those who had received their commission directly from the Lord. See the note 'on the name and office of an Apostle' in *Galatians*, p. 92 sq.

συνεργὸν τοῦ Θεοῦ] 'a fellow worker with God,' as the usage of συνεργὸς with the genitive elsewhere requires, e.g. Rom. xvi. 3, 9, 21, Phil. ii. 25, iv. 3, Philem. 1, 24. The same expression occurs in 1 Cor. iii. 9 Θεοῦ γάρ ἐσμεν συνεργοί. It was so startling however that the copyists here have tampered with the text in order to get rid of it, some (as B) omitting τοῦ Θεοῦ, others (as ℵ) substituting διάκονον for συνεργόν.

παρακαλέσαι] Not to 'comfort,' as E.V.; but rather to 'exhort' or 'encourage,' for the opposition to σαίνεσθαι (ver. 3) requires this meaning. 'We sent Timotheus,' the Apostle explains, 'not only to confirm you in your present conduct (στηρίξαι), but also to exhort you to fresh efforts (παρακαλέσαι).' See the note on ii. 11.

ὑπὲρ τῆς πίστεως ὑμῶν] 'for the establishment, furtherance of your faith.' Here, as in many other passages, the less usual ὑπὲρ has been altered by the scribes into περί. Though ὑπὲρ in the later stages of the language approaches nearer to περὶ in meaning, it does not (at least in the Greek of the New Testament) entirely lose its proper sense of 'interest in.' See the note on Gal. i. 4 περὶ τῶν ἁμαρτιῶν.

3. τὸ μηδένα σαίνεσθαι] The reading of this passage presents some difficulty. Τοῦ, τῷ and τὸ are all possible constructions with the infinitive —the *genitive* expressing the motive, 'with a view to,' the *dative* expressing the instrument, 'by means of,' the *accusative* expressing the end or result, 'that so as a consequence.' This distinction is in accordance with the well-known characteristics of the three cases in Greek, motion from, rest at, motion towards. In the present instance the reading of the Textus Receptus τῷ, rejected on the ground of MS. authority, is moreover incapable of any satisfactory grammatical explanation. If it could stand at all, it must mean 'in no one's being moved,' a sort of dative of the manner or means of accomplishment. On the other hand, both τὸ and τοῦ give good sense, the difference consisting in this that the genitive views the result definitely as the motive of the action, which the former does not. Manuscript evidence however is decisive in favour of τὸ μηδένα σαίνεσθαι. The expression is sometimes explained as in apposition with τὸ στηρίξαι κ.τ.λ. and so governed by εἰς. But it is more correctly taken as dependent on the clause εἰς τὸ στηρίξαι...ὑμῶν, or perhaps better the whole

sentence from ἐπέμψαμεν...ὑμῶν describing the result or consequence. Translate 'to the end that,' and compare iv. 6 τὸ μὴ ὑπερβαίνειν with the note.

σαίνεσθαι] '*be led astray, allured from the right path.*' Σαίνειν (derived from σάω, σείω, see Blomfield on *Sept. c. Theb.* 378 and Donalds. *Cratyl.* § 473) is originally 'to shake or wag,' e.g. Hes. *Theog.* 771 οὐρῇ τε καὶ οὔασιν of a dog : hence it is used especially of a dog wagging the tail (Hom. *Od.* xvi. 4, 6, 10, comp. the words σαίνουρος, σαινουρὶς in Hesych.), and frequently even with an accusative of a person 'to wag the tail at, to fawn upon.' Hence σαίνειν gets to signify 'to fondle, caress, flatter, coax, wheedle, allure, fascinate, deceive' (Æsch. *Choeph.* 186, Pind. *Olymp.* iv. 7), and even 'to avoid' (Æsch. *Sept. c. Theb.* 378, 701). This seems to be the meaning here; 'that no one, in the midst of these troubles, desert the rough path of the truth, drawn aside and allured by the enticing prospect of an easier life.' This is the temptation alluded to in ver. 5. Observe also it is ἐν ταῖς θλίψεσιν ταύταις, not ὑπὸ τῶν θλίψεων τούτων. Comp. *Mart. Ign.* 9 (p. 356, ed. Dressel) πολὺς ἦν ὑποσαίνων καὶ καταψῶν said of Trajan.

On the other hand it is taken by some in the sense 'to be disturbed, disquieted' (e.g. Chrysostom and Theophylact θορυβεῖσθαι), with a reference to its root σείειν ; but the history of the word, showing that its derivation was entirely lost sight of in its later usage, is quite averse to this interpretation, nor can any passages be produced where it bears this meaning. Those commonly adduced may be otherwise interpreted, e.g. Diog. Laert. VIII. 41 σαινόμενοι τοῖς λεγομένοις ἐδάκρυον καὶ ὤμωζον, cited by Ellicott from Elsner, where the sense of 'under the influence of' is adequate. Again in Eur. *Rhes.* 55 the idea is rather of encouragement, or at least attraction, than of disquietude, and so Soph. *Antig.* 1214. Lachmann reads ἀσαίνεσθαι in the sense of 'to be disgusted,' a verb connected with ἀσάομαι from ἄση fastidium (see Steph. *Thes.* s. v. ἀσάομαι). Hesychius explains ἀσαίνων as ὑβρίζων, λυπῶν, and ἀσαίνεσθαι as λυπεῖσθαι. See also Cobet, *Præf. ad Cod. Vat.* p. xc. Severianus in Cramer's Catena explains as τὸ μηδένα ξενίζεσθαι. Theodore of Mopsuestia is here translated 'cedere.'

ἐν ταῖς θλίψεσιν ταύταις] '*in the midst of these afflictions which befal us and you alike.*'

αὐτοὶ] i.e. 'without my repeating it.'

εἰς τοῦτο] i.e. τὸ θλίβεσθαι.

κείμεθα] '*we are appointed, ordained*' ; see the note on Phil. i. 16 κεῖμαι.

4. πρὸς ὑμᾶς] The use of πρὸς with the accusative is not uncommon after verbs implying rest ; comp. 2 Thess. ii. 5, Gal. i. 18, 1 Cor. xvi. 6, Mark vi. 3.

ὅτι μέλλομεν θλίβεσθαι] 'we are about to,' or perhaps better, for the οἴδατε seems to require it, 'are destined to suffer persecution.' Μέλλομεν is used rather than ἐμέλλομεν, because the Apostle's words are given in the oratio recta, for which we are prepared by ὅτι. See e.g. Acts xv. 5 ἐξανέστησάν τινες λέγοντες ὅτι δεῖ περιτέμνειν and other examples given by Winer (§ xli. p. 376).

For the whole passage compare Acts xiv. 22, where it is said of Paul and Barnabas ἐπιστηρίζοντες τὰς ψυχὰς τῶν μαθητῶν, παρακαλοῦντες ἐμμένειν τῇ πίστει καὶ ὅτι διὰ πολλῶν θλίψεων δεῖ ἡμᾶς εἰσελθεῖν εἰς τὴν βασιλείαν τοῦ Θεοῦ. Observe here, beyond the general resemblance to the passage in the Thessalonian Epistle, the occurrence of the same words (ἐπι)στηρίζειν, παρακαλεῖν, πίστις, θλίψεις, and of ὅτι introducing the direct narrative in the same way as here. The completeness of the parallel is an undesigned coincidence of no ordinary importance. And it does not stand alone. It recurs, with more or less marked emphasis, wherever St Luke reports St Paul's words, showing that he repeats them with the accuracy of an ear-witness. In this case, as the Apostle tells us in this verse, the language employed had been often used to the Thessalonian converts; St Paul had dwelt on this topic (ὅτε πρὸς ὑμᾶς ἦμεν προελέγομεν).

μέλλομεν] i.e. all Christians, as the parallel passage just cited shows.

καθὼς καὶ ἐγένετο καὶ οἴδατε] 'as indeed it came to pass and ye have learnt from bitter experience.' It is better not to take καὶ...καὶ as correlative 'both...and,' because that would imply a greater distinction between ἐγένετο and οἴδατε than the sense of the passage warrants.

5. διὰ τοῦτο] i.e. 'because these persecutions had already befallen you.' κἀγὼ] 'I on my part,' seeing what you were suffering. Compare the note on ii. 13, where καὶ ἡμεῖς is used in the same way. Κἀγὼ here is not intended to limit the plural of ver. 1 μηκέτι στέγοντες to St Paul himself, but simply to give greater prominence to the part which he took in despatching Timothy, though Silvanus acquiesced in and sympathized with the project. Exactly in the same spirit he adds ἐγὼ μὲν Παῦλος καὶ ἅπαξ καὶ δὶς after the plural ἠθελήσαμεν in ii. 18.

μήπως ἐπείρασεν...καὶ...γένηται] For the change of moods compare Gal. ii. 2 μήπως εἰς κενὸν τρέχω ἢ ἔδραμον, where τρέχω is the subjunctive, see the note there. The indicative ἐπείρασεν describes a past action, now inevitable, which St Paul could not have affected in any way; γένηται a possible future consequence of that past action, hence is strictly a hypothetical mood. It is unnecessarily harsh to assign different meanings to μήπως in the two clauses, as though it meant 'an forte,' 'to see whether' when applied to ἐπείρασεν, and 'ne forte' 'to prevent by any chance' as applied to γένηται (Fritzsche, Opusc. p. 176). Comp. Eur. Phœn. 92 ἐπίσχες ὡς ἂν προὐξερευνήσω στίβον, Μή τις πολιτῶν ἐν τρίβῳ φαντάζεται, Κἀμοὶ μὲν ἔλθῃ φαῦλος, ὡς δούλῳ, ψόγος, Σοὶ δ' ὡς ἀνάσσῃ. Here too the first clause represents something out of the control of the speaker, the second a contingency still future, which could be guarded against. See too Arist. Eccles. 495 and Winer § lvi. p. 633 sq.

εἰς κενὸν γένηται] The expression εἰς κενὸν is not unfrequent in St Paul, occurring twice with his favourite metaphor of τρέχειν (Gal. ii. 2, Phil. ii. 16), and three times elsewhere (2 Cor. vi. 1 εἰς κενὸν δέξασθαι, Phil. ii. 16 εἰς κενὸν ἐκοπίασα and in the present passage). It is found in the LXX. (Is. xxix. 8, xlv. 18, Jer. vi. 29, xviii. 15, Mic. i. 14, Hab. ii. 3), especially of fruitless labour (Job xxxix. 16, Is. lxv. 23, Jer. li. 53), and occurs in post-classical Greek, e.g. Lucian, *Epigr.* 32 εἰς κενὸν ἐξέχεας, Heliodor. x. 30. For a similar weakening of εἰς in adverbial expressions compare εἰς κοινόν, εἰς καιρόν (Bernhardy, *Synt.* V. 2, p. 221).

6. ἄρτι δὲ ἐλθόντος Τιμοθέου] Ἄρτι denotes simultaneity and may apply either (1) to the actual moment of reference, 'at this very time,' i.e. 'just now' or 'just then' (as the case may be), e.g. Matth. ix. 18; 1 Cor. xiii. 12; or (2) to a preceding moment, 'a short time ago' or 'a short time before'; but never (3) to a future time, 'a short time hence or after.' See Lobeck, *Phryn.* p. 18. This limitation pointed out by Phrynichus is strictly observed in the New Testament. Ellicott (*ad loc.*) appears to confine the first of the two meanings given above to later Greek; but the word is not unfrequently used of present time by classical writers, e.g. Pind. *Pyth.* iv. 158 σὸν δ᾽ ἄνθος ἥβας ἄρτι κυμαίνει, Æsch. *Sept. c. Theb.* 534 στείχει δ᾽ ἴουλος ἄρτι διὰ παρηίδων, Soph. *Aj.* 9, occasionally with the addition of νῦν, e.g. Arist. *Lys.* 1008 ἄρτι νυνὶ μανθάνω.

It is more natural here to take ἄρτι with ἐλθόντος, which immediately follows, than with παρεκλήθημεν, which is far distant and has moreover an 'adjunct' (Ellicott) of its own in διὰ τοῦτο.

It seems to be generally assumed that ἄρτι ἐλθόντος Τιμοθέου must mean 'Timotheus having arrived not long ago,' i.e. 'not long before the present time, when I am writing this letter,' thus furnishing a chrono-logical datum. But may not it signify 'Timotheus having just arrived' (comp. μεταξύ, ἅμα etc.), i.e. 'as soon as Timotheus arrived we were comforted'; for ἄρτι need not be 'a short time ago' referring to the actual present, but may also be 'a short time *before*' in relation to some other point of time (here that of παρεκλήθημεν) to which everything is referred. Cf. Philo, *Vit. Moys.* i. § 9 (II. p. 88, *ed.* Mangey) ἄρτι πρῶτον ἀφιγμένος ἂν ἐσπούδασεν (cited by Lobeck, l. c.) and see also Rost and Palm, s. v. And this seems to me the more natural interpretation, as the prominent time of reference in the passage is that of παρεκλήθημεν. Perhaps a feeling of this awkwardness has led to the substitution of παρακεκλήμεθα in A and one or two cursives.

εὐαγγελισαμένου] This word is not elsewhere used by St Paul in any other sense than that of preaching the Gospel; and rarely by any other New Testament writer (Luke i. 19 is an exception). Chrysostom remarks on this passage οὐκ εἶπεν ἀπαγγείλαντος, ἀλλ᾽ εὐαγγελισαμένου· τοσοῦτον ἀγαθὸν ἡγεῖτο τὴν ἐκείνων βεβαίωσιν καὶ τὴν ἀγάπην.

τὴν πίστιν καὶ τὴν ἀγάπην] i.e. yours was not a speculative, intellectual faith only, but a working principle of love: comp. Gal. v. 6 πίστις δι᾽ ἀγάπης ἐνεργουμένη.

ἀγαθὴν] 'that ye retain a kindly remembrance of us always,' for this seems to be the force of ἀγαθήν: comp. 1 Pet. ii. 18, Tit. ii. 5, and Rom. v. 7, where the point of the sentence seems to depend on this sense of ἀγαθός (see the note on this last passage).

ἐπιποθοῦντες] Stronger than ποθοῦντες: for though the preposition is not strictly intensive, but points out the direction (e.g. Ps. xlii. 1 ἐπιποθεῖ ἡ ἔλαφος ἐπὶ τὰς πηγὰς τῶν ὑδάτων, and see Fritzsche on Rom. i. 11), still the very expression of this direction 'yearning after' has the same effect as an intensive preposition. The simple words πόθος, ποθεῖν etc. do not occur in the New Testament, see the notes on Phil. i. 8, ii. 26.

7. διὰ τοῦτο] i.e. 'on account of this good news.'

ἀνάγκῃ καὶ θλίψει] The same metaphor underlies both of these words; ἀνάγκη (a word akin to ἄγχω, 'angor,' 'anxious,' 'Angst,' etc.) 'the choking, pressing care' and θλίψις 'the crushing trouble.' But ἀνάγκη is especially applied to physical privations, while θλίψις refers to persecution, and generally to positive sufferings inflicted from without. The inverted order of the words in the Textus Receptus, though insufficiently supported, is in accordance with 2 Cor. vi. 4, where see Stanley's note. On the difference between θλίψις and another kindred word στενοχωρία, see Trench, N. T. Syn. § lv. The two latter words are perhaps to be distinguished as the temporary and the continuous. Θλίψις, though extremely common in the LXX., occurs very rarely in classical writers even of a late date, and in these few passages has its literal meaning. The same want in the religious vocabulary, which gave currency to θλίψις, also created 'tribulatio' as its Latin equivalent. On the accent of θλίψις see Lipsius, Gramm. Unters. p. 35.

8. νῦν ζῶμεν] 'For now that we have received good tidings of your faith and love, we live, if only you stand firm, do not fall off from your present conversation, as thus reported to us.' Or the meaning of νῦν may be 'now, this being so'; for in a case like this it is almost impossible to distinguish the temporal sense of νῦν ('now') from the ethical ('under these circumstances'). The one meaning shades off imperceptibly into the other.

ζῶμεν] 'we live once more' i.e. in spite of this distress and affliction. In his outward trial 'he died daily' (1 Cor. xv. 31), but the faith of his converts inspired him with new life. Compare Horace, Epist. I. 10. 8 'vivo ac regno.'

στήκετε] 'stand fast': comp. Phil. i. 27, iv. 1, Gal. v. 1. Στήκειν, a later form derived from the perfect ἕστηκα, and not found earlier than the New Testament, is a shade stronger than ἑστάναι, involving an idea of fixity— 'stehen bleiben,' not 'stehen' simply. This idea however is not always very prominent; see Mark xi. 25 ὅταν στήκετε προσευχόμενοι, the only passage out of St Paul in the New Testament where the word occurs, unless, as is probable, ἕστηκεν is to be read for ἕστηκεν in John viii. 44 ἐν τῇ ἀληθείᾳ οὐκ ἕστηκεν. The reading στήκετε (for στήκητε) is generally

regarded as a solecism, but it certainly has overwhelming manuscript
authority here and in other passages (Acts viii. 31, Luke xix. 40, 1 John
v. 15), and ἐὰν seems certainly to be found with an indicative in later
writers, and very probably the usage may have come in before this time:
see Winer § xli. p. 369, and on the similar use of ὅταν with the indicative
§ xlii. p. 388.

St Paul speaks with some hesitation here 'if so be ye stand fast.'
Their faith was not complete (ver. 10). There was enough in the fact
that they had been so recently converted, enough in the turn which
their thoughts had recently taken, absorbed so entirely in the contemplation of the future state, to make the Apostle alarmed lest their faith
should prove only impulsive and transitory. Such appears to be the
connexion of the thought with what follows.

9. τίνα γὰρ] 'I call it *life*, for it is our highest blessing. There is
nothing for which we have greater reason to thank God, nothing for
which our gratitude must give a more inadequate return.'

ἀνταποδοῦναι] '*to give back as an equivalent*'—not 'to repay' simply
(ἀποδοῦναι) but 'to recompense.' Comp. Rom. xii. 17 μηδενὶ κακὸν ἀντὶ
κακοῦ ἀποδιδόντες with xii. 19 ἐμοὶ ἐκδίκησις ἐγὼ ἀνταποδώσω, where the
words in the E. V. would be better if interchanged. The ἀντὶ is important, for it implies the adequacy of the return. 'What sufficient
thanks can we repay?' ἀνταπόδοσις is 'retaliation, exact restitution, the
giving back as much as you have received.' Compare especially Arist.
Eth. Nic. ix. 2 (IX. p. 177, *ed.* Bekker), where we have δοῦναι, ἀποδοῦναι,
ἀνταποδοῦναι, and Herod. i. 18 οὗτοι δὲ τὸ ὅμοιον ἀνταποδιδόντες ἐτιμώρεον.
Philo marks the difference between δοῦναι and ἀποδοῦναι, *Vit. Moys.* iii.
§ 31, II. p. 172 (*ed.* Mangey). See also Luke xiv. 12, 14.

ᾗ χαίρομεν] As χαίρειν χαρὰν (Matt. ii. 10) is a construction equally
admissible with χαίρειν χαρᾷ (John iii. 29), we might take ᾗ as by attraction for ἥν. But the other construction (with the dative) is perhaps
better both as being simpler and more forcible, for in ᾗ χαίρομεν the verb
dwells anew upon the rejoicing, whereas ἣν χαίρομεν is little more expressive than ἣν ἔχομεν.

δι' ὑμᾶς] '*for your sakes*,' expressing a less selfish interest in the object
of their rejoicing than the more common phrase χαίρειν ἐπί τινι. Comp.
John iii. 29 χαρᾷ χαίρει διὰ τὴν φωνὴν τοῦ νυμφίου.

ἔμπροσθεν τοῦ Θεοῦ] 'Our rejoicing is of that pure and unselfish kind,
that we dare lay it bare before the searching eye of God.'

10. ὑπερεκπερισσοῦ] The expression ἐκ περισσοῦ or ἐκ περιττοῦ is
classical and occurs several times in Plato, 'abundantly, superfluously,'
e.g. *Protag.* 25 B ὁ γὰρ ὅμοιος ἡμῖν ὅμοια καὶ ποιήσει ὥστε ἐκ περιττοῦ
ᾑρήσεται. The compound ὑπερεκπερισσοῦ occurs once in the LXX., Dan.
iii. 23 (Theodot.) ἡ κάμινος ἐξεκαύθη ὑπερεκπερισσοῦ. The fondness of
St Paul for cumulative compounds in ὑπὲρ has often been noticed, and is
especially remarkable in the second chronological group of his Epistles,

written in what may be regarded as the most intense period of his life. Ellicott on Eph. iii. 20 draws attention to the fact that of the twenty-eight words compounded with ὑπέρ found in the New Testament, twenty-two occur in St Paul's Epistles, and twenty of them there alone. Instances are ὑπεραυξάνειν (2 Thess. i. 3), ὑπερλίαν (2 Cor. xi. 5), ὑπερνικᾶν (Rom. viii. 37), ὑπερπερισσεύειν (Rom. v. 20), ὑπερυψοῦν (Phil. ii. 9). See further on Rom. v. 20.

δεόμενοι] is not to be attached to τίνα εὐχαριστίαν δυνάμεθα (ver. 9), but to χαίρομεν, with which it is more easily connected in the train of thought which may be supposed to have passed through the Apostle's mind. The mention of his joy in his converts reminds him of the prayerful desire he has to see them face to face and to assist them. Thus the attachment of δεόμενοι to χαίρομεν is not of an argumentative kind, but is simply due to the association of ideas.

εἰς τὸ ἰδεῖν] 'to the end that': comp. 2 Thess. ii. 2 εἰς τὸ μὴ ταχέως σαλευθῆναι ὑμᾶς.

καταρτίσαι] The prominent idea in this word is 'fitting together'; and its force is seen more especially in two technical uses. (1) It signifies 'to reconcile factions,' so that a political umpire who adjusts differences between contending parties is called καταρτιστήρ; e.g. Herod. v. 28 ἡ Μίλητος...νοσήσασα ἐς τὰ μάλιστα στάσι μέχρι οὗ μιν Πάριοι κατήρτισαν· τούτους γὰρ καταρτιστῆρας ἐκ πάντων Ἑλλήνων εἵλοντο οἱ Μιλήσιοι (comp. iv. 161). (2) It is a surgical term for 'setting bones': e.g. Galen, Op. xix. p. 461 (ed. Kühn) καταρτισμός ἐστι μεταγωγὴ ὀστοῦ ἢ ὀστῶν ἐκ τοῦ παρὰ φύσιν τόπου εἰς τὸν κατὰ φύσιν. In the New Testament it is used, (1) literally, e.g. Mark i. 19 καταρτίζοντας τὰ δίκτυα: but (2) generally metaphorically, especially by St Paul and the author of the Epistle to the Hebrews, sometimes with the meaning of 'correct, restore,' the idea of punishment being quite subordinate to that of amendment (see the note on Gal. vi. 1 καταρτίζετε τὸν τοιοῦτον ἐν πνεύματι πραΰτητος), sometimes with the sense of 'prepare, equip' (Rom. ix. 22, 1 Cor. i. 10, Heb. x. 5, xi. 3, xiii. 21), sometimes, as here, in the sense of ἀναπληροῦν, a word which either simply or compounded occurs in five other passages closely connected with ὑστέρημα (1 Cor. xvi. 17, 2 Cor. ix. 12, xi. 9, Phil. ii. 30, Col. i. 24). This sense of completion is borne out by a not uncommon application of καταρτίζειν to military and naval preparation, e.g. in Polybius, where it is used of manning a fleet (Polyb. i. 21. 4, 29. 1, iii. 95. 2), of supplying an army with provisions (i. 36. 5) etc.

τὰ ὑστερήματα] 'the shortcomings,' from ὑστερεῖσθαι 'to be left behind. These ὑστερήματα were both practical and spiritual. For the wish expressed comp. Rom. i. 11. Ὑστέρημα is opposed to περίσσευμα, 2 Cor viii. 14.

v. *The Apostle's prayer for the Thessalonians* (iii. 11—13).

11—13. The first great division of the Epistle closes with a supplication suggested by the main topics which have been touched upon. The second division likewise concludes in the same way (v. 23, 24), the prayer in each instance commencing with the same words Αὐτὸς δὲ ὁ Θεός. In both cases there is a reference to the Lord's Advent, and a wish that the Thessalonians may appear *blameless* on that great day.

11. **αὐτὸς δὲ ὁ Θεός**] Comp. v. 23, 2 Thess. iii. 16, 2 Cor. x. 1, which passages show that in αὐτὸς δὲ we are not to look for a strong or direct contrast to anything in the context, as for instance to δεόμενοι; but that it is simply an outburst of the earnest conviction which was uppermost in the Apostle's mind of the utter worthlessness of all human efforts without the divine aid. 'But after all said and done, it is for God Himself to direct our path' etc. Ὁρᾷς τὴν μανίαν τῆς ἀγάπης τὴν ἀκάθεκτον τὴν διὰ τῶν ῥημάτων δεικνυμένην; Πλεονάσαι, φησί, καὶ περισσεῦσαι, ἀντὶ τοῦ αὐξῆσαι. Ὡς ἂν εἴποι τις ἐκ περιουσίας πως ἐπιθυμεῖ φιλεῖσθαι παρ' αὐτῶν is the comment of Chrysostom. In 2 Thess. ii. 16 on the other hand the context supplies a direct antithesis (if such were needed) in ἡμῶν (ver. 15). See the note on the passage.

πατὴρ ἡμῶν] suggesting the divine attribute of mercy (see the note on i. 3).

καὶ ὁ Κύριος ἡμῶν Ἰησοῦς] It is worthy of notice that this ascription to our Lord of a divine power in ordering the doings of men occurs in the earliest of St Paul's Epistles, and indeed probably the earliest of the New Testament writings: thus showing that there was no time, however early, so far as we are aware, when He was not so regarded, and confirming the language of the Acts of the Apostles, which represents the first converts appealing to Him, as to One possessed of divine power. The passage in 2 Thess. ii. 16 of the same kind, is even more remarkable in that ὁ Κύριος ἡμῶν is placed before ὁ Θεὸς καὶ πατήρ. The employment of the singular (κατευθύναι) here enforces this fact in a striking way; comp. παρακαλέσαι 2 Thess. ii. 16, 17 and see the note on the passage.

κατευθύναι τὴν ὁδὸν ἡμῶν] '*direct our path to you, make a straight path from us to you,* by the levelling or removal of those obstacles with which Satan has obstructed it.' The metaphor here is the same with that of ἐνέκοψεν ii. 18 (see note there).

12. **πλεονάσαι καὶ περισσεύσαι**] '*increase you and make you to abound,*' where περισσεῦσαι is stronger than πλεονάσαι, and the two together are equivalent to 'increase you to overflowing.' Πλεονάζειν has no reference to increase in outward numbers, but both it and περισσεύειν refer to spiritual enlargement, and τῇ ἀγάπῃ is attached to both.

Πλεονάσαι and περισσεύσαι are naturally taken as optatives, like κατευθύναι. In this case they are both transitives, contrary to ordinary usage. Πλεονάζειν however is so found in LXX. as e.g. Numb. xxvi. 54, Ps. xlix. 19, lxx. 21, 1 Macc. iv. 35 etc., though never in St Paul. Περισσεύειν also occurs as a transitive verb in 2 Cor. ix. 8 δυνατεῖ ὁ Θεὸς πᾶσαν χάριν περισσεῦσαι, and perhaps in 2 Cor. iv. 15 τὴν εὐχαριστίαν περισσεύσῃ, but always with an accus. of the *thing* made to abound. Otherwise we might accentuate περισσεῦσαι, and take both words to be infinitives, understanding ὑμᾶς δὲ δῴη πλεονάσαι καὶ περισσεῦσαι—such an ellipse being common in prayers or wishes in classical writers, see Jelf § 671 b, p. 338. But this or any similar use of the infinitive (e.g. χαίρειν and Phil. iii. 16 τῷ αὐτῷ στοιχεῖν) is too rare in the New Testament to encourage the adoption of it here. See Winer, § xliii. p. 397.

εἰς ἀλλήλους καὶ εἰς πάντας] Had it been εἰς ἀλλήλους only, it would have been φιλαδελφία. But they were to extend their love to all, in St Peter's words (2 Pet. i. 7) to add to 'their brotherly kindness charity.' Compare the directions on φιλαδελφία given below (iv. 9).

ἡμεῖς εἰς ὑμᾶς] We may supply the ellipsis by some general word as διετέθημεν (Theodoret); or more precisely from the context by πλεονάζομεν καὶ περισσεύομεν, for in support of the change from the transitive to the intransitive meaning in the same passage there is authority in 2 Cor. ix. 8 περισσεῦσαι χάριν followed by ἵνα περισσεύητε. But why should we attempt in such cases to discuss the exact expression to be supplied, when it is at least not improbable that the thought did not shape itself in words in the Apostle's mind?

13. εἰς τὸ στηρίξαι] '*to the end that He may stablish,*' i.e. ὁ Κύριος above, comp. 2 Thess. ii. 17; not 'that *we* may stablish.' For the addition of the words ἔμπροσθεν τοῦ Θεοῦ κ.τ.λ. need not lead us to look for a different subject in στηρίξαι in a writer like St Paul, and the whole point of the passage requires that Christ should be regarded as the sole author of the spiritual advancement of the Thessalonians.

τὰς καρδίας] '*your hearts.*' Something more than an outward sanctity is required.

ἀμέμπτους κ.τ.λ.] '*so that they may be blameless in holiness in the sight of God at the coming of Christ.*' For this proleptic use comp. 1 Cor. i. 8 ἀνεγκλήτους, Phil. iii. 21 σύμμορφον, and below v. 23 ὁλοτελεῖς.

ἁγιωσύνη] The correct form, not ἁγιοσύνη. In such compounds the o is lengthened or not, according as the preceding syllable is short or long, thus ἀσχημοσύνη, σωφροσύνη, but ἀγαθωσύνη, μεγαλωσύνη, ἱερωσύνη.

Ἁγιότης is the abstract quality (Hebr. xii. 10); ἁγιωσύνη the state or condition, i.e. the exemplification of ἁγιότης working; ἁγιασμὸς is the process of bringing out a state of ἁγιότης, and sometimes the result, but always with a view to a certain process having been gone through. The distinction between the three words roughly corresponds to that between 'sanctitas,' 'sanctitudo' and 'sanctificatio.' Compare the difference between ἀγαθωσύνη and ἀγαθότης. It is worth notice that in the New Testament forms in -σύνη are much more frequent than those in -ότης.

There is a reference in ἐν ἁγιωσύνῃ to πάντων τῶν ἁγίων, as if he had said, 'in sanctity that ye may be prepared to join the assembly of the saints, who will attend the Lord at His coming.'

ἔμπροσθεν τοῦ Θεοῦ κ.τ.λ.] to be attached to ἀμέμπτους ἐν ἁγιωσύνῃ 'that your holiness may not only pass the scrutiny of men, but may be pronounced blameless by God, Who is all-seeing.'

πάντων τῶν ἁγίων] 'all His saints.' Not only the spirits of just men made perfect, but the angels of heaven also. For though the angels are never called simply οἱ ἅγιοι in the New Testament, yet the term is found in Ps. lxxxix. 5, Zech. xiv. 5, Dan. iv. 10 (13), and the imagery of Daniel has so strongly coloured the apocalyptic passages of the Thessalonian Epistles, that this passing use of the expression is not surprising. The presence of the angels with the returning Christ is expressly stated in several passages (Matt. xiii. 41 sq., xxv. 31, Mark viii. 38, Luke ix. 26, 2 Thess. i. 7), and in two of these (Mark l. c., Luke l. c.) the epithet ἅγιοι is applied to them in this connexion.

αὐτοῦ] i.e. τοῦ Κυρίου Ἰησοῦ, as the close proximity of the word demands. Compare 2 Thess. i. 7 μετ᾽ ἀγγέλων δυνάμεως αὐτοῦ.

CHAPTER IV

3. HORTATORY PORTION, iv. 1—v. 24.

i. *Warning against impurity* (iv. 1—8).

1. **Λοιπὸν οὖν κ.τ.λ.**] 'Now then that I have finished speaking of our mutual relations, it remains for me to urge upon you some precepts.' Λοιπὸν 'for the rest' here marks the transition from the first or narrative portion of the Epistle to the second and concluding part, which is occupied with exhortations. On this peculiar province of λοιπὸν and τὸ λοιπὸν thus to usher in the conclusion see the note on Phil. iii. 1. In the passage before us this conclusion is extended over two chapters; in the Philippian Epistle the Apostle is led on by his affectionate earnestness so far that he has, so to speak, to commence his conclusion afresh (Phil. iii. 1 compared with Phil. iv. 8). It is strange that the Greek commentators here give a temporal sense to λοιπὸν 'continually,' 'from this time forward.' The E. V., which elsewhere rightly renders the word 'finally,' translates it here 'furthermore,' which is misleading. Τὸ λοιπὸν is slightly stronger than λοιπόν, as will be seen by a comparison of such passages as 2 Thess. iii. 1 and Phil. ll. cc. with 1 Cor. i. 16, 2 Cor. xiii. 11, 2 Tim. iv. 8. On the difference between τὸ λοιπὸν and τοῦ λοιποῦ see the note on the latter word on Gal. vi. 17.

οὖν] if indeed the word is not to be omitted with B and some early versions, may perhaps be explained by what immediately precedes, 'seeing that we shall have to face the scrutiny of an all-seeing God, I entreat you etc.' But inasmuch as the change of subject is very complete here, it is better not to attach οὖν to any single clause or sentence, but to the main subject of the preceding portion of the Epistle: 'seeing that such has been our mutual intercourse, that we have toiled so much, and ye have suffered for the Gospel's sake, that God has done so much for you.'

ἐρωτῶμεν] 'we ask, request you,' a signification which ἐρωτᾶν never bears in classical Greek, being always used of asking a question, 'interrogare' not 'rogare.' Ἐρωτᾶν however in the New Testament is not exactly equivalent to αἰτεῖν, but denotes greater equality, more familiarity, differing from αἰτεῖν as 'rogare' from 'petere.' See Trench, *N. T. Syn.* § xl. p. 143.

ἐρωτῶμεν καὶ παρακαλοῦμεν] 'We entreat you as friends, nay, we exhort you with authority in the Lord'; ἐν Κυρίῳ Ἰησοῦ perhaps belonging only to παρακαλοῦμεν, as Lünemann suggests.

παρελάβετε] The word is used here of practical precepts, not of doctrinal tenets. See the note on 2 Thess. ii. 15 παράδοσις.

τὸ πῶς] '*the lesson how.*' The article τὸ gives precision and unity to the words which it introduces. Compare Acts iv. 21 μηδὲν εὑρίσκοντες τὸ πῶς κολάσωνται αὐτούς, Mark ix. 23 εἶπεν αὐτῷ τό εἰ δύνῃ, and Winer § xviii. p. 135.

περιπατεῖν καὶ ἀρέσκειν Θεῷ] equivalent to περιπατοῦντας ἀρέσκειν Θεῷ, '*how ye ought to walk so as to please God.*'

καθὼς καὶ περιπατεῖτε] The continuity of the sentence is broken after ἀρέσκειν Θεῷ, and the apodosis is confused. The irregularity is twofold. (1) Feeling that the bare command might seem to imply a condemnation of the present conduct of the Thessalonians, he alters the sentence from οὕτω καὶ περιπατῆτε into καθὼς καὶ περιπατεῖτε with his usual eagerness to praise and encourage where praise and encouragement are due. (2) This change of form involves the substitution of περισσεύητε for περιπατῆτε in the apodosis, and the repetition of ἵνα in order to resume the main thread of the sentence, which has been suspended by the lengthening out of the parenthesis. For the repetition of ἵνα compare the repetition of ὅτι, 1 John iii. 20 ἐν τούτῳ...πείσομεν τὴν καρδίαν ἡμῶν ὅτι ἐὰν καταγινώσκῃ ἡμῶν ἡ καρδία ὅτι μείζων ἐστὶν ὁ Θεὸς τῆς καρδίας ἡμῶν, Eph. ii. 11 μνημονεύετε ὅτι ποτὲ ὑμεῖς...ὅτι ἦτε τῷ καιρῷ ἐκείνῳ χωρὶς Χριστοῦ. The transcribers, not appreciating the spirit of the passage, have altered the text in various ways to reduce it to grammatical correctness; thus the Textus Receptus strikes out the first ἵνα and the sentence καθὼς καὶ περιπατεῖτε. For a similar irregularity see Col. i. 6 with the notes.

περισσεύητε μᾶλλον] sc. ἐν τῷ οὕτω περιπατεῖν—'advance more and more in this path of godliness in which you are walking.'

2. οἴδατε γὰρ] 'The lesson which ye received of us, I say, *for* ye know what precepts we gave you : commands not of our own devising, but prompted by the Lord Jesus Himself (διὰ τοῦ Κυρίου Ἰησοῦ).'

3. τοῦτο γὰρ] '*For this—this precept which I am going to mention.*' Τοῦτο is the subject and θέλημα τοῦ Θεοῦ the predicate, ὁ ἁγιασμὸς ὑμῶν being in apposition with τοῦτο. The following words, ἀπέχεσθαι κ.τ.λ., are added in explanation of ὁ ἁγιασμὸς ὑμῶν.

θέλημα τοῦ Θεοῦ] '*a thing willed of God*': comp. Col. iv. 12 ἐν παντὶ θελήματι τοῦ Θεοῦ (with the note). 'Non subjective facultatem aut actionem, qua deus vult [θέλησις], sed objective id quod deus vult, designat,' Fritzsche on Rom. ii. 18, xii. 2. Both θέλησις and θέλημα are words of the Alexandrian period, and are not found in classical authors.

They are related to each other as the action to the result, and are always used in the New Testament with proper regard to their terminations. See Lobeck, *Phryn.* pp. 7, 353; Pollux 5. 165.

The omission of the article before θέλημα is to be explained on the ground that the sanctification of the Thessalonians is not coextensive with the whole will of God; compare Bengel, 'multae sunt voluntates.' The grammarians (see Ellicott *ad loc.*) notice the fact that the article is omitted frequently 'after verbs substantive or nuncupative,' but do not offer any explanation of this. On the difference between θέλειν and βούλεσθαι see the note on Philem. 13.

ἁγιασμὸς] is used almost as the direct opposite to ἀκαθαρσία (see ver. 7), inasmuch as 'purity' is so large an ingredient in holiness of character.

ἀπέχεσθαι κ.τ.λ.] This ἁγιασμὸς is explained negatively in the clause ἀπέχεσθαι κ.τ.λ., and positively in the phrase εἰδέναι ἕκαστον κ.τ.λ.

πορνείας] Compare the language of the Apostolic ordinance Acts xv. 20 τοῦ ἀπέχεσθαι τῶν ἀλισγημάτων τῶν εἰδώλων καὶ τῆς πορνείας κ.τ.λ. The Apostolic decree was only issued a year or two before the present Epistle was written, and St Paul had subsequently been distributing copies of it among the Churches of Asia Minor (Acts xvi. 4). To this fact may perhaps be referred the similarity of expression here; it is sufficiently natural though to have occurred accidentally.

In both passages the sin is somewhat unexpected. It is clear that those addressed were only too ready to overlook its heinousness. If in the Acts we are startled to find it prohibited among things indifferent in themselves and forbidden only because the indulgence in them would breed dissension, it is scarcely less surprising here to find that the Apostle needed to warn his recent converts, whose very adhesion to the Gospel involved a greater amount of self-denial than we can well realize, against a sin, which the common voice of society among ourselves strongly reprobates.

The contrast to the Christian idea presented by the Roman Empire at the time when St Paul wrote can be seen from the passages from classical writers quoted by Wordsworth *ad loc.*, and by Jowett's Essay 'On the State of the Heathen World,' *St Paul's Epistles*, II. p. 74 sq. On the consecration of this particular sin in religious worship something has been said already in the note to ii. 3.

See too Seneca *de Ira* ii. 8, a passage cited by Koch (p. 306) below on ver. 5.

4. εἰδέναι] 'to know,' i.e. to learn to know; for purity is not a momentary impulse, but a lesson, a habit (μαθήσεως πρᾶγμα, see Chrysostom). Σημείωσαι καὶ τὸ εἰδέναι· δείκνυσι γὰρ ὅτι ἀσκήσεως καὶ μαθήσεώς ἐστι τὸ σωφρονεῖν, Theophylact.

For this sense of εἰδέναι comp. Soph. *Ajax* 666 (quoted by Koch) τοιγὰρ τὸ λοιπὸν εἰσόμεσθα μὲν θεοῖς Εἴκειν.

τὸ ἑαυτοῦ σκεῦος κτᾶσθαι] Two interpretations are given of σκεῦος κτᾶσθαι, between which it is difficult to make a choice, not because both are equally appropriate, but because neither is free from serious objections.

(1) Σκεῦος means 'the body.' This interpretation is as early as Tertullian (*de Resurr. Carnis* 16 'Caro...vas vocatur apud Apostolum, quam jubet in honore tractari'; comp. *adv. Marc.* v. 15), and is adopted by Chrysostom, Theodoret, John Damascene, Œcumenius, Ambrosiaster, Pelagius, Rabanus Maurus, Primasius and others. This sense of σκεῦος is unobjectionable ; for though there is no exact parallel to it in the New Testament, the expression in 2 Cor. iv. 7 ἔχομεν τὸν θησαυρὸν τοῦτον ἐν ὀστρακίνοις σκεύεσιν (comp. 1 Cor. vi. 18) is sufficiently near, and the term 'vessel of the soul, vessel of the spirit,' which is commonly applied to the body by moralists (e.g. Lucret. iii. 441 'corpus quod vas quasi constitit ejus' sc. animae, Philo, *quod det. pot. ins.* § 46 I. p. 223 τὸ τῆς ψυχῆς ἀγγεῖον τὸ σῶμα, *de Migrat. Abrah.* § 36 I. p. 467, who interprets τοῖς σκεύεσι of 1 Sam. xxi. 5 as bodies, τοῖς ἀγγείοις τῆς ψυχῆς, Hermas, *M.* v. 1, Barnabas, *Ep.* §§ 7, 11 τὸ σκεῦος τοῦ πνεύματος, § 21 ἕως ἔτι τὸ καλὸν σκεῦός ἐστι μεθ᾽ ὑμῶν), is a fair illustration ; nor is a qualifying adjective or genitive needed, as the sense suggests itself at once. But the real difficulty lies in κτᾶσθαι, which cannot possibly have the meaning 'to possess or keep' (κέκτησθαι) as the sense would require, if σκεῦος were so interpreted. Seeing this difficulty, Chrysostom and others have explained κτᾶσθαι as equivalent to 'gain the mastery over,' 'to make it our slave.' Ἡμεῖς αὐτὸ κτώμεθα, ὅταν μένῃ καθαρὸν καὶ ἔστιν ἐν ἁγιασμῷ, ὅταν δὲ ἀκάθαρτον, ἁμαρτία· εἰκότως, οὐ γὰρ ἃ βουλόμεθα πράττει λοιπὸν ἀλλ᾽ ἃ ἐκείνη ἐπιτάττει.   Comp. Luke xxi. 19 ἐν τῇ ὑπομονῇ ὑμῶν κτήσεσθε ('ye shall win') τὰς ψυχὰς ὑμῶν. This interpretation introduces a new difficulty, as ἐν ἁγιασμῷ κ.τ.λ. is not adapted to such a meaning of κτᾶσθαι.

(2) Σκεῦος means 'wife.' This is the interpretation of Theodore of Mopsuestia, and of Augustine (*contra Julian.* iv. 56 and other references given by Wordsworth), and is mentioned by Theodoret as held by some. In favour of this interpretation it is urged (1) that κτᾶσθαι is used of marrying a wife, e.g. in the LXX. Ruth iv. 10, Ecclus. xxxvi. 24 ὁ κτώμενος γυναῖκα ἐνάρχεται κτήσεως (see Steph. *Thes.* s.v. κτᾶσθαι), and (2) that σκεῦος is found in this sense in Rabbinical writers—as *Megilla Esther* fol. 12 (II. p. 827 *ed.* Schöttgen) 'vas meum quo ego utor, neque Medicum, neque Persicum est, sed Chaldaicum,' and *Sohar Levit.* fol. 38, col. 152. See *Clem. Recogn.* p. 39, l. 14 (Syr.) ܐܢܬܬܐ ܕܝܠܟ, and Shakespeare, *Othello* IV. Sc. 2, l. 83 'If to preserve this vessel for my lord' etc. The passage in 1 Pet. iii. 7 ὡς ἀσθενεστέρῳ σκεύει τῷ γυναικείῳ ἀπονέμοντες τιμὴν ought not to be adduced in favour of this interpretation, for the woman is there called σκεῦος not in reference to her husband, but to the Holy Spirit whose instrument she is. This interpretation certainly clears the general sense of the passage, which will then be 'that ye abstain from illicit

passions, and that each man among you (who cannot contain) marry a wife of his own.' Compare esp. 1 Cor. vii. 2 διὰ δὲ τὰς πορνείας ἕκαστος τὴν ἑαυτοῦ γυναῖκα ἐχέτω, where marriage is set forth as the appointed remedy for incontinence in language closely resembling this. Nor is it any valid argument against this interpretation that the Apostle's precept would thus apply to men only: for the corresponding obligation on the part of the woman is inferentially implied in it.

The real objection to this view of the passage is that by using such an expression as σκεῦος κτᾶσθαι in this sense the Apostle would seem to be lowering himself to the low sensual view of the marriage relation, and adopting the depreciatory estimate of the woman's position which prevailed among both Jews and heathen at the time, whereas it is his constant effort to exalt both the one and the other.

Possibly however the term σκεῦος did not suggest any idea of depreciation or contempt as used in later writers; and at least any impression of the kind that might be conveyed by it is corrected by the following words, ἐν ἁγιασμῷ καὶ τιμῇ κ.τ.λ.

De Wette does not overcome the difficulty, when he says that the wife is called τὸ σκεῦος not as a wife absolutely, 'sondern vom Werkzeuge zur Befriedigung des Geschlechtstriebes.' For the question then arises, why present her in this depreciatory light?

τιμῇ] On the other hand ἀτιμάζεσθαι is used of unbridled desire; Rom. i. 24 τοῦ ἀτιμάζεσθαι τὰ σώματα αὐτῶν ἐν αὐτοῖς. The honour due to the body as such is one of the great contrasts which Christianity offers to the loftiest systems of heathen philosophy (e.g. Platonism and Stoicism) and is not unconnected with the doctrine of the resurrection of the body.

5. **ἐν πάθει ἐπιθυμίας**] Lust has at first the guise of a temptation from without, but at length the indulgence of it assumes the character of an inward habit, 'a passion,' or affection of the man's nature. In this case it is πάθος ἐπιθυμίας. Then sin is said 'to reign in our bodies that we obey its lusts' (Rom. vi. 12). Thus though πάθος and πάθημα are generally distinguished from ἐπιθυμία, as the passive from the active principle (e.g. Gal. v. 24, Col. iii. 5, where see the notes), here the two are combined as is the case frequently, e.g. Athenagoras, *Legat.* 21 πάθη ὀργῆς καὶ ἐπιθυμίας of the passions of the heathen gods.

καὶ τὰ ἔθνη] The appearance of καὶ is very frequent after comparative clauses where a comparison is affirmed or commanded: e.g. Eph. v. 23 ὅτι ἀνήρ ἐστιν κεφαλὴ τῆς γυναικὸς ὡς καὶ ὁ Χριστὸς κεφαλὴ τῆς ἐκκλησίας, where Ellicott rightly remarks that the fact of being head is common to both ἀνήρ and Χριστός, though the bodies to which they are so are different. The insertion however is much more rare where, as here, a comparison is prohibited or denied. Compare however iv. 13 ἵνα μὴ λυπῆσθε καθὼς καὶ οἱ λοιποὶ οἱ μὴ ἔχοντες ἐλπίδα.

τὰ μὴ εἰδότα τὸν Θεόν] '*that know not God.*' For the expression εἰδέναι Θεὸν see 2 Thess. i. 8, Gal. iv. 8. In what qualified sense the

heathen are said here to know not God appears from Rom. i. 19, 28.
He was present to them in the works of His creation: and they could
not but recognize Him there; yet they did not glorify Him as such, they
turned to idols, did not retain Him in knowledge, and so He gave them
over to lust and dishonour. The same idea, which is there developed at
length, is briefly hinted at here: viz. that the profligacy of the heathen
world was due to their ignorance of the true God, and to their idolatrous
and false worship. St Paul knows nothing of the common (but shallow)
distinction of religion and morality. He regards the two as inseparable.
See Jowett's Essay 'On the Connexion of Immorality and Idolatry,' in
St Paul's Epistles, II. p. 70 sq. 'Ignorantia impudicitiae origo,' says Bengel.

6. τὸ μὴ ὑπερβαίνειν κ.τ.λ.] '*so as not to go beyond etc.*' For this
use of τὸ in the sense of ὥστε see the note on iii. 3 above, and comp. Phil.
iv. 10 and Winer § xliv. p. 406. This is better than taking τὸ μὴ ὑπερβαίνειν
κ.τ.λ. in apposition with ὁ ἁγιασμὸς ὑμῶν; for (1) the insertion of the
article before ὑπερβαίνειν when it is omitted before ἀπέχεσθαι and εἰδέναι
is not easily explicable, if the clauses are parallel; and (2) the special
aspect of the sin presented in τὸ μὴ ὑπερβαίνειν as an act of fraud is much
more appropriate as an appendage to τὸ ἑαυτοῦ σκεῦος κτᾶσθαι, than as
an independent clause brought prominently forward and emphasized by
the unexpected insertion of the article.

ὑπερβαίνειν] The subject of ὑπερβαίνειν is ἕκαστον ὑμῶν, or rather
perhaps a subject understood from ἕκαστον ὑμῶν such as τινα. Ὑπερβαίνειν
may either be taken (1) absolutely, in the sense, 'exceeds the proper
limit' or 'to transgress'; compare e.g. Hom. *Il.* ix. 501 ὅτε κέν τις ὑπερβήῃ
καὶ ἁμάρτῃ, Soph. *Antig.* 663 ὅστις δ' ὑπερβὰς ἢ νόμους βιάζεται, or (2) it
may possibly govern τὸν ἀδελφόν. But ὑπερβαίνειν with an accusative of
a person has the sense rather of 'to get the better of, to override.'
Compare Demosth. *adv. Aristocr.* p. 645 ἔτι τοίνυν πέμπτον δικαστήριον
ἄλλο θεάσασθε οἷον ὑπερβέβηκε, Plutarch *de Amore*, Prol. p. 439. Thus the
sense of the passage is in favour of the absolute use, though our first
impulse is to consult the continuity of the sentence and adopt the second
alternative. The paraphrase of Jerome well gives the meaning of ὑπερβαίνειν (on Ephes. v. 3) 'transgredi [?] concessos fines nuptiarum.'

πλεονεκτεῖν] '*to overreach*,' '*defraud*.' He who is guilty of fornication
sins only against the law of purity: but the adulterer in addition to
this is guilty of a breach of the law of honesty also, for he defrauds
his neighbour of that which is rightfully his. This connexion between
πλεονεξία and ἀκαθαρσία is an accidental one arising from the context,
and there is no ground for the assertion that πλεονεξία is used in
the sense of impurity. The case is the same in Ephes. iv. 19 ἑαυτοὺς
παρέδωκαν εἰς ἐργασίαν ἀκαθαρσίας πάσης ἐν πλεονεξίᾳ. On this whole
question see the note on Col. iii. 5 τὴν πλεονεξίαν ἥτις ἐστὶν εἰδωλολατρεία,
and the *Journal of Classical and Sacred Philology*, III. 97. On connexions of πλεονεξία illustrating the passages in the New Testament see

Theoph. *ad Autol.* i. 14, where it is named between sins of impurity and idolatry, μοιχείαις καὶ πορνείαις καὶ ἀρσενοκοιτίαις καὶ πλεονεξίαις καὶ ταῖς ἀθεμίτοις εἰδωλολατρείαις, and *Test. xii. Patr.* Nepth. 3 μὴ σπουδάζετε ἐν πλεονεξίᾳ διαφθεῖραι τὰς πράξεις ὑμῶν. The position of πλεονεξία in its ordinary sense in the catalogue of sins, Eph. v. 3—5, Col. iii. 5, is as natural as in other instances (e.g. 1 Cor. v. 10, 11, vi. 10). In Eph. iv. 19 εἰς ἐργασίαν ἀκαθαρσίας πάσης ἐν πλεονεξίᾳ and in the passage before us the notion of sensuality is, as I have said, contained in the context, not in the word itself. Thus it is surely arbitrary to assign here this special sense to πλεονεκτεῖν and not to ὑπερβαίνειν. On the assumption that conversely ἀκαθαρσία is used for πλεονεξία see the notes above on ii. 3, 5. It is strange that several able commentators have supposed that the sin of 'avarice' is here reproved.

ἐν τῷ πράγματι] '*in the matter*,' the meaning of which is sufficiently defined by the context. This expression is suggested by a delicacy of feeling leading to the suppression of a plainer term: see 2 Cor. vii. 11 ἐν τῷ πράγματι. A somewhat similar use is cited from Isæus *de Ciron. hered.* § 44 (p. 116 ed. Schömann) ὃς μοιχὸς ληφθεὶς...οὐδ᾽ ὡς ἀπαλλάττεται τοῦ πράγματος.

The translators of the E.V. at first sight seem to have read τῷ (=τινι) for τῷ, but there appears to be no support for this except perhaps the Armenian version; and it is perhaps better to suppose that both here and in 1 Cor. xv. 8 ὡσπερεὶ τῷ (others ὡσπερεί τῳ) ἐκτρώματι the rendering arises from an imperfect acquaintance with the Greek article (see *On a Fresh Revision of the English New Testament*, p. 107 sq.). There seems to be no instance of του, τῷ for τινος, τινι in the New Testament. See Winer, § vi. p. 60 sq.

τὸν ἀδελφὸν αὐτοῦ] Not 'his Christian brother,' but 'his neighbour.' For the brotherhood intended must be defined by the context, and this is a duty which extends to the universal brotherhood of mankind, and has no reference to the special privileges of the close brotherhood of the Gospel.

ἔκδικος] Compare Rom. xiii. 4 ἔκδικος εἰς ὀργὴν τῷ τὸ κακὸν πράσσοντι. In the older Greek writers ἔκδικος is used in the sense of 'unjust,' e.g. Soph. *Œd. Col.* 917 οὐ γὰρ φιλοῦσιν ἄνδρας ἐκδίκους τρέφειν. The meaning 'an avenger' occurs first in Diocles, *epigr.* i. 3 ἥξει τις τούτου χρόνος ἔκδικος (Antholog. II. p. 167 ed. Jacobs), followed by Herodian, vii. 4 εἴ τινες ἢ στρατιωτῶν ἢ δημοτῶν αὐτοῖς ἐπίοιεν ἔκδικοι τοῦ γενησομένου ἔργου, Aristænet. i. 27 etc. In this sense it is found as a Latin word, e.g. Pliny, *Ep.* x. 111 'Ecdicus Amisenorum civitatis.' It is found instead of the more usual ἐκδικητὴς in the Apocryphal books of the Old Testament, Wisd. xii. 12 and Ecclus. xxx. 6. It seems to mean 'one who elicits justice or satisfaction,' and is appropriate here in connexion with the words ὑπερβαίνειν καὶ πλεονεκτεῖν.

περὶ πάντων τούτων] i.e. all these sins, which fall under the general head of ἀκαθαρσία.

For the construction ἔκδικος περὶ compare 1 Macc. xiii. 6 ἐκδικήσω περὶ τοῦ ἔθνους μου.

διεμαρτυράμεθα] '*earnestly protested.*' On the meaning of μαρτύρεσθαι and its distinction from μαρτυρεῖν see above ii. 12 and the note on Gal. v. 3.

7. οὐ γὰρ ἐκάλεσεν] 'Impurity is disobedience to God's commands : *for* He called us etc., and therefore it will bring down His vengeance.' It is better perhaps thus to connect this verse with what immediately precedes (ἔκδικος περὶ πάντων τούτων) than with θέλημα τοῦ Θεοῦ, ver. 3.

ἐπὶ ἀκαθαρσίᾳ, ἀλλ' ἐν ἁγιασμῷ] The change of the preposition is significant : 'not for uncleanness, but in sanctification.' Holiness is to be the pervading element in which the Christian is to move. 'Εν ἁγιασμῷ after ἐκάλεσεν is a natural abbreviation for ὥστε εἶναι ἡμᾶς ἐν ἁγιασμῷ, as the sense requires. Compare 1 Cor. vii. 15 ἐν δ' εἰρήνῃ κέκληκεν ὑμᾶς ὁ Θεός, Eph. iv. 4, and see Winer, § 1. p. 518 sq. Possibly ἐν ἁγιασμῷ καὶ τιμῇ ver. 4 may be so taken, but see the note there.

8. οὐκ ἄνθρωπον ἀθετεῖ, ἀλλὰ τὸν Θεόν] 'rejecteth not any individual man, but the one God.' On the article comp. Gal. i. 10 ἄρτι γὰρ ἀνθρώπους πείθω ἢ τὸν Θεόν; where Bengel pointedly remarks : '*ἀνθρώπους, homines*; hoc sine articulo : at mox τὸν Θεόν, *Deum*, cum articulo. Dei solius habenda est ratio.' Compare also Gal. iv. 31 οὐκ ἐσμὲν παιδίσκης τέκνα, ἀλλὰ τῆς ἐλευθέρας with the note.

τὸν διδόντα τὸ πνεῦμα κ.τ.λ.] 'This gift of the Spirit leaves you in a different position with regard to God from that which you held before. It is a witness in your souls against impurity.   It is a token that He has consecrated you to Himself.   It is an earnest of vengeance, if you defile what is no longer your own.' The appeal is the same in effect here as in 1 Cor. iii. 16 'Know ye not that ye are the temple of God, and that the Spirit of God dwelleth in you? If any man defile the temple of God, him shall God destroy; for the temple of God is holy, which temple ye are.' Compare also 1 Cor. vi. 19.

τὸν διδόντα] i.e. who is ever renewing this witness against uncleanness in fresh accessions of the Holy Spirit.

If τὸν καὶ δόντα be retained, καὶ will refer to ἐκάλεσεν, 'who not only called you to be sanctified, but also gave you His Spirit.' But the manuscript evidence alike and the context are against the reading of the Textus Receptus.   The gift of the Spirit by one decisive act (δόντα) does not suit the argument.

τὸ πνεῦμα αὐτοῦ τὸ ἅγιον] St Paul uses this stronger form in preference to the more usual πνεῦμα ἅγιον or τὸ ἅγιον πνεῦμα, as being more emphatic, and especially as laying stress on τὸ ἅγιον in connexion with the ἁγιασμὸs which is the leading idea of the passage. Compare Clem. Rom. 30 Ἁγίου οὖν μερὶς ὑπάρχοντες ποιήσωμεν τὰ τοῦ ἁγιασμοῦ πάντα.

εἰς ὑμᾶς] is better than εἰς ἡμᾶς, for it brings the general statement (ὁ ἀθετῶν κ.τ.λ.) more directly home to the Thessalonians themselves.

ii. *Exhortation to brotherly love and sobriety of conduct* (iv. 9—12).

9. φιλαδελφίας] Not 'brotherly love,' as E.V., but '*love of the brethren*,' i.e. the Christian brotherhood, and thus narrower than ἀγάπη which extends to all mankind. See 2 Pet. i. 7; and comp. Rom. xii. 9, 10 and the note on 1 Thess. iii. 12.

οὐ χρείαν ἔχετε] is probably the right reading as being the best supported, though it may have arisen from v. 1. The very fact that ἔχετε introduces a grammatical irregularity is in its favour, for it was less likely to be substituted for ἔχομεν than conversely. Comp. Heb. v. 12 πάλιν χρείαν ἔχετε τοῦ διδάσκειν ὑμᾶς for a somewhat analogous instance; but there the construction of διδάσκειν requires a different subject to be understood from that of ἔχετε. In the passage before us, the construction with τινα supplied before γράφειν, though irregular, is quite tenable, and in a writer like St Paul ought to create no difficulty. The more natural usage occurs a few verses lower down, v. 1 οὐ χρείαν ἔχετε ὑμῖν γράφεσθαι.

αὐτοὶ γὰρ] 'for of yourselves, without our intervention.'

θεοδίδακτοι] '*taught of God.*' The word occurs Barnab. *Ep.* § 21, Athenag. *Leg.* § 11, Theoph. *ad Autol.* ii. 9. Compare also the expression διδακτοὶ [τοῦ] Θεοῦ in John vi. 45, and 1 Cor. ii. 13 ἐν διδακτοῖς πνεύματος.

This word θεοδίδακτοι has no reference to any actual saying of our Lord, such for instance as that recorded in John xiii. 34, or to any external instruction: but it signifies the spiritual teaching of the heart, which supersedes all external precepts, though in the first instance it may have been conveyed by the medium of such. Both elements of the compound are emphatic: (1) the θεο- is brought out by what precedes, in contrast to ἡμᾶς understood, (2) the -δίδακτοι by what follows in the ποιεῖτε. The prophecy of Isaiah liv. 13 here receives its fulfilment, καὶ πάντας τοὺς υἱούς σου διδακτοὺς Θεοῦ: comp. Jer. xxxi. 34.

εἰς τὸ ἀγαπᾶν ἀλλήλους] i.e. to cultivate this φιλαδελφία, for ἀλλήλους is applied to the Christian brotherhood. See iii. 12 τῇ ἀγάπῃ εἰς ἀλλήλους καὶ εἰς πάντας, v. 15 and Rom. xii. 10 τῇ φιλαδελφίᾳ εἰς ἀλλήλους φιλόστοργοι.

10. καὶ γὰρ] '*for also, for indeed.*' The καὶ marks this statement as an advance upon the preceding one. 'You are not only taught the lesson, but you also practise it, and that, to every one of the brethren throughout Macedonia, i.e. all the brethren with whom you can possibly come in contact.'

αὐτὸ] i.e. τὸ ἀγαπᾶν ἀλλήλους.

ὅλῃ τῇ Μακεδονίᾳ] The history of the Acts only records the foundation
of three Churches in Macedonia previously to this time, viz. those of
Philippi, Thessalonica and Berea. It is probable, however, that in the
interval between St Paul's departure from Macedonia and the writing of
this letter other Christian communities were established, at least in the
larger towns, such as Amphipolis, Pella, etc., either by the instrumentality
of the more active of his recent Macedonian converts, such perhaps as
Aristarchus (Acts xix. 29, xx. 4), or by missionaries of his own sending,
such as Luke, Silvanus, and Timotheus, all of whom seem to have been
actively engaged in Macedonia during this interval. See the essay on
the Churches of Macedonia in *Biblical Essays*, p. 237 sq.

περισσεύειν μᾶλλον] See above on ver. 1.

11. καὶ φιλοτιμεῖσθαι] It is clear from the form of the sentence
(contrast the καὶ here with δὲ ver. 9) that this injunction had some
close connexion in the Apostle's mind with that which goes before.
What this connexion was it is impossible to say. A thorough knowledge of the condition of the early Thessalonian Church would alone
enable us to supply the missing links in the chain of thought with any
degree of confidence. We may however conjecture that the large and
ready charities of the richer brethren had caused some irregularities :
that there were those who availed themselves of these means of support
to the neglect of their lawful occupations ; and that thus relieved from
the necessity of working, they went about preaching fantastic doctrines
and exciting feverish anxieties and thus disturbing the simpler and purer
faith of others. It is probable that they asserted the immediate coming
of Christ (see the notes on ver. 13 and 2 Thess. ii. 2). That there were
such idlers in the Thessalonian Church appears from the Second Epistle,
where St Paul condemns in plain terms those 'which walk among you
disorderly, working not at all, but are busybodies' (2 Thess. iii. 11 μηδὲν
ἐργαζομένους, ἀλλὰ περιεργαζομένους), language which seems to imply that
the evil had gained ground in the interval. And the assumption made
above in accordance with the requirements of the context that these were
spiritual busybodies is very natural in itself, and is further borne out
by Tit. i. 10, 11 (though the form which the evil assumes there is
grosser).

What evils the extensive charity of the early Christians might, and
probably did, to some extent, give rise to, may be seen from Lucian's
satire of Peregrinus, see especially §§ 12, 13 ἤ γε ἄλλη θεραπεία πᾶσα οὐ
παρέργως ἀλλὰ σὺν σπουδῇ ἐγίγνετο...εἶτα δεῖπνα ποικίλα εἰσεκομίζετο....Καὶ
δὴ καὶ τῷ Περεγρίνῳ πολλὰ τότε ἧκε χρήματα παρ' αὐτῶν ἐπὶ προφάσει
τῶν δεσμῶν καὶ πρόσοδον οὐ μικρὰν ταύτην ἐποιήσατο κ.τ.λ.

φιλοτιμεῖσθαι] The original idea of φιλοτιμία 'the pursuit of honour,
the love of distinction' (typical of Athens, see Pericles' speech in Thuc.
ii. 44 τὸ φιλότιμον ἀγήρων μόνον) is more or less obscured in its later

usages (e.g. Rom. xv. 20, 2 Cor. v. 9) and the verb comes to signify 'to
make the pursuit of a thing one's earnest endeavour,' 'to strive restlessly
after' a thing, and the substantive 'restless energy' (see e.g. Athenag. *de
resurr.* § 18 οὐ γὰρ φιλοτιμίας τὸ κατάγειν ἢ διαιρεῖν νῦν). Thus though the
meaning 'ambition' would well suit the context here, it is unsafe to
press it.

The oxymoron however of φιλοτιμεῖσθαι ἡσυχάζειν is equally strong
whichever meaning we attach to φιλοτιμεῖσθαι, and the verbal paradox
reminds us forcibly of the Horatian 'strenua inertia,' of Grotius'
complaint that he had spent his life 'operose nihil agendo,' and of
Pericles' estimate of woman's true ambition (Thuc. ii. 45) μεγάλη ἡ δόξα
ἧς ἂν ἐπ' ἐλάχιστον ἀρετῆς πέρι ἢ ψόγου ἐν τοῖς ἄρσεσι κλέος ᾖ. For other
examples of παρὰ προσδοκίαν in St Paul compare Rom. xiii. 8 μηδενὶ μηδὲν
ὀφείλετε, εἰ μὴ τὸ ἀλλήλους ἀγαπᾶν, and see the note on Phil. iv. 7 ἡ εἰρήνη
τοῦ Θεοῦ φρουρήσει τὰς καρδίας ὑμῶν.

πράσσειν τὰ ἴδια] For the juxtaposition compare Plato, *Rep.* 496 D
ἡσυχίαν ἔχων καὶ τὰ αὑτοῦ πράττων, Dion Cassius lx. 27 τὴν ἡσυχίαν ἄγων
καὶ τὰ ἑαυτοῦ πράττων.

ταῖς χερσὶν] The word ἰδίαις has been wrongly inserted by some
authorities both here and in the parallel passage Eph. iv. 28 ἐργαζόμενος
ταῖς [ἰδίαις] χερσὶν τὸ ἀγαθόν, where however the authority for its retention
is somewhat stronger. On this characteristic interpolation see the note
on ii. 15 καὶ τοὺς προφήτας.

12. **ἵνα περιπατῆτε κ.τ.λ.**] This is a precept dictated by prudence,
and does not fall under the head of φιλαδελφία or ἀγάπη : but it was
doubtless suggested by this topic, for St Paul was led from it to speak of
the one flaw which disfigured their 'love of the brotherhood,' and hence
to consider how it would affect their dealings with the heathen. They
were not to appear as worthless vagabonds and beggars. The precept
has nothing to do with their conduct towards heathen magistrates, as
Wordsworth imagines. Luther's comment, quoted by Koch, is very
characteristic, 'Nähret euch selber und lieget nicht den Leuten auf dem
Halse, wie die faulen Bettelmönche, Wiedertäufer, Landläufer, denn
solche sind unnütze Leute und ärgern die Ungläubigen.'

εὐσχημόνως] *'decorously'*; vulg. 'honeste.' The E.V. has 'honestly,'
which is rather an archaism than a mistranslation : comp. Rom. xiii. 13,
where εὐσχημόνως is similarly rendered.

τοὺς ἔξω] *'the unbelievers,'* opposed to οἱ ἔσω, 'the Christian brethren.'
See the note on Col. iv. 5.

μηδενὸς χρείαν ἔχητε] It is not easy to say whether μηδενὸς is neuter
or masculine here. Perhaps the fact that χρείαν ἔχειν is frequently used
with a genitive of the thing will turn the scale in favour of the neuter.
In Rev. iii. 17 however the right reading is πεπλούτηκα καὶ οὐδὲν (not
οὐδενὸς) χρείαν ἔχω. Otherwise it would be a decisive instance. In either
case the meaning is the same. The Apostle is enforcing the necessity of

manual labour, in order that his converts may have sufficient for the wants of life, and may not appear before the unbelievers in the light of needy idlers.

iii.   *The Advent of the Lord* (iv. 13—v. 11).

(a)   *The dead shall have their place in the Resurrection* (iv. 13—18).

13. Though there is an apparent change of subject here, the new topic is not entirely unconnected with the old. The restlessness which agitated the Church of Thessalonica, and led to a neglect of the occupations of daily life, was doubtless due to their feverish anticipations of the immediate coming of Christ; see *Biblical Essays*, 264 sq. This view can scarcely be considered a mere conjecture, supported as it is by 2 Thess. ii. 2; but, even if it were, the supposition is so natural as to commend itself, and we are not without instances of the disturbing effects of such an unchastened anticipation in later ages of the Church. In the tenth century for instance the expectation of the approaching end of the world in or about the year 1000 A.D. was almost universal. This event was to usher in the seventh sabbatical period of a thousand years, the preceding six millennia being calculated as five between Adam and Christ, and one after the Nativity. See on this matter Trithemius, *Chronic. Hirsaug.* ad ann. 960, Glaber Rudulphus, *Hist.* iv. 6. Again, amidst the plagues and famines of the fourteenth century the Flagellantes were prominent in their announcements of the speedy approach of the end.

The anticipation of Christ's coming then is the connecting link between the former subject and the present. It reminds the Apostle that he has to meet a difficulty respecting the position of the dead at the coming of Christ. This can scarcely be an imaginary difficulty which the Apostle has here started, and yet on the other hand from the indirect way in which the subject is introduced it does not seem to have been formally propounded to him by the Thessalonians. In this respect it presents a contrast to 1 Cor. vii. 1. The intermediate view is the most probable, that Timotheus had learnt during his visit to Thessalonica that this question agitated the Church, and had reported the fact to St Paul. That such questions were propounded in the early Church is evident from the interrogation put by Clement to St Peter in the *Clem. Recogn.* (I. 52), 'Si Christi regno fruentur hi quos justos invenerit ejus adventus, ergo qui ante adventum ejus defuncti sunt, regno penitus carebunt?'

It is not necessary to suppose any lengthened existence of the Church of Thessalonica at the time when this letter was written, in order to account for this difficulty. If only one or two of the converts had died meanwhile, it was sufficient to give rise to the question. Indeed it is one much more likely to be started in an early stage of the Church's growth than at a later period.

Οὐ θέλομεν δὲ ὑμᾶς ἀγνοεῖν] An emphatic expression of St Paul, characteristic of his earlier Epistles, and used especially when he is correcting false impressions, or solving difficult questions (e.g. Rom. xi. 25, 1 Cor. x. 1, xii. 1), or dwelling on personal matters (e.g. Rom. i. 13, 2 Cor. i. 8 ; comp. Col. ii. 1 θέλω γὰρ ὑμᾶς εἰδέναι): never it would appear without a special reference to something which had occurred.

It is frequently used with γάρ; but it does not even with δὲ necessarily imply an abrupt transition, but generally introduces a subject more or less connected with what precedes. See the passages above referred to, e.g. Rom. i. 13.

κοιμωμένων] '*lying asleep*.' The reading is somewhat doubtful, external testimony being divided between κοιμωμένων and κεκοιμημένων. However κοιμωμένων is the more probable, for (1) it is favoured by the older manuscripts, including אB ; (2) it is more likely to have been altered into κεκοιμημένων than conversely, the latter being the usual expression, comp. Matt. xxvii. 52, 1 Cor. xv. 20 ; (3) it is a more expressive term, pointing forward to the future awakening and so implying the Resurrection more definitely than κεκοιμημένων. This last consideration no doubt it was which induced the transcriber of D to substitute κοιμᾶται for κεκοίμηται in John xi. 12 εἰ κεκοίμηται, σωθήσεται.

καθὼς καὶ οἱ λοιποὶ] This sentence has been taken, after Augustine (*Serm.* 172) and Theodoret, to express not a total prohibition of grief, but only of such excessive grief as the heathen indulged in, and is accordingly translated 'may not grieve to the same extent as the heathen.' The Greek is thus strained to obtain a more humane interpretation. That St Paul would not have forbidden the reasonable expression of sorrow at the loss of friends we cannot doubt. But here, as elsewhere, he states his precept broadly, without caring to enter into the qualifications which will suggest themselves at once to thinking men. On καὶ see the note on iv. 5 καὶ τὰ ἔθνη.

οἱ λοιποὶ] i.e. 'the heathen'; as Ephes. ii. 3 καὶ ἤμεθα τέκνα φύσει ὀργῆς ὡς καὶ οἱ λοιποί : comp. Rom. xi. 7.

οἱ μὴ ἔχοντες ἐλπίδα] The contrast between the gloomy despair of the heathen and the triumphant hope of the Christian mourner is nowhere more forcibly brought out than by their monumental inscriptions. The contrast of the tombs, for instance, in the Appian Way, above and below ground, has often been dwelt upon. On the one hand there is the dreary wail of despair, the effect of which is only heightened by the pomp of outward splendour from which it issues. On the other the exulting psalm of hope, shining the more brightly in all ill-written, ill-spelt records amidst the darkness of subterranean caverns. This is a more striking illustration than any quotations from literature which could be produced. Yet such testimony is readily available also. Such is the passage in

Catullus v. 4 'Soles occidere et redire possunt, Nobis, cum semel occidit brevis lux, Nox est perpetua una dormienda,' or the lament of Moschus (iii. 106 sq.) over the death of his friend Bion, if possible even more pathetic in its despair, Aἴ, aἴ, ταὶ μαλάχαι μὲν ἐπὰν κατὰ κᾶπον ὄλωνται, Ἢ τὰ χλωρὰ σέλινα, τό τ' εὐθαλὲς οὖλον ἄνηθον, Ὕστερον αὖ ζώοντι καὶ εἰς ἔτος ἄλλο φύοντι· Ἄμμες δ', οἱ μεγάλοι καὶ καρτεροὶ ἢ σοφοὶ ἄνδρες, Ὁππότε πρᾶτα θάνωμες, ἀνάκοοι ἐν χθονὶ κοίλᾳ Εὔδομες εὖ μάλα μακρὸν ἀτέρμονα νήγρετον ὕπνον. In these and similar passages we cannot fail to observe how the very objects in nature, which Christian philosophers, e.g. Butler (*Analogy*, Pt. I. ch. 1), have adduced as types and analogies of the resurrection of man, as for instance the rising and setting of the sun, and the annual resuscitation of plants, presented to the heathen only a painful contrast, enforcing the inferiority of man to the inanimate creation. This triumphant application of natural phenomena by Christian writers to support the doctrine of immortality begins at once. In a striking passage Clement of Rome employs the succession of day and night, the rotation of crops, etc. as analogies pointing to the Resurrection (καιροὶ ἐαρινοὶ καὶ θερινοὶ καὶ μετοπωρινοὶ καὶ χειμερινοὶ ἐν εἰρήνῃ μεταπαραδιδόασιν ἀλλήλοις κ.τ.λ. § 20).

Had St Paul been addressing a Jewish population, he could not have spoken so strongly. If the doctrine of the Resurrection is not brought prominently forward in the Old Testament, still the Messianic hopes, there suggested, could not but tend to its taking deep root in the minds of the people. There was an instinctive feeling that the coming of Messias was not a national revival only, but that it must have some reference to themselves individually, that they were to partake in it. Hence the distinctness, with which the doctrine of the Resurrection presented itself to the Jewish people, kept pace with the growth of the expectation of a coming Deliverer.

14. οὕτως καὶ ὁ Θεὸς κ.τ.λ.] The apodosis to be in conformity with the protasis ought to have run οὕτως δεῖ πιστεύειν κ.τ.λ. ; but the protasis having been stated in a hypothetical form '*if* we believe etc.,' St Paul is instinctively led to correct any impression of uncertainty, by throwing the apodosis into the form of a direct assertion and thus clinching the truth on which he is dwelling.

διὰ τοῦ Ἰησοῦ] Though there is some difficulty in explaining διὰ if we connect these words with τοὺς κοιμηθέντας (as Chrysostom and apparently Ambrosiaster), yet the arguments in favour of this connexion are so strong that it is to be preferred to the otherwise simpler construction attaching them to ἄξει σὺν αὐτῷ. For (1) the parallelism of the sentence (and consequently the sense which is guided by this parallelism) requires that the words should be so taken—Ἰησοῦς ἀπέθανε being answered by τοὺς κοιμηθέντας διὰ τοῦ Ἰησοῦ, and [Ἰησοῦς] ἀνέστη by ἄξει σὺν αὐτῷ. (2) It was necessary in some way to limit and define τῶν κεκοιμημένων so as to show that not all the dead were meant, but only 'the dead in Christ.'

How then is διὰ to be explained? Such passages as 1 Cor. xv. 18 οἱ κοιμηθέντες ἐν Χριστῷ (comp. Apoc. xiv. 13) only illustrate generally the meaning : for the difficulty is in assigning its proper signification of instrumentality to the preposition. Such expressions as 'to live through Christ,' 'to be raised through Christ' are natural enough of Him who is the Resurrection and the Life ; but 'to die through Christ' is startling, for He is always represented in St Paul as in direct antagonism to death (e.g. 1 Cor. xv. 26). The justification of διὰ however is probably to be sought in the fact that κοιμηθῆναι is not equivalent to θανεῖν, but implies moreover the idea *first* of peacefulness, and *secondly* of an awakening. It was Jesus who transformed their death into a peaceful slumber. Or it may be the case that διὰ here is not the διὰ of instrument, but the διὰ of passage. As a state of spiritual condition is ἐν Χριστῷ, so a transition from one state to another is διὰ Χριστοῦ.

Professor Jowett (on ver. 13) speaks of κοιμᾶσθαι as 'a euphemism for the dead which is used in the Old Testament and sometimes in classical writers.' But indeed it is more than a euphemism in the New Testament, which speaks also of their awakening : compare August. *Serm.* 93 ' Quare dormientes vocantur ? nisi quia suo die resuscitabuntur ' cited by Wordsworth, and a remarkable passage in Philo, *Fragm.* II. p. 667 *ed.* Mangey. Photius (*Quaest. Amphil.* 168) remarks ἐπὶ μὲν οὖν τοῦ Χριστοῦ θάνατον καλεῖ, ἵνα τὸ πάθος πιστώσηται· ἐπὶ δὲ ἡμῶν κοίμησιν, ἵνα τὴν ὀδύνην παραμυθήσηται.   ἔνθα μὲν γὰρ παρεχώρησεν ἡ ἀνάστασις θαρρῶν καλεῖ θάνατον· ἔνθα δὲ ἐν ἐλπίσιν ἔτι μένει κοίμησιν καλεῖ κ.τ.λ.

ἄξει σὺν αὐτῷ] is best explained by vv. 17, 18. It is not a pregnant expression for 'will take so as to be with Him': but 'will lead with Him ' to His eternal abode of glory. 'ἄξει *ducet*, suave verbum : dicitur de viventibus,' Bengel. For the general sentiment compare 2 Cor. iv. 14, Ign. *Trall.* 9 ὃς καὶ ἀληθῶς ἠγέρθη ἀπὸ νεκρῶν...κατὰ τὸ ὁμοίωμα ὃς καὶ ἡμᾶς τοὺς πιστεύοντας αὐτῷ οὕτως ἐγερεῖ ὁ πατὴρ αὐτοῦ ἐν Χριστῷ Ἰησοῦ.

15. ἐν λόγῳ Κυρίου] This expression has been explained as a reference to some recorded saying of our Lord, transmitted either in writing or orally. The nearest approach to the passage here in the canonical Gospels is found in Matt. xxiv. 31, where however the similarity is not great enough to encourage such an inference. It is perhaps more probable that St Paul refers to a direct revelation, which he had himself received from the Lord. The use of the phrase ' the word of the Lord ' in the Old Testament is in favour of this meaning. On the expression λόγος Κυρίου generally, see the note on i. 8. See also below on v. 2 ἀκριβῶς οἴδατε. The same question arises with reference to 1 Cor. vii. 10 οὐκ ἐγὼ ἀλλὰ ὁ Κύριος, and it ought probably to be decided in the same way.

ἡμεῖς οἱ ζῶντες] This expression suggests the question to what extent and in what sense it may be said that St Paul and the Apostles generally looked for the speedy approach of the advent of Christ. It is difficult in attempting an answer to this question to avoid exaggerating on one side or the other, but the facts seem to justify the following remarks.

(1) It should create no difficulty, if we find the Apostles ignorant of the time of the Lord's coming. However we may extend the limits of inspiration, this one point seems to lie without those limits. This is indeed the one subject on which we should expect inspiration to exercise a reserve. It is 'I, not the Lord,' who speaks here. For we are told that the angels of heaven—and even the Son Himself, otherwise than as God— are excluded from this knowledge (Mark xiii. 32). On this subject then we might expect to find the language of the Apostles vague, inconstant and possibly contradictory.

(2) The Apostles certainly do speak as though there were a reasonable expectation of the Lord's appearing in their own time. They use modes of expression which cannot otherwise be explained. Such is the use of the plural here: comp. 1 Cor. xv. 51 according to the received text, which seems to retain the correct reading. Nor does it imply more than a reasonable expectation, a probability indeed, but nothing approaching to a certainty, for it is carefully guarded by the explanatory οἱ ζῶντες, οἱ περιλειπόμενοι, which may be paraphrased, " When I say 'we,' I mean those who are living, those who survive to that day." Bengel says very wisely and truly : ' Sic τὸ nos hic ponitur, ut alias nomina Caius et Titius: idque eo commodius, quia fidelibus illius aetatis amplum temporis spatium usque ad finem mundi nondum distincte scire licuit. Tempus praesens in utroque participio est praesens pro ipso adventu Domini, uti Act. x. 42, et passim.'

(3) On the other hand, they never pledge themselves to a positive assurance that He will so come: but on the contrary frequently qualify their expression of anticipation by declaring that the time is uncertain (as 1 Thess. v. 1, 2); and sometimes when pressed even guard against the idea that the day is immediate (as 2 Thess. ii. 2), or justify the delay by reference to the attributes of God (as 2 Pet. iii. 8).

(4) With regard to St Paul it is scarcely true to say that the expectation grows weaker in his later Epistles, that in these he seems to delay the coming of the Lord (for see e.g. Phil. iv. 5, 1 Cor. xvi. 22). It is rather that the expectation remains about where it was, but is not brought so prominently forward, and this for two reasons. *First.* The Apostle's own dissolution in the ordinary course of things was drawing nearer, and therefore his own chance of being alive at the time was diminished. *Secondly.* The doctrine of Christ's coming, essentially and necessarily brought forward in the Apostle's teaching to the Church in its earliest stages in connexion with the Resurrection and the Judgment, resigns its special prominence at a later period to other great doctrines of the Faith. See the Essay 'On the chronology of St Paul's life and Epistles' in *Biblical Essays*, p. 215 sq., esp. p. 228.

(5) There is no ground for the assumption that ecclesiastical organi-

zation was deferred in the infancy of the Church owing to this belief. This organization appears to have kept pace with the growing needs of the Church and not to have received any unnatural check. Moreover such a supposition would be little in accordance with the tone always maintained by St Paul in speaking of the Lord's coming; for he urges the sober application to the ordinary duties of life, and deprecates any restless extravagances built upon the supposition of its near approach. Whatever the converts may have done, the Apostles themselves seem never to have given way to any such feeling. It is significant here for instance that obedience to rulers follows after this explanation about the Lord's day.

(6) The tone and temper exhibited by the Apostles in relation to this great event is intended as an example to the Church in all ages. She is to be ever watchful for the Advent of her Lord, and yet ever to pursue the daily avocations of life in calmness and sobriety.

οὐ μὴ φθάσωμεν] '*shall in no wise prevent, or be before.*' On οὐ μὴ in the New Testament see Winer § lvi. p. 634 sq.

16. αὐτὸς ὁ Κύριος] '*The Lord Himself,*' i.e. not by any intermediate agency, but in His own person He will come. '*αὐτὸς Ipse*, grandis sermo' Bengel.

There is nothing more certain than that the New Testament represents the general judgment of mankind as ushered in by an actual visible appearance of our Lord on earth. 'This same Jesus, which is taken up from you into heaven, shall so come in like manner as (οὕτως ἐλεύσεται ὃν τρόπον) ye have seen Him go into heaven' (Acts i. 11). And the announcement of the angels is not more explicit on this point than the universal language of the New Testament. Indeed, independently of revelation, it would be not unreasonable to infer that, as the redemption of mankind had an outward historical realization in His appearance in the flesh, so also the judgment of mankind should be manifested outwardly in the same way in time and space by His coming in person— that in short there should exist the analogy suggested by the angels' announcement. But in filling in the details of this great event, into which even the Apostles themselves saw but dimly, we are apt to be led into idle and unprofitable fancies; and in interpreting individual expressions, it is perhaps safer to content ourselves with pointing out parallels from apocalyptic imagery, than to attempt to realize and define figurative language with too great minuteness.

ἐν κελεύσματι] Κέλευσμα (from κελεύειν 'to summon') is a classical word used (1) generally of 'commands' e.g. Æsch. *Eum.* 226 Λοξίου κελεύσμασιν ἥκω, Soph. *Antig.* 1198, (2) 'a shout of encouragement' Thuc. ii. 92 ἀπὸ ἑνὸς κελεύσματος ἐμβοήσαντες, with special reference to the encouragement of rowers by the κελευστής, e.g. Æsch. *Pers.* 397, or of horses, dogs etc., e.g. Xen. *Cyrop.* vi. 20, (3) 'a summons for the purpose of gathering together,' e.g. Diod. iii. 15 τὸ πλῆθος ἀθροίζεται καθάπερ ἀφ' ἑνὸς κελεύσματος. It occurs once in the LXX. of the marshalling of the

locusts, Prov. xxx. 27 (xxiv. 62) στρατεύει ἀφ' ἑνὸς κελεύσματος εὐτάκτως.
The nearest approach to the meaning of the passage before us is perhaps
Philo de praem. et poen. § 19, II. p. 427 ἀνθρώπους ἐν ἐσχατιαῖς ἀπῳκισμένους
ῥᾳδίως ἂν ἑνὶ κελεύσματι συναγάγοι Θεὸς ἀπὸ περάτων. It would seem then
that the κέλευσμα of which St Paul speaks is the summons to all, both
living and dead, to meet their Lord. Such a summons is expressed in
figurative language in Matt. xxv. 6 'Behold the bridegroom cometh, go
ye out to meet him.'

The preposition ἐν signifies the attendant circumstances rather than
the time (1 Cor. xv. 52 ἐν τῇ ἐσχάτῃ σάλπιγγι); see Winer § xlviii. p. 482.

φωνῇ ἀρχαγγέλου] i.e. of one of the leaders of the heavenly host. Later
Judaism busied itself with idle speculation about the number and names
and functions of the angelic host, see Gfrörer, Jahrb. der Heil. I. p. 352 sq.:
but St Paul gives no encouragement to such speculations, though his language necessarily takes its colour from the imagery which was common
in his day, e.g. Ephes. i. 21, Col. i. 16.

ἐν σάλπιγγι Θεοῦ] The same figure, if it be a figure, is repeated in
1 Cor. xv. 52 ἐν τῇ ἐσχάτῃ σάλπιγγι· σαλπίσει γὰρ κ.τ.λ. The trumpet was
the signal of the approach of the Lord at the giving of the law (Exod.
xix. 16); see also Zech. ix. 14, which suggests the doubt whether the
expression is more than an image here.

οἱ νεκροὶ ἐν Χριστῷ] The whole phrase is to be kept together. On
the omission of the article see the notes on i. 1 ἐν Θεῷ πατρί and ii. 14. The
question how are the dead raised is touched upon in 1 Cor. xv., where the
change from corruption to incorruptibility is described as coincident with
their rising (ver. 52).

πρῶτον] 'first,' in relation to ἔπειτα which follows. There is no reference here to the 'first resurrection' (Apoc. xx. 5).

17. ἅμα] is not to be taken apart from σὺν αὐτοῖς in the sense 'at the
same time, together with them'; for the combination ἅμα σὺν is too
common to allow of the separation of the two words (see v. 10, and comp.
e. g. Eur. Ion 717 νυκτιπόλοις ἅμα σὺν βάκχαις). The distinction of
Ammonius (quoted by Ellicott) ἅμα μέν ἐστι χρονικὸν ἐπίρρημα, ὁμοῦ δὲ
τοπικόν may be correct, but does not decide the construction here or in
Rom. iii. 12. On the other hand Moeris (p. 272) states ὁμόσε, ἅμα, ὁμόθεν
τόπου δηλωτικά· τὸ μὲν γὰρ ἅμα ἐν τῷ αὐτῷ δηλοῖ, τὸ δὲ ὁμόσε εἰς τὸ αὐτό, τὸ
δὲ ὁμόθεν ἐκ τοῦ αὐτοῦ. In Matt. xiii. 29 the sense seems to require that
ἅμα αὐτοῖς should be interpreted of place rather than of time, and instances
of a local meaning are frequent in the classics, e.g. Herod. vi. 138 τοὺς
ἅμα Θόαντι, Thuc. vii. 57 τοὺς ἅμα Γυλίππῳ, Appian. Hisp. vi. 8 ὁ δῆμος
ἅμα τοῖς κατηγοροῦσιν ἐγίγνετο.

ἐν νεφέλαις] 'in clouds,' on which as on a chariot they would be borne
aloft. Compare the expression in Acts i. 9 νεφέλη ὑπέλαβεν αὐτὸν ἀπὸ
τῶν ὀφθαλμῶν αὐτῶν. Christ is represented as coming 'on the clouds of
heaven' ἐπὶ τῶν νεφελῶν (Matt. xxiv. 30, xxvi. 64). In Apoc. i. 7 the idea
is somewhat different (μετὰ τῶν νεφελῶν); the clouds are the accompani-

ment not the throne, and according to Trench (*Commentary on the Epistles to the Seven Churches* ad loc.) 'belong not to the glory and gladness, but to the terror and anguish of that day.' He compares Ps. xcviii. 2, Nah. i. 3.

ἀπάντησιν v. l. ὑπάντησιν] The distinction commonly given between ἀπάντησις and ὑπάντησις, viz. that the former signifies a casual, the latter a premeditated meeting (see Bornemann on Xen. *Cyrop.* i. 4. 22), is only approximately true. It would be more correct to say that ἀπάντησις is a meeting absolutely, whereas ὑπάντησις involves a notion of 'looking out for,' 'waiting for,' 'waylaying.' In most places where either word occurs there is the same variety of reading, συνάντησις being also found as a variant. The comparison of authorities shows that ἀπάντησις is to be preferred in Matt. xxv. 6, Acts xxviii. 15 and here, ὑπάντησις in Matt. viii. 34, Matt. xxv. 1 and John xii. 13. The two passages in Matt. xxv. are significant of the variety in meaning of the two words.

εἰς ἀέρα] '*into the air.*' The distinction in classical writers between αἰθήρ 'the pure æther,' and ἀήρ 'the atmosphere with the clouds etc.' is strictly observed. Compare e.g. Hom. *Il.* viii. 558 οὐρανόθεν δ' ἄρ' ὑπερράγη ἄσπετος αἰθήρ, xvii. 371 (where εὔκηλοι ὑπ' αἰθέρι is distinguished from *Od.* viii. 562 ἠέρι καὶ νεφέλῃ), Plato *Phaedo* III. Β ὁ δὲ ἡμῖν ὁ ἀήρ, ἐκείνοις τὸν αἰθέρα, and as late as Plutarch *de esur. carn.* or. 1 § 2 (p. 230 ed. Hutten) ἔτι μὲν οὐρανὸν ἔκρυπτεν. So too in Christian writers, e.g. Athenag. *Leg.* 5 τὸν δὲ ἀπὸ τῶν ἔργων ὄψει τῶν ἀδήλων νοῶν τὰ φαινόμενα, ἀέρος, αἰθέρος, γῆς. In the New Testament indeed the word αἰθήρ does not occur, but still ἀήρ seems to be used in its proper sense : e.g. Eph. ii. 2 τὸν ἄρχοντα τῆς ἐξουσίας τοῦ ἀέρος, an expression which we cannot well explain unless ἀήρ presented some contrast to the pure heaven, the οὐρανός, which is the abode of God and of Christ. Thus then εἰς ἀέρα here denotes that the Lord will descend into the immediate region of the earth, where He will be met by His faithful people. Of the final abode of His glorified saints nothing is said here ; for the Apostle closes, as soon as he has fulfilled his purpose of satisfying his Thessalonian readers that the dead will participate in Christ's coming. The comment however of Augustine (*de civit. Dei* xx. 20. 2) is worth recording : 'non sic accipiendum est tanquam in aere nos dixerit semper cum Domino mansuros, quia nec ipse utique ibi manebit, quia veniens transiturus est ; venienti quippe ibitur obviam, non manenti' ; comp. Origen *de princ.* ii. 11 (I. p. 104).

οὕτως] '*accordingly,*' i.e. 'having thus joined our Lord.' 'Paulus, quum quae scribi opus erat ad consolandum scripsit, maximas res hac brevitate involvit.' Bengel.

18. ἐν τοῖς λόγοις] '*with these words,*' i.e. 'this my account of the Lord's coming.' The instrumental use of ἐν is noticeable, the action being 'conceived of as existing in the means' (Ellicott *ad loc.*, who refers to Wunder on Soph. *Philoct.* 60).

CHAPTER V

(*b*) *The time however is uncertain* (v. 1—3).

1. **τῶν χρόνων καὶ τῶν καιρῶν**] '*the times and the seasons*.' Compare Acts i. 7 οὐχ ὑμῶν ἐστιν γνῶναι χρόνους ἢ καιρούς, 1 Pet. i. 11, and Dan. ii. 21, Wisd. viii. 8, Eccles. iii. 1. Also Demosth. *Olynth.* 3 § 32 τίνα γὰρ χρόνον ἢ τίνα καιρόν, ὦ ἄνδρες Ἀθηναῖοι, τοῦ παρόντος βελτίω ζητεῖσθε; and Ign. *Polyc.* 3 τοὺς καιροὺς καταμάνθανε· τὸν ὑπὲρ καιρὸν προσδόκα, τὸν ἄχρονον (with the notes). The common distinction that χρόνος means a longer, καιρὸς a shorter period of time is erroneous, though it contains an element of truth. The real difference is correctly given by Ammonius p. 80 ὁ μὲν καιρὸς δηλοῖ ποιότητα, χρόνος δὲ ποσότητα. In fact χρόνος denotes a period of time whether long or short, and hence in reference to any particular event 'the date.' Καιρὸς on the other hand applies equally to place as to time (perhaps primarily to place rather than to time, as is generally the case), and signifies originally 'the fit measure' (compare the use of καίριος, e.g. Æsch. *Agam.* 1343 πέπληγμαι καιρίαν πληγήν). Hence in reference to time it is 'the right moment,' 'the opportunity for doing, or avoiding to do, anything,' involving the idea of *adaptation*. Now the opportunity for doing a thing is generally of brief duration (Demosth. *Fals. Leg.* p. 343. 1 πολλάκις συμβαίνει πολλῶν πραγμάτων καὶ μεγάλων καιρὸν ἐν βραχεῖ χρόνῳ γίγνεσθαι), and hence καιρὸς may frequently signify 'a short period of time'; but this is accidental, and it is best distinguished from χρόνος (as by Ammonius) as pointing to *quality* rather than *quantity*. There are some good passages in Trench, *N. T. Syn.* p. 209 *s. vv.*, but he does not seem quite to hit off the distinction. Augustine *Epist.* 197 (quoted by Wordsworth) draws attention to the inadequacy of the Latin language to express the distinction between the two words 'ibi (Acts i. 7) Graece legitur χρόνους ἢ καιρούς. Nostri utrumque hoc verbum *tempora* appellant, sive χρόνους sive καιρούς, cum habeant haec duo inter se non negligendam differentiam, καιροὺς quippe appellant Graece tempora quaedam...quae in rebus ad aliquid opportunis vel importunis sentiuntur...χρόνους autem ipsa spatia temporum vocant.' Tertullian's translation (*de resur. carn.* 24. 19) 'de temporibus autem et temporum spatiis' is utterly misleading.

Here χρόνοι denotes the period which must elapse before and in the consummation of this great event, in other words it points to the date: while καιροὶ refers to the occurrences which will mark the occasion, the signs by which its approach will be ushered in (comp. Matt. xvi. 3 τὰ σημεῖα τῶν καιρῶν).

2. **ἀκριβῶς οἴδατε**] The resemblance in this passage to the saying of our Lord recorded in two of the Evangelists (Matt. xxiv. 43, Luke xii. 39) makes it probable that St Paul is referring to the very words of Christ. The introductory words ἀκριβῶς οἴδατε seem to point to our Lord's authority. There is no ground however for supposing the existence of a written gospel at this time, since the same facts which were afterwards committed to writing would naturally form the substance of St Paul's oral gospel. Had such a written gospel existed and been circulated by St Paul, in the manner which has sometimes been supposed, he could scarcely have referred to his oral teaching in preference five years later in 1 Cor. xi. 23 sq., xv. 1, when a reference to the written document would have been decisive. There is probably the same reference to our Lord's saying in 2 Pet. iii. 10 ἥξει δὲ ἡμέρα Κυρίου ὡς κλέπτης, for several such are embedded in St Peter's Epistles.

ἡμέρα Κυρίου] In this expression, which is derived from the Old Testament, the word ἡμέρα seems originally to have involved no other notion than that of *time*. It is of frequent occurrence in the prophets to designate the time of the manifestation of God's sovereignty in some signal manner by the overthrow of His enemies (e.g. Is. ii. 12, Jer. xlvi. 10, Ezek. vii. 10), and thus is used specially of the judgment day, of which these lesser imitations are but types. So Joel (ii. 31) distinguishes 'the great and terrible day of the Lord' from ordinary visitations. As the day of the Lord was the day *par excellence*, we find ἡ ἡμέρα (Rom. xiii. 12, Heb. x. 25) and ἡ ἡμέρα ἐκείνη (2 Thess. i. 10, 2 Tim. i. 12, 18, iv. 8) without the distinguishing Κυρίου or κρίσεως, of the judgment day. From this accidental connexion of meaning, ἡμέρα is sometimes used in the sense of *judgment* or *verdict*: 1 Cor. iv. 1 ὑπὸ ἀνθρωπίνης ἡμέρας, a meaning the currency of which would be facilitated by the analogy of the Latin 'diem dicere,' see Stanley *ad loc.* Compare Acts xvii. 31 ἔστησεν ἡμέραν κ.τ.λ. i.e. appointed a day to vindicate Himself. On the collateral idea which has attached itself to ἡ ἡμέρα, see the note on ver. 4.

The omission of the article, which the received text has inserted on inferior authority, is justified by Phil. i. 10, ii. 16 ἡμέρα Χριστοῦ, where see the notes, and 2 Pet. iii. 10 ἡμέρα Κυρίου, where there is the same variation of reading as here.

ἐν νυκτί] On the ecclesiastical tradition see Jerome on Matt. xxv. 6 cited by Lünemann, p. 135, and compare *Biblical Essays* p. 153 for the Jewish expectation of the midnight appearance of the Messiah.

ἔρχεται '*cometh.*' The present tense denotes rather the certainty of its arrival, than the nearness. Similar instances of this usage are 1 Cor.

iii. 13 ἀποκαλύπτεται, Heb. viii. 8 ἰδοὺ ἡμέραι ἔρχονται (cited from Jer. xxxi. 31), 1 John ii. 18 ἀντίχριστος ἔρχεται, 1 John iv. 3. See further on 2 Thess. ii. 9 οὗ ἐστὶν ἡ παρουσία. It is akin to the prophetic present. See Winer § xl. p. 331 sq.

3. ὅταν λέγωσιν] It is difficult to explain the δὲ of the Textus Receptus before λέγωσιν, supposing it to be genuine. It cannot well mark the opposition between the faithful Thessalonians, who were waiting for the coming of the Lord, and the careless who would be taken by surprise; for the absence of any expressed subject to λέγωσιν shows that the antithesis is not that of persons. If the conjunction is to be retained, the meaning is rather this: 'though men have been warned that the Lord cometh as a thief in the night and should therefore be watchful and prepared, yet they will be taken by surprise.' On the whole however manuscript evidence is rather in favour of omitting the word.

If, as seems not unlikely, the sentence is a direct quotation from our Lord's words, the reference implied in the word αὐτοῖς is to be sought for in the context of the saying from which St Paul quotes.

εἰρήνη καὶ ἀσφάλεια] Compare Ezek. xiii. 10, Jerem. vi. 14.

τότε αἰφνίδιος αὐτοῖς κ.τ.λ.] The resemblance of this passage to one of the apocalyptic discourses of our Lord recorded by St Luke (xxi. 34, 36) has not escaped observation, προσέχετε ἑαυτοῖς.. μὴ...ἐπιστῇ ἐφ᾽ ὑμᾶς αἰφνίδιος ἡ ἡμέρα ἐκείνη...ἵνα κατισχύσητε ἐκφυγεῖν ταῦτα πάντα. This is only one out of several special points of coincidence between St Paul's Epistles and the Third Gospel, where it diverges from the others. Compare for instance the account of the institution of the Eucharist (1 Cor. xi. 23—26) with Luke xxii. 19, 20, and the Lord's appearance to St Peter (1 Cor. xv. 5) with Luke xxiv. 34; also the maxim in 1 Tim. v. 18 with Luke x. 7, where St Luke unites with St Paul in reading τοῦ μισθοῦ, as distinct from the τῆς τροφῆς of Matt. x. 10. This confirms the tradition that the compiler of that Gospel was a companion of St Paul, and committed to writing the Gospel which the Apostle preached orally.

ὠδίν] 'the birth-throe of some new development,' a frequent metaphor in the Old Testament: e.g. Psalm xlviii. 6, Jerem. vi. 24.

The dissimilarity which this verse presents to the ordinary style of St Paul is striking. We seem suddenly to have stumbled on a passage out of the Hebrew prophets. This phenomenon appears frequently in the New Testament writers where they are dealing with Apocalyptic questions and with denunciations of woe, and in fact explains anomalies of style which otherwise would create considerable difficulty. The writers fall naturally into the imagery and the language. Such is the case in some degree with the second chapter of the Second Epistle to the Thessalonians (see also 2 Thess. i. 7); and to a still greater extent with a large portion of St Peter's Second Epistle, where the Apocalyptic portion is so different in style from the rest, that some have thought to settle the question of its genuineness by rejecting this portion and retaining the remainder. It explains also to a great extent the marked difference in style between the Revelation of St John and his other writings.

(c)   Watchfulness therefore is necessary (v. 4—11).

4. 'Ye are living in the daylight now. Therefore there will be no sudden change for you. You will not be surprised by the transition from darkness to light, when the secret sins of men shall be revealed.'

ὑμεῖς δέ] '*but ye*,' as opposed to the careless and unbelieving of the former verse. Compare Eph. iv. 20 ὑμεῖς δὲ οὐχ οὕτως ἐμάθετε τὸν Χριστόν. The opposition is still further enforced by the emphatic position of ὑμᾶς below, preceding the verb which governs it.

ἵνα] It is possible to assign to ἵνα here its original force of purpose or design, 'in order that'; and to explain it as used in reference to the counsels of God. But the word is better taken here as simply expressing the result or consequence, a meaning which in the decline of the Greek language gradually displaced its original signification. An analogous case is Gal. v. 17 ταῦτα γὰρ ἀλλήλοις ἀντίκειται, ἵνα μὴ ἃ ἐὰν θέλητε ταῦτα ποιῆτε : see also above ii. 16 (with the note).

ἡ ἡμέρα] '*the day*' of judgment, '*the day*' *par excellence*. As we have seen above, the primary meaning of 'the day' as applied to the coming of the Lord involved only a notion of time (see note on ver. 2): but the word came naturally to imply an idea of revelation, enlightenment (1 Cor. iv. 5), and thus to suggest a contrast between the darkness of the present world and the light of the future—the one being related to the other as night to day. This is the predominant notion of ἡ ἡμέρα here. See 1 Cor. iii. 13 ἡ γὰρ ἡμέρα δηλώσει, Rom. xiii. 12 ἡ νὺξ προέκοψεν, ἡ δὲ ἡμέρα ἤγγικεν (the whole passage strongly resembling this), compared with Heb. x. 25 τοσούτῳ μᾶλλον ὅσῳ βλέπετε ἐγγίζουσαν τὴν ἡμέραν. In the first of these passages the further notion of 'fire' comes in (see the note on 1 Cor. iii. 13 ὅτι ἐν πυρὶ ἀποκαλύπτεται).

κλέπτας] The reading κλέπτας, though perhaps insufficiently supported by external authority (being read only by AB and the Egyptian versions), has a claim to preference on the ground of its being the more difficult and on internal grounds is rendered probable. It is extremely unlikely that a transcriber would alter κλέπτης into κλέπτας, while (in face of ver. 2) the converse is highly probable, and indeed natural. The inversion of the metaphor in κλέπτης, κλέπτας is quite after St Paul's manner. See the note on ii. 7 and the examples collected there.

The Apostle's way of dealing with metaphors may be still further illustrated by the different lights in which ἡμέρα is presented here, and by the double figurative application of γρηγορεῖν, καθεύδειν, first to the spiritually watchful and careless in ver. 6, and then to the physically living and the dead in ver. 10. Nothing, in short, is farther from his aim than to present a simple and consistent metaphor. No application which suggests itself is discarded on rules of rhetoric. All things are lawful to him, if only they are expedient; and wherever a great spiritual lesson is to be enforced, the first instrument which comes to hand is made use of, even though it might offend the more refined and exact taste of some. This, we may suppose, was one of the characteristics of his eloquence which made him appear 'rude of speech' (2 Cor. xi. 6) to the critical ears of a Greek audience.

Moreover the reading κλέπτας is better adapted to what follows : 'that the day should surprise you as if ye were thieves : for ye are all *sons of light* etc.' For the whole idea see a remarkable coincidence in Euripides (*Iph. in Taur.* 1025, 6) ΙΦ. ὡς δὴ σκότος λαβόντες ἐκσωθεῖμεν ἄν ; OP. κλεπτῶν γὰρ ἡ νύξ, τῆς δ᾽ ἀληθείας τὸ φῶς.

5. **υἱοὶ φωτός ἐστε**] '*sons of light*,' as opposed to the unenlightened, whether heathen or Jews; but to the former especially, see Eph. v. 8 ἦτε γάρ ποτε σκότος, νῦν δὲ φῶς ἐν Κυρίῳ· ὡς τέκνα φωτὸς περιπατεῖτε. For the expression υἱοὶ φωτός compare also Luke xvi. 8 (where οἱ υἱοὶ τοῦ φωτὸς are opposed to οἱ υἱοὶ τοῦ αἰῶνος τούτου), and John xii. 36. Is the expression found, and, if found, is it at all common previously to the New Testament? In the earliest utterances which usher in the new dispensation, the songs of Zachariah (Luke i. 78) and of Simeon (Luke ii. 32), the idea of the Messiah as a light is impressively dwelt upon; though there, as might be expected, from an Israelite pre-Christian point of view, as one 'to lighten the Gentiles,' the contrast being rather between the Jews and the heathen, than between the believer in Christ and the unbeliever.

υἱοὶ ἡμέρας] This is a slight advance upon υἱοὶ φωτός. 'Not only have ye an illumination of your own, but you are also living and moving in an enlightened sphere.' Christ is the φῶς; the Church or (in the frequent language of scripture) the kingdom of God is the ἡμέρα, of the believer.

To the believer the boundary-line between darkness and light is the time of his being brought to the knowledge of Christ. Here, rather than at the moment of his dissolution, or of the Second Advent of Christ, is the great change wrought. From this time forward he is living in the light. And the revelation of a future state presents no such contrast of light and darkness as that which he had already passed. The view which St Paul here presents of ἡμέρα, first in the revelation of Christ at His Second Advent, and then as the present illumination of the faithful, is exactly akin to the double significance of ἡ βασιλεία τοῦ Θεοῦ (or τῶν οὐρανῶν) which runs through the New Testament.

νυκτὸς οὐδὲ σκότους] '*we belong not to night, neither to darkness.*' σκότους corresponding to φωτός, and νυκτὸς to ἡμέρας by the figure called chiasm. For this diagonal correspondence see Jelf *Gr.* 904. 3, Madvig *Lat. Gr.* 473 a, Winer § l. p. 511, § lix. p. 658.

6. In this passage the metaphor of 'sleep' is applied to the careless

and indifferent, that of 'drunkenness' to the reckless and profligate. The one is to the other as negative to positive sin.

ἐσμέν] In the preceding verse ἔστε had been employed. For a similar interchange of the first and second persons see Gal. iii. 25, 26 ἐλθούσης δὲ τῆς πίστεως οὐκέτι ὑπὸ παιδαγωγόν ἐσμεν· πάντες γὰρ υἱοὶ Θεοῦ ἐστέ κ.τ.λ. Other examples are given in the note on Col. ii. 13. Here as there St Paul is eager to share with his disciples the responsibilities entailed by his Christian privileges.

ἄρα] in classical usage never commences an independent sentence. But in later Greek it assumes a more strictly argumentative sense than in the earlier language, and so frequently occupies the first place. The combination ἄρα οὖν is frequent in St Paul, especially in the Romans (e.g. v. 18, vii. 3 etc.). On the difference between ἄρα and ἆρα see the note on Gal. ii. 17.

ὡς καὶ οἱ λοιποί] See the note on iv. 5.

γρηγορῶμεν καὶ νήφωμεν] For the collocation see 1 Pet. v. 8 νήψατε, γρηγορήσατε.

7. οἱ γὰρ καθεύδοντες κ.τ.λ.] No figurative meaning is to be attached to this verse. It is simply a general explanation of the circumstances employed in the metaphor. 'Night is the time when men sleep and are drunken.'

μεθυσκόμενοι...μεθύουσιν] *'those who get drunk...are drunk.'* Bengel remarks rightly: 'Μεθύσκομαι notat actum, μεθύω statum vel habitum.' The difference of meaning however between the two words is scarcely perceptible and does not affect the sense of the passage. Elsewhere the distinction between the action of becoming drunk and the state of being drunk is obvious: e.g. Luke xii. 45 πίνειν καὶ μεθύσκεσθαι, Acts ii. 15 οὐ... οὗτοι μεθύουσιν : and so in the classics Plutarch *Symp.* iii. qu. 3 (p. 650 A) διὰ τί γυναῖκες ἥκιστα μεθύσκονται, τάχιστα δὲ οἱ γέροντες; Aristoph. *Plut.* 1047 μεθύων ὡς ἔοικεν ὀξύτερον βλέπει.

8. ἐνδυσάμενοι θώρακα] The train of thought which suggested the transition from the mention of sobriety to that of the Christian armour is not very obvious. And yet there is exactly the same connexion in Rom. xiii. 12, 13 Ἡ νὺξ προέκοψεν, ἡ δὲ ἡμέρα ἤγγικεν· ἀποθώμεθα οὖν τὰ ἔργα τοῦ σκότους, καὶ ἐνδυσώμεθα τὰ ὅπλα τοῦ φωτός· ὡς ἐν ἡμέρᾳ, εὐσχημόνως περι- πατήσωμεν. Perhaps the mention of vigilance suggested the idea of a sentry armed and on duty.

With this account of the parts of the Christian armour, compare Ephes. vi. 13—17, where the metaphor is more fully drawn out. The differences between the two passages are such as to show that it would be unsafe to lay too much stress on the individual weapons in applying the lesson. Corresponding to the 'breast-plate of faith and love,' we have in Ephesians 'the breast-plate of righteousness' and a little lower down 'the shield of faith,' love not being mentioned at all. Answering to περικεφαλαίαν ἐλπίδα σωτηρίας, the Ephesian epistle has περικεφαλαίαν τοῦ σωτηρίου. Perhaps without attempting any minute application of the metaphor, we may still go so far as to recognize the common distinction of heart and head, the seat of the feelings and affections, and the seat of the intellect. Compare Philo *Leg. All.* i. § 22 I. p. 57, *ed.* Mangey.

The base of both passages is to be found in Isaiah lix. 17 ἐνεδύσατο δικαιοσύνην ὡς θώρακα καὶ περιέθετο περικεφαλαίαν σωτηρίου ἐπὶ τῆς κεφαλῆς. Compare also a kindred passage, Wisdom v. 17 sq λήμψεται πανοπλίαν τὸν ζῆλον αὐτοῦ, καὶ ὁπλοποιήσει τὴν κτίσιν εἰς ἄμυναν ἐχθρῶν. ἐνδύσεται θώρακα δικαιοσύνην καὶ περιθήσεται κόρυθα κρίσιν ἀνυπόκριτον· λήμψεται ἀσπίδα ἀκαταμάχητον ὁσιότητα, ὀξυνεῖ δὲ ἀπότομον ὀργὴν εἰς ῥομφαίαν κ.τ.λ. The language of St Paul is loosely imitated by Ignatius *Polyc.* 6, who says ἡ πίστις ὡς περικεφαλαία, ἡ ἀγάπη ὡς δόρυ, ἡ ὑπομονὴ ὡς πανοπλία κ.τ.λ., a passage which corresponds more closely to Ephes. vi. than to the verses under discussion.

On the mention of the triad of Christian virtues, and the position occupied by ἐλπὶς see the note on i. 3.

πίστεως καὶ ἀγάπης] For faith is not fulfilled except by love. For this connexion which exists between faith and love and thus accounts for their conjunction here, compare Gal. v. 6 πίστις δι' ἀγάπης ἐνεργουμένη (with the note).

9. **ὅτι**] 'which hope is reasonable, for God appointed us not to wrath etc.'

εἰς περιποίησιν σωτηρίας] This expression is capable of two interpretations.

First. It may mean 'for the acquisition of salvation,' i.e. that we may obtain salvation, the περιποίησις being regarded as our own act. This has the advantage of simplicity here, as also in 2 Thess. ii. 14, Heb. x. 39, in which latter passage perhaps it is necessary.

Secondly. It may be rendered 'for the adoption of salvation,' the περιποίησις being the act of God, and σωτηρίας signifying 'which consists in salvation.' In favour of this may be urged the almost technical sense which the words περιποιεῖσθαι, περιποίησις bear in the New Testament, being used to denote the act of God in purchasing, or setting apart, for Himself a peculiar people. Compare Acts xx. 28 τὴν ἐκκλησίαν τοῦ Θεοῦ, ἣν περιεποιήσατο διὰ τοῦ αἵματος τοῦ ἰδίου, 1 Pet. ii. 9 λαὸς εἰς περιποίησιν, and Ephes. i. 13, 14 ἐσφραγίσθητε...εἰς ἀπολύτρωσιν τῆς περιποιήσεως (which passage is further useful as illustrating the use of the genitive σωτηρίας here, see the note). Thus περιποίησις is almost equivalent to ἐκλογή. See the Old Testament usage also, Isaiah xliii. 21 λαόν μου ὃν περιεποιη-σάμην, Mal. iii. 17 καὶ ἔσονταί μοι...εἰς περιποίησιν. On the LXX. equivalent of סְגֻלָּה, which is rendered by the two phrases εἰς περιποίησιν and περιούσιος, see the discussion on the words περιούσιος, περιουσιασμὸς in Appendix I. of the work *On a Fresh Revision of the English New Testament* p. 260 sq (3rd ed. 1891).

διὰ τοῦ Κυρίου κ.τ.λ.] to be taken with εἰς περιποίησιν σωτηρίας.

10.   This verse is remarkable as enunciating the great Christian doctrine of the Redemption, to which elsewhere there is no allusion in the Epistles to the Thessalonians, though it forms the main subject of St Paul's teaching in the second chronological group of his Epistles. It is presented moreover, as it is there, in its double aspect: *first*, as implying an act on the part of Christ (τοῦ ἀποθανόντος περὶ ἡμῶν); and *secondly*, as involving the union of the believer with Christ (ἵνα...ἅμα σὺν αὐτῷ ζήσωμεν). On this double aspect of the scheme of the Redemption, and on the position occupied by the doctrine in St Paul's teaching generally, see *Biblical Essays*, p. 229 sq.

Here the mention of it is important as showing that in his earliest writings this doctrine was present to St Paul's mind, though he has busied himself generally in these Epistles with other matters. It was not therefore, as has been maintained, an aftergrowth of his maturer reflections.

τοῦ ἀποθανόντος περὶ ἡμῶν] describing the means by which this salvation is obtained for us. As the preposition is περί, not ἀντί, the sense of a *vicarious* death cannot be insisted upon here. It is otherwise in 1 Tim. ii. 6 δοὺς ἑαυτὸν ἀντίλυτρον ὑπὲρ πάντων, where see the note. But the whole passage points to the death of Christ as being the one essential act by which eternal life was purchased for us. On the fundamental difference between περί and ὑπέρ see the note on Gal. i. 4 τοῦ δόντος ἑαυτὸν περὶ τῶν ἁμαρτιῶν ἡμῶν. Here, as there, there is a strongly supported variant ὑπέρ; but περί is read by אB, and should be preferred.

εἴτε γρηγορῶμεν εἴτε καθεύδωμεν] i.e. 'whether we are alive or whether we are dead at the time of His appearing.' In these words St Paul again reverts to the difficulty felt by the Thessalonians relative to the dead (iv. 13) whence this whole paragraph arose. Thus the resemblance to Rom. xiv. 8 ἐάν τε οὖν ζῶμεν, ἐάν τε ἀποθνήσκωμεν, τοῦ Κυρίου ἐσμέν is rather one of expression than of substantial meaning.

Observe in γρηγορῶμεν, καθεύδωμεν an entirely different application of the metaphor from that which applied to ver. 6. It is not now of the spiritual slumber that the Apostle speaks, but of the slumber of death. See the extract from Photius quoted on iv. 14 διὰ τοῦ Ἰησοῦ.

εἴτε] The use of εἰ with a subjunctive is extremely rare in Attic Greek, but becomes more common at a later epoch. A few authenticated instances may be produced from the New Testament: e.g. in the Pauline Epistles, Phil. iii. 11 εἴ πως καταντήσω (where see the note) and 1 Cor. xiv. 5 ἐκτὸς εἰ μὴ διερμηνεύῃ. In other alleged examples the future is probably to be read: e.g. Rom. i. 10, 1 Cor. ix. 11. Here however the subjunctive may perhaps be explained by a sort of attraction to the subjunctive ζήσωμεν of the clause on which this depends. See Moulton in Winer § xli. p. 368, who explains the passage here as I have done.

ἅμα σὺν αὐτῷ] '*together with Him.*' Ἅμα can scarcely be separated from σὺν αὐτῷ: see the note on iv. 17.

11.   **διό**] '*wherefore*,' referring to the main lesson of the paragraph (iv. 13—v. 11) respecting the condition of the dead at the coming of the Christ.   This lesson has been accidentally summed up in the concluding words of the preceding verse, ἵνα, εἴτε γρηγορῶμεν εἴτε καθεύδωμεν, ἅμα σὺν αὐτῷ ζήσωμεν.

παρακαλεῖτε] '*comfort*,' not 'exhort,' this being in fact a reiteration of the precept in iv. 18.

οἰκοδομεῖτε] '*edify, build up*,' as a temple for the Holy Spirit; see the note on 1 Cor. iii. 12.   This metaphor runs throughout the different chronological groups of St Paul's Epistles, the figure of a temple being applied sometimes to the individual believer (1 Cor. vi. 19), sometimes to the collective church, each individual being a stone in the building (Ephes. ii. 20—22).   The passage last cited well illustrates the metaphor: see the notes there.

εἰς τὸν ἕνα] Compare 1 Cor. iv. 6.   It is a rather late, though not unclassical, expression for ἀλλήλους (iv. 18), than which however it is somewhat stronger.   The earliest writer in whom any analogous expression seems to occur is Theocr. xxii. 65 εἰς ἑνὶ χεῖρας ἄειρον.   The passages cited by Winer (p. 217) from Herod. iv. 50, and by Ellicott *ad loc.* from Plat. *Legg.* i. p. 626 C, are scarcely to the point.   The occurrence however of the phrase in classical Greek shows that it is not sufficient to explain the expression here and 1 Cor. iv. 6 εἰς ὑπὲρ τοῦ ἑνός as an Aramaism with Hoffmann (*Gramm. Syr.* III. p. 330) and others; though this may account for the kindred phrase, Ezek. xxiv. 23 παρακαλέσετε ἕκαστος τὸν ἀδελφὸν αὐτοῦ, which is a translation of אִישׁ אֶל אָחִיו, and Jer. xxxi. (xxxviii.) 34, quoted in Heb. viii. 11.

καθὼς καὶ ποιεῖτε] Compare iv. 1, 10, where similar encouragement is given to the Thessalonians.   St Paul again guards himself against seeming to rebuke, while he intends but to exhort.

iv.   *Exhortation to orderly living and the due performance of social duties* (v. 12—15).

12.   The thread of connexion with the last topic, though slender, may yet be traced.   Having charged his converts to edify one another, the Apostle is reminded of those on whom the office of instruction especially devolved, and is led to speak of the duty of the whole body of Christians towards these their teachers.   St Chrysostom however goes too far in representing the connexion with the preceding verses as one of contrast, as if St Paul would say, 'while you edify one another, do not usurp the functions of your appointed ministers.'   Such an interpretation smacks rather of later ecclesiastical feeling, and is scarcely suited to the very primitive condition of the Thessalonian Church.   The train of thought is rather a return to the subject of the restlessness of the Thessalonians connected with the immediate expectation of the Second Advent.

εἰδέναι] '*to know,*' with a pregnant meaning, i.e. 'to see in their true character, to recognize the worth of, to appreciate, to value.' Compare the expression εἰδέναι τὸν Θεόν, εἰδέναι τὸν πατέρα, and with the same meaning as here 1 Cor. xvi. 18 ἐπιγινώσκετε οὖν τοὺς τοιούτους. This sense of 'appreciation' probably underlies the verb εἰδέναι in such passages as 1 Cor. ii. 2 οὐ γὰρ ἔκρινά τι εἰδέναι ἐν ὑμῖν εἰ μὴ Ἰησοῦν Χριστόν, and 12 ἵνα εἰδῶμεν τὰ ὑπὸ τοῦ Θεοῦ χαρισθέντα ἡμῖν. A similar phrase is found in Ign. *Smyrn.* 9 καλῶς ἔχει Θεὸν καὶ ἐπίσκοπον εἰδέναι. The Hebrew verb ידע is used in the same sense, e.g. Job ix. 21.

τοὺς κοπιῶντας...καὶ προϊσταμένους...καὶ νουθετοῦντας] The fact that the article is not repeated here before προϊσταμένους and νουθετοῦντας makes it probable that some single office is thus designated. If so, it can scarcely be any other than that of the presbytery, which would involve all the duties specified in κοπιῶντας, προϊσταμένους, νουθετοῦντας. Compare especially 1 Tim. v. 17 οἱ καλῶς προεστῶτες πρεσβύτεροι διπλῆς τιμῆς ἀξιούσθωσαν, μάλιστα οἱ κοπιῶντες ἐν λόγῳ καὶ διδασκαλίᾳ, (for there is no reason for supposing that the offices of ruling and of teaching were in separate hands), and the functions of the ἐπίσκοποι (i.e. πρεσβύτεροι) as described in 1 Timothy and Titus. See *Philippians* p. 194 sq on these twofold duties of the presbyters. It is probable also that St Paul intended to designate the presbytery collectively in Ephes. iv. 11 under the term τοὺς δὲ ποιμένας καὶ διδασκάλους, where again the article is not repeated before the second title. See the note on that passage, and compare Schaff *History of the Apostolic Church*, i. p. 134 sq (1876). It is much more likely that local officers, such as the presbyters, are here intended, than any other spiritual functionaries, such as prophets or evangelists (Ephes. iv. 11, 1 Cor. xii. 28).

We read of 'presbyters' in the church of Jerusalem, some seven or eight years before this time (Acts xi. 30). And on St Paul's first Apostolic journey we find him ordaining elders in every church (Acts xiv. 23), though these churches had been only recently founded during this same journey, and can have been in existence only a few months at most.

κοπιῶντας] is a general term, which is further explained by προϊσταμένους ὑμῶν and νουθετοῦντας ὑμᾶς, these two functions corresponding roughly to those assigned to the presbyters in Ephes. iv. 11 ποιμένας καὶ διδασκάλους, the duties namely of ruling and of teaching.

ἐν Κυρίῳ] to show that he is speaking here of their spiritual, not of their political rulers.

13. καὶ ἡγεῖσθαι αὐτοὺς κ.τ.λ.] The sentence may be taken in two ways, according as ἐν ἀγάπῃ or ὑπερεκπερισσοῦ is attached to ἡγεῖσθαι—

(1) Ἡγεῖσθαι ἐν ἀγάπῃ 'to hold (or to esteem) in love.' This construction however is deficient in support. For Job xxxv. 2 τί τοῦτο ἡγήσω ἐν κρίσει is a parallel in form only and not in meaning, ἡγήσω being there equivalent to 'cogitasti': and in Thuc. ii. 18 ἐν ὀργῇ ἔχειν τινα the parallelism vanishes in the difference of the verbs, for the real difficulty

here consists in attaching its proper significance to ἡγεῖσθαι ('to hold,' in the sense of 'to consider, regard') in connexion with ἐν ἀγάπῃ.

(2) Ἡγεῖσθαι ὑπερεκπερισσοῦ 'to esteem very highly'—in which case ἡγεῖσθαι assumes something more than a neutral meaning, and implies more or less the 'looking with favour upon.' Compare Thuc. ii. 42 τὸ ἀμύνεσθαι καὶ παθεῖν μᾶλλον ἡγησάμενοι ἢ τὸ ἐνδόντες σώζεσθαι 'preferring rather to suffer in self-defence etc.'; where, as here, ἡγεῖσθαι is found with an adverb. On the whole this interpretation is perhaps better than the former, but it were to be wished that other parallels could be produced.

εἰρηνεύετε ἐν ἑαυτοῖς] St Paul here glides off from special precepts into a general and comprehensive one. So below, ver. 14 μακροθυμεῖτε πρὸς πάντας, ver. 22 ἀπὸ παντὸς εἴδους πονηροῦ κ.τ.λ. Perhaps the correction εἰρηνεύετε ἐν αὐτοῖς, which has the support of אD and was read by Chrysostom and Theodoret, arose from not appreciating this fact, and from a desire to restrict the precept to the matter in hand. At all events it can scarcely mean what it is interpreted by some to mean : ' Be at peace in your intercourse with them' (διὰ τὸ ἔργον αὐτῶν εἰρηνεύετε ἐν αὐτοῖς Chrysostom, μὴ ἀντιλέγειν τοῖς παρ' αὐτῶν λεγομένοις Theodoret).

14. παρακαλοῦμεν δὲ ὑμᾶς κ.τ.λ.] The Greek commentators regard these exhortations as addressed to the presbyters ; but there is nothing in the form of the sentence to indicate this restriction. On the contrary the terms of the appeal are exactly the same as in ver. 12. Such a change of subject lays an undue stress on ὑμᾶς.

In illustration of the three special points in this exhortation, we may refer (1) for νουθετεῖτε τοὺς ἀτάκτους to 2 Thess. iii. 6, 11, and the note on iv. 11, where the nature of this ἀταξία is discussed ; (2) for παραμυθεῖσθε τοὺς ὀλιγοψύχους to iv. 13, 18, and (3) for ἀντέχεσθε τῶν ἀσθενῶν to iii. 3, 5 (see especially the note on σαίνεσθαι). At the same time the exhortations do not apply to these alone ; for there could be other disorderly members, others faint-hearted, and others weak in the faith, besides those who are hinted at in these passages.

ἀτάκτους] is properly a military term, 'one who leaves his rank.' See the note on 2 Thess. iii. 6 ἀτάκτως.

ὀλιγοψύχους] Compare LXX. Is. lvii. 15 ; Ecclus. vii. 10, Prov. xviii. 14.

ἀσθενῶν] i.e. the spiritually weak ; as in Rom. iv. 19 μὴ ἀσθενήσας τῇ πίστει, xiv. 1, 2, 1 Cor. viii. 7—12, ix. 22. For the difference between ἀσθενὴς and πτωχὸς see the note on Gal. iv. 9.

ἀντέχεσθε] 'lay hold of,' i.e. 'remain firm towards, stand by, give support to.' The word is used of the man who endeavours to serve two masters 'he will hold to the one' (ἑνὸς ἀνθέξεται Matt. vi. 24, Luke xvi. 13): so of steadfastness to doctrine (Tit. i. 9).

15. For this passage compare Rom. xii. 17—19, 1 Pet. iii. 9. The repetition of the phrase μὴ ἀποδιδόναι κακὸν ἀντὶ κακοῦ in all three passages would seem to point to some saying of our Lord as the original.

τὸ ἀγαθὸν] Not 'what is absolutely good, good in a moral point of view,' which would be τὸ καλόν; but what is beneficial, as opposed to κακὸν in the sense of injury or harm. See iii. 6, and the note on ἀγαθὴν there; also the contrast below, ver. 21 τὸ καλὸν κατέχετε.

εἰς ἀλλήλους καὶ εἰς πάντας] 'to the Christian brotherhood and to mankind generally.' Compare iii. 12, iv. 9 with the notes. On the heathen view of retaliation, of which the exhortation above is the direct denial, see Soph. *Antig.* 643, 4 ὡς καὶ τὸν ἐχθρὸν ἀνταμύνωνται κακοῖς, καὶ τὸν φίλον τιμῶσιν ἐξ ἴσου πατρί.

v. *Injunctions relating to prayer and spiritual matters generally* (v. 16—22).

16.   πάντοτε χαίρετε] This precept again may have been suggested by the preceding, though the connexion between the two is not very close. The maxim of universal well-doing just enunciated leads the Apostle's thoughts to the frame of mind which naturally results from it.

There is something startling in the command πάντοτε χαίρετε. It is strange that the disciples of Him, Who was preeminently 'a man of sorrows and acquainted with grief,' should be bidden to 'rejoice always.' Yet 'joy' is elsewhere no less distinctly attributed to the Christian character—'joy in the Holy Ghost' (Rom. xiv. 17). Admitted to a fuller insight into the dispensations of providence, the Christian sees the token of God's goodness in all things, even in persecution and sickness. This is a never-failing source of joy to him. On the other hand, it may be said no less truly that sorrow is especially the Christian's heritage. For with a fuller sense of the exceeding sinfulness of sin, of the fearful significance of death, he has more abundant matter for sorrow in the scenes amidst which he moves, than those whose convictions are less deep. Yet the two attitudes are not antagonistic. They may, and do, coexist. How much of the purest joy is mingled with the most heartfelt sorrow in the higher types of Christian mourning! On this injunction to rejoice see further on Phil. ii. 18, iii. 1, iv. 4.

17.   ἀδιαλείπτως προσεύχεσθε] It is not in the moving of the lips, but in the elevation of the heart to God, that the essence of prayer consists. Thus amidst the commonest duties and recreations of life it is still possible to be engaged in prayer. And in this sense the command to pray without ceasing must receive its noblest and most real fulfilment ; for though from a necessary condition of our nature the duty of expressing our aspirations to God in words is laid upon us, yet this is only as a means to an end or as the letter to the spirit. It is in the spirit alone that it is possible to 'pray without ceasing.' Origen remarks characteristically, περὶ εὐχῆς 12, ἀδιαλείπτως προσεύχεται...ὁ συνάπτων τοῖς δέουσιν ἔργοις τὴν εὐχὴν καὶ τῇ εὐχῇ τὰς πρεπούσας πράξεις. οὕτω γὰρ μόνως τὸ ἀδιαλείπτως

προσεύχεσθε ἐκδέξασθαι δυνάμεθα ὡς δυνατὸν ὂν εἰρημένον, εἰ πάντα τὸν βίον τοῦ ἁγίου μίαν συναπτομένην μεγάλην εἴποιμεν εὐχὴν κ.τ.λ. See the whole passage, and compare Tertullian *de Oratione*, 29.

ἀδιαλείπτως] This adverb occurs above, i. 2, ii. 13, and Rom. i. 9: the adjective, Rom. ix. 2, 2 Tim. i. 3. Both are peculiar to St Paul in New Testament writings. The adverb however is found four times in the Maccabees (e.g. 1 Macc. xii. 11, 2 Macc. iii. 26), and there only of the LXX. The form, which is a late one, occurs in Plutarch more than once, e.g. *ad Apoll.* 10 (p. 106 E), 37 (121 E), the adverb being frequently applied to military attack, e.g. Josephus *B. J.* v. 6. 4, 7. 2 etc. St Paul's employment of the words made them popular in early Christian writings, and the expression ἀδιαλείπτως προσεύχεσθαι is found in Ignatius (*Eph.* 10, comp. *Polyc.* 1 προσευχαῖς σχόλαζε ἀδιαλείπτοις) and Hermas (*Sim.* ix. 11. 7 ἀδιαλείπτως προσηυχόμην).

18. **ἐν παντὶ εὐχαριστεῖτε**] '*in every thing give thanks*'; for there is no event of our lives, which has not its bright side as well as its dark; no incident which may not be turned to good account, and therefore nothing for which we have not reason to thank God, if we view it in a right spirit.

This is one form of St Paul's constant practice of referring all our thoughts and actions, all the dispensations of providence, to the glory of God, as their ultimate end and aim: e.g. Rom. xv. 6, 7, 1 Cor. x. 31, Ephes. i. 6, 12, 14. For what is thanksgiving but a recognition of His Majesty, and a tribute to His divine power? This is St Paul's view markedly in 2 Cor. iv. 15, ix. 11, 12. On εὐχαριστεῖν see the note on i. 2.

τοῦτο γὰρ] It is difficult to decide whether τοῦτο refers to the three preceding precepts, or to the last only. But as these three precepts are so closely connected together both in form and in purport, it is perhaps better to include them all under τοῦτο.

ἐν Χριστῷ Ἰησοῦ] 'For the will of God is manifested in Christ, not only by His life and death in the flesh, but also because through Him all God's government of the world (whether moral or physical) is carried on.' See John i. 3, 18.

εἰς ὑμᾶς] '*to you-ward.*'

19. **τὸ πνεῦμα μὴ σβέννυτε**] Having dwelt on duties which are especially of a spiritual character, St Paul naturally turns to speak of the obligations of his converts to the Holy Spirit generally.

It has been thought strange however that the exhortation not to 'quench the Spirit' should be needed. On the contrary, much more danger might reasonably be apprehended from an unchastened enthusiasm in the first flush of their devotion to the Gospel. To meet this difficulty it is supposed that a reaction had taken place among the more sober-minded against the spiritual ἀταξία which beset the Church, and that among such there was a disposition to disregard the gifts of the Spirit.

It is perhaps better however to give the exhortation a wider signi-ficance. We need not assume a direct reference to the special manifes-tations (χαρίσματα) of the Apostolic age. The meaning may well be : ' Quench not the Spirit, whether by carelessness, or hardness of heart, or immorality.' Compare Ephes. iv. 30 καὶ μὴ λυπεῖτε τὸ πνεῦμα τὸ ἅγιον τοῦ Θεοῦ, ἐν ᾧ ἐσφραγίσθητε κ.τ.λ. In this case we need not seek to account for the precept in any special circumstances of the Thessalonian Church, and we may compare the Apostle's injunction to Timothy ἀναμιμνήσκω σε ἀναζωπυρεῖν τὸ χάρισμα τοῦ Θεοῦ (2 Tim. i. 6). Bengel's view is not quite clear. He begins : 'τὸ πνεῦμα spiritum i.e. charismata.' In the next note however he appears to give a wider interpretation to the metaphor : 'spiritus, ubi est, ardet: ideo non exstinguendus, nec in nobis, nec in aliis.'

20. From the general mention of the Spirit, the Apostle passes on to speak of one of the special gifts of the Spirit.

προφητείας μὴ ἐξουθενεῖτε] It would seem that there was the same tendency among the Thessalonians to underrate ' prophecy ' in comparison with other more striking gifts of the Spirit, which St Paul condemns in writing to the Corinthians. See especially 1 Cor. xiv. 1 ζηλοῦτε τὰ πνευματικά, μᾶλλον δὲ ἵνα προφητεύητε, 2—5, 22, 24, 25, 39.

In the words πρόφημι, προφήτης, προφητεία etc., according to their classical usage, the meaning is that of *forth-telling* rather than of *fore-telling*. The προφήτης was one who pronounced or enunciated to men the will or command of the deity whose minister he was. Though he might at times be charged with the prediction of future events, as the manifestation of that will, and thus be a 'prophet' in the common acceptance of the term, still this was only an accident of his office. The Hebrew term *nabi* (which is translated by προφήτης in the LXX.) originally signified nothing more, though the idea of prediction is most frequently associated with it. See Gesenius s. v. נביא and especially Stanley's *Jewish Church* (first series), Lecture xix. p. 415 sq. In the New Testament the notion of foretelling is kept in the background ; rarely appearing (as Acts xi. 28 of Agabus), except in reference to the prophets of the Old Dispensation. When any of these words are used by St Paul of the special gift of the Spirit, there is not the slightest allusion to the anticipation of future events. 'Prophesying' is closely connected with 'praying' (1 Cor. xi. 4, 5). 'He that prophesieth, speaketh unto men edification and exhortation and comfort' (*ib.* xiv. 3). The conviction of sin, the manifestation of the secrets of the heart, are attributed to this gift as its work (*ib.* xiv. 24, 25). Prophecy is in short the impassioned and inspired utterance of the deep things of God.

The Greek προφητεία is sometimes rendered in the Authorized Trans-lation by 'prophecy,' sometimes by 'prophesying.' In this passage all the early English Versions seem to have ' prophesyings.' And the word would convey quite the correct idea, as it was used in the English of the time.   The religious revivals or 'prophesyings' of the reign of Elizabeth are a matter of history, and Taylor's *Liberty of Prophesying* is a storehouse of information as regards the interpretations put upon the word and idea in his own and in earlier times.

21.   πάντα δὲ δοκιμάζετε] '*yet at the same time prove, test, all things*': i.e. 'do not be led away by counterfeits.' The disjunctive particle δὲ is almost necessary for the sense; and, where omitted, as in Aℵ, may have been absorbed in the following syllable.

'The simple fact of a preternatural inspiration is not enough to establish the claims of a spirit to be heard.   There are inspirations from below as well as from above.' With such a conviction at least the injunction here is given, and St John says more explicitly μὴ παντὶ πνεύματι πιστεύετε, ἀλλὰ δοκιμάζετε τὰ πνεύματα εἰ ἐκ τοῦ Θεοῦ ἐστίν, ὅτι πολλοὶ ψευδοπροφῆται ἐξεληλύθασιν εἰς τὸν κόσμον (1 John iv. 1). And such also is the universal language of the early Church in relation to spiritual manifestations. Witness the case of miracles to which Justin Martyr makes allusion (*Apol.* I. § 14, *Trypho* §§ 7, 69, 85).

The test, of which St Paul speaks here, however, is not that of an intellectual criticism or a balance of evidences.   He is contemplating not so much a logical as a spiritual criterion.   It is by a spiritual standard that things spiritual are to be tried (πνευματικοῖς πνευματικὰ συνκρίνοντες 1 Cor. ii. 13 and see the whole passage in which this expression is embedded).   The discrimination of spirits (διάκρισις πνευμάτων) was no less a spiritual gift of the Spirit than 'prophesying' (προφητεία) itself. See 1 Cor. xii. 10.

πάντα] Not πάντα τὰ πνεύματα 'all spirits,' or πάντα τὰ τῆς προφητείας 'all kinds of prophesyings'; but 'all things whatsoever,' for a general precept is required to introduce the following words τὸ καλὸν κατέχετε, ἀπὸ παντὸς εἴδους πονηροῦ ἀπέχεσθε.   The sentence might be paraphrased thus: 'Quench not the Spirit, nor despise prophesyings: but on the other hand do not rashly give heed without testing them.   In fact test all things.   This is an universal law from which spiritual experiences are not exempt.' The possibility of a ψευδοπροφητεία (see Chrysostom) is alluded to also in the Second Epistle (2 Thess. ii. 2 μήτε διὰ πνεύματος μήτε διὰ λόγου μήτε δι' ἐπιστολῆς ὡς δι' ἡμῶν).   Thus the admonition, though called forth to meet the special case of spirits, assumes a general form.

δοκιμάζετε] '*test*,' a metaphor probably derived from assaying precious metal, as the word is frequently used in this sense; e.g. Isocrates *Panathen.* p. 240 D τὸν χρυσὸν θεωροῦμεν καὶ δοκιμάζομεν ἕτερα παραδεικνύοντες. The metaphorical use also is classical; e.g. Plato *Resp.* viii. p. 546 E ἄρχοντες οὐ πάνυ φυλακικοὶ καταστήσονται πρὸς τὸ δοκιμάζειν τὰ Ἡσιόδου τε καὶ τὰ παρ' ὑμῖν γένη, χρυσοῦν τε καὶ ἀργυροῦν καὶ χαλκοῦν καὶ σιδηροῦν, Xen. *Cyrop.* viii. 4. 30 etc.   From this notion of 'proving' come the further ideas of 'approval' (Plutarch *Mor.* p. 18 F ταῦτα οὐκ ἐπαινοῦντες οὐδὲ δοκιμάζοντες), of 'choice, selection' (Plut. *de Instit.* p. 3 D σπουδαίους τίτθας δοκιμαστέον ἐστί), and of 'expression of an opinion' (Thuc. ii. 35 ἐπειδὴ τοῖς πάλαι οὕτως ἐδοκιμάσθη ταῦτα καλῶς ἔχειν). All these senses, except the last, occur in the New Testament (see Trench *N. T. Syn.* § lxxiv. p. 278 sq.); viz. 'testing' (1 Cor. iii. 13), 'approving' (1 Thess. ii. 4), 'choosing' (Rom. i. 28); and there is perhaps a further sense of 'allowing, suffering' (Rom. xiv. 22). See the note on ii. 4 δεδοκιμάσμεθα.

The passage under consideration has been not inaptly connected by early Christian writers with the saying traditionally attributed to our Lord, though not contained in the canonical Gospels, γίνεσθε δόκιμοι τραπεζῖται, a saying which is well supported by external testimony and bears in itself the marks of genuineness (see Westcott, *Introduction to the Study of the Gospels*, p. 453 sq. ed. 5). The one passage is rarely quoted without the other, and the two were so closely associated in the mind of early writers that Dionysius of Alexandria for instance (in Euseb. vii. 7) quotes the second as an 'apostolic saying' (ἀποστολικῇ φωνῇ), and Cyril of Alexandria (*Com. in Isai.* iii. 4, p. 56) cites it as from St Paul γίνεσθε δόκιμοι τραπεζῖται· πάντα δοκιμάζετε, τὸ καλὸν κατέχετε (and so again *Com. in Johan.* lib. IV. ch. v. p. 407, though not *op. cit.* lib. IV. ch. iii. p. 374). In the same way Clement of Alexandria (*Strom.* i. 28. 177, p. 425 Potter), though he does not name the author, connects it with the context here. Basil also (*Com. in Isai.* v. 20, p. 503) with an obvious reminiscence of the saying writes δοκίμου τραπεζίτου (ἐστὶ) τὸ καλὸν κατέχειν ἀπὸ δὲ παντὸς εἴδους πονηροῦ ἀπέχεσθαι, deriving the context from this epistle: compare also *in princ. Proverb.* § 6, p. 103, where 1 Thess. v. is again quoted. So too Athanasius (*Hom. in Matth.* xxi. 8, II. p. 662), Ambrose (*Com. in Luc.* i. 1, p. 1265) and others. Cyril of Jerusalem also (*Catech.* vi. 36), who converts it into the singular γίνου δόκιμος τραπεζίτης, continues in the language of the Epistle τὸ καλὸν κατέχων ἀπὸ παντὸς εἴδους πονηροῦ ἀπεχόμενος. On the other hand, Origen ascribes the saying to our Lord by name and connects it with St Paul's teaching (*in Evang. Johan.* xix. II. p. 153 ed. Lommatzsch), τηρούντων τὴν ἐντολὴν Ἰησοῦ λέγουσαν Δόκιμοι τραπεζῖται γίνεσθε· καὶ τὴν Παύλου διδαχὴν φάσκοντος Πάντα δοκιμάζετε, τὸ καλὸν κατέχετε, ἀπὸ παντὸς εἴδους πονηροῦ ἀπέχεσθε, and he is followed in this ascription by Cassianus (*Collat.* i. 20, p. 186), Cæsarius and others. Epiphanius (*Haer.* xliv. 2, p. 382) gives Apelles as his authority for the attribution of the saying to our Lord; while in the *Pistis Sophia* the utterance is our Lord's to the Virgin Mary, but it is followed as usual by the Pauline admonition 'bonum suscipite, malum ejicite' (ed. Schwartz and Petermann 1851, p. 353). In the *Clementine Homilies* it is quoted no less than three times (*Clem. Hom.* ii. 51, iii. 50, xviii. 20), and in every case is ascribed to our Lord by the interlocutor St Peter; in the Syriac *Didascalia Apostolorum* edited by Lagarde (p. 42) it is included among the admonitions to bishops, and it reappears in the *Apostolical Constitutions* (ii. 36).

τὸ καλὸν κατέχετε] '*hold fast the good.*' The metaphor of assaying coin, which was discernible in δοκιμάζετε, is not to be pressed upon these or the following words. The expression is quite general, and none of the terms used have any connexion with money.

Τὸ καλόν is used in Aristotle in two distinct senses arising from the twofold aspect of the word physical and moral; e.g. Arist. *Rhet.* i. 7. 24, p. 1364 τὸ καλόν ἐστιν ἤτοι τὸ ἡδὺ ἢ τὸ καθ' αὑτὸ αἱρετόν. In the moral aspect of the word, with which alone we are concerned here, it differs from τὸ ἀγαθὸν in that it regards the good in itself, τὸ ἀγαθὸν rather in its results, Arist. *Rhet.* i. 9. 3, p. 1366 καλόν ἐστιν ὃ ἂν δι' αὑτὸ αἱρετὸν ὂν ἐπαινετὸν ᾖ. Contrast with this Plato *Hipp. Major* 296 E τοῦ ἀγαθοῦ ἆρ' αἴτιόν ἐστι τὸ καλόν and the whole passage. This distinction between the two adjectives is common in the classics; e.g. Xen. *Memor.* iii. 5. 28 καί σοι καλὸν ἔσται καὶ τῇ πόλει ἀγαθόν. Hence the definition of the two qualities which combined make up the true gentleman (τὸν καλὸν κἀγαθόν), where τὸ μὲν καλὸς ἐπὶ τῆς ἐν σώματι ὥρας· τὸ δὲ ἀγαθὸς ἐπὶ τῆς ἐν ψυχῇ (Suidas) has no application here.

Perhaps it is not merely idle fancy to dwell on the change of expression from τὸ καλὸν 'the good' to παντὸς εἴδους πονηροῦ 'every evil form, or every form of evil'; for 'the good' is one and the same essentially, while vice is manifold and variable. The change would suggest itself instinctively to the writer. Comp. Arist. *Eth. Nic.* ii. § 5, IX. p. 32 ἔτι τὸ μὲν ἁμαρτάνειν πολλαχῶς ἐστιν (τὸ γὰρ κακὸν τοῦ ἀπείρου, ὡς οἱ Πυθαγόρειοι εἴκαζον, τὸ δ' ἀγαθὸν τοῦ πεπερασμένου), τὸ δὲ κατορθοῦν μοναχῶς.

22. ἀπὸ παντὸς εἴδους πονηροῦ] In the interpretation of this phrase two questions arise; *first*, what is the meaning of εἴδους, and *secondly*, is πονηροῦ to be taken as an adjective with εἴδους, or as a substantive after it? As the answer to the first question seems to depend in some measure on the solution of the second, the second will best be considered first. The absence of the article before πονηροῦ is in itself no argument against the word being taken substantively. Compare Plato *Resp.* ii. 358 C τρίτον εἶδος ἀγαθοῦ, Heb. v. 14 πρὸς διάκρισιν καλοῦ τε καὶ κακοῦ, Gen. ii. 9. But though πονηροῦ might without offence be taken as equivalent to πονηρίας in the expression πᾶν εἶδος πονηροῦ, the case is somewhat different in παντὸς εἴδους πονηροῦ where such a construction would sever πονηροῦ from the preceding genitive with which we instinctively connect it. Πονηροῦ is therefore probably an adjective with εἴδους. For the order compare Rom. iii. 4 πᾶς ἄνθρωπος ψεύστης, Ephes. i. 3 ἐν πάσῃ εὐλογίᾳ πνευματικῇ, iv. 29, 1 Tim. v. 10, 2 Tim. ii. 21, iii. 16, 17, Tit. i. 16, iii. 1, and especially 2 Tim. v. 18 ῥύσεταί με ὁ Κύριος ἀπὸ παντὸς ἔργου πονηροῦ. For the first part of the expression *Epist. Vien. et Lyon.* πᾶν εἶδος ὀνειδισμοῦ (Routh *R. S.* I. p. 296). On the whole question of the use of [ὁ] πονηρὸς in the New Testament see Appendix II. 'on the Last Petition of the Lord's Prayer' printed in *A Fresh Revision of the English New Testament*, 3rd ed., 1891, p. 269 sq., especially p. 277 where this passage is referred to.

Εἴδους may mean either (1) 'the outward form,' 'that which is presented to view,' 'appearance'; in this sense without any notion of unreality, comp. Luke iii. 22, ix. 29, John v. 37, and so probably 2 Cor. v. 7, διὰ πίστεως...οὐ διὰ εἴδους. Or it may mean (2) 'appearance,' i.e. semblance, as opposed to the reality, as the E. V. seems to take it, i.e. not only were they to abstain from any actual evil, but from anything which men might consider evil, and which might thus give offence, see 2 Cor. viii. 21 προνοοῦμεν γὰρ καλὰ οὐ μόνον ἐνώπιον Κυρίου ἀλλὰ καὶ ἐνώπιον ἀνθρώπων. This interpretation however lays a stress upon εἴδους which there is perhaps nothing in the context to justify. (3) We may translate the word 'sort, kind, species,' comparing Joseph. *Ant.* x. 3. 1 πᾶν εἶδος πονηρίας and the passage from the letter of the Churches of Vienne and Lyons quoted above. Εἶδος will thus be used in its very frequent quasi-philosophical sense; for it would be absurd to assign to the word here its strictly technical meaning of 'species' as opposed to 'genus' (see Grote, *Plato* II. 467). In support of the first interpretation is the fact that it is more in accordance with the usage of εἶδος elsewhere in the New Testament; and if πονηροῦ is to be taken as an adjective, this seems to be decisive in its favour, at least as against the last of the three alternatives.

23. αὐτὸς δὲ ὁ Θεὸς] 'Yet without God all your strivings will be in vain: therefore I pray that God Himself may interpose to sanctify you.' The particle δὲ recals the minds of his hearers to the true Author and Source of all spiritual progress. For the expression see the note on iii. 11.

τῆς εἰρήνης] God is further specified as the God of peace, inasmuch as peace is the end and fulfilment of all blessings.

ὁλοτελεῖς] This word is sometimes taken as equivalent to ὅλους, in the sense of 'every part of you.' But though ὑμᾶς ὅλους might bear this meaning, it will not apply equally well to ὑμᾶς ὁλοτελεῖς, for ὁλοτελεῖς not only implies entirety (which exhausts the meaning of ὅλους), but involves the further idea of completion. It is therefore better to consider ὁλοτελεῖς as proleptic, in the sense of ὥστε ὁλοτελεῖς εἶναι 'may He sanctify you so that ye be entire,' in a qualitative rather than a quantitative sense. The connexion with what follows is then: 'May God not only make you perfect, but keep you so.' Ὁλοτελεῖς occurs in Plut. *Mor.* 909 B, and ὁλοτελῶς in Aquila's version of Deut. xiii. 17.

ὁλόκληρον] The distinction between this word and τέλειος is traced by Trench *N. T. Syn.* § xxii. p. 74 sq. The two adjectives occur together in James i. 4. While ὁλόκληρος denotes the presence of all the parts, τέλειος signifies the full development, perfect growth of the whole. Like τέλειος the epithet ὁλόκληρος is applied especially to sacrifices; e.g. Philo *de Vict.* § 4 (II. p. 240 ed. Mangey) θυσίαν ὁλοκλήρῳ καὶ παντελεῖ (θεῷ) μηδὲν ἐπιφερομένην τῆς θνητῆς φιλαυτίας ὁλόκληρον καὶ παντελῆ, *ib.* § 14, p. 250 ὁλόκληρον καὶ παντελῆ διάθεσιν, ἧς ἡ ὁλόκαυτος θυσία σύμβολον, *de Agricult.* § 29, I. p. 320, *Cherub.* § 28, in all of which passages ὁλόκληρος and παντελὴς occur together. So also *de Vict. Off.* § 1, 11. p. 251 and Plato *Tim.* 44 C ὁλόκληρος, ὑγιής τε παντελῶς, and doubtless St Paul had here also the image of a sacrifice in his mind. Compare Rom. xii. 1.

'Ολόκληρον is to be taken with τηρηθείη 'be preserved entire'; not as the E.V. 'your whole spirit,' which is objectionable both on account of the order of the words and also as identifying ὁλόκληρον in meaning with ὅλον.

The epithet, though applying to the three substantives by a sort of attraction, agrees with the first only. This peculiarity of construction, together with the fact of the singular verb τηρηθείη, expresses the integrity of each part separately.

τὸ πνεῦμα καὶ ἡ ψυχὴ καὶ τὸ σῶμα] Human nature is most frequently spoken of in the New Testament as consisting of two parts—the flesh, or body, and the soul, or spirit—i.e. the material and the immaterial part. Thus, for example, in Matt. x. 28 the opposition is σῶμα, ψυχή; in Rom. viii. 10, 13, 1 Cor. v. 3, vii. 34, James ii. 26 σῶμα, πνεῦμα; in 2 Cor. vii. 1, Matt. xxvi. 41, John vi. 63, Rom. i. 3, viii. 4 sq., 1 Cor. v. 5, Gal. iii. 3, v. 16 sq., vi. 8, Col. ii. 5, 1 Pet. iii. 18 σὰρξ and πνεῦμα; in Rom. vii. 25 σὰρξ and νοῦς. But sometimes, as here, a tripartite division is recognized, σῶμα, ψυχὴ and πνεῦμα; the immaterial part being subdivided into the lower part, ψυχή, including the feelings, impulses etc., and the ruling faculty, the πνεῦμα (sometimes νοῦς), by which alone communication is maintained with God. Ψυχή and πνεῦμα are distinguished in Hebr. iv. 12 ἄχρι μερισμοῦ ψυχῆς καὶ πνεύματος (see also Phil. i. 27), and ψυχικὸς is markedly opposed to πνευματικὸς as the natural to the spiritual in 1 Cor. ii. 14 sq., xv. 44—46. And not in St Paul only; compare also James iii. 15 οὐκ...ἡ σοφία ἄνωθεν κατερχομένη ἀλλ' ἐπίγειος, ψυχική, Jude 19 οὗτοί εἰσιν ψυχικοί, πνεῦμα μὴ ἔχοντες: and in the Old Testament, Ecclus. v. 2 μὴ ἐξακολούθει τῇ ψυχῇ σου καὶ τῇ ἰσχύϊ σου, τοῦ πορεύεσθαι ἐν ἐπιθυμίαις καρδίας σου, and xviii. 30.

Such a threefold division of the nature of man is not peculiar to Christianity. It appears in the heathen philosophers, as for instance in Plato *Timœus* 30 B νοῦν μὲν ἐν ψυχῇ, ψυχὴν δὲ ἐν σώματι ξυνιστὰς τὸ πᾶν ξυνετεκταίνετο (ὁ θεός), and in the Neoplatonists as Plotinus (see Nemesius *ap.* Wetstein); and in the Stoics (see Marc. Anton. iii. 16 σῶμα, ψυχή, νοῦς· σώματος αἰσθήσεις, ψυχῆς ὁρμαί, νοῦ δόγματα κ.τ.λ.).

It was familiar also to Jewish speculators, whether of the Rabbinical type or of the Alexandrian School. See Eisenmenger's *Entdecktes Judenthum*, I. p. 887, cited by Ellicott. Philo indeed sometimes speaks of human nature as twofold, body and soul (or mind), e.g. *Leg. Alleg.* ii. § 55, I. p. 119 M. δύο ἐστὶν ἐξ ὧν συνέσταμεν, ψυχή τε καὶ σῶμα κ.τ.λ.; sometimes he subdivides the soul into three parts after Plato, the λογικόν, the θυμικὸν and the ἐπιθυμητικὸν (λόγος or νοῦς, θυμός, ἐπιθυμία), e.g. *Leg. Alleg.* i. §§ 22, 23, I. pp. 57, 58 (where there is a reference to Plato's chariot in the *Phædo*), *de Concupisc.* § 2, II. p. 350; sometimes he makes four elements of man's nature, *de Somn.* i. § 5, I. p. 624 σῶμα, αἴσθησις, λόγος, νοῦς. But he frequently considers the soul as composed of two parts, *de Vict.* § 5, II. p. 241 τὸ μὲν λογικὸν τῆς ἄρρενος γενεᾶς ἐστιν, ὅπερ νοῦς καὶ λογισμὸς κεκλήρωται, τὸ δὲ ἄλογον τῆς γυναικῶν, ὅπερ ἔλαχεν αἴσθησις. The same is essentially the division in *Fragm.* II. p. 668 M., though confusedly stated there. This would make human nature threefold. The division however is not exactly the same as in St Paul, inasmuch as αἴσθησις could scarcely fall under ψυχή, but under σῶμα as in Marc. Anton. l. c. On Philo see Gfrörer *Philo* I. c. xii. p. 373 sq. and Dähne *Gesch. Darstell. d. jüd. alexr. Relig. Philos.* I. p. 317 sq.

We are not surprised to find that this threefold organization, sanctioned by such scriptural authority, was generally recognized by the Early Fathers. See especially Iren. v. 6 and Origen *Comm. in Joann.* ii. p. 433 ed. Lommatzsch and other passages cited by Ellicott, pp. 169, 170. On the use to which Origen applied it see Neander, *Church History* II. p. 365 sq. (Bohn). When Apollinaris made it subservient to his own heresy (see Neander IV. p. 101), it began to be looked upon with disfavour.

On the whole question see Ellicott's *Sermons* v. and notes, Delitzsch *Psychology*, English version, p. 109 sq., Beck *Bibl. Seelenl.*, *Introduction to the Epistles by a Bishop's Chaplain*, p. 88, Trench *N. T. Syn.* § lxxi., and especially Olshausen *de naturæ humanæ trichotomia* given in his *Opusc.* p. 157.

Even if it be granted that the Apostle here had no intention of laying down a metaphysical distinction, yet still less are the words here to be treated as a mere rhetorical expression. The spirit, which is the ruling faculty in man and through which he holds communication with the unseen world—the soul, which is the seat of all his impulses and affections, the centre of his personality—the body, which links him to the material world and is the instrument of all his outward deeds—these all the Apostle would have presented perfect and intact in the day of the Lord's coming.

ἀμέμπτως] is added to strengthen ὁλόκληρον τηρηθείη 'be preserved entire beyond the reach of complaint.' Μέμφεσθαι (differing from ψέγειν) signifies properly 'to find fault with,' i.e. 'to blame as defective,' and thus ἀμέμπτως is appropriately used to define ὁλόκληρον.

ἐν τῇ παρουσίᾳ] The preposition ἐν, where εἰς might be expected, is probably to be explained by a brachylogy, 'be preserved entire and be found so in the day etc.' Cf. I Cor. xi. 18 συνερχομένων ὑμῶν ἐν ἐκκλησίᾳ.

24. πιστὸς ὁ καλῶν ὑμᾶς κ.τ.λ.] 'The fact that you were called by God to a knowledge of the Gospel should be an assurance to you that He is ready to sanctify and perfect you to the coming of the Lord. If His first work is rendered fruitless, it must be in spite of Him.'

ὁ καλῶν ὑμᾶς] *'your caller,'* ὁ καλῶν, not ὁ καλέσας, because the Apostle is dwelling rather on the person, than on the act. See the similar expression in Gal. v. 8 (with the note).

ὃς καὶ ποιήσει] '*who besides calling you will also do it.*' The meaning of ποιήσει is to be sought in the whole sentence from ἁγιάσαι ὑμᾶς to τηρηθείη.

4. PERSONAL INJUNCTIONS AND BENEDICTION, v. 25—28.

25. This and the remaining verses form a sort of postscript to the Epistle. See the note on τὴν ἐπιστολὴν ver. 27. It is questioned whether vv. 26, 27 are addressed to the whole Thessalonian Church, or to the Elders only. This will depend in part on the meaning assigned to πάντες οἱ ἀδελφοὶ in these verses. If it is restricted to the Christians who were in the habit of assembling at Thessalonica, as in the case of the Colossian Epistle which was to be read by the Laodiceans (Col. iv. 16), then the injunction must be addressed to the Elders only; if it signifies the whole body of Christians, then the entire church of Thessalonica may be addressed. But the latter interpretation of πάντες οἱ ἀδελφοὶ seems to be excluded by ἐν φιλήματι ἁγίῳ (ver. 26), which implies personal intercourse. Thus then, though there is no notification of the restriction, ἀσπάσασθε, ἐνορκίζω ὑμᾶς must refer solely to those to whom the letter was directly sent, i.e. probably the Elders. See verse 12.

26. ἀσπάσασθε κ.τ.λ.] The expression, as found elsewhere, is slightly different, ἀσπάσασθε ἀλλήλους ἐν φιλήματι ἁγίῳ (Rom. xvi. 16, 1 Cor. xvi. 20, 2 Cor. xiii. 12) or ἐν φιλήματι ἀγάπης (1 Pet. v. 14); but in all these passages it occurs in close juxtaposition with personal salutations sent from the writer, or from his friends, to the church addressed or to individual members of it. This fact perhaps points to a pregnant meaning in the expression as used here. 'Salute all the brethren *from me* with a holy kiss, and let this kiss be a token of brotherly love among yourselves.' There seems to be no direct reference to any liturgical rite, though the kiss of love would naturally be exchanged on the first day of the week, when they met together for prayer and for celebrating the Holy Communion. Hence it is not surprising that the 'holy kiss,' thus accidentally connected with it in the first instance, should in the next age be incorporated in the eucharistic ceremony. See Justin Mart. *Apol.* i. 65 ἀλλήλους φιλήματι ἀσπαζόμεθα παυσάμενοι τῶν εὐχῶν, Tertull. *de Orat.* 18 'osculum pacis, quod est signaculum orationis,' and *ad Uxor.* ii. 4, *Const. Apost.* ii. 57 τὸ ἐν Κυρίῳ φίλημα and viii. 11. Comp. Cyril of Jerusalem *Catech.* xxiii., *Myst.* v. 3, Chrysost. passim e.g. Hom. xx. *in Matth.* p. 205, Clem. Alex. *Paedag.* iii. 11, § 81 (p. 301 ed. Potter) ἀγάπη δὲ οὐκ ἐν φιλήματι ἀλλ᾿ ἐν εὐνοίᾳ κρίνεται· οἱ δὲ οὐδὲν ἀλλ᾿ ἢ φιλήματι καταψοφοῦσι τὰς ἐκκλησίας τὸ φιλοῦν ἔνδον οὐκ ἔχοντες· αὐτὸ with evident allusion to this custom. See on its use in the Eucharist Bingham *Ant.* viii. 10. 9, xv. 3. 3, and Stanley on 1 Cor. xvi. 20. It was also given at baptisms (Bingham xii. 4. 5), at the ordination of bishops (Bingham ii. 11. 10) and priests (Bingham ii. 19. 17), and at espousals (Bingham xxii. 3. 6).

27. It has been found difficult to account for the strength of the Apostle's language here. The explanation is perhaps to be sought, not in any supposed differences existing between the Elders and the laity of the Thessalonian Church (comp. vv. 12, 13) which might lead to the suppression of the letter; but in a sort of presentiment or suspicion, which St Paul may be supposed to have entertained, that a wrong use might be made of his name and authority. Such a suspicion was entirely justified by subsequent occurrences (2 Thess. ii. 2; see *Biblical Essays.* p. 265 sq.), and doubtless sufficient grounds for it had already appeared. Hence it was of infinite importance that his views should be known to all. The same feeling is exhibited in the second Epistle in the Apostle's anxiety to authenticate his letter (iii. 17). In its solemnity this closing adjuration may be compared with the εἴ τις οὐ φιλεῖ τὸν Κύριον, ἤτω ἀνάθεμα of 1 Cor. xvi. 21, or τοῦ λοιποῦ, κόπους μοι μηδεὶς παρεχέτω of Gal. vi. 17.

ἐνορκίζω] This, the better supported reading, is not found elsewhere except in a Cephallenian inscription, Boeckh, *C. I. G.* II. no. 1933, though ἐνορκοῦν occurs in an obscure place (Schol. Lucian. *Catapl.* 23). In Tobit ix. 20 the reading is ἐνόρκως. It is probably stronger than ὁρκίζω 'I appeal to you by an oath,' which occurs twice in the New Testament (Mark v. 7, Acts xix. 13) and is read by the bulk of manuscripts here. Thus the compound form will signify 'I bind you by an oath.' Of the forms ὁρκοῦν and ὁρκίζειν, the former is more strictly Attic, the latter belongs rather to late Greek. See Lobeck, *Phryn.* pp. 360, 361.

τὴν ἐπιστολὴν] '*the letter*'; not 'this letter' (τήνδε τὴν), for the Epistle is regarded as already concluded, and these words occur in the postscript. Compare Rom. xvi. 22 ἐγὼ Τέρτιος ὁ γράψας τὴν ἐπιστολήν, Col. iv. 16. On the other hand in 1 Cor. v. 9 the sentence ἔγραψα ὑμῖν ἐν τῇ ἐπιστολῇ cannot refer to the first epistle itself, occurring as it does in the main body of the letter. See the note there. On the significance of 2 Thess. iii. 14 διὰ τῆς ἐπιστολῆς see the note on the passage.

28. The main body of the Epistle would probably be written by an amanuensis, and the Apostle would here take up his pen and add the benediction (ἡ χάρις τοῦ Κυρίου κ.τ.λ.) in his own handwriting. See the note on the conclusion of the Second Epistle.

The salutation as here given may be regarded as the typical form in St Paul's Epistles. The longest form occurs in 2 Cor. xiii. 13, the shortest in most of the later Epistles as Colossians, 1 and 2 Timothy and Titus. In all however the ascription of grace is the leading feature. St Paul seems to have regarded this salutation as his characteristic token (see 2 Thess. iii. 17); and it was adopted after him by those especially who were his companions or disciples, as by the inspired writer of the Epistle to the Hebrews (xiii. 25), and by Clement in his Epistle to the Romans.   Compare likewise the conclusion of the Epistle of Barnabas ὁ Κύριος τῆς δόξης καὶ πάσης χάριτος μετὰ τοῦ πνεύματος ὑμῶν.   Afterwards it became the common salutation or benediction of the Church in her liturgies.

THE EPISTLES OF ST PAUL

II

THE SECOND APOSTOLIC JOURNEY

2

SECOND EPISTLE TO THE THESSALONIANS

Ye men of Galilee,
why stand ye gazing up into heaven?

In quietness and in confidence shall be your strength.

I shall see Him, but not now: I shall behold Him,
but not nigh.

ANALYSIS

I.   SALUTATION.   i. 1, 2.

II. THANKSGIVING AND DOCTRINAL PORTION.   i. 3—ii. 17.

A general expression of thankfulness and interest, leading up to the difficulty about the Lord's Advent.

  i.   The Apostle pours forth his thanksgiving for their progress in the faith; he encourages them to be patient under persecution, reminding them of the Judgment to come, and prays that they may be prepared to meet it.   i. 3—12.

  ii. He is thus led to correct the erroneous idea that the Judgment is imminent, pointing out that much must happen first.   ii. 1—12.

  iii. He repeats his thanksgiving and exhortation, and concludes this portion with a prayer.   ii. 13—17.

III. HORTATORY PORTION.   iii. 1—16.

  i.   He urges them to pray for him, and confidently anticipates their progress in the faith.   iii. 1—5.

  ii. He reproves the idle, disorderly and disobedient, and charges the faithful to withdraw from such.   iii. 6—15.

  iii. Prayer to the Lord of Peace.   iii. 16.

IV. SPECIAL DIRECTION AND BENEDICTION.   iii. 17, 18.

CHAPTER I

1. SALUTATION, i. 1, 2.

1, 2. The commencement of this Epistle is identical with that of the former, except that in the first verse ἡμῶν is inserted here after πατρὶ and in the second verse the clause ἀπὸ Θεοῦ πατρὸς...Ἰησοῦ Χριστοῦ, which is more than doubtful in the first Epistle, is genuine here. For the explanation of these verses see the note on the opening of the first Epistle.

2. THANKSGIVING AND DOCTRINAL PORTION, i. 3—ii. 17.

i. *Encouragement to patience from thoughts of the Judgment to come* (i. 3-12).

3. εὐχαριστεῖν] See the note on 1 Thess. i. 2.

καθὼς ἄξιόν ἐστιν] The addition of this phrase after ὀφείλομεν illustrates St Paul's vehemence of language, leading him to accumulate cognate expressions, where an ordinary writer would adopt a simple form; compare e.g. Phil. i. 9, 14, 23, ii. 2, iii. 9, iv. 1, 2, 17 with the notes. Still the sentence is not strictly speaking pleonastic. We may say that ὀφείλομεν points rather to the divine, καθὼς ἄξιόν ἐστι to the human side of the obligation. We may paraphrase thus: 'It is not only a duty, which our conscience prescribes as owed to God; but it is also merited by your conduct.' In the words of our Anglican Liturgy, 'It is very meet, right, and our bounden duty that we should at all times and in all places give thanks.' As expressed in the Greek Liturgies the original of these words does not show much correspondence with the language of St Paul given above; see Swainson, *The Greek Liturgies*, 1884, pp. 28, 80, 128, 267.

ὅτι] Two grammatical questions arise here. *First*, Is ὅτι to be taken with εὐχαριστεῖν ὀφείλομεν, or with καθὼς ἄξιόν ἐστι? *Secondly*, if the former construction is to be preferred, has the conjunction a definitely causal signification 'because,' or is it merely objective describing the matter of εὐχαριστεῖν, 'that'? In answer to the first question, we may say that καθὼς ἄξιόν ἐστι seems to be parenthetical, so that ὅτι is attached to εὐχαριστεῖν ὀφείλομεν. The flow of the language appears to require this connexion. There would be a certain halt in the sentence, if εὐχαριστεῖν ὀφείλομεν, the emphatic clause, were unexplained, and the explanation attached to the subordinate καθὼς ἄξιόν ἐστι. Besides, the construction of εὐχαριστεῖν with ὅτι is confirmed by the parallel passages, Rom. i. 8, 1 Cor. i. 4, 5.

The second question is more difficult. The causal signification of ὅτι runs almost imperceptibly into the objective. By translating the two into different words ('because' and 'that') in English, we give a distinctness to them which a Greek probably would not recognize. The only distinction in Greek can have been one of emphasis, the causal being the more emphatic, the objective the less so. As ὅτι here seems to be very unemphatic, we may assume that it leans to the objective meaning, and is best translated by 'that.' On the other hand, if ὅτι were attached to καθὼς ἄξιόν ἐστι, it must signify 'because.'

ὑπεραυξάνει] It has been thought that a reproof is implied in ὑπεραυ-ξάνει, as if the Apostle would warn his converts that their zeal had outrun their discretion. Such however is not the necessary or even the general meaning of compounds with this preposition, as used by St Paul, see the note on 1 Thess. iii. 10 ὑπερεκπερισσοῦ. Nor indeed would he speak of any one as having an excess of faith. The words ὑπεραυξάνει and πλεονάζει are carefully chosen; the former implying an internal, organic growth, as of a tree; the other a diffusive, or expansive character, as of a flood irrigating the land. For St Paul's habit of rapid transition in metaphor compare the note on Col. ii. 6 περιπατεῖτε ἐρριζωμένοι καὶ ἐποικοδομούμενοι.

Αὐξάνειν is elsewhere a transitive verb in St Paul, though generally intransitive in the other New Testament writers. The future intransitive αὐξήσω in Ephes. iv. 15 may come from αὔξω, which is also intransitive in Ephes. ii. 21.

εἰς ἀλλήλους] These words are perhaps better taken with πλεονάζει than with ἡ ἀγάπη ἑνὸς ἑκάστου πάντων ὑμῶν. Compare the phrase περισ-σεύειν εἰς τινὰ in Rom. v. 15, 2 Cor. i. 5, Ephes. i. 8.

4. ὥστε κ.τ.λ.] In this clause St Paul loses sight of πλεονάζει ἡ ἀγάπη, and dwells exclusively on the former head ὑπεραυξάνει ἡ πίστις. On the collocation of πίστις and ἀγάπη see the note on 1 Thess. i. 3.

αὐτοὺς ἡμᾶς] 'we ourselves'; i.e. Paul, Silvanus and Timotheus, who, as the human instruments through whom this change had been wrought, would be backward to sound the praises of the Thessalonians, lest they should seem to be boasting of themselves.

ἐνκαυχᾶσθαι] Though supported by אABP only against the bulk of manuscripts, ἐνκαυχᾶσθαι, a word which occurs here only in the New

Testament, is the most expressive reading and is certainly to be preferred to the simple καυχᾶσθαι. The preposition of the compound corresponds to ἐν ὑμῖν, not to ἐν ταῖς ἐκκλησίαις. In other words it describes the sphere of the boasting of St Paul and his companions. Compare ἐνοικεῖν ἐν (2 Cor. vi. 16), ἐνδημεῖν ἐν (2 Cor. v. 6), ἐμμένειν ἐν (Heb. viii. 9); but ἐνεργεῖν ἐν is somewhat different, see the notes on Phil. ii. 13, Gal. ii. 8.

ἐν ταῖς ἐκκλησίαις] As St Paul, after leaving Macedonia, seems not to have travelled out of the province of Achaia before writing this letter, he must here allude chiefly to the Church of Corinth and the affiliated communities, see 2 Cor. i. 1 τῇ ἐκκλησίᾳ τοῦ Θεοῦ τῇ οὔσῃ ἐν Κορίνθῳ σὺν τοῖς ἁγίοις πᾶσιν τοῖς οὖσιν ἐν ὅλῃ τῇ Ἀχαίᾳ, though by letter and by other than direct personal communication he may have boasted also to distant churches. See the note on 1 Thess. i. 8.

Polycarp undoubtedly had this passage in mind, when, writing to the Philippians, he says 'Ego autem nihil tale sensi in vobis vel audivi, in quibus laboravit beatus Paulus qui estis in principio epistolae eius (comp. 2 Cor. iii. 2): de vobis etenim *gloriatur in* omnibus *ecclesiis*, quae solae tunc Dominum cognoverant' (*Philip.* 11). A little lower down he quotes 2 Thess. iii. 15. He may have confused the Epistles to Philippi and to Thessalonica; or, as Wordsworth suggests, he may have 'regarded the Epistles to Thessalonica, the capital of Macedonia, as addressed to all the Macedonian Churches, and therefore to Philippi.'

πίστεως] '*faith*,' which was especially manifested in their patient endurance under affliction. Ὑπομονὴ is generally connected with ἐλπὶς (see on 1 Thess. i. 3), but here with πίστις. The line of separation between the two is not easily drawn.

διωγμοῖς, θλίψεσιν] The former is a special term for external persecutions inflicted by the enemies of the Gospel; the latter is more general, and denotes tribulation of any kind. See the notes on 1 Thess. i. 6, iii. 2, Phil. i. 17.

αἷς ἀνέχεσθε] The construction of ἀνέχεσθαι with a dative is quite possible (see Eur. *Androm.* 980 ξυμφοραῖς δ' ἠνειχόμην); but we have here doubtless an attraction for ἅς or rather ὧν ἀνέχεσθε, the genitive being the case with which the verb is always found in the New Testament: e.g. 2 Cor. xi. 1, 19, Eph. iv. 2, Col. iii. 13.

The first Epistle speaks of the persecutions attending their first acceptance of the Gospel as past, i. 6, ii. 14. Here the Apostle alludes, not perhaps to any fresh definite outbreak of rigorous persecution, but rather to the daily trials which as Christians they had to endure.

5. ἔνδειγμα τῆς δικαίας κρίσεως κ.τ.λ.] For the sentence compare Phil. i. 28 καὶ μὴ πτυρόμενοι ἐν μηδενὶ ὑπὸ τῶν ἀντικειμένων · ἥτις ἐστὶν αὐτοῖς ἔνδειξις ἀπωλείας, ὑμῶν δὲ σωτηρίας, καὶ τοῦτο ἀπὸ Θεοῦ· ὅτι ὑμῖν ἐχαρίσθη τὸ ὑπὲρ Χριστοῦ, οὐ μόνον τὸ εἰς αὐτὸν πιστεύειν, ἀλλὰ καὶ τὸ ὑπὲρ αὐτοῦ πάσχειν, another point of coincidence between the Thessalonian and Philippian Epistles. See the notes on 1 Thess. i. 1 Παῦλος, 2.

This parallel passage shows that ἔνδειγμα τῆς δικαίας κρίσεως here refers not to their being subject to persecution (i.e. not to αἷς ἀνέχεσθε solely), but to their *patience* under persecution, i.e. to the whole sentence ὑπὲρ τῆς ὑπομονῆς...ἀνέχεσθε. It still however remains a question whether ἔνδειγμα is a nominative or an accusative case. If it is a nominative, the sentence is elliptical, and may be supplied ὅτι (or ὅπερ) ἐστὶν ἔνδειγμα on the model of the passage from the Philippians. But the word is more probably an accusative by a loose sort of construction not without a parallel in classical writers, the sentence with which it is in apposition having assumed an objective form. Compare Rom. xii. 1 τὴν λογικὴν λατρείαν, 1 Tim. ii. 6 τὸ μαρτύριον καιροῖς ἰδίοις. Winer however (§ lix. p. 669) prefers to consider ἔνδειγμα a nominative.

What then is meant by the δικαία κρίσις of God? and what is the ἔνδειγμα of it? The δικαία κρίσις involves (1), and prominently, the law of compensation by which the sufferers of this world shall rest hereafter and the persecutors of this world shall suffer hereafter. Compare our Lord's saying in the parable (Luke xvi. 25): 'Thou in thy lifetime receivedst thy good things, and likewise Lazarus evil things : but now he is comforted, and thou art tormented.' Contrast the offensive form in which the thought is expressed in Tertullian (*de Spectac.* 30 praesides persecutores dominici nominis saevioribus quam ipsi flammis saevierunt insultantibus contra Christianos liquescentes, and the whole chapter). But (2) the simple suffering does not in itself constitute a claim to future joy. The suffering must come of faith. The sufferer must endure for the kingdom of God's sake (ὑπὲρ ἧς καὶ πάσχετε).

The ἔνδειγμα, the 'evidence' or 'token' of this just judgment of God, is found in the confident endurance and patient waiting of the Thessalonians. This strong practical belief in the judgment was *pro tanto* a proof of its truth. Compare the parallel expression in the Philippian Epistle (l.c.) πτυρόμενοι ἐν μηδενὶ...ἥτις ἐστὶν ἔνδειξις κ.τ.λ.

ἔνδειγμα] This word occurs here only in the New Testament. On the analogy of other substantives in -μα formed from the passive perfect, ἔνδειγμα must have a passive sense. It must signify not 'a thing proving,' but 'a thing proved,' 'a proof.' See the note on πλήρωμα *Colossians* p. 257 sq., where other examples of this form are adduced. On the other hand ἔνδειξις, which is more usual with St Paul (Rom. iii. 25, 26, 2 Cor. viii. 24, Phil. i. 28), lays stress rather on the act or process of proving. The E.V., which translates ἔνδειγμα here 'a manifest token,' renders ἔνδειξις in Phil. l.c. 'an evident token.' So in Acts i. 3 it translates τεκμήριον 'an infallible proof.' Ἀπόδειξις occurs once in the New Testament, 1 Cor. ii. 4 ἐν ἀποδείξει πνεύματος καὶ δυνάμεως. It differs from ἔνδειξις as considering the proof rather from the point of view of its acceptance by others, than of its inherent truth ; thus it means 'demonstration.' Compare the technical senses of the word both in mathematics and dialectic : Pollux iv. 33 μέρη τοῦ ῥητορικοῦ λόγου προοίμιον, διήγησις, πίστις, ἀπόδειξις.

εἰς τὸ καταξιωθῆναι] The only construction which renders the sentence logically smooth, though slightly awkward grammatically, is that which connects these words with δικαίας κρίσεως. If ἔνδειγμα τῆς δικαίας κρίσεως τοῦ Θεοῦ is treated as a parenthesis and εἰς τὸ καταξιωθῆναι attached to any part of the preceding verse, a new awkwardness is introduced in εἴπερ δίκαιον, which is thus deprived of its proper reference to δικαίας κρίσεως. The preposition εἰς will therefore denote either the result or the purpose (see note on 1 Thess. ii. 16) of the δικαία κρίσις, 'the just judgment of God which contemplates your being counted worthy etc.'

τῆς βασιλείας τοῦ Θεοῦ] *'the kingdom of God,'* the new order of things as established under Christ, though with a special reference to its final and perfect development in His future kingdom.

ὑπὲρ ἧς] Not 'to gain which,' but 'for the establishment, promotion and maintenance of which.' Compare again the passage in the Philippians (i. 29) cited above, ὑμῖν ἐχαρίσθη τὸ ὑπὲρ Χριστοῦ...πάσχειν.

καὶ πάσχετε] The καὶ still further enforces the connexion between present suffering and future glory. Compare 2 Tim. ii. 12 εἰ ὑπομένομεν, καὶ συμβασιλεύσομεν.

6. **εἴπερ**] i.e. 'assuming that it is just in the sight of God.' The word is purely hypothetical and in itself seems to imply neither probability nor improbability. So far is it from implying the latter, that wherever it occurs in the New Testament, it is used of what the writer regards as the true or probable hypothesis: comp. Rom. viii. 9, 17, 1 Cor. viii. 5, except perhaps 1 Cor. xv. 15 εἴπερ ἄρα νεκροὶ οὐκ ἐγείρονται, where the introduction of ἄρα refers the assumption to the opinion of others, who took it for granted. On the difference between εἴπερ and εἴγε see the note on Gal. iii. 4 εἴ γε καὶ εἰκῆ, and compare 2 Cor. v. 3, where the reading varies. Consult also Hermann *ad Viger.* p. 834, Klotz *Devar.* II. pp. 308, 528 and Winer § liii. p. 561.

εἴπερ δίκαιον παρὰ Θεῷ] This clause is to be referred to δικαίας κρίσεως τοῦ Θεοῦ εἰς τὸ καταξιωθῆναι ὑμᾶς κ.τ.λ. Thus the sense of the passage will be: 'the just judgment of God which purposes your admission to His kingdom, granting that it is just in the sight of God etc.'

7. **ἄνεσιν**] *'relief.'* The word is properly used here, as elsewhere, in opposition to θλίψις. See 2 Cor. vii. 5, viii. 13 and compare 2 Cor. ii. 13 οὐκ ἔσχηκα ἄνεσιν τῷ πνεύματι with ii. 4 ἐκ πολλῆς θλίψεως καὶ συνοχῆς καρδίας ἔγραψα. So too *Act. Paul. et Thecl.* § 37. Ἄνεσις is 'a slackening, relaxation, relief,' just as θλίψις is 'a crushing, a constraint.' On θλίψις and words of similar import such as στενοχωρία, ἀνάγκη, συνοχή see the note on 1 Thess. iii. 7.

μεθ' ἡμῶν] *'with us,'* the writers of the Epistle, Paul, Silvanus and Timotheus. Their community in present suffering was an earnest of their community in future glory. In the same spirit St Paul elsewhere associates the sufferings of his converts with his own. So especially 2 Cor. i. 7 εἰδότες ὅτι ὡς κοινωνοί ἐστε τῶν παθημάτων, οὕτως καὶ τῆς παρακλήσεως, and Phil. i. 30 τὸν αὐτὸν ἀγῶνα ἔχοντες οἷον εἴδετε ἐν ἐμοί, a continuation of the passage which has already been quoted on ver. 5 as a close parallel to this.

ἐν τῇ ἀποκαλύψει] On the resemblance of apocalyptic passages in point of language and imagery to the Old Testament see the note on 1 Thess. v. 3.

In the passage before us we have chiefly to notice the fearlessness with which the Apostle applies the phenomena represented in the Old Testament as the symbols of the divine presence, the attendant angels (Ps. lxviii. 17) and the flame of fire (Ex. iii. 2, xix. 18, Deut. iv. 11, Ps. civ. 4, Is. lxvi. 15, Mal. iv. 1, also Dan. vii. 9, 10 where both images are found combined), to the Appearing of our Lord. In some cases the very expressions used in the Hebrew prophets of God have been adopted by St Paul in speaking of Christ. We have a remarkable instance of this in the words ἀπὸ προσώπου τοῦ Κυρίου καὶ ἀπὸ τῆς δόξης τῆς ἰσχύος αὐτοῦ borrowed from Isaiah (ii. 10, 19, 21, xix. 16, cited by Jowett).

The term ἀποκάλυψις is used here of the Lord's coming, as 1 Cor. i. 7 and 1 Pet. i. 7, 13, iv. 13, in place of the more usual word παρουσία. The common term for this great event in the Pastoral Epistles is ἐπιφάνεια (see note below on ii. 8), neither ἀποκάλυψις nor παρουσία occurring in them.

μετ' ἀγγέλων δυνάμεως αὐτοῦ] 'with the angels, the ministers of His power.' This expression is translated in the E.V. and by others 'with his mighty angels,' δυνάμεως being made to serve the turn of an epithet according to the common Hebrew idiom. Jowett who supports this view instances υἱοὶ δυνάμεως (Judges xviii. 2, 1 Sam. xviii. 17, 2 Chron. xxv. 13), ἄρχοντες δυνάμεως (1 Kings xv. 20, 2 Kings xxv. 23). But the interpretation must be discarded, though the Hebraic tinge of the passage is pro tanto in favour of it; for the position of αὐτοῦ would thus be rendered extremely awkward. Moreover on this supposition the Apostle would dwell rather on the power of subordinate beings than of the Lord Himself.

8. ἐν πυρὶ φλογὸς] This is probably the true reading in this passage and in Exod. iii. 2 of which it is a reminiscence. On the other hand ἐν φλογὶ πυρὸς is on the whole to be preferred in Acts vii. 30. There is a similar variation of reading in all three passages.

Whether these words are to be attached to the preceding or the following sentence is doubtful. The flow of the sentence seems to be in favour of the second alternative, and the sense is somewhat assisted by this construction. In this case the 'flame of fire' will be regarded at one and the same time as a revelation of the divine presence, and as an instrument of vengeance, though ἐν is not to be taken in the instrumental sense. Compare Malachi iii. 2, iv. 1, 2. This double aspect will hold equally whether the 'fire' be taken in a literal or a figurative sense: for the revelation of Christ will in itself inflict the severest punishment on the wicked, by opening their eyes to what they have lost.

διδόντος ἐκδίκησιν] '*awarding retribution.*' Again an expression
borrowed from the Old Testament and there applied to God. See
Ezek. xxv. 14 ἐπιγνώσονται τὴν ἐκδίκησίν μου, λέγει Κύριος.

τοῖς μὴ εἰδόσι κ.τ.λ.] That two distinct classes are here meant is
clear, from the repetition of the article. These classes are generally
taken to correspond to the unbelieving heathen and the unbelieving Jew
respectively. But if by τοῖς μὴ εἰδόσι Θεὸν are meant the heathen who
rejected the Gospel when offered to them, they are not distinct from τοῖς
μὴ ὑπακούουσι; and if on the other hand the heathen world generally is
signified, this is opposed to the doctrine which St Paul teaches in
Romans ii. The classification seems to be somewhat different, viz. 'those
who, not having the Gospel offered to them, yet reject the light of natural
religion, which in a certain sense reveals God to them; and those who,
whether Jews or Gentiles, hearing the Gospel preached yet refuse to
accept it.' This seems to give a more adequate explanation of τοῖς μὴ
εἰδόσι Θεὸν (compare Rom. i. 18, 28); and the two classes will then
correspond to those condemned in the opening chapters of the Epistle to
the Romans. On τοῖς μὴ εἰδόσι compare Gal. iv. 8, 1 Thess. iv. 5 with
the notes, and on εἰδέναι see 1 Thess. v. 12.

9. οἵτινες] '*men who.*' While the simple οἱ would define the persons
themselves, οἵτινες regards them as members of a class, and points to
their class characteristics. It may be paraphrased, 'for they and such as
they.' See further on Gal. iv. 24 ἥτις ἐστὶν Ἄγαρ, Phil. i. 28 ἥτις ἐστὶν
αὐτοῖς ἔνδειξις ἀπωλείας, iv. 3 αἵτινες συνήθλησάν μοι with the notes; and
comp. Rom. ii. 15, vi. 2, Gal. iv. 26, v. 19, Phil. ii. 20, 1 Tim. i. 4, etc.

ὄλεθρον] Lachmann's reading ὀλέθριον, if better supported by external
authority, would deserve some consideration; for the accumulation of
epithets compare 1 Tim. i. 17.

ἀπὸ προσώπου κ.τ.λ.] It has been questioned what sense should be
assigned to ἀπό, whether it should be taken 'by reason of,' or 'shut out
from, removed from.' The latter is grammatically much more probable,
and on all accounts to be preferred. The expression is borrowed from
Isaiah ii. 10, 19, 21 ἀπὸ προσώπου τοῦ φόβου Κυρίου καὶ ἀπὸ δόξης τῆς
ἰσχύος αὐτοῦ ὅταν ἀναστῇ κ.τ.λ., as was observed by Tertullian (*adv.
Marc.* v. 16 'quos ait poenam luituros exitialem, aeternam, a facie Domini
et a gloria valentiae eius'), and there ἀπὸ is clearly in this sense. It is
thought that the second clause ἀπὸ τῆς δόξης is in favour of the other
meaning 'by reason of'; but δόξα is here used, as elsewhere, of the
visible glory, the bright light which is the symbol of the divine presence.
Compare 2 Cor. iii. 7 sq., Luke ii. 9 δόξα Κυρίου περιέλαμψεν, 1 Cor. xv. 41
ἄλλη δόξα ἡλίου, and more especially 1 Kings viii. 11 ἔπλησε δόξα Κυρίου τὸν
οἶκον. The opinion of some critics that ἀπὸ in the sense of 'apart from'
should be accentuated ἄπο seems not to rest on sufficient grounds.

The severest punishment of the wicked is here represented to be
exclusion from the presence of God. Compare Luke xiii. 27 'Depart

from me, all ye workers of iniquity,' and the corresponding phrase in St Matthew viii. 12 τὸ σκότος τὸ ἐξώτερον (so Matt. xxii. 13, xxv. 30). The idea is not confined to the New Testament: it is met with in the Old Testament also; see Ps. li. 11 and other passages quoted by Lünemann *ad loc.* Whatever may be meant by the 'worm that dieth not and the fire that is not quenched' (Mark ix. 48 quoted from Isaiah lxvi. 24), we are at least led by such passages as these to hold the essence of the future punishment of the wicked, as indeed seems to be the case in the present world also, to consist rather in a moral and spiritual condition than in any physical sufferings undergone.

10. ἐνδοξασθῆναι] Used with a reference to ἀπὸ τῆς δόξης of the preceding verse. 'The object of His coming is that He may be glorified in His saints; and yet from that glory the wicked, your persecutors, will be shut out. Thus have they hindered the high purposes of God, and been untrue to the end for which they were created.'

ἐν τοῖς ἁγίοις αὐτοῦ] Not 'amidst,' nor yet 'by,' 'through' (ἐν instrumental), but '*in His saints.*' They are the mirror in which His glory shines. His infinite perfections are reflected in those finite beings exalted and purified through Him. Similarly the Father is said to be glorified in the Son (John xiv. 13), though in a far higher sense, because there the mirror is perfect, and the reflection is 'the express image of His person' (Hebr. i. 3).

That this is the meaning of the preposition is shown by the compound ἐνδοξασθῆναι. Though only used in the New Testament here and ver. 12, the word is not uncommon in LXX.: compare Exod. xiv. 4 ἐνδοξασθήσομαι ἐν Φαραώ, Ecclus. xxxviii. 6 ἐνδοξάζεσθαι ἐν τοῖς θαυμασίοις αὐτοῦ etc.

τοῖς ἁγίοις αὐτοῦ] See note on 1 Thess. iii. 13.

ἐν πᾶσιν τοῖς πιστεύσασιν] The preposition ἐν here clearly has the same meaning as in the parallel clause ἐν τοῖς ἁγίοις. 'His marvellous attributes are displayed in the believers.' But for the parallelism of the clauses, a different interpretation might have been assigned to θαυμασθῆναι ἐν πᾶσιν τοῖς πιστεύσασιν.

πιστεύσασιν] The word πιστεύειν signifies not merely 'to believe,' as a continuous state of mind, but also 'to accept the Gospel,' as a single definite act. Compare 1 Cor. xv. 2, 11, 2 Cor. iv. 13 (from LXX.). Hence the past ὁ πιστεύσας is 'one who has accepted the Gospel, a believer,' as e.g. in Acts iv. 32, xi. 17. It is simpler so to explain it, than to suppose that the past tense is used here to denote that faith would then have been absorbed in sight and ceased to be. The correction πιστεύουσιν adopted by the Textus Receptus probably arose from an inability to grasp this meaning of the aorist. Compare similar usages in Madv. *Gr. Syn.* § III. Rem. *d.* p. 90, as ἐβασίλευσε, ἐβούλευσε etc., who however confines it to the aorist; see also Donaldson *Gr. Gr.,* p. 411 sq. (ed. 3).

ὅτι ἐπιστεύθη] '*because it was believed.*' The sentence is elliptical.

If completed it would have run, 'in all them that believed, and *therefore in you*, for our testimony was believed by you.' The suppressed clause naturally supplies itself from what has gone before, the participation of the Thessalonians in the glories of Christ's coming being the leading idea of the context; see especially ver. 7 ὑμῖν τοῖς θλιβομένοις ἄνεσιν. Moreover πᾶσιν points to the ellipsis, as if he had said: 'for all, you included'; and perhaps still further the dead, as well as the surviving, see 1 Thess. iv. 13 sq.

ἐφ' ὑμᾶς] is generally taken strictly] with τὸ μαρτύριον ἡμῶν, 'our testimony addressed to you was believed'; but the point of the sentence is rather 'you believed,' than 'you had the Gospel offered to you' as this construction would make it. In other words, we look for a direct connexion between the Thessalonians and a *belief* in the Gospel rather than between the Thessalonians and the *preaching* of the Gospel. Nor is the construction ἐπιστεύθη ἐφ' ὑμᾶς grammatically indefensible. The preposition has a notion of 'direction towards,' 'belief in our testimony directed itself to reach you.' Compare 2 Cor. ii. 3 πεποιθὼς ἐπὶ πάντας ὑμᾶς ὅτι ἡ ἐμὴ χαρὰ πάντων ὑμῶν ἐστὶν and the construction ἐλπίζειν ἐπί, 1 Pet. i. 13, 1 Tim. v. 5. The language of Bengel however 'ad vos usque, in occidente,' goes too far.

ἐν τῇ ἡμέρᾳ ἐκείνῃ] '*in that day*'; to be attached to ἐνδοξασθῆναι κ.τ.λ., the clause ὅτι ἐπιστεύθη...ἐφ' ὑμᾶς being parenthetical. This suspension of ἐν τῇ ἡμέρᾳ ἐκείνῃ, giving it greater emphasis by making it clinch the sentence, is in accordance with the pervading tone and purport of the Thessalonian Epistles, which enforce the duty of waiting for the Lord's coming. On the expression ἡμέρα ἐκείνη see the notes on 1 Thess. v. 2, 4.

11.   εἰς ὅ] '*to which end*,' i.e. εἰς τὸ καταξιωθῆναι ὑμᾶς (ver. 5).

ἵνα ὑμᾶς κ.τ.λ.] This still further defines the meaning of εἰς ὅ. The particle ἵνα seems to be used here rather in its classical sense, denoting the purpose, 'in order that,' than to imply simply the substance of the prayers 'pray that God may etc.' according to the meaning which it bears in later Greek. But the one meaning shades off into the other, and it is often difficult to discriminate between them. See the notes on 1 Thess. ii. 16, v. 4.

τῆς κλήσεως] As the verb ἀξιοῦν never signifies 'to make worthy,' but always 'to account worthy,' τῆς κλήσεως cannot denote 'calling' according to the accepted meaning of the term (i.e. the being included in the fold of Christ), as it is usually found (e.g. 2 Tim. i. 9); but must refer to something future. It is in fact capable of the same differences of meaning as ἐκλογὴ (see the note on 1 Thess. i. 4), and is here used of 'final acceptance.' The Apostle's prayer therefore for his converts is that God may deem them worthy to be called to the kingdom of His glory. This higher and future 'calling' differs rather in degree than in kind from the calling whereby they have been already called, and therefore is denoted by the same word. Just so the βασιλεία τοῦ Θεοῦ of the future is but a higher development of the βασιλεία τοῦ Θεοῦ of the present.

ὁ Θεὸς ἡμῶν] '*the God of us all.*' By the pronoun the Apostle once more asserts his fellowship with his converts. Compare ver. 7, ἄνεσιν μεθ' ἡμῶν, and the note on 1 Thess. v. 6 ἐσμέν.

καὶ πληρώσῃ] After the mention of τῆς κλήσεως we might have expected some reference to external happiness or to outward glories. But it is not so. The essence of their 'calling' consisted in their being perfected morally and spiritually. The end of it was that the Lord might be glorified in them (ver. 12).

εὐδοκίαν ἀγαθωσύνης] '*delight in well-doing.*' If the phrase had stood alone, we should naturally have translated it 'the good pleasure of His goodness,' referring both εὐδοκίαν and ἀγαθωσύνης to God ; as the E.V. in accordance with the common usage of εὐδοκεῖν, εὐδοκία of the divine will. But its parallelism with ἔργον πίστεως, which cannot be interpreted here of God but must apply to the Thessalonians, shows that it must be taken in the same way, 'all delight, all gladness in well-doing.' It is something to do good, but it is a higher stage of moral progress to delight in doing good. For the opposite to this compare Rom. i. 32, οὐ μόνον αὐτὰ ποιοῦσιν ἀλλὰ καὶ συνευδοκοῦσι τοῖς πράσσουσιν. On ἀγαθωσύνη and its difference from ἀγαθότης and χρηστότης see the notes on 1 Thess. iii. 13 and Gal. v. 22 respectively. On εὐδοκία see the note on Phil. i. 25, and compare Eph. i. 5.

ἔργον πίστεως] '*work, activity of faith.*' It must not be simply a passive, dead faith. See James ii. 18, and the note on 1 Thess. i. 3.

ἐν δυνάμει] '*powerfully, effectively,*' referring to πληρώσῃ above.

12.   τὸ ὄνομα τοῦ Κυρίου] In this expression we have another instance of the adoption of the language of the Old Testament originally referring to Jehovah, and its application to our Lord, see vv. 8, 9. The name of the Lord (יהוה שֵׁם) is a frequent periphrasis for 'the Lord.' In this expression, 'the name' seems to imply idea of 'title, dignity, majesty, power,' better than of 'personality.' Indeed 'the name' (הֵשּׁם) and sometimes even without the article, שֵׁם) is at times found absolutely for 'the Lord,' e.g. Levit. xxiv. 11, 16; compare also Deut. xxviii. 58, φοβεῖσθαι τὸ ὄνομα τὸ ἔντιμον καὶ τὸ θαυμαστὸν τοῦτο, Κύριον τὸν Θεόν σου (LXX.). From a misinterpretation of these passages of Leviticus came the superstitious fear of the Jews of pronouncing the word Jehovah. See Drusius on *Ecclus.* li. 4 cited by Schleusner *Vet. Test.* s. v. ὄνομα. It does not appear that a similar periphrasis is used in the Old Testament of any other person, or office. Instances like τὸ ὄνομα τοῦ βασιλέως, or τὸ ὄνομα τοῦ Δαρείου for ὁ βασιλεύς or ὁ Δαρεῖος are not parallels; and so far the expression may be regarded as one confined to the Divine Being. On the 'name' belonging to our Lord compare Phil. ii. 9 ἐχαρίσατο αὐτῷ τὸ ὄνομα τὸ ὑπὲρ πᾶν ὄνομα, Heb. i. 4 ὅσῳ διαφορώτερον παρ' αὐτοὺς κεκληρονό-μηκεν ὄνομα, and for a remarkable and reiterated use of the periphrasis

applied to Him, Acts iii. 16 τῇ πίστει τοῦ ὀνόματος αὐτοῦ τοῦτον ὃν θεωρεῖτε...ἐστερέωσεν τὸ ὄνομα αὐτοῦ. For more on this subject see the notes on Phil. ii. 9 τὸ ὄνομα and 10 ἐν τῷ ὀνόματι.

καὶ ὑμεῖς ἐν αὐτῷ] The similarity in spirit and expression here to St John has not escaped notice. Compare John xvii. 1, 10, 21—26. κατὰ τὴν χάριν] i.e. 'the source, whence all glorification springs.' An instance of St Paul's anxiety to exclude human merit. This desire appears frequently (Rom. iv. 16, xi. 5, 6, Ephes. ii. 5, 8).

Κυρίου 'Ιησοῦ Χριστοῦ] Since Κυρίου may be regarded as a proper name and therefore frequently stands without the article, it is not safe to take Θεοῦ and Κυρίου as referring to the same Person because the article is not repeated. The translation of the E. V. is rendered much more probable by the common connexion of Κύριος 'Ιησοῦς Χριστός. See the matter fully discussed in Middleton *ad loc.*

CHAPTER II

ii. *Much must happen before the Judgment* (ii. 1—12).

1. Ἐρωτῶμεν] '*we beseech you.*' On the sense which this word bears in the New Testament, see the note on 1 Thess. iv. 1.

δὲ] The Apostle had spoken of the day, when the Thessalonians should be glorified and their persecutors punished. He now turns aside (δὲ) to correct any mistakes which his mention of this day may have occasioned, to calm any feverish desires which it may have excited. He bids his converts be aware that, though come it will, yet it will not come yet. Their persecutions must be endured yet awhile. They must not give up their patient watchfulness, their sober judgment.

ὑπὲρ] The E. V., following the Vulgate and the Latin authorities generally, translates this as a particle of adjuration, '*by* the coming.' But there is no support for this sense in the New Testament. Ὑπὲρ is here almost equivalent to περί, to which however it superadds an idea of advocacy (see the note on Gal. i. 3) more or less prominent in different passages, and here probably very faint. Roughly and broadly paraphrased, ὑπὲρ τῆς παρουσίας would be, 'to correct mistaken notions,' or 'to advocate the true view of the coming.'

ἐπισυναγωγῆς] The verb ἐπισυνάγειν is used in the Gospels of the gathering together of the elect at the Lord's coming (Matt. xxiv. 31, Mark xiii. 27), and the substantive ἐπισυναγωγὴ seems to have acquired a precise and definite meaning in relation to the great event, corresponding to that attached to παρουσία. It has this sense in 2 Macc. ii. 7, though there the ἐπισυναγωγὴ is regarded from a Jewish point of view, as the gathering into a temporal kingdom of Messiah.

2. ταχέως] Not 'soon' (i.e. 'after so short a time') in regard to a previous point of time, as e.g. their conversion; but '*hastily,*' '*readily,*' 'unhesitatingly,' describing the manner of σαλευθῆναι. Compare 1 Tim. v. 22, and so perhaps the word is used in Gal. i. 6 θαυμάζω ὅτι οὕτως ταχέως μετατίθεσθε 'I marvel that ye are so ready in changing.' See the note there.

σαλευθῆναι] i.e. 'not to be driven by feverish expectations from your sober senses, as a ship drifts away under a tempest from its moorings. The E. V. 'shaken in mind' is quite wrong. The phrase σαλεύεσθαι ἐπὶ ἀγκύρας is not an uncommon one, signifying 'to ride at anchor.' The opposite to it is ἀποσαλεύειν ἀγκύρας, or σαλεύειν ἀπὸ ἀγκύρας. Compare especially Plut. *Op. Mor.* ii. p. 493 D ὄρεξιν τοῦ κατὰ φύσιν ἀποσαλεύουσαν, followed almost immediately by ὡς ἐπ' ἀγκύρας τῆς φύσεως σαλεύει.

τοῦ νοὸς] *'judgment, reason, sober sense,'* as opposed to any fit of enthusiasm, or any feverish anxieties and desires. Νοῦς is here used in a similar sense to 1 Cor. xiv. 15 προσεύξομαι τῷ πνεύματι, προσεύξομαι δὲ καὶ τῷ νοΐ. Generally in St Paul πνεῦμα and νοῦς are regarded as closely allied, and almost convertible, being opposed to σάρξ or σῶμα ; but in 1 Cor. l. c., as here, the intellectual element in νοῦς is the prominent one. See the note on 1 Thess. v. 23.

μηδὲ] is the best supported reading. Nor indeed does μήτε suit the context, where the disjunctive, not the adjunctive, negative is required. There is the same variation of reading, with a similar preponderance of authority in favour of the more grammatical particle, in Eph. iv. 27 μηδὲ δίδοτε τόπον τῷ διαβόλῳ. On the difference between οὐδέ, μηδέ, and οὔτε, μήτε see the notes on Gal. i. 12, and 1 Thess. ii. 3. The same phenomenon of μηδὲ followed by a triple μήτε occurs in the Epistle on the Martyrs of Lyons and Vienne given in Eusebius *H. E.* v. 1. 20 ὥστε μηδὲ τὸ ἴδιον κατειπεῖν ὄνομα μήτε ἔθνους μήτε πόλεως ὅθεν ἦν μήτε εἰ δοῦλος κ.τ.λ., where again μήτε is found as a variant for μηδέ.

θροεῖσθαι] *'nor yet be confused,'* without actually losing your mind. Θροεῖσθαι seems to be weaker, not stronger, than σαλευθῆναι ἀπὸ τοῦ νοός ; and this we might expect after μηδέ.

ὡς δι' ἡμῶν] It is questioned whether these words refer to ἐπιστολῆς only, or to λόγου and ἐπιστολῆς, or to all the three πνεύματος, λόγου, ἐπιστολῆς. The sense seems to require us to extend the reference to λόγου as well as ἐπιστολῆς 'oral tidings no less than the written letter'; and having done this we are almost forced by the parallelism of the clauses to include πνεύματος also. Nor is διὰ πνεύματος incapable of an explanation, when connected with ὡς δι' ἡμῶν. There are three ways in which the pretended authority of the Apostle might be brought forward by false or mistaken teachers. They might represent his opinion as communicated to them by some spiritual revelation (διὰ πνεύματος) ; or they might report a conversation pretended to have been held with him (διὰ λόγου) ; or they might produce a letter purporting to come from him (δι' ἐπιστολῆς). In this way διὰ πνεύματος might as well be used of spiritual communication, as opposed to διὰ λόγου, δι' ἐπιστολῆς, the instruments of outward intercourse. Nor need this πνεῦμα have been a fabrication of the false teachers ; but they may have been deceived themselves by spiritual hallucinations which they mistook for true revelations, the διάκρισις πνευμάτων being indispensable in the Early Church, and Paul having himself warned the Thessalonians that they must try the spirits.   See the notes on 1 Thess. v. 19—21.

Do the words δι' ἐπιστολῆς here refer to the First Epistle to the Thessalonians, some passages of which (as iv. 13 sq) being misunderstood might not unnaturally give rise to the expectation that the day of the Lord was close at hand? Or do they point to a forged epistle circulated in the Apostle's name? The former opinion is maintained and lucidly set forth by Paley (*Horæ Paulinæ* c. x. § 3) who accordingly translates 'quasi nos quid tale aut dixerimus aut scripserimus.' But the words will scarcely bear this interpretation: for as no mention has gone before of the *purport* of the tidings or letter, the expression ὡς δι' ἡμῶν, 'as if coming from us,' cannot be intended to throw discredit on the interpretation of this purport, but on the letter or tidings themselves. The expression is different where he confessedly speaks of his own letter, as below, ii. 15.

We have therefore to fall back upon the supposition of a forged letter. Whether St Paul actually knew that such a letter had been forged, it is impossible to say. If he had, probably he would have spoken more strongly; and the whole sentence is couched in the vague language of one who suspected rather than knew. But he must at least have had reasons for believing that an illicit use had been made of his authority in some way or other: and the suspicion of a possible forgery seems to have crossed his mind at an earlier date, when he wrote the first epistle (see the note on 1 Thess. v. 27); and he guards against it at the close of this epistle also (iii. 17).

ὡς ὅτι] '*representing that.*' The expression in this passage throws discredit on the statement. Compare 2 Cor. xi. 21 κατὰ ἀτιμίαν λέγω ὡς ὅτι ἡμεῖς ἠσθενήκαμεν, Isocr. *Busir.* Arg. p. 220 κατηγόρουν αὐτοῦ ὡς ὅτι καινὰ δαιμόνια εἰσφέρει, Xenophon *Hell.* iii. 2. 14 etc. The idea of misrepresentation or error is not however necessarily inherent in the combination of particles ὡς ὅτι; but the ὡς points to the subjective statement as distinguished from the objective fact, and thus this idea of untruth is frequently implied. It is not however universal: see 2 Cor. v. 19 ὡς ὅτι Θεὸς ἦν ἐν Χριστῷ κόσμον καταλλάσσων ἑαυτῷ.

ἐνέστηκεν] '*is imminent.*' For τὰ ἐνεστῶτα 'things present' as opposed to τὰ μέλλοντα 'things future' see Rom. viii. 38, 1 Cor. iii. 22, and for ἐνεστὼς in the sense of 'present' compare 1 Cor. vii. 26, Gal. i. 4.

The Apostle then does not deny that the day of the Lord may be near. He asserts that it is not imminent. Certain events must take place before it arrives; and though they may be crowded into a short space of time, still they demand the lapse of some appreciable period.

ἡ ἡμέρα τοῦ Κυρίου] See the notes on 1 Thess. v. 2, 4.

3. κατὰ μηδένα τρόπον] i.e. whether by the means specified in the preceding verse, or in any other way.

ὅτι] '*for (the day shall not come).*' We have here an instance of the ellipsis so common in St Paul. Another instance occurs just below, ver. 7

II. 3]   SECOND EPISTLE TO THE THESSALONIANS.   III

μόνον ὁ κατέχων ἄρτι κ.τ.λ.   Other examples are Gal. i. 20 ἰδοὺ ἐνώπιον τοῦ Θεοῦ ὅτι, ii. 4 διὰ δὲ τοὺς παρεισάκτους ψευδαδέλφους κ.τ.λ., ii. 9 ἵνα ἡμεῖς εἰς τὰ ἔθνη (and of ellipse after ἵνα again 1 Cor. i. 31, 2 Cor. viii. 13, Rom. iv. 16), v. 13 μόνον μὴ τὴν ἐλευθερίαν εἰς ἀφορμὴν τῇ σαρκί, 1 Cor. iv. 6 μὴ ὑπὲρ ἃ γέγραπται, v. 1 τοιαύτη πορνεία ἥτις οὐδὲ ἐν τοῖς ἔθνεσιν, xi. 24 τὸ σῶμα τὸ ὑπὲρ ὑμῶν, 2 Cor. ix. 7 ἕκαστος καθὼς προῄρηται τῇ καρδίᾳ, Rom. xiii. 7 etc.

Another interpretation attaches ὅτι to ἐξαπατήσῃ 'let no man deceive you by saying that,' sc. the day will not be delayed.   But this is extremely harsh, as obviously the words ἐὰν μὴ ἔλθῃ κ.τ.λ. suggest a different way of supplying the ellipsis.

ἡ ἀποστασία] '*the revolt, rebellion.*'   The word implies that the opposition contemplated by St Paul springs up from within rather than from without.   In other words, it must arise either from the Jews or from apostate Christians, either of whom might be said to fall away from God. On the other hand it cannot refer to Gentiles.   This consideration alone will exclude many interpretations given of the 'man of sin.'   The word ἀποστασία is a later form for ἀπόστασις.   See Lobeck, *Phryn.* p. 528.

καὶ ἀποκαλυφθῇ] It is impossible to pronounce on mere grammatical grounds whether this 'revelation' is spoken of as the consequence and crowning event of the ἀποστασία, or is the same incident regarded from another point of view.   The interpretation will depend mainly on the conception entertained of ὁ ἄνθρωπος τῆς ἀνομίας as denoting a person or otherwise.

One of the important features in this description is the parallel drawn between Christ and the adversary of Christ.   Both alike are 'revealed,' and to both alike the term 'mystery' is applied.   From this circumstance, and from the description given in ver. 4 of his arrogant assumption, we cannot doubt that the man of sin in St Paul is identical with the ἀντίχριστος of St John, the preposition in the latter term expressing the idea of antagonistic claims.

ὁ ἄνθρωπος τῆς ἀνομίας, ὁ υἱὸς τῆς ἀπωλείας] The one term expresses the intrinsic character, the other the ultimate destination of the person or thing intended.   The expression ὁ ἄνθρωπος τῆς ἀνομίας is to be traced originally to the Hebrew idiom, where the genitive supplies the place of epithet.   Ὁ υἱὸς τῆς ἀπωλείας again is a Hebraism : e.g. 'the son of death,' 1 Sam. xx. 31 (LXX. ὅτι υἱὸς θανάτου οὗτος, i.e. 'destined to die'), 'son of stripes,' Deut. xxv. 2.   So arrows are called 'sons of the quiver,' 'sons of the bow,' Lam. iii. 13, Job xli. 20 (28).

Yet these expressions, when transferred to the Greek, would have a depth and freshness of significance, which from having become idiomatic they had probably lost in the original Hebrew.   The Apostle, we may suppose, would employ them (1) as being more forcible than the idiomatic expressions corresponding to them in the Greek ; (2) because speaking in a prophetic view he would naturally fall into the language of the Hebrew prophets: see especially the note on 1 Thess. v. 3. (3) It is not improbable that St Paul is adopting the recognised phraseology in reference to the events of the last day. Thus Judas is called ὁ υἱὸς τῆς ἀπωλείας, John xvii. 12.

Does the Apostle intend an actual person by these expressions, or do they represent the impersonation of some evil principle or movement? The first is the *primâ facie* view, but there are good reasons for preferring the latter.

(1) The 'man of sin' is obviously distinguished from Satan (ver. 9), and yet it is difficult to see how any other person could be spoken of in such terms. (2) From the interchange of τὸ κατέχον and ὁ κατέχων we may infer that in this case at least a principle, not a person, is meant, inasmuch as it is much more natural to personify a principle than conversely. And this suggests that ὁ ἄνθρωπος τῆς ἀνομίας may be a personification also. (3) The language which St John uses in 1 Joh. ii. 18, where he speaks of 'many Antichrists,' apparently as elements of ὁ ἀντίχριστος, seems to point to the same result. (4) The 'man of sin' is spoken of as existing and working at the time when St Paul wrote, though still unrevealed (ὁ ἀντικείμενος καὶ ὑπεραιρόμενος κ.τ.λ.).

Perhaps St Paul may have seen in some actual adversary of the Gospel a type of the antichristian spirit and working; and this may have facilitated the personification.

4. ὁ ἀντικείμενος] Not to be taken with ἐπὶ πάντα κ.τ.λ., but absolutely 'the adversary.' It is equivalent to ὁ ἀντίχριστος.

ὑπεραιρόμενος ἐπὶ] Not to be translated as E. V., but '*exalteth himself exceedingly against.*' The verb ὑπεραίρεσθαι occurs in the sense 'to be exalted above measure' in 2 Cor. xii. 7 διὸ ἵνα μὴ ὑπεραίρωμαι, ἐδόθη μοι σκόλοψ τῇ σαρκί. The images and to a certain extent the expressions are drawn from Dan. xi. 36 καὶ ὁ βασιλεὺς ὑψωθήσεται καὶ μεγαλυνθήσεται ἐπὶ πάντα θεὸν καὶ λαλήσει ὑπέρογκα κ.τ.λ., referring primarily at least to Antiochus Epiphanes.

πάντα λεγόμενον θεὸν] i.e. whether the true God, or so-called gods of heathendom. St Paul inserts the word λεγόμενον, where Daniel has simply πάντα θεόν, lest he should seem to allow the claim and so derogate from the majesty of the true God. Compare 1 Cor. viii. 5 καὶ γὰρ εἴπερ εἰσὶ λεγόμενοι θεοί...ἀλλ᾽ ἡμῖν εἷς Θεὸς ὁ πατὴρ κ.τ.λ. The writer of the Clementine Homilies (xi. 12, 13, 15) uses σεβάσματα and λεγόμενοι θεοὶ in close connexion, possibly having this passage in his mind. Elsewhere he employs the words separately, λεγόμενοι θεοί v. 29, ix. 15, x. 9, 11, σέβασμα iv. 8, ix. 18, x. 8, 21, 22. See also Polybius xxxi. 3, 13, Clem. Alex. *Strom.* vii. 1 § 2 (p. 829 ed. Potter), σεβάσματι.

ἢ σέβασμα] '*or object of reverence.*' A more comprehensive expression than λεγόμενον θεόν, since it includes things as well as persons. Σέβασμα only occurs elsewhere in the New Testament in St Paul's speech on the Areopagus (Acts xvii. 23), which was nearly coincident in point of time with the writing of this Epistle.   In the E.V. of Acts l. c. σεβάσματα is wrongly translated 'devotions.'

The epithet λεγόμενον does not refer to σέβασμα, but is confined to Θεόν.

ὥστε αὐτὸν...καθίσαι] The verb καθίζειν is here intransitive as generally in the New Testament.   In 1 Cor. vi. 4, Eph. i. 20 it is transitive, and possibly in John xix. 13 also.

ὥστε] denotes here not the purpose of ὑπεραιρόμενος, in which case αὐτὸν would be inadmissible; but the result, '*so that it ends in his sitting* etc.'

εἰς τὸν ναὸν τοῦ Θεοῦ] The figure may have been suggested by the insane attempt of the emperor Caius to set up his statue in the temple at Jerusalem (Joseph. *Ant.* xviii. 8. 2).   But the actual temple can scarcely under any circumstances be meant here, as has been supposed by many from Irenæus (*Haer.* v. 30. 4) downwards.   Indeed if the 'man of sin' be regarded merely as a personification, such a view is at once precluded.

Naòs is properly the shrine, the inner sanctuary, as opposed to ἱερὸν which would include all the outer buildings.   The expression ὁ ναὸς τοῦ Θεοῦ is always figurative elsewhere in St Paul, e.g. 1 Cor. iii. 16, 17 (comp. vi. 19), 2 Cor. vi. 16, and see Ephes. ii. 21.

τοῦ Θεοῦ] After these words the received text adds ὡς Θεόν, which however must be rejected on the testimony of the ancient authorities.

ἀποδεικνύντα ἑαυτὸν] The word ἀποδεικνύναι is used frequently to denote either the nomination of a person to office, or the proclamation of a sovereign on his accession.   Compare Philo *in Flacc.* § 3 (II. p. 518 ed. Mangey) Γαίου δὲ ἀποδειχθέντος αὐτοκράτορος, together with the passages quoted in Wetstein.   The word seems to have attained this technical sense at a later than the classical period.

ὅτι ἐστὶν Θεός] The deification of the Roman Emperor may to a certain extent have supplied the image here; see the note on εἰς τὸν ναὸν τοῦ Θεοῦ above.   Wetstein mentions a coin of Julius Cæsar, having on the one side his head with the inscription θεός, on the other the word Θεσσαλονικέων.

5.   μνημονεύετε] On this verb see the note on 1 Thess. i. 3.

ἔτι ὢν πρὸς ὑμᾶς] That the purport of St Paul's preaching at Thessalonica had mainly reference to the second coming of Christ, appears also from Acts xvii. 7, 'These all do contrary to the decrees of Cæsar, saying that there is another king, one Jesus.'   See more fully in *Biblical Essays* p. 260 sq.   For the construction εἶναι πρός τινα see the note on 1 Thess. iii. 4.

6.   καὶ νῦν] The νῦν appears on the whole to be logical and not temporal: '*Well then*, ye know.'   These particles are frequently so used. Instances are Acts vii. 34 (LXX.), x. 5, xiii. 11, xx. 22, xxii. 16, 1 John i. 28 (in all of which passages the temporal sense of νῦν is more or less eclipsed).   This usage is particularly noticeable with οἶδα following, e.g.

Acts iii. 17 καὶ νῦν, ἀδελφοί, οἶδα ὅτι κατὰ ἄγνοιαν ἐπράξατε and probably xx. 25 καὶ νῦν ἰδοὺ ἐγὼ οἶδα ὅτι οὐκέτι ὄψεσθε κ.τ.λ.

It is possible however that νῦν may be temporal here as opposed not to ἔτι ὤν, which would give no good sense, but to ἐν τῷ αὐτοῦ καιρῷ. For though in this case we should naturally expect τὸ νῦν κατέχον, the displacement of νῦν is to be explained by the desire of emphasizing the adverb : 'and *as to the present time* ye know what it is that restraineth.' Compare John iv. 18 καὶ νῦν ὃν ἔχεις οὐκ ἔστιν σου ἀνήρ, where the more natural order would certainly be ὃν νῦν ἔχεις. See instances of displacement especially in temporal adverbs given in Winer § lxi. p. 692 sq. Observe this is a very different thing from saying that νῦν τὸ κατέχον is equivalent to τὸ νῦν κατέχον. In the case before us the νῦν is taken absolutely.

τὸ κατέχον] '*the restraining power*,' afterwards personified in ὁ κατέχων. The Apostle seems to intend some intermediate power, between Christ and Antichrist, which, without being directly Christian, acts as a check upon Antichrist ; such as the principle of law or order, civil government and the like. Of this restraining principle he would find a type in the Roman Empire.

εἰς τὸ ἀποκαλυφθῆναι] The preposition signifies the purpose of God : 'to the end that he, the man of sin, may be revealed at his proper, destined, season, and not before it.'

7. **τὸ γὰρ κ.τ.λ.**] 'Revealed, I say, rather than called into existence ; for in fact the evil is already working, though in secret.' Τὸ μυστήριον τῆς ἀνομίας may be contrasted with τὸ μυστήριον τῆς εὐσεβείας in 1 Tim. iii. 16 and with τὸ μυστήριον τῆς πίστεως in 1 Tim. iii. 9, by which terms St Paul describes the Christian dispensation with especial reference to the revelation of God in the Incarnation. The parallelism between Christ and Antichrist is thus kept up: see especially ver. 9. Compare also Joseph. *B. J.* i. 24. 1 τὸν Ἀντιπάτρου βίον οὐκ ἂν ἁμάρτοι τις εἰπὼν κακίας μυστήριον. On the word μυστήριον see the note on Col. i. 26.

ἐνεργεῖται] See the note on 1 Thess. ii. 13.

τῆς ἀνομίας] The genitive is thrown back to the end of the sentence, in order to give priority to the words of logical importance in the sentence—viz. 'mystery,' 'already,' 'is active'; in antithesis to 'revealed,' 'in his own time,' 'that which hindereth.'

μόνον κ.τ.λ.] The sentence is elliptical, but the ellipsis is supplied in the wrong place in the E. V. which renders 'only he that now letteth (will let), until he be taken out of the way.' The true ellipsis is after μόνον, and ὁ κατέχων ἄρτι is connected with what follows as the nominative to γένηται. Render : '*Only it must work in secret, must be unrevealed, until he that restraineth now be taken out of the way.*' For an exact parallel both to the ellipsis after μόνον, and to the position of ὁ κατέχων ἄρτι before the relative word ἕως for the sake of emphasis, see Gal. ii. 10 μόνον τῶν πτωχῶν ἵνα μνημονεύωμεν with the note.

ὁ κατέχων ἄρτι] The hindrance which was before spoken of as a principle (τὸ κατέχον) is here personified. If a person were contemplated, it is extremely improbable that the neuter gender would have been used in the other passage, whereas conversely it is a natural figure of speech in all languages to ascribe a personality to a thing. In this instance the way was paved for such personification by the fact that one of the contending powers is embodied in a person in Christ.

On ἄρτι see the note on 1 Thess. iii. 6.

ἕως γένηται] The omission of ἂν with ἕως and the conjunctive seems to be more frequent in later writers than in earlier; see Winer § xli. p. 370. The distinction which Hermann gives (de Partic. ἂν pp. 103, 109), that the insertion of the ἂν makes the time more indefinite and therefore in many cases the action less immediate or less certain, is just in principle, and the passages in the New Testament, if they do not strongly confirm it, seem to be not inconsistent with it. The English expressions 'until it be removed' and 'until it may be removed' would represent ἕως γένηται and ἕως ἂν γένηται here respectively.

8. ὁ ἄνομος] The same with ὁ ἄνθρωπος τῆς ἀνομίας of ver. 3, and probably a personification like ὁ κατέχων.

ὁ Κύριος] The word Ἰησοῦς is omitted in the received text with BKL and several other MSS. The weight of authority however, especially of the versions, is in its favour ; it is retained in אA and D primâ manu, and it was perhaps omitted on the supposition that St Paul was quoting directly from Is. xi. 4 (see the next note) instead of, as is the case, paraphrasing the passage.

ἀνελεῖ] This reading is much better supported than the received ἀναλώσει and is the reading in Is. xi. 4 καὶ πατάξει γῆν τῷ λόγῳ τοῦ στόματος αὐτοῦ (originally בשבט פיו 'by the scourge of his mouth') καὶ ἐν πνεύματι διὰ χειλέων ἀνελεῖ ἀσεβῆ. Moreover ἀναλώσει is more likely to be a gloss than ἀνελεῖ, being the more definite word. It is however worth consideration whether the ἀναλοῖ of the Sinaitic manuscript be not the original reading, since it explains both variants. The Hebrew is ימית 'he shall slay.' It is a question here whether τῷ πνεύματι τοῦ στόματος αὐτοῦ is to be taken (1) as a single phrase, 'by His mere command': or (2) as an image of power, 'by the breath of His lips.' The former seems to be certainly the sense in the original passage of Isaiah, judging by the parallelism. Indeed it was a common Hebrew expression in this sense: see the Rabbinical passages cited in Wetstein. On the other hand, the latter is the image present to the mind of the Apostle, if we are to be guided by the context. The phrases 'the breath of His lips,' 'the brightness of His presence,' will point to some physical manifestation of the Divine power. For the image compare Plautus Mil. Glor. i. 1. 16 sq. 'nempe illum dicis cum armis aureis, Quoius tu legiones difflavisti spiritu, quasi ventus folia.'

καταργήσει] A word more than once used by St Paul in opposition to 'light' as if with a sense of 'darkening,' 'eclipsing': e.g. 2 Tim. i. 10 καταργήσαντος μὲν τὸν θάνατον, φωτίσαντος δὲ ζωὴν καὶ ἀφθαρσίαν, 2 Cor. iii.

7 διὰ τὴν δόξαν τοῦ προσώπου αὐτοῦ τὴν καταργουμένην, 1 Cor. ii. 7 σοφίαν οὐ...τῶν ἀρχόντων τοῦ αἰῶνος τούτου τῶν καταργουμένων· ἀλλὰ...σοφίαν...ἣν προώρισεν ὁ Θεὸς...εἰς δόξαν ἡμῶν with the notes on the last passage. For the word καταργεῖν generally see Vaughan on Rom. iii. 3.

τῇ ἐπιφανείᾳ τῆς παρουσίας αὐτοῦ] The word ἐπιφάνεια is a recognized term even in heathen writers for the appearance of a God at a critical moment. Compare especially Wesseling on Diod. Sic. i. 25. In the New Testament it is used by St Paul alone, and with this single exception only in the Pastoral Epistles, referring either to the First (2 Tim. i. 10) or the Second Advent (1 Tim. vi. 14, 2 Tim. iv. 1, 8, Tit. ii. 13) of our Lord. Hence it became a common word with the Fathers in this signification. It is moreover sometimes applied in ecclesiastical writers to saints or martyrs : see Greg. Naz. *Orat.* iii. p. 77 A (cited by Wesseling). For more on the word ἐπιφάνεια and the corresponding θεοφάνεια (or -νια) see Suicer s. vv.

The word seems always to involve an idea of that which is striking and conspicuous, and so ultimately of splendour or glory—an idea to a certain extent implied in the compound ἐπιφαίνω (comp. Tit. ii. 11 ἐπεφάνη γὰρ ἡ χάρις τοῦ Θεοῦ and iii. 4, of the revelation of God's purpose in Christ). And this is further enforced here by the accumulation of words τῇ ἐπιφανείᾳ τῆς παρουσίας. See the note on καταργήσει above, which points to brightness as a prominent idea in the word here. The language of Milton (*Par. Lost* vi. 768) 'Far off His coming shone' is appositely quoted by Alford.

παρουσίας] The word παρουσία of the Lord's Advent occurs in St Paul only in the Thessalonian Epistles and possibly 1 Cor. xv. 23. In 1 Cor. i. 8 the right reading is ἡμέρᾳ. Elsewhere it is found in St James, the Second Epistle of St Peter and 1 John. It would seem to be the strictly Jewish term; while ἐπιφάνεια appealed more directly to the Greek mind, and was used more frequently by St Paul, when he became more thoroughly busied with the conversion of the Greeks.

It will be observed that St Paul here, speaking in prophetic language, falls instinctively into the characteristic parallelism of Hebrew poetry. For St Paul's change of style in apocalyptic passages see above on 1 Thess. v. 3 ὠδίν, 2 Thess. i. 7.

9. The counterfeit character of the Antichrist, which has been alluded to before (especially vv. 3, 4), is still further enforced here. He too like the true Christ has an Advent; he too works in obedience to a superior power; he too has his miracles and signs.

ἐστὶν] The present tense is used here, as below in πέμπει ver. 11, in accordance with the ordinary language of prophecy. See the note on 1 Thess. v. 2 ἔρχεται.

Σατανᾶ] See the note on 1 Thess. ii. 18.

ἐν πάσῃ δυνάμει κ.τ.λ.] Both πάσῃ and ψεύδους seem to refer to all the three substantives, binding them, as it were, together. For a similar instance see ver. 17 ἐν παντὶ ἔργῳ καὶ λόγῳ ἀγαθῷ. For the combination of terms δυνάμει καὶ σημείοις καὶ τέρασιν, compare Acts ii. 22 δυνάμεσι καὶ τέρασι καὶ σημείοις and 2 Cor. xii. 12 σημείοις καὶ τέρασιν καὶ δυνάμεσιν, Hebr. ii. 4 σημείοις τε καὶ τέρασιν καὶ ποικίλαις δυνάμεσιν, Rom. xv. 19 ἐν δυνάμει σημείων καὶ τεράτων. Of these three words the first (δύναμις) points to the author of the miracle, absolutely ; while the two last relate to the impression made on the witness, whether as enlightening his understanding (σημεῖα), or as arresting his moral sense (τέρατα). Thus σημεῖα and τέρατα are connected closely together where they occur, while δύναμις (-εις) is independent of either. For a full discussion of these words see Trench *On the Miracles* ch. 1 and *N. T. Syn.* § xci.

10. ἀδικίας] Here used in its most general sense of wrong-doing. Any act which disturbs the moral balance is an act of ἀδικία. Compare the account of the ὅλη ἀδικία given by the Aristotelian author of Bk V. of the *Nicomachean Ethics* ch. 1 *ad fin.* αὕτη μὲν οὖν ἡ δικαιοσύνη οὐ μέρος ἀρετῆς ἀλλ᾿ ὅλη ἀρετή ἐστιν· οὐδ᾿ ἡ ἐναντία ἀδικία μέρος κακίας ἀλλ᾿ ὅλη κακία. This comprehensive sense of δικαιοσύνη and ἀδικία would be adopted the more naturally in the New Testament from the technical meaning attached to δίκαιος as one who fulfilled the law.

τοῖς ἀπολλυμένοις] The participle is connected closely with ἀπάτῃ, for the ἐν of the received text is to be rejected on overwhelming authority. For the present tense of ἀπολλυμένοις see the note on 1 Cor. i. 18, where the same phrase occurs.

ἀνθ᾿ ὧν] '*because*,' the sense which it always bears in the New Testament except Luke xii. 3. It will signify either 'because' or 'wherefore,' according as the relative is supposed to contain the antecedent in itself, or is referred to the preceding clause as its antecedent.

τὴν ἀγάπην τῆς ἀληθείας] Stronger than τὴν ἀλήθειαν simply, and corresponding therefore to the εὐδοκήσαντες τῇ ἀδικίᾳ of ver. 12. For the different gradations which would be expressed by τὴν ἀλήθειαν and τὴν ἀγάπην τῆς ἀληθείας compare Rom. i. 32 οὐ μόνον αὐτὰ ποιοῦσιν, ἀλλὰ καὶ συνευδοκοῦσιν τοῖς πράσσουσιν. Not only did they reject the truth, but they have no desire to possess it.

11. Three stages are here described in the downward career of the wicked. *First*, their obstinately setting themselves against the truth: this is their own act (τὴν ἀγάπην τῆς ἀληθείας οὐκ ἐδέξαντο). *Secondly*, the judicial infatuation which overtakes them at a certain point: they are then scarcely their own masters, it is a *divine* judgment (διὰ τοῦτο πέμπει αὐτοῖς ὁ Θεὸς ἐνέργειαν πλάνης). *Thirdly*, their final punishment, for which the second stage was an ordained preparation (ἵνα κριθῶσιν πάντες κ.τ.λ.).

The same three stages are portrayed in the description of the heathen world in the first chapter of the Romans, the second being there dwelt on with a fearful earnestness and, as here, represented as a visitation from God; διὸ παρέδωκεν αὐτοὺς ὁ Θεὸς ἐν ταῖς ἐπιθυμίαις τῶν καρδιῶν αὐτῶν εἰς ἀκαθαρσίαν (ver. 24).

For the discussion of this and similar expressions see the notes on the
Epistle to the Romans *ad loc.*

διὰ τοῦτο] i.e. because they did not welcome the love of the truth.

πέμπει] the prophetic present (see note on ἐστὶν ver. 9), which not
having been understood is altered into πέμψει in the received text.

ἐνέργειαν πλάνης] A strong expression which it is difficult to render
adequately in English. It is not only that they resign themselves passively
to the current of deceit. They are active as the champions of falsehood.
They begin by closing their hearts to the truth. They end by being
strenuous promoters of error.

εἰς τὸ πιστεῦσαι] The phrase sets forth the immediate purpose of their
delusion, as ἵνα κριθῶσιν describes its ultimate end and object. It is of
little consequence here to enquire how far the particular expression εἰς τὸ
πιστεῦσαι denotes a purpose of the divine agent, and how far merely
a result (see note on 1 Thess. ii. 16 εἰς τὸ ἀναπληρῶσαι). It is clear that
the main sentence implies a divine leading, and such moreover is the
language elsewhere used by St Paul of this judicial blindness.

τῷ ψεύδει] '*the lie.*' The universe is divided between the false and
the true, the one ranged against the other. Hence τὸ ψεῦδος is opposed
to ἡ ἀλήθεια.

The frequency in St Paul, and more especially in St John, of the
representation of the contrast between belief and disbelief as one of truth
and falsehood suggests two reflections. (1) Inasmuch as ἡ ἀλήθεια is
not in itself an obvious term for a particular dispensation or system, its
adoption is a token of the deep impression which the Gospel made upon
the Apostles, as answering to their natural cravings and satisfying their
difficulties, thus producing the conviction of its truthfulness. (2) The
use of these words is a striking example of the New Testament doctrine
of the connexion between faith and practice.. To believe is to act.
'Truth' and 'falsehood' are terms belonging not more to the intellectual
than to the moral world. Wrong-doing is a lie, for it is a denial of
God's sovereignty; right-doing is a truth, for it is a confession of the
same. Compare especially for this thought Rev. xxii. 15 πᾶς φιλῶν
καὶ ποιῶν ψεῦδος, and again Ephes. iv. 25 διὸ ἀποθέμενοι τὸ ψεῦδος, λαλεῖτε
ἀλήθειαν ἕκαστος μετὰ τοῦ πλησίον αὐτοῦ where the Apostle is speaking
chiefly of profligacy of life. In short, 'truth' and 'falsehood' cover the
whole domain of morality. So it is here more the moral than the
intellectual aspect which is contemplated, as the opposition in the next
verse shows, 'who believed not the truth, but had pleasure in unrighteous-
ness.'

12. **κριθῶσι**] '*be judged,*' '*called to account,*' and so condemned. On
the Pauline use of κρίνειν and its compounds and the distinction in
meaning between them see *On a Fresh Revision of the English New
Testament* (ed. 3 p. 69 sq.).

εὐδοκήσαντες τῇ ἀδικίᾳ] The weight of authority is in favour of omitting ἐν before τῇ ἀδικίᾳ, and probably it should be omitted. The constructions of the word in the LXX. are τι and ἔν τινι frequently, ἐπί τινι (Judith xv. 11) and τινι (1 Macc. i. 45), these last two constructions apparently only once each. In the New Testament we find generally ἔν τινι, εἴς τι once (2 Pet. i. 17), τι twice (Matth. xii. 18 and Heb. x. 6, both being quotations from the Old Testament), but never simply τινι. On the other hand the simple dative is ͵the common use in profane writers. Thus there is no improbability in εὐδοκήσαντες τῇ ἀδικίᾳ here, and perhaps the preposition was added to conform to the ordinary New Testament usage.

iii.   *Thanksgiving and exhortation repeated; a prayer for their strengthening in the faith* (ii. 13—17).

13. 'But far different is our fortune. While they are awaiting their condemnation, it is our business to rejoice over your salvation.'

ἡμεῖς δὲ] '*we*,' i.e. Paul and Silvanus and Timotheus. The more natural opposition to τοῖς ἀπολλυμένοις would have been ὑμεῖς, yet the interests were sufficiently identified with those of their converts to admit of the language in the text.

ἠγαπημένοι ὑπὸ Κυρίου] i.e. 'the Lord Jesus Christ,' as seems probable both (1) from the fact that the word Κύριος is almost universally so applied by St Paul ; and (2) from its occurrence here between τῷ Θεῷ and ὁ Θεός. If on the other hand in 1 Thess. i. 4 the expression is ἀδελφοὶ ἠγαπημένοι ὑπὸ Θεοῦ, this will not weigh strongly, the love of God in giving His own Son and the love of Christ in dying for us equally affording matter for contemplation, and the latter being introduced even more frequently than the former at least by St Paul. Compare Rom. viii. 37, 2 Cor. v. 14, Gal. ii. 20, Ephes. iii. 19, v. 2, 25, as against Rom. v. 8, 2 Cor. xiii. 13, Ephes. ii. 4.

εἵλατο] The word does not occur elsewhere in the New Testament in this meaning, which is generally expressed by ἐκλέγεσθαι or προορίζειν. Indeed αἱρεῖσθαι is a rare word in any sense, being found only in two other passages, Phil. i. 22, Heb. xi. 25. It is not common in the LXX. either: compare however Deut. xxvi. 18.

On the Alexandrian form εἵλατο, which is probably correct here, see Lobeck, *Phryn.* pp. 183, 724, Winer § xiii. p. 86. Other examples found in St Paul are ἐξέλθατε (2 Cor. vi. 17), and the aorist of πίπτειν and its compounds ἔπεσαν (1 Cor. x. 8), ἐπέπεσαν (Rom. xv. 3), ἐξεπέσατε (Gal. v. 4).

ἀπ᾽ ἀρχῆς] is perhaps the best supported reading, and on the whole is better suited to the context, bringing out the distinction between the original purpose of God and the historical fulfilment of that purpose. The phrase itself however does not occur elsewhere in St Paul, who expresses the eternal decrees of God by such phrases as πρὸ τῶν αἰώνων (1 Cor. ii. 7), πρὸ καταβολῆς κόσμου (Ephes. i. 4) and the like. On the other hand, the reading ἀπαρχὴν has very considerable support, including B, and is very unlikely to have been substituted for ἀπ' ἀρχῆς, if the latter had stood in the original text. The Thessalonians converted on this his first visit (of which he speaks elsewhere as ἀρχὴ τοῦ εὐαγγελίου Phil. iv. 15) might fairly be classed among the 'firstfruits' of Macedonia or of Europe, no less than those Philippians whose conversion preceded that of the Thessalonians by a few weeks. For ἀπαρχὴ (a rather favourite word with St Paul) compare 1 Cor. xvi. 15 ἀπαρχὴ τῆς Ἀχαίας, and Rom. xvi. 5 ἀπαρχὴ τῆς Ἀσίας, where the Codex Bezæ has ἀπ' ἀρχῆς primâ manu and is followed in this by some western authorities.

ἐν ἁγιασμῷ κ.τ.λ.] The sentence is to be connected with εἵλατο εἰς σωτηρίαν, describing wherein the call to salvation consisted.

ἐν ἁγιασμῷ πνεύματος] 'in sanctification of (or by) the Spirit': πνεῦμα being here the Holy Spirit, an interpretation to which the absence of the article will offer no impediment. Such appears certainly to be the meaning of the same expression in 1 Pet. i. 2, a passage which has many points of resemblance with this, ἀπόστολος...κατὰ πρόγνωσιν Θεοῦ πατρός, ἐν ἁγιασμῷ πνεύματος, εἰς ὑπακοὴν καὶ ῥαντισμὸν αἵματος Ἰησοῦ Χριστοῦ, where the mention of the three Persons of the Holy Trinity cannot fail to be noticed. Moreover, if the expression be so interpreted here, the difficulty in the order of the words vanishes. The operation of the Spirit is first mentioned (ἐν ἁγιασμῷ πνεύματος), then the reception of the truth on the part of the person influenced (ἐν πίστει ἀληθείας).

ἀληθείας] is the objective genitive; 'the faithful acceptance of the truth,' in contrast to οἱ μὴ πιστεύσαντες τῇ ἀληθείᾳ ver. 12, thus explaining the opposition expressed in ἡμεῖς δέ.

14. εἰς ὃ] 'whereunto,' 'to which state,' referring to the whole expression εἰς σωτηρίαν ἐν ἁγιασμῷ κ.τ.λ.

ἐκάλεσεν] 'called you,' as the fulfilment of the fore-ordained purpose expressed in εἵλατο. The Gospel preached by us was the instrument whereby He accomplishes His purpose. Compare Rom. viii. 30 οὓς δὲ προώρισεν, τούτους καὶ ἐκάλεσεν.

ὑμᾶς] The authority in favour of ἡμᾶς (Lachmann's reading) is somewhat strong: but the context so obviously requires ὑμᾶς and the confusion between the two words is so frequent, that we can scarcely hesitate to retain ὑμᾶς with the received text. Lachmann places a comma after ἡμᾶς, and this is necessary if we adopt this reading; but in any case διὰ τοῦ εὐαγγελίου ἡμῶν does not go so well with εἰς σωτηρίαν κ.τ.λ. as with ἐκάλεσεν.

τοῦ εὐαγγελίου ἡμῶν] 'the gospel which we preach.' See the references given in the note to 1 Thess. i. 5. The term εὐαγγέλιον seems first to have been applied to a written Gospel by Irenæus (Haer. iii. 11. 8).

ἡμῶν] i.e. of Paul, Silvanus and Timotheus. The different usage of τὸ εὐαγγέλιόν μου and τὸ εὐαγγέλιον ἡμῶν in St Paul is a crucial test of the force of his first person plural: see the note on 1 Thess. ii. 4 τὰς καρδίας ἡμῶν.

εἰς περιποίησιν δόξης] This may mean either (1) 'in order that we might obtain the glory,' or (2) 'in order that He might adopt us into, invest us with, the glory.' For the expression itself see the note on 1 Thess. v. 9 εἰς περιποίησιν σωτηρίας.

The three stages here enumerated are (1) the predestination on the part of God (εἵλατο); (2) the historical fulfilment of that purpose (ἐκάλεσεν); (3) the glorious consummation (εἰς περιποίησιν δόξης). The same gradations occur, with steps interpolated, in Rom. viii. 29, 30 (part of which has been already quoted) οὓς προέγνω καὶ προώρισεν...οὓς δὲ προώρισεν τούτους καὶ ἐκάλεσεν· καὶ οὓς ἐκάλεσεν, τούτους καὶ ἐδικαίωσεν· οὓς δὲ ἐδικαίωσεν, τούτους καὶ ἐδόξασεν. See the notes on Eph. i. 4—11, a passage which presents many affinities with the above.

15. **ἄρα οὖν στήκετε**] For ἄρα οὖν see the note on 1 Thess. v. 6: for στήκετε the note on 1 Thess. iii. 8.

The drift of the Apostle's 'therefore' is best apprehended by Phil. ii. 12, 13 'work out your own salvation with fear and trembling, for it is God which worketh in you both to will and to work etc.' 'Your election should be an encouragement to you in well-doing, and not an occasion of carelessness.'

τὰς παραδόσεις] The passage before us is a direct negative of the distinction which gained ground in later times between the written word and oral tradition, as if the authority of the latter were sanctioned by the use of παράδοσις in scripture. 'Tradition' in the scriptural sense of the word may be either written or oral. It is a synonyme for 'teaching,' implying on the part of the teacher a confession that he was not expressing his own ideas, but *delivering* or *handing on* a message that he had received from heaven. Compare the use of the words παραδιδόναι, παραλαμβάνειν, παραγγέλλειν (the last being used in classical Greek of transmitting the word of command); and see especially 1 Cor. xi. 23 ἐγὼ γὰρ παρέλαβον ἀπὸ τοῦ Κυρίου, ὃ καὶ παρέδωκα, of the institution of the Eucharist. The prominent idea of παράδοσις then in the New Testament is that of an authority external to the teacher himself. The opposition between παράδοσις, as ἄγραφος, and γραφὴ does not exist in the word itself, and is not sanctioned by the New Testament usage. Such an opposition in fact was impossible under the circumstances of the case before the era of the written Gospels, when instruction was still mainly conveyed by word of mouth. The matter of a παράδοσις would be various. What class of subjects were included under the term may be seen from 1 Cor. xi. 23, already cited, or 1 Cor. xi. 2 (of certain practical regulations), xv. 3 (of the facts of the Resurrection). On the ecclesiastical sense of the word see Suicer s. v. Ellicott (*ad loc.*) refers to Möhler's *Symbolik* § 38, p. 361 sq. for a defence of the Roman Catholic doctrine. See also his other references.

εἴτε διὰ λόγου κ.τ.λ.] Not as E. V. 'whether by word or our epistle, for ἡμῶν refers to both substantives: render '*whether by word or by letter of ours.*' Ἐπιστολῆς may refer solely to our first Epistle, but in itself is quite general. On the question whether any of St Paul's Epistles have been lost see the note on iii. 17 ἐν πάσῃ ἐπιστολῇ, and a fuller treatment of the subject in *Philippians*, p. 13 sq. Observe the difference of expression here and ii. 2 ἐπιστολῆς ὡς δι' ἡμῶν.

16. **αὐτὸς δὲ**] is opposed to ἡμῶν. The Apostle suddenly checks himself. 'All our instructions,' he says, 'will be in vain, unless the Lord Himself stablish you.' With αὐτὸς δὲ here compare 1 Thess. iii. 11, v. 23, and 2 Thess. iii. 16, and see the note on the first of these passages.

We cannot fail to be struck with the similarity of structure between the first and second Epistles. Both are divided into two parts, the first being chiefly narrative or explanatory, and the second hortatory: the second part in both commences in much the same way (compare 1 Thess. iv. 1 λοιπὸν οὖν, ἀδελφοὶ κ.τ.λ. with 2 Thess. iii. 1 τὸ λοιπὸν προσεύχεσθε, ἀδελφοί): and each part in both Epistles concludes with a prayer couched in similar language, αὐτὸς δὲ κ.τ.λ.

There are considerable variations in the MSS., chiefly as to the position of the articles: but on the whole the weight of evidence is in favour of reading ὁ Κύριος ἡμῶν Ἰησοῦς Χριστὸς καὶ Θεὸς ὁ πατὴρ ἡμῶν. Lachmann still further inserts the article before Χριστὸς on the slenderest authority (A and one cursive), apparently for the sake of the parallelism Ἰησοῦς ὁ Χριστὸς and Θεὸς ὁ πατὴρ. But the chiasm in the reading adopted, ὁ Κύριος ἡμῶν answering to ὁ πατὴρ ἡμῶν and Θεὸς corresponding to Ἰησοῦς Χριστὸς, is much more after St Paul's manner. Of the variants the insertion of the article before Θεὸς is the most worthy of consideration, and has the support of B K and D *primâ manu*.

The usual order of the names of the Father and Son is reversed here, as in the apostolic benediction ἡ χάρις τοῦ Κυρίου Ἰησοῦ Χριστοῦ καὶ ἡ ἀγάπη τοῦ Θεοῦ κ.τ.λ. (2 Cor. xiii. 13).

ὁ πατὴρ ἡμῶν] When ἡμῶν is added there seems always to be a more emphatic reference to His fatherly tenderness and protection, as here.

ὁ ἀγαπήσας ἡμᾶς] These words ought probably to be referred to Θεὸς ὁ πατὴρ ἡμῶν alone; though it is difficult to see how St Paul could otherwise have expressed his thought, if he had intended it to refer to the Son, as well as the Father. There is probably no instance in St Paul of a plural adjective or verb, where the two Persons of the Godhead are mentioned. At least both here and in 1 Thess. iii. 11 the singular verb is, as it would seem, designedly employed. See also the note on 1 Thess. l. c.

The aorist ἀγαπήσας (not ἀγαπῶν) refers to the act of His love in giving His Son to die for us. Compare John iii. 16 οὕτως γὰρ ἠγάπησεν ὁ Θεὸς τὸν κόσμον, ὥστε κ.τ.λ. This act is the source of all our consolation and hope.

παράκλησιν, ἐλπίδα] 'consolation and encouragement in the present, hope for the future.'

αἰωνίαν] '*never-failing*, '*inexhaustible*.' Αἰώνιος is generally an adjective of two terminations, Hebr. ix. 12 being the only other exception in the New Testament.

ἐν χάριτι] 'as an act of grace,' i.e. without any claims or deserving on our part. These words refer to the whole clause ὁ ἀγαπήσας ἡμᾶς καὶ δοὺς κ.τ.λ. They are used in this sense in Rom. v. 15, 2 Cor. i. 12, Gal. i. 6. Other passages however, as Col. iii. 16, iv. 6, 2 Tim. ii. 1, 2 Pet. iii. 18, perhaps suggest a different interpretation, 'by the possession of grace,' as a Christian virtue, and possibly the E. V. intended this by the rendering 'through grace.' The former interpretation however is more natural.

17. στηρίξαι] A furtherance and confirmation of the work begun in παρακαλέσαι. On παρακαλεῖν see the note on 1 Thess. ii. 11.

παντὶ ἔργῳ καὶ λόγῳ ἀγαθῷ] Here the adjectives παντὶ and ἀγαθῷ refer to both the intervening nouns. For a similar instance of a sentence bound together by the first and last words see ver. 9 above.

The order ἔργῳ καὶ λόγῳ is much better supported than that of the received text which reverses the words, and is capable of an easy explanation. 'May the grace of God extend not to your works only, but to your words also,' i.e. be exhibited in minor as in greater matters.

CHAPTER III

3. HORTATORY PORTION, iii. 1—16.

i. *Exhortation to prayer, and anticipation of their progress in faith* (iii. 1—5).

1. **Τὸ λοιπὸν**] *'Finally.'* On the meaning of this phrase and the position it occupies in St Paul's Epistles, as ushering in the conclusion, see the note on 1 Thess. iv. 1.

προσεύχεσθε περὶ ἡμῶν] literally *'make us the subject of your prayers';* and so the phrase becomes equivalent to, though slightly weaker than, προσεύχεσθε ὑπὲρ ἡμῶν.

ὁ λόγος τοῦ Κυρίου] See the note on 1 Thess. i. 8.

τρέχῃ καὶ δοξάζηται] *'may have a triumphant career.'* Τρέχῃ 'may speed onward,' with an allusion apparently to Ps. cxlvii. 15 ἕως τάχους δραμεῖται ὁ λόγος αὐτοῦ. Δοξάζηται 'may be received with honour.' See Acts xiii. 48 ἐδόξαζον τὸν λόγον τοῦ Θεοῦ, of the heathen population of the Pisidian Antioch.

2. **ἵνα ῥυσθῶμεν**] It is surely a mistaken zeal for the honour of the Apostle, which refuses to see in this prayer a 'shrinking of the flesh,' in other words an instinct of self-preservation. No one else would be blamed for praying to be delivered from his enemies, irrespectively of any great work which depended on his life ; and it is not easy to see how such a desire is unworthy of an Apostle. That the personal feeling does come in here appears from the form of the sentence ἵνα...τρέχῃ... καὶ ἵνα ῥυσθῶμεν. If the Apostle had had no further motive in wishing to live than the furtherance of the Gospel, we might expect the words to run ἵνα ῥυσθῶμεν...καὶ τρέχῃ. For the form and purport of this prayer compare Rom. xv. 30, 31.

ἀτόπων] The word signifies 'out of place,' and hence in later writers 'impracticable, perverse, irregular, outrageous.' Hence ἄτοπα ποιεῖν and πράττειν is not an uncommon phrase in later Greek for 'to commit an outrage,' both in profane writers and in the LXX. Indeed this moral sense of ἄτοπος seems to be the common one in the later Greek. See Philo *Leg. Alleg.* iii. § 17, I. p. 97 (ed. Mangey) ἄτοπος λέγεται εἶναι ὁ φαῦλος· ἄτοπον δέ ἐστι κακὸν δύσθετον, and other references given in Ellicott.

οὐ γὰρ πάντων ἡ πίστις] '*for the faith*,' i.e. the Gospel, '*is not the portion of all.*' The ordinary usage of ἡ πίστις in the New Testament seems to require this translation here, e.g. Gal. vi. 10 τοὺς οἰκείους τῆς πίστεως. See the note there, and for a discussion of the word πίστις, *Galatians*, p. 154 sq. The expression 'not all' is a common litotes in all languages for 'the few,' as in the proverbial expression οὐ παντὸς ἀνδρὸς εἰς Κόρινθον ἐσθ' ὁ πλοῦς.

To what enemies does St Paul here allude? The answer must be supplied by a comparison of the passage before us with the notices in the Acts relating to this period of the Apostle's life. (1) The enemies here spoken of are without the pale of the Church. They are not of 'the household of the faith.' There is no reason to suppose that St Paul had much to fear at this early stage from the Judaizing Christians, from whom he suffered so much persecution subsequently; nor is it probable that their hostility, though systematically attacking his influence, ever endangered his life. It is arbitrary to explain οὐ πάντων ἐστὶν ἡ πίστις 'all who profess Christianity are not genuine believers'; and still more unjustifiable to interpret οἱ ἀπειθοῦντες ἐν τῇ Ἰουδαίᾳ (Rom. xv. 31) of Judaizing Christians. (2) The narrative in the Acts points to the Jews, as the authors of St Paul's sufferings during this visit to Greece. They persecuted him at Thessalonica itself (xvii. 5) and Berea (xvii. 13). His preaching at Corinth, from which city this letter was written, was likewise interrupted, and his life endangered, by them (Acts xviii. 12 sq.). And throughout these Epistles it is evident that St Paul regards them, rather than the heathen, as the most determined opponents of the Gospel. See 1 Thess. ii. 14 and the notes there.

3. πιστὸς δὲ] Suggested by the foregoing οὐ γὰρ πάντων ἡ πίστις 'Men may be faithless, but God is faithful.' Compare 2 Tim. ii. 13 εἰ ἀπιστοῦμεν, ἐκεῖνος πιστὸς μένει, Rom. iii. 3 μὴ ἡ ἀπιστία αὐτῶν τὴν πίστιν τοῦ Θεοῦ καταργήσει; At the same time, this opposition should not lead us to give to ἡ πίστις in the preceding verse the sense of 'fidelity,' while other considerations are strongly in favour of the objective sense 'the faith.' For (1) the Gospel is a life, and the objective ('the faith') and subjective ('faith') are so closely bound together that the one more or less involves the other. (2) Even setting aside this indirect antagonism of meaning, the appeal to the ear would be sufficient to recommend this paronomasia, as a means of riveting attention. For instances of this imperfect connexion in sense in St Paul, compare 1 Cor. iii. 17 εἴ τις τὸν ναὸν τοῦ Θεοῦ φθείρει, φθερεῖ τοῦτον ὁ Θεός, xi. 29 κρίμα ἑαυτῷ ἐσθίει καὶ πίνει, μὴ διακρίνων τὸ σῶμα. See also the note below on ver. 11.

καὶ φυλάξει] i.e. 'He will not only place you in a firm position, but also maintain you there against assaults from without.'

ἀπὸ τοῦ πονηροῦ] It is questioned whether this phrase should be rendered 'from evil' or 'from the Evil One.' The latter seems the more probable rendering, for as in an Attic writer the genius of the language

would at once point to τὸ πονηρὸν 'evil' as a principle; so on the other
hand in the New Testament the frequency of ὁ πονηρὸς compared with τὸ
πονηρὸν is strongly in favour of the masculine. There are but two certain
instances of the neuter, Luke vi. 45 ὁ πονηρὸς ἐκ τοῦ πονηροῦ προφέρει τὸ
πονηρὸν and Rom. xii. 9 ἀποστυγοῦντες τὸ πονηρόν, where in both cases it
is directly opposed to τὸ ἀγαθόν. On the other hand the masculine is
certainly employed in no less than eight passages (Matt. v. 37, xiii. 19,
38, 49, Eph. vi. 16, 1 Joh. ii. 13, 14, iii. 12, v. 18, 19). In Matt. v. 39 μὴ
ἀντιστῆναι τῷ πονηρῷ (E. V. 'that ye resist not evil') the context seems to
support the rendering 'the evil man' (comp. 1 Joh. v. 19), for it goes on
ἀλλ' ὅστις κ.τ.λ. In John xvii. 15 ἵνα τηρήσῃς αὐτοὺς ἐκ τοῦ πονηροῦ, as in the
present passage, there seems to be an indirect allusion to the Lord's prayer.

The rendering adopted in the clause of the Lord's prayer ought
probably to decide the meaning in these two last cases; but here again
there is an ambiguity. The question must be decided mainly on two
issues: (1) the comparison of any Jewish formularies, which our Lord
may be found to have sanctioned and embodied in this compendium of
prayer; and (2) the traditional interpretation of the prayer itself, for this
is exactly an instance in which tradition would be especially valuable and
might be expected to be tolerably consistent. With regard to Jewish
formularies the passages collected in Wetstein on Matth. vi. 13 are on
the whole in favour of the masculine. That the expression 'the Evil One'
was not uncommon in early Rabbinical writings is evidenced from its use
in such passages as *Midrash Shemoth Rabbah* c. 21 'God delivered me
over to the Evil One,' *Midrash Debarim Rabbah* c. 11 'the Evil One, the
head of all Satanim,' and *Baba Bathra* 16a, where Job ix. 24 is quoted
'the earth is given into the hands of the Evil One.' And this seems also
to have been the traditional interpretation. Among Greek writers there
is absolute unanimity on this point: see *Clem. Hom.* xix. 2, Origen, *de
Orat.* 30 (I. p. 265), *Sel. in Psalm.* ii. § 3 (II. p. 661), Dionysius of
Alexandria, *Fragm.* (p. 1601 ed. Migne), Cyril of Jerusalem, *Catech.* xxiii.
19 (p. 331), Gregory of Nyssa, *de Orat. Dom.* 5 (I. p. 760), Didymus of
Alexandria, *in* 1 *Johan.* v. 19 (p. 1806 ed. Migne), *c. Manich.* 11 (p. 1100),
Chrysostom, *in Matt. Hom.* xix. (VII. p. 253), Isidore of Pelusium, *Epist.*
iv. 24 (p. 425). With the Latin fathers there is not the same agreement.
But the two great ante-Nicene Western fathers treat the word as
masculine; e.g. Tertullian in *de Orat.* § 8 and *de fuga* § 2, and Cyprian in
de Domin. Orat. 25. The other interpretation was apparently started by
Augustine (*Epist.* 130, *de Serm. Dom.* ii. 35 etc.) and spread through his
influence. Again, the evidence of early versions (the Syriac and Sahidic
certainly, the Memphitic and Old Latin probably) and of the Eastern
Liturgies points decisively to the masculine rendering. On all these
grounds therefore it is highly probable that τοῦ πονηροῦ is here 'the Evil
One.' See the subject treated at length in Appendix II. of the work *On
a Fresh Revision of the English New Testament* (ed. 3) p. 269 sq.

The 'Evil One' is the father of the 'evil men' of ver. 2. Their assaults are instigated by him. On the manner in which St Paul turns from himself to his converts, see Calvin here: 'de aliis magis quam de se anxium fuisse Paulum, ostendunt haec ipsa verba.'

4. πεποίθαμεν δέ] 'But if we have enjoined you to pray for us, it is not from any distrust of your doing so.'

The most common constructions with πεποιθέναι in the New Testament are τινα and ἐπί τινι: but the verb also takes ἐπί τινα (2 Cor. ii. 3), εἰς τινα (Gal. v. 10) and ἔν τινι (Phil. iii. 3, 4 ἐν σαρκὶ πεποιθέναι) of the objects of trust. This being the case, two constructions are possible here. (1) We may consider ἐν Κυρίῳ as the more immediate object of trust (compare ἐν σαρκὶ Phil. l. c.), and paraphrase: 'I put my trust in the Lord, this trust being directed towards you.' Or (2) we may take ἐφ' ὑμᾶς as giving the more immediate object of πεποιθέναι, while ἐν Κυρίῳ describes the element in which it is exercised according to the common New Testament usage of ἐν Κυρίῳ, ἐν Χριστῷ, removing trust from the domain of worldly calculations and motives. Thus the sentence becomes almost equivalent to 'my trust in you comes from the Lord.' Compare Rom. xiv. 14 οἶδα καὶ πέπεισμαι ἐν Κυρίῳ. The order is perhaps in favour of the former connexion: the parallel passage in Gal. v. 10 πέποιθα εἰς ὑμᾶς ἐν Κυρίῳ ὅτι κ.τ.λ. supports the latter.

ἃ παραγγέλλομεν] i.e. the charge just given that they should pray for him.

The received text is probably correct, except that external authority (including אBD) is strongly in favour of the omission of ὑμῖν. Lachmann introduces the words ὑμῖν καὶ ἐποιήσατε καὶ in brackets after παραγγέλλομεν on the strength of two important manuscripts (B and F); but the insertion is not justified either on external or internal grounds of probability.

5. ὁ δὲ Κύριος κ.τ.λ.] The force of the particle may be expressed somewhat as follows: 'In this, as in other things, I trust you: only may the Lord be your guide.'

κατευθύναι] On the metaphor conveyed in this word see the note on 1 Thess. iii. 11.

τοῦ Θεοῦ, τοῦ Χριστοῦ] Are the genitive cases here subjective or objective? In other words: does 'the love of God' signify 'the love which God has shown towards them,' or 'the love which they should feel towards Him,' or something between the two? By 'the patient waiting of Christ' does the Apostle mean 'such patient endurance under persecution as Christ exhibited in the flesh,' or 'the patient waiting for the coming of Christ'?

May we not say with regard to the first of these expressions ἡ ἀγάπη τοῦ Θεοῦ, that the Apostles availed themselves, either consciously or unconsciously, of the vagueness or rather comprehensiveness of language, to express a great spiritual truth: that they use the expression 'the love of God,' not only of that which is external to us of the divine attribute itself, but also of that same principle as imparted to us and so reflected back on its author, as 'love towards God': and that these senses are so combined and interwoven, that it is very seldom possible, where the expression occurs, to separate the one from the other? So only can we explain the language of St Paul and St John, where the two senses of 'the love of God,' as God's love towards us and our love towards God, are regarded as logically convertible. Any one who will compare 1 John ii. 5 ἐν τούτῳ ἡ ἀγάπη τοῦ Θεοῦ τετελείωται, 15 ἐάν τις ἀγαπᾷ τὸν κόσμον, οὐκ ἔστιν ἡ ἀγάπη τοῦ πατρὸς ἐν αὐτῷ, iii. 16 ἐν τούτῳ ἐγνώκαμεν τὴν ἀγάπην ὅτι, 17 πῶς ἡ ἀγάπη τοῦ Θεοῦ μένει ἐν αὐτῷ; and especially iv. 7—12, 16—19, v. 3, will feel the difficulty of separating between the two usages. A signal instance of this we have in St John himself, who, from being 'the beloved disciple,' became himself the great preacher of love.

That the same comprehensive significance may attach to the expression in St Paul will, I think, appear from Rom. v. 5 ἡ ἀγάπη τοῦ Θεοῦ ἐκκέχυται ἐν ταῖς καρδίαις compared with its context, and from Rom. viii. 35, 39. Compare also Ephes. iii. 19, 2 Cor. v. 14. In the same wide sense should probably be taken ἡ ἀγάπη τοῦ πνεύματος (Rom. xv. 30), and ἡ ἀγάπη τοῦ Θεοῦ in the benediction (2 Cor. xiii. 13).

Thus then ἡ ἀγάπη τοῦ Θεοῦ here will signify 'the love of God,' not only as an objective attribute of deity, but as a ruling principle in our hearts; including perhaps the idea of love towards God, this however not being the most prominent idea.

Analogously to this, ἡ ὑπομονὴ τοῦ Χριστοῦ will be best explained not exactly as 'patience like that of Christ,' which would not exhaust its meaning; but 'the patience of Christ,' in which the believer participates. Compare the expression in 2 Cor. i. 5 περισσεύει τὰ παθήματα τοῦ Χριστοῦ εἰς ἡμᾶς, exemplifying the close union of the believer with Christ, ἡ δικαιοσύνη τοῦ Χριστοῦ, and kindred phrases. The interpretation of the E.V. however 'the patient waiting for Christ,' in the same sense as τῆς ὑπομονῆς τῆς ἐλπίδος τοῦ Κυρίου (1 Thess. i. 3), accords well with the tone of the whole Epistle, and is not to be hastily rejected. But there is no instance of this use of ὑπομονή, the verb employed to express this meaning being ἀναμένειν (1 Thess. i. 10), not ὑπομένειν: and the reference to the coming of Christ, the leading topic of these Epistles, is implied, though less directly, in the more natural interpretation of ὑπομονή. See Ignat. *Rom.* 10 (with the note) ἔρρωσθε εἰς τέλος ἐν ὑπομονῇ Ἰησοῦ Χριστοῦ, where probably the expression is derived from St Paul. On ὑπομονή in its connexion with ἐλπὶς see the note on 1 Thess. i. 3, and on the word generally see on Col. i. 11.

ii. *Reproof of the idle, disorderly and disobedient* (iii. 6—15).

6. The comparison of St Paul's language here with his brief charge on the same subject in the first Epistle (v. 13, 14) is instructive. What was at the earlier date a vague suspicion is now an ascertained fact. The

disorderly conduct of certain members has become patent. Hence the stress laid on the charge here, both in the solemn adjuration with which it is introduced, and in the greater length with which he dwells on the subject. On the nature of this ἀταξία see the notes on 1 Thess. iv. 13, and v. 13.

παραγγέλλομεν] We cannot altogether lose sight of the classical sense of παραγγέλλειν here, as referring to 'the word of command,' in connexion with the ἀτάκτως which follows. Ignatius has this same form of adjuration *Polyc.* 5 ὁμοίως καὶ τοῖς ἀδελφοῖς μου παράγγελλε ἐν ὀνόματι Ἰησοῦ Χριστοῦ ἀγαπᾶν τὰς συμβίους. See the note on ἀτάκτως below.

The passage may be paraphrased thus. 'Your title of brethren should remind you of your mutual obligations. The name of the Lord Jesus Christ should be your watchword of unity.' Compare the note on 1 Cor. i. 10, where exhorting the Corinthians to unity in the same way he says: παρακαλῶ δὲ ὑμᾶς, ἀδελφοί, διὰ τοῦ ὀνόματος τοῦ Κυρίου ἡμῶν Ἰησοῦ Χριστοῦ, ἵνα τὸ αὐτὸ λέγητε πάντες.

στέλλεσθαι] The active verb στέλλειν (and sometimes the middle form στέλλεσθαι also) is used especially of furling sails (Hom. *Il.* i. 433) and of girding up a robe (Ap. Rhod. *Argon.* iv. 45). Thus στέλλεσθαι absolutely signifies 'to gather oneself together,' 'to shrink into oneself,' and so 'to hold back, withdraw.' The metaphor then is not directly nautical, though ὑποστέλλεσθαι is very common in this sense. It occasionally takes an accusative of the object shunned, as in 2 Cor. viii. 20 στελλόμενοι τοῦτο, μή τις ἡμᾶς μωμήσηται: on the other hand ὑποστέλλεσθαι with this construction is found not unfrequently in classical writers. For στέλλεσθαι ἀπὸ compare Malachi ii. 5 ἀπὸ προσώπου ὀνόματός μου στέλλεσθαι αὐτόν.

παντὸς ἀδελφοῦ] with a slight reference to ἀδελφοὶ above. 'Your duty to the brotherhood requires you to withdraw from a disorderly brother, because he is a brother.' Compare 1 Cor. v. 11 ἐάν τις ἀδελφὸς ὀνομαζόμενος ᾖ πόρνος...τῷ τοιούτῳ μηδὲ συνεσθίειν.

ἀτάκτως] '*disorderly*' ; a metaphor borrowed more especially from military discipline, ἀταξία meaning 'insubordination.' It may be worth while to compare the address (παράγγελμα) of Germanicus to the army on the occasion of the mutiny related in Tacitus (*Ann.* i. 43) 'discedite a contactu, ac dividite turbidos: id stabile ad paenitentiam, id fidei vinculum erit,' where the terms used present affinities to St Paul's language here. The same must be the conduct of the Christian soldier (2 Tim. ii. 3), however different the character of his στρατεία (2 Cor. x. 4).

κατὰ τὴν παράδοσιν κ.τ.λ.] For παράδοσις and παραλαμβάνειν see the note on ii. 15.

There is great diversity in reading here, the authorities varying between παρελάβοσαν, ἐλάβοσαν, παρέλαβον, παρελάβετε, παρέλαβε. The choice lies ultimately between παρελάβοσαν and παρελάβετε, the other readings having obviously been derived from one or other of these. Where the weight of authority on either side is very evenly balanced, it seems better to choose the third person παρελάβοσαν, for the frequent occurrence of παρελάβετε (e.g. 1 Thess. iv. 1) was likely to suggest the alteration.

On the form παρελάβοσαν see Winer § xiii. p. 91. Other examples in the New Testament are εἴχοσαν (John xv. 22, 24), ἐδίδοσαν (John xix. 3) and ἐδολιοῦσαν (Rom. iii. 13), the last a quotation from the LXX., where the use is not uncommon. It may perhaps have been suggested by a striving after conformity with the first aorist; though probably it does not differ very much from the original termination of the 3rd plur. 2nd aorist, the first and second aorists having grown out of the same primary form.

7. **αὐτοὶ γὰρ κ.τ.λ.**] 'For you know of yourselves by your own observation, without my urging it upon you.' The γάρ is probably explained by ὅτι. For the expression see 1 Thess. ii. 1 with the note.

πῶς δεῖ μιμεῖσθαι ἡμᾶς] an abridged expression for 'how ye ought to walk, so as to imitate us' (πῶς δεῖ ὑμᾶς περιπατεῖν ὥστε μιμεῖσθαι ἡμᾶς).

ὅτι] seems here to be 'for,' explaining αὐτοὶ γὰρ οἴδατε. This construction is simpler than taking the last clause ὅτι οὐκ ἠτακτήσαμεν κ.τ.λ. in the sense 'how that,' as an explanation of πῶς δεῖ μιμεῖσθαι ἡμᾶς. Perhaps however such indirectly analogous instances as 1 Thess. i. 4, 5 εἰδότες τὴν ἐκλογὴν ὑμῶν ὅτι, which are frequent in St Paul, may seem to favour the other construction.

8. **οὐδὲ**] '*we were not disorderly, nor yet were we idle.*'

παρά τινος] To be taken with the whole sentence δωρεὰν ἄρτον ἐφάγομεν—an expression equivalent to δωρεὰν ἄρτον ἐλάβομεν ὃν ἐφάγομεν 'did we receive the bread we ate,'—rather than with either δωρεὰν or ἄρτον singly. On δωρεάν see Gal. ii. 21 with the note.

ἐν κόπῳ καὶ μόχθῳ] For these words see the note on 1 Thess. ii. 9; as also for the order νύκτα καὶ ἡμέραν and for the subject of St Paul's manual labour.

The words here are almost a repetition of the language in that passage. The motive however in introducing the subject is different: there the Apostle is dwelling on his labour as a sign of his disinterestedness, here, as an example to be followed by others.

νύκτα καὶ ἡμέραν] The reading νυκτὸς καὶ ἡμέρας has the support of the two oldest MSS. (אB); but it may have been introduced to conform to 1 Thess. ii. 9. The accusative cases are stronger than the genitives, implying the uninterruptedness of the labour.

9. The anxiety with which the writer guards against misapprehension as if the work of the ministry should be gratuitous, is characteristic of St Paul. See especially 1 Cor. ix. 3—18, where the assertion of his right, and the waiving of his claim in the particular case, are dwelt upon side by side with great force.

ἐξουσίαν] St Paul speaks of this same right as ἐξουσία in the parallel passage referred to in the last note (see 1 Cor. ix. 4, 12). The word ἐξουσία, which originally signified merely 'liberty to act' whether conferred by law or not, shifted its meaning, and as time advanced obtained more and more the signification of a definite, positive and acknowledged right, implying control over others. For power over means follows as a necessary consequence upon liberty of action. This meaning, which is perceptible in classical writers, is more definitely stamped on the word in the New Testament, e.g. Luke xxiii. 7.

ἀλλ' ἵνα] *'but we waived it that'*; another of St Paul's ellipses. See the note on ii. 3, 7, where examples are given.

τύπον δῶμεν] In another connexion, and probably with no reference to this passage, Clement of Rome (§ 5) says of St Paul ὑπομονῆς γενόμενος μέγιστος ὑπογραμμός.

εἰς τὸ μιμεῖσθαι ἡμᾶς] On the other hand a different preposition is used above: πρὸς τὸ μὴ ἐπιβαρῆσαι. Something has been said on the distinction between the two words in the note on Philemon 5. The fact seems to be that, while πρὸς always denotes a purpose (at least in the New Testament), εἰς points to the end of the action; whether as implying a purpose (as is frequently the case, here for instance), or not. See the note on 1 Thess. ii. 16 εἰς τὸ ἀναπληρῶσαι. In two passages, Ephes. vi. 11, James iii. 3, in both of which a purpose is implied, the reading varies between πρὸς and εἰς, πρὸς being more strongly supported in the first case, εἰς in the second. This distinction between the two prepositions arises out of the composition of the words, since πρὸς contains a reference to the source of the action (προ-τι see *New Crat.* § 171) which is not directly involved in εἰς (ἐν-s). Thus Aristotle's category of 'relation' (Donalds. *Gr. Gr.* § 486) is expressed by πρός τι not by εἴς τι.

10. καὶ γὰρ] *'for also'*; i.e. 'not only did we set before you our own example, but we gave you a positive precept to this effect, when at Thessalonica.'

εἴ τις οὐ θέλει κ.τ.λ.] St Paul seems to be repeating a favourite maxim of the Rabbins. See the passages in Wetstein, especially *Bereshith R.* ii. 2 'ego vero si non edo,' xiv. 12 'ut, si non laborat, non manducet.' This book however dates in the fourth century A.D., and possibly the form which the precept has taken may have been derived from St Paul. In spirit at least this honourable feature in the teaching of the Rabbins accords with St Paul: see the notes on 1 Thess. ii. 9 ἐργαζόμενοι, and on τὸν ἑαυτῶν ἄρτον below (ver. 12).

For the change to the direct narrative, the exact words as spoken being introduced by ὅτι, compare Acts xiv. 22 παρακαλοῦντες ἐμμένειν τῇ πίστει καὶ ὅτι διὰ πολλῶν θλίψεων δεῖ ἡμᾶς εἰσελθεῖν εἰς τὴν βασιλείαν τοῦ Θεοῦ, xxiii. 22, Gal. i. 23 (with the note), and see the examples given in Winer § lx. p. 683.

οὐ θέλει] *'is unwilling, refuses.'* 'Nolle vitium est' is Bengel's comment.

11. μηδὲν ἐργαζομένους ἀλλὰ περιεργαζομένους] Compare Afer's saying

reported by Quintilian (vi. 3. 54) of Mallius Sura, a bustling lawyer, 'non agere dixit sed satagere' (quoted by Jowett), and Demosthenes *Phil.* iv. p. 150 σοὶ μὲν ἐξ ὧν ἐργάζῃ καὶ περιεργάζῃ τοὺς ἐσχάτους ὄντας κινδύνους. For other instances of this play on words see the note on Phil. iii. 3 κατατομή, περιτομή: and add the following examples from St Paul, 1 Cor. vii. 31 οἱ χρώμενοι τὸν κόσμον ὡς μὴ καταχρώμενοι, 2 Cor. i. 13 ἃ ἀναγινώσκετε ἢ καὶ ἐπιγινώσκετε, iii. 2 γινωσκομένη καὶ ἀναγινωσκο-μένη, vi. 10 ὡς μηδὲν ἔχοντες καὶ πάντα κατέχοντες, x. 12 οὐ τολμῶμεν ἐνκρῖναι ἢ συνκρῖναι ἑαυτούς, and from the Epistle to the Hebrews (v. 8) ἔμαθεν ἀφ' ὧν ἔπαθεν τὴν ὑπακοήν (comp. 'where pain ends, gain ends too').

12. **καὶ παρακαλοῦμεν**] sc. αὐτούς: '*yea, and we even entreat them.*'

ἐν Κυρίῳ Ἰησοῦ Χριστῷ] This is by far the best supported reading; and as there was no more likelihood of its being substituted for διὰ τοῦ Κυρίου ἡμῶν Ἰησοῦ Χριστοῦ than conversely, it must be adopted in place of the reading of the received text.

ἵνα] See the notes on 1 Thess. ii. 16, v. 4. Παρακαλεῖν and παραγγέλ-λειν ἵνα are very frequent combinations, and link together the later use of ἵνα with the earlier. Compare 1 Cor. i. 10, xvi. 12, 15, 2 Cor. viii. 6, xii. 8, 1 Thess. iv. 1 etc.

μετὰ ἡσυχίας ἐργαζόμενοι] The direct opposite to μηδὲν ἐργαζομένους ἀλλὰ περιεργαζομένους, μετὰ ἡσυχίας being opposed to περιεργαζομένους.

τὸν ἑαυτῶν ἄρτον] A Rabbinical phrase apparently, like the precept in ver. 10. Compare the references in Wetstein and Schöttgen.

13. 'On the other hand, we exhort the rest of you, who have hitherto lived soberly, to persevere in your honourable course.'

μὴ ἐγκακήσητε] Wherever the word ἐγκακεῖν or ἐνκακεῖν occurs in the New Testament (Luke xviii. 1, 2 Cor. iv. 1, 16, Gal. vi. 9, Eph. iii. 13), it is always with the form ἐκκακεῖν as a various reading; the same authorities substantially being ranged on either side, but the weight of testimony being in favour of ἐγκακεῖν. The form ἐκκακεῖν indeed seems to be later, though it was in use in the time of the Greek commentators, Chrysostom etc. (see Tischendorf on 2 Cor. iv. 1); and, it may be conjectured, arose in the first instance from a faulty pronunciation, rather than as a distinct compound. There can be little doubt that ἐγκακεῖν is correct, and it is supported by the analogous use of ἐν in ἐλλείπειν. Ἐγκακεῖν occurs in the versions of Symmachus (Gen. xxvii. 46, Numb. xxi. 5) and of Theodotion (Prov. iii. 11), and in Polybius iv. 19, 10. The word ἀποκακεῖν, which is found once in the LXX. (Jer. xv. 9) as equivalent to 'exspiro,' might seem to favour ἐκκακεῖν.

καλοποιοῦντες] '*in well-doing,*' i.e. 'in your honourable course': a ἅπαξ λεγόμενον in the New Testament. It must not be rendered, as it is sometimes taken, even by Chrysostom and the Greek commentators generally, 'in your charitable course'—a restricted sense which ἀγαθοποιεῖν frequently has, but which καλοποιεῖν could not admit. In Levit. v. 4 the reading seems to be καλῶς ποιῆσαι. The substantive καλοποιΐα occurs in

Theophyl. *ad Autol.* i. 3.   Compare Gal. vi. 9 τὸ δὲ καλὸν ποιοῦντες μὴ ἐγκακῶμεν.

14. **διὰ τῆς ἐπιστολῆς**] must be attached to τῷ λόγῳ ἡμῶν '*our charge conveyed by our letter.*'   The insertion of the article τῷ διὰ τῆς ἐπιστολῆς would define the construction more precisely, but its absence is no objection to this rendering in the Greek of the New Testament.   See the note on 1 Thess. i. 1 ἐν Θεῷ πατρὶ and the references given there.   On the other hand it is proposed by some to attach διὰ τῆς ἐπιστολῆς to what follows, 'mark him in (or 'by') your letter.'   But this is doubly objectionable, (1) as laying an emphasis on the letter, which is not easy of explanation ; and (2) because '*your* letter,' where we should expect 'a letter,' assumes a reply on the part of the Thessalonians, which assumption is not borne out by any hint in this Epistle.   It is better therefore to suppose that ἡ ἐπιστολὴ refers to the present Epistle, as it does elsewhere ; though generally, as here, only at the close of the letter (comp. 1 Thess. v. 27, Rom. xvi. 22, Col. iv. 16).   On the other hand, this explanation will not apply to 1 Cor. v. 9 (see the note there).

The words διὰ τῆς ἐπιστολῆς are added, because the Apostle feared that the unruly members might presume on his absence : comp. 1 Cor. v. 3, 2 Cor. x. 11.   His written commands, he would say, are of equal authority with his personal commands.   The New Testament writers nowhere betray any consciousness, either on their own part, or on the part of their hearers, that their written teaching was inspired in any higher sense than their oral teaching.

σημειοῦσθε] '*set your mark on.*'   The word σημειοῦσθαι, in itself neutral, got to imply more or less the idea of disapprobation, though not so definitely as the corresponding Latin word 'notare,' 'to brand,' 'reprobate.'   Compare Dion. Hal. *de adm. vi dic. Dem.* p. 1127 ed. Reiske οἱ δ' ὡς ἁμάρτημα τοῦ ῥήτορος ἐσημειώσαντο, Polyb. v. 78 of a sinister omen, σημειωσάμενοι τὸ γεγονός.   The form σημειοῦσθαι is condemned by the Atticists (Thomas Mag. p. 791, Herodian p. 420 ed. Koch, these references are from Ellicott), who gave ἀποσημαίνεσθαι as the correct Attic word ; and probably with justice, for the derivation of σημειοῦσθαι from a secondary substantive (σημεῖον from σῆμα) points to a later origin.   Compare the old 'acknow' with the modern 'acknowledge.'   Σημειοῦσθαι however occurs as early as Theophrastus at least (*Caus. Plant.* i. 21. 7 προσεπιλέγει τοῖς εἰρημένοις καὶ τὰ τοιαῦτα σημειούμενος ὅτι κ.τ.λ. if the present text may be depended upon).   I cannot trace the reference to Hippocrates given in De Wette.   The language of Aristotle and Theophrastus often forms a link between the pure Attic and the κοινὴ of later writers.

It is difficult to decide between the claims of the readings μὴ συναναμίγνυσθαι (omitting καὶ) and καὶ μὴ συναναμίγνυσθε.   The former on the whole is the more probable, the weight of external testimony (אABD³ copt.) being in its favour.   The order of the variants would then be (1) σημειοῦσθε μὴ συναναμίγνυσθαι, (2) σημειοῦσθε μὴ συναναμίγνυσθε, the ordinary error between ε and αι, (3) σημειοῦσθε καὶ μὴ συναναμίγνυσθε, the καὶ being added in order to obviate the abruptness. If this be so, the reading of some few MSS. (as D*F) σημειοῦσθε καὶ μὴ συναναμίγνυσθαι is to be regarded as a mere transcriptional error, -σθαι for -σθε, arising out of (3). Otherwise it would point to καὶ μὴ συναναμίγνυσθε as the original reading.

μὴ συναναμίγνυσθαι] 'so as not to mix freely with them.' The double compound is expressive; the first preposition σὺν denoting 'combination,' the second ἀνὰ 'interchange.' It is used in the same connexion in 1 Cor. v. 9, 11, and never elsewhere in the New Testament. It is found however in a quotation from Clearchus given in Athenæus (Deipn. vi. 68, p. 256) of professional flatterers moving about among the townsfolk (συναναμιγνύμενοι τοῖς κατὰ τὴν πόλιν) in order to report what they heard to their patrons.

15. καὶ] The use of καί, where we should expect ἀλλά, is easily explained, if we regard νουθετεῖτε as the leading word of the sentence, and the rest as qualifying it. The sense will thus be, 'and reprove him, but as you would reprove a brother, not regarding him as an enemy.' The anxiety of St Paul to soften the severity of his censure has led to a confusion in the form of the sentence; the qualifying clause, which ought to have been subordinate, taking the first place. Νουθετεῖν implies a greater or less shade of blame, meaning 'to remind another of his duty,' but always with some idea of 'admonition.' Compare Tit. iii. 10 μίαν καὶ δευτέραν νουθεσίαν, and see Trench, N. T. Syn. § xxxii. p. 111 sq.

For the spirit of the charge given to the Thessalonians here, compare the analogous case of the Corinthian offender (2 Cor. ii. 6, 7). The συναναμίγνυσθαι seems not itself to mean the absolute ignoring of the delinquent, but the refusal to hold free intercourse or have familiar dealings with him. In 1 Cor. v. 11 the separation was much more strict, and so it is enforced by adding τῷ τοιούτῳ μηδὲ συνεσθίειν.

Polycarp repeats the words of St Paul when dealing with the case of some offenders at Philippi (Phil. 11 'non sicut inimicos tales existimetis, sed sicut passibilia membra et errantia eos revocate').

iii. *Prayer to the Lord of Peace* (iii. 16).

16. αὐτὸς δὲ] 'only may the Lord of peace Himself.' The disjunctive particle δέ is slightly corrective of the preceding. It implies: 'Yet without the help of the Lord all your efforts will be in vain'; see the note on 1 Thess. v. 23, where the same phrase occurs in the corresponding position in the Epistle.

It is doubtful whether by ὁ Κύριος here is meant 'God the Father,' or the 'Lord Jesus Christ.' In favour of the former may be urged the corresponding ὁ Θεὸς τῆς εἰρήνης at the close of the first Epistle (v. 23): in favour of the latter the almost universal meaning of Κύριος in St Paul.

ἐν παντὶ τόπῳ v. l. τρόπῳ] The external authority is evenly balanced between τόπῳ and τρόπῳ, though somewhat favouring the latter reading.

But on the whole τόπῳ is perhaps to be preferred as suiting the context somewhat better, 'at all times, in all places,' i.e. 'wheresoever you are.' For ἐν παντὶ τόπῳ comp. 1 Cor. i. 2, 2 Cor. ii. 14, 1 Thess. i. 8, 1 Tim. ii. 6. On the other hand it may be argued that the original reading was ἐν παντὶ τρόπῳ, altered by transcribers into τόπῳ to conform to a common expression. The preposition ἐν however is awkward where the simple παντὶ τρόπῳ (Phil. i. 18), or even κατὰ πάντα τρόπον (Rom. iii. 2, cf. 2 Thess. ii. 3), would be more natural.

μετὰ πάντων ὑμῶν] *with you all,* not excluding those who are walking disorderly.

4. SPECIAL DIRECTION AND BENEDICTION, iii. 17, 18.

17.   St Paul here takes the pen from the amanuensis, and adds the two last verses containing the salutation in his own handwriting. 'By this,' he says, 'they may know that the letter is his own and not a forgery. This is his practice in every Epistle.'

ὁ ἀσπασμὸς τῇ ἐμῇ χειρὶ Παύλου] seems to be incorrectly rendered in the E.V., apparently as if Παύλου were the genitive with ἀσπασμός. It should be *by the hand of me Paul,* according to the common Greek idiom, e.g. Soph. Œd. Col. 344 τἀμὰ δυστήνου κακά, and other references given in Matthiæ *Gr.* § 466. 1, Jelf *Gr.* § 467. 4.   The same words occur in 1 Cor. xvi. 21, Col. iv. 18.

ὅ ἐστιν σημεῖον] What is the token by which his letters may be known?   Not surely the insertion of the notice ὁ ἀσπασμὸς τῇ ἐμῇ χειρὶ Παύλου which is found in only three of his Epistles, though this seems to be the interpretation put on the words by most commentators ; but the fact of the salutation being written by himself, whether he called direct attention to the fact, or not.   See the following note.

ἐν πάσῃ ἐπιστολῇ] Two questions of some interest arise out of this expression.

First.   How far does St Paul adhere to this rule in his extant Epistles?   The case seems to be this.   Most of his letters, if not all, were written by an amanuensis (see Rom. xvi. 22).   It was the practice of the Apostle himself to take up the pen at the end, and add a few words in his own handwriting to vouch for the authenticity of the letter.   The salutation was always so written, but the Apostle not unfrequently added some words besides.   Thus in 1 Cor. xvi. 22 an anathema is appended ('If any man love not' etc.) ; in Col. iv. 18 an appeal to their compassion ('remember my bonds'); in Galatians vi. 11—17 an earnest protest against Judaizing tendencies, and in Romans xvi. 25—27 perhaps the ascription of praise as a kind of afterthought.   It was only rarely that St Paul called attention to the fact that the conclusion was in his own handwriting (as here, 1 Cor. xvi. 21, Col. iv. 18, and comp. Gal. vi. 11).   When he did so, we may suppose that he had some special motive. As here, for instance, he had regard to the forgeries which he suspected to have been circulated in his name. See the notes on 1 Thess. v. 19, 20, 2 Thess. ii. 2.

It is generally assumed that only those letters contained his autograph salutations in which he calls attention to the fact (as here and in 1 Corinthians and Colossians): and an explanation is sought for its absence in other cases in the fact that no such attestation was necessary, either owing to the circumstances of the letters themselves (e.g. the circular character of the letter to the Ephesians, and the letters addressed to private individuals): or to their having been delivered by accredited messengers (as 2 Corinthians by Timothy, and Philippians by Epaphroditus): or in other ways. But the assumption is in itself unwarrantable, and is only consistent with a somewhat strained interpretation of the expression ἐν πάσῃ ἐπιστολῇ.

Secondly. Is the expression 'in every letter' capable of explanation, except on the supposition that the Apostle wrote many Epistles which have not been preserved to us? This question must be answered in the negative. The Epistles to the Thessalonians were written A.D. 52, 53. See *Biblical Essays*, p. 222 sq. The active labours of the Apostle must have commenced not later than A.D. 45. Yet there is no extant Epistle written before the Epistles to the Thessalonians. The first Epistle to the Corinthians was written A.D. 57. This was the next in chronological order of all the extant letters after those to Thessalonica. Is it to be supposed that these two brief Epistles are the sole utterances of the Apostle, standing isolated in the midst of a period of twelve years, during which the Apostle was holding constant communications with the Gentile churches far and wide? If this were conceivable in itself, it is quite irreconcilable with the expression in the text. How could he speak of 'every letter,' if with the single exception of the first Epistle to the Thessalonians he had written nothing for the eight years preceding, and was destined to write nothing for five years to come? On the whole question of lost letters of St Paul see *Philippians*, p. 138 sq.

οὕτως γράφω] The words probably refer to the handwriting itself: *'this is my handwriting.'* Compare Gal. vi. 11, where he calls attention to the size of the characters, Ἴδετε πηλίκοις ὑμῖν γράμμασιν ἔγραψα τῇ ἐμῇ χειρί. Otherwise οὕτως γράφω might be interpreted either (1) generally: 'this is my practice in writing,' i.e. to add the salutation in my own hand; or (2) referring specially to the formula used: 'these are the words I use.' But in this latter case it ought surely not to be referred to ὁ ἀσπασμὸς κ.τ.λ., but to the salutation itself. See the note on ὅ ἐστιν σημεῖον κ.τ.λ.

18. On the form of salutation see the note on 1 Thess. v. 28. There is only this difference that πάντων is not found in the first Epistle. St Paul had a special reason for inserting it here. He would not run the risk of seeming to exclude those members whose conduct he had reprobated. See the note above on μετὰ πάντων ὑμῶν ver. 16.

THE EPISTLES OF ST PAUL

II
THE THIRD APOSTOLIC JOURNEY

I
FIRST EPISTLE TO THE CORINTHIANS

ANALYSIS

I. INTRODUCTION. i. 1—9.

    i. Salutation. i. 1—3.

    ii. Thanksgiving. i. 4—9.

II. BODY OF THE LETTER. i. 10—xv. 58.

    i. *Divisions.* i. 10—iv. 21.

        (*a*) He describes and deprecates these divisions. i. 10—16.

        (*b*) The unhealthy craving after σοφία. God's folly triumphant over man's wisdom. The true and the false wisdom contrasted. The wisdom of God spiritually discerned. The Corinthians incapacitated by party spirit from discerning it. i. 17—iii. 3.

        (*c*) Their preference of Paul or of Apollos criminal. Paul and Apollos only human instruments. Human preferences worthless: the divine tribunal alone final. iii. 4—iv. 5.

        (*d*) Contrast between the self-satisfied temper of the Corinthians and the sufferings and abasement of the Apostles. This said not by way of rebuke but of fatherly exhortation. His own intentions respecting them. The mission of Timothy and his own proposed visit. iv. 6—21.

    ii. *The case of incest.* v. 1—vi. 20.

        (*a*) The incest denounced. The offender to be cast out of the Church. Reference to the Apostle's letter in which he had recommended them to treat similar offences in the same way. v. 1—13.

        (*b*) [Episode. The Corinthian brethren apply to heathen courts to decide their disputes. This is monstrous.] vi. 1—9.
        Altogether their spirit, whether of sensuality or of strife and overreaching, is inconsistent with heirship in the kingdom of heaven. vi. 10, 11.

(*c*) The distinction between license and liberty. Fornication and Church-membership a contradiction in terms. The members of Christ cannot be made the members of an harlot. vi. 12—20.

[(i) and (ii) are the result of reports received by St Paul. Now follow two answers to questions raised in a letter from the Corinthians.]

iii. *Marriage.* vii. 1—40.

(*a*) To marry, or not to marry? The Apostle's answer. vii. 1, 2.

(*b*) About those already married. Mutual duties of husband and wife. vii. 3—7.

(*c*) About the unmarried, the widows, the separated. Let them remain as they are. vii. 8—11.

(*d*) On the marriage relations of the believer wedded with the unbeliever. Let them not do any violence to their conjugal duties. vii. 12—16.

And generally, do not be eager to alter the condition of life in which God has placed you. vii. 17—24.

(*e*) On virgins specially. Are they to be given in marriage or not? The case to be decided on the same principles as before. Two principles to be kept in view: (1) to preserve continence, (2) to keep the soul disentangled 'because of the present necessity.' vii. 25—38.

(*f*) On widows specially. vii. 39, 40.

iv. *Meats offered to idols.* viii. 1—xi. 1.

(*a*) Meats offered to idols are indifferent in themselves: they are only important as they affect (1) our own consciences, (2) the consciences of others. viii. 1—13.

(*b*) [Episode on Apostolic claims. St Paul asserts (1) his claim to support, and his disinterested renunciation of the claim: (2) his freedom and yet his accommodation to the needs of all: (3) his preaching to others and his discipline of self. ix. 1—27.

This is an interruption to the argument, suggested we know not how. Perhaps the letter was broken off. Something then may have occurred meanwhile; some outward event or some inward train of thought, of which when the letter was resumed the Apostle must first disburden himself, before he took up the thread where he had dropped it.]

(*c*) The Israelites a type to us. All like you had the same spiritual privileges. They all were baptized like you: they all partook of their Eucharistic feast. And yet some perished for their fornication and idolatry. x. 1—12.

(*d*) Therefore be on your guard against the abuse of this liberty. Do not entangle yourselves in idolatry. Do not cause offence to any. x. 13—xi. 1.

CHAPTER I

1. INTRODUCTION, i. 1—9.

i. *Salutation* (i. 1—3).

BESIDES the standard commentaries on this Epistle, the following contributions to the study of some of its problems, from German periodical literature chiefly, will well repay investigation: Klöpper *exegetisch-kritische Untersuchungen über den zweiten Brief des Paulus an die Gemeinde zu Korinth*, Göttingen, 1869, Hausrath *der Vier-Capitel-Brief an die Korinther*, Heidelberg 1870, Weizsäcker *Paulus und die Gemeinde in Korinth* in the *Jahrb. f. deutsche Theol.* 1876 xxi. p. 603 sq., Delitzsch on Lightfoot's *Hor. Hebraic.* in the *Zeitsch. f. Luth. Theol.* 1877 p. 209 sq., Hilgenfeld *die Christus-Leute in Korinth* in the *Zeitsch. f. wiss. Theol.* 1865 viii. p. 241 sq., 1872 xv. p. 200 sq., *die Paulusbriefe und ihre neusten Bearbeitungen* ibid. 1866 ix. p. 337 sq., *Paulus und die Korinth. Wirren* ibid. 1871 xiv. p. 99 sq., *Paulus und Korinth* ibid. 1888 xxxi. p. 159 sq., Holsten *zur Erklärung von 2 Kor.* xi. 4—6 ibid. 1873 xvii. p. 1 sq., Heinrici *Christengemeinde Korinths* ibid. 1876 xix. p. 465 sq., Holtzmann *das gegenseitige Verhältniss der beiden Korintherbriefe* ibid. 1879 xxii. p. 455 sq., Curtius *Studien zur Geschichte von Korinth* in *Hermes* 1876 x. p. 215 sq. There are also articles by Dickson in the *Academy* ii. p. 37, and by P. Gardner in the *Journal of Hellenic Studies* ix. p. 47 sq. (*Countries and Cities in Ancient Art*, esp. p. 61 sq.).

1. On the general form and special modifications of the superscriptions and greetings of St Paul's Epistles see the notes on 1 Thess. i. 1, 2.

κλητὸς ἀπόστολος] '*a called Apostle*'; i.e. one whose apostleship is due not to himself, but to God. The translation of the E. V. 'called to be an Apostle' is as near as the English idiom will permit. The expression is not to be regarded as polemical, that is to say, as directed against

those who denied St Paul's apostleship. For in this case the words
employed would probably have been much stronger, as in Gal. i. 1
ἀπόστολος οὐκ ἀπ' ἀνθρώπων οὐδὲ δι' ἀνθρώπου. That this is so may be
seen (1) from a comparison with the opening of the Epistle to the
Romans, where the same expression is used and no polemical meaning
can be attributed to it, inasmuch as St Paul had no adversaries to attack
in that Epistle; and (2) from the parallelism with the clause following,
κλητοῖς ἁγίοις (ver. 2). His apostleship and their churchmembership were
both alike to be traced to the same source, to the merciful call of God,
and not to their own merits. There is the same parallelism in the
opening words of the Epistle to the Romans, where Παῦλος δοῦλος Ἰησοῦ
Χριστοῦ κλητὸς ἀπόστολος (ver. 1) is followed by ὑμεῖς κλητοὶ (ver. 6).

This preliminary consideration disposed of, we may say further that
the phrase κλητὸς ἀπόστολος is here opposed not so much to human
authorisation or self-assumption, as to personal merit. Both ideas indeed
have their correspondences in the Pauline Epistles. For a reference to
God as the source of all honours and privileges we may compare Rom.
ix. 16 οὐ τοῦ θέλοντος οὐδὲ τοῦ τρέχοντος ἀλλὰ τοῦ ἐλεῶντος Θεοῦ. But a
closer parallel, as it seems to me, occurs in the context of the passage
from the Romans, οὐκ ἐξ ἔργων ἀλλ' ἐκ τοῦ καλοῦντος (Rom. ix. 11). This
feeling of self-abasement, though pervading all St Paul's Epistles, is
especially strong in those belonging to this chronological group. On the
other hand, a strong polemical sense would be more in place in the
second group than in the first. The significance of κλητὸς is still further
enforced by the words following, διὰ θελήματος Θεοῦ. See the note on
Eph. i. 1.

Bengel sees a double direction in St Paul's language, combining these
two last views: 'Ratio auctoritatis, ad ecclesias; humilis et prompti
animi, penes ipsum Paulum. Namque mentione *Dei* excluditur auctora-
mentum humanum, mentione *voluntatis Dei*, meritum Pauli.' But for
the reasons above stated, the assertion of authority, if it is to be
recognized at all, must be quite subordinate and secondary.

Σωσθένης] The mention of Sosthenes naturally takes our thoughts
back to the scene recorded in the Acts (xviii. 12—17) where the name
occurs (ver. 17). By identifying the Sosthenes of the Acts with the
Sosthenes of this Epistle, the notices of him hang together. He was a
Jew by birth and ruler of the synagogue at Corinth. At the time when
St Paul was brought before Gallio, he had either actually declared himself
a Christian, or at least shown such a leaning towards Christianity as to
incur the anger of his fellow-countrymen, who set upon him and beat
him. It is not improbable that he retired from Corinth in consequence :
and it may be conjectured that the hostility with which he was regarded
there was a special inducement to St Paul to recommend him favourably
to the Corinthians in this unobtrusive way, by attaching his name to his
own in the opening salutation. It is of course impossible according to

this view that he could have been one of the Seventy in accordance with an early tradition given by Eusebius (*H. E.* i. 12). But patristic writers exercised so much ingenuity in making up the list of the Seventy (comp. the list published in the works of Hippolytus) that such a tradition is worthless. Thus e.g. Silas is distinguished from Silvanus, and Luke is included in the number (Hippol. *Spur.* in Migne *P. G.* x. p. 955). See also Tillemont I. p. 26, and Baronius, *s. ann.* 33, I. p. 113 (1738).

We may at least infer that Sosthenes was well known to the Christians of Corinth, both from the position which his name occupies and from the designation ὁ ἀδελφός. The definite article implies some distinction, something more than 'one of the brotherhood.' The term appears to have been used in those cases where the person named, though distinguished, had no claim to a higher title, as e.g. Apostle. Thus for instance it is applied to Apollos (1 Cor. xvi. 12), Timothy (2 Cor. i. 1, Col. i. 1, Philem. 1, Heb. xiii. 23), and Quartus (Rom. xvi. 23).

Sosthenes may or may not have been St Paul's amanuensis. The fact of his name occurring here proves nothing. For instance, Tertius (Rom. xvi. 22) is not named in the heading of the Roman letter. Again Timothy and Silvanus (1 Thess. i. 1, 2 Thess. i. 1) were not probably amanuenses of the Epistles to the Thessalonians. On the degree of participation in the contents of the letter implied by his being thus mentioned, see the note on 1 Thess. i. 1. In this letter Sosthenes is named and apparently disappears at once. St Paul immediately returns to the singular (εὐχαριστῶ ver. 4) and loses sight of him.

2. τῇ ἐκκλησίᾳ τοῦ Θεοῦ] On this expression see the notes to 1 Thess. i. 1, ii. 14.

ἡγιασμένοις ἐν Χριστῷ Ἰησοῦ] The authority of the best Greek MSS. must decide the question whether these words shall precede or follow the clause τῇ οὔσῃ ἐν Κορίνθῳ. In a case like this, where for purposes of interpretation there was every temptation to change the order, no great stress must be laid on the versions and citations from the fathers. But even if we decide in favour of the more awkward arrangement of interjecting ἡγιασμένοις ἐν Χριστῷ Ἰησοῦ between τῇ ἐκκλησίᾳ τοῦ Θεοῦ and τῇ οὔσῃ ἐν Κορίνθῳ, the dislocation is quite characteristic of St Paul. The mention of God as the source of spiritual blessings does not satisfy the Apostle, unless supplemented by the parallel mention of Christ as the *medium* of that life. Consequently grammar is disregarded in his anxiety not to postpone this reference to our Lord. Again, there was another reason for inserting the words thus early. The expression ἡ ἐκκλησία τοῦ Θεοῦ might be applied equally well to the Jews ; and consequently, whenever St Paul uses it, he is careful to guard against this ambiguity. See 1 Thess. ii. 14, Gal. i. 22. There was therefore a double motive for the insertion of some such clause as ἡγιασμένοις ἐν Χρ. Ἰησ., and the eagerness of the Apostle to bring this in has disturbed the sequence of the sentence. This parallel reference to the Source from Whom, and the Means through

Whom is too frequent in St Paul, where he has occasion to use terms like ἐκκλησία ἐκλεκτοὶ κλητοὶ and the like, to need special illustration. See however the notes on 1 Thess. l. c.

A somewhat similar instance of the disturbance of grammatical order occurs just below in αὐτῶν καὶ ἡμῶν (ver. 2).

κλητοῖς ἁγίοις] corresponds to κλητὸς ἀπόστολος, as in Rom. i. 7. See the note on ver. 1.

On the words κλητός, ἐκλεκτὸς and the corresponding substantives, as used by St Paul, see the notes on 2 Thess. i. 11 and Col. iii. 12. In this connexion words such as ἡγιασμένοις, ἁγίοις denote the consecrated people, the Christians, as they denoted the Jewish people under the old dispensation. Compare 1 Pet. ii. 9, where many terms formerly applied to the Jews are transferred to the Christians. See also the note on Phil. i. 1.

The ascription of 'holiness' to a community guilty of such irregularities as that of Corinth, reiterated in the words ἡγιασμένοις ἐν X. 'I. κλητοῖς ἁγίοις, is strikingly significant of St Paul's view of the Christian Church, and of his modes of appeal. He addresses the brethren not as the few, but as the many. He delights to take a broad and comprehensive ground. All who are brought within the circle of Christian influences are in a special manner Christ's, all who have put on Christ in baptism are called, are sanctified, are holy. Let them not act unworthily of their calling. Let them not dishonour and defile the sanctity which attaches to them. He is most jealous of narrowing the pale of the Gospel, and this righteous jealousy leads him to the use of expressions which to the 'unlearned and unstable' might seem to betoken an excessive regard for the outward and visible bond of union, and too much neglect of that which is inward and spiritual.

The same liberal and comprehensive spirit is traced in his remarks on the alliance of the believer and unbeliever (vii. 12 sq.), and in his illustration drawn from the practice of baptism (xii. 2 sq.).

σὺν πᾶσι τοῖς ἐπικαλουμένοις] 'as also to all those who invoke.' This clause cannot be attached to κλητοῖς in the sense of 'saints called together with all that invoke etc.' For though this construction would obviate considerable difficulty in interpreting what follows, it is grammatically harsh, if not untenable, and would require a participle for κλητοῖς, or at all events a different order of words.

There still remains the difficulty of interpreting σὺν πᾶσι τοῖς ἐπικαλουμένοις κ.τ.λ. ἐν παντὶ τόπῳ. A comparison with the opening of the second Epistle, σὺν τοῖς ἁγίοις πᾶσιν τοῖς οὖσιν ἐν ὅλῃ τῇ 'Αχαίᾳ would suggest the restriction of 'every place' to 'all the churches of Achaia': but though the expression ἐν παντὶ τόπῳ elsewhere (e.g. 1 Thess. i. 8, 2 Cor. ii. 14) must be taken with certain natural limitations, still the very definite restriction to 'every place in Achaia' receives no sanction from such examples. We must suppose then that St Paul associates the whole Christian Church with the Corinthians in this superscription. This

association would refer more especially to the benediction which immediately follows, but in some degree also to the main contents of
the letter, which, though more special and personal than perhaps any
other of St Paul's Epistles, yet founds its exhortations on great general
principles applying to all alike. It perhaps arose out of the idea of unity
prominent in the Apostle's mind, and was suggested by the dissensions
which divided the Corinthian Church.

For a similar superscription compare the Epistle of the Church of
Smyrna on the death of Polycarp...τῇ ἐκκλησίᾳ τοῦ Θεοῦ τῇ παροικούσῃ ἐν
Φιλομηλίῳ καὶ πάσαις ταῖς κατὰ πάντα τόπον τῆς ἁγίας καὶ καθολικῆς
ἐκκλησίας παροικίαις, ἔλεος καὶ εἰρήνη καὶ ἀγάπη κ.τ.λ. See also the close
of St Clement's Epistle to the Corinthians, Ἡ χάρις τοῦ Κ. ἡμῶν Ἰησ. Χρ.
μεθ' ὑμῶν καὶ μετὰ πάντων πανταχῇ τῶν κεκλημένων ὑπὸ τοῦ Θεοῦ κ.τ.λ. (§ 65).

ἐπικαλουμένοις τὸ ὄνομα τοῦ Κυρίου] A phrase which in the O.T. e.g.
Gen. iv. 26, xiii. 4 etc., is applied to Jehovah, and therefore seems to
imply a divine power and attributes. For the expression τὸ ὄνομα τοῦ
Κυρίου see the notes on 2 Thess. i. 12, Phil. ii. 9, 10, and generally for
the application to our Lord of phrases applied in the O.T. to God see
on 2 Thess. i. 7, 9. The practice is illustrated by the testimony of Pliny
(*Ep.* xcvi.) 'carmen Christo quasi Deo dicere secum invicem.'

αὐτῶν καὶ ἡμῶν] Is this clause to be taken with ἐν παντὶ τόπῳ or with
τοῦ Κυρίου ἡμῶν? The former is the interpretation adopted by most
modern commentators after the Vulgate, which translates it 'in omni loco
ipsorum et nostro,' as also do some other ancient versions. But all
possible interpretations of the words so connected are extremely harsh.
Thus it is explained by some to mean 'both in Achaia (αὐτῶν) and in
Asia' (ἡμῶν, for St Paul was writing from Ephesus); by others 'in every
part of Achaia, which Achaia belongs to us, as well as to them, inasmuch
as we are their spiritual teachers.' Other interpretations are still more
arbitrary.

It is better therefore to attach αὐτῶν καὶ ἡμῶν to τοῦ Κυρίου, as taking
up the foregoing ἡμῶν. This is the view of all the Greek commentators,
from a sense, I suppose, of the fitness of the Greek. The words are an
after-thought, correcting any possible misapprehension of ἡμῶν. 'Our
Lord, did I say?—their Lord and ours alike.' There is a covert allusion
to the divisions in the Corinthian Church, and an implied exhortation to
unity. The particle τε after αὐτῶν if genuine (as is probably not the
case) would assist this interpretation; but even in its absence this is far
less harsh than the alternative construction.

3. χάρις ὑμῖν καὶ εἰρήνη] See notes on 1 Thess. i. 1.

ii. *Thanksgiving* (i. 4—9).

4. εὐχαριστῶ κ.τ.λ.] On the thanksgivings at the openings of St Paul's
Epistles and on the Hellenistic use of the word εὐχαριστῶ see the notes

on 1 Thess. i. 2. In this instance St Paul bears in mind a subject which will occupy a prominent place in the body of the Epistle, the spiritual gifts of the Corinthians.

δοθείσῃ, ἐπλουτίσθητε] *'which was given...ye were enriched.'* The aorists point back to the time of their baptism into the Christian Church, and generally of their admission to the privileges of the Gospel. The phrase ὅτι ἐν παντὶ ἐπλουτίσθητε is an epexegesis of ἐπὶ τῇ χάριτι τῇ δοθείσῃ.

ὅτι] *'in that,'* used after εὐχαριστῶ, as in Rom. i. 8, 2 Thess. i. 3.

ἐν Χριστῷ Ἰησοῦ, ἐν αὐτῷ] *'in Christ Jesus,' 'in Him'*; not as the E.V. 'by Jesus Christ,' 'by Him.' God is represented here, as generally, as the 'Giver of all good gifts.' Christ is the medium through whom and the sphere in which these gifts are conferred. It is by our incorporation in Christ that they are bestowed upon us.

5. ἐν παντὶ λόγῳ καὶ πάσῃ γνώσει] The distinction between these words is differently given, as follows. (1) Λόγος is the lower, γνῶσις the higher knowledge, a distinction which is without sufficient foundation. (2) Λόγος refers to the gift of tongues, γνῶσις to that of prophecy. But the restriction to 'special gifts' seems not to be warranted by the context: see the conclusion of the note. (3) Λόγος is the teaching of the Gospel as offered to the Corinthians, γνῶσις their hearty acceptance of the same. But against this view it may be urged that the words τῇ χάριτι τῇ δοθείσῃ, ἐπλουτίσθητε ἐν παντὶ κ.τ.λ., as well as the parallelism of λόγος with γνῶσις, point to some personal and inward gift, as the meaning of λόγος. (4) Λόγος is the outward expression, γνῶσις the inward conviction; as the E.V. 'all utterance and all knowledge.'

The last is probably the correct interpretation. Not only were the Corinthians rich in the knowledge of the truths of the Gospel, but they were also gifted with the power of enunciating them effectively. St Chrysostom says (*ad loc.*) καὶ νοῆσαι καὶ εἰπεῖν ἱκανοί, perhaps having in his mind the expression which Thucydides uses of his teacher Antiphon (viii. 68) κράτιστος ἐνθυμηθῆναι γενόμενος καὶ ἃ ἂν γνοίη εἰπεῖν. This distinction of λόγος and γνῶσις is partially illustrated by 2 Cor. viii. 7, xi. 6 εἰ δὲ καὶ ἰδιώτης τῷ λόγῳ ἀλλ' οὐ τῇ γνώσει. The order here need not stand in the way of this interpretation; for though γνῶσις is prior to λόγος, and so might be expected to stand first, it is reserved for the last as being of superior and essential importance.

St Paul is doubtless alluding in part to the special gifts of the Spirit, which seem to have been bestowed so lavishly on the Corinthian Church (see chaps. xii, xiv). And thus λόγος would include the gift of tongues, γνῶσις the gifts of discerning spirits and interpreting tongues (comp. especially 1 Cor. xiii. 1, 2 ἐὰν ταῖς γλώσσαις τῶν ἀνθρώπων λαλῶ...κἂν ἔχω προφητείαν καὶ εἰδῶ τὰ μυστήρια πάντα καὶ πᾶσαν τὴν γνῶσιν κ.τ.λ.). Thus the λόγος of the Corinthians comes prominently forward in speaking of the gift of tongues—the γνῶσις in condemning their divisions and rebuking their self-sufficiency. St Paul here gives thanks for their use: he afterwards condemns their abuse.

But it would be a mistake to confine the allusion to these. It is obvious from the context that the Apostle is referring chiefly to those more excellent gifts, the spiritual graces which make up the Christian character. In the same spirit in which he has addressed his Corinthian converts 'as sanctified in Christ Jesus,' he goes on to express his thankfulness for their advance in true holiness. He loses sight for a moment of the irregularities which had disfigured the Church at Corinth, while he remembers the spiritual blessings which they enjoyed. After all deductions made for these irregularities, the Christian community at Corinth must have presented as a whole a marvellous contrast to their heathen fellow-citizens—a contrast which might fairly be represented as one of light and darkness. See further on χάρισμα (ver. 7). On the distinction between γνῶσις and σοφία see the note on Col. ii. 3, and compare 1 Cor. xii. 8.

6. καθὼς] 'according as,' 'in this respect that,' 'inasmuch as,' and so almost equivalent to 'seeing that.' It explains the manner of ἐν παντὶ ἐπλουτίσθητε κ.τ.λ. For this use of καθὼς introducing an epexegesis of what has preceded, compare 1 Thess. i. 5.

τὸ μαρτύριον τοῦ Χριστοῦ] 'the testimony borne to Christ' by the Apostles and preachers; and thus equivalent to 'the Gospel as preached to you,' Χριστοῦ being the objective genitive. Compare 2 Tim. i. 8 μὴ οὖν ἐπαισχυνθῇς τὸ μαρτύριον τοῦ Κυρίου ἡμῶν, Rev. i. 2, 9, and see the note on ii. 1 below.

ἐβεβαιώθη ἐν ὑμῖν] This might mean either (1) 'received confirmation in your persons,' i.e. commended itself to others by the effect it produced on your character; or (2) 'was confirmed in you,' 'produced a deep conviction in your hearts.' The latter sense is to be preferred, as being more in accordance with the use of καθὼς as explained above, and also as better adapted to the statement ὃς καὶ βεβαιώσει ὑμᾶς which follows.

7. ὥστε] is best attached to what immediately precedes. Otherwise καθὼς...ἐν ὑμῖν is to be treated as parenthetical, and ὥστε referred to the previous clause ἐν παντὶ ἐπλουτίσθητε. But this is not so good. It is more in St Paul's manner thus to string the clauses together one after the other.

μὴ ὑστερεῖσθαι ἐν μηδενὶ χαρίσματι] 'so that ye fall short in no spiritual gift.' The expression signifies more than μηδενὸς χαρίσματος. The latter would mean 'not to be without any gift' (comp. Rom. iii. 23); the former 'not to possess it in less measure than others.' For the wish compare James i. 4, 19, and Ign. Pol. 2 ἵνα μηδενὸς λείπῃ καὶ παντὸς χαρίσματος περισσεύῃς.

χαρίσματι] The term χάρισμα. though sometimes applied especially to the extraordinary gifts of the Spirit (such as tongues etc.), is not so confined. It includes all spiritual graces and endowments. The greatest χάρισμα of all the Apostle declares elsewhere to be eternal life (Rom. vi. 23). That it is here used in this wider sense, is clear from the context, which shows that St Paul is dwelling especially on moral gifts, as for instance on holiness of life.

It would probably be correct to say that St Paul himself was conscious of no such distinction as that of the ordinary and extraordinary gifts of the Spirit. At all events in his enumeration he classes together those endowments which we commonly speak of as miraculous and special, and such as belong generally to the Christian character. See chap. xii. And in some cases, as for instance the χάρισμα of 'prophesying,' it is difficult to say where the non-miraculous ceases and the miraculous begins; or to point to any distinction in kind between its manifestation in the Apostolic times and its counterpart in later ages of the Church.

ἀπεκδεχομένους] 'as you eagerly expect.' The significance of this clause in connexion with the context is best illustrated by 1 Joh. iii. 2, 3 'we know that, when He shall appear, we shall be like Him...and every man that hath this hope in Him purifieth himself, even as He is pure': and by 2 Pet. iii. 11, 12 'what manner of persons ought ye to be in all holy conversation and godliness, looking for and hasting the coming of the day of God.' In other words, the very expectation is productive of that advance in Christian grace and knowledge which was spoken of before. The word ἀπεκδέχεσθαι does not necessarily signify 'awaiting hopefully, desiring'; but the double preposition implies a degree of earnestness and an intensity of expectation which is quite inconsistent with the careless-ness of the godless. Hence it is never used in the New Testament in reference to the coming of Christ, except of the 'faithful.' See Rom. viii. 23, 25 (and comp. ver. 19), Gal. v. 5, Phil. iii. 20, and especially Heb. ix. 28 ἐκ δευτέρου χωρὶς ἁμαρτίας ὀφθήσεται τοῖς αὐτὸν ἀπεκδεχομένοις εἰς σωτηρίαν.

8. ὃς καί] i.e. 'Who also will go on with this process of strengthening even unto the end, so that ye may be blameless.' This relative is referred either to Θεός or to Χριστός as its antecedent. The latter is to be preferred, as immediately preceding, while Θεός must be sought far back in the sentence. And then again a new subject seems to be introduced in Θεός below (verse 9). The repetition of τοῦ Κ. ἡμ. Ἰησ. Χρ., where we might expect αὐτοῦ, is no valid argument against referring ὅς to Χριστός. Such a repetition of the substantive has its parallel even in classical Greek, and is common in the New Testament. See 1 Thess. iii. 13, 2 Tim. i. 18, Gen. xix. 24; and compare Winer § xxii. p. 180 sq. There is a special fascina-tion in that 'name which is above every name,' leading St Paul to dwell upon it, and reiterate it. Compare also in this respect ver. 21.

ὃς καὶ βεβαιώσει] to be referred to ἐβεβαιώθη ἐν ὑμῖν, on which see the note. Compare also 2 Cor. i. 10 ἐρρύσατο ἡμᾶς καὶ ῥύσεται εἰς ὃν ἠλπίκα-μεν ὅτι καὶ ἔτι ῥύσεται, Phil. i. 18 ἐν τούτῳ χαίρω· ἀλλὰ καὶ χαρήσομαι.

ἕως τέλους] with a reference to ἀπεκδεχομένους.

ἀνεγκλήτους] 'so that ye may be blameless': proleptic. See the instances given on 1 Thess. iii. 13 ἀμέμπτους.

ἐν τῇ ἡμέρᾳ] See the notes on 1 Thess. v. 2, 4, and compare iv. 3 below, ὑπὸ ἀνθρωπίνης ἡμέρας.

9. The sequence of thought is as follows. 'The fact that you have been called through God to a communion with Christ, is an earnest assurance to you that Christ will bring this good work to a favourable issue. For reliance can be placed on God. This calling was not intended to be illusory or vain.' Here again St Paul takes the broad and comprehensive view of God's dealings. See the notes above on vv. 2, 4. For the same thought compare Phil. i. 6 'Being confident of this very thing that He which hath begun a good work in you will perform it until the day of Jesus Christ'; and see the notes on the verse.

πιστὸς ὁ Θεὸς] Compare 1 Cor. x. 13, 2 Cor. i. 18, 1 Thess. v. 24 πιστὸς ὁ καλῶν ὑμᾶς ὃς καὶ ποιήσει, 2 Thess. iii. 3.

δι' οὗ] 'through Whom,' not as E.V. 'by whom,' which is ambiguous, 'by' being here an archaism. We may speak of God the Father, either as the source from whom, or the means, instrumentality through which all things arise and are. Compare Rom. xi. 36 ἐξ αὐτοῦ καὶ δι' αὐτοῦ καὶ εἰς αὐτὸν τὰ πάντα. He is at once beginning, middle and end. Most commonly He is regarded as the Source (ἐξ οὗ); but sometimes as the Means (δι' οὗ) as here and Heb. ii. 13 ἔπρεπεν γὰρ αὐτῷ, δι' ὃν τὰ πάντα καὶ δι' οὗ τὰ πάντα κ.τ.λ. Compare Gal. i. 1 and note. Whenever God the Father and Christ are mentioned together, origination is ascribed to the Father, and mediation to Christ in things physical as well as spiritual. See especially 1 Cor. viii. 6 εἷς Θεός, ὁ πατήρ, ἐξ οὗ τὰ πάντα καὶ ἡμεῖς εἰς αὐτόν, καὶ εἷς Κύριος Ἰησοῦς Χριστός, δι' οὗ τὰ πάντα καὶ ἡμεῖς δι' αὐτοῦ. This distinction is as precise in St Paul as in St John, though dwelt upon more fully by the latter. We should nowhere find such an expression as ἐξ οὗ τὰ πάντα applied to Christ.

The preceding note suggests two remarks. (1) It is important to observe how early and with what exactness the doctrine of the person of Christ was maintained. The genuineness of this Epistle is not questioned even by the severest negative criticism, and yet here it is as distinctly stated as in the Fourth Gospel, which that same criticism condemns as the forgery of a later age. (2) We should not fail to observe the precision with which St Paul uses the preposition, as a token of his general grammatical accuracy.

κοινωνίαν] including both spiritual communion with Christ in the present life and participation in His glory hereafter, without which this communion would be incomplete. The κοινωνία τοῦ υἱοῦ αὐτοῦ is coextensive in meaning with the βασιλεία τοῦ Θεοῦ. On the uses of the word in St Paul's Epistles see the note on Phil. i. 5 ἐπὶ τῇ κοινωνίᾳ ὑμῶν εἰς τὸ εὐαγγέλιον.

2. BODY OF THE LETTER, i. 10—xv. 58.

i. DIVISIONS, i. 10—iv. 21.

(a) He describes and deprecates these divisions (i. 10—17).

10. **παρακαλῶ δὲ**] The participle is slightly corrective. 'Though I have commended your progress in the Gospel, yet I must rebuke you for your divisions.'

ἀδελφοί] i.e. 'ye who profess to be held together in the bond of brotherhood.' The repetition of the term in the following verse, ἀδελφοί μου, points to its significance here. For the use of this term in similar appeals compare Gal. vi. 1, 18 (with the notes). See also especially 1 Cor. vi. 5, 6.

διὰ τοῦ ὀνόματος τοῦ Κ. ἡμῶν Ἰ. Χ.] The exhortation to unity is still further strengthened. 'I intreat by that one name which we all bear in common, that ye assume not divers names, as of Paul, and Apollos etc.' For the adjuration comp. 2 Thess. iii. 6.

ἵνα] It is difficult in this passage, as elsewhere, to discriminate between the two senses of ἵνα as denoting the purpose, design, or simply the object, consequence. Compare the notes on 1 Thess. ii. 16, v. 4.

τὸ αὐτὸ λέγητε] We have here a strictly classical expression. It is used of political communities which are free from factions, or of different states which entertain friendly relations with each other. Thus τὸ αὐτὸ λέγειν is 'to be at peace,' or 'to make up differences'; see Thuc. iv. 20 ἡμῶν καὶ ὑμῶν ταὐτὰ λεγόντων, v. 31 Βοιωτοὶ δὲ καὶ Μεγαρῆς τὸ αὐτὸ λέγοντες ἡσύχαζον, Arist. *Polit.* ii. 3. 3, Polyb. ii. 62, v. 104 etc. Here the second idea to make up differences is the prominent one, and is carried out in κατηρτισμένοι below, where the same political metaphor is used. On the application of classical terms relating to the body politic to the Christian community by the N. T. writers, see the note on τῶν ἐκκλησιῶν 1 Thess. ii. 14.

The marked classical colouring of such passages as this leaves a much stronger impression of St Paul's acquaintance with classical writers than the rare occasional quotations which occur in his writings. Compare especially the speech before the Areopagus (Acts xvii.). The question of St Paul's general education is discussed in *Biblical Essays*, p. 201 sq., see especially p. 205 sq.

σχίσματα] This is said to be the earliest passage in which the word occurs of a 'moral division' (Stanley, *Corinthians* ad loc.). It is here used as almost synonymous with ἔριδες, and in a later passage (1 Cor. xi. 18) it is distinguished from αἱρέσεις, the latter denoting a more complete separation than σχίσματα. See the passage. The word does not occur elsewhere in the N. T. in this sense, except in St John's Gospel (vii. 43, ix. 16, x. 19). In St Clement's Epistle to the Corinthians it occurs frequently, as might be expected, with more or less of reference to this Epistle. See §§ 2, 49, 54 and especially § 46 ἵνα τί ἔρεις καὶ θυμοὶ καὶ διχοστασίαι καὶ σχίσματα πόλεμός τε ἐν ὑμῖν, where the words are arranged in an ascending scale. Θυμοὶ are 'outbursts of wrath,' διχοστασία is weaker than σχίσμα, as it is stronger than στάσις : as στάσις developes into διχοστασία, so διχοστασία widens into σχίσμα. See the notes on this passage, and on Gal. v. 20, 21. The word is apparently not found elsewhere in the Apostolic Fathers.

κατηρτισμένοι] On this word see the note on 1 Thess. iii. 10. It is especially appropriate here with reference to σχίσματα (Matt. iv. 21, Mark i. 19).

ἐν τῷ αὐτῷ νοΐ καὶ ἐν τῇ αὐτῇ γνώμῃ] Of these words νοῦς denotes the frame or state of mind, γνώμη the judgment, opinion or sentiment, which is the outcome of νοῦς. The former denotes the general principles, the latter the special applications of those principles. The form νοΐ is peculiar to St Paul in the N. T., but not uncommon with him (Rom. vii. 25, xiv. 5, 1 Cor. xiv. 15). It is confined to late writers (Winer § viii. p. 72).

11. ὑπὸ τῶν Χλόης] The expression may mean either (1) 'the children,' or (2) 'the servants,' or (3) 'the relations of Chloe.' We learn a good deal of the social condition of the early Christians from their names. Judging from her name, Chloe was probably a freedwoman. At least the name does not denote any exalted rank. Compare Horace *Od.* iii. 9. 9 'me nunc Thressa Chloe regit.' Chloe is an epithet of the Goddess Demeter (Aristoph. *Lysistr.* 835, compare εὔχλοος Soph. *O. C.* 1600); and it is not improbable that, as a proper name, it was derived from this use. Slaves and by consequence freedmen seem very frequently to have borne the Greek names of heathen divinities. Compare the instances of Phœbe (Rom. xvi. 1), of Hermes (xvi. 14), and of Nereus (xvi. 15).

Perhaps however the name is to be referred to the primary meaning of the word, as in the case of Stachys (στάχυς) (Rom. xvi. 9) and Chloris. On either supposition it would point to a servile origin, from which class a large number of the early converts to Christianity appear to have been drawn. Compare ver. 26, and see the notes on Cæsar's household in *Philippians*, p. 171 sq.

The position of importance occupied by women in the Christian Church, even at this early date, is a token of the great social revolution which the Gospel was already working. See *Philippians*, p. 55 sq. for the development of this feature in Macedonia especially.

It is possible that Stephanas, Fortunatus and Achaicus (xvi. 17) are included in οἱ Χλόης ; but there is no ground for the supposition, and all such identifications are hazardous.

12. λέγω δὲ τοῦτο ὅτι] '*I refer to the fact that,*' '*my meaning is this*

that'; not as E.V., 'now this I say that.' Compare Gal. iii. 17,
1 Thess. iv. 15, and see [Clem. Rom.] ii. §§ 2, 8, 12 τοῦτο λέγει 'he
means this.'

ἔκαστος ὑμῶν] i.e. 'there is not one of you, but has his party leader.
The whole body is infected with this spirit of strife.'

'Ἀπολλῶ] The name Apollos is contracted either from Apollonius, or
Apollodorus, probably the first. So at least it is written in full in Codex D
(Acts xviii. 24), and the variation seems to point to some very early
tradition. Apollos was an Alexandrian (Acts l. c.), and the name Apollonius was common in Alexandria, probably owing to the fact 'that the
first governor left by Alexander in his African province was so called'
(Arrian *Anab.* iii. 5). On the contracted names in -ὠς and -ᾶς, so frequent
in the N. T., see Winer § xvi. p. 127, and the note on 1 Thess. i. 1
Σιλουανός. This particular contraction is found elsewhere, though rarely;
see Conybeare and Howson, p. 364.

We first hear of Apollos residing at Ephesus about the time of
St Paul's first visit to Corinth (A.D. 52, 53). Here he is instructed in
the Gospel by Aquila and Priscilla. From Ephesus he crosses over to
Corinth, where he preaches to the Corinthians and makes a deep
impression upon the Corinthian Church. After his departure St Paul
arrives at Ephesus, and remains there three years (from A.D. 54 to 57).
See Acts xviii. 24—xix. 1. There is no notice of the return of Apollos
from Corinth to Ephesus; but he was with St Paul or in the neighbour-
hood when this Epistle was written, i.e. about or after Easter 57 (see xvi.
12). For his subsequent movements see Tit. iii. 13; and on the subject
generally Heymann in *Sächs. Stud.* (1843), II. p. 222 sq., Pfizer *de
Apollone doctore apostol.* Altorf (1718), Bleek *Hebr.* p. 394 sq., Meyer
on Acts xviii. 24 and Stanley *Corinthians* ad loc.

Κηφᾶ] The Aramaic word כֵּיפָא corresponding to the Greek Πέτρος
(John i. 42). St Paul seems to have employed both forms indifferently.
In this Epistle he always speaks of Κηφᾶς; in the Epistle to the Galatians,
sometimes of Κηφᾶς (Gal. i. 18, ii. 9, 11, 14), sometimes of Πέτρος (Gal. ii.
7, 8). Here, as repeating the language of the Judaizers, he would
naturally use Cephas.

The question occurs, had St Peter been at Corinth before this time?
Apollos had been there, but there is no indication that St Peter had been.
In ix. 5 there is an allusion to him which points to his moving about at
this time. The Rómanist story of St Peter's twenty-five years episcopate
at Rome (A.D. 42 to 67), if true, would cover the time of St Paul's im-
prisonment at Rome, and also the period of the Epistles to and from
Rome, so that the entire absence of any allusion to his being at Rome at
this time is quite inexplicable, if he were there. Besides, St Paul speaks
(Rom. xv. 20) as though no Apostle had previously visited it. It does not
seem at all necessary that St Peter should have been at Corinth in order
that his name should be taken by a party. He was naturally head of the

Church of the circumcision. See the essay entitled 'Saint Peter in Rome' in *Apostolic Fathers*, Part I., vol. II. p. 481 sq. (1890).

Observe the delicacy evinced by St Paul in treating of this subject. His ascending scale is Paul, Apollos, Cephas, Christ. He places himself in the lowest grade, next, that teacher who was especially associated with him, and highest of human instructors the Apostle who was represented as his direct antagonist. Again, when he wants to enforce the opposition between the servant and the master, between the human instrument and the divine source, he selects his own name, as the meanest of all, and therefore the best antithesis : μεμέρισται ὁ Χριστός· μὴ Παῦλος ἐσταυρώθη ὑπὲρ ὑμῶν; so also in iii. 5 (τί οὖν ἐστιν Ἀπολλώς; τί δέ ἐστιν Παῦλος;) there is no mention of Cephas. His well-known friendly relations with Apollos allowed him, both here and in iv. 6, as it were to take liberties with his name. On the other hand, a true gentlemanly feeling led him to abstain from appearing to depreciate Cephas, his supposed adversary. This is an instance of his fine appreciation of what was due to his fellow-men.

In the Epistle to the Galatians, where it was necessary for him to assert his Apostleship, his language is different.

13. μεμέρισται ὁ Χριστός;] Lachmann omits the note of interrogation, as is done apparently in most of the ancient versions. Yet the sentence is more forcible taken interrogatively. Nor does the absence of μὴ in one clause, whilst it is present in the other, form any objection to this way of taking it. The form of the interrogative is purposely varied, because the reply suggested in each case is different. Μὴ interrogative implies a negative answer, whereas the omission of μὴ allows an affirmative answer. 'Has Christ been divided?' This is only too true. 'Was Paul crucified for you?' This is out of the question. On μὴ interrogative as implying a negative answer see Winer § lvii. p. 641. The opposition in the form of the interrogative would have been still stronger, if St Paul had written οὐ μεμέρισται;

In what sense did the Apostle mean that Christ had been divided? Christ is here identified with the body of believers. Thus 'Has Christ been divided?' is in effect 'Have you by your dissensions rent Christ's body asunder, tearing limb from limb?' Compare 1 Cor. xii. 12, 13 'For as the body is one, and hath many members and all the members of that one body, being many, are one body : so also is Christ. For by one Spirit are we all baptized into one body.' Compare also xii. 27. This passage seems to leave no doubt as to the interpretation here ; and so Clement of Rome evidently understands it, for speaking of the later factions at Corinth, he says (§ 46) ἵνα τί διέλκομεν καὶ διασπῶμεν τὰ μέλη τοῦ Χριστοῦ; with an evident reference to St Paul's language here. Immediately afterwards he alludes directly to this Epistle ἀναλάβετε τὴν ἐπιστολὴν τοῦ μακαρίου Παύλου τοῦ ἀποστόλου...ἐπέστειλεν ὑμῖν περὶ αὐτοῦ τε καὶ Κηφᾶ τε καὶ Ἀπολλὼ κ.τ.λ. For an equally strong instance of the use of the metaphor see Hebr. vi. 6 ἀνασταυροῦντας ἑαυτοῖς τὸν υἱὸν τοῦ Θεοῦ καὶ παραδειγματίζοντας.

Some would give to μεμέρισται the sense of 'assigned as a share' ('Has Christ become the badge of a party?'), in which case the words would refer solely to the section described as ἐγὼ δὲ Χριστοῦ. It does not appear however that μερίζειν absolutely could well have this meaning; though in certain connexions, as in the construction μερίζειν τινί τι, it would be natural enough.

μὴ Παῦλος ἐσταυρώθη] 'surely Paul was not crucified for you.' The appeal is not simply to their gratitude towards one who has laid down his life for them, but to their sense of justice. 'You were not purchased by the blood of Paul, you have not become the property of Paul.' Compare 1 Cor. vi. 19, 20, vii. 23, where this idea of ownership is brought out. The idea will of course be more strongly implied here if the reading is ὑπέρ, than if περί. The balance of evidence is slightly in favour of ὑπέρ.

εἰς τὸ ὄνομα Παύλου] 'into the name of,' not 'in the name of' as in the E.V. The preposition implies both 'subjection to and communion with' another. The phrase is sometimes ἐπὶ τῷ ὀνόματι (Acts ii. 38 v. l.), sometimes ἐν τῷ ὀνόματι (Acts x. 48), but more frequently the stronger εἰς τὸ ὄνομα (Matt. xxviii. 19, Acts viii. 16, xix. 5).

It is unsafe to infer from such expressions as this (comp. Acts x. 48, xix. 5 and Hermas V. iii. 7. 3 θέλοντες βαπτισθῆναι εἰς τὸ ὄνομα τοῦ Κυρίου) that the formula of baptism in the name of the Trinity (as commanded Matt. xxviii. 19) was dispensed with, and the name of Jesus alone pronounced. Baptism in or into the name of Jesus is to be regarded as an abridged expression to signify Christian baptism, retaining the characteristic element in the formula. Justin Martyr at least recognises only baptism in the name of the Trinity (Apol. i. § 61, p. 94 A) and see Clem. Recogn. iii. 67, Tertull. c. Praxean § 27. Certain heretics however baptized solely in the name of Christ, and in the discussion on rebaptism it was a question whether such baptism was valid. See a full account in Bingham's Christian Antiquities, XI. c. iii. § 1 and comp. Neander. Pfl. u. Leit. § 276, Ch. Hist. (Bohn's translation), II. pp. 430, 446 sq., who however leans to the opinion that baptism in the name of Christ alone is intended in these passages of Scripture, as did St Ambrose also de Spir. Sanct. i. 3.

14. Κρίσπον] The ruler of the synagogue whose whole household was converted, probably among the earliest Corinthian converts. Crispus (like Cincinnatus, etc. referring originally to the hair) is a common Roman cognomen, and occurs frequently also as a Jewish name. See the passages cited by Lightfoot and Wetstein here.

Γάϊον] St Paul (Rom. xvi. 23) speaks of Gaius as 'mine host and of the whole Church,' so that he would appear to have lodged with him during his (now approaching) third visit to Corinth. Several persons

of the name appear in the N.T.   It was an ordinary praenomen among
the Romans, and being common to several distinguished members of the
Imperial family, like Julius, Claudius etc., was probably more in vogue than
ever at this epoch.   Whether this is the same with the Gaius addressed in
3 John, it is impossible to say.   They are both commended in similar
terms for their hospitality: comp. 3 John 5, 6.   But the Gaius of St John
seems to be spoken of as a younger man or at least a young disciple,
whereas the Gaius of St Paul cannot have been either when St John
wrote.   The correct pronunciation and probably the correct form in Latin
is Gaius, as it is always written in Greek.   The same character in Latin
originally stood for C and G : comp. Donaldson *Varron.* vii. § 3, p. 291.

15. ἵνα μή τις εἴπῃ] is to be connected with the whole sentence
εὐχαριστῶ...ἐβάπτισα, not with οὐδένα ἐβάπτισα alone.   ' I am thankful it
was so, that no one may have it in his power to say.'   It is not meant
that St Paul at the time abstained from baptizing, foreseeing this result,
but that afterwards he was glad that it was so.   ' Providentia Dei regnat
saepe in rebus, quarum ratio postea cognoscitur' Bengel.

εἰς τὸ ἐμὸν ὄνομα] as certain heretics actually did, or are reputed to
have done, e.g. Menander (in Pseudo-Tertull. *adv. omn. Hær.* c. 1.) and
others.   See the references in Bingham, XI. c. iii. § 5.

ἐβαπτίσθητε] the correct reading, not ἐβάπτισα.

16. The verse was an afterthought.   He was perhaps reminded of the
omission by his amanuensis, who may have been Stephanas himself or one
of his household, for they were with him at the time (1 Cor. xvi. 15, 17).
Perhaps Fortunatus and Achaicus were members of his household.   The
house of Stephanas is spoken of in 1 Cor. l. c. as the first-fruits of Achaia.
This will account for their being baptized by the Apostle's own hand.

On the undesigned coincidences between the Acts and Epistles
lurking under these names see Paley *Hor. Paul.* III. § 8.

17. οὐ γὰρ ἀπέστειλε] Baptism might be performed by a subordinate.
It presupposed no extraordinary gifts on the part of the performer, for
its efficacy consisted in the spirit of the recipient and the grace of God, ἡ
γὰρ προαίρεσις τοῦ προσιόντος λοιπὸν ἐργάζεται τὸ πᾶν, καὶ ἡ τοῦ Θεοῦ χάρις :
but successful preaching requires special gifts.

Hence we find that our Lord did not baptize Himself, but left this
work to His disciples (John iv. 1, 2).   And the Apostles followed this
precedent, as St Peter (Acts x. 48), and St Paul here.   St Paul was
generally attended by one or more of the brethren, who ministered to
him and on whom this office would devolve (Acts xiii. 5 εἶχον Ἰωάννην
ὑπηρέτην, xix. 22 δύο τῶν διακονούντων αὐτῷ Τιμόθεον καὶ Ἔραστον, both
phrases pointing to a recognised position, more or less official).

οὐκ ἐν σοφίᾳ λόγου] St Paul is eager to obviate any misapprehension
which might arise from his exaltation of the ordinance of preaching.
There were many members of the Corinthian Church who would eagerly
seize hold of this concession as they would regard it.   It is not as a mere

display of rhetoric, or of logical subtlety that he exalts it.   This might require special gifts, but not the gifts of the Spirit.

It is questioned whether ἐν σοφίᾳ λόγου refers to the form or the matter of the teaching.   So far as it is possible to separate the two, this question is best answered by determining against which party the implied rebuke is directed.   We can scarcely be wrong in assuming this to be the party which affected to follow Apollos the man of eloquence (ἀνὴρ λόγιος, Acts xviii. 24).   If so, the reference must be mainly to form, through the natural tendency of the Corinthian mind to attach too much importance to the graces of diction: for the substance of Apollos' teaching cannot have differed from that of St Paul in any such degree as to have been exaggerated into a party question.   The σοφία λόγου then will refer not only to the luxuriant rhetoric, but also to the dialectic subtleties of the Alexandrian method, which we find to an exaggerated degree in the writings of Philo and some of the Alexandrian fathers.

κενωθῇ] '*be emptied*,' i.e. 'dwindle to nothing, vanish under the weight of rhetorical ornament and dialectic subtlety.'   For κενοῦν compare I Cor. ix. 15, 2 Cor. ix. 3.

(*b*)   *The unhealthy craving after* σοφία.   *God's folly triumphant over man's wisdom* (i. 18—ii. 5).

18.   Through this incidental allusion to preaching St Paul passes to a new subject.   The dissensions in the Corinthian Church are for a time forgotten, and he takes the opportunity of correcting his converts for their undue exaltation of human eloquence and wisdom.   He returns from this digression to his former theme almost imperceptibly at the beginning of the third chapter.   The link of connexion in both cases is equally subtle.

ὁ λόγος γὰρ κ.τ.λ.] The connexion is as follows : 'For the preaching with which we are concerned—the preaching of the Cross—is the very antithesis to σοφία λόγου.   It has no triumphs of rhetoric or subtleties of dialectic to offer to those whose hearts are set on such trifles.   To such it appears to be but foolishness : and this is a sign that they are on the way of destruction.'   On the repetition of λόγος see note ii. 6 σοφίαν.

ὁ λόγος ὁ τοῦ σταυροῦ] here used as co-extensive with the preaching of the Gospel, just as ὁ σταυρὸς τοῦ Χριστοῦ in the previous verse denotes the substance of the Gospel.   This expression shows clearly the stress which St Paul laid on the death of Christ, not merely as a great moral spectacle and so the crowning point of a life of self-renunciation, but as in itself the ordained instrument of salvation.

ἀπολλυμένοις, σωζομένοις] '*those who are in the path of destruction, of salvation.*'   'In the language of the New Testament salvation is a thing of the past, a thing of the present, and a thing of the future.   St Paul says sometimes "Ye (or we) were saved" (Rom. viii. 24), or "Ye have been saved" (Ephes. ii. 5, 8), sometimes "Ye are being saved" (I Cor. xv. 2), and sometimes "Ye shall be saved" (Rom. x. 9, 13). It is important to observe this, because we are thus taught that σωτηρία involves a moral condition which must have begun already, though it will receive its final accomplishment hereafter. Godliness, righteousness, is life, is salvation. And it is hardly necessary to say that the divorce of morality and religion must be fostered and encouraged by failing to note this, and so laying the whole stress either on the past or on the future—on the first call or on the final charge.' *On a Fresh Revision*, p. 104, *ed.* 3 (1891). For ἀπολλυμένοις compare 2 Cor. ii. 15, iv. 3, 2 Thess. ii. 10; for σωζομένοις 2 Cor. ii. 15, Acts ii. 47; see also Luke xiii. 23 εἰ ὀλίγοι οἱ σωζόμενοι. Comp. also Clem. Rom. § 58, *Clem. Hom.* xv. 10, *Apost. Const.* viii. 5, 7, 8. The idea of final acceptance or rejection is obviously excluded in the present tense : nor is it at all necessarily implied by the past tense, if we remember that the knowledge of God is in itself σωτηρία, and those who are brought to that knowledge are σεσωσμένοι; just as they are said to belong to the βασιλεία τοῦ Θεοῦ, though they may not attain to the blissful consummation of their salvation, and may be excluded from the future kingdom of Christ by falling away. For St Paul's way of speaking compare the note on ver. 2 ἡγιασμένοις and ver. 9 κοινωνία.

τοῖς δὲ σωζομένοις ἡμῖν] This order, which is somewhat unnatural, is adopted in order to bring out the opposition between οἱ ἀπολλύμενοι and οἱ σωζόμενοι sharply. At the same time it serves to smooth down the prominence of ἡμῖν.

δύναμις Θεοῦ] The direct opposition to μωρία would require σοφία Θεοῦ, but the word δύναμις is instinctively substituted to show that it is not the intellectual excellence so much as the moral power of the doctrine of the Cross on which the Apostle lays stress. At the same time, inasmuch as μωρία involves the notion of vainness, inefficiency, δύναμις is no unnatural opposition.

19. ἀπολῶ κ.τ λ.] A quotation from Isaiah xxix. 14. By this appeal to Scripture St Paul enforces the two points, which are brought out in the preceding verse : *first*, the opposition between the wisdom of the world and the power of God, and *secondly*, the destruction of the wise of this world. Compare ἀπολῶ with τοῖς ἀπολλυμένοις of ver. 18.

The passage is taken from the LXX. with this difference that St Paul has substituted ἀθετήσω for κρύψω. In the Hebrew the sentence is in a passive form : 'the wisdom of their wise shall perish etc.' The spirit of the application here is in exact accordance with the original context of the passage. The opposition there is between the ἐντάλματα ἀνθρώπων καὶ διδασκαλίας (ver. 13, a passage cited by our Lord Matt. xv. 8, 9) and the power of God which shall be exerted to the ruin of those who trust in human teaching. The original reference however is to a temporary calamity, the invasion of Sennacherib; and the application which St Paul makes of the passage, in a spiritual and more comprehensive sense, is after the common analogy of the New Testament writers.

σοφίαν, σύνεσιν] On the distinction between these two terms see the note on Col. i. 9. They are explained in Arist. *Eth. Nic.* vi. 7, 10. The first is a creative, the second a discerning faculty.

20. ποῦ σοφός; κ.τ.λ.] These words are a loose paraphrase of Isaiah xxxiii. 18. They are certainly not intended as a quotation, for the language diverges too much both from the Hebrew and LXX. The original passage describes the overthrow of Sennacherib, who had attacked the people of God. It runs in the LXX. ποῦ εἰσιν οἱ γραμματικοί; ποῦ εἰσιν οἱ συμβουλεύοντες; ποῦ ἐστιν ὁ ἀριθμῶν τοὺς τρεφομένους μικρὸν καὶ μέγαν λαόν; perhaps translated from a corrupt text. The meaning of the Hebrew is given in Bishop Lowth's translation : 'Where is now the accomptant? where the weigher of tribute? where is he that numbereth the towers?' The annihilation of the officers of Sennacherib's army is intended by these words. In place of these St Paul substitutes the leaders in the world of thought, who war against the spiritual Israel. From this it will be seen that the passage in Isaiah will not aid us to the interpretation of the individual words σοφός, γραμματεύς, συνζητητής, the form of the sentence only being the same and the general application analogous, while the similarity of γραμματικοὶ of the LXX. in Isaiah and γραμματεὺς in St Paul is merely accidental, or at best suggested the paraphrase by its appeal to the ear.

σοφός, γραμματεύς, συνζητητής] Two explanations of these words deserve consideration. *First*, σοφὸς is the general term including both the Jewish and Greek teachers, γραμματεὺς is the Jewish scribe, συνζητητὴς the Greek philosopher. But against this interpretation it may be urged (1) that σοφὸς more fitly designates the Greek philosopher than συνζητητής, being the word specially reserved for this meaning among the Greeks themselves; see Theodoret (ad loc.) καλεῖ σοφὸν τὸν τῇ Ἑλληνικῇ στωμυλίᾳ κοσμούμενον, Clem. Alex. *Strom.* I. 3. 23, p. 329, and above all Rom. i. 23 φάσκοντες εἶναι σοφοὶ ἐμωράνθησαν. Compare also the Jewish proverb quoted by Lightfoot (*H. H.* ad loc.) 'Cursed is he that herdeth hogs, and cursed is he that teacheth his son Grecian wisdom.' (2) This interpretation seems to require τοῦ αἰῶνος τούτου to be taken with all three words, whereas the repetition of ποῦ separates the clauses. For these reasons it is better, *secondly*, to take σοφὸς as the Greek philosopher, γραμματεὺς as the Jewish scribe, and συνζητητὴς τοῦ αἰῶνος τούτου as the comprehensive term, a general expression comprehending both, τοῦ αἰῶνος τούτου being confined to the last of the three. The use of σοφία just below in the phrase τὴν σοφίαν τοῦ κόσμου, as including both, is not a sufficient reason for discarding this interpretation. A stronger argument in favour of this explanation might be drawn from ver. 22, where σοφία is used of the Greeks alone.

Both these senses recognise a special mention of Jew and Greek severally, and this seems to be required by the sequel ἐπειδὴ καὶ Ἰουδαῖοι... καὶ Ἕλληνες (ver. 22). This in itself is decisive in favour of rejecting other distinctions, as for instance that σοφὸς is the ethical and meta-physical philosopher, γραμματεὺς the historian and literary man, συνζητητὴς the naturalist and man of science—a distinction which has quite a modern smack. Moreover γραμματεὺς can only be a learned man when applied to the Jewish scribe: in the ordinary Greek vocabulary it denotes a civil officer, 'a town-clerk' or 'secretary,' e.g. Acts xix. 35; Ecclus. xxxviii. 24 σοφία γραμματέως ἐν εὐκαιρίᾳ σχολῆς is not an exception.

The Jewish writers (see the passages in Wetstein) included in their general picture of the corruption of the age at the time of Messiah's coming the failing of Rabbinical wisdom, apparently with a reference to Isaiah xxxiii. 18. With regard to the heathen, we have here the germ of the thought which St Paul afterwards expands so strikingly in the first chapter of the Epistle to the Romans, especially vv. 21, 22 ἐματαιώθησαν ἐν τοῖς διαλογισμοῖς αὐτῶν καὶ ἐσκοτίσθη ἡ ἀσύνετος αὐτῶν καρδία· φάσκοντες εἶναι σοφοὶ ἐμωράνθησαν, καὶ ἤλλαξαν κ.τ.λ. See also the notes on οὐχὶ ἐμώρανεν ὁ Θεὸς below and on ἐν τῇ σοφίᾳ τοῦ Θεοῦ in the next verse. For a similar instance of an expansion see xv. 56.

τοῦ αἰῶνος τούτου] On this expression, as opposed to ὁ αἰὼν ὁ μέλλων or αἰὼν ἐκεῖνος 'Messiah's reign,' compare Usteri Paul. Lehrb. p. 327 sq. The phrase had a temporal meaning, as originally employed by the Jews; but as St Paul uses it, it is rather ethical in its signification, there being no sharp division in time between 'the age of the world' and 'the age of Messiah.'

οὐχὶ ἐμώρανεν ὁ Θεὸς] 'did not God render vain'; and this in two ways, (1) by exhibiting its intrinsic worthlessness and corrupt results, and (2) by the power of the Cross set in opposition to it and triumphing over it, as explained in the following verse. The process of this μωραίνειν in the case of the Gentiles is portrayed in the passage from the Romans quoted above. The hand of God is there distinctly rècognised, διὸ παρέδωκεν αὐτοὺς ὁ Θεὸς ἐν ταῖς ἐπιθυμίαις κ.τ.λ. 'While the reason strove to raise itself,' remarks Neander, 'above Polytheism, it was betrayed into Pantheism only to fall at last into scepticism.' Yet it is rather their moral degradation, as resulting from their idolatry, that St Paul must have had in his mind, as the passage in the Epistle to the Romans shows.

τοῦ κόσμου] Omit τούτου, which has been introduced to conform to τοῦ αἰῶνος τούτου above; κόσμος is in itself 'the existing order of things,' and needs no specification like αἰών. We never find ὁ κόσμος ὁ μέλλων. Κόσμος is used as synonymous with αἰών, as in 1 Cor. iii. 18, 19: compare also 1 Cor. ii. 6 with ii. 12 and Eph. ii. 2, where we have κατὰ τὸν αἰῶνα τοῦ κόσμου τούτου. So far as there is any difference between the two words, αἰὼν would seem, like 'sæculum,' to refer to the prevailing ideas and feelings of the present life, and κόσμος to its gross, material character; and the two would be contrasted, though not so sharply, in the same way as 'the world' and 'the flesh.'

21. ἐπειδὴ γὰρ] explaining the manner of ἐμώρανεν in the preceding verse.

ἐν τῇ σοφίᾳ τοῦ Θεοῦ] is explained in two ways. (1) 'When the world failed to recognise God in the works of His wisdom': σοφία denoting the wisdom of God as displayed in the works of creation to the Gentiles and in the Mosaic dispensation to the Jews. Or (2) 'when owing to the wise dispensation of God the world failed to recognise Him etc.' The first interpretation produces indeed a stronger resemblance to Rom. i. 18 sq. of which this passage is the germ; compare especially ver. 20 τὰ γὰρ ἀόρατα αὐτοῦ ἀπὸ κτίσεως κόσμου τοῖς ποιήμασιν νοούμενα καθορᾶται κ.τ.λ., and see Wisd. xiii. 1. But everything else is in favour of the second rendering. For *first*, it is harsh to attribute to σοφία a concrete sense, as 'the works of His intelligence'; *secondly*, the position of ἐν τῇ σοφίᾳ τοῦ Θεοῦ points to it, as giving the explanation of οὐκ ἔγνω ὁ κόσμος κ.τ.λ.: and *thirdly*, the sense suits the context better, as accounting for ἐμώρανεν ὁ Θεὸς which idea it assists the following εὐδόκησεν διὰ τῆς μωρίας in carrying out. Even the corruption of the world was in a certain sense God's doing, inasmuch as He permitted it with a providential end in view: comp. Rom. xi. 32.

ὁ κόσμος] here includes Jew as well as Gentile. The Pharisee, no less than the Greek philosopher, had a σοφία of his own, which stood between his heart and the knowledge of God.

διὰ τῆς σοφίας] is taken either of 'the wisdom of God,' or of 'the wisdom of the world.' The latter is probably correct, as it presents the same opposition to διὰ τῆς μωρίας τοῦ κηρύγματος which runs through the context.

τοῦ κηρύγματος] '*of the thing preached*,' 'the proclamation'; not τῆς κηρύξεως. It refers therefore to the subject, not to the manner of the preaching. There is only the very slightest approach in classical writers to this sense of the words κηρύσσειν, κήρυγμα etc., as denoting 'instruction,' 'teaching.' The metaphor, if it can be called a metaphor, is perhaps derived from the Jewish theocracy, and involves the notion of heralding the approach of a king (Matt. iii. 1, iv. 17), or of proclaiming an edict of a sovereign. But it seems to be very rarely used in a sense approaching to this, even in the LXX.

22. The following verses (22—25) contain a confirmation and amplification of the assertion in ver. 21, in its twofold bearing. They maintain *first*, that the preaching of the gospel is directly opposed to the wisdom of the world, whether displayed in the sign-seeking of the Jews, or the philosophical subtleties of the Greeks (the σοφία *par excellence*); and *secondly*, that this foolishness of God triumphs over the wisdom of the world.

καὶ Ἰουδαῖοι...καὶ Ἕλληνες] i.e. 'the Jews no less than the Gentiles have gone astray.' Compare Rom. iii. 9 προῃτιασάμεθα γὰρ Ἰουδαίους τε καὶ Ἕλληνας πάντας ὑφ' ἁμαρτίαν εἶναι. The particles καὶ...καὶ correspond to each other, and attach the two sentences together. The absence of a μὲν in this clause, answering to ἡμεῖς δέ, is to be accounted for by supposing that the Apostle had not cast the form of the latter part of the sentence in his mind, when he commenced it.

Ἰουδαῖοι, Ἕλληνες] The absence of the article shows that they are spoken of rather with a view to their attributes than to their individuality, 'Jews as Jews,' 'Greeks as Greeks.'

σημεῖα] the correct reading, for which the received text has σημεῖον. The whole force of the passage here comes from the meaning 'miraculous sign' as applied to σημεῖον. Compare Matt. xii. 38 sq., xvi. 1 sq., John ii. 18, vi. 30, incidents to which St Paul may be alluding indirectly, though doubtless the Apostles were frequently met by the Jews with the demand 'give us a sign,' as our Lord had been. It is not difficult to conjecture in what sense the Jews asked for 'signs.' Signs were vouchsafed in plenty, signs of God's power and love, but these were not the signs which they sought. They wanted signs of an outward Messianic Kingdom, of temporal triumph, of material greatness for the chosen people. See *Biblical Essays*, p. 150 sq., for Jewish expectation of signs to be wrought by the Messiah, and the references in Wetstein on Matt. xvi. 1. With such cravings the gospel of a 'crucified Messiah' (Χριστὸν ἐσταυρωμένον) was to them a stumbling-block indeed.

Ἕλληνες σοφίαν] This characteristic of the Greeks was noted by Anacharsis in Herod. iv. 77, Ἕλληνας πάντας ἀσχόλους εἶναι πρὸς πᾶσαν σοφίην. He excepts however the Lacedaemonians.

αἰτοῦσιν, ζητοῦσιν] The same accurate appreciation of the difference between Jew and Gentile as regards the reception of the Gospel, which dictated the whole passage, is visible in these words. All the terms are carefully chosen. The importunity of the Jews is expressed by αἰτεῖν, the curious speculative turn of the Greeks by ζητεῖν.

23. An instructive commentary on this passage is furnished by the different arguments which Justin Martyr employs in combating Jewish and Greek assailants in the Apologies and the Dialogue with Trypho. See Blunt *Church in the First Three Centuries* (1861), p. 120 sq.

The Jews looked to material, outward privileges, the Greeks sought satisfaction for their intellectual cravings. The preaching of the Cross commended itself to neither. It is a moral and spiritual power.

ἡμεῖς δὲ κηρύσσομεν] '*but we preach*,' i.e. 'we do not discuss or dispute.'

Χριστὸν ἐσταυρωμένον] '*a crucified Messiah*,' not as the E. V., 'Christ crucified.' The expression is a sort of oxymoron. It is not so much the person as the office which is denoted here by Χριστός. By suffering He was to redeem; by suffering He was to make many perfect. His Messiahship and His Cross were necessarily connected. To the Jew however Χριστὸς ἐσταυρωμένος was a contradiction in terms: to the Greek it would be simply meaningless. The great difficulty of the Jews in overcoming the idea of a crucified Messiah appears from the very first.

See Acts xxvi. 23, where St Paul states that one of the main theses which
he had to maintain was that the Christ was to suffer. Consequently we find
that the Apologists in arguing with the Jews had to explain this difficulty
(Ariston of Pella in Routh *R. S.* I. p. 95, Justin Martyr *Dial. c. Tryph.*
c. 69, p. 323 C, Tertull. *adv. Judaeos* § 10). On this point see further
in *Galatians*, p. 152 sq. An illustration of this difficulty we have in
the fact that the later Jews, recognising the prediction of the prophets
that the Messiah should suffer, were driven to the expedient of supposing
two Christs, both a suffering and a glorified Redeemer, called respectively Ben Joseph and Ben David. There is no trace however of this
distinction until Christian arguments from prophecy forced it upon
Jewish apologists. See Bertholdt *Christol.* § 17, p. 75 sq., Gfrörer *Jahr.
des Heils* II. p. 318 sq., and compare Stanley, p. 51. With regard to the
general abhorrence of the Cross by the Gentiles see Cicero *pro Rabirio*,
c. 5 'nomen ipsum crucis absit non modo a corpore civium Romanorum,
sed etiam a cogitatione, oculis, auribus,' comp. *Verr.* v. 64. That this
'stumbling-block of the cross' existed not only in the apostolic age but
that it continued for generations later appears from many indications.
Thus Lucian (*de morte Peregr.* c. 13) speaks of our Lord as 'the gibbeted
sophist,' τὸν ἀνεσκολοπισμένον ἐκεῖνον σοφιστήν; but perhaps the best
illustration of the popular feeling is the well-known caricature of a
slave falling down before an ass hanging on a gibbet with the inscription
Ἀλεξαμενος σεβετε θεον, found in the Paedagogium on the Palatine, and
now in the Museo Kircheriano. So Celsus (Orig. *c. Cels.* iv. 7) speaks of
the Christians as 'actually worshipping a dead man' (ὄντως νεκρὸν σέβον-
τας), a *reductio ad absurdum* in his opinion. The Emperor Julian after
his apostasy uses similar language. See also the note on Phil. ii. 8.

σκάνδαλον] Σκάνδαλον corresponds to σημεῖα, μωρίαν to σοφίαν. Instead
of finding signs or tokens of the approach of Messiah's Kingdom,
finger-posts guiding them thereto, they found a hindrance to their belief
in that approach.

24. αὐτοῖς δὲ τοῖς κλητοῖς] '*but to the believers themselves,*' whatever
it might be to others. 'Though they see that those around them regard
the cross as a stumbling-block or as foolishness, yet they themselves
know it to be' etc. This is the force of αὐτοῖς, which is added because
the passage is expressed from the standpoint of the believer. The
meaning of αὐτοῖς would have been more clear if St Paul had said αὐτοῖς
δὲ ἡμῖν, but he avoids the first person because he wishes no longer to
restrict the application to the preachers (ἡμεῖς δὲ κηρύσσομεν) of whom
he has been speaking hitherto. Αὐτοῖς δὲ τοῖς κλητοῖς cannot mean, 'to
them, viz. the called'; *first*, because this is very questionable Greek,
and *secondly*, because there is nothing nearer than τοὺς πιστεύοντας
(ver. 21) to which to refer the pronoun. On τοῖς κλητοῖς see ver. 2
above.

Χριστὸν] The repetition of this word is emphatic. 'Christ crucified' of the former clause is now 'Christ the power of God and the wisdom of God.'

δύναμιν] corresponds to σημεῖα of ver. 22, as σοφίαν does to σοφίαν. The analogy between δύναμις and σημεῖα will appear, if we remember that the signs, which the Jews sought, were manifestations of kingly power.

The terms δύναμις and σοφία applied to our Lord are suggested by what has gone before. He is the reality of that power of which the Jews were pursuing the shadow, of that wisdom for which the Greeks were substituting a counterfeit. At the same time they have a deeper meaning. They appeal to the theosophy of the day, and declare Christ to be the Eternal Word of God. For both δύναμις (Θεοῦ) and σοφία (Θεοῦ) are synonyms for Λόγος in the phraseology of Jewish speculators. For δύναμις in the sense of an emanation of the Godhead see Acts viii. 10, for σοφία see Luke xi. 49.

25. τῶν ἀνθρώπων] St Paul in abridging the comparison is only following a common Greek idiom: e.g. Eur. *Med.* 1342, 3 λέαιναν, οὐ γυναῖκα, τῆς Τυρσηνίδος Σκύλλης ἔχουσαν ἀγριωτέραν φύσιν. See Jelf, *Gr.* § 781 d, Winer, § xxxv. p. 307. At the same time the expression here is more forcible than if it had been written in full τῆς σοφίας (τῆς ἰσχύος) τῶν ἀνθρώπων. The very foolishness of God is wiser than men and all that is in man.

Tertullian's comment is 'Quid est stultum Dei sapientius hominibus, nisi crux et mors Christi? Quid infirmum Dei fortius homine, nisi nativitas et caro Dei?' (c. *Marcion.* v. 5). The separation however in this comment is not justified by the text.

26. 'Is not this in accordance with your own experience? Thus not only in the means of redemption, but in the persons of the redeemed, is the weakness of God declared to be stronger than men. Not only is the power of God seen in the effect of the preaching of a crucified Messiah: it is evidenced also in the fact that preachers and believers alike are chiefly drawn from the weak and the despised of the world.'

βλέπετε γὰρ] '*for look at your calling*,' the circumstances under which ye were called to Christianity. Not an indicative but an imperative mood: compare viii. 9, x. 12, 18, xvi. 10, Phil. iii. 2 and frequently in St Paul. The passage is more vigorous when thus taken: 'excitat quasi torpentes ad rem ipsam considerandam' says Calvin. And the emphatic position of βλέπετε seems to require it. Otherwise the order would probably have been τὴν κλῆσιν ὑμῶν βλέπετε, as in 2 Cor. x. 7 τὰ κατὰ πρόσωπον βλέπετε.

τὴν κλῆσιν ὑμῶν] '*the manner of your calling*'; here and elsewhere with a special reference to their station in life at the time of their calling. This idea however is not contained in the word κλῆσις itself, but is derived from the context, as also in vii. 20. Κλῆσις in itself never signifies a 'vocation' or 'calling in life.' It is the calling to the knowledge of the Gospel, and it may or may not, according to the context, have reference to the circumstances under which the calling took place. On the Pauline interchange of κλῆσις and ἐκλογή see on Col. iii. 12 ὡς ἐκλεκτοὶ τοῦ Θεοῦ, and compare 1 Thess. i. 4, 2 Thess. i. 11. It will be observed here that St Paul uses the verb ἐξελέξατο in ver. 27 as corresponding to the substantive κλῆσιν.

ὅτι] '*how that.*' For this construction compare the note on 1 Thess. i. 5 (a passage which is mistranslated in the E. V.). It is the ὅτι, which introduces the idea of manner or circumstances into κλῆσις.

κατὰ σάρκα] should probably be taken with all three words σοφοί, δυνατοί, εὐγενεῖς. The position of the qualifying phrase after the first of the three is much more in favour of this conjuncture than if it had been placed after the last, as for instance in ver. 20. Besides it applies equally well to all three. There is a spiritual δύναμις and a spiritual εὐγένεια, as well as a spiritual σοφία. The Bereans are examples of this spiritual nobility (οὗτοι ἦσαν εὐγενέστεροι τῶν ἐν Θεσσαλονίκῃ Acts xvii. 11). Lastly, τοῦ κόσμου is repeated with the opposites of all three in the next verse.

οὐ πολλοί] '*not many.*' The phrase is not equivalent to οὐδείς, for there were some few exceptions. In the Church of Corinth Erastus 'the chamberlain of the city' (Rom. xvi. 23) might perhaps be reckoned among the δυνατοί. That the majority of the first converts from heathendom were either slaves or freedmen, appears from their names. Compare especially the salutations in the last chapter of the Roman Epistle (see on this *Philippians*, p. 171 sq.), and the remarks of Merivale, *History of the Romans* (1858), vol. VI. p. 265 sq.

The sentence is elliptical and a verb must be understood from the context. The reference however in οὐ πολλοί κ.τ.λ. is probably to be confined neither to the teachers as such, nor to the taught as such (as different commentators have maintained); but to be extended to the converts generally. Accordingly some less precise term is needed than ἐκλήθησαν or ἐξελέχθησαν, though in one sense ἐκλήθησαν is applicable, for teachers and taught alike are 'called.' On the brachylogies of St Paul see the note on ver. 31, and on this passage Dr Ainslie in the *Journal of Philology* (1868) II. p. 158.

This fact of the social condition of the early Christians is the constant boast of the first Apologists as the glory of Christianity. See especially Justin Martyr *Apol.* ii. 9 Χριστῷ οὐ φιλόσοφοι οὐδὲ φιλόλογοι μόνον ἐπείσθησαν, ἀλλὰ καὶ χειροτέχναι καὶ παντελῶς ἰδιῶται καὶ δόξης καὶ φόβου καὶ θανάτου καταφρονήσαντες, ἐπειδὴ δύναμίς ἐστι τοῦ ἀρρήτου Πατρὸς κ.τ.λ.; and Origen *c. Cels.* II. 79 καὶ οὐ θαυμαστὸν εἰ τῶν φρονίμων· ἀλλὰ καὶ τῶν ἀλογωτάτων καὶ τοῖς πάθεσιν ἐγκειμένων...ἀλλ' ἐπεὶ δύναμις τοῦ Θεοῦ ὁ Χριστὸς ἦν καὶ σοφία τοῦ Πατρός, διὰ τοῦτο ταῦτα πεποίηκεν καὶ ἔτι ποιεῖ κ.τ.λ.

27, 28. ἀλλὰ κ.τ.λ.] Μωρά, ἀσθενῆ, ἀγενῆ καὶ τὰ ἐξουθενημένα are the

opposites of σοφοί, δυνατοί, εὐγενεῖς. See the note on the reading καὶ τὰ
μὴ ὄντα below. The omission of the words ἵνα καταισχύνῃ τοὺς σοφούς, καὶ
τὰ ἀσθενῆ τοῦ κόσμου ἐξελέξατο ὁ Θεὸς in some uncial MSS. probably arises
out of a confusion due to the repetition of the same words ἐξελ. ὁ Θεός.
Origen is guilty of a different error. He omits from the first to the third
ἐξελ. ὁ Θεός. The neuters (e.g. τὰ μωρὰ for οἱ μωροὶ) are adopted in
preference to the masculines, as sinking the individuality and conveying
an idea of meanness in the objects, and thus bringing out the point of
the contrast more strongly.

The repetition of ἐξελέξατο ὁ Θεὸς is emphatic. The effect is the same
as in the reiteration of κλητὸς ver. 1 (where see the note). St Paul is
penetrated with the intense conviction that our calling is not of ourselves
but of God; and expresses himself accordingly. Thus he is already
preparing us for the precept with which he closes the paragraph, Ὁ
καυχώμενος ἐν Κυρίῳ καυχάσθω.

28. τὰ μὴ ὄντα] The omission of the particle καὶ before τὰ μὴ ὄντα
is justifiable on external authority alone, though the evidence in its favour
(אBC³D³L) is considerable. It is however not found in אAC¹D¹FG and
several of the early fathers. Certainly the sense gains by the omission.
The three classes which are the opposites to σοφοί, δυνατοί, εὐγενεῖς have
been already enumerated (though in the last the supplementary clause
ἵνα καταισχύνῃ τὰ εὐγενῆ is not expressed and has to be supplied by the
reader). The strong expression τὰ μὴ ὄντα is now added as at once a
climax and a summary of what has gone before.

The negative μὴ is generally explained here as denoting not the
objective fact (τὰ οὐκ ὄντα) but the subjective impression, 'things reputed
non-existent.' So apparently Winer § lv, p. 608. This however would
weaken the force of the contrast, and it is probable that it denotes
simply the class-attributes, 'such things as are not,' according to its
ordinary usage. Compare Xen. Anab. iv. 4. 15 οὗτος γὰρ ἐδόκει καὶ
πρότερον πολλὰ ἤδη ἀληθεῦσαι τοιαῦτα, τὰ ὄντα τε ὡς ὄντα καὶ τὰ μὴ ὄντα ὡς
οὐκ ὄντα, where the sense is obvious and has nothing to do with the
subjective impression. See also Jelf, Gr. § 746. 2, and Eur. Troad. 608
(cited by Alford) Ὁρῶ τὰ τῶν θεῶν, ὡς τὰ μὲν πυργοῦσ' ἄνω Τὰ μηδὲν
ὄντα, τὰ δὲ δοκοῦντ' ἀπώλεσαν. In fact τὰ μὴ ὄντα is much more usual
than τὰ οὐκ ὄντα in the sense of 'things not existing.'

καταργήσῃ] 'annihilate, reduce to non-entity.' This strong expression
is substituted for the weaker καταισχύνῃ, as the opposition to τὰ μὴ ὄντα
requires.

29. ὅπως μὴ καυχήσηται πᾶσα σάρξ] 'that no flesh may boast,' 'that all
flesh may be prevented from boasting.' Compare Acts x. 14 οὐδέποτε
ἔφαγον πᾶν κοινὸν 'I have always avoided eating everything common,'
Rom. iii. 20 οὐ δικαιωθήσεται πᾶσα σὰρξ ἐνώπιον αὐτοῦ. In such cases the
negative is attached closely to the verb which it immediately precedes.
This seems to be scarcely a classical usage of πᾶς with the negative,

and the analogy of the classical οὐ πάνυ (with which on the other hand compare οὐ πάντως Rom. iii. 9) is apparent, rather than real. It is a common Hebraism, and the corresponding Hebrew (כל־בשׂר), showing that πᾶσα σάρξ are to be regarded as one word, assists to explain how πᾶσα is unaffected by the negative which refers solely to the verb.

ἐνώπιον τοῦ Θεοῦ] The preposition conveys an idea of boldness and independence. As Bengel says; 'Non *coram* illo, sed *in* illo gloriari possumus.' See ver. 31.

30. 'Nay, so far from there being any place for boasting, ye owe your existence as Christians to Him, as the Author of your being.'

The words ἐξ αὐτοῦ ὑμεῖς ἐστε ἐν Χριστῷ Ἰησοῦ are differently taken. Either (1) 'From Him ye have your being (ἐξ αὐτοῦ ἐστε), ye are born of Him in Christ Jesus,' 'ye are His children in Christ Jesus.' So Chrysostom (ἐκείνου παῖδές ἐστε διὰ τοῦ Χριστοῦ τοῦτο γενόμενοι), and in the same way the other Greek commentators. Compare xi. 8, 12, xii. 15. Or (2) 'For it is His doing (ἐξ αὐτοῦ) that ye are in Christ Jesus, are members of Christ (ἐστε ἐν Χριστῷ Ἰησοῦ).' The latter of these interpretations is open to two objections; *first*, that the sense attributed to ἐξ αὐτοῦ is unusual at least in the New Testament, and *secondly*, the emphatic position of ἐστε would scarcely be explicable, for the natural order would certainly be ἐν Χριστῷ Ἰησοῦ ἐστε. It was probably from an instinctive feeling of the requirements of the Greek that the Greek commentators seem all to have adopted the other interpretation. For the sentiment and even the form in which it is expressed, compare Gal. iii. 26 πάντες γὰρ υἱοὶ Θεοῦ ἐστε διὰ τῆς πίστεως ἐν Χριστῷ Ἰησοῦ. If the idea of a regeneration and spiritual sonship appears most frequently in St John, it was certainly not unknown to St Paul.

ἐστέ] Possibly an allusion to the preceding τὰ μὴ ὄντα 'you, who were not, now are.' But in any case, ἐστε is here best taken as a predicate, and accentuated, as in Lachmann's edition.

ἐγενήθη] '*became*' (i.e. by His incarnation); not 'was made.' See the note on 1 Thess. i. 5 ἐγενήθημεν. 'He showed us the way to all true knowledge, the knowledge of God and of our own salvation. He by taking upon Him our nature was manifested to us as the impersonation of all wisdom,' or perhaps better 'the representative of the wise dispensation of God.'

ἀπὸ Θεοῦ] To be taken with ἐγενήθη σοφία, not with σοφία alone. St Paul accumulates words to intensify the leading idea of the sentence that everything comes of God.

δικαιοσύνη τε καὶ ἁγιασμὸς καὶ ἀπολύτρωσις] '*that is to say, righteousness and sanctification and redemption.*' These three words are an epexegesis of σοφία. Owing to the absence of any connecting particle between σοφία and δικαιοσύνη, and especially considering the interposition of ἀπὸ Θεοῦ, it is impossible to coordinate the four words, as is done in the English version and by many commentators.

The connecting particles τε καὶ...καὶ perhaps imply a close connexion between δικαιοσύνη and ἁγιασμός, whereas ἀπολύτρωσις stands rather by itself. 'By becoming wisdom He became both righteousness and sanctification and also redemption.' Compare Hom. *Od.* xv. 78 ἀμφότερον, κῦδός τε καὶ ἀγλαΐη, καὶ ὄνειαρ, Herod. vii. 1 καὶ νέας τε καὶ ἵππους καὶ σῖτον καὶ πλοῖα: and see Jelf, *Gr.* § 758, Hartung, *Partikeln*, i. 103.

The order of the words δικαιοσύνη, ἁγιασμός is what might be expected. Δικαιοσύνη is used in its peculiar Pauline sense as 'righteousness before God,' 'justification'; differing however from δικαίωσις (Rom. iv. 25, v. 18) in that the latter is the verdict of God which pronounces a man righteous. Ἁγιασμός is the natural following up of δικαιοσύνη and is illustrated by Rom. vi. 19 παραστήσατε τὰ μέλη ὑμῶν δοῦλα τῇ δικαιοσύνῃ εἰς ἁγιασμόν. On the terminations -σύνη, -σις, -σμός see 1 Thess. iii. 13. On the other hand we are scarcely prepared to find ἀπολύτρωσις following these words which we might expect it to precede, as e.g. Rom. iii. 24 δικαιούμενοι δωρεὰν τῇ αὐτοῦ χάριτι διὰ τῆς ἀπολυτρώσεως τῆς ἐν Χριστῷ Ἰησοῦ. But 'redemption' is really used in two ways. Calvin very justly says, 'Redemptio primum Christi donum est quod inchoatur in nobis, et ultimum quod perficitur'; and here the word is used not so much of the initiative act (the death of Christ, cf. Eph. i. 7), as of redemption consummated in our deliverance from all sin and misery. In this sense it is almost equivalent to ζωὴ αἰώνιος and is therefore rightly placed last. For the sense of ἀπολύτρωσις see especially Eph. iv. 30 εἰς ἡμέραν ἀπολυτρώσεως and compare Rom. viii. 23, Eph. i. 14.

This is the earliest indication in St Paul's Epistles of the doctrine which occupies so prominent a place in the Epistles to the Romans and Galatians, and in St Paul's teaching generally. See *Biblical Essays*, p. 224 sq.

31. ἵνα καθὼς γέγραπται κ.τ.λ.] '*in order that it may be according to the language of Scripture.*' The sentence is frequently explained as an anacoluthon, as if St Paul had retained the imperative mood of the original (καυχάσθω) instead of substituting καυχήσηται. But it is more in accordance with St Paul's usage to regard it as an ellipsis ἵνα (γένηται) καθὼς γέγραπται κ.τ.λ. His ellipses are often very abrupt (see the instances collected on 2 Thess. ii. 3), and have occasioned much trouble to the transcribers, who are at much pains to supply them. See a note in *Journal of Philology* iii. p. 85. Of the ellipsis of a verb after ἵνα we have examples in Rom. iv. 16 διὰ τοῦτο ἐκ πίστεως ἵνα κατὰ χάριν, Gal. ii. 9 ἵνα ἡμεῖς εἰς τὰ ἔθνη, αὐτοὶ δὲ εἰς τὴν περιτομήν, 2 Cor. viii. 13 οὐ γὰρ ἵνα ἄλλοις ἄνεσις, ὑμῖν θλίψις. Whichever explanation is given, the sentence in form very much resembles Rom. xv. 3 ἀλλὰ καθὼς γέγραπται· Οἱ ὀνειδισμοὶ τῶν ὀνειδιζόντων σε ἐπέπεσον ἐπ' ἐμέ, and 1 Cor. ii. 9 below.

ὁ καυχώμενος κ.τ.λ] is not a direct quotation, but abridged from Jeremiah ix. 23, 24 μὴ καυχάσθω ὁ σοφὸς ἐν τῇ σοφίᾳ αὐτοῦ καὶ μὴ καυχάσθω ὁ ἰσχυρὸς ἐν τῇ ἰσχύϊ αὐτοῦ καὶ μὴ καυχάσθω ὁ πλούσιος ἐν τῷ πλούτῳ αὐτοῦ, ἀλλ' ἢ ἐν τούτῳ καυχάσθω ὁ καυχώμενος, συνιεῖν καὶ γινώσκειν ὅτι ἐγώ εἰμι Κύριος ὁ ποιῶν ἔλεος, combined with 1 Sam. ii. 10 μὴ καυχάσθω ὁ φρόνιμος ἐν τῇ φρονήσει αὐτοῦ καὶ μὴ καυχάσθω ὁ δυνατὸς ἐν τῇ δυνάμει αὐτοῦ καὶ μὴ καυχάσθω ὁ πλούσιος ἐν τῷ πλούτῳ αὐτοῦ, ἀλλ' ἢ ἐν τούτῳ καυχάσθω ὁ καυχώμενος συνιεῖν καὶ γινώσκειν τὸν Κύριον καὶ ποιεῖν κρίμα καὶ δικαιοσύνην ἐν μέσῳ τῆς γῆς. It will be observed that the three classes, the wise, the strong and the wealthy, correspond roughly to the three enumerated in the passage above in ver. 26, and the reference is peculiarly apt here.

St Paul repeats the words ὁ καυχώμενος ἐν Κυρίῳ καυχάσθω in 2 Cor. x. 17, and St Clement of Rome (§ 13) quotes the passage from the LXX. with the conclusion thus ἀλλ' ἢ ὁ καυχώμενος ἐν Κυρίῳ καυχάσθω, τοῦ ἐκζητεῖν αὐτὸν καὶ ποιεῖν κρίμα καὶ δικαιοσύνην, words which, though diverging considerably from the corresponding passage in Jeremiah, approach nearly to the conclusion of 1 Sam. ii. 10 given above.

The resemblance of St Clement's language to St Paul may be explained in two ways; either (1) St Paul does not quote literally but gives the sense of one or other passage (1 Sam. ii. 10 or Jer. ix. 23 sq); and Clement, writing afterwards, unconsciously combines and confuses St Paul's quotations with the original text; or (2) a recension of the text of Jeremiah (or Samuel) was in circulation in the first century which contained the exact words ὁ καυχώμενος ἐν Κυρίῳ καυχάσθω. The former is the more probable hypothesis. Iren. *Haer.* iv. 17. 3 quotes Jer. ix. 24 as it stands in our texts. In neither passage does the Hebrew aid in solving the difficulty. In 1 Sam. ii. 10 it is much shorter than and quite different from the LXX. Lucifer *de Athan.* ii. 2 (Hartel, p. 148) quotes it 'non glorietur sapiens in sua sapientia...nec glorietur dives in divitiis suis, sed in hoc glorietur qui gloriatur, inquirere me et intelligere et scire in Deum gloriari, quia ego sum Dominus qui facio misericordiam et judicium et justitiam super terram.' As Cotelier (on Clem. Rom. § 13) remarks, he seems to have read ἐκζητεῖν with Clement, for he has 'inquirere' three times in this context, but the coincidence may be accidental. On the other hand Antioch. Palæst. *Hom.* xliii. (*Bibl. Vet. Patr.* p. 1097, Paris 1624) quotes directly from 1 Sam. ii. 10 and betrays no connexion with Clement's language. For St Paul's quotations see further on ii. 9.

CHAPTER II.

1. 'And this divine rule was illustrated in my case also. Just as God has ordained the weakness of the cross as the means of salvation (i. 22—25), just as He has chosen the weak of this world as the objects of salvation (i. 26—31), so I too observed the same rule among you.' And this in two ways (introduced by κἀγώ). 'Humility characterised my preaching (ii. 1, 2). Humility was stamped upon my person and penetrated my feelings (ii. 3).'

ἐλθών...ἦλθον] Perhaps the aorist ἐλθών is to be explained by supposing that the sentence was begun with the idea of ending it οὐ καθ' ὑπεροχὴν κ.τ.λ. κατήγγελλον, and the form was abruptly changed after ἀδελφοί. For repetitions however somewhat analogous to this see Jelf, Gr. § 705. 3, and better still Matth. § 558, especially the instance from Plato Euthyd. p. 288 D τίνα ποτ' οὖν ἂν κτησάμενοι ἐπιστήμην ὀρθῶς κτησαίμεθα; At all events it is not to be compared with the Hebraism ἰδὼν εἶδον.

οὐ καθ' ὑπεροχὴν λόγου ἢ σοφίας] 'not in excess of eloquence or wisdom,' i.e. not in excellence of rhetorical display or of philosophical subtlety. The two are united lower down in ver. 4 ἐν πειθοῖς σοφίας λόγοις. 'Corinthia verba' was a proverbial expression for elaborate language (Wetstein on 1 Cor. ii. 4). The phrase here is better taken with καταγγέλλων than with ἦλθον.

καταγγέλλων] A present participle, instead of the future which generally accompanies verbs of motion to express the object of the verb (Matth. § 566. 6). As we find however that this exception occurs so frequently in the case of ἀγγέλλειν and its compounds, we are led to look for the explanation in the special meaning of this verb, which is not so much 'to announce, declare,' as 'to bear tidings.' Compare Xen. Hell. ii. 1. 29 ἐς τὰς Ἀθήνας ἔπλευσεν ἀγγέλλουσα τὰ γεγονότα, Thucyd. i. 116 οἰχόμεναι περιαγγέλλουσαι βοηθεῖν, Eur. Med. 372; and so Acts xv. 27 ἀπεστάλκαμεν...αὐτοὺς...ἀπαγγέλλοντας.

τὸ μαρτύριον] 'the testimony.' He spoke in plain and simple language, as became a witness. Elaborate diction and subtlety of argument would only discredit his testimony. The various reading μυστήριον, though strongly supported (אAC Syr. Memph. and some fathers), has probably crept in from ver. 7.

τοῦ Θεοῦ] Τοῦ Θεοῦ here is perhaps the subjective genitive, 'the testimony proceeding from God,' as τοῦ Χριστοῦ in i. 6 (τὸ μαρτύριον τοῦ Χριστοῦ) is the objective genitive, 'the testimony borne to Christ.' The expression of St John (1 Joh. v. 9) 'This is the witness of God which He hath testified of His Son' links the two together. It is the testimony borne by God (τοῦ Θεοῦ) to Christ (τοῦ Χριστοῦ).

Μαρτυρία and μαρτύριον differ as 'the giving evidence' and 'the evidence given.' But it is not easy in this case to separate the ἔργον from the ἐνέργεια.

2. οὐ γὰρ ἔκρινά τι εἰδέναι] '*I had no intent, no mind to know anything.*' It does not mean therefore 'I steadfastly excluded all other knowledge,' but simply ' I did not trouble myself about the knowledge of anything else.' For this sense of κρίνειν compare vii. 37, 2 Cor. ii. 1, Acts xv. 19, Rom. xiv. 13. The other rendering 'I determined not to know' (E.V.) cannot be supported by the analogy of the common idiom οὐ φημί ('I non-say it,' 'I say no to it'); unless it can be shown that οὐ κρίνω is commonly so used. Thus e.g. οὐ λέγω would not be equivalent to οὐ φημί. Οὐκ ἐῶ again presents no correspondence, it being simply a softened expression for 'I forbid.' It is not necessary to understand ἐξεῖναι with οὐκ ἔκρινα ('I did not judge it allowable'), as Lobeck contends (*Phryn.* p. 753).

τι εἰδέναι] in a pregnant sense, 'to exhibit the knowledge of, recognise'; resembling its use in 1 Thess. v. 12 (see note there) and ver. 12 below. The reading of the received text τοῦ εἰδέναι τι is a legitimate construction in late Greek (cf. Acts xxvii. 1 ἐκρίθη τοῦ ἀποπλεῖν ἡμᾶς), but is destitute of textual support here.

Ἰησοῦν Χριστὸν] i.e. both the Person (Ἰησοῦν) and the office (Χριστὸν) of our Lord.

καὶ τοῦτον ἐσταυρωμένον] i.e. and Him too not in His glory, but in His humiliation; that the foolishness of the preaching might be doubly foolish, and the weakness doubly weak. The Incarnation was in itself a stumbling-block; the Crucifixion was much more than this.

3. κἀγὼ] 'as in my ministerial teaching, so also in my own person, weakness was the distinguishing mark.' For the repetition of κἀγὼ... κἀγὼ compare Juvenal *Sat.* i. 15, 16 'et nos ergo manum ferulae subduximus, et nos Consilium dedimus Sullae.'

ἐν ἀσθενείᾳ] The meaning of ἀσθένεια should not be arbitrarily restricted to any one form of weakness. Whatever enhanced in the Apostle's mind the contrast between the meanness and inability of the preacher, and the power and efficacy of the Gospel, would be included under ἀσθένεια. Thus it would comprehend (1) the physical malady, under which he was labouring at the time (see Gal. iv. 13 ἀσθένεια τῆς σαρκός), which is in all probability the same as 'the thorn in the flesh' mentioned 2 Cor. xii. 7 and in reference to which see *Galatians* p. 186 sq : (2) the meanness of his personal appearance (2 Cor. x. 10) with which he was taunted, and which perhaps was the result of his complaint : (3) his inability as a speaker, whether this arose from imperfection of the physical organs or from some other cause (see again 2 Cor. x. 10) : (4) a sense of loneliness, from which we may suppose him suffering before the arrival of Silvanus and Timotheus (Acts xvii. 15, xviii. 5 ὡς δὲ κατῆλθον...συνείχετο τῷ λόγῳ i.e. perhaps 'he grew more bold'), analogous to the feelings which oppressed him at a later date during the absence of Titus (2 Cor. ii. 13) : (5) his unprotected condition, when assailed by persecution : and (6) his general inability to deliver his message worthily.

ἐν φόβῳ καὶ ἐν τρόμῳ πολλῷ] Each word is an advance upon the other. The sense of weakness produced fear. The fear betrayed itself in much trembling. Φόβος καὶ τρόμος is a not unfrequent combination in St Paul, 2 Cor. vii. 15, Eph. vi. 5, Phil. ii. 12. See the note on the last named passage. Here the expression denotes the Apostle's nervous apprehension that he might not fulfil his ministry aright : i.e. fear and trembling in the sight of God rather than of man.

ἐγενόμην] may be taken either (1) with ἐν ἀσθενείᾳ κ.τ.λ. 'I manifested weakness and fear, in my intercourse with you'; or (2) with πρὸς ὑμᾶς 'I arrived among you in weakness and fear.' There is the same ambiguity of construction in 1 Thess. i. 5 (see the note on that passage). Here probably the former is the preferable construction, not only as being the more usual, but also as better suited to the context.

4. λόγος, κήρυγμα] are not to be distinguished as his private and public instruction respectively : nor yet exactly as the form and the matter of his preaching; though the latter is not far from the right distinction. While κήρυγμα (not 'my preaching' as E.V., which would be κήρυξις, see on i. 21) signifies the facts of the Gospel, e.g. the Incarnation, Crucifixion, Resurrection etc.; λόγος is the teaching built upon this, whether in the way of exhortation or of instruction.

πειθοῖς] '*persuasive, plausible.*' The word πειθός, which is equivalent to πιθανός, is not found elsewhere in Greek literature, but was probably a colloquial form. Thus the word unconsciously illustrates the very fact which the Apostle states. It is formed on the analogy of φειδός (from φείδομαι), which is apparently found only in the comic writers, βοσκός from βόσκω, etc. Eusebius and Origen (though not consistently) quote the passage ἐν πειθοῖ σοφίας λόγων, and so apparently do some versions. On πειθός see the references in Meyer, also Lobeck *Phryn.* p. 434, Winer § xvi. p. 119. The whole expression includes both the rhetorical (λόγοις) and the philosophical (σοφίας) element, the two together producing πειθώ (so ver. 1 ὑπεροχὴ λόγου ἢ σοφίας). The received text inserts ἀνθρωπίνης before σοφίας without sufficient authority.

ἐν ἀποδείξει κ.τ.λ.] Here ἀπόδειξις 'demonstration' is opposed to
πειθώ (in πειθοῖς) 'plausibility'; and πνεῦμα καὶ δύναμις to λόγοι σοφίας.
Of these last, πνεῦμα is opposed to λόγος as the inward spirit to the
mere superficial expression; and δύναμις to σοφία as moral power to
intellectual subtlety. Δύναμις is not to be taken in the sense of 'miracle-
working.' There is the same opposition, and in very similar language, in
1 Thess. i. 5 τὸ εὐαγγέλιον ἡμῶν οὐκ ἐγενήθη εἰς ὑμᾶς ἐν λόγῳ μόνον, ἀλλὰ
καὶ ἐν δυνάμει καὶ ἐν πνεύματι ἁγίῳ καὶ πληροφορίᾳ πολλῇ.

It is questioned whether πνεύματος καὶ δυνάμεως is a subjective or an
objective genitive, i. e. whether it is 'the demonstration which comes of
spirit and of power,' or 'the demonstration which exhibits spirit and
power.' The former is the more probable meaning; both because the
form of the substantive ἀπόδειξις (a ἅπαξ λεγόμενον in the N.T.) rather
points to this, and also (which is a stronger reason) because the parallelism with σοφίας λόγοις seems to require it.

We are reminded by these words of the criticism of Longinus (Fragment
I. ed. Weiske p. 113), who describes St Paul as πρῶτον...προϊστάμενον
δόγματος ἀναποδείκτου. It was moral, not verbal, demonstration at which
he aimed. See Loesner Obs. p. 363 on Col. ii. 1, and compare the
expression of Ignatius (Rom. § 3) οὐ πεισμονῆς τὸ ἔργον ἀλλὰ μεγέθους κ.τ.λ.

5. ἐν σοφίᾳ ἀνθρώπων] The preposition denotes the object of their
faith, 'that your faith may not repose in the wisdom of men.' For this
use of πίστις with ἐν compare Rom. iii. 25 διὰ πίστεως ἐν τῷ αὐτοῦ αἵματι,
Gal. iii. 26, Eph. i. 15, 1 Tim. iii. 13, 2 Tim. i. 13, iii. 15.

*The true and the false wisdom. The former is spiritually
discerned* (ii. 6—16).

6. 'Though we eschew the wisdom of men, yet we have a wisdom of
our own which we communicate with the perfect.' For the manner in
which the word σοφία is taken up here, compare λόγος in i. 17, 18 οὐκ
ἐν σοφίᾳ λόγου...ὁ λόγος γὰρ ὁ τοῦ σταυροῦ κ.τ.λ.

ἐν τοῖς τελείοις] Τέλειος is properly that of which the parts are fully
developed, as distinguished from ὁλόκληρος, that in which none of the
parts are wanting. See James i. 4 where the words occur, Trench N.T.
Syn. § xxii. p. 74 sq, and the passages quoted on 1 Thess. v. 23. Hence
it signifies 'full-grown,' and accordingly τέλειος is used by St Paul as
opposed to νήπιος or παιδία, though in a moral sense as τέλειοι ἐν Χριστῷ.
Compare xiv. 20 τῇ κακίᾳ νηπιάζετε, ταῖς δὲ φρεσὶ τέλειοι γίνεσθε, Eph. iv.
13, Phil. iii. 15, Heb. v. 14. That it is used in this sense here will appear
also from iii. 1 ὡς νηπίοις ἐν Χριστῷ. The distinction is somewhat the
same as that which St John makes, dividing his hearers into πατέρες and
νεανίσκοι or παιδία (1 Joh. ii. 13, 14). Pythagoras also is said to have
distinguished his disciples as τέλειοι and νήπιοι.

But besides this meaning of 'full development,' the term here most probably bears the collateral sense of 'initiated' according to its classical usage, illustrating ἐν μυστηρίῳ below.   See this side of the question treated fully in the notes on Col. i. 28 διδάσκοντες πάντα ἄνθρωπον ἐν πάσῃ σοφίᾳ ἵνα παραστήσωμεν πάντα ἄνθρωπον τέλειον ἐν Χριστῷ, a passage where, as here, both μυστήριον and σοφία occur in the context.

These words have been the subject of much dispute.   On the one hand they have been adduced to justify the distinction of an exoteric and an esoteric doctrine, as though there were certain secrets withheld from the generality.   This idea of a higher and a lower teaching seems early to have gained ground even among orthodox writers, and Clement of Alexandria (Eus. *H.E.* v. 11) especially says that Christ communicated the inner γνῶσις to a few chosen disciples.   This distinction became the starting-point of Gnosticism : see Lechler *Ap. Zeit.* p. 500 and note on Col. l.c.   The difference between γνῶσις and σοφία is discussed on Col. ii. 3.

On the other hand several modern commentators, seeing how entirely opposed this system of religious castes is to the genius of Christianity and to the teaching of St Paul elsewhere, have avoided any semblance of it here, by putting a forced construction on the passage σοφίαν λαλοῦμεν ἐν τοῖς τελείοις 'we teach a doctrine which is wisdom in the judgment of the perfect.'   But to say nothing of the harshness of this construction, it is clear from the whole context, especially iii. 1, 2, that St Paul was speaking of an actual distinction in the teaching addressed to the less and the more advanced believer.   What is implied by the contrast between 'babes' and 'grown men' may be seen from iii. 1.   It is the distinction of less or greater spirituality.   What is meant by the σοφία may be gathered from a comparison of St Paul's earlier with his later Epistles.   The σοφία will involve especially the ampler teaching as to the Person of Christ and the eternal purpose of God.   Such 'wisdom' we have in the Epistles to the Ephesians and Colossians especially, and in a less degree in the Epistle to the Romans.   This 'wisdom' is discerned in the Gospel of St John, as compared with the other Evangelists. Compare the note on γάλα οὐ βρῶμα (iii. 2).

τῶν ἀρχόντων τοῦ αἰῶνος τούτου] i.e. the great men of this world, as the whole context seems imperatively to demand ; the princes whether in intellect or in power or in rank, so that οἱ ἄρχοντες κ.τ.λ. would include the σοφοί, δυνατοί, εὐγενεῖς of i. 26.   See further the note on ver. 8.

On the other hand some of the fathers (e.g. Origen *Homil.* IV. *in Matth.*, IX. *in Genes.*) understood it of the powers of evil, comparing Eph. vi. 12 πρὸς τοὺς κοσμοκράτορας τοῦ σκότους τούτου, πρὸς τὰ πνευματικὰ τῆς πονηρίας ἐν τοῖς ἐπουρανίοις.   In this sense the Gnostics availed themselves of it to support their Dualism, see Tert. *adv. Marc.* v. 6.   And it would almost seem as if St Ignatius were referring to this passage in *Ephes.* § 19 ἔλαθεν τὸν ἄρχοντα τοῦ αἰῶνος τούτου ἡ παρθενία Μαρίας καὶ ὁ τοκετὸς αὐτῆς, ὁμοίως καὶ ὁ θάνατος τοῦ Κυρίου, τρία μυστήρια κραυγῆς, where however ἔλαθεν is probably intended as a paraphrase of οὐδεὶς τῶν ἀρχόντων τοῦ αἰῶνος τούτου ἔγνωκεν (ver. 8). At all events, the meaning is quite out of place here; and 'the princes of this world' are to be understood as great men according to the world's estimate of greatness.

τῶν καταργουμένων] is best explained by i. 28 τὰ μὴ ὄντα ἵνα τὰ ὄντα καταργήσῃ: i.e. who are brought to nought by the power of Christ, whose glory wanes before the advance of Messiah's kingdom; ὁ αἰὼν οὗτος being the direct opposite of ἡ βασιλεία τοῦ Χριστοῦ, 'Messiah's kingdom' in its widest sense. Compare *Martyr. Vienn.* c. 8 (in Routh *R.S.* I. p. 305) καταργηθέντων δὲ τῶν τυραννικῶν κολαστηρίων ὑπὸ τοῦ Χριστοῦ διὰ τῆς τῶν μακαρίων ὑπομονῆς. See also the note on δόξαν ἡμῶν in the next verse.

7. Θεοῦ σοφίαν] is the correct order, Θεοῦ being emphatic: 'a wisdom not of this world, but of God.' The received text has σοφίαν Θεοῦ on the slenderest authority.

ἐν μυστηρίῳ] '*the wisdom which consists in a mystery.*' The phrase must be taken either (1) with σοφίαν or (2) with λαλοῦμεν. Perhaps the former is preferable. For the omission of the article see the note on I Thess. i. 1 ἐν Θεῷ πατρί, and references there. If ἐν μυστηρίῳ is taken with λαλοῦμεν, the sense will be much the same ; 'We speak a wisdom of God, while declaring a mystery.' On the Pauline use of the word μυστήριον, as something which would not have been known without revelation, and its connexion with words denoting publication (as here ἡμῖν γὰρ ἀπεκάλυψεν ὁ Θεὸς ver. 10) see the note on Col. i. 26. See also the note on 2 Thess. ii. 7 : from the passage in Josephus there quoted, μυστήριον appears to have the subordinate sense of something extraordinary and portentous.

τὴν ἀποκεκρυμμένην] The article is frequently placed thus between the substantive and the accompanying adjective or participle when it is intended to give a definite reference to an indefinite statement. 'A wisdom of God, that wisdom I mean, which was etc.' Compare Gal. iii. 21 νόμος ὁ δυνάμενος, with the note.

ἣν προώρισεν] '*which God foreordained*' ; absolutely. It is not necessary to understand ἀποκαλύψαι or any word of the kind. The σοφία Θεοῦ is the scheme of redemption.

εἰς δόξαν ἡμῶν] i.e. the glory of inward enlightenment as well as of outward exaltation; for the word δόξα (like βασιλεία τοῦ Θεοῦ) involves the complex idea. Compare 2 Cor. iii. 8—18. Here there is an opposition between δόξαν ἡμῶν and τῶν ἀρχόντων τοῦ αἰῶνος τούτου, τῶν καταργουμένων, 'Our glory increases, while their glory wanes.' This use of καταργεῖσθαι in connexion with δόξα is illustrated by the passage from 2 Corinthians already referred to, and by 2 Thess. ii. 8 καταργήσει τῇ ἐπιφανείᾳ τῆς παρουσίας αὐτοῦ (where see the notes).

8. ἣν] i.e. σοφίαν.
ἔγνωκεν] '*hath discerned.*'
τὸν Κύριον...ἐσταύρωσαν] As types and representatives of the princes of this world, St Paul takes the Jewish and heathen rulers who crucified

the Lord (comp. Acts iv. 27). Yet the rebuke is not confined to these; and he rightly says οὐδεὶς τῶν ἀρχόντων, for all alike who oppose themselves to the spread of the Gospel, all the princes of this world, as such, do in a certain sense 'crucify the Lord afresh' (Heb. vi. 6).

τῆς δόξης] The contrast present to the Apostle's mind is that between the shame of the Cross (Heb. xii. 2) and the glory of the Crucified, between the ignominy which they seemed to be inflicting on Him and the honour which was intrinsically His.

9. ἀλλὰ καθὼς γέγραπται] '*but it has come to pass according to the words of Scripture.*' The sentence is elliptical. For an exact parallel in form see Rom. xv. 3, and compare the note on 1 Cor. i. 31.

ἃ ὀφθαλμὸς κ.τ.λ.] The composition of the sentence is somewhat loose. Like 1 Tim. iii. 16 ὃς ἐφανερώθη κ.τ.λ. it begins with a relative, so that the construction is broken. The grammar also is irregular, ἃ being the accusative after εἶδεν and ἤκουσεν, and the nominative to ἀνέβη; and ὅσα (the correct reading for the second ἃ of the received text) in apposition with ἃ. Another construction is proposed which makes ἡμῖν δὲ ἀπεκάλυψεν (ver. 10) the apodosis, introduced by the particle δέ; but this, even if γὰρ is not to be read for δέ, seems not to be after St Paul's manner, being too elaborate and indeed requiring ταῦτα δὲ ἡμῖν. The whole of verse 10 is best considered to be the Apostle's own addition to the quotation. For ἀνέβη ἐπὶ τὴν καρδίαν, a Hebrew expression (עלה על לב), see Acts vii. 23, Jerem. iii. 16, xliv. 21, li. 50.

The distinction here is between things perceived by the senses, and things apprehended by the understanding. Compare the lines of Empedocles οὕτως οὔτ' ἐπιδερκτὰ τάδ' ἀνδράσιν, οὔτ' ἐπακουστά, οὔτε νόῳ περίληπτα in Sext. Empir. *adv. Math.* vii. 123 (Ritter and Preller, p. 126).

The quotation, the words of which are not found in the existing text of the Old Testament, is generally considered to be a combination of Is. lxiv. 4, which runs in the LXX. ἀπὸ τοῦ αἰῶνος οὐκ ἠκούσαμεν οὐδὲ οἱ ὀφθαλμοὶ ἡμῶν εἶδον Θεὸν πλὴν σοῦ καὶ τὰ ἔργα σοῦ, ἃ ποιήσεις τοῖς ὑπομένουσιν ἔλεον, but more nearly in the Hebrew, 'From eternity they have not heard, they have not hearkened, neither hath eye seen a god [or 'O God'] save thee (who) worketh [or '(what) He shall do'] to him that awaiteth Him' (see Delitzsch *ad loc.*), and Is. lxv. 16, 17 οὐκ ἀναβήσεται αὐτῶν ἐπὶ τὴν καρδίαν...οὐ μὴ ἐπέλθῃ αὐτῶν ἐπὶ τὴν καρδίαν. The passage, if we may trust St Jerome, occurred as given by St Paul, both in the *Ascension of Isaiah* and in the *Apocalypse of Elias* (Hieron. *in Is.* lxiv. 4, IV. p. 761; *Prol. in Gen.* IX. p. 3). And Origen, *in Matth.* xxvii. 9 (III. p. 916), says that St Paul quotes from the latter, 'In nullo regulari libro hoc positum invenitur, nisi (εἰ μή, 'but only') in Secretis Eliae prophetae.' This assertion is repeated also by later writers (see Fabricius *Cod. Ps. V. T.* I. p. 1073) doubtless from Origen, but combated by Jerome (ll. cc. and *Epist.* lvii. § 9, I. p. 314), who refers the quotation to Is. lxiv. 4. There does not seem any reason for doubting that the quotation occurs as Origen states, especially as Jerome, making a savage onslaught on this opinion, tacitly allows the fact ; see more below.   If it could be shown that these apocryphal books were prior to St Paul, this solution would be the most probable ; but they would appear to have been produced by some Christian sectarians of the second century, for Jerome terms them 'Iberae naeniae' and connects them with the Basilideans and other Gnostics who abounded in Spain (ll. cc. ; see also *c. Vigil.* II. p. 393, and comp. Fabricius, p. 1093 sq.).   If so, they incorporated the quotation of St Paul, as also another missing quotation (Eph. v. 14, see below), in order to give verisimilitude and currency to their forgeries.   At all events both these works appear from the extant remains to have been Christian.   For the *Apocalypse of Elias* see Epiphan. *Haer.* xlii. (p. 372), who says that the quotation in Eph. v. 14 (which is obviously Christian) was found there; and for the *Ascension of Isaiah*, this same father *Haer.* lxvii. 3 (p. 712), where he quotes a passage referring to the Trinity.   Indeed there is every reason to believe that the work known to Epiphanius and several other fathers under this name, is the same with the *Ascension and Vision of Isaiah* published first by Laurence in an Æthiopic Version and subsequently by Gieseler in a Latin.   The two versions represent different recensions ; and the passage 'Eye hath not seen, etc.' appears in the Latin (xi. 34) but not in the Æthiopic (see Jolowicz, *Himmelfahrt u. Vision des Propheten Iesaia,* p. 90, Leipzig, 1854).   The Latin recension therefore must have been in the hands of Jerome ; though this very quotation seems to show clearly that the Æthiopic more nearly represents the original form of the work (see Lücke *Offenbarung d. Johannes,* p. 179 sq.).   Both recensions alike are distinctly Christian.

Still in favour of Jerome's view it may be said that St Paul's quotations are often very free as e.g. in i. 31, and that there is no instance in St Paul of a quotation from an apocryphal writing being introduced by καθὼς γέγραπται.   The quotation from a Christian hymn in Eph. v. 14 is introduced by λέγει, which is quite general.   It is just possible moreover that some Greek version, with which St Paul was acquainted, gave a different rendering from the LXX. and more resembling the quotation in the text.

It is at least remarkable that St Clement of Rome (§ 34) gives the quotation in almost the same words, though approaching somewhat nearer to the LXX.   He reads τοῖς ὑπομένουσιν αὐτὸν for St Paul's τοῖς ἀγαπῶσιν αὐτόν, and is followed by the *Martyr. Polyc.* § 2 ἀνέβλεπον τὰ τηρούμενα τοῖς ὑπομείνασιν ἀγαθά, ἃ οὔτε οὓς ἤκουσεν, οὔτε ὀφθαλμὸς εἶδεν, οὔτε ἐπὶ καρδίαν ἀνθρώπου ἀνέβη, passages which seem to suggest an original lying somewhere between the present LXX. rendering in Isaiah, and the quotation of St Paul, though nearer to the latter.   In the other places where the quotation occurs, 2 [Clem.] §§ 11, 14, *Clem. Ep. ad Virg.* i. 9, it does not reach the point where Clement and St Paul diverge.

An additional interest attaches to this passage from the words ascribed to Hegesippus in a passage of Stephanus Gobarus ap. Photium *Bibl.* 232 (see Routh *R. S.* I. 219), who after quoting this passage says Ἡγήσιππος μέντοι, ἀρχαῖός τε ἀνὴρ καὶ ἀποστολικός, ἐν τῷ πέμπτῳ τῶν ὑπομνημάτων οὐκ οἶδ' ὅ τι καὶ παθὼν μάτην μὲν εἰρῆσθαι ταῦτα λέγει, καὶ καταψεύδεσθαι τοὺς ταῦτα φαμένους τῶν τε θείων γραφῶν καὶ τοῦ κυρίου λεγόντος, Μακάριοι οἱ ὀφθαλμοὶ ὑμῶν οἱ βλέποντες, καὶ τὰ ὦτα ὑμῶν τὰ ἀκούοντα καὶ ἑξῆς. Stephanus seems to regard this (at least Baur and Schwegler do so) as an attack on St Paul and a proof that Hegesippus was an Ebionite ; but he has probably misunderstood the drift of Hegesippus' words. Hegesippus was attacking, not the passage itself, but the application which was made of it by certain Gnostics, who alleged it in support of an esoteric doctrine (see Routh *R. S.* I. p. 281 and *Galatians* p. 334). We know from Hippolytus (*Haer.* v. 24, 26, 27, vi. 24) that it was a favourite text with these heretics and that the Justinians even introduced it into their formula of initiation. Perhaps *the Revelation of Elias* may have been an early Gnostic work itself, and embodied this quotation from St Paul for doctrinal purposes. In favour of this view, it may be remarked that Hegesippus elsewhere (*ap.* Euseb. *H. E.* iii. 32) in attacking the Gnostic heresy avails himself of St Paul's own words ψευδώνυμος γνῶσις (1 Tim. vi. 20), and seems to have commended the Epistle of Clement and to have been satisfied with the orthodoxy of the Corinthian Church (Euseb. *H. E.* iv. 22, comp. iii. 16).

10. ἡμῖν] '*to us who believe*' ; not to the Apostles specially, but to believers generally.

ἀπεκάλυψεν ὁ Θεὸς] This order is perhaps better than that of the received text ὁ Θεὸς ἀπεκ., and is strongly supported (אABCD). The 'revelation' is the emphatic idea in the sentence. The aorist (ἀπεκάλυψεν) is on a par with many aorists in St Paul. Its force is, 'revealed it to us when we were admitted into the Church, when we were baptized.' Ἀποκάλυψις implies an extraordinary revelation, while φανέρωσις is the general term, including e.g. the revelation of God in nature.

τὸ γὰρ πνεῦμα] i.e. the Spirit of God given to us. If we know the things of God, it is only by His Spirit dwelling in us. See Rom. viii. 9—27, where the same idea occurs in several forms and with several applications.

καὶ τὸ βάθη] '*even the depths*,' which are manifold, the plural being stronger than the singular. On the other hand we have τὰ βαθέα τοῦ Σατανᾶ (Apoc. ii. 24).

11. 'For as a man's self-consciousness reveals man's nature to him, so it can be nothing else but the Spirit of God dwelling in him which reveals to him the nature and dealings of God.' Τὰ τοῦ ἀνθρώπου are 'the things of man' generally, of human nature. The emphatic repetition of ἀνθρώπων, ἀνθρώπου, ἀνθρώπου and of Θεοῦ, Θεοῦ is intended to enforce the contrasts.

ἔγνωκεν] is the correct reading for the second οἶδεν of the received text. The words are carefully chosen. Οἶδεν 'knoweth' denotes direct knowledge, while ἔγνωκεν 'discerneth' involves more or less the idea of a process of attainment. Compare e.g. 1 Joh. ii. 29 ἐὰν εἰδῆτε ὅτι δίκαιός ἐστιν, γινώσκετε ὅτι πᾶς ὁ ποιῶν τὴν δικαιοσύνην ἐξ αὐτοῦ γεγέννηται, where γινώσκετε implies an inference. In this passage the distinction is not so marked, but the ἔγνωκεν seems to place τὰ τοῦ Θεοῦ a degree more out of reach than οἶδεν does τὰ τοῦ ἀνθρώπου. Compare also 2 Cor. v. 16, and see for γινώσκειν the notes on Gal. iii. 7, iv. 9, for εἰδέναι 1 Thess. v. 12.

The examination of the passages, where the two words are found in the First Epistle of St John, shows most clearly that they were employed with the same precision of meaning as in the classical age. While οἶδα is simple and absolute, γινώσκω is relative, involving more or less the idea of a process of examination. Thus while οἶδα is used of the knowledge of the facts and propositions in themselves, γινώσκω implies reference to something else, and gives prominence to either the acquisition of the knowledge or the knowledge of a thing in its bearings. It surely cannot be by chance, that where St John wishes to place in bold relief the fundamental facts of our religious conviction in and by themselves, he uses οἶδα (see ii. 20, 21, iii. 2, 5, 14, 15, and especially v. 18, 19, 20); that where he speaks of our knowledge not as direct but as derived from something prior to it, he almost always employs γινώσκω, both in the phrase ἐν τούτῳ γινώσκειν, which occurs repeatedly (ii. 3, 5, iii. 19, 24, iv. 2, 13, v. 2, cf. iii. 16 ἐν τούτῳ ἐγνώκαμεν: not once ἐν τούτῳ εἰδέναι), and in other expressions (ii. 18 ὅθεν γινώσκομεν, iii. 1 οὐ γινώσκει ἡμᾶς ὅτι, iv. 6 ἐκ τούτου γινώσκομεν, cf. iv. 7, 8); and that when the two words γινώσκειν and εἰδέναι are found together, as in the passage already quoted (comp. John xxi. 17, Eph. v. 5), they stand to each other in the relation which the distinction given above would lead us to expect. If there are also passages in which the difference of meaning is not so plain, the induction seems still to be sufficiently large to establish the facts.

οὐδείς...εἰ μή] i.e. 'no man, as man, knoweth, but only the Spirit of God.' Οὐδείς (sc. ἀνθρώπων) as τίς ἀνθρώπων above. For this use of εἰ μή (ἐὰν μή) see on Gal. i. 7, 19, ii. 16.

τὸ πνεῦμα τοῦ Θεοῦ] Not τὸ πνεῦμα τὸ ἐν αὐτῷ according to the analogy of the preceding part of the verse; for though the spirit of man is in him, a similar expression would not correctly apply to the Spirit of God. This change of phraseology may be regarded as a caution to us not to press the analogy beyond the point to illustrate which it was introduced. It may be true that the spirit of man takes cognizance of the things of man, just as the Spirit of God does of the things of God ; but it does not follow that the spirit of man has the same relation to man as the Spirit of God has to God.

12. ἡμεῖς δέ] *'but we received not the spirit of the world, but the*

Spirit which cometh from God.' Ἡμεῖς includes the believers generally, but refers especially to the Apostles, as Paul and Apollos : for the reference is mainly to the teachers in the following verse.

τὸ πνεῦμα τοῦ κόσμου] The interpretation of this expression will depend on the view taken of τῶν ἀρχόντων τοῦ αἰῶνος τούτου (ver. 6); see the note there. It seems therefore to be simply the spirit of human wisdom, of the world as alienated from God.

ἐλάβομεν] '*received,*' i.e. when we were admitted to the fold of Christ. The aorist τὰ χαρισθέντα below refers to the same time. St Paul regards the gift as ideally summed up when he and they were included in the Christian Church, though it is true that the Spirit is received constantly.

ἵνα εἰδῶμεν κ.τ.λ.] i.e. 'that we may be conscious of, may realize the spiritual blessings and hopes conferred upon us.' For this sense of εἰδέναι see ii. 2 and the note on 1 Thess. v. 12. Here τὰ χαρισθέντα will include miraculous gifts; but, like χάρισμα itself, the expression extends to all blessings conferred by the Gospel. See i. 7 above.

13. ' Nor do we keep this knowledge to ourselves. As it is revealed to us, so also (καὶ) do we communicate it to others. And the manner of our communication is in accordance with the matter. Spiritual truths are expressed in spiritual language.' The expression ἃ καὶ λαλοῦμεν is in a measure corrective of any impression which might have been left by the foregoing words, that the mysteries of the Gospel were the exclusive property of a few. The emphatic word in the sentence is λαλοῦμεν, as the order shows ; and the mention of the manner of communication (οὐκ ἐν διδακτοῖς κ.τ.λ.) is quite subordinate.

σοφίας] is the genitive governed by διδακτοῖς, as the form of the ellipsis in the corresponding clause ἐν διδακτοῖς πνεύματος shows. Compare John vi. 45 (from Is. liv. 13) πάντες διδακτοὶ Θεοῦ. This construction of the genitive with verbal adjectives of passive force is in classical Greek confined to poetry; e.g. Soph. *Electra* 343 ἅπαντα γάρ σοι τἀμὰ νουθετήματα κείνης διδακτά, Pind. *Ol.* ix. 152 (100) διδακταῖς ἀνθρώπων ἀρεταῖς.

'There is no display of human rhetoric in our preaching. The language, no less than the matter, is inspired.' Indeed the notion of a verbal inspiration in a certain sense is involved in the very conception of an inspiration at all, because words are at once the instruments of carrying on and the means of expressing ideas, so that the words must both lead and follow the thought. But the passage gives no countenance to the popular doctrine of verbal inspiration, whether right or wrong.

πνευματικοῖς πνευματικὰ συγκρίνοντες] '*combining the spiritual with the spiritual,*' i.e. applying spiritual methods to explain spiritual truths. It is excellently explained by Theod. Mops. here : διὰ τῶν τοῦ πνεύματος ἀποδεί-ξεων τὴν τοῦ πνεύματος διδασκαλίαν πιστούμεθα. This is the proper meaning of συγκρίνειν 'to combine,' as διακρίνειν is 'to separate.' Συγκρίνειν, it is true, sometimes gets the sense of 'comparing,' as in 2 Cor. x. 12; but it does not suit the context here, whether explained, as by Chrysostom and others, of comparing the types of the Old Testament with the tidings of the New, or more generally. Others again, taking πνευματικοῖς to be masculine, translate it 'explaining spiritual things to spiritual men.' Against this it may be urged, (1) that though συγκρίνειν is frequently used of interpreting dreams (cf. Gen. xl. 8, 22, xli. 12, Dan. v. 12), yet the leading notion which it involves is that of 'finding out,' 'comparing' the phenomena of the dream with the phenomena of common life (so κρίνειν, ἐγκρίνειν are used of dreams), which notion is out of place here: (2) the combination πνευματικοῖς πνευματικά points to the neuter gender, as otherwise we should rather expect πνευματικὰ τοῖς πνευματικοῖς: (3) the dative is naturally governed by the σὺν of συγκρίνοντες, and (4) the qualifications of the recipient seem to be introduced first in the following verse by ψυχικὸς δέ.

14. 'Though we communicate our knowledge freely, yet being, as I said, spiritual—spiritual in form as well as in matter—it addresses itself only to spiritual hearers, and therefore the natural man is excluded from it.' The verse is connected with ver. 12, and St Paul comes round to the subject of ver. 6 once more.

ψυχικὸς] '*the natural man*,' as opposed to πνευματικός, and closely allied to σαρκικός. See note on 1 Thess. v. 23, where the triple division of man's nature into σῶμα, ψυχή, and πνεῦμα is discussed.

οὐ δέχεται] '*rejects*,' '*does not receive*'; not 'is incapable of' (a strictly classical usage of δέχεσθαι which would be expressed in the N.T. by οὐ χωρεῖ). The meaning which I have given is the universal sense of δέχεσθαι in the New Testament and is moreover better suited to the explanation μωρία γὰρ κ.τ.λ., which includes more than the incapacity of the hearer, and implies a disinclination also.

ὅτι πνευματικῶς ἀνακρίνεται] '*for they*' (sc. τὰ τοῦ πνεύματος) '*are spiritually discerned*,' i.e. the investigation is a spiritual process. This is an explanation of the whole sentence from μωρία...γνῶναι, and not of the latter clause only.

15. 'On the other hand, the spiritual man is placed on a vantage-ground. He can survey and duly estimate the relative proportion of all things. He has a standard by which to measure others, but they have no standard which they can apply to him.'

ἀνακρίνει μὲν πάντα] '*examineth*,' '*sifteth everything*,' e.g. in the matter of meats or of the observance of days. In any case the same translation of the verb ought to have been preserved in the English version here, as in ver. 14. The leading idea of ἀνακρίνειν is that of examination, investigation, sifting, while κρίνειν implies more prominently the pronouncing a verdict. The word adopted by the A.V. as an equivalent is unfortunate; for, besides being a mistranslation of ἀνακρίνεται, it is quite untrue in fact to say that the spiritual man 'is judged by no one.' So ὑπ' οὐδενὸς ἀνακρίνεται means 'he is a riddle to the natural man; they can make nothing out of him, cannot bring him to book at all.'

"St Paul especially delights to accumulate" the compounds of κρίνειν, "and thus by harping upon words (if I may use the expression) to emphasize great spiritual truths or important personal experiences. Thus, he puts together συγκρίνειν, ἀνακρίνειν" here, "κρίνειν, ἀνακρίνειν, 1 Cor. iv. 3, 4; ἐγκρίνειν, συγκρίνειν, 2 Cor. x. 12; κρίνειν, διακρίνειν, 1 Cor. vi. 1—6; κρίνειν, διακρίνειν, κατακρίνειν, Rom. xiv. 22, 23, 1 Cor. xi. 29, 31, 32; κρίνειν, κατακρίνειν, Rom. ii. 1. Now it seems impossible in most cases, without a sacrifice of English which no one would be prepared to make, to reproduce the similarity of sound or the identity of root; but the distinction of sense should always be preserved. How this is neglected in our English version, and what confusion ensues from this neglect, the following instances will show. In 1 Cor. iv. 3, 4, 5, the word ἀνακρίνειν is translated throughout 'judge'; while in 1 Cor. ii. 14, 15, it is rendered indifferently 'to discern' and 'to judge.' But ἀνακρίνειν is neither 'to judge,' which is κρίνειν, nor 'to discern,' which is διακρίνειν; but 'to examine, investigate, enquire into, question,' as it is rightly translated elsewhere, e.g. 1 Cor. ix. 3, x. 25, 27; and the correct understanding of 1 Cor. iv. 3, 4, 5 depends on our retaining this sense. The ἀνάκρισις, it will be remembered, was an Athenian law term for a preliminary investigation (distinct from the actual κρίσις or trial), in which evidence was collected and the prisoner committed for trial, if a true bill was found against him. It corresponded in short *mutatis mutandis* to the part taken in English law proceedings by the grand jury. And this is substantially the force of the word here. The Apostle condemns all these impatient human *praejudicia*, these unauthorised ἀνακρίσεις, which anticipate the final κρίσις, reserving his case for the great tribunal where at length all the evidence will be forthcoming and a satisfactory verdict can be given. Meanwhile this process of gathering evidence has begun; an ἀνάκρισις is indeed being held, not however by these self-appointed magistrates, but by One who alone has the authority to institute the enquiry, and the ability to sift the facts (ὁ δὲ ἀνακρίνων με Κύριός ἐστιν). Of this half-technical sense of the word the New Testament itself furnishes a good example. The examination of St Paul before Festus is both in name and in fact an ἀνάκρισις. The Roman procurator explains to Agrippa how he had directed the prisoner to be brought into court (προήγαγον αὐτόν) in order that, having held the preliminary enquiry usual in such cases (τῆς ἀνακρίσεως γενομένης), he might be able to lay the case before the Emperor (Acts xxv. 26). Again, in 1 Cor. xiv. 24 ἀνακρίνεται ὑπὸ πάντων, the sense required is clearly 'sifting, probing, revealing,' and the rendering of our translators 'he is judged of all' introduces an idea alien to the passage." *On a Fresh Revision of the English N. T.* p. 69 sq. (3rd edit.).

πάντα] The article should be omitted, but the omission does not affect the sense, because πάντα must still be taken as neuter. Τὰ πάντα would express with slightly increased force the comprehensiveness of the spiritual man. 'All things whatsoever—even those out of his own sphere—not πνευματικὰ only but ψυχικὰ also.'

16. 'For the mind in us is the mind of the Lord. Our spirits are one with His spirit: and we have Scriptural authority for saying that no one can penetrate and understand the mind of the Lord.'

τίς γὰρ ἔγνω κ.τ.λ.] '*for who hath perceived or apprehended* etc.' From the LXX. of Is. xl. 13 τίς ἔγνω νοῦν Κυρίου; καὶ τίς αὐτοῦ σύμβουλος ἐγένετο, ὃς συμβιβᾷ αὐτόν; The middle clause is omitted in the quotation as being somewhat foreign to St Paul's purpose. On the other hand, in Rom. xi. 34, where the same quotation occurs, the first two clauses appear and not the third, as they bear on his argument there.

νοῦν Κυρίου] For the distinction between πνεῦμα and νοῦς see Usteri *Paul. Lehrb.* p. 384. In a man there might be an opposition between the νοῦς and the πνεῦμα (1 Cor. xiv. 14), but in God the νοῦς would be identical with, or at least in perfect accordance with, the πνεῦμα. It should be observed also that the original here translated νοῦν is רוח which is the common word for πνεῦμα. Compare 1 Esdr. ii. 9, where ἐγείρειν τὸν νοῦν is equivalent to ἐγείρειν τὸ πνεῦμα of the preceding verse. Thus νοῦς was the familiar form in the ears of his hearers owing to the influence of the LXX.

ὃς συμβιβάσει] '*so that he shall instruct him.*' Compare Matth. *Gr. Gr.* § 479, Obs. 1.

Συμβιβάζειν in classical Greek generally means 'to put together so as to draw an inference from, to conclude'; but here it is 'to instruct,' the sense which it usually bears in the LXX., where it occurs frequently. It thus represents the classical ἐμβιβάζειν.

νοῦν Χριστοῦ] equivalent to the νοῦν Κυρίου of the preceding verse. The 'Spirit of God' and the 'Spirit of Christ' are convertible terms here as in Rom. viii. 9 εἴπερ πνεῦμα Θεοῦ οἰκεῖ ἐν ὑμῖν. εἰ δέ τις πνεῦμα Χριστοῦ οὐκ ἔχει κ.τ.λ. (cf. Gal. iv. 6). And the substitution of Χριστοῦ for Κυρίου in this passage and for Θεοῦ in the Romans has the same point: it suggests a practical test. 'Ask yourselves whether the mind of Christ is in you.' (Compare Phil. ii. 5.)

CHAPTER III

The Corinthians incapable of discerning the wisdom of God (iii. 1—3).

1. The manner in which his readers are brought round after a long digression to their dissensions is characteristic of St Paul. One topic suggests another and he seems entirely to have lost sight of their subject: till accidentally, as one might say, the course of thought brings him within the range of its attraction, and he flies back to it at once. Thus the mention of party watchwords (in i. 12) leads him to speak of his abstaining from baptizing. He was sent not to baptize but to preach. What was the nature of his preaching? It was foolishness in the sight of the world. Yet it contained the truest wisdom. This wisdom however could not be revealed in all its depths, save to the spiritual. 'But ye are not spiritual, so long as these dissensions last.' And so he comes back to what he left.

κἀγώ] 'And I, individually, was subject to the prohibition implied in the general rule of ii. 6, σοφίαν λαλοῦμεν ἐν τοῖς τελείοις. I was obliged to withhold from you the treasures of wisdom, which I possessed in myself.'

σαρκίνοις] Unquestionably the reading here, as σαρκικοὶ in ver. 3 where it occurs twice. Considering the strong tendency to alter one or other word for the sake of conformity, the consistency of the MSS. is the more remarkable and must decide the readings.

Σάρκινος is 'fleshy, made of flesh,' 'carneus'; while σαρκικὸς is 'fleshly, partaking of the characteristics of flesh, associated with flesh,' 'carnalis.' Hence σαρκικὸς is scarcely a classical word, because the idea is not classical. As an illustration of the difference of meaning in the two terminations -ικος and -ινος, compare τὸ δερματικὸν 'the tax on hides' with δερμάτινον, which could mean nothing else but 'made of hides.' On these terminations cf. Matth. *Gr. Gr.* § 108, 110, Meyer's reff. *ad loc.* and Buttm. § 119. III, Fritzsche *ad Rom.* II. p. 46. The proper meaning of σάρκινος is seen in 2 Cor. iii. 3 οὐκ ἐν πλαξὶν λιθίναις ἀλλ᾽ ἐν πλαξὶν καρδίαις σαρκίναις, and that of σαρκικὸς in 1 Cor. ix. 11 εἰ ἡμεῖς ὑμῖν τὰ πνευματικὰ ἐσπείραμεν, μέγα εἰ ἡμεῖς ὑμῶν τὰ σαρκικὰ θερίσομεν; (cf. Rom. xv. 27), in neither of which passages there is a various reading, and in neither of which the other word would be suitable. In Heb. vii. 16, though we should expect σαρκικῆς, the νόμος ἐντολῆς σαρκίνης is intelligible because the commandment was, as it were, a part of the flesh, and thus of hereditary descent from the body of Aaron. See also Rom. vii. 14, where σάρκινος is certainly right.

ὡς σαρκίνοις] '*to men of flesh.*' For the vigour of the expression compare Matt. xvi. 17 σὰρξ καὶ αἷμα οὐκ ἀπεκάλυψέν σοι. While σάρκινος here points rather to their original nature when St Paul first preached to them, σαρκικοί (ver. 3) expresses their moral tendencies, their hankerings, even after their conversion, and implies more of a rebuke, though the less strong word in itself.

νηπίοις ἐν Χριστῷ] the opposite to which is τέλειοι ἐν Χριστῷ, Col. i. 28. See note on τέλειος ii. 6.

2. γάλα, οὐ βρῶμα] Apparently a favourite image with the Rabbinical teachers, who styled their scholars 'sugentes' or 'lactentes' (see Wetst. on 1 Pet. ii. 2). Compare Heb. v. 12 sq. γεγόνατε χρείαν ἔχοντες γάλακτος, οὐ στερεᾶς τροφῆς· πᾶς γὰρ ὁ μετεχὼν γάλακτος, ἄπειρος λόγου δικαιοσύνης· νήπιος γάρ ἐστιν· τελείων δέ ἐστιν ἡ στερεὰ τροφή, where the resemblances are so close as to suggest that the writer of the Epistle to the Hebrews had seen this Epistle and 1 Pet. ii. 2. The metaphor however was a common one at this time, see Philo *de Agricult.* § 2, I. p. 301 (ed. Mangey), ἐπεὶ δὲ νηπίοις μέν ἐστι γάλα τροφή, τελείοις δὲ τὰ ἐκ πυρῶν πέμματα, Pinytus *ap.* Routh *R. S.* I. p. 184

ἐπότισα, οὐ βρῶμα] For the zeugma compare Hesiod, *Theog.* 640 νέκταρ τ' ἀμβροσίην τε, τά περ θεοὶ αὐτοὶ ἔδουσι, Luke i. 64.

ἐδύνασθε] is probably to be taken absolutely here, '*for ye were not strong enough,*' a sense in which it appears to be not infrequently used in the LXX., e.g. Jerem. v. 4, xxxviii. 5, Ps. cxxviii. 2.

ἀλλ'] 'Why should I say ye were not strong enough; nay ye are not strong enough even now'; for ἀλλά in this sense cf. Winer *Gr.* § liii. p. 551 sq.

οὐδὲ ἔτι νῦν] An interval of about five years had elapsed since St Paul first visited them. He seems to make no allusion here to his *second* visit, which was probably of short duration, and in which he had few opportunities of instructing them.

We are led to enquire what teaching St Paul signified by γάλα and βρῶμα respectively. Obviously the doctrine of Christ crucified belonged to the former, as he himself says that he made the preaching of this his sole object on this occasion (ii. 3). This was the basis of his teaching. The best comment on this passage is furnished by Heb. v. 11—vi. 2, where the writer, laying down the same distinction between γάλα and στερεὰ τροφή, describes the former thus: 'not laying again the foundation of repentance from dead works, and of *faith towards God*, of the doctrine of *baptisms* and of *laying on of hands*, and of *resurrection of the dead*, and of *eternal judgment.*' And thus the teaching of the Thessalonian Epistles, which does not go beyond this, may be taken as a sample of the 'milk' for babes. The doctrine of justification by faith, which, as lying at the foundation of Christian teaching, would fall under the term γάλα, might still in its more complex aspects be treated as βρῶμα, and so it is in the Epistle to the Romans. If it be asked again whether St Paul is speaking of doctrinal or spiritual truths, our reply is that the two cannot be separated in Christianity. Christianity, it is said, is a life, not a creed. It could be more truly called 'a life in a creed.' See more on this subject in note on σοφία ii. 11.

3. ὅπου] introduces a condition. In itself it puts the case as purely hypothetical, and the fulfilment of the condition here is implied from the context, as in 2 Pet. ii. 11.

ζῆλος καὶ ἔρις] 'ζῆλος cogitatione, ἔρις verbis, διχοστασίαι opere. Sall. *Catil.* ix. 2 Jurgia, discordias, simultates,' Wetstein. A regular sequence: 'emulation' engenders 'strife,' and 'strife' produces 'divisions.' Cf. ii. 3. But the words καὶ διχοστασίαι of the Textus Receptus should be omitted. For the terms see the notes on Gal. v. 20; and for a more complete sequence Clem. Rom. § 3 ζῆλος καὶ φθόνος, καὶ ἔρις καὶ στάσις, διωγμὸς καὶ ἀκαταστασία, πόλεμος καὶ αἰχμαλωσία (with the notes).

It is instructive to observe how ζῆλος has been degraded in Christian ethics from the high position which it holds in classical Greek as a noble emulation (ἐπιεικές ἐστιν ὁ ζῆλος καὶ ἐπιεικῶν Arist. *Rhet.* ii. 11), so that it is most frequently used in a bad sense of quarrelsome opposition. Compare especially Clem. Rom. §§ 4, 5. Similar to this is the degradation of εὐτραπελία (Eph. v. 4 contrasted with Arist. *Eth. Nic.* ii. 7, iv. 14) and the exaltation of ταπεινοφροσύνη (e.g. 1 Pet. v. 5 compared with Arist. (?) *Eth. Eudem.* iii. 3 cited by Neander *Pfl. u. Leit.* ii. p. 759).

κατὰ ἄνθρωπον] '*with merely human motives or feelings*': i.e. your walk in life conforms to a merely human standard. Compare Rom. iii. 5, 1 Cor. xv. 32, Gal. i. 11, iii. 15. The expression is confined to the Epistles of this group. The preposition denotes the measure or standard.

(c) *Paul and Apollos human instruments merely* (iii. 4—23).

4. ἐγὼ μὲν, ἕτερος δὲ] Observe the irregular position of the particles μὲν and δὲ, which correspond logically though not grammatically. On the omission of St Peter's name here, see the note on i. 12.

ἄνθρωποί ἐστε] '*are ye not mere men?*' 'Is not the divine principle— the principle of love and unity—obliterated in you?' The word is much more forcible than σαρκικοί, the reading of the Textus Receptus introduced from ver. 3 above, and links on better with the foregoing κατὰ ἄνθρωπον. The distinction of meaning between ἄνθρωπος, the lower, and ἀνήρ, the higher aspect of man, would be as present to St Paul's mind, as it would to that of a Greek of the classical age. See Xen. *Anab.* vi. 1. 26 ἐγώ, ὦ ἄνδρες, ἥδομαι μὲν ὑπὸ ὑμῶν τιμώμενος, εἴπερ ἄνθρωπός εἰμι, Philostratus *Vita*

Apoll. i. 7. 4 τοὺς ἐν τῇ χώρᾳ ἀνθρώπους ὑμῶν δὲ ἀνδρῶν ὄντων, i. 19. Ἄνθρωπος is equivalent to the Heb. אדם and ἀνήρ to איש, as in the LXX. of
Is. ii. 9, v. 15, xxxi. 8.

5. **τί οὖν...τί δέ**] 'Are Apollos and Paul then lords over God's
vintage, that you exalt them to party-leaders? No; they are but
servants.' Τί is the right reading both times, being much more emphatic
than τίς : it expresses greater disdain. 'As though Apollos or Paul
were anything.'

Ἀπολλώς, Παῦλος] This, the correct order, is perhaps to be explained
as a mark of respect to Apollos ; or it may be that St Paul here, as
elsewhere (e.g. iv. 10), picks up the last word from the preceding verse
first—'I am of Apollos, why what is Apollos?' and then adds 'and
what is Paul?' lest he should seem to exalt himself at the expense of
Apollos.

Ἀλλ' ἤ must be omitted on strong external testimony, though grammatically quite correct. This is one out of many instances where the
received text enfeebles the style of St Paul, by smoothing his abrupt-
nesses.

διάκονοι] '*mere servants,*' not leaders at all. The word is opposed to
the Great Master (ὁ Κύριος), Who is mentioned just below.

δι' ὧν] i.e. the instruments only, not the objects of your faith ; 'per quos,
non in quos,' as Bengel says. Therefore do not pin your faith on them.

ἐπιστεύσατε] '*ye were converted, ye accepted the faith.*' This use of the
aorist is common : see the note on 2 Thess. i. 10 πιστεύσασιν.

ἑκάστῳ] The construction is καὶ ἕκαστος (not ἐπίστευσεν but διηκόνει)
ὡς ὁ Κύριος ἔδωκεν αὐτῷ : comp. vii. 17, Rom. xii. 3. That the reference is
here to the teachers and not to the taught, appears from the following
words explaining the different ministrations assigned to each, ' I planted,
Apollos watered,' and from ἕκαστος below, ver. 8.

ὁ Κύριος] '*the Lord,*' 'the Master of the universe and of themselves';
opposed to οἱ διάκονοι. We have the same play upon the word, so to
speak, in Col. iii. 22, 23, where δοῦλοι is opposed to τοῖς κατὰ σάρκα κυρίοις,
and then immediately follows φοβούμενοι τὸν Κύριον and in the next
verse again τῷ Κυρίῳ Χριστῷ δουλεύετε. See also Eph. vi. 5—9. Κύριος,
which in Attic Greek is chiefly used for 'a master' with a technical legal
meaning, is in the N.T. the common word rather than δεσπότης, which
occurs comparatively seldom. On both words see Trench *N. T. Syn.*
§ xxviii.

6. **ἐγὼ ἐφύτευσα κ.τ.λ.**] This is entirely in accordance with the
account given in the Acts of the part taken by St Paul and Apollos
respectively in the foundation of the Church of Corinth : Acts xviii. 1—18
with regard to St Paul, xviii. 24—xix. 1 with regard to Apollos.

The Fathers put a very curious interpretation upon this passage : in
order to refer ἐπότιζεν to baptism they applied ἐφύτευσα to the work of
educating the catechumens. Thus Gregory Nyssen *c. Eunom.* ii. (p. 565)

φυτεύει μὲν διὰ τῆς κατηχήσεως ὁ ἀπόστολος, ποτίζει δὲ βαπτίζων ὁ Ἀπολλώς, Optatus, 'de pagano catechumenon feci : ille catechumenon baptizavit,' and Petilianus *ap.* Aug. iii. 53, and Augustine himself, *Epist.* 48. The interpretation is instructive, as showing a general fault of patristic exegesis, the endeavour to attach a technical sense to words in the N.T. which had not yet acquired this meaning.

ηὔξανεν] Observe the change of tense from the aorist ἐφύτευσα, ἐπότισεν, to the imperfect. 'God ever gave the increase,' this being a continuous and gradual process.

7, 8. The argument is as follows : 'Paul and Apollos are *nothing*: therefore you ought not to make them lords over you (ver. 7). Again, Paul and Apollos are *one thing*: therefore they ought not to be the occasion of dissension among you (ver. 8).' Every word, especially in these earlier chapters, is charged with meaning.

7. ὥστε] is explained by ἀλλ' ὁ Θεὸς ηὔξανεν. It is as if the Apostle had said, 'What are the planting and watering without the principle of growth? Therefore you ought not to regard the planter and waterer etc.' The contrast is implied in the adversative ἀλλά.

ἐστίν τι] For εἶναί τι see Gal. ii. 6, vi. 15, Acts v. 36, viii. 9.

ὁ αὐξάνων Θεός] i.e. τὰ πάντα ἐστι. Notice the order : 'but He that giveth the increase, which is God.'

8. ὁ φυτεύων δὲ] The particle either marks the opposition to ὁ αὐξάνων Θεός which has just preceded, or introduces the second application 'but again.'

ἕν εἰσιν] '*are one thing,*' i.e. 'are working for one and the same end, are part of the same administration : and therefore ought not to be the cause of divisions.' Observe how their independence is sunk in the form of the expression (ἕν).

ἕκαστος δὲ] Here the particle is corrective : 'though they are one, yet they will *each* severally etc.' Just as their individuality had been ignored in ἕν εἰσιν of the former clause, so now it is especially emphasized in this new aspect by ἕκαστος and by the repetition of τὸν ἴδιον, 'congruens iteratio, antitheton ad *unum*' Bengel.

9. Θεοῦ γάρ ἐσμεν συνεργοί] It is better to refer γὰρ to the first clause in the preceding verse and to treat ἕκαστος δὲ...κόπον as parenthetical. 'We are a part of one great scheme, for we are fellow-workers with God.' Observe the emphatic Θεοῦ—emphatic both from its position and from its repetition. All things are referred to Him.

συνεργοί] '*labourers together with God,*' '*fellow-labourers with God,*' as the E.V., not, as others take it, 'fellow-labourers in the service of God.' See note on 1 Thess. iii. 2, where the transcribers have altered the text in order to get rid of so startling an expression as 'fellow-workers with God.'

Θεοῦ γεώργιον, Θεοῦ οἰκοδομή ἐστε] The former of these metaphors has been already applied (*vv.* 6—8): and now the latter is expanded (*vv.*

10—17). Thus 'God's husbandry, God's building' is the link which connects the two paragraphs together. Of the two images γεώργιον implies the organic growth of the Church, οἰκοδομή the mutual adaptation of its parts. Οἰκοδομή is a later form of οἰκοδόμημα: see Lobeck *Phryn.* p. 481 sq., Buttm. *Gr.* § 121.

10. St Paul had hitherto dwelt on the metaphor of the husbandry; he now turns to that of the building. The former metaphor was best adapted to develope the essential unity of the work, the latter to explain the variety of modes in which the workmen might carry out the labour.

κατὰ τὴν χάριν τοῦ Θεοῦ] This is not a mere empty form of words. It is emphatic from its position. 'If I laid the foundation, I cannot take to myself the credit of the work. The honour is due to God.' St Paul is still dwelling on the same idea, which he brings out in the thrice repeated Θεοῦ of the preceding verse.

For the expression itself and for the emphatic position in which it is placed compare Acts xv. 11 ἀλλὰ διὰ τῆς χάριτος τοῦ Κυρίου 'Ιησοῦ πιστεύομεν σωθῆναι. Where it is necessary for him to speak of his work, he is careful to exclude boasting at the outset. Χάρις is the watchword of St Paul. It is the objective element, the divine counterpart, corresponding to the subjective element, the human correlative πίστις; cf. Eph. ii. 8 τῇ γὰρ χάριτί ἐστε σεσωσμένοι διὰ τῆς πίστεως. It is opposed to νόμος (Rom. vi. 14), as πίστις is to ἔργα.

σοφὸς] 'skilful,' the correct epithet to apply to proficiency in any craft or art. Cf. Arist. *Eth. Nic.* vi. 7 τὴν δὲ σοφίαν ἐν ταῖς τέχναις τοῖς ἀκριβεστάτοις τὰς τέχνας ἀποδίδομεν· οἷον Φειδίαν λιθουργὸν σοφὸν καὶ Πολύκλειτον ἀνδριαντοποιόν. The expression σοφὸς ἀρχιτέκτων occurs in Is. iii. 3.

θεμέλιον] The dictum of Moeris θεμέλια καὶ θεμέλιον οὐδετέρως, ἀττικῶς· θεμέλιοι καὶ θεμέλιος, κοινῶς (cf. Thom. Magister) is not borne out by its usage in extant passages. For an instance of the neuter in the κοινή see Acts xvi. 26, and of the masculine in Attic see Thucyd. i. 93. The singular masculine and neuter seem equally rare in Attic writers (no instances given in the common lexicons), though not uncommon in the κοινή (cf. e.g. Polyb. I. 40. 9, not cited in the lexx.). The word is properly an adjective and therefore when used in the masc. λίθος is understood. Cf. Aristoph. *Av.* 1137 γέρανοι θεμελίους καταπεπωκυῖαι λίθους.

ἔθηκα] the better supported reading, is more appropriate here. The more absolute τέθεικα 'I have laid' would savour somewhat of arrogance, and would better describe the office of God than of the human agent. See the note on κείμενον ver. 11.

ἄλλος δέ] The reference is not solely to Apollos, for he was only one out of many teachers who had built up the Corinthian Church. Cf. ἕκαστος δέ. At the same time, occurring as it does so soon after the mention of Apollos (ver. 6), it suggests the idea that St Paul feared that Apollos might not be quite free from blame : that he might have conceded too much to the cravings of the ears and intellect of the Corinthians.

πῶς ἐποικοδομεῖ] '*what is the character of the building he erects thereupon*'; including the character of the materials, which are specified afterwards, but not restricted to them. 'My caution,' says St Paul, 'has reference to the building up, for the superstructure may be built up in many ways (and therefore care is needed): but only one foundation is possible.'

St Paul refuses to conceive the possibility of any professedly Christian teacher laying any other foundation. The foundation is already laid for him. In exactly the same spirit he speaks of the impossibility of there being more than one Gospel in Gal. i. 6, 7 θαυμάζω ὅτι οὕτως ταχέως μετατίθεσθε...εἰς ἕτερον εὐαγγέλιον ὃ οὐκ ἔστιν ἄλλο κ.τ.λ. The word δύναται here must not be emptied of its meaning.

11. παρὰ τὸν κείμενον] '*besides that which lieth*,' stronger than τὸν τεθέντα which ἔθηκα (ver. 10) would lead us to expect, or even than τὸν τεθειμένον. The foundation is already laid, when the workman begins his work. Τὸν κείμενον asserts the position of the foundation stone to be absolutely independent of human interference.

St Paul is here inconsistent in his language only that he may bring out the truth more fully. He had before spoken of himself as a skilful architect. Now he says that no one could have done otherwise than he has done. He had before asserted that he had laid the foundation stone. Now he affirms that the foundation stone was already laid for him.

'Ιησοῦς Χριστός] The one only foundation stone is the personal Saviour, the historical Christ. Observe that it is not Χριστός alone—no ideal Christ—no theories or doctrines about Christ—not faith in Christ—but Jesus Christ himself, 'the same yesterday, to-day, and for ever' (Heb. xiii. 8).

Our Lord is here represented as the foundation stone (θεμέλιος), elsewhere the chief corner stone, ἀκρογωνιαῖος (Eph. ii. 20). He is the basis on which the Church rests, and the centre of her unity.

12.   In the passage which follows there seems to be a clear allusion to the prophecy of Malachi iii. 1 sq. ἐξαίφνης ἥξει εἰς τὸν ναὸν ἑαυτοῦ κύριος ...καὶ τίς ὑπομενεῖ ἡμέραν εἰσόδου αὐτοῦ...διότι αὐτὸς εἰσπορεύεται ὡς πῦρ χωνευτηρίου...καὶ καθιεῖται χωνεύων καὶ καθαρίζων ὡς τὸ ἀργύριον καὶ ὡς τὸ χρυσίον, iv. 1 διότι ἰδοὺ ἡμέρα ἔρχεται καιομένη ὡς κλίβανος καὶ φλέξει αὐτοὺς καὶ ἔσονται...οἱ ποιοῦντες ἄνομα καλάμη καὶ ἀνάψει αὐτοὺς ἡ ἡμέρα ἡ ἐρχομένη, i.e. the fire shall purify the nobler materials, the silver and gold, and consume the baser material, the stubble. The application of the metaphor of the 'fire' and the 'day' here however is somewhat different.

εἰ δέ τις] i.e. but on the other hand the character of the superstructure may vary, and these varieties will be made manifest.

χρυσίον κ.τ.λ.] i.e. durable materials as gold, silver and costly stones, or perishable materials as wood, hay and stubble. The words go in threes, of a palace on the one hand, of a mud hovel on the other. The idea of splendour however seems to be included in the first triad. The structure is at once a palace adorned with gold and silver and precious stones no less than a palace firmly built of gold and silver and costly marbles. Tibull. iii. 3. 16 'Quidve domus prodest Phrygiis innixa columnis, Aurataeque trabes, marmoreumque solum?'

Χρυσίον, ἀργύριον, which represent the right reading here, differ from χρυσός, ἄργυρος (gold and silver simply) in signifying gold or silver made up in some way, as in coins, plate etc. The λίθοι τίμιοι are perhaps 'costly marbles.' Perhaps however 'precious stones, jewels' may be meant, and the description here is not intended to apply to any actual building, but to an imaginary edifice of costly materials as the New Jerusalem. Cf. Rev. xxi. 18, 19 καὶ ἡ πόλις χρυσίον καθαρὸν...οἱ θεμέλιοι τοῦ τείχους τῆς πόλεως παντὶ λίθῳ τιμίῳ κεκοσμημένοι. The LXX. use of the expression appears to vary between these two meanings. Thus in 2 Sam. xii. 30 τάλαντον χρυσίου καὶ λίθου τιμίου it is employed of a king's crown, in 1 Kings x. 2, 2 Chron. ix. 1, 9 of the Queen of Sheba's gifts. In other passages (1 Kings x. 11, 2 Chron. ix. 10) it seems to refer to marbles. Cf. also Ezek. xxvii. 12, 22 and esp. Dan. xi. 38.

ξύλα, χόρτον, καλάμην] A hovel of which the supports would be of wood, and the hay and straw would be employed either to bind the mud or plaster together, or to thatch the roof. Compare Seneca *Ep.* xc. 10, 17 'Culmus liberos texit...non quaelibet virgea in cratem texuerunt manu et vili obleverunt luto, deinde stipula aliisque silvestribus operuere fastigium?'

The question is raised here whether 'the building' represents 'the body of believers,' or 'the body of doctrine taught.' In favour of the first view is the direct statement Θεοῦ οἰκοδομή ἐστε (ver. 9): in favour of the second, the whole context, which certainly has some reference to the character of the teaching. Perhaps we should say that neither is excluded, that both are combined. The building is the Church as the witness of the truth. Thus it is the doctrine exhibited in a concrete form.

From the metaphor is derived the use of οἰκοδομή (-μεῖν -μία -μησις) in the sense of 'instruction,' 'edification.' This meaning seems not to occur in the LXX., and probably not in the classical writers. Indeed in the New Testament it is not found out of St Paul with the exception of Acts ix. 31 (for in Acts xx. 32 it occurs in a speech of St Paul); and therefore the prevalence of this metaphor of 'edification' is probably due to the influence of his phraseology. See on 1 Thess. v. 11.

The idea of an allusion in the whole passage to the conflagration of Mummius is too far fetched to commend itself.

13. ἑκάστου κ.τ.λ.] The apodosis is framed, as if the protasis had

run otherwise—εἴτε τις ἐποικοδομεῖ χρυσίον κ.τ.λ....εἴτε ξύλα κ.τ.λ. 'whether the superstructure has been raised of durable or of perishable materials.'

τὸ ἔργον] The plural τὰ ἔργα is frequently used in a special sense of buildings, or 'works' as we say. That sense is less defined in the singular, but there may perhaps be a tinge of it here. Cf. e.g. Thuc. i. 90.

ἡ ἡμέρα] '*the day.*' See the notes on 1 Thess. v. 2, 4.

ὅτι ἐν πυρὶ ἀποκαλύπτεται] The idea of manifestation, which is faintly involved in ἡμέρα, having been more definitely insisted upon in φανερὸν γενήσεται and δηλώσει, the *manner* of this manifestation is declared : 'it is revealed in fire'—a reference to Malachi l.c. Cf. also 2 Thess. i. 8.

ἐν πυρὶ] The idea of fire here is the connecting link between the idea of illumination which has hitherto prevailed and that of burning which now takes its place. By its destructive property the fire will test the stability of the work, purifying the better material and consuming the baser. The application is thus to a certain extent different from that in Malachi l. c.

ἀποκαλύπτεται] For this use of the present see the note on 1 Thess. v. 2 ἔρχεται, and to the references there given add Luke xvii. 30.

ἑκάστου τὸ ἔργον] may either be the accusative case after δοκιμάσει, this being the more idiomatic construction ; or on the other hand a suspended nominative. Rom. xii. 2 εἰς τὸ δοκιμάζειν ὑμᾶς τί τὸ θέλημα is in favour of the nominative here ; but a single passage should not weigh much, and the order of the words is against this construction.

αὐτὸ] Though omitted in the T.R., αὐτὸ is probably genuine, the weight of authority slightly preponderating in its favour. It is taken by Meyer closely with πῦρ 'the fire itself,' but it is not easy to see the force of the expression. Rather should it be considered as referring to ἑκάστου τὸ ἔργον, the pronoun being added by a pleonasm not uncommon in the N. T. 'The fire shall test it.' This idiomatic use will account for its omission. Similar omissions of the pleonastic pronoun occur in some MSS. on Matt. ix. 27, xxvi. 71, Luke viii. 27, xvii. 7. In other passages the stumbling block is removed by altering the form of the sentence.

14. μένει] It is a question whether this verb is present or future. Though the future would accord with the following κατακαήσεται, yet on the other hand the present is the more forcible here, the notion of permanence being better expressed by it. Compare John viii. 35, xii. 34, 1 Cor. xiii. 13 for μένειν in this tense.

15. ζημιωθήσεται] '*shall be mulcted of his reward,*' sc. τὸν μισθὸν understood from the previous verse. Cf. Deut. xxii. 19, Exod. xxi. 22, where ζημιοῦν is used with an accusative of the fine inflicted. The idea can be illustrated by 2 Joh. 8 ἵνα μὴ ἀπολέσητε ἃ ἠργασάμεθα ἀλλὰ μισθὸν πλήρη ἀπολάβητε.

αὐτὸς δὲ] opposed to μισθόν. His reward shall be lost, but his person shall be saved.

οὕτως δὲ ὡς διὰ πυρός] '*but only as one passing through fire is saved*' : i.e. with such a narrow escape. 'Prope ambustus evaserat' Livy xxii. 35. Much has been built on this passage. The Romish doctrine of purgatory has been supposed to be supported by it. But we must not press οὕτως ὡς as though the expression necessarily implies any actual fire. It is used equally to express a fact and a similitude. Thus in 1 Cor. iv. 1 οὕτως ἡμᾶς λογιζέσθω ἄνθρωπος ὡς ὑπηρέτας Χριστοῦ it expresses a fact, they were ministers; on the other hand in 1 Cor. ix. 26 οὕτως πυκτεύω ὡς οὐκ ἀέρα δέρων it introduces a metaphor. But the context decides the meaning to be metaphorical here. From beginning to end we cannot treat any part as literal to the exclusion of the rest (the ξύλα, χόρτος, καλάμη). There is no stopping at one point. If any further argument were needed, it would be found in the fact that a moral and not a physical agency is obviously required here. It would be rash to deny that St Paul conceived of the Lord appearing amidst an actual flame of fire: but the outward appearance is only the symbol of a spiritual power. Thus the light which accompanies the Lord's appearing is a symbol of that light which He will shed on the thoughts and deeds of all men, the revelation of the hidden things of darkness: the flame of fire, which surrounds Him, betokens the powerful agency which consumes the inefficient work, and spares only the substantial labour. Here St Paul sees the thing symbolized in the symbol. See the notes on 1 Thess. iv. 16, 17.

Διὰ πυρὸς is here local, not instrumental; cf. e.g. Rom. xv. 28 δι' ὑμῶν εἰς Σπανίαν, and see Winer § 51, p. 452. For it is clearly an allusion to the proverbial expression of 'passing through fire.' This expression is equally common in classical Greek (compare Eur. *Andr.* 487 διὰ πυρὸς ἐλθεῖν, Eur. *Electr.* 1182 διὰ πυρὸς μολεῖν) and in the Old Testament. See Is. xliii. 2, Ps. lxv. 12 διελθεῖν διὰ πυρός, Zech. xiii. 9 διάγειν διὰ πυρός, and for similar phrases Zech. iii. 2 ὡς δαλὸς ἐξεσπασμένος ἐκ πυρός, 1 Pet. iii. 20 διεσώθησαν δι' ὕδατος. There is therefore no idea of purifying 'by means of fire' implied in the passage here. It simply denotes a hairbreadth escape.

That the Apostle does not intend any purgatorial fire by this expression will appear from the following considerations. (1) Fire is here simply regarded as a destructive agency. There is no trace here of the idea of refining or purging, an attribute elsewhere given to it, as in Malachi iii. 3, though even there the prophet seems to speak of purging the whole nation by destroying the wicked, not of purging sin in the individual man. (2) The whole image implies a momentary effect and not a slow, continuous process. The Lord shall appear in a flash of light and a flame of fire. The light shall dart its rays into the innermost recesses of the moral world. The flame shall reduce to ashes the superstructure raised by the careless or unskilful builder. The builder himself shall flee for his life. He shall escape, but scorched and with the marks of the flame about him.

16. **οὐκ οἴδατε**] The warning and the metaphor seem to come in somewhat abruptly, but there is a link of connexion, for ναὸς is only a definition of the previous metaphor οἰκοδομή (ver. 9). The building has now become a temple. Compare Eph. ii. 20—22, where we have the same transition, first the building (ἐποικοδομηθέντες), then that building defined as a temple (εἰς ναὸν ἅγιον), lastly that temple described as the permanent abode (εἰς κατοικητήριον) of God in the spirit. Here ναὸς is more immediately suggested by the passage of Malachi which the Apostle has in his mind throughout, the temple there being one of the leading ideas (Mal. iii. 1).

ναὸς Θεοῦ] '*God's temple,*' not 'a temple of God.' The Apostle is speaking of the community, not of the individual Christian. There is an allusion in these verses to the dissensions which are a corrupting of God's temple. The metaphor is not from the many temples of the heathen, but from the one temple of Jerusalem. So Philo *Monarch.* ii. 1 (II. p. 223 *ed.* Mangey) προενόησε δὲ ὡς οὔτε πολλαχόθι οὔτ᾽ ἐν ταὐτῷ πολλὰ κατασκευασθήσεται ἱερὰ δικαιώσας ἐπειδὴ εἷς ἐστι Θεὸς καὶ ἱερὸν εἶναι μόνον.

οἰκεῖ] The ναός, the inward shrine or sanctuary, was regarded as the abode of the deity (from ναίειν 'to dwell'). Of course this was the case with heathen deities, but in a certain sense it was also true of the temple at Jerusalem; for though God 'dwelleth not in temples made with hands' (Acts xvii. 24), yet the symbol of His presence, the Shechinah, was there. Hence St Luke (xi. 51) calls the inner temple the οἶκος, where another evangelist has ναὸς (Matt. xxiii. 35). Observe however that, in the case of the Christian community, the word is appropriate not because the image of the deity was there, as in heathen temples, nor the symbol, as in the Jewish temple, but because the Spirit of God was the Indweller.

17. **φθείρει, φθερεῖ**] The same word is studiously kept to show that the offender is requited in kind. Compare Acts xxiii. 2, 3 ἐπέταξεν τύπτειν αὐτοῦ τὸ στόμα...Τύπτειν σε μέλλει ὁ Θεός, where we must recollect that St Paul is speaking. The same English word then ought to have been preserved at all hazards in the A. V. For the metaphor compare Ign. *Eph.* § 16 μὴ πλανᾶσθε, ἀδελφοί μου, οἱ οἰκοφθόροι βασιλείαν Θεοῦ οὐ κληρονομήσουσιν ,κ.τ.λ., following immediately after § 15 πάντα οὖν ποιῶμεν ὡς αὐτοῦ ἐν ἡμῖν κατοικοῦντος, ἵνα ὦμεν αὐτοῦ ναοί.

A comparison with vi. 19 is instructive. Here it is a subtle and disputatious spirit, there moral impurity, which violates the temple of the Spirit. The two passages together condemn the leading vicious tendencies of the Corinthian character.

18. **δοκεῖ**] '*seemeth to himself.*' This is the usual (though perhaps not the universal) sense of δοκεῖν in St Paul: comp. vii. 40, viii. 2, x. 12, xiv. 37 etc.

ἐν τῷ αἰῶνι τούτῳ] The idea is not temporal, but ethical, moral: the mundane order of things as opposed to the eternal, the heavenly.

19. ὁ δρασσόμενος κ.τ.λ] '*he that seizeth the wise*'; a quotation from Job v. 13, the only quotation from Job in the N.T. The Apostle however translates from the Hebrew himself, substituting two more forcible expressions for the LXX. ὁ καταλαμβάνων σοφοὺς ἐν τῇ φρονήσει αὐτῶν. St Paul's rendering of עָרַם by πανουργία is the more correct, as the adjective עָרוּם is generally translated πανοῦργος in the LXX.

The words, it will be observed, are the words of Eliphaz, but they are appropriated because of their intrinsic truth. Compare Gal. iv. 30, where the language of Sarah is cited as Scripture (ἡ γραφή), and Matt. xix. 5, where apparently the words of Adam are quoted as the voice of God.

20. καὶ πάλιν] Taken from the LXX. of Ps. xciv. (xciii.) 11, τῶν σοφῶν however being substituted for τῶν ἀνθρώπων. Here the LXX. follows the Hebrew more closely, but 'there seems to be a reminiscence of the original in the next words ἐν ἀνθρώποις' (Stanley).

διαλογισμοὺς] '*the reasonings*,' '*thoughts*': not 'the disputations.' This is the sense of the word in the original and therefore is decisive for us here, besides being the usual meaning of διαλογισμοὶ in the N.T. See the note on Phil. ii. 14.

21. ἐν ἀνθρώποις] i.e. 'in human teachers,' returning to what he has said in i. 31.

πάντα γὰρ ὑμῶν ἐστίν] The whole universe, as it were, lies at the feet of the true disciple of Christ. Compare Rom. viii. 28, where the same idea is expressed in not quite such strong language. This mode of speaking is perhaps borrowed from Stoic phraseology; but though the Stoics certainly talked in this way, the application is different. Zeno (*ap.* Diog. Laert. vii. I. 25) may say καὶ τῶν σοφῶν δὲ πάντα εἶναι, Cicero (*Acad.* ii. 44) 'omnia, quae ubique essent, sapientis esse,' Seneca (*de Benef.* vii. 2, 3) 'emittere hanc dei vocem Haec omnia mea sunt'; but though the Stoic and Christian phraseology may be the same, how striking the real contrast of sentiment! Instead of assigning all virtues to the wise, it is just to the wise that St Paul denies them. They belong, so to speak, to the fools (οἱ μωροί). Again, instead of assigning this universal dominion to the isolation of self, he bestows it upon the negation of self, the absorption or incorporation of self in Christ (ἐν Χριστῷ). All things are the believer's; but they are only his, in so far as he is Christ's, and because Christ is God's. See *Philippians*, p. 304 sq.

22. Παῦλος, Ἀπολλώς, Κηφᾶς] He begins with the human teachers. 'They *all* belong to you, they are your slaves; you each individually take one of them as a party-leader, but they are *all* yours.' He starts from this, as being the point at issue: and then he goes on, 'Indeed the whole universe, the whole order of things is yours.' Here κόσμος is best taken by itself, the rest hanging together in pairs. 'Whether life or death.' Again an exhaustive division, but this time with reference to the subjective state. Life and death are antagonistic to each other, are

mutually exclusive; yet either state ministers alike to the good of the faithful. Compare Rom. viii. 38, Phil. i. 21, and for ἐνεστῶτα, μέλλοντα see the note on Gal. i. 4.

23. ὑμεῖς δὲ Χριστοῦ] 'But this mastery of the universe is only yours by virtue of your incorporation in Christ, your participation in His sovereignty.'

Χριστὸς δὲ Θεοῦ] It is not the human but the divine nature of Christ to which the Apostle alludes. This interpretation is necessary for the proper understanding of the Nicene Creed; necessary for the preservation of the Unity of the Godhead, while confessing the divinity of Christ. Compare St John xvii. 7, 8, 21—23.

CHAPTER IV

Human preferences worthless: the divine tribunal alone final
(iv. 1—5).

1. οὕτως] The adverb does not go with what precedes 'this being so,' 'therefore'; but is to be taken closely with ὡς : comp. iii. 15, ix. 26, 2 Cor. ix. 5, Eph. v. 33. The order of the words seems imperatively to demand this, because otherwise we can give no account of the position of ἡμᾶς, which then becomes the principal word in the sentence. Eph. v. 28 οὕτως ὀφείλουσιν καὶ οἱ ἄνδρες ἀγαπᾶν τὰς ἑαυτῶν γυναῖκας ὡς τὰ ἑαυτῶν σώματα has a very different order and force. 'So ought the husbands also to love their wives as their own bodies.' If οὕτως be taken as the principal word and joined with ὡς, ἡμᾶς falls at once into insignificance, as the sense demands.

οἰκονόμους] '*stewards of the mysteries,*' i.e. teachers of the revealed truths. The church is the οἶκος (1 Tim. iii. 15), God the οἰκοδεσπότης (Matt. xiii. 52), the members the οἰκεῖοι (Gal. vi. 10, Eph. ii. 19, where see the notes). See also especially the notes on οἰκονομίαν Col. i. 25, Eph. i. 10.

2. ὧδε] This reading has the vast preponderance of evidence. The same change into ὁ δὲ has been made in Luke xvi. 25, where it is quite impossible to connect with the previous sentence, as the reading ὁ δὲ would require. Compare also Rev. xiii. 18, xvii. 9. Ὧδε never has any other than a local sense in the N.T., 'here,' 'in this matter'; but it must be taken with what follows, as is distinctly done by the principal versions (Vulg. Pesh. Memph.).

λοιπὸν κ.τ.λ.] '*for the rest, it is required* (generally the force of ζητεῖν) *that a man be found trustworthy*' (passive, see *Galatians*, p. 155).

3. ἐμοὶ δὲ κ.τ.λ.] '*but to me it amounts to the smallest of all matters that I should be examined by you or by man's day.*' For εἰς after εἶναι in the sense of 'it comes to' compare vi. 16 ἔσονται...εἰς σάρκα μίαν. Somewhat different is the expression in Col. ii. 22 ἅ ἐστιν εἰς φθορὰν ' destined to,' where see the note. On the technical sense of ἀνακρίνειν here see above on ii. 15.

ἀνθρωπίνης ἡμέρας] The A. V. somewhat boldly translates 'man's judgment'; but the word is put here because it is in opposition to ἡ ἡμέρα of iii. 13 'the Lord's day.' The meaning is 'by any day fixed by man.' The idea of a day as implying judgment is common in Hebrew, and would be directly assisted by such expressions as 'diem dicere,' 'to fix a day for judgment.' Compare the English 'daysman,' which contains the same idea (Wright's *Bible Word Book* s. v.).

4. οὐδὲν γὰρ κ.τ.λ.] '*for though I know nothing against myself, yet.*' It is important to see exactly what the Apostle's meaning is. It is simply a hypothetical case. 'For supposing I am conscious of no guilt in myself, yet am I not thereby justified.' The most saintly of men are the most conscious of guilt in themselves, and St Paul would be the last to make an absolute statement to the contrary. The sentence means 'on the supposition that I am not conscious, though I am.' Other instances of the second sentence qualifying the first are (1) Rom. vi. 17, where the force of the passage is 'Thanks be to God that though we were slaves to sin, we have obeyed,' (2) Matt. xi. 25 'that while thou hast concealed these things from the wise and prudent, thou hast revealed them' etc., and (3) John iii. 19, where it is not true to say that the judgment consisted in the fact of the light coming into the world, but, light having come into the world, the judgment is this that men loved darkness rather than light. Here then the sentence is put as a pure hypothesis.

'I know nothing by myself' is simply an archaism: compare Cranmer's letter to Henry VIII. quoted in Wright's *Bible Word Book*, 'I am exceedingly sorry that such faults can be proved by the queen.' For the idea cf. Horace *Epist.* i. 1. 61 'nil conscire sibi, nulla pallescere culpa.'

ἀλλ' οὐκ] Comp. Ign. *Rom.* 5 ἀλλ' οὐ παρὰ τοῦτο δεδικαίωμαι, a reminiscence of this passage.

5. πρὸ καιροῦ] i.e. 'do not therefore anticipate the great judgment (κρίσις) by any preliminary investigation (ἀνάκρισις), which must be futile and incomplete.'

ὁ Κύριος] There seems to be here a secondary allusion to the technical sense of κύριος as the properly constituted authority, e.g. Plato *Legg.* viii. p. 848 C κύριος ἔστω τῆς νομῆς, Arist. *Pol.* ii. 9 (p. 1270 *ed.* Bekker) κύριος εἶναι κρίσεων μεγάλων, ii. 11 (p. 1273) ἀλλὰ κύριοι κρίνειν εἰσί. See also the note on iii. 5 and cf. vii. 22.

ὃς καὶ φωτίσει κ.τ.λ.] i.e. 'Who will reveal all the facts, bring all the evidence to light; thus superseding the necessity of this human ἀνάκρισις; and will make manifest the counsels of men's hearts, and then shall his due praise accrue to each one from God.' Ὁ ἔπαινος is 'the praise due to him,' whether small or great, whether much or none. Compare Rom. ii. 29 οὗ ὁ ἔπαινος οὐκ ἐξ ἀνθρώπων ἀλλ' ἐκ τοῦ Θεοῦ, where the force of the article is lost in the A. V.

(d) Contrast between the self-satisfied temper of the Corinthians
and the sufferings and abasement of the Apostles (iv. 6—21).

6. ταῦτα δὲ κ.τ.λ.] 'But though I have spoken only of Paul and
Apollos, you must not suppose that the remarks refer to these solely
or chiefly. I used the name of Paul and Apollos: but I alluded especially
to others'—the Judaizing factions doubtless, with whom probably the
party-spirit, as such, was strongest.

μετεσχημάτισα] 'I transferred by a figure to myself and Apollos, that
taking us as an illustration ye might learn not to exceed what is written
in scripture.'
We find from both Greek and Latin writers that σχῆμα (schema) was
used at this time especially (and almost exclusively) to imply a rhetorical
artifice, by which, either from fear or respect or some other motive, the
speaker veiled the allusion to individuals under an allegory or a feigned
name or in any other way. Thus Quintilian says (ix. 2) 'Jam ad id genus
...veniendum est in quo per quandam suspicionem, quod non dicimus
accipi volumus...quod et supra ostendi jam fere solum schema a nostris
vocatur et inde controversiae figuratae dicuntur.' It appears therefore
that this sense of a 'covert allusion' had almost monopolized the meaning
of schema in Quintilian's day: compare Martial iii. 68. 7 'schemate nec
dubio sed aperte nominat illam.' Another Latin term equivalent to
'schema' was 'figura.' Suetonius Dom. 10 'occidit Hermogenem Tar-
sensem propter quasdam in historia figuras,' and this explains the
'controversiae figuratae' above. St Paul therefore says, 'I have applied
these warnings to myself and Apollos for the purpose of a covert allusion,
and that for your sakes, that ye may learn this general lesson.'

ἐν ἡμῖν] 'in our case,' 'by our example,' i.e. 'by this μετασχηματισμὸς to
ourselves.'

μὴ ὑπὲρ ἃ γέγραπται] 'not to go beyond what is written in scripture' ;
apparently a proverb, or at any rate in a proverbial form ; hence its
elliptical dress : compare Terence Andr. I. 1. 61 'id arbitror Adprime in
vita esse utile ut ne quid nimis.' The insertion of φρονεῖν after μὴ in the
Textus Receptus illustrates the tendency to smooth down these ellipses
of St Paul by insertions: see v. 1 ὀνομάζεται, xi. 24 κλώμενον, and the notes
on 2 Thess. ii. 3 ὅτι, 1 Cor. i. 26 οὐ πολλοί, 31 ἵνα καθὼς γέγραπται.
Passages in the Apostle's mind would doubtless be those quoted by him
on i. 19, 31, iii. 19, 20.

φυσιοῦσθε] For the present indicative after ἵνα comp. Gal. iv. 17 ἵνα
αὐτοὺς ζηλοῦτε with the note. It is conceivable however that in both
these cases we have a dialectic form of the conjunctive of verbs in -οω.

7. τίς γάρ σε διακρίνει ;] 'for who is he that maketh a difference in
thee ?' 'who differentiates thee from another?'

8. The Apostle bursts out in impassioned irony. 'You, it appears, are
to be exalted by the Christian dispensation. You are eager to seize all

the advantages, to aim at all the elevation ; but you will leave to us all the hard work, all the indignities, all the sufferings.   It is a very easy thing to claim all the privileges of your calling.'

κεκορεσμένοι] An allusion probably to Deut. xxxi. 20 καὶ φάγονται καὶ ἐμπλησθέντες κορήσουσι καὶ ἐπιστραφήσονται ἐπὶ θεοὺς ἀλλοτρίους, comp. Deut. xxxii. 15.   They are filled and (as the Apostle implies) have waxed wanton.

ἐπλουτήσατε, ἐβασιλεύσατε] The aorists, used instead of perfects, imply indecent haste.   Here we meet with Stoic phraseology once more : see the note on iii. 21.

συμβασιλεύσωμεν] For their triumph, supposing it to be genuine, would be his triumph also.   They were his στέφανος καυχήσεως.   Genuine however it was not: this is the force of the aorist after ὄφελον without ἄν.

9.   δοκῶ γὰρ] 'As it is, so far from being kings, we are the refuse of society.   For, I fancy, God exhibited us, the Apostles, last of all as condemned criminals : for we were made a spectacle to the whole world, aye to angels and men.'

τοὺς ἀποστόλους] He adds the words not to claim this position for himself alone.

ἀπέδειξεν] a technical word here, like the Latin 'edere' (Suet. *Aug.* 45 'edere gladiatores,' Livy xxviii. 21 'munus gladiatorium ').   'He brought us out in the arena of this world's amphitheatre.'   We have the same metaphor in xv. 32 ἐθηριομάχησα.   Tertullian (*de pudic.* 14) takes up the idea 'velut bestiarios.'

ἐσχάτους] '*last of all*,' i.e. to make the best sport for the spectators. The Apostles were brought out to make the grand finale, as it were.   The reference to ἔσχατοι would be to the prophets and martyrs under the Old Covenant (Heb. xi. 33 sq., esp. *vv.* 39, 40).

ἐπιθανατίους] '*condemned criminals.*'   In this sense Dionysius of Halicarnassus, speaking of the Tarpeian Rock, says (*A. R.* vii. 35) ὅθεν αὐτοῖς ἔθος βάλλειν τοὺς ἐπιθανατίους.

θέατρον]   The Greek word may mean (1) the place, (2) the spectators, (3) the actors in the spectacle, or (4) the spectacle itself.   The last meaning is the one used here and is the rarest (Hesych. θέατρον· θέαμα ἢ σύναγμα).

καὶ ἀγγέλοις]   Καὶ is not exclusive of what went before, but singles out the ἄγγελοι for special attention.   Compare ix. 5 οἱ λοιποὶ ἀπόστολοι καὶ οἱ ἀδελφοὶ τοῦ Κυρίου καὶ Κηφᾶς, Acts i. 14 σὺν γυναιξὶν καὶ Μαριάμ.   For the angels as interested spectators of man's doings see xi. 10, 1 Tim. v. 21.

12.   ἐργαζόμενοι]   He had done this at Corinth before (Acts xviii. 3) ; he was doing it at Ephesus when he wrote (Acts xx. 34).

13.   δυσφημούμενοι]   A rare word, and like γυμνιτεύομεν, ἀστατοῦμεν above and περικαθάρματα, περίψημα below, a ἅπαξ λεγόμενον in the N. T. Hence the change in many MSS. to the common word βλασφημούμενοι. It occurs however in 1 Macc. vii. 41

περικαθάρματα] '*sweepings, offscourings.*'   This is the primary meaning of the word. But the Apostle is carrying on the metaphor of ἐπιθανατίους above. Both περικαθάρματα and περίψημα were used especially of those condemned criminals of the lowest classes who were sacrificed as expiatory offerings, as scapegoats in effect, because of their degraded life. It was the custom at Athens to reserve certain worthless persons who in case of plague, famine or other visitations from heaven, might be thrown into the sea, in the belief that they would cleanse away, or wipe off, the guilt of the nation. Hence they were called κάθαρμα. The word sometimes corresponds to φαρμακοί, those slaves who were sacrificed for the good of the state, as being too vile to live (see Hermann *Griech. Alterth.* Gottesdienst, § 60). Though the simple form is more common, περικάθαρμα occurs in Epictetus (iii. 22. 78) of Priam ὁ πεντήκοντα γεννήσας περικαθάρματα, see also Prov. xxi. 18 περικάθαρμα δικαίου ἄνομος.

τοῦ κόσμου, πάντων] These genitives refer to the people both from whom and for whom the lives are sacrificed.

περίψημα] On this word see the note on Ign. *Eph.* 8. It is not uncommon in the writings of the sub-apostolic age (Ign. *Eph.* 8. 18, *Ep. Barn.* 4, 6).

15. παιδαγωγούς] See the note on Gal. iii. 24.

17. ἔπεμψα] Probably a little before the letter, as xvi. 10 seems to imply. The aorist however is not decisive, nor is the notice in Acts xix. 22. Timothy appears not to have reached Corinth. On his movements at this time and those of Titus see *Biblical Essays*, p. 273 sq. 'The Mission of Titus to the Corinthians' (especially p. 276 sq.).

21. ἐν ῥάβδῳ] The Hebraism is the more natural, as it is an O.T. phrase, 1 Sam. xvii. 43 σὺ ἔρχῃ ἐπ᾽ ἐμὲ ἐν ῥάβδῳ, 2 Sam. vii. 14, xxiii. 21, Ps. ii. 9, lxxxviii. 32. The Apostle offers the alternative: shall he come as a father or as a παιδαγωγός?

CHAPTER V

ii. THE CASE OF INCEST, v. 1—vi. 20.

(a) *The incest denounced: the offender to be cast out of the Church* (v. 1—13).

1. We have come now to the main pivot of the letter, the leading motive of the Apostle in writing it. The Second Epistle likewise arises altogether out of this case and the way in which the Corinthians received St Paul's rebuke.

Who then was St Paul's informant? Possibly the household of Chloe (i. 11), but more probably Stephanas and his household mentioned in xvi. 15 sq. For we notice an evident anxiety to shield them from the displeasure of the Corinthians. Hence the suppression of the informants' names here. But this is pure conjecture.

The connexion of this chapter with what precedes is twofold : (1) the condemnation of their vanity, involving the contrast between the spiritual pride of the Corinthians and the state of their Church, comp. iv. 18, 19 with v. 2 ; and (2) the character of his intended visit, should it be made in love or not, comp. iv. 18, 19, 21 with v. 3.

ὅλως] '*altogether*,' '*most assuredly*': almost equivalent to πάντως, 'prorsus.' That ὅλως bears this sense in the N. T. appears from vi. 7, xv. 29, Matt. v. 34, the only passages where the word occurs. It is not a common meaning in itself, but is found in classical writers also, e.g. Plato *Philebus* 36 B ἀλγοῦνθ' ὅλως ἢ χαίροντα, Arist. *Top*. Θ. 1. p. 152 l. 24 *ed.* Bekker κἂν ὅλως χρήσιμον ᾖ.

ἀκούεται] '*is reported*,' i.e. is commonly known to exist : ἐν ὑμῖν to be connected with ἀκούεται rather than with πορνεία.

πορνεία] The context enables us to form some idea of what the crime was. (1) It was a lasting, not a momentary relation. This is inferred, not, as some take it, from πράξας (ver. 2) or κατεργασάμενον (ver. 3), but from ἔχειν (ver. 1). It might have been concubinage or marriage. (2) The former husband and father was still living : see 2 Cor. vii. 12 τοῦ ἀδικηθέντος. (3) There had been a divorce or separation. The crime is called πορνεία, not μοιχεία. (4) As no censure is uttered on the woman in either Epistle, it may be inferred that she was not a Christian.   Thus she was one of 'those without,' whom God would judge (ver. 13).

ἥτις οὐδὲ] On this ellipse see iv. 6 above.   If a word had to be supplied, ἀκούεται would be preferable to ὀνομάζεται of the Textus Receptus ; but probably nothing so definite was intended.   'Ονομάζεται comes apparently from Eph. v. 4.

ἔθνεσιν] The heinousness of this form of sin among the Gentiles is well illustrated from Cicero *pro Cluentio* v. 14 'nubit genero socrus...o mulieris scelus incredibile, et praeter hanc unam...inauditum.'   See other passages given in Wetstein *ad loc.*   We may well ask how was this crime possible?   It was probably due to the profligacy of the Corinthian Church, but it may be accounted for in another way.   The Mosaic Law was very stringent on this point (Lev. xx. 11, Deut. xxii. 30).   But some of the Rabbis had invented a subterfuge to escape its stringency.   They allowed such a connexion in the case of a proselyte.   He had, as it were, they said, undergone a new birth ; he had thus been taken out of his old relationships, and thus this intercourse was allowable (so Rabbi Akibah).   It is quite possible that some subterfuge of this kind may have had its influence in excusing this crime to the man himsel and to the church.

2.   ὑμεῖς πεφυσιωμένοι στέ] 'You vaunt your higher wisdom, you are proud of your spiritual gifts, you are puffed up ; while this plague-spot is eating like a canker at the vitals of the church.'   The ὑμεῖς prepares us for the following ἐγὼ μὲν (ver. 3).

ἐπενθήσατε] '*ye ought rather to have put on mourning,*' i.e. when it came to your ears.   Observe the change of tenses.   'Επενθήσατε is more than ἐλυπήθητε.   It involves the idea of the outward exhibition of humiliation and grief, and is especially used of funerals : see Matt. ix. 15 and Gen. l. 10 ἐποίησε τὸ πένθος τῷ πατρὶ αὐτοῦ.   'Ye should have clothed yourselves with sackcloth : ye should have humbled yourselves before God.'

τὸ ἔργον τοῦτο πράξας] This is the reading, not ποιήσας, which is weaker and less technical ; comp. ἐν τῷ πράγματι 1 Thess. iv. 6 (with the note).   Πράξας brings out the moral aspect of the deed.   The whole expression is a sort of euphemism.

3.   ἐγὼ μὲν γάρ] '*for I for my part.*'   He contrasts his feelings with theirs.

ἀπὼν] '*albeit absent,*' i.e. 'notwithstanding my absence, while you on the spot condoned the offence.'   The ὡς of the Textus Receptus is to be left out before ἀπών.   It enfeebles the sense, and manuscript evidence is against it.   For παρὼν δὲ τῷ πνεύματι comp. Col. ii. 5.

ἤδη κέκρικα ὡς παρὼν] '*have already decided as though I were present.*'   The proper punctuation is to put a colon after παρών, and to take τὸν κατεργασάμενον as a prospective accusative, governed by παραδοῦναι and resumed in τὸν τοιοῦτον.   For κέκρικα absolutely 'I am resolved,' a frequent use, see Pliny *Ep.* i. 12 'dixerat sane medico admonenti cibum

κέκρικα,' Epict. ii. 15 etc.   The form of the sentence can be illustrated
by Acts xv. 38 Παῦλος δὲ ἠξίου τὸν ἀποστάντα ἀπ' αὐτῶν ἀπὸ Παμφυλίας καὶ
μὴ συνελθόντα αὐτοῖς εἰς τὸ ἔργον μὴ συνπαραλαμβάνειν τοῦτον, where we
seem almost to hear the Apostle's own words.

οὕτως]   The word aggravates the charge, 'under circumstances such
as these.'

4.   Of all the various possibilities enumerated by Meyer, the connexion
of words suggested by the order appears most natural and best accords
with the sense.   By it ἐν τῷ ὀνόματι τοῦ K. 'I. is to be taken with συναχθέν-
των ὑμῶν, and σὺν τῇ δυνάμει τοῦ K. ἡμῶν 'I. with παραδοῦναι.   Thus the
inauguration of the proceedings, the gathering together, is in the name of
the Lord, in accordance with Matt. xviii. 20; the action as the result is
accompanied by His power.   In the picture given, an imaginary court is
formed and the Apostle's spirit is represented as presiding.   That some
such a tribunal was actually held and the offender condemned appears
from 2 Cor. ii. 6, where we learn the result in 'the penalty inflicted by the
majority.'   The bearing of this passage on the question of direct apostolic
supervision in the earliest stage of the Church's history is drawn out in
Philippians, p. 198.

5.   παραδοῦναι τὸν τοιοῦτον] '*that we* (or *ye*) *should deliver so rank an
offender as this.*'   He is described in the same vague way in 2 Cor. ii. 6, 7.
The Apostle forbears to give his name.

τῷ Σατανᾷ]   We have just the same expression in 1 Tim. i. 20.   Satan
is here spoken of as the instrument of physical suffering, just as in
2 Cor. xii. 7 St Paul's own malady is described as ἄγγελος Σατανᾶ.   This
delivery to Satan is by virtue of the extraordinary power given to St Paul
as an Apostle, and has its analogy in the cases of Ananias and Sapphira
(Acts v. 1 sq.) and Elymas (Acts xiii. 8 sq.).   He alludes to this power
again in 2 Cor. xiii. 10.   That physical suffering of some kind is implied,
the purpose being remedial, appears from 2 Cor. ii. 6, 7, 1 Tim. i. 20,
2 Cor. xiii. 10 εἰς οἰκοδομὴν καὶ οὐκ εἰς καθαίρεσιν.   Thus the instrumentality
of Satan is used for a divine end.   Of the two forms, Σατᾶν and Σατανᾶς,
the first is the Hebrew word; the second, a Grecised form of the Aramaic,
is alone employed by St Paul: see on 1 Thess. ii. 18.

εἰς ὄλεθρον τῆς σαρκὸς]   Not merely a crushing of fleshly lusts, though
this is involved in the expression; but physical suffering also.

6.   τὸ καύχημα ὑμῶν] '*the subject of your boasting.*'   What St Paul
means is this: 'there is nothing in you worth boasting about, as long as
this plague-spot remains; all your intellectual insight is worth nothing, is
no matter of self-congratulation.'   For the contrast with καύχησις see the
notes on Gal. vi. 4, Phil. i. 26.

μικρὰ ζύμη]   On the application of this proverb see the note on Gal. v. 9,
where it occurs again.   That ζύμη here is not the sinner, but the sin or
sinfulness, appears from ver. 8.   Philo *de vict. off.* 6 (II. p. 256 *ed.* Mangey)
takes leaven as the symbol of inflation, pride (φυσηθεὶς ὑπ' ἀλαζονείας).

This idea however is not present to St Paul's mind here. Though pride is condemned in the context, yet the leaven here represents not the pride but the profligacy of the Corinthian Church. Elsewhere (*de congr. erud. gr.* 28 I. p. 542) Philo explains the metaphor otherwise τὸ μὴ οἰδεῖν καὶ ἀναζεῖν ταῖς ἐπιθυμίαις, which, he says, constitutes ἑορτὴ διανοίᾳ φιλάθλῳ.

ζυμοῖ] A various reading δολοῖ occurs both here and in Gal. v. 9, chiefly in western authorities. Hence Jerome (on Gal. l. c.) says 'male in nostris codicibus habetur modicum fermentum totam massam *corrumpit.*' The accusation of the Greeks against the Latins (see Mich. Cerul. in Tischendorf), that they read φθείρει, seems to be founded on a mistake. They retranslated 'corrumpit,' which was really a rendering, not of φθείρει, but of δολοῖ. Tertullian (*de pudic.* 13, 18, *adv. Marc.* I. 2) has 'desipit.'

7. **ἐκκαθάρατε**] A new turn is given to the metaphor, the mention of leaven suggesting the Paschal Feast. The reference is to the purging out the leaven on the eve of the Passover (Exod. xii. 15, xiii. 7). The word in Ex. xii. 15 (LXX.) ἀφανιεῖτε ζύμην is very strong, 'ye shall make it to vanish.' With what exactness this injunction was carried out appears from a passage in Chrysostom (p. 177 *ed.* Field μυῶν ὀπὰς περιεργάζονται, 'they even scrutinise mouse-holes to see that there is no leaven in them'), and is confirmed by statements quoted in Lightfoot *H. H.* I. p. 953 and Edersheim *Temple*, p. 188. The passage in Zeph. i. 12 was considered to authorise a search with candles on this occasion.

νέον] On the distinction between νέος and καινὸς see the note on Col. iii. 10, and for the contrast between the old and the new, comp. also 2 Cor. v. 17, Eph. iv. 22 sq.

καθώς ἐστε ἄζυμοι] '*even as ye are unleavened,*' i.e. 'by the very terms of your Christian profession'; in other words, 'that ye may fulfil the idea of your being,—may be, as ye profess to be, καινὴ κτίσις.'

Vain attempts have been made to give ἄζυμοι the sense of 'eating unleavened bread.' These destroy the point of the image. There is a double application of the metaphor here. The Corinthians are (1) the φύραμα itself, the lump which is leavened (*vv.* 6, 7), (2) then they become the keepers of the festival (*vv.* 7, 8), and the Apostle characteristically passes from the one to the other. Examples of these sudden inversions of metaphors have already been given in the note on 1 Thess. ii. 7. So here the Apostle has turned the metaphor about to find some new lesson which he could draw from it.

καὶ γὰρ] '*for besides.*' Here another analogy is introduced. Not only is there a Christian putting away of the leaven, but also a Christian paschal sacrifice. The passage gains much by the omission (with the best authorities) of the words ὑπὲρ ὑμῶν, which blunt the point of the Apostle's reference. All we want here is the fact of the sacrifice.

τὸ πάσχά] '*the paschal lamb*': as frequently in the Gospels, Matt. xxvi.

17 φαγεῖν τὸ πάσχα, Mark xiv. 12 τὸ πάσχα ἔθυον...ἵνα φάγῃς τὸ πάσχα, comp. ver. 14, Luke xxii. 7, 11, 15.

ἐτύθη] 'was sacrificed' on the Cross. The A. V. loses the point by translating as a present or perfect. The reference is not to the passover as a type of Christ's sacrifice, but rather to this sacrifice under the figure of the Paschal Feast. It is not the old as signifying the new, but the Paschal Lamb of the new dispensation.

Χριστός] 'even Christ.'

8. ἑορτάζωμεν] 'let us keep perpetual feast.' Chrysostom grasps the point when he says (p. 175) ἑορτῆς ἄρα ὁ παρὼν καιρός...δεικνὺς ὅτι πᾶς ὁ χρόνος ἑορτῆς ἐστι καιρὸς τοῖς Χριστιανοῖς διὰ τὴν ὑπερβολὴν τῶν δοθέντων ἀγαθῶν. There is some resemblance to St Paul's language here in Philo de sacrif. Abel. et Cain. 33 (I. p. 184 sq.) τὸ τοίνυν φύραμα...ἡμεῖς ἐσμεν αὐτοί...μόνος δὲ ἑορτάζει τὴν τοιαύτην ἑορτὴν ὁ σοφὸς κ.τ.λ., but he is not speaking of the passover.

κακίας καὶ πονηρίας] 'malice and villainy.' Κακία is the vicious disposition, πονηρία the active exercise of it. The words occur together in Rom. i. 29. See Trench N. T. Syn. § xi. p. 37 sq. and the note on Col. iii. 8 κακίαν.

ἀληθείας] In the widest sense of the word: comp. John iii. 21 ὁ ποιῶν τὴν ἀλήθειαν. This exercise of truth extends throughout all the domain of moral life: see Eph. iv. 15 ἀληθεύοντες ἐν ἀγάπῃ 'holding the truth' i.e. speaking and doing the truth. We have parallel applications of the metaphor in the sub-Apostolic age: Ign. Magn. 10 (where it applies to the leaven of Judaism) ὑπέρθεσθε οὖν τὴν κακὴν ζύμην τὴν παλαιωθεῖσαν, καὶ ἐνοξίσασαν, καὶ μεταβάλεσθε εἰς νέαν ζύμην ὅς ἐστιν Ἰησοῦς Χριστός, Just. Mart. Dial. 14 p. 114 τοῦτο γάρ ἐστι τὸ σύμβολον τῶν ἀζύμων, ἵνα μὴ τὰ παλαιὰ τῆς κακῆς ζύμης ἔργα πράττητε κ.τ.λ., Clem. Hom. viii. 17 ὁ Θεὸς αὐτοὺς ὥσπερ κακὴν ζύμην ἐξελεῖν ἐβούλετο. For εἰλικρινίας see on Phil. i. 10 εἰλικρινεῖς.

It has been suggested with great probability that we have in this verse a hint of the season of the year when the Epistle was written. This was, we know, towards the end of the Apostle's stay at Ephesus, which place he hoped to leave about Pentecost (1 Cor. xvi. 8). It is thus probable that the Jewish Paschal Feast was actually impending. The natural way, however, in which the mention of the Passover arises here out of the proverb just quoted, deprives this suggestion of much of its force. Similarly a passage in the Second Epistle may have been suggested by the Feast of Tabernacles. The reference in 2 Cor. v. 1 sq. seems to be a comparison between the removal into their permanent dwellings after the destruction of the temporary booths, and our removal to a 'house not made with hands' after the destruction of 'our earthly house of the tabernacle.' If we follow the narrative in the Acts, we see that the Second Epistle would probably have been written about the time of the Feast of Tabernacles.

9. **ἔγραψα κ.τ.λ.**] '*I wrote unto you in my letter.*' The Apostle is reminded here of general instructions which he had sent them in a former communication, and in the spirit of which he asks them now to act. The expression imperatively demands the hypothesis of a previous letter. This necessity does not lie in the word ἔγραψα, which might stand equally in the beginning or middle of a letter as at the end: see the note on Gal. vi. 11 πηλίκοις ὑμῖν γράμμασιν ἔγραψα, where the question of the epistolary aorist is gone into and instances given, Philemon 19, 21 ἔγραψα, Col. iv. 8 ἔπεμψα with the notes, and *Biblical Essays*, p. 275 (note 1). In the *Martyrdom of Polycarp* for example immediately after the salutation occurs (§ 1) an epistolary aorist ἐγράψαμεν ὑμῖν, ἀδελφοί, τὰ κατὰ τοὺς μαρτυρήσαντας καὶ τὸν μακάριον Πολύκαρπον κ.τ.λ., giving the purport of the letter of which it is the opening sentence. But the theory of a previous letter is rendered necessary by the words ἐν τῇ ἐπιστολῇ, which are quite meaningless if applied to our extant Epistle. It is true that ἡ ἐπιστολή is a phrase used sometimes of the letter itself in which it occurs (Rom. xvi. 22, 1 Thess. v. 27, Col. iv. 16, and probably 2 Thess. iii. 14, see the notes on the last three passages); but in all these cases the expression occurs in a postscript, when the Epistle is considered as already at an end. These instances therefore are not to the point, and the same can be said of *Martyrdom of Polycarp* § 20 τὴν ἐπιστολὴν διαπέμψασθε, where the document is regarded as concluded. But we have no example of the phrase occurring in the middle of a letter as here. Nor is the case met by the theory propounded by Stanley of a postscript note consisting of 1 Cor. v. 9—13 subsequently incorporated in the middle of the Epistle. For apart from the awkwardness of this hypothesis, the whole passage hangs together in close connexion of thought: ver. 9 μὴ συναναμίγνυσθαι πόρνοις arising naturally out of the mention of the leaven in *vv.* 6—8, and vi. 1 κρίνεσθαι being directly suggested by the κρίνειν, κρίνετε of *vv.* 12, 13. These links would not exist, if that theory were true. The hypothesis of a previous letter is as old as the first Latin commentator Ambrosiaster, and is accepted by Calvin, Beza, Estius, Grotius, Bengel, Meyer and many others. It is likewise borne out by other expressions of St Paul to the Corinthians, viz. 2 Cor. vii. 8 εἰ καὶ ἐλύπησα ὑμᾶς ἐν τῇ ἐπιστολῇ, where the words cannot refer to the letter which he was inditing, but require a previous communication; and especially 2 Cor. x. 10, 11, where the acknowledgement of the Corinthians that his 'letters are weighty and powerful' together with his own reply 'Such as we are by letters when absent etc.' cannot be explained quite satisfactorily by the single extant Epistle written before this date. See the whole question of lost letters of St Paul treated in *Philippians*, p. 138 sq. There are extant two letters, one purporting to be from St Paul to the Corinthians, the other from the Corinthians to St Paul, both obviously spurious, but held as canonical by the Armenian Church (see Stanley *Corinthians*, p. 591 sq. and my note on vii. 1 below).

10. οὐ πάντως] 'assuredly I did not mean.' The πάντως qualifies the οὐ, not the οὐ the πάντως. This is at least an allowable meaning (probably the general meaning) in classical Greek, see Cope's Appendix to *Gorgias*, p. 139 sq., who however shows that οὐ πάνυ (we may extend the term to οὐ πάντως) need not necessarily mean 'not at all'; and it becomes still more prominent in Biblical Greek as coinciding with a common Hebraism (Mark xiii. 20, Acts x. 14, 1 Joh. ii. 21, Apoc. vii. 16 etc., and 1 Cor. i. 21 above). Compare *Clem. Hom.* xix. 9 καὶ ὁ Πέτρος, Οὐ πάντως· ὁρῶμεν γὰρ πολλοὺς τῶν ἀνθρώπων ἀγαθοὺς ὄντας, *Epist. ad Diogn.* 9 οὐ πάντως ἐφηδόμενος τοῖς ἁμαρτήμασιν ἡμῶν ἀλλ' ἀνεχόμενος, where it would be impossible to give the sentence the meaning that God was 'not altogether pleased' with sin. Taken by itself the passage before us is not decisive, and might imply 'it was not altogether my meaning'; but with the examples cited it is better to render it, as above, in the sense 'it was altogether not, assuredly not, my meaning': compare Rom. iii. 9.

ἢ τοῖς πλεονέκταις καὶ ἅρπαξιν ἢ εἰδωλολάτραις] Καὶ is the right reading. On the false interpretation of πλεονέκταις here to denote sins of sensuality see the note on Col. iii. 5. The καὶ connects πλεονέκταις with ἅρπαξιν, which together form one notion; εἰδωλολάτραις introduces another, though a kindred, idea, see Col. l. c. and Eph. v. 5.

εἰδωλολάτραις] Here again Stanley without sufficient reason attempts to put into this word a reference to sins of sensuality. The fact is there was a strong temptation for Christians living among heathen to play fast and loose with idolatrous rites. These rites might be licentious or not, but this further idea is not conveyed by the word itself. We have a prospective reference here to the discussion which is introduced subsequently (ch. viii.) upon εἰδωλόθυτα (see esp. x. 21 τραπέζης δαιμονίων). That this danger of idolatry even in the Christian Church was not an imaginary one appears from the warning given in 1 Joh. v. 21 τεκνία, φυλάξατε ἑαυτὰ ἀπὸ τῶν εἰδώλων.

The word εἴδωλον has a curious history. It originally means 'a phantom, shadow,' and so 'unreality' as opposed to genuine truth. This is the sense in which Bacon uses the word 'idols' in his *Novum Organum*, implying idle phantoms which lead men astray. It was then happily applied in the LXX. to false gods, as a translation, among other words, of the Hebrew אֱלִיל, 'nothingness.' In the next stage, the word was applied to anything used as a representation of these false gods, and thus had attached to it an idea the very reverse of its original meaning, viz. a tangible, material god as opposed to the Invisible God. The passage before us marks the first appearance of the compound εἰδωλολάτρης.

ἐπεὶ ὠφείλετε ἄρα] The imperfect is the correct reading both from a vast preponderance of textual authorities and from the sense. 'Ye ought to have done something, which has not been done,' is the meaning of the imperfect, 'ye ought to do something,' of the present. The ἄρα declares the ἐπεὶ to be conditional. 'Since in that case it would have been your duty, which it is not, to leave the world wholly.' See vii. 14 below, and comp. xv. 15 εἴπερ ἄρα.

11. νῦν δὲ] is ethical not temporal, 'as matters stand,' 'the world being what it is.' Comp. Rom. iii. 21, and esp. 1 Cor. vii. 14 ἐπεὶ ἄρα...νῦν δὲ, Heb. ix. 26 ἐπεὶ ἔδει...νυνὶ δὲ ἅπαξ. The misinterpretation of ἔγραψα (ver. 9) has been partly aided by taking νῦν in its primary temporal sense.

ἀδελφὸς ὀνομαζόμενος] 'called a brother,' but not really deserving the name: comp. Rom. ii. 17 Ἰουδαῖος ἐπονομάζῃ.

λοίδορος] Here again Stanley (on vi. 10) sees a reference to sins of sensuality; but there is no indication of any such connexion in the N. T., see esp. 1 Pet. iii. 9.

μέθυσος] This is an instance of the not unfrequent phenomenon of a word used first in a comic sense, which in later times becomes part of the common stock of language, having lost its original ludicrous character. This is what is meant by grammarians who say that in Attic the word is never applied to men but to women. Pollux vi. 25 ἡ δὲ γυνὴ μεθύση καὶ μεθύστρια παρὰ Θεοπόμπῳ τῷ κωμικῷ · ὁ γὰρ μέθυσος ἐπὶ ἀνδρῶν Μενάνδρῳ δεδόσθω, which we may illustrate from Meineke Comm. Fragm., Menander IV. p. 88 πάντας μεθύσους τοὺς ἐμπόρους ποιεῖ, quoted originally in Athen. x. p. 442 D. Thus it was originally 'tipsy,' rather than 'a drunkard'—Lucian Timon 55 μέθυσος καὶ πάροινος οὐκ ἄχρις ᾠδῆς καὶ ὀρχηστύος μόνον ἀλλὰ καὶ λοιδορίας καὶ ὀργῆς. Other examples of words casting off all mean associations in the later language are ψωμίζειν (1 Cor. xiii. 3) and χορτάζειν (Phil. iv. 12): see also other instances in Lobeck Phryn. p. 151 sq. The elevation of ταπεινοφροσύνη under Christian influence is noticed in the note on Phil. ii. 3.

12. τοὺς ἔξω] 'those outside the pale' of the Church: see on Col. iv. 5.

οὐχὶ κ.τ.λ.] Two points in the punctuation of this passage require a notice. (1) Is οὐχὶ to be taken separately 'nay, not so,' in which case κρίνετε would become an imperative? No; for (a) wherever οὐχὶ is so taken in the N. T., it is always followed by ἀλλά (Luke xii. 51, xiii. 3, 5, xvi. 30, Rom. iii. 27): (b) the sentence is not a direct answer to τί γάρ μοι κ.τ.λ. Οὐχὶ therefore is best taken with τοὺς ἔσω. (2) Is κρινεῖ to be read or κρίνει? The present tense is probably right, (a) because more suited to the context, preserving the parallelism better; (b) because more emphatic and more in accordance with usage, comp. vi. 2 κρίνεται, Rom. ii. 16, John viii. 50 ὁ ζητῶν καὶ κρίνων.

13. ἐξάρατε κ.τ.λ.] An adaptation of the command given Deut. xvii. 7 καὶ ἐξαρεῖτε τὸν πονηρὸν ἐξ ὑμῶν αὐτῶν, and repeated elsewhere (with variations ἐξαρεῖς, τὸ πονηρὸν) of sins akin to this (Deut. xxii. 21 sq.). On ἐξ ὑμῶν αὐτῶν Bengel remarks 'antitheton externos.'

CHAPTER VI

(b)   *The Corinthian brethren apply to heathen courts to decide
their disputes* (vi. 1—9).

1.   The close of the last paragraph suggests a wholly different subject.
The Apostle had incidentally spoken of the right and wrong tribunals for
judging offences against purity.   Hence he passes to the question of
litigation in heathen courts.

Τολμᾷ τις ὑμῶν πρᾶγμα ἔχων] 'Τολμᾷ grandi verbo notatur laesa
majestas Christianorum' says Bengel.   Πρᾶγμα is the proper technical
term for a lawsuit: for its forensic sense see the references in Meyer,
and compare the technical sense of 'negotium' and 'res.'

κρίνεσθαι] '*to go to law,*' as in Matt. v. 40 τῷ θέλοντί σοι κριθῆναι   The
propriety of the forensic terms used here by St Paul is noteworthy : it is
otherwise in Gal. iv. 1 sq., where see the notes.

τῶν ἀδίκων, τῶν ἁγίων] The word ἄδικοι is borrowed from Jewish
phraseology, just as δίκαιος was a faithful Israelite.   It is chosen here
rather than any other word, (1) because it enhances the incongruity of the
whole action of seeking justice at the hands of the unjust : (2) because of
the alliteration: see the note on Phil. ii. 2.   On the rabbinical prohibition,
which was based on Ex. xxi. 1, see Meyer, p. 163.

2.   τὸν κόσμον κρινοῦσιν]   A reminiscence of Wisdom iii. 7, 8 ἐν καιρῷ
ἐπισκοπῆς αὐτῶν ἀναλάμψουσιν...κρινοῦσιν ἔθνη καὶ κρατήσουσιν λαῶν, of the
souls of the righteous, which is decisive in favour of the future here :
compare for the idea Daniel vii. 22 τὸ κρίμα ἔδωκεν ἁγίοις ὑψίστου.   This
office the saints will hold by virtue of their perfected ἐπίγνωσις, their completed communion with the judgments of the Great Judge.   This is a necessary part of the ultimate triumph of good over evil.   Just as the faithful shall
reign with Christ as kings (2 Tim. ii. 12, Rev. xxii. 5), so shall they sit with
Him as judges of the world.   The thought is an extension of the promise
made to the Apostles (Matt. xix. 28, Luke xxii. 30): comp. Rev. xx. 4.

ἐν ὑμῖν] '*before you, among you,*' 'in consessu vestro.'   This is a
common use of ἐν when speaking of tribunals: see Aristides *de Socrat.* 1.

p. 128 ἐν ἡμῖν πρώτοις ὁ Φίλιππος ἐκρίνετο, Thuc. i. 53. 1 ἐν δικασταῖς, and other references given in Wetstein and Meyer.

κρίνεται] The present tense denotes the certainty of the event. With Him is no before and no after: see the note on 1 Thess. v. 2 ἔρχεται.

ἀνάξιοί ἐστε κ.τ.λ.] i.e. unworthy to sit in the most trivial tribunals.

κριτηρίων] The word κριτήριον is said by grammarians to have two meanings, (1) 'a tribunal, court of judicature' (so in the LXX. Dan. vii. 10, Judg. v. 10), (2) 'a trial'; but no passage quoted appears to demand this latter sense. Such instances as Lucian *in accus.* 25 οὐδὲν ἡγεῖται κριτήριον ἀληθὲς εἶναι can readily bear the meaning of a 'court of justice.' St Paul's injunction here is echoed in *Apost. Const.* ii. 45 μὴ ἐρχέσθω ἐπὶ κριτήριον ἐθνικόν.

3. μήτιγε] An elliptical sentence, 'let me not say,' and so, 'much more.' See the references collected in Winer § lxiv. p. 746 and Wetstein *ad loc.* It is frequent in the classics : e.g. Demosthenes *Olynth.* B. p. 24 οὐδὲ τοῖς φίλοις ἐπιτάττειν ὑπὲρ αὐτοῦ τι ποιεῖν, μήτιγε δὴ τοῖς θεοῖς.

βιωτικά] '*things of this life.*' The word occurs also in Luke xxi. 34 μερίμναις βιωτικαῖς, comp. *Clem. Hom.* i. 8 βιωτικὰ πράγματα, Marc. Anton. vi. 2 τῶν βιωτικῶν πράξεων. There is an important difference between βίος and ζωή. Ζωή signifies the principle of life, βίος the circumstances and accidents of life; thus ζωή is vita qua vivimus, βίος vita quam vivimus. With Aristotle βίος is the more important word of the two. He calls it λογικὴ ζωή : hence it follows that his conception of life was a low one. But when we come to the N. T., the principle of life is no longer physical but spiritual : accordingly ζωή is exalted, while βίος remains at its former level. In the N. T. ζωή is commonly, but not universally, used of the higher spiritual life, βίος is always employed of the lower earthly life, e.g. Luke viii. 14 τῶν ἡδονῶν τοῦ βίου, 2 Tim. ii. 4 ταῖς τοῦ βίου πραγματίαις, 1 Joh. ii. 16 ἡ ἀλαζονία τοῦ βίου, that is to say of the external concomitants of life. Thus βίος expresses the means of subsistence (Luke xv. 12, 30, xxi. 4, and 1 Joh. iii. 17, where it is contrasted with the ζωή of two verses earlier). For the contrast of the two words compare Origen *c. Cels.* iii. 16 περὶ τῆς ἑξῆς τῷ βίῳ τούτῳ ζωῆς προφητεύσαντος, *Clem. Hom.* xii. 14 τοῦ ζῆν τὸν βίον μεταλλάξαι. See also the note on Ign. *Rom.* 7.

4. τοὺς ἐξουθενημένους] Several modern commentators take the sentence as though καθίζετε were an indicative interrogative, and τοὺς ἐξουθενημένους ἐν τῇ ἐκ. equivalent to 'the heathen.' But apart from the awkwardness of the interrogative coming at the end of so long a sentence, this rendering is open to two serious objections : (1) the force of μὲν οὖν 'nay rather' is obscured, and equally so if we take μὲν merely to correspond to an unexpressed δέ, (2) τοὺς ἐξουθενημένους is a strong phrase to apply to the heathen without any further explanation. It appears best to render as the E. V., and to consider the clause to mean 'those possessed of high spiritual gifts are better employed on higher matters than on settling petty wrongs among you, and thus serving tables.' Compare

Origen *c. Cels.* iii. 29 *ad fin.* τίς γὰρ οὐκ ἂν ὁμολογήσαι καὶ τοὺς χείρους τῶν ἀπὸ τῆς ἐκκλησίας καὶ συγκρίσει βελτιόνων ἐλάττους πολλῷ κρείττους τυγχάνειν τῶν ἐν τοῖς δήμοις ἐκκλησιῶν ; and the Jewish dictum (*Sanhedr.* fo. 32 *a*) 'omnes idonei sunt ut judicent lites pecuniarias.'

5.   οὕτως] 'has it come to this that,' 'is it to such a degree true that?' The rendering of Meyer and others 'things being so' is less forcible.

ἔνι] '*is found*,' stronger than ἐστι : see on Gal. iii. 28.   Οὐδεὶς σοφὸς ὅς, i.e. 'no one with sufficient wisdom to.'

ἀνὰ μέσον τοῦ ἀδελφοῦ αὐτοῦ] '*to decide between his brothers.*' The sentence is much abridged : ordinary Hebraic usage would require at least the insertion of ἀδελφοῦ καὶ after ἀνὰ μέσον.   The word τοῦ ἀδελφοῦ αὐτοῦ conveys a reproach : 'must his brothers go before strangers?' This reproach is driven home in the next verse : 'not only this, but brother goes to law with brother.' Thus the very idea of brotherhood is outraged and a scandal caused in the sight of unbelievers.

7.   ἤδη] '*to begin with*,' i.e. prior to the ulterior question of the fitness of Gentile courts.   See Kühner II. p. 675, and comp. Xen. *Cyr.* iv. 1. 2 ἐγὼ μὲν ξύμπαντας ὑμᾶς ἤδη ἐπαινῶ.

μὲν] to be separated from οὖν.   It suggests a suppressed clause with δέ, which would have run somewhat in this vein, 'but ye aggravate matters by going before the heathen.'

ὅλως] '*altogether*,' i.e. 'before whomsoever they are tried'; or perhaps 'under any circumstances,' i.e. 'whatever the decision may be.'

ἥττημα ὑμῖν ἐστιν] '*it is a loss to you, a defeat.*' 'You trust to overreach, to gain a victory: it is really a loss, a defeat, before the trial even comes on.'   In Is. xxxi. 8 the word ἥττημα is equivalent to 'clades': in Rom. xi. 12 it is opposed to πλοῦτος : thus the two ideas given above can be predicted of it.

μεθ' ἑαυτῶν] '*with yourselves.*'   The Apostle does not say μετ' ἀλλήλων, for though the pronouns are often interchanged, the reciprocal ἑαυτῶν differs from the reciprocal ἀλλήλων in emphasizing the idea of corporate unity.   See the passage from Xen. *Mem.* (iii. 5. 16) quoted on Col. iii. 13.   Ἀλλήλων here would bring out the idea of diversity of interest, ἑαυτῶν emphasizes that of identity of interest : 'you are tearing yourselves to pieces.'

8.   ὑμεῖς] Emphatic : 'you, Christians though you are.'

9.   Θεοῦ βασιλείαν] The order, though unusual, is right here and adds to the force of the passage.   'God is essentially just : unjust men may inherit the kingdom of this world, but God's kingdom they cannot inherit.'   A similar transposition for the sake of emphasis occurs in Gal. ii. 6 πρόσωπον Θεὸς ἀνθρώπου οὐ λαμβάνει.

Their spirit, whether of sensuality or strife, is inconsistent with heirship in the kingdom of heaven (vi. 10, 11).

11. **ἀλλὰ ἀπελούσασθε**] '*but ye washed yourselves*' : a reference to baptism. They were voluntary, conscious, agents: comp. Acts xxii. 16 ἀναστὰς βάπτισαι καὶ ἀπόλουσαι τὰς ἁμαρτίας σου, where St Paul is narrating the circumstances of his own conversion.

ἡγιάσθητε] '*ye were consecrated.*' The word is not to be taken in the technical theological sense of sanctification ; but in that of e.g. 1 Cor. vii. 14 ἡγίασται γὰρ ὁ ἀνὴρ ὁ ἄπιστος ἐν τῇ γυναικί, comp. i. 2. This appears from the order of the words.

ἐδικαιώθητε] '*ye were justified,*' i.e. by incorporation into Christ. The verb is used in Rom. vi. 7 also in connexion with the initial entrance into the Church by baptism. We have put ourselves in a new position: we are justified not simply by imputation, but in virtue of our incorporation into Christ.

ἐν τῷ ὀνόματι, ἐν τῷ πνεύματι] There is a reference here to the external and to the internal essentials of baptism. Comp. Acts x. 48, xix. 5, 1 Cor. i. 13.

(c) *The distinction between license and liberty applied to sins of the flesh* (vi. 12—20).

12. The new subject arises out of the preceding. Certain members of the Corinthian Church defend their moral profligacy on the ground of Christian liberty. Such a contention seems to us extraordinary; but the glaring immorality of Corinth, where sensuality was elevated into a *cultus*, may partly account for it. It was thus difficult for converts to realize their true position, and they ran into the danger of extending the Pauline doctrine of ἀδιάφορα so as to cover these vital questions. The case of incest mentioned above obviously did not stand by itself (see 2 Cor. xii. 21): the sin of sensuality was the scourge of the Corinthian Church. In his reply the Apostle opposes the true principle of liberty to the false, the Christian to the heathen.

πάντα μοι ἔξεστιν] This is the principle pleaded by his opponents. The Apostle admits the principle, but qualifies it by the words ἀλλ' οὐ πάντα συμφέρει. The opponents then return to the charge; and again the Apostle replies ἀλλ' οὐκ ἐγὼ κ.τ.λ. This ἐγὼ points to a different person as being supposed to assert the principle. St Paul has an imaginary opponent before him. Not that St Paul denies the principle πάντα μοι ἔξεστιν: he himself asserts it quite as strongly. But the πάντα, he says, are πάντα ἀδιάφορα, and he disputes the application to sins of the flesh by examining this qualifying word.

What then are ἀδιάφορα? Two principles, he contends, are to be observed with regard to them: (1) scandal to others is to be avoided, (2) self-discipline is to be maintained. These are the main, though not the sole, considerations in the two replies; (1) οὐ πάντα συμφέρει, i.e. expedient especially with regard to their effect on others, (2) οὐκ ἐξουσιασθήσομαι ὑπό τινος, i.e. I shall not allow myself to be tyrannised over by any habit. This second idea therefore is the effect produced on one's own moral character by the weakening of self-discipline. In x. 23 the same maxim is urged in the same form: but there both συμφέρει and οἰκοδομεῖ refer to the effect produced on others, as the context seems to show (he is speaking of εἰδωλόθυτα); here the words are chosen so as to balance one aspect of the question with the other. Similarly, when the case of εἰδωλόθυτα is discussed at length (viii. 1—13), neither side is neglected : (1) οὐ συμφέρει (viii. 9—13), (2) οὐκ ἐξουσιασθήσομαι (viii. 1—8).

ἐξουσιασθήσομαι] The active ἐξουσιάζω occurs in Luke xxii. 25 with a genitive, the active in LXX. (Neh. ix. 37, Eccles. ix. 17, x. 4). The present however is the only place where the passive appears, and in fact the use must be regarded as a slight straining of the Greek language. As a general rule we only find the passive of verbs which in the active take an accusative after them; but this rule has numerous exceptions in later Greek : e.g. διακονεῖσθαι (Matt. xx. 28), δογματίζεσθαι (Col. ii. 20). The subtle paronomasia ἔξεστι, ἐξουσιασθήσομαι should be noticed: 'All are within my power; but I will not put myself under the power of any one of all things.'

13. These half-converted Gentiles mixed up questions which were wholly different in kind, and classed them in the same category; viz. meats and drinks on the one hand, and sins of sensuality on the other. We have traces of this gross moral confusion in the circumstances which dictated the Apostolic Letter (Acts xv. 23—29), where things wholly diverse are combined, as directions about meats to be avoided and a prohibition of fornication. It was not that the Apostle regarded these as the same in kind, but that the Gentiles, for whom the rules were framed, did so. St Paul here carefully separates the two classes. The cases are quite different, he says. *First,* as regards meats, there is a mutual adaptation, βρώματα and κοιλία, each made for the other and both alike perishable. *Secondly,* as regards fornication, we have on the contrary, the body not made for fornication but for the Lord: the body, again, not perishable but with an existence after death.

βρώματα] This may have here a threefold application. (1) To εἰδω-λόθυτα (chs. viii. ix.). (2) To the Mosaic distinction of meats. These had been abrogated for the Christian and he enjoyed liberty. (3) To certain ascetic prohibitions which appeared early in the Church, such as drinking no wine and eating no flesh (Col. ii. 16, 21 with the notes and *Colossians,* pp. 86 sq., 104 sq.). We have other traces of the same ascetic tendency at this time in Rom. xiv. 2 λάχανα ἐσθίει, and in ver. 21 of that chapter the Apostle deals with it on the principle laid down in this Epistle. Which thought then was uppermost in St Paul's mind here? The large space which the εἰδωλόθυτα occupy in the latter part of the Epistle points more especially to these, and the repetition of the same maxim (x. 23) in connexion with meats sacrificed to idols confirms this view. But there is no reason to suppose that he is alluding to them solely. There was certainly an appreciable section of Judaizers in the Corinthian Church, and possibly there were ascetic Essene tendencies also. To all these alike the maxim would apply.

καὶ ταύτην καὶ ταῦτα] The same argument is used in Col. ii. 20—22.

τὸ δὲ σῶμα κ.τ.λ.] The case, argues the Apostle, is different here. It is the body and the Lord which stand to each other in the same relation as the βρώματα and κοιλία. They are each for the other.

The argument depends upon the Christian doctrine of the resurrection of the body, and would be discussed more appropriately in connexion with ch. xv. Two remarks will suffice here. *First*, the idea of the resurrection of the body is in reality not a philosophical difficulty but a philosophical necessity to us. As far as we know of man, the union of the soul of man with an external framework is essential. We cannot conceive of man as not working through some such instrument. Hence the Christian doctrine commends itself to true philosophy. But, *secondly*, we must not suppose that the resurrection-body is like our present body. St Paul guards against this confusion (1 Cor. xv. 35 sq.); but it does add to the difficulty of most people that they cannot dissociate the idea of a body from the idea of flesh and blood. The resurrection-body need not have any particle the same as the present body. All we can say about it is that it must be a body which, if not imperishable, is at all events capable of constant renewal. Of its form, structure, size etc. we cannot form any conception. But we may affirm that it must be an external instrument through which the man acts, an instrument which has its position in space. Many of our difficulties arise from forgetting that St Paul carefully guards against any supposition that it resembles our material body. The κοιλία, with its eating and drinking, with its gratification of the senses, is perishable : the σῶμα will live on always.

The moral import of this doctrine of the resurrection of the body is sufficiently obvious. It was the fashion of the Platonists and Stoics to speak contemptuously of the body, but in Christian theology the body is glorified because destined to be conformed to Christ's glorified body (Phil. iii. 21). This moral aspect has had great influence in banishing such sins as the Apostle is contemplating here.

It is noticeable that these three verses (12—14) contain the germ of very much which follows in the Epistle: (1) the great principle which is to guide the Christian conduct, (2) the question of εἰδωλόθυτα involved in βρώματα, (3) the conflict with sensual indulgences, (4) the doctrine of the resurrection of the dead.

τῷ Κυρίῳ] The Apostle does not argue this point. It is an axiom which has its roots in the Christian consciousness. It is involved in the very profession of a Christian.

14. **καὶ τὸν Κύριον...καὶ ἡμᾶς**] corresponding to the *καὶ ταύτην καὶ ταῦτα* of the preceding verse. 'Ημᾶς 'and therefore our bodies,' for the body is a part of the man.

ἐξεγερεῖ] The manuscripts present some interesting variants : (1) *ἐξεγερεῖ* אCD³EKL f vulg. (but see below), Pesh. Harcl. Memph. Arm. Æth., Iren. (transl.), Tert. Archel. Method. Athan. etc., (2) *ἐξεγείρει* AD*PQ 37, 93 (but P 37, 93 *ἐξεγειρεῖ*) d e suscitat. (3) *ἐξήγειρεν* B 67 *am. fuld. harl.* suscitavit (but the confusion with suscitabit was easy). The choice must lie between the aorist and the future. If we prefer the former, we may compare Eph. ii. 6, Col. ii. 12, 13. This idea however, though strictly Pauline, is not the idea wanted here : for it is not the past resurrection of the spirit, but the future resurrection of the body, on which the argument turns, in accordance with other passages (as ch. xv. throughout, 2 Cor. iv. 14, Rom. viii. 11, 1 Thess. iv. 14). Still *ἐξήγειρεν* is not impossible in this connexion. The past spiritual resurrection might be regarded here as elsewhere, e.g. Rom. vi. 5, viii. 11, as an earnest and an initiation of the future bodily resurrection. But on the whole *ἐξεγερεῖ* is the more likely reading and has the best documentary support.

αὐτοῦ] The pronoun probably refers to Christ : comp. 1 Thess. iv. 14 *διὰ τοῦ Ἰησοῦ* (in 2 Cor. iv. 14 the right reading is *σὺν Ἰησοῦ*). We have both *δύναμις Θεοῦ* frequently, and *δύναμις Χριστοῦ* (e.g. 2 Cor. xii. 9). The use of *διὰ* here rather points to the mediation of Christ in our resurrection, but it cannot be considered as in any way decisive.

15. **μέλη Χριστοῦ**] The earliest application of this metaphor which plays so important a part in this and later Epistles.

ἄρας] Not as the A. V. 'take' (which would be *λαβών*), but *'take away.'* It is robbing Christ of what is His own. Αἴρειν 'tollere' is (1) either 'to take up,' e.g. Mark ii. 9 *ἆρον τὸν κράβαττόν σου*, Luke ix. 23 *ἀράτω τὸν σταυρὸν αὐτοῦ*, John xi. 40 *ἦραν οὖν τὸν λίθον*: or (2) 'to take away,' e.g. Luke vi. 29 *αἴροντός σου τὸ ἱμάτιον*, xi. 52 *ἤρατε τὴν κλεῖδα τῆς γνώσεως* ; but never simply 'to take.'

μὴ γένοιτο] On this expression see Gal. ii. 17, vi. 14. Like *οὐκ οἴδατε* (of this and the following verse) it is confined to this chronological group of St Paul's Epistles, where it occurs thirteen times ; but it is found also in Luke xx. 16.

16. **τῇ πόρνῃ**] The article marks the fact that she is considered no longer as an individual, but as the representative of a class. Compare John x. 12 *ὁ μισθωτός*, 1 Tim. iii. 2, Tit. i. 7 *ὁ ἐπίσκοπος* etc.

ἔσονται γὰρ κ.τ.λ] Taken from Gen. ii. 24. Several points require notice here. (1) As to the text. St Paul follows the LXX., for the Hebrew text has not the words *οἱ δύο* nor have the older Targums. The additional phrase however appears, not only in the LXX., but also in the Samaritan

Pentateuch, the Targum of Jonathan, the Peshito, in Philo (*Leg. Allegor.* § 14, I. p. 75 ed. Mangey, *de Gigant.* § 15, I. p. 272, *Lib.* I *in Genes.* § 29. 22 ed. Aucher), and invariably in the N. T. quotations (Matt. xix. 5, Mark x. 8, Eph. v. 31), and perhaps in some Rabbinical quotations also (e.g. possibly *Beresh. Rab.* 18). Still no such variant is at present known to exist in any Hebrew manuscript (see De Rossi *Var. Lect. Vet. Test.* I. p. 4). But from this great number of independent authorities which contain the words we are disposed to think that they had a place at some time in the Hebrew text. (2) As to the interpretation. It is impossible to weaken the meaning of ἔσονται εἰς here so as to make it imply less than the Hebrew idiom ל היו 'they shall become': see esp. Matt. xix. 5, 6 ἔσονται οἱ δύο εἰς σάρκα μίαν, where our Lord's comment is explicit ὥστε οὐκέτι εἰσὶν δύο ἀλλὰ σὰρξ μία. (3) As to the application. In Genesis l.c. the words are used of man and wife, the legitimate connexion of male and female. But, so far as regards the question at issue, there is no difference between the two cases. What applies to the one applies to the other also, for as Athanasius says ἐν γὰρ καὶ τοῦτο κἀκεῖνο τῇ φύσει τοῦ πράγματος. (4) Lastly, as to the authority assigned to the passage. What are we to understand by φησίν? Is ὁ Θεὸς to be supplied or ἡ γραφή? To this question it is safest to reply that we cannot decide. The fact is that, like λέγει, φησὶν when introducing a quotation seems to be used impersonally. This usage is common in Biblical Greek (λέγει Rom. xv. 10, Gal. iii. 16, Eph. iv. 8, v. 14: φησὶν Heb. viii. 5, 2 Cor. x. 10 v. l.), more common in classical Greek. Alford, after Meyer, objects to rendering φησὶν impersonal here, as contrary to St Paul's usage. But the only other occurrence of the phrase in St Paul is 2 Cor. x. 10, where he is not introducing scripture, but the objections of human critics and of more than one critic. If then φησὶν be read there at all, it must be impersonal. The Apostle's analogous use of λέγει points to the same conclusion. In Eph. v. 14 it introduces a quotation which is certainly not in scripture, and apparently belonged to an early Christian hymn. We gather therefore that St Paul's usage does not suggest any restriction here to ὁ Θεὸς or ἡ γραφή. But we cannot doubt from the context that the quotation is meant to be authoritative. In the original the words are Adam's; but Adam is here the mouthpiece of God. Compare Gal. iv. 30 where Sarah's words are adopted in the same way, and the quotation from Job v. 13 given above (ch. iii. 19).

17. ἐν πνεῦμα] The union is an inner spiritual union (Eph. iv. 4). The converse truth appears in Eph. v. 30.

18. πᾶν ἁμάρτημα] i.e. 'every other sin.' Even drunkenness and gluttony are in a certain sense ἐκτὸς τοῦ σώματος.

εἰς τὸ ἴδιον σῶμα] which is unnatural. See Eph. v. 29.

19. ἢ οὐκ οἴδατε] Of the ten occasions on which this expression is found in this Epistle, six occur in this chapter. The others are iii. 16, v. 6, ix. 13, 24. It is used only twice elsewhere by St Paul

(Rom. vi. 16, xi. 2) and then in an Epistle of this group : but it appears in James iv. 4.

The same truth is enunciated in iii. 16 in almost the same words : see the note there. The difference in application is mainly twofold: *first*, here the expression τὸ σῶμα ὑμῶν means 'the body of each one of you' individually, while in iii. 16 the whole Christian brotherhood is regarded collectively as the shrine; *secondly*, there the sins attacked are hatred, strife and vainglory, here sensuality.

20. ἠγοράσθητε γὰρ τιμῆς] '*for ye were bought with a price.*' The aorist shows that the ransom was paid once for all: compare vii. 23, where the metaphor is developed. In the ordinary form of the metaphor, Christ's blood is a λύτρον (Matt. xx. 28, Mark x. 45) or ἀντίλυτρον (1 Tim. ii. 6); and the process of redemption, ἀπολύτρωσις (Rom. iii. 24, Eph. i. 7, Col. i. 14, Heb. ix. 15), or simply λύτρωσις (Heb. ix. 12). It is thus a ransom from slavery, from captivity, the purchase-money of our freedom. Here on the other hand it is spoken of as τιμή, that is to say, a transference to another master, the purchase by which a new owner acquires possession of us, by which we become his slaves. In Rom. vi. 18, 22 the two ideas are combined, ἐλευθερωθέντες δὲ ἀπὸ τῆς ἁμαρτίας ἐδουλώθητε τῇ δικαιοσύνῃ...ἐλευθερωθέντες ἀπὸ τῆς ἁμαρτίας δουλωθέντες δὲ τῷ Θεῷ.

δή] The word is hortatory, 'now,' 'verily,' 'surely'; not 'therefore' as the A. V. renders it, which would be οὖν in N. T. language. For this use of δή compare Luke ii. 15 διέλθωμεν δή, Acts xiii. 2 ἀφορίσατε δή μοι, xv. 36 ἐπιστρέψαντες δὴ κατηγγείλαμεν.

ἐν τῷ σώματι ὑμῶν] So the Apostle's genuine words end, as his argument requires. The addition of the T. R. καὶ ἐν τῷ πνεύματι ὑμῶν ἅτινά ἐστιν τοῦ Θεοῦ is condemned by the vast preponderance of ancient authority. But how came it to be added? I venture to think from some ancient liturgical use of the passage, thus: V. δοξάσατε δὴ τὸν Θεὸν ἐν τῷ σώματι ὑμῶν. R. καὶ ἐν τῷ πνεύματι ὑμῶν ἅτινά ἐστιν τοῦ Θεοῦ. The response would then be incorporated in the text by scribes who remembered the versicle. The influence of liturgical forms on the reading of the N. T. appears in the doxology added to the Lord's Prayer in Matt. vi. 13, and the baptismal formula in Acts viii. 37. The early and curious Latin reading 'glorificate et portate' (or 'tollite') found in g, in Tertullian, Cyprian, Lucifer and the Vulgate, may perhaps be traced to a similar source, or may have arisen from a reading ἄραγε (comp. Acts xvii. 27, Matt. vii. 20, xvii. 26) which was confused with ἄρατε: see Reiche *Comm. Crit.* I. p. 165, and the reading of Methodius, ἀρά γε δοξάσατε (δὴ omitted), which goes far to justify this suggestion. Chrysostom (*in* 1 *Cor. hom.* xviii. § 2, p. 153 E) reads δοξάσατε δὴ ἄρατε τὸν Θεόν, if his text is to be trusted (Saville read ἄρα τε); but lower down (*hom.* xxvi. § 1, p. 227 D) δοξάσατε δὴ ἄρα τὸν Θεόν, which probably represents more nearly his true text in both passages.

CHAPTER VII

3. MARRIAGE, vii. 1—40.

(*a*) *To marry or not to marry.* (*b*) *Duties of those already married.*
(*c*) *Advice to the unmarried, the widows, the separated* (vii. 1—11).

1. Περὶ δὲ ὧν ἐγράψατε] Here we have the first reference to the letter written by the Corinthians to St Paul. This letter must obviously have reached him later than the date of the Apostle's letter to the Corinthians to which he alludes in v. 9: otherwise it would have received an answer in that letter. We may form a fairly complete idea of the contents of this letter of the Corinthians. It raised questions relating to marriage under various circumstances (see vii. 1); it contained a reference to εἰδωλόθυτα, for we may infer from the way in which that topic is introduced that they had consulted St Paul about it (comp. viii. 1 περὶ δὲ τῶν εἰδωλοθύτων with vii. 25 περὶ δὲ τῶν παρθένων: it is as though the Apostle were taking in detail the heads of their letter); it consulted him as to the conduct of women in church (xi. 2 shows that the connecting link is an allusion to something which the Corinthians had related); it raised the question of spiritual gifts. This also may be inferred from the form of the introduction of this topic in xii. 1 (περὶ δὲ τῶν πνευματικῶν). We may suppose that the letter was brought by Stephanas, Fortunatus and Achaicus, who by their presence 'supplemented the deficiency' of the Church (xvi. 17 τὸ ὑμέτερον ὑστέρημα οὗτοι ἀνεπλήρωσαν), that is, explained more fully the condition of things by word of mouth.

As I have already said (see on v. 9), there is extant in Armenian a spurious correspondence consisting of an epistle from the Corinthians to St Paul and of an epistle from St Paul to the Corinthians. These are included in the canon of the Armenian Church, and the translations which we have are made from the Armenian. They are given in Stanley's *Corinthians* (ed. 4) p. 593 sq. in the English translation made in 1817 from the Armenian by Lord Byron assisted by Aucher. See also Meyer, p. 6 and Fabricius *Cod. Apocr. N. T.* p. 918 sq. It is remarkable that though this correspondence consists of two letters, and though St Paul mentions just two such letters, yet there is no analogy between the two sets of letters.   There is no reason at all for believing that the forger intended to supply the lack; or at least, if his work was suggested by the notices in 1 Corinthians, he has certainly performed it in a most slovenly way.

Let us first take the spurious letter addressed by the Corinthians to St Paul.   It begins in the name of Stephanus and the elders with him, no doubt intended to represent Stephanas and his companions (1 Cor. xvi. 17).   They write to consult St Paul about certain heretics who are troubling the Church.   Of these Simon (probably Magus) and Cleophas are mentioned by name.   The heresies are described and St Paul's advice asked.   The Apostle is supposed to receive the letter at Philippi and to be a prisoner at the time.   Thus the topics have nothing in common with the topics of the real letter of the Corinthians, and the circumstances are different, for the real letter must have been received by the Apostle at Ephesus.

The so-called letter from St Paul to the Corinthians exhibits just the same divergencies from the real facts of the case.   The one topic which we know for certain that St Paul's letter must have contained is the direction quoted in 1 Cor. v. 9 μὴ συναναμίγνυσθαι πόρνοις.   There is however no reference whatever to this subject.   The spurious letter of St Paul is an answer to the spurious letter to St Paul.   The writer meets the case of the heresies by a declaration of the true doctrine of the Resurrection, and concludes with a warning against false teachers. Thus not only are the topics quite dissimilar from what we might have expected, but the order of the letters is reversed.   The lost letter of the Corinthians was later in time than the lost letter of St Paul, whereas in the forged correspondence the letter of the Corinthians comes first in chronological order.

Yet there is no flagrant anachronism in the Epistles.   The heresies might very well be those of the end of the first or the beginning of the second century.   In *Ep. Paul. ad Cor.* 30 'but these cursed men hold the doctrine of the serpent,' there is probably an allusion to the Ophites; but I have given elsewhere reasons for supposing that this form of heresy was closely connected with that combated by St Paul in the Pastoral Epistles, and if so it must have been widely prevalent in the latter half of the first century.   See the excursus in *Biblical Essays* (p. 411 sq.), where this question is fully discussed.   This spurious correspondence then was an early forgery probably of the second century, but a very obvious forgery.   Its genuineness however is maintained by Rinck (*das Sendschr. d. Kor. an d. Apost. Paul.* Heidelb. 1823) who is answered by Ullmann in the *Heidelb. Jahrb.* 1823.

καλὸν] '*good,*' '*right,*' comp. ver. 26; not 'convenient.'   There is no qualification in the word itself; the qualifications are added afterwards in the context. They are twofold. (1) With what limitations is celibacy good? These limitations are given in verses 2 and 9. Thus it is not good in all cases. (2) For what reasons is it good? These appear in vv. 26, 32 sq. Celibacy therefore is only so far better than marriage in proportion as it fulfils these conditions. It may not however fulfil them in the case of particular men ; and so with them it is not better than marriage, but the reverse. Further, the passage must not be taken alone, but in connexion with what the Apostle says elsewhere, Eph. v. 22—33, where he exalts marriage as a type of the union of Christ with the Church. In Heb. xiii. 4 τίμιος ὁ γάμος ἐν πᾶσιν κ.τ.λ. the first clause is an imperative 'let marriage be respected among all,' as appears from the true reading of the next sentence πόρνους γάρ ; it can therefore only be adduced as an argument here by a misinterpretation. In the passage before us καλὸν is not employed for καλὸν μέν: the statement is made absolutely and the limitation διὰ δὲ κ.τ.λ. comes in as an after consideration.

2. **τὰς πορνείας**] The phrase hints at the profligacy of all kinds which prevailed in the dissolute city (2 Cor. xii. 21).

ἕκαστος, ἑκάστη] An incidental prohibition of polygamy. Such a prohibition was by no means unnecessary at this time, when polygamy was recklessly encouraged by the Jewish rabbis : see Justin Martyr, *Dial.* 134 and the note on 1 Tim. iii. 2 μιᾶς γυναικὸς ἄνδρα. The variation of the form τὴν ἑαυτοῦ γυναῖκα, τὸν ἴδιον ἄνδρα is noticeable, the husband being, as it were, considered the lord of the wife. If this passage stood alone, it would be unsafe to build upon it : but this difference of expression pervades the whole of the Epistles ; e.g. Eph. v. 28, τὰς ἑαυτῶν γυν., 31 τὴν γυν. αὐτοῦ, 33 τὴν ἑαυτοῦ γυν., as contrasted with Eph. v. 22, Tit. ii. 5, 1 Pet. iii. 1, 5 τοῖς ἰδίοις ἀνδράσιν, 1 Cor. xiv. 35 τοὺς ἰδίους ἄνδρας.

3. **τὴν ὀφειλὴν**] Not a classical word in any sense : for though stated in Etym. Magn. to be used in Xenophon περὶ πόρων, it does not occur in the present text of the treatise : see Steph. *Thes.* s.v. It is found in Matt. xviii. 32, Rom. xiii. 7.

5. **εἰ μήτι ἄν**] If ἄν is to be retained here, we must supply γένηται 'it should take place,' see Winer § xlii. p. 380. For ἄν for ἐὰν see Winer § xli. p. 364, who quotes John xiii. 20, xvi. 23, xx. 23. The use is classical also, e.g. Eur. *Alc.* 181 σώφρων μὲν οὐκ ἂν μᾶλλον, εὐτυχὴς δ' ἴσως, quoted by Alford.

σχολάσητε] '*may devote yourselves to*,' literally, 'may have leisure for.' Thus the secondary meaning has eclipsed the primary, and σχολή which originally meant 'leisure' becomes 'work,' 'school' (as in Acts xix. 9). Σχολάζειν takes the dative (1) of the subject studied, φιλοσοφίᾳ, στρατείᾳ, μαθήμασιν, τοῖς φίλοις, τῇ τοῦ λόγου διακονίᾳ (Chrysost. *de sacris*); or (2) of the person teaching, Σωκράτει, Πλάτωνι, etc. It is used absolutely in Matt. xii. 44, Luke xi. 25 in its primary sense.

τῇ προσευχῇ] The words τῇ νηστείᾳ καί, which precede τῇ προσευχῇ in the T. R., are to be omitted by the vast preponderance of ancient

authorities.   There are three other passages where similar insertions are
made, supported by varying degrees of evidence.   In the case of Matt.
xvii. 21 the whole verse should be omitted; it is wanting in אB, some
old Latin authorities (e ff), the Curetonian and Jerusalem Syriac, the
Thebaic, in manuscripts of the Memphitic, and in the Eusebian Canons,
a combination of authorities which shows decisively that the passage has
been transferred from Mark ix. 29.   In Acts x. 30 the words νηστεύων καὶ
are omitted in אBAC etc., the Vulgate, Memphitic, Armenian, etc., and
where they occur are found in different positions, e.g. in D*, the oldest
manuscript which contains them, νηστεύων τὴν ἐνάτην τε καὶ προσ.   Here
again there can be not a shadow of a doubt that they are an insertion.
In Mark ix. 29 the case is somewhat different.   The words καὶ νηστείᾳ are
omitted in אBk, a small but very formidable combination ; and here
again authorities which contain them present them in different positions
as ἐν νηστείᾳ καὶ προσευχῇ (Pesh. Arm. Æthiop.).   Hence, if retained, the
phrase should certainly be bracketed as doubtful.

The four passages represent what may be called an ascetic addition of
later scribes.   Yet too much must not be made of this fact.   Though the
tendency of a later age was to exalt fasting to a level with prayer, yet the
highest authorities for the practice itself still remain in the example
(Matt. iv. 2) and directions of our Lord (Matt. vi. 16– 18), and in the
custom of the Apostles (Acts xiii. 2, 3, xiv. 23) in pursuance of our Lord's
prophecy (Matt. ix. 15, Mark ii. 20, Luke v. 35).   We must not however
adduce in this connexion such passages as 2 Cor. vi. 5, xi. 27, because
the context shows that in both cases ἐν νηστείαις denotes involuntary
fastings, like νῆστεις in Matt. xv. 32, Mark viii. 3.   Thus the practice of
fasting has abundant sanction in the New Testament ; but it holds a
subordinate place to prayer, with only a secondary value in so far as it
promotes self-discipline or conduces to spiritual growth.

ἀκρασίαν]   We must carefully distinguish two words spelt in the
same way, (1) ἀκρᾱσία, a rare word, derived from κεράννυμι and akin
to ἄκρατος 'unmixed,' 'untempered,' used (Theophr. C. P. iii. 2. 5) of
the climate or sky as opposed to εὐκρασία and equivalent to the Latin
'intemperies' ; and (2) ἀκρᾰσία, which we have here and in Matt. xxiii.
25, the character of the ἀκρατής (from κρατεῖν), opposed to ἐγκράτεια,
and expressed in Latin by 'impotentia,' 'the absence of self-restraint.'
That this is the word meant here is evident from the juxtaposition of
ἐγκρατεύονται (ver. 9).   It is common in classical Greek (see Steph.
Thes. s.v., Wetstein ad loc., Lobeck Phryn. p. 524), and found in
passages which set at rest the question of its derivation, e.g. Xen.
Mem. iv. 5. 7 τῷ ἀκρατεῖ...αὐτὰ γὰρ δήπου τὰ ἐναντία σωφροσύνης καὶ
ἀκρασίας ἔργα ἐστί, Arist. Eth. Nic. vii. 1 passim where it is contrasted
again and again with ἐγκράτεια and associated with ἀκρατὴς and ἀκρατεύεσθαι.   It is apparently the usual form in Aristotle, though ἀκράτεια
appears also (de virt. et vit. p. 1250 ll. 1, 22 ed. Bekker).   It is found

likewise in Plutarch (*Mor.* p. 446 B) associated with ἀκρατής. A similar form is γυναικοκρασία which occurs side by side with γυναικοκρατία. Owing to their similarity of sound and meaning ἀκρᾶσία and ἀκρᾶσία are frequently confused: see Steph. *Thes.* s.v.

6. τοῦτο δὲ λέγω] To what does the Apostle refer? Not to the previous verse only, or to part of it; but to the general terms of the preceding paragraph (vv. 2, 3, 4, 5), especially to verse 2 as involving the rest, to the recommendation, that is to say, of the marriage state with all its obligations.

κατὰ συγγνώμην οὐ κατ' ἐπιταγὴν] '*by way of concession, not by way of command.*' It is permissive, not imperative. 'I do not give this as a binding rule (e.g. γυναῖκα ἐχέτω). I state it as what is allowable. If I had my way, I should desire all men to live a celibate life in continence like myself.'

The rendering of the A. V. 'by permission, not by commandment' seems to imply 'though I have no command from God, yet I am permitted by God to speak this'; accordingly ver. 25 ἐπιταγὴν Κυρίου οὐκ ἔχω γνώμην δὲ δίδωμι is frequently referred to in the margin of English bibles to illustrate this verse. It is conceivable that the translators of the Authorised Version intended this to be the meaning, though the passage is otherwise and, as I think, correctly explained in a note in the Geneva Version. This interpretation however in itself is hardly possible, much less probable. True, it has in its favour ver. 25 quoted above, also κατ' ἐπιταγὴν used elsewhere (Rom. xvi. 26, 1 Tim. i. 1, Tit. i. 3) of the divine commands. But neither the verb συγγινώσκω nor the substantive συγγνώμη is used of God in either the LXX. or the N.T., nor would it be an appropriate word to employ, for it contains by implication the notion of fellow-feeling and the like. Nor does this meaning suit what follows θέλω δὲ κ.τ.λ. On these grounds therefore it is better to explain the passage in the sense given above.

7. θέλω δὲ] '*on the contrary I desire.*' Δὲ is undoubtedly the correct reading, γὰρ being a correction for the purpose of simplification. While γὰρ would connect this verse with the whole preceding sentence, δὲ attaches it more particularly with the last clause οὐ κατ' ἐπιταγήν.

ὡς καὶ ἐμαυτὸν] '*as myself*': comp. ver. 9 ὡς κἀγώ. The obvious interpretation of this and similar passages is that St Paul was unmarried. On the other hand Clement of Alexandria (*Strom.* iii. 6, p. 535 ed. Potter) states the opposite; but then he gives his reasons. He is arguing against the Encratites and referring to Phil. iv. 3 says ἐν τινι ἐπιστολῇ τὴν αὐτοῦ προσαγορεύειν σύνζυγον: he then goes on to add that though the Apostle had a wife, he did not 'lead her about,' as he had a perfect right to do (1 Cor. ix. 5). It is clear therefore that Clement's view had no support from tradition, but was an inference from St Paul's own language. Tertullian (*ad Uxor.* ii. 1) and almost all the other fathers speak of St Paul as unmarried. Origen (on *Rom.* I. p. 461 ed. Delarue) characteristically gives both explanations (Paulus ergo sicut quidam tradunt cum uxore vocatus est de qua dicit ad Philippenses, etc.) and follows his master Clement but with hesitation (si vero ut aliis videtur sine uxore etc.). To say nothing of the grammatical difficulty of the masculine form γνήσιε σύνζυγε being applied to a woman, the verse we are considering is fatal to that interpretation of the passage, and the contention of Clement and Origen therefore falls to the ground (see the note on Phil. l.c.). In these latter years of his life the Apostle certainly had not a wife living. There is however one argument which needs consideration in favour of his having been married earlier in life and being at this time a widower. It was a maxim of the rabbis, at all events of a later date, that no one could be a member of the Sanhedrin or sit in judgment on a capital offence, except one who was not only a married man but a father (*Sanh.* fo. 36 *b*); because such a one was more likely to take a merciful view of an offence. Now St Paul says (Acts xxvi. 10) expressly that he recorded his vote against those who were condemned to death on the charge of Christianity. Hence it is contended that at that time he must have been a married man. But this inference depends on two points both very precarious: (1) that κατήνεγκα ψῆφον is to be taken literally, (2) that the regulations laid down by the later Talmudists held good at the time of which we are speaking. Against this highly precarious hypothesis we may set two considerations, (*a*) that wife and children are never once hinted at, but everything points the opposite way: he goes about as one entirely free from such ties: (*b*) the whole passage before us implies that the Apostle lived a celibate life throughout, and lived it in continence.

χάρισμα] It was such, for it was an instrument for preaching the Gospel. Others might have other gifts, might serve God in other ways; but this which enabled him to keep himself free from all earthly ties was to the Apostle a special grace. Comp. xii. 4, Rom. xii. 6, 1 Pet. iv. 10, and for the wide use in St Paul the notes on i. 7 above and Rom. i. 11.

οὕτως, οὕτως] The maxim therefore is thrown into a general form. It is quite comprehensive: each man has his own qualifications for serving God and it is his business to realize them. On οὕτως οὕτως see Judg. xviii. 4, 2 Sam. xi. 25, xvii. 15, 2 Kings v. 4, references given in Meyer.

8. τοῖς ἀγάμοις] i.e. the unmarried of both sexes; not to be rendered 'widowers' as though corresponding to ταῖς χήραις.

9. οὐκ ἐγκρατεύονται] The negative belongs closely to the verb and the phrase is to be treated as one word; otherwise it would be μή. Grammarians tell us that ἀκρατεύεσθαι is a solecism, though used by many, as Menander (Lobeck *Phryn.* p. 442 ἀκρατεύεσθαι· ἀδοκίμῳ ὄντι οἵγε πολλοὶ χρῶνται τούτῳ τῷ ὀνόματι καὶ Μένανδρος· Λέγε οὖν οὐκ ἐγκρατεύεσθαι). Ἀκρατεύεσθαι however occurs several times in Aristotle (see index to the Nicomachean Ethics). On the other hand there is no such classical authority for ἐγκρατεύεσθαι. St Paul would doubtless have used

ἀκρατεύεσθαι, if it had served his purpose ; but it would have conveyed a darker shade of meaning than he intended. Ἐγκρατεύεσθαι occurs in Gen. xliii. 30, 1 Sam. xiii. 12.

10. οὐκ ἐγὼ ἀλλὰ ὁ Κύριος] The common conception of this phrase is quite wrong. It is generally thought that the distinction on which St Paul insists is the distinction between Paul inspired and Paul speaking of himself, between an utterance *ex cathedrâ* and a private opinion. The real difference is between the words of Paul the inspired Apostle and the express command of Christ Himself. We are expressly told that our Lord did prohibit divorce (Matt. v. 32, xix. 9, Mark x. 9, 11, 12, Luke xvi. 18). The nearest approach to St Paul's language is Mark x. 9 ὃ οὖν ὁ Θεὸς συνέζευξεν ἄνθρωπος μὴ χωριζέτω. In Matt. v. 32 an exception to the rule is allowed παρεκτὸς λόγου πορνείας; but St Paul does not think it necessary to add this qualification, because it would be understood of itself. Indeed it is not found in the other Gospel passages, except possibly in Matt. xix. 9 where it occurs in the common text.

μὴ χωρισθῆναι, μὴ ἀφιέναι] For this distinction see the quotation from Bengel given on ver. 13.

11. ἐὰν δὲ...καταλλαγήτω] The sentence is parenthetical : a caution being introduced as an afterthought. Compare ver. 15 εἰ δὲ ὁ ἄπιστος χωρίζεται χωριζέσθω, and ver. 21 ἀλλ' εἰ καὶ δύνασαι ἐλεύθερος γενέσθαι μᾶλλον χρῆσαι, where a great deal depends on the interpretation of this one clause : see the note there.

(d) On the marriage relations of the believer wedded with the unbeliever, and on change of condition generally (vii. 12—24).

12. τοῖς δὲ λοιποῖς] Hitherto St Paul had spoken solely to Christians (in vv. 8, 9 to the unmarried, in vv. 10, 11 to the married). Now he turns to speak of mixed marriages between Christian and heathen. The use of οἱ λοιποὶ here of the Gentiles is akin to the use elsewhere in St Paul (Eph. ii. 3, 1 Thess. iv. 13, v. 6).

λέγω ἐγὼ] This is the right order of the two words ; it corresponds with what goes before, παραγγέλλω οὐκ ἐγὼ ἀλλὰ ὁ Κύριος (ver. 10), and it is more emphatic in itself, comp. Gal. ii. 20.

αὕτη] is preferable to αὐτὴ here, because of οὗτος which succeeds in the next verse.

συνευδοκεῖ] The compounding preposition shows that the man's consent is assumed.

13. μὴ ἀφιέτω] '*Separatur* pars ignobilior, mulier; *dimittit* nobilior, vir: inde conversa ratione etiam mulier fidelis dicitur *dimittere*: et vir infidelis, *separari*, vv. 13, 15.' Bengel on ver. 10.

τὸν ἄνδρα] This, the correct reading, is stronger than αὐτόν. 'Let her not dismiss him, for he still remains her husband.'

14. ἡγίασται] Observe the large and liberal view which the Apostle here adopts. The lesser takes its character from the greater, not the

greater from the lesser.   God does not reject the better because of its
alliance with the worse, but accepts the worse on account of its alliance
with the better.   On this feature in St Paul's theology see the note on i. 2
κλητοῖς ἁγίοις.

ἐπεὶ ἄρα] i.e. 'since on the contrary supposition it follows that your
children are unclean,' a thing not to be thought of.   This argumentative
ἐπεὶ 'since otherwise' (which can stand alone without ἄρα) is not uncommon in St Paul (xv. 29, Rom. iii. 6, xi. 6, 22) and elsewhere (Heb. ix.
26, x. 2), and is followed by the indicative.

νῦν δὲ ἅγιά ἐστιν] '*but, as it is, they are holy.*'   St Paul regards this as
an axiom.   'It is allowed on all sides that the children of these mixed
marriages are holy.'   The sense of the passage is clear enough, but to
what objective fact does it correspond?   Plainly the children of mixed
marriages were regarded as in some sense Christian children.   We
cannot say more or less than this.

It has been affirmed that this passage tells against the supposition of
Infant Baptism as a practice of the Early Church at this time.   Thus
Meyer says, 'weil darum die ἁγιότης der Christenkinder einen andern
Grund gehabt habe.'   But this is a mere *petitio principii*.   How do we
know that it was not the very token of their ἁγιότης that such children
were baptized as Christians?   This at all events was a definite overt act
to which the Apostle might well make his appeal, as showing that they
were regarded as holy.   The passage is not to be pressed on either side.
The Jews indeed had a maxim, that the child of a proselytess need not be
baptized (*Jebamoth* f. 78, 'si gravida fit proselyta, non opus est ut bapti-
zetur infans quando natus fuerit: baptismus enim matris ei cedit pro
baptismo').   But this proves nothing, because it proves too much.   If
valid at all, it would be valid against ever baptizing one born of Christian
parents.   As a matter of fact, the baptism of the Christian corresponded
not to the baptism of the proselyte, but to the circumcision of the Jew,
which was required of all alike.   Thus no inference can be drawn here
against the practice of Infant Baptism.   On the contrary the expression
tells rather in its favour.   Certainly it enunciates the principle which leads
to infant baptism, viz. that the child of Christian parents shall be treated
as a Christian.

15. **εἰ δὲ κ.τ.λ.**]   By parity of reasoning this includes by implication
the unbelieving woman as well as the unbelieving man.

ἐν δὲ εἰρήνῃ κ.τ.λ.] '*but in peace hath God called us.*'   This is not to be
connected with what immediately precedes, as though it meant, 'they are
not bound to a compulsory connexion which would be fatal in their peace.'
The words refer to the whole tenour of these directions, the first part of
ver. 15 being a parenthetical limitation.   What St Paul says is this : 'Do
not let any jar or conflict in the family relations arise out of your
Christianity.   Live peaceably with the heathen husband or wife who
wishes to live with you.   If a discussion is urged on their part, do not

refuse it. The Christian is not so enslaved by such an alliance that he or she may not thus be set free. But let the liberation be the work of another. Do not foster dissensions, do not promote a separation. Do nothing to endanger peace: peace is the very atmosphere of your calling in Christ, the very air which you breathe as Christians.'

16. τί γὰρ οἶδας κ.τ.λ.] This passage again is often wrongly interpreted as though it meant, 'separate yourself, for you cannot be sure that by continuing the connexion you will convert the unbelieving husband (or wife).' Thus Stanley (p. 105) speaks of the injunction as 'a solemn warning against the gambling spirit which intrudes itself even into the most sacred matters,' and 'a remarkable proof of the Apostle's freedom from proselytism.' But surely the Apostle would not have admitted this interpretation of his words. For (1) such a motive—the conversion of the partner—was not likely to be urged by the Corinthian Christians for remaining in this state of enforced wedlock; nor (2) was the Apostle likely to give prominence to the uncertainty of the result as a reason for seeking freedom. What he is really advising is the sacrificing of much for the possible attainment of what is a great gain though an uncertain one. If we look at the sense we see that though the possibility of succeeding in the conversion would be a highly adequate reason for continuing the connexion, yet on the other hand the possibility of failure would be a highly inadequate reason for closing the connexion. The interpretation of the passage depends upon the meaning to be assigned to εἰ in the phrase τί οἶδας, τίς οἶδεν etc. As a matter of fact, whether we should have expected it beforehand or not, these expressions, so far from emphasizing a doubt, express a hope: e.g. 1 Sam. xii. 22 τίς οἶδεν εἰ ἐλεήσει με Κύριος implying that there is a reasonable chance (comp. Esther iv. 14, Jonah iii. 9, Joel ii. 14, the only passages in the LXX. under οἶδα which illustrate the meaning). We therefore conclude that the whole sentence expresses a hope, and that St Paul's meaning is that this saving of the husband (or wife) is worth any temporal inconvenience.

17. εἰ μὴ κ.τ.λ.] A general maxim arising out of a special case, and illustrated below by the examples, *first*, of circumcision (vv. 18, 19), *secondly*, of slavery (vv. 20, 21). These illustrations are a digression which arises out of the general maxim. Εἰ μὴ never stands for ἀλλά; it is here as elsewhere in the sense of πλήν 'only': see Rom. xiv. 14, Jelf G. G. § 860, Winer § liii. p. 566, and the notes on Gal. i. 7, 19.

ὡς μεμέρικεν ὁ Κύριος, ὡς κέκληκεν ὁ Θεὸς] Two variations from the reading of the T. R. are necessary. (1) The substantives should be interchanged in accordance with the vast majority of ancient authorities and St Paul's own usage. For in all cases (1 Thess. iv. 7, Rom. iv. 17, viii. 30, 2 Tim. i. 9) it is God Who calls; on the other hand to assign external positions in the Church falls naturally to Him Who is the Head of the Church and is elsewhere associated with the distribution of such gifts (xii. 5 διαιρέσεις διακονιῶν εἰσὶν καὶ ὁ αὐτὸς Κύριος, Eph. iv. 11).

(2) Μεμέρικεν, though only read by אB, is preferable to ἐμέρισεν ; as balancing the perfect which follows, and as being in itself a rare form. The sense also is improved by the change of tense, 'has assigned his lot in life once for all.' The word here refers entirely to the external conditions of life : Ecclus. xlv. 20 ἀπαρχὰς πρωτογενημάτων ἐμέρισεν αὐτοῖς, 2 Macc. viii. 28.

18. ἐπισπάσθω] '*become as uncircumcised,*' efface the signs of his Judaism. This was done literally by renegade Jews, e.g. in the time of Antiochus (1 Macc. i. 15), comp. Joseph. *Ant.* xii. 5. 1. See Buxtorf, p. 1274 s.v. משׁוּך, Wetstein here and Schöttgen I. p. 1159 sq. Here however the term is used as the symbol of a much wider application, e.g. the observance of sabbaths, festivals, etc.

κέκληται] The change of tense from the aorist of the preceding clause may have been guided by the fact that as a rule the conversions of the Jews were earlier than the conversions of the Gentiles.

19. We have the same sentiment expressed in Gal. v. 6, vi. 15. On independent grounds we know that our Epistle was the earlier one, and this quite accords with the evidence of the three passages considered together. The passage before us gives the original form. The maxim is two-edged, and both edges are used here. On the other hand, in Galatians ll. cc. it is applied only against the Gentiles who would become as Jews. Stanley rightly draws attention to the double assertion of the maxim in St Paul's own conduct: the circumcision of Timothy as a child of one Jewish parent (Acts xvi. 3), the non-circumcision of Titus as a Greek (Gal. ii. 3). In its wider application the maxim reconciles the Apostle's own conduct as a Jew among Jews (Acts xxi. 21 sq.) with his assertion of Gentile freedom (e.g. in the Epistle to the Galatians). It condemns those in our own time who insist on the absolute rejection of forms and those who maintain the absolute necessity of retaining them, as equally opposed to the liberty of the Gospel.

τήρησις ἐντολῶν Θεοῦ] In the corresponding passages the requisites are πίστις δι' ἀγάπης ἐνεργουμένη (Gal. v. 6) and καινὴ κτίσις (Gal. vi. 15): see the notes there. Those who would contrast the teaching of St Paul with that of St James, or who would exaggerate his doctrine of justification by faith, should reflect on this τήρησις ἐντολῶν Θεοῦ.

20. ἐν τῇ κλήσει] From this passage comes the common usage of the word 'calling' or 'vocation,' for our profession in life regarded as sanctified, as given to us by God. The sentiment which underlies this thought is essentially right, but as an interpretation of the Apostle's words here it is quite wrong. Here, as always in the N. T., κλῆσις is the summons to the knowledge of God, to membership in the Church, to the kingdom of Christ. Κλῆσις is a good classical word, meaning (1) a designation or appellation, (2) an invitation, e.g. to a supper, (3) a summons or citation to appear as a witness or advocate in court. These last two senses form a connecting link with the N. T. use of the expression.

The calling of Christians into the kingdom is represented under the image of an invitation to a feast (Matt. xxii. 3, 4, 8, 11 : comp. the technical use of καλεῖν in Luke xiv. 7). But more than this, the language of Epictetus i. 29 § 46 μάρτυς ὑπὸ τοῦ Θεοῦ κεκλημένος and § 49 ταῦτα μέλλεις μαρτυρεῖν καὶ καταισχύνειν τὴν κλῆσιν ἣν κέκληκεν [ὁ Θεός] reminds us forcibly of St Paul's language here (cf. Eph. iv. 1, 2 Tim. i. 9), which the Stoic philosopher seems elsewhere to have caught (see *Philippians*, p. 313 sq.), though here he has put another meaning into it. In the N.T. the substantive occurs chiefly, but not solely (see Heb. iii. 1, 2 Pet. i. 10) in St Paul's writings, and is applied both to the act and (as here) to the circumstances of calling. But the circumstances represent not the external condition to which God called us, but the external conditions in which God called us to a knowledge of Himself.

21. ἀλλ' εἰ καὶ κ.τ.λ.] '*but if it should be in thy power to become a free man, the rather avail thyself of the opportunity.*' Two opposite interpretations have been put upon this passage: (1) 'even though it is in thy power to be set free, prefer to continue in slavery'; (2) 'if it should be in thy power etc., prefer this freedom to remaining in slavery.' In the first case the sentence (vv. 21, 22) is continuous; in the latter, the clause ἀλλ' εἰ καὶ...μᾶλλον χρῆσαι is parenthetical, 'in giving you this injunction I do not mean to prevent you from becoming free if opportunity offers.'

Of earlier commentators, Origen (in Cramer's *Catena*, p. 140) explains the slavery metaphorically of marriage and seems to take the phrase as recommending liberty. He mentions that οἱ λοιποὶ ἑρμηνευταὶ interpret the passage of subjection to the ordinances of the law. Of those who explain the sentence literally and naturally, Severianus (in Cramer) takes it to recommend liberty; Photius slavery, and so Theodoret with qualifications. Hilary (Ambrosiaster) is doubtful. Chrysostom mentions the interpretation which recommends liberty (τινὲς τὸ μᾶλλον χρῆσαι περὶ ἐλευθερίας φασὶν εἰρῆσθαι), but prefers the contrary view. Thus the tendency of patristic interpretation is on the side of a continuance in slavery; and this we should expect, for while slavery was an existing institution, there would be a temptation to explain the passage as recommending the *status quo*.

Turning now to the language, we may safely say that εἰ καὶ may bear both senses. It may mean 'although,' 'even though,' as in Phil. ii. 17 ἀλλ' εἰ καὶ σπένδομαι, Col. ii. 5, Luke xi. 8 etc.; or it may mean 'if,' as in Luke xi. 18 εἰ καὶ ὁ Σατανᾶς...διεμερίσθη : comp. ἐὰν καὶ (vii. 11, Gal. vi. 1). When however we come to consider the phrase μᾶλλον χρῆσαι, it is much more natural to supply τῇ ἐλευθερίᾳ out of the ἐλεύθερος of the immediate sentence, than τῇ δουλείᾳ out of the δοῦλος of a more distant clause. Again χρῆσαι in the sense of 'to avail oneself of an opportunity offered' is an idiomatic usage which occurs elsewhere in this Epistle, ix. 12 ἀλλ' οὐκ ἐχρησάμεθα τῇ ἐξουσίᾳ ταύτῃ, 15 οὐ κέχρημαι οὐδενὶ τούτων, and is thus characteristic and forcible.

But the main argument in favour of the translation adopted in these notes is the extreme improbability that St Paul would have taken any other view. From the nature of the case the free man was in a much more advantageous position for doing God's work than a slave who was fettered at every turn. Again, the Apostle's own practice in his own case shows how strong was the sense of freedom which he carried with him. This he exhibits when he asserts more than once his rights as a Roman citizen (Acts xvi. 37, xxii. 25 sq.).

Thus we conclude that the passage is parenthetical, a qualification of the Apostle's general statement which precedes it, added lest he should be misunderstood. 'In saying this, I do not mean but that, if you have the opportunity of gaining your freedom, you should avail yourself of the more advantageous position in which you will then be placed.' Whatever the nature of the freedom may be, it is generally to be preferred to the slavery whatever it may be, if it come in a natural and lawful way. Compare the parentheses in vv. 11, 15. Thus the substantive to be supplied is τῇ ἐλευθερίᾳ.

22. ὁ γὰρ...δοῦλος] '*for he that is called in the Lord being a slave*'; comp. ver. 21. The expression ἐν Κυρίῳ καλεῖν, though unusual, occurs in 1 Pet. v. 10, but not in Eph. i. 11, where ἐκληρώθημεν is the correct reading.

ἀπελεύθερος] '*freedman.*' A double process is indicated here. Christ first buys us from our old master, sin, and then sets us free. For this enfranchisement see Rom. viii. 2, Gal. v. 1. But observe that a service is still due from the *libertus* to his *patronus*. This was the case in Roman Law (see Becker and Marquardt, v. p. 211), which required the freedman to take his patron's name, live in his patron's house, consult his patron's will etc. Compare the language of Ignatius (*Rom.* 4) ἐκεῖνοι ἐλεύθεροι, ἐγὼ δὲ μέχρι νῦν δοῦλος· ἀλλ' ἐὰν πάθω, ἀπελεύθερος Ἰησοῦ Χριστοῦ, καὶ ἀναστήσομαι ἐν αὐτῷ ἐλεύθερος. See the note on vi. 20 ἠγοράσθητε γὰρ τιμῆς above, where the double aspect of the Redemption, as an emancipation and as a transference of ownership, is drawn out. This second aspect is hinted at here in the word Κυρίου representing the great Lord of all (see the note on iii. 5, above). But in effect freedom in Christ and slavery to Christ merely represent two sides of the same moral truth: for subjection to Christ is freedom from sin (Rom. vi. 18, 22).

23. τιμῆς ἠγοράσθητε] See the note on vi. 20.

μὴ γίνεσθε] '*become not*': for it would be a change of state if they were to become slaves once more. Comp. Gal. iv. 31, v. 1.

δοῦλοι ἀνθρώπων] What is the reference here? There is nothing in the context which points to the meaning, and we have to look for the idea elsewhere in the Epistle. The allusion is probably to the insolent tyranny of their party-leaders (i. 12, iii. 4, 21); and if so, it can be well illustrated by 2 Cor. xi. 20 ἀνέχεσθε γὰρ εἴ τις ὑμᾶς καταδουλοῖ.

24. In this verse St Paul repeats again the general maxim formulated in ver. 17, emphasizing the saving clause, 'in the sight of God,' παρὰ Θεῷ.

(e) *On virgins specially* (vii. 25—38).

25. **περὶ δὲ τῶν παρθένων**] This commences a new subject and (from the way in which it is introduced) probably another of the topics of the Corinthian letter (see on vii. 1).

A preliminary question has to be settled. Does παρθένοι include both sexes? The use of the word in Rev. xiv. 4 is not decisive; for obviously the term there was not a recognised term : otherwise St John would not have said further παρθένοι γάρ εἰσιν—an addition which shows that he used the phrase καταχρηστικῶς. There is apparently no indication of this use until a much later period, unless *Pistis Sophia*, p. 146, be an example in Syriac (see Payne Smith, *Thes. Syr.* p. 624 sq.). But, it will be said, St Paul does immediately afterwards (vv. 26—28, 29—33) speak of both sexes. That is true; but the facts seem to be that the Corinthians consulted him about the special case of giving virgin daughters in marriage; whereupon St Paul generalised, first stating the guiding principle (ver. 27), then applying it to both sexes (vv. 28—35), and finally dealing with the special point which the Corinthians had put to him (vv. 36—38).

ἐπιταγὴν Κυρίου] i.e. an express command, whether a directly recorded saying of our Lord (as in ver. 10), or a direct intimation to the Apostle by revelation.

ἠλεημένος] Compare 1 Tim. i. 13, 16.

26. **τοῦτο καλὸν ὑπάρχειν**] '*this is good to begin with.*' It is thus the fundamental axiom, the starting-point, of the discussion that follows. Καλὸν is used in the same sense as in ver. 1, and the sentiment is nearly the same. 'Ανθρώπῳ here includes both sexes.

ἐνεστῶσαν] '*present,*' not 'imminent.' On this word see on Gal. i. 4, where this passage is referred to.

ἀνάγκην] Persecution was impending. There were signs of a coming storm. The man, who kept himself free from the entanglement of earthly ties, would save himself from many a bitter conflict: he would not have to face the terrible alternative—the most terrible to sensitive minds—between duty to God and affection to wife and children. He was altogether more free to do and to suffer for Christ. A man who is a hero in himself becomes a coward when he thinks of his widowed wife and his orphaned children. The ἀνάγκη, of which the Apostle speaks, might or might not be the beginning of the ἀνάγκη μεγάλη (Luke xxi. 23).

ὅτι καλὸν κ.τ.λ.] Governed, like the preceding clause, by νομίζω, but a new construction.

οὕτως] '*just as he is,*' i.e. 'unmarried,' for he is speaking of them. For οὕτως compare ver. 40, Rom. ix. 20, John iv. 6.

27. **λέλυσαι**] '*art thou set free from a wife*': not implying that the person addressed was ever married. It is complementary to δέδεσαι

above. That this sense is legitimate appears from Xen. *Cyr.* i. 1. 4 (quoted by Meyer) ἔτι καὶ νῦν αὐτόνομα εἶναι λέγεται καὶ λελύσθαι ἀπ᾽ ἀλλήλων.

28. **γαμήσῃς, γήμῃ**] If this distinction is intentional, it certainly is not the distinction of classical usage between γαμεῖν for the man and γαμεῖσθαι of the woman (Lobeck *Phryn.* p. 742, Porson on *Medea* l. 264, Pollux iii. 45); for here the aorist active is used of the woman also ἐὰν γήμῃ ἡ παρθένος. So too ver. 34 ἡ γαμήσασα, 1 Tim. v. 11 γαμεῖν θέλουσιν (χῆραι), 14 βούλομαι νεωτέρας γαμεῖν. In all these cases the verb is used absolutely, but in Mark x. 12 ἐὰν αὐτὴ γαμήσῃ ἄλλον (the right reading) it governs an accusative. On the other hand the classical distinction is preserved below in ver. 39 ἐλευθέρα ἐστὶν ᾧ θέλει γαμηθῆναι. There is a tendency in scribes to alter the voice in order to bring it into conformity with the classical idiom; see Mark l.c. and Ign. *Pol.* 5 where πρέπει δὲ τοῖς γαμοῦσι καὶ ταῖς γαμούσαις has been corrected by the interpolator into πρέπει δὲ τοῖς γαμοῦσι καὶ ταῖς γαμουμέναις (see the note there). Ἔγημα (from γάμω) is an older form than ἐγάμησα (from γαμέω), which however is found in Menander and Lucian; both occur elsewhere in the N. T., ἔγημα in Matt. xxii. 25, Luke xiv. 20, ἐγάμησα in Matt. xix. 9, Mark vi. 17, x. 11, and ver. 9 above. For the occurrence of an older and a later form side by side in the N. T., comp. κερδήσω, κερδανῶ (1 Cor. ix. 21, 22), ἐλεῶντος, ἐλεεῖ (Rom. ix. 16, 18), and see Lobeck *de orthograph. Graec. inconst. (Path.* II. 341 sq.).

ἡ παρθένος] taken as a typical case: comp. vi. 16 τῇ πόρνῃ. But the article here is doubtful.

ἐγὼ δὲ κ.τ.λ.] i.e. 'my object in giving this advice is to spare you suffering as far as possible.'

29. **συνεσταλμένος**] The verb συνστέλλεσθαι is commonly used of persons to signify 'to be depressed,' 'dejected'; as in 1 Macc. iii. 6 συνεστάλησαν οἱ ἄνομοι ἀπὸ τοῦ φόβου αὐτῶν, v. 5 συνέστειλεν αὐτούς, 2 Macc. vi. 12 μὴ συνστέλλεσθαι διὰ τὰς συμφοράς, see also examples in Steph. *Thes.* s.v. The question then arises, is συνεσταλμένος here temporal or moral, of the contracted time or of the pressure of calamity? Perhaps both ideas are implied in the phrase, but in the light of the context the temporal cannot be excluded (comp. Rom. xiii. 11). For στέλλεσθαι see the note on 2 Thess. iii. 6, and for the Apostle's views as to the approach of the Second Advent the note on 1 Thess. iv. 15.

ἐστίν, τὸ λοιπόν] This is the right reading: not τὸ λοιπόν ἐστιν, nor λοιπόν ἐστιν. How then is the expression τὸ λοιπόν to be taken, with what precedes or with what follows? To connect it with what follows in the sense given by the A. V. 'it remains therefore that' becomes impossible as soon as the true reading τὸ λοιπὸν for λοιπὸν is established. Two possibilities therefore remain : (1) to connect with the preceding sentence 'the season is short henceforth,' which is flat and unmeaning; or (2) to consider the phrase as belonging to the subordinate clause ἵνα...ὦσιν, but misplaced for the sake of emphasis, 'the season is short, so that henceforth' etc.   Such an anticipation of words for purposes of emphatic statement is characteristic of St Paul (see Winer § lxi. p. 685 sq.), especially with clauses introduced by ἵνα: see Rom. xi. 31, 2 Cor. ii. 4, Gal. ii. 10, Col. iv. 16 and comp. John xiii. 29: and is on the whole to be preferred here.

30.   Sorrows and joys alike are temporary, are transient.   In a moment all may be changed.   Therefore to one who judges rightly, earthly grief is not over grievous and earthly joy not over joyous.

ὡς μὴ κατέχοντες] i.e. as not sure of absolute ownership.   Compare 2 Cor. vi. 10, and for the metaphor Lucr. iii. 971 'Vitaque mancipio nulli datur, omnibus usu.'

31.   οἱ χρώμενοι κ.τ.λ.]   The accusative (τὸν κόσμον) is very rare after χρᾶσθαι except in quite late writers (Malalas p. 5, Theophan. p. 314): it has very slight support in Acts xxvii. 17 βοηθείαις (v. l. -as) ἐχρῶντο, but occurs in Wisdom vii. 14 θησαυρὸς...ὃν οἱ χρησάμενοι (where the variant κτησάμενοι is rejected by Tischendorf and Fritzsche).   The construction however is found in a Cretan inscription of the second or third century B.C. (Boeckh *C. I. G.* II. p. 405).   In the passage before us the accusative may have been influenced by the καταχρώμενοι which follows ; καταχρᾶσθαι often taking an accusative (A. Buttmann p. 157, Meyer *ad loc.*), even in classical writers.   It occurs however below with a dative, ix. 18, εἰς τὸ μὴ καταχρήσασθαι τῇ ἐξουσίᾳ μου.

καταχρώμενοι] '*using up*,' 'using to the full,' comp. 'abuti' in Latin, which often takes this meaning.   'Misusing' would be παραχρώμενοι: 'abusing' of the A. V., though an archaism, well preserves the alliteration.

33, 34.   The interesting question of the reading of this passage falls under two heads.   (1) καὶ μεμέρισται καὶ is undoubtedly the reading at the end of ver. 33, the omission of the first καὶ in some manuscripts having been assisted by the fact that γυναικὶ immediately precedes it.   (2) As regards ver. 34 three groups of reading present themselves: (*a*) η γυνη η αγαμος και η παρθενος η αγαμος supported by אAF 17, Memph., (*b*) η γυνη η αγαμος και η παρθενος, BP Vulg. Bashm. Euseb. and others, (*c*) η γυνη και η παρθενος η αγαμος DFG 37, 47 *fuld.* Pesh. Harkl. Method.   These variants originated probably in the accident that in some very early manuscript, through the carelessness of the scribe or amanuensis, the words η αγαμος were written above the line or in the margin, and so were inserted subsequently in different places of the text.   The choice seems to lie between (*b*) and (*c*).   If we choose the first of these two alternatives, then we punctuate after καὶ μεμέρισται and render 'and he is distracted,' i.e. his allegiance is divided; a rendering for which Achilles Tatius v. 24 p. 343 may be quoted ἐμεμέριστο πολλοῖς ἅμα τὴν ψυχήν, αἰδοῖ καὶ ὀργῇ καὶ ἔρωτι καὶ ζηλοτυπίᾳ.   The γυνὴ ἡ ἄγαμος is then 'the widow,' one who was once married and remains unmarried.   If however we prefer the second alternative, we punctuate after γυναικὶ and after παρθένος: and in this case μεμέρισται has a different meaning 'there is a distinction between' (as the

A. V. renders it). I venture to prefer this latter reading, though supported chiefly by Western authorities, from internal evidence; for the sentences then become exactly parallel. There is just the same distinction between the married woman and the virgin, as between the married and the unmarried man. The other view throws sense and parallelism into confusion, for καὶ μεμέρισται is not wanted with ver. 33 which is complete in itself. It also necessitates the awkward phrase ἡ γυνὴ καὶ ἡ παρθένος μεριμνᾷ. The reading η γυνη η αγαμος και η παρθενος η αγαμος illustrates the habitual practice of scribes to insert as much as possible, and may be neglected.

35. βρόχον ἐπιβάλω] The rendering of the A. V. 'cast a snare' conveys a false impression as to the Apostle's meaning, because it suggests temptation instead of constraint: St Paul's desire is not to fetter their movements, the metaphor being that of the halter. Compare Prov. vi. 21 (quoted by Meyer) ἐγκλοίωσαι ἐπὶ σῷ τραχήλῳ and Philo *Vita Moys*. iii. 34 (II. p. 173) βλέπω (τὴν ἐκ Θεοῦ βοήθειαν) βρόχους τοῖς αὐχέσι περιβάλλουσαν κατὰ τῶν ἀντιπάλων ἕλκει κατὰ τῆς θαλάσσης κ.τ.λ.

εὐπάρεδρον] A rarer word than εὐπρόσεδρον of the T. R., and better supported here. Similarly παρεδρεύοντες is the right reading in ix. 13. The form πάρεδρος occurs in Wisd. ix. 4 τὴν τῶν σῶν θρόνων πάρεδρον σοφίαν 'the wisdom which is attendant on thy throne.' Like ἀπερισπάστως it is found here only in the N. T.

36. ὑπέρακμος] '*of full age*,' rather than 'past the flower of her age.'

37. These directions of St Paul must be judged in the light of two considerations. *First*, the recognized power of the father over his daughter, the 'patria potestas,' on which see Becker and Marquardt, v. 3 sq. *Secondly*, the way in which St Paul makes the question depend not on the wishes of the daughter but of the father, points doubtless to the form in which the matter was submitted to him in the letter of the Corinthians, viz. with special reference to the attitude of the father in such cases.

(*f*)   *On widows specially* (vii. 39, 40).

39, 40. It is impossible to say what led St Paul to add these last two verses. It is conceivable that we have here an answer to a question raised in the Corinthian letter, or the subject may have sprung from something which has gone before. But however this may be, we have here the origin of the metaphor which was worked out a few months later in the Epistle to the Romans (vii. 1—3). A parallel case has been noted already on ver. 19 with regard to the Epistle to the Galatians. The influence of the passage in the Roman letter is traceable in the interpolation of νόμῳ after δέδεται from Rom. vii. 2, where it comes in naturally, the legal aspect underlying the whole passage.

39. μόνον ἐν Κυρίῳ] This expression is generally interpreted to imply that she must marry a Christian husband, if she marry at all. But the expression cannot be so pressed. It will only signify that she must remember that she is a member of Christ's body; and not forget her Christian duties and responsibilities, when she takes such a step. Marriage with a Christian only does not seem to be contained in the words, though that might be the consequence of her attempt to fulfil those duties.

40. οὕτως] For οὕτως see on ver. 26: for δοκῶ the note on iii. 18 δοκεῖ.

THE EPISTLES OF ST PAUL

II
THE THIRD APOSTOLIC JOURNEY

4
EPISTLE TO THE ROMANS

ANALYSIS

I.   INTRODUCTION. i. 1—15.

    i.   *Salutation.* i. 1—7.

        Paul called to be an Apostle to the Romans called as believers. Grace and peace in Jesus Christ.

    ii. *Personal explanations.* i. 8—15.

        His thanksgivings for them and his interest in them. His desire to see them and to impart some spiritual gift to them. His obligation to preach the Gospel to all men. He is not ashamed of the Gospel.

II. DOCTRINAL PORTION. i. 16—xi. 36.

    i.   *What is the Gospel?* i. 16—18.

        A righteousness of God to every one that believeth, to the Jew first and then to the Greek. A righteousness by faith, just as the wrath of God falls on all impiety and unrighteousness.

    ii. *State of the Gentile world.* i. 19—32.

        They might have seen God through His works. They refused to see Him. They disputed, and they blinded their hearts. They worshipped men and beasts.

        Therefore they were delivered over to impurity. Their shameless lusts. Their violent and unruly passions. Their lack of all natural affection. They not only did these things; but they took delight in those who did them.

    iii. *State of the Jewish people.* ii. 1—29.

        The Jews condemn the Gentiles and yet do the same things. Their wrong-doing and stubbornness will be equally punished. As the Jew has a priority of knowledge, so also he has a priority of condemnation. Those without the law and those under the law will both be judged by the standard under which they lived. The natural conscience is to the heathen as a rule.

        The Jew has God's law, and is proud of his privileges. Yet he violates the law. Thus his circumcision is no better than the uncircumcision of the heathen. The mere outward token is worth nothing.

iv. *But if so, what is the meaning of the covenant?*   iii. 1—20.

In other words, in what does the privilege of the Jew consist? It is great in many ways. First of all, the oracles of God were entrusted to the Jews.

But what if they disbelieved? Do you say that then the Jews have no preference? No, none at all. Their own Scriptures condemn them, as having sinned one and all. By the works of the law no flesh shall be justified before Him.

v. *To meet this universal failure, a universal remedy is found.*   iii. 21—31.

This remedy is 'a righteousness of God by faith in Jesus Christ,' accorded to all, to Jew and Gentile alike. Past sins of the world have been overlooked, that now God might shew His righteousness.

We do not annihilate law by this : we confirm law.

vi. *But our father Abraham—what is the meaning of the covenant made with him?*   iv. 1—25.

He is an example of this very principle, for he was justified through faith. For he that believeth in God Who justifieth the impious—his faith is counted for righteousness. Such is the language of the Psalms. Remember that Abraham was still uncircumcised at this time. It was not through circumcision, still less through law, that he was justified. Law worketh wrath, for it creates transgression.

Thus Abraham is the father of the faithful. He hoped against hope, and so was justified. This was written for our sakes, who believe on Him Who raised up Jesus our Lord from the dead.

vii. *The results of this position of righteousness through faith.*   v. 1—11.

(*a*) Peace before God.
(*b*) Confident boasting.
(*c*) Patience under affliction.

The love of God has been manifested through the death of Christ : and this is an assurance that, as we have been reconciled through Christ's death, so we shall be saved, shall live, in Christ's life.

viii. *The terms 'life' and 'death' explained.*   v. 12—21.

The parallel of the First and Second Adam. Through the First Adam death came into the world : through the Second, life. The death passed over all : so *a fortiori* the life.

The law only interposed to heighten the sense of sin, and so to increase the effect of grace.

ix. *What is to be the influence of all this on our conduct?*   vi. 1—14.

Are we to continue in sin that grace may abound? This is a contradiction of the very conception of our position. We have been crucified, have died, with Christ, to sin ; we have risen, have been made alive to God, to righteousness.

Therefore we must recognize this death, this life, in our conduct. 'Sin shall be no longer your master, for ye are not under law, but under grace.'

x. *But if so, we are under grace, and not under law, shall we commit sin?* vi. 15—23.

No : you were slaves once to sin : now you are slaves to righteousness. What came of your former slavery? Death. What of your present slavery? Eternal life.

xi. *The assertion substantiated, 'Ye are not under law.'* vii. 1—6.

The obligation of the law in the case of a contract is cancelled by death. The wife is free to marry when her husband dies.

So in Christ's body, death has interposed between you and the law, the law is dead to you and you to the law. The newness of the Spirit is substituted for the oldness of the letter.

xii. *But is not all this tantamount to saying that the law is sin?* vii. 7—24.

On the contrary, sin is revealed and condemned by the law. Sin is dormant and dead, until it is quickened by the law. Sin is then revived and I am slain. But the purpose of the law is life, though the actual result may be death to me. The object of the law is to deepen sin ; and the conflict within myself vindicates the spirituality, the holiness, of the law.

True, I sin through the law ; but I sin against my conscience, and therefore I testify to the holiness of the law. The holiness of the law is thus vindicated ; but woe is me, wretched sinner, how shall I be rescued ?

xiii. *Thanks to God through Christ, there is no condemnation to those in Christ.* vii. 25—viii. 11.

Through Christ, God has freed us from sin and death. We have been transferred from the domain of the flesh to the domain of the Spirit. It is the Spirit of Christ that quickens our spirits, and it will quicken our mortal bodies also.

xiv. *Therefore we are bound to live after the Spirit.* viii. 12—39.

The Spirit witnesses that we are sons and heirs. Thus present afflictions sink into insignificance : while we yearn for the future redemption. We hope and we trust, even where we cannot see.

For God hath foreknown and foreordained us ; and if He is with us, who can oppose us ? No sufferings, therefore, no sorrows, shall separate us from the love of God in Christ.

xv. *But what about the Jews?* ix. 1—13.

I have unspeakable sorrow on their behalf, bearing in mind their great privileges. Yet God's word is true : not all Israel shall be saved. The Scriptures always speak of a part, e.g. in Isaac, and again in Jacob.

xvi. *It is as God foreordains, not as man likes.* ix. 14—33.

So in Pharaoh's case. Yet what man shall impugn the purpose of God, Who moulds us as the potter his clay ? The gathering-in of the Gentiles as well as the saved remnant of the Israelites is foretold by the prophets. Heathendom has attained unto righteousness, Israel has stumbled on the rock of offence.

xvii. *Thus the zeal of the Jews has been ineffectual, for they have sought righteousness in a false way.* x. 1—21.

Righteousness is of faith, which believes in Christ's death and Christ's ascension. Here Jew and Gentile are on a level. The Gospel must be preached to all, but all will not listen to the preaching. This too was foretold by the prophets. The Gentiles, it was predicted, should excite Israel to emulation.

xviii. *Has God then rejected His people?* xi. 1—16.

No, it is now as of old. The faithful are few, and the apostates many. But their apostasy has brought salvation to the Gentiles. And ultimately the faith of the Gentiles will re-act and draw the Jews into the fold.

xix. *Meanwhile the Gentiles have no ground for boasting.* xi. 17—36.

They are simply the wild graft on the cultivated tree. Their superiority is but for a time. Israel at length will be saved with them. Thus God hath concluded all under unbelief that He may have mercy upon all. Marvellous is the wisdom of God, to Whom be glory for ever.

III. PRACTICAL EXHORTATIONS. xii. 1—xv. 13.

Present your bodies a living sacrifice. Ye are limbs of Christ's body. The metaphor implies diversities of functions. Let each do his own work.

Observe charity in all forms. Overcome evil with good.

Be obedient to the temporal powers. They are God's delegates. Render to all their due, i.e. love thy neighbour as thyself. Love is the fulfilling of the law.

Let each man look to himself, and each respect the conscience of another.

So in the observance of days. So also in the observance of meats.

Let the strong especially deal tenderly with the scruples of the weak, and put no stumblingblock in his way.

We must not please ourselves, but each his neighbour.

God grant that you may so live in harmony, that with one accord with one mouth ye may glorify God.

Receive one another therefore, as Christ received you. For Christ came as a minister of the circumcision, that through Him the Gentiles also might be brought into the fold ; and the prophecies might be fulfilled which spoke of the joint tribute of praise of Jews and Gentiles.

This do, and God will fill you with all joy in believing.

IV. PERSONAL EXPLANATIONS. xv. 14—xvi. 27.

 i. *The Apostle's motive in writing the letter.* xv. 14—21.

This I am persuaded you will do ; but I have written to remind you, as your Apostle, as the Apostle of the Gentiles. As such I have preached the Gospel far and wide, not building on other men's foundations.

 ii. *His intention of visiting them.* xv. 22—33.

For this reason I have been prevented from visiting you. But I hope to see you on my way to Spain. At present I am bound to Jerusalem, as bearer of alms for the poor brethren. Pray that I may be delivered from the unbelieving Jews there and may be free to visit you. I am persuaded that the blessing of God will attend my visit.

 iii. *Greetings.* xvi. 1—20.

I commend you to Phebe, the bearer of this letter.
Salute all the saints by name. The Churches of Christ salute you.
I charge you to avoid divisions and offences. So will the God of peace crush Satan under your feet.
The grace of our Lord Jesus Christ be with you.

 iv. *Postscript.* xvi. 21—27.

Timothy, Lucius, Jason, Sosipater salute you.
I, Tertius, the amanuensis, salute you.
Gaius, my kind host, salutes you : so do Erastus and Quartus.
The Doxology.

CHAPTER I

I. INTRODUCTION, i. 1—15.

1. **δοῦλος**] This is the earliest Epistle in which St Paul styles himself a 'bond servant' in the opening sentence. But in the Epistle which immediately precedes this (see *Galatians* p. 36 sq.), the note of bondage is struck early (Gal. i. 10 Χριστοῦ δοῦλος οὐκ ἂν ἤμην) and is repeated at the close (Gal. vi. 17 τὰ στίγματα τοῦ 'Ιησοῦ). In the 'brands' which are the badges of ownership we see the marks which he bore of persecution undergone in the service of Christ. Perhaps his late sufferings have something to do with the prominence here given to the word δοῦλος.

κλητὸς] The word is a protest not against those who denied his Apostleship, but against those who upheld human merit: see the note on 1 Cor. i. 1. As such it sounds the keynote of the Epistle, for it has its counterpart in the spiritual position of his hearers also (vv. 6, 7 κλητοὶ 'Ιησοῦ Χριστοῦ, κλητοῖς ἁγίοις). 'To the calling of God I owe my office, to the same calling you owe your place within the Christian fold': comp. Rom. ix. 11, 12, 16.

ἀφωρισμένος] The word may refer either (1) to the fore-ordained purpose of God as in Gal. i. 15, or (2) to the conversion and potential call to the Apostleship (Acts ix. 15), or again (3) to the actual call and consecration to the Apostleship (Acts xiii. 2) ; or lastly it may include all three ideas. The word is actually used elsewhere of the first (Gal. i. 15) and of the third (Acts xiii. 2) of these events. Probably however the first idea would be more prominent in the Apostle's mind when he used the expression here : carrying out as it does the sense of κλητὸς above, the origination as derived from God.

εἰς εὐαγγέλιον] i.e. to learn and to teach the Gospel: for the two were not separated in the minds of the earliest disciples and ought not ever to be.

2. **ὃ προεπηγγείλατο**] The two leading ideas as regards the results, in what follows are (1) the fulfilment of the Jewish expectations, and (2) the comprehension of the Gentiles. These two thoughts run through the Epistle in various forms and are gathered up in the final doxology (xvi. 25—27), where the words διά τε γραφῶν προφητικῶν are inserted

almost out of place in order to bring in the first, the fulfilment of the promise to the Jews. They are thus introduced in the salutation to show the purpose of the Epistle, which is conciliation, see *Biblical Essays*, p. 315. The description begins with a recognition of God's special office as regards the Jews, and expands into a declaration of this relation to the Gentiles (comp. i. 16, ii. 9, 10).

The force of the word προεπηγγείλατο lies in its prepositions, which show that salvation is something quite independent of human merit, the promise being at once *previous* and *absolute*. On ἐπαγγελία in the N. T. and its distinction from ὑπόσχεσις see the note on Gal. iii. 14.

διὰ τῶν προφητῶν] The preposition (διὰ) implies the divine source, the substantive (προφήτης not μάντις) the conscious, human agent. As connected with the words which follow (ἐν γραφαῖς ἁγίαις), διὰ signifies the immediate vehicle, ἐν the permanent repository.

3. περὶ τοῦ υἱοῦ] to be connected closely with εὐαγγέλιον.

τοῦ γενομένου] Compare the contrast in the language of Phil. ii. 6, 7 ἐν μορφῇ Θεοῦ ὑπάρχων...ἐν ὁμοιώματι ἀνθρώπων γενόμενος, where see the notes. Here then the word γενόμενος implies a prior existence of the Son before the Incarnation.

ἐκ σπέρματος Δαυεὶδ κατὰ σάρκα] i.e. Who on His human side fulfilled the condition, as the promised Messiah of the Jews; Who on His divine side etc. His Messiahship was after all only the lower aspect of His Person (κατὰ σάρκα). His personality as the Divine Word, the Teacher of Gentile as well as Jew, was His higher aspect. The reference to the descent from David occurs, as we might expect, most frequently in the Judaic Gospel (Matt. i. 1, 6, 20 : ix. 27, xii. 23, xv. 22, xx. 30, 31, xxi. 9, 15, xxii. 42 sq.) ; and in that part of St Luke's narrative which from internal evidence and external probability must have been derived from Jewish information (Luke i. 27, 32, 69, ii. 4, 11); but it is also found elsewhere, though rarely (John vii. 42, Acts xiii. 23, 2 Tim. ii. 8).

4. τοῦ ὁρισθέντος] '*determined*,' not absolutely but relatively ; that is to say, with regard not to God's counsels, but to man's understanding ; not 'constituted,' but 'defined,' 'declared.'

ἐν δυνάμει] i.e. power over the moral and the physical world, with a reference to His miracles (δυνάμεις) but not confined to these. The A.V. 'with power' is somewhat misleading.

κατὰ πνεῦμα ἁγιωσύνης] Is this expression to be taken as the anti-thetical clause to κατὰ σάρκα above? Probably ; for though the parallelism is somewhat obscured by the interposition of ἐν δυνάμει and by the addition of ἁγιωσύνης, yet it is the emphatic part of the sentence, at least as antithetical to κατὰ σάρκα. In any case πνεῦμα is here not objective but subjective, and 'a spirit of holiness' would be a better rendering than that of the A.V.

ἐξ ἀναστάσεως νεκρῶν] The force of the preposition is 'out of,' and therefore 'owing to,' by reason of.' Though St Paul singles out this one incident, he cannot mean to exclude other exhibitions of power. The Resurrection was the one crowning, decisive act which manifested His Sonship. It is also the crowning spiritual agency. Hence it sums up both the preceding phrases ἐν δυνάμει and κατὰ πνεῦμα ἁγιωσύνης. See the note on Phil. iii. 10 τὴν δύναμιν τῆς ἀναστάσεως αὐτοῦ. This prominence given to the doctrine of the Resurrection is a leading idea of the Roman letter (iv. 24, vi. 4, viii. 11, x. 9), and of St Paul elsewhere (Acts xvii. 31, xxvi. 23). The phrase here however is not ἐξ ἀναστάσεως αὐτοῦ ἐκ νεκρῶν, but the general resurrection of the dead is meant, which was implied in His Resurrection and of which His Resurrection was the firstfruits and the assurance. The expression is to be explained by St Paul's conception that the truth of man's resurrection stands or falls with the truth of Christ's Resurrection (1 Cor. xv. 12 sq.).

5. δι' οὗ] not ἀφ' οὗ. It is the preposition used of Christ, as the Logos, the expression of the Father (see on Gal. i. 1). Ἀπὸ is however used of the Son when the names of Father and Son are attached together (see ver. 7 below), and so conversely is διὰ (Gal. l.c.).

ἐλάβομεν] we, i.e. the Apostles. St Paul never uses the epistolary plural: see on 1 Thess. ii. 4. The plural here serves a double purpose, excluding egotism, and forming a contrast to ὑμεῖς in the next verse.

χάριν καὶ ἀποστολὴν] The conjunction may be regarded as epexegetical, 'the gracious privilege of the Apostleship,' or 'the grace which fits for the Apostleship.' The Apostleship is itself the χάρις, as in Gal. ii. 9, Eph. iii. 2, 7, 8.

εἰς ὑπακοὴν πίστεως] 'unto obedience which springs from faith.' Compare xvi. 26, where again the doxology is suggested by the introduction. The rendering of the two passages in the A. V. is inconsistent, 'obedience to the faith' (here), but 'the obedience of faith' (xvi. 26). Another instance of the subjective genitive after ὑπακοή in this Epistle occurs in xv. 18 εἰς ὑπακοὴν ἐθνῶν. For the meaning here compare Heb. xi. 8 πίστει καλούμενος Ἀβραὰμ ὑπήκουσεν. The expression is chosen to describe the true character of the Gospel: thus πίστις, like χάρις and κλητὸς (-τοὶ), is a keyword.

ἐν πᾶσιν τοῖς ἔθνεσιν] i.e. extending far beyond the Jews, by virtue of the higher personality of our Lord.

ὑπὲρ τοῦ ὀνόματος αὐτοῦ] Involving the idea of person, dignity, authority: see on Phil. ii. 9 τὸ ὄνομα.

6. κλητοὶ Ἰησοῦ Χριστοῦ] 'called to be Jesus Christ's'; not 'called by Jesus Christ,' for the call is always ascribed to God the Father.

7. πᾶσιν] An allusion perhaps to the extensive and straggling character of the Church of the metropolis; or an endeavour to bind together the two sections of that Church (see on Phil. i. 4, and Biblical Essays, p. 312 sq.): 'to all, whether Jews or Gentiles; I make no difference.'

ἐν Ῥώμῃ] On the omission of these words in some texts and the inferences therefrom see Biblical Essays, p. 287 sq.

ἀγαπητοῖς] The variant ἐν ἀγάπῃ has apparently arisen out of a combination of the two readings τοῖς οὖσιν ἐν ῾Ρώμῃ ἀγαπητοῖς Θεοῦ and τοῖς οὖσιν ἐν ἀγάπῃ Θεοῦ : see *Biblical Essays*, p. 288. For ἁγίοις see the notes on Phil. i. 1, Col. i. 2 ; for χάρις ὑμῖν καὶ εἰρήνη the note on 1 Thess. i. 1.

8. πρῶτον μὲν] The antithetical clause which should commence ἔπειτα δὲ (Heb. vii. 2), or at least ἔπειτα (James iii. 17), is lost in the crowd of thoughts which clamour for expression in the Apostle's mind ; as e.g. Rom. iii. 2, 1 Cor. xi. 18, in both which cases the subsequent clauses are strung together continuously, as here, chiefly by the connecting particle γάρ. For a similar example in sub-apostolic literature see [Clem. Rom.] ii. § 3 πρῶτον μὲν ὅτι ἡμεῖς οἱ ζῶντες κ.τ.λ. where there is no balancing sentence.

εὐχαριστῶ] See the note on 1 Thess. i. 2.

τῷ Θεῷ μου κ.τ.λ.] For the sense of close personal relationship expressed in the singular μου, see the notes on Phil. i. 3, Gal. ii. 20. For the difference between περὶ (which is the reading here) and ὑπὲρ see on Gal. i. 4. For the hyperbole ἐν ὅλῳ τῷ κόσμῳ compare 1 Thess. i. 8 ἐν παντὶ τόπῳ with the note.

9. μάρτυς γάρ κ.τ.λ.] The same force of attestation occurs in Phil. i. 8 : see also 2 Cor. i. 23, 1 Thess. ii. 5, 10.

λατρεύω] St Paul contrasts the formal and the spiritual λατρεία here and elsewhere in this Epistle (Rom. xii. 1 τὴν λογικὴν λατρείαν ὑμῶν). For the technical sense of the terms λατρεία, λατρεύειν see the note on Phil. iii. 3, where, as here, πνεύματι occurs in the immediate context.

ἐν τῷ πνεύματί μου ἐν τῷ εὐαγγελίῳ] The first ἐν denotes the subjective atmosphere, the second the external sphere. For the repetition of ἐν, which is frequent in St Paul, see Phil. i. 20, 26, iv. 19, Col. i. 29, ii. 7, iii. 16 etc. 'My λατρεία,' says the Apostle, 'is not a ritual, but a spiritual service ; a service rendered not through the works of the law, but through the preaching of the Gospel. I am not less diligent than the straitest of my fellow-countrymen, but the sphere and the spirit of my diligence are different.'

ὡς ἀδιαλείπτως κ.τ.λ.] As πάντοτε cannot stand in the same clause with ἀδιαλείπτως, the stop must be placed after ποιοῦμαι. For ἀδιαλείπτως and μνείαν ποιοῦμαι see the notes on 1 Thess. v. 17 and 1 Thess. i. 2 respectively. The two phrases occur together in this latter passage.

10. εὐοδωθήσομαι] '*my way shall be made plain.*' The word is always found in the N.T. in the passive (1 Cor. xvi. 2, 3 Joh. 2). It soon loses its literal sense and becomes a metaphor. Here however, considering the subject, the primary meaning can hardly be obliterated : comp. Gen. xxiv. 21, 40, 42, 56 where it takes the cognate accusative τὴν ὁδόν, but elsewhere (Gen. xxiv. 27, 48) it governs the accusative of the person directed.

11. ἐπιποθῶ] See the notes on Phil. i. 8, ii. 26. St Paul frequently uses the verb with ἰδεῖν following, 1 Thess. iii. 6, 2 Tim. i. 4.

χάρισμα πνευματικὸν] What gifts and graces may be included under this term may be seen from 1 Cor. xii. 1 sq. They include (1) moral and spiritual (as πίστις, προφητεία), (2) intellectual (as λόγος σοφίας, ἑρμηνεῖαι γλωσσῶν), (3) physical gifts (as χαρίσματα ἰαμάτων, ἐνεργήματα δυνάμεων). They are thus comprehensive alike in character and in the domain in which they are exercised. St Paul makes no difference between the natural and supernatural: 'all these,' he tells us, 'worketh the one and the same Spirit.' See further on 1 Thess. i. 7. There is nothing in the context which strictly limits χάρισμα here. It might include ἐνεργήματα δυνάμεων, supposing the Apostles had power to communicate such (Acts viii. 14 sq.). The spirit of the passage however points rather to moral and spiritual gifts in a stricter sense: comp. εἰς τὸ στηριχθῆναι ὑμᾶς, διὰ τῆς ἐν ἀλλήλοις πίστεως, and such are enumerated below, xii. 6.

12. τοῦτο δέ ἐστιν] '*I would rather say.*' This, not τοῦτ' ἔστιν, is the true reading here. The difference is important. Τοῦτο δέ ἐστιν is corrective as well as explanatory, τοῦτ' ἔστιν is explanatory merely. St Paul wishes to substitute something more appropriate for what he has just said. On second thoughts, he seems to himself to have arrogated too much in desiring to communicate some spiritual gift, to strengthen them. He has put himself in a position of superiority, from which he hastens to depose himself. 'I should not speak so,' he says in effect: 'you are not the only gainers, I the only benefactor; the gain, the benefaction, is mutual.' Whereas τοῦτ' ἔστιν occurs frequently in the N.T. (Rom. vii. 18, Philem. 12, Heb. ix. 11, xi. 16, xiii. 15 etc.), τοῦτο δέ ἐστιν is found here only.

συνπαρακληθῆναι] sc. ἐμέ. The subject cannot be either (1) ὑμᾶς, as the construction of the preceding στηριχθῆναι would suggest, or (2) ἡμᾶς (i.e. ὑμᾶς καὶ ἐμέ) as Dr Vaughan takes it. The ἐν ὑμῖν excludes both alike. The former would require ἐν ἐμοί, the latter ἐν ἑαυτοῖς or ἐν ἀλλήλοις. The force of the prepositions is, 'that I may be comforted (strengthened, encouraged) with and in you,' the συν- preparing the way for διὰ τῆς ἐν ἀλλήλοις πίστεως.

ὑμῶν τε καὶ ἐμοῦ] Added to emphasize the mutual character of the benefit. This is introduced in the συν-, still further enforced in the ἐν ἀλλήλοις, and finally emphasized by ὑμῶν τε καὶ ἐμοῦ. And not only so, the addition rectifies the balance in another way. The usual Greek order would be ἐμοῦ τε καὶ ὑμῶν (for in classical language grammar swayed the order, just as on the other hand in modern parlance courtesy overrules the grammar). St Paul however departs from the natural order, that so he may give superior prominence to the faith of the Romans over his own.

13. οὐ θέλω] The variant οὐκ οἴομαι (D*G) is perhaps connected with the abridgment of the Epistle: see *Biblical Essays*, p. 319.

πολλάκις προεθέμην] The first indication of this purpose is to be found in Acts xix. 21, perhaps half a year or more before this Epistle was written; but the expression there (δεῖ με καὶ ʽΡώμην ἰδεῖν) implies a fixed, and probably a long-cherished, intention of visiting Rome. This intention may have gained definiteness from the moment when he fell in with Aquila and Priscilla at Corinth, six or seven years before he wrote this Epistle. They had left Rome because of Messianic disturbances there (Acts xviii. 2).

καὶ ἐκωλύθην ἄχρι τοῦ δεῦρο] I prefer to take this sentence independently and parenthetically, and not to connect it with οὐ θέλω: 'albeit I was prevented.' Compare 1 Thess. ii. 18. The καὶ thus becomes a quasi-Hebraism. The hindrance of which he speaks was the necessity of completing his work in Greece and the East (Rom. xv. 22, 23).

τινὰ καρπὸν σχῶ] For the metaphor compare Phil. i. 22, 1 Cor. iii. 6 sq., John iv. 36.

καθὼς καὶ] For the repetition of καὶ see on Col. iii. 13, 1 Thess. ii. 14, and comp. Eph. v. 23.

14. ῞Ελλησίν τε καὶ βαρβάροις] A comprehensive description of the Gentile world. St Paul does not here mention the Jew; for the Jew was the special charge of the Apostles of the Circumcision: he only fell incidentally to St Paul. Therefore we need not ask whether in the Apostle's mind the Jew is reckoned as ῞Ελλην or βάρβαρος. He employs the latter word twice elsewhere. In Col. iii. 11 (where its exaggeration is Σκύθης) the Jew is obviously not included: in 1 Cor. xiv. 11 the word is used of a person speaking an unintelligible tongue and contains no idea of nationality. If it be asked under which head St Paul classes the Romans, we may reply that doubtless, had the question been put to him, he would have included them under ῞Ελληνες: but perhaps he did not put the question definitely to himself. The circumstances of the Roman Church, which for two centuries was mainly Greek-speaking, did not require him to do so. For a full discussion of the word βάρβαρος see Col. iii. 11.

σοφοῖς τε καὶ ἀνοήτοις] This division is almost coincident with the former (comp. 1 Cor. i. 22): but while that regards civilisation as the line of demarcation, this makes intellectual progress the criterion of distinction.

ὀφειλέτης εἰμί] Another way of expressing the ἀνάγκη of 1 Cor. ix. 16.

οὕτω τὸ κατ᾽ ἐμὲ πρόθυμον] 'in pursuance of this principle (or in fulfilment of this obligation), my part is ready.' Πρόθυμον cannot be taken as a substantive, and rendered, 'there is readiness on my part.' The absence of the article and of the substantive verb is fatal to this interpretation. For τὸ κατ᾽ ἐμὲ compare τὰ κατ᾽ ἐμὲ Eph. vi. 21, Col. iv. 7, Phil. i. 12, Tobit x. 8, Esdr. i. 22.

II. DOCTRINAL PORTION, i. 16—xi. 36.

i. *What is the Gospel?* (i. 16—18).

16. **οὐ γὰρ ἐπαισχύνομαι κ.τ.λ.**] The motive of ἐπαισχύνομαι here is explained by 1 Cor. i. 21, the context of which passage contains the expression δύναμις Θεοῦ twice used, as here, of the Gospel (1 Cor. i. 18, 24). The words τοῦ Χριστοῦ of the Textus Receptus after εὐαγγέλιον should be omitted, and ἐν αὐτῷ in the next paragraph referred to τὸ εὐαγγέλιον.

Ἰουδαίῳ τε πρῶτον] Compare ii. 9, 10, where the same phrase occurs. Here however the word πρῶτον is suspicious, as it is omitted in BG and Tertullian, and may have been interpolated from ii. 9, 10. If it be retained, it must refer to priority of time; for absolutely there is no distinction, as St Paul elsewhere states (ch. x. 12). Thus it will be explained by St Paul's language to the Jews at Antioch (Acts xiii. 46 ὑμῖν ἦν ἀναγκαῖον πρῶτον λαληθῆναι τὸν λόγον τοῦ Θεοῦ) and by his constant practice everywhere. Even at Rome itself he did not act otherwise (Acts xxviii. 17, 28). In verse 17 of that passage τοὺς ὄντας τῶν Ἰουδαίων πρώτους is translated in the A. V. 'the chief of the Jews,' and this seems to be the universal interpretation. But may it not be 'he called together first those who were of the Jews'? in which case for the use of the genitive we may compare Acts v. 17, ix. 2, 1 Tim. i. 20, 2 Tim. i. 15, ii. 17.

17. **δικαιοσύνη Θεοῦ**] The expression is common in St Paul (see iii. 5, 21, 22, x. 3, 2 Cor. v. 21: comp. James i. 20). The genitive should be rendered 'coming from God,' compare the phrase ὀργὴ Θεοῦ in the next verse, to which it is opposed. Similarly in the passage cited from St James ὀργὴ ἀνδρὸς is the antithesis to δικαιοσύνη Θεοῦ. In ch. x. 3 it is opposed to τὴν ἰδίαν (δικαιοσύνην) and must bear this meaning (see also a similar phrase and contrast in Phil. iii. 9, and Luke xvi. 15). The contrast then is between a righteousness appointed by God and a righteousness of our own making, and it may be illustrated by the parable of the publican and the Pharisee (esp. Luke xviii. 14). It cannot therefore mean here 'righteousness in the sight of God,' which is the meaning in iii. 20.

ἐκ πίστεως εἰς πίστιν] Faith is the starting point, and faith the goal. For the phrase compare 2 Cor. iii. 18 ἀπὸ δόξης εἰς δόξαν, Rom. vi. 19 τῇ ἀνομίᾳ εἰς τὴν ἀνομίαν, John i. 16 χάριν ἀντὶ χάριτος.

ὁ δὲ δίκαιος κ.τ.λ.] From Habak. ii. 4. The passage is quoted also in Gal. iii. 11 (where see the notes), and Heb. x. 38. I cannot doubt that ἐκ πίστεως is to be taken with ζήσεται, not with ὁ δίκαιος. For (1) the original seems certainly so to intend it; and in the LXX., whether we read μου ἐκ πίστεως or ἐκ πίστεώς μου (see *Galatians*, p. 156 note 4), it

appears so to be taken. This is also the construction in the Targum
Jonathan. (2) Ἐκ πίστεως here corresponds to ἐκ πίστεως in the former
part of the verse, where it belongs, not to the predicate, but to the subject.
It is here separated from ὁ δίκαιος, as it is there separated from δικαιοσύνη.
(3) Ὁ δίκαιος ἐκ πίστεως is not a natural phrase, and, I think, has no
parallel in St Paul. (4) The other construction takes the emphasis off
'faith,' which the context shows to be the really emphatic word, and lays
it on the verb 'live.' In Gal. iii. 11 the context is still more decisive.
For the Old Testament meaning of faith see *Galatians*, p. 154 sq., where
this passage is discussed with others. The construction ζῆν ἐκ may be
illustrated from 2 Cor. xiii. 4, where the phrase occurs twice.

18. ἀποκαλύπτεται γὰρ] 'A righteousness of God is revealed, being
required for the state of mankind; *for* a wrath of God is revealed and
extends to all.' Thus the opening words of this verse correspond to the
opening words of the last. Here however ἀποκαλύπτεται is placed first,
and is emphatic, 'for there has been also another revelation.' In the
individual, as in the race, this revelation must precede the other. The
sense of sin, the sense of God's displeasure at sin, the sense that God
will not overlook sin—this is the revelation of the ὀργὴ Θεοῦ.

ἀπ' οὐρανοῦ] to be taken with ἀποκαλύπτεται. It is added to give
solemnity to the facts. The heavens open, as it were, and reveal the
Righteous Judge (2 Thess. i. 7).

πᾶσαν] Extending to Jew as well as Gentile (comp. ii. 1, 9, 10),
though the remaining part of the chapter refers specially to the Gentiles.

ἀσέβειαν καὶ ἀδικίαν] Ἀσέβεια against God, ἀδικία against men. The
first precedes and entails the second: witness the teaching of this
chapter.

τὴν ἀλήθειαν] The word involves two ideas; first, the confession of
the One True God, as opposed to idols; secondly, the acknowledgment
of Christ, as the manifestation of God the Father. The first is the
prominent idea here; the second perhaps in St John.

κατεχόντων] '*grasping, possessing*': comp. 1 Cor. xi. 2, xv. 2, Luke
viii. 15, and see the antithesis of ἔχειν, κατέχειν in 2 Cor. vi. 10. The
preposition κατὰ is no objection to this rendering. The strength of the
word is its recommendation. They did grasp, did possess the truth
potentially. Compare καθορᾶται below (ver. 20) and γνόντες (ver. 21).
There was no doubt about the truth: at least there ought to have been
none. They could not plead that it was slippery, that it eluded their
grasp. Thus the preposition is really expressive here. Against the
other interpretation, 'restraining, keeping down,' I would urge, first
that τὴν ἀλήθειαν ἐν ἀδικίᾳ is an awkward expression in this sense; and
secondly, that we want some statement here of the fact that they had
the truth.

ii. *State of the Gentile world* (i. 19—32).

19. διότι] ' I say possessing, because' etc.

τὸ γνωστὸν] This may mean either 'known' or 'knowable.' The word however seems always to have the first sense in the N. T. For this passage compare Acts xv. 18. There are unseen truths behind all this, but the one essential thing was a known thing.

ἐν αὐτοῖς] '*among them*'; rather than ' in them,' in the sense of 'in their hearts.' Comp. 1 Cor. xi. 19 ἵνα οἱ δόκιμοι φανεροὶ γένωνται ἐν ὑμῖν.

20. τὰ γὰρ ἀόρατα κ.τ.λ.] All which follows in this chapter shows a remarkable correspondence with Wisdom chs. xiii.—xv., a passage which St Paul must have had in his mind. See especially Wisdom xiii. 1, 5, 7, 10, 13, 14, xiv. 11, 12, 15, 23—27, xv. 11, xvi. 1. We must remember that the Book of Wisdom was written in Egypt where animals were worshipped. The general thought is well illustrated in ps.-Aristotle *de Mundo* 6 πάσῃ θνητῇ φύσει γενόμενος ἀθεώρητος ἀπ' αὐτῶν τῶν ἔργων θεωρεῖται ὁ Θεός.

ἀπὸ κτίσεως κόσμου] i.e. 'from the very beginning'; to be taken with καθορᾶται, not with τὰ ἀόρατα αὐτοῦ. For 'the invisible things,' i.e. His Person and attributes, are in themselves independent of time. On the vicissitudes of the word κόσμος see the note on Eph. ii. 2; on κτίσις the note on Col. i. 15.

καθορᾶται] '*are clearly discerned*' : the only passage where the word occurs in the N. T. The force of the preposition is shown in Job x. 4 ἢ ὥσπερ βροτὸς ὁρᾷ καθορᾷς; 'or is Thy clear vision like the vision of a mortal?'

θειότης] On this word and its distinction from θεότης see the note on Col. ii. 9.

εἰς τὸ εἶναι] '*so that they are.*' The proper distinction between εἰς τὸ and πρὸς τὸ seems to be that εἰς denotes 'result,' πρὸς 'design' or 'purpose': but of course purpose may be indirectly implied in εἰς here.

ἀναπολογήτους] Arraigned before the bar of divine justice they have nothing to say. The same word is applied also to the Jew (ii. 1). It is a forensic term, not uncommon in the age of Polybius and later; but it is not found elsewhere in the LXX. and N. T. Cicero uses it (*ad Att.* xvi. 7) 'sed hoc ἀναπολόγητον.'

21. ἐδόξασαν ἢ ηὐχαρίστησαν] The first term denotes the objective worship, the second the reflexive feeling. On the duty of εὐχαριστία, as the crown of Christian worship in St Paul's teaching, see on 1 Thess. i. 2, v. 16.

ἐματαιώθησαν] See 2 Kings xvii. 15, Jerem. ii. 5, passages which the Apostle may be supposed to have had in his mind. At all events the train of thought is the same here. 'They followed foolishness (τὰ μάταια) and became foolish (μάταιοι) themselves.' Comp. Wisdom xiii. 1 μάταιοι μὲν γὰρ πάντες ἄνθρωποι φύσει οἷς παρῆν Θεοῦ ἀγνωσία, Ps. xciv. 11 (quoted on 1 Cor. iii. 20, an Epistle written not long before this) Κύριος γινώσκει τοὺς διαλογισμοὺς αὐτῶν ὅτι εἰσὶ μάταιοι, where the correspondence to ἐν τοῖς διαλογισμοῖς αὐτῶν is noticeable.

διαλογισμοῖς] Here 'inward questionings': as generally in the N.T.; though not universally, see 1 Tim. ii. 8 and the note on Phil. ii. 14.

ἐσκοτίσθη] Of the three forms found in the LXX. σκοτάζω, σκοτίζω and σκοτόω, the second is the more usual in the N.T. (Matt. xxiv. 29, Mark xiii. 24, Rom. xi. 10, all however quotations, here and Rev. viii. 12); but the last is found (Eph. iv. 18 the true reading, Rev. ix. 2). Σκοτάζω does not occur. The celebrated passage in Clement of Rome (§ 36) διὰ τούτου ἡ ἀσύνετος καὶ ἐσκοτωμένη διάνοια ἡμῶν ἀναθάλλει εἰς τὸ φῶς is a combination of this passage with Eph. iv. 18: accordingly we are not surprised to find a diversity of reading; ἐσκοτωμένη being read there, but the passage from Clement as quoted by Clement of Alexandria (Strom. iv. 16, p. 613) having ἐσκοτισμένη. See A. Jahn's Methodius II. p. 77, note 453.

23. ἤλλαξαν τὴν δόξαν ἐν ὁμοιώματι] An embedded quotation from Ps. cvi. (cv.) 20 (comp. Jer. ii. 11). The variant ἠλλάξαντο seems to have come from the original passage, which, as being in the Psalms, would be well remembered. For a similar embedded quotation involving a similar motive see Phil. ii. 15. The whole context here is full of Old Testament phraseology, ἡ ἀσύνετος αὐτῶν καρδία (comp. Ps. lxxvi. 6), σοφοὶ ἐμωράνθησαν (comp. Is. xix. 11).

δόξαν] i.e. His attributes as manifested to men in His works, whether by the revelation of nature, or by the revelation of grace. On the other hand, the great manifestation, the culminating exhibition of His δόξα, in the Person and Life of Christ (John i. 14), was not vouchsafed to them.

ὁμοιώματι εἰκόνος] For the difference between these words, ὁμοίωμα implying a resemblance which may be accidental, εἰκὼν presupposing an archetype of which it is a copy, see on Col. i. 15. The distinction however has no very important bearing on this passage, and the genitive is the genitive of apposition or explanation, 'a likeness which consists in an image or copy.'

φθαρτοῦ ἀνθρώπου κ.τ.λ.] Ἀνθρώπου as in the mythologies of Greece and Rome, including the worship of the Emperor; πετεινῶν, τετραπόδων, ἑρπετῶν as in Assyria and especially Egypt. For this latter class of idolatry see Deut. iv. 17 sq., and Wisdom xiii. ll. cc. which was probably the composition of an Alexandrian Jew. The cult of the crocodile, ibis, cat etc. was a theme of ridicule for Roman satirists (like Juvenal Sat. xv. 1 sq. 'qualia demens Ægyptus portenta colit? crocodilon adorat Pars haec, illa pavet saturam serpentibus ibim' etc.), as well as for Jewish writers (like Philo who is very severe Legatio ad Caium § 20 (II. p. 566) οἱ κύνας καὶ λύκους καὶ λέοντας καὶ κροκοδείλους καὶ ἄλλα πλείονα θηρία καὶ ἔνυδρα καὶ χερσαῖα καὶ πτηνὰ θεοπλαστοῦντες, ὑπὲρ ὧν βωμοὶ καὶ ἱερὰ καὶ ναοὶ καὶ τεμένη κατὰ πᾶσαν Αἴγυπτον ἵδρυνται, § 25 Θεοῦ κλῆσις οὕτως ἐστὶ σεμνὸν παρ' αὐτοῖς ὥστε καὶ ἴβεσι καὶ ἰοβόλοις ἀσπίσι ταῖς ἐγχωρίοις καὶ πολλοῖς ἑτέροις τῶν ἐξηγριωμένων αὐτῆς θηρίων μεταδεδώκασιν), and Christian (as the Sibylline Oracles see *proem.* vv. 60, 65 sq., iii. 29, 30 ματαίως δὲ πλανᾶσθε προσκυνέοντες ὄφεις τε καὶ αἰλούροισι θύοντες).

24. **διὸ παρέδωκεν αὐτοὺς**] So ver. 26 διὰ τοῦτο παρέδωκεν αὐτούς, and again ver. 28 παρέδωκεν αὐτούς. Two facts must be noticed here. (1) This delivering up, this hardening the heart, is the second stage in the downward fall, not the first, in the language of Scripture. The first is in the man's own power. (2) This is not represented as a negative result of God's dealings, not as a permissive act, a passive acquiescence on His part. There is a stage in the downward course when by God's law sin begets more sin and works out its own punishment in the degradation of the whole man. Thus there are moral laws of God's government just as there are physical laws. This fact was perceived by thoughtful men even without the assistance of Christian teaching. See the celebrated passage of Persius *Satir.* iii. 35 sq. 'Magne pater divum, saevos punire tyrannos Haud alia ratione velis, quum dira libido Moverit ingenium, ferventi tincta veneno: Virtutem videant intabescantque relicta,' and compare the Jewish proverb *Pirke Aboth* iv. 5 'Merces praecepti praeceptum est et transgressionis transgressio.' Quite apart from revelation, all experience shows that this is a moral law.

ἐν ταῖς ἐπιθυμίαις] '*in their lusts*'; not 'to their lusts,' which Dr Vaughan suggests as a possible rendering. True the LXX. by a common Hebraism has the construction παραδιδόναι ἐν as equivalent to παραδιδόναι εἰς: but here we have the thing to which the deliverance over is made expressed in a separate phrase εἰς ἀκαθαρσίαν. Ἐν ταῖς ἐπιθυμίαις must therefore represent 'the field or region in which the abandonment acted,' as Vaughan prefers to take it.

ἀτιμάζεσθαι] Compare in this sense ver. 26 εἰς πάθη ἀτιμίας and 1 Thess. iv. 4 τὸ ἑαυτοῦ σκεῦος κτᾶσθαι ἐν ἁγιασμῷ καὶ τιμῇ. On the Christian reverence for the body see note on 1 Cor. vi. 13.

αὐτῶν ἐν αὐτοῖς] The correct reading, not αὐτῶν ἐν αὐτοῖς. On the other hand ἐν αὐτοῖς is the reading three verses below.

25. **τῷ ψεύδει**] '*the lie, the falsehood.*' An expression used for an idol, both in the Old Testament (Hab. ii. 18) and in the New Testament (Rev. xxi. 27, xxii. 15). The idol is a lie in two senses; for it professes to be what it is not, and it leads others astray.

ἐσεβάσθησαν] '*took as the objects of their devotion*' (their σεβάσματα, comp. Acts xvii. 23). Σεβάζεσθαι is thus stronger than σέβεσθαι. For the connexion of idolatry and profligacy see the note on 1 Thess. ii. 3. It was the necessary consequence of deifying human passions. Fetish worship produces fetish morality. Unbelief or wrong-belief in religious matters will ultimately degrade morality.

26. **διὰ τοῦτο**] '*for this reason it was.*' Very emphatic, taking up

and emphasizing the διὸ παρέδωκεν αὐτοὺς of ver. 24. A later stage in the downward course is reached in ver. 28.

27. κατεργαζόμενοι] A very strong and a favourite word with St Paul at this time, occurring in this Epistle no less than eleven times, and eight times in the Epistles to the Corinthians.

28. ἐδοκίμασαν] On this word see the notes on 1 Thess. ii. 4, v. 21. The metaphor is that of testing coin, and the counterpart appears in ἀδόκιμον below. Just as they would not accept the knowledge of God as standard coin, so God refused to accept their minds. Compare Jerem. vi. 30 ἀργύριον ἀποδεδοκιμασμένον καλέσατε αὐτούς, ὅτι ἀπεδοκίμασεν αὐτοὺς Κύριος. Ἀδόκιμον thus becomes equivalent to κίβδηλον, and the two adjectives are found in close connexion elsewhere, e.g. Greg. Naz. *Orat.* iv. 10 (I. p. 82) οὐ κίβδηλον ᾠδὴν οὐδὲ ἀδόκιμον. For the construction of ἔχειν after δοκιμάζειν 'so as to have,' comp. 1 Thess. ii. 4.

παρέδωκεν αὐτοὺς] There are two stages, not three, described in God's abandonment of the wicked. *First,* they persisted in worshipping false gods, whereupon God let them follow their own flagitious passions (ver. 24 repeated in ver. 26). *Secondly,* they steeped themselves in flagitious passions, whereupon God suffered their mind to be wholly perverted and reprobate (ver. 28).

νοῦν] As ἀδόκιμον corresponds to the preceding ἐδοκίμασαν, so does νοῦν to the preceding ἐν ἐπιγνώσει. Vaughan well quotes Tit. i. 16. This is the aggravation of their moral state. This is the second and final stage in their abandonment by God. The higher part of their nature is gone.

29. πεπληρωμένους, μεστοὺς] The wrong-doing, the degrading passion, is not now occasional. It is they, and they are it. Comp. Plato *Gorgias* § 80, p. 525 A ὑπὸ ἐξουσίας καὶ τρυφῆς καὶ ὕβρεως καὶ ἀκρατίας τῶν πράξεων ἀσυμμετρίας τε καὶ αἰσχρότητος γέμουσαν τὴν ψυχὴν εἶδεν, *Respubl.* ix. § 6, p. 579 E φόβου γέμων διὰ παντὸς τοῦ βίου, σφαδασμῶν τε καὶ ὀδυνῶν πλήρης.

πάσῃ ἀδικίᾳ κ.τ.λ.] There are many variants in the list of sins which follow. The word πορνείᾳ at all events ought to be struck out of the text for two reasons. (1) It seems to have been introduced as an explanation (and a wrong one) of πλεονεξίᾳ. (2) It is out of place here. The sins here enumerated are of a different kind. In the former part St Paul had spoken of passions which degrade the man himself. Here he speaks of vices which make him intolerable to others. The resemblance in form to πονηρίᾳ which precedes, assisted in the corruption of the text. The most probable reading is πάσῃ ἀδικίᾳ πονηρίᾳ πλεονεξίᾳ κακίᾳ, or possibly the order of the last two terms should be reversed. Thus we obtain a natural grouping. First come the outward acts, ἀδικία, πονηρία, πλεονεξία 'injustice, rascality, graspingness.' Then follows the inward disposition, κακία, 'viciousness.' Κακία denotes the pleasure taken in injuring others, where vice has become habitual, and where injury is done to others, not for the sake of gain but for its own sake. For the distinction between κακία and πονηρία see on Col. iii. 8, and for πλεονεξία Col. iii. 5. Πλεονεξία is the disposition which is ever ready to sacrifice one's neighbour to oneself in all things, not in money dealings merely.

φθόνου, φόνου] See the note on Gal. v. 21 φθόνοι, φόνοι where φόνοι is of doubtful authority. The alliteration decided the juxtaposition here, as in ἀσυνέτους, ἀσυνθέτους (ver. 30).

ψιθυριστάς, καταλάλους] The secret and the open detractors respectively. See Tac. *Ann.* vi. 7 'cum primores senatus infimas etiam delationes exercerent, alii propalam, multi per occultum.' It seems probable that St Paul here had the 'delatores' in his mind. He is especially dwelling on heathen vices, and at this time 'delatio' was among the most prominent and crying vices of Rome. For the combination comp. 2 Cor. xii. 20, 1 Pet. ii. 1.

30. **θεοστυγεῖς**] '*hateful to God*,' rather than 'God-haters.' There seems indeed to be no authority for the active meaning. The phrase is explained in Clement of Rome § 35 ταῦτα γὰρ οἱ πράσσοντες στυγητοὶ τῷ Θεῷ ὑπάρχουσιν, a passage which is a reminiscence of Rom. i. 29 sq., and can be illustrated from Wisdom xiv. 9 μισητὰ Θεῷ καὶ ὁ ἀσεβῶν καὶ ἡ ἀσέβεια αὐτοῦ, a work of which (as I have remarked before, see on ver. 20) the context is full. Philo, *ap.* Joh. Damasc. *Sacr. Parall.* p. 436 D, speaking of informers calls them διάβολοι καὶ θείας ἀπόπεμπτοι χάριτος θεοστυγεῖς τε καὶ θεομισεῖς πάντῃ.

ὑβριστάς, ὑπερηφάνους, ἀλαζόνας] The first term implies disregard for others, the second and third terms exaltation of self; with this distinction however that ὑπερηφάνους means 'arrogant in thought,' ἀλαζόνας 'braggarts in words and gestures.'

The rendering of ὑβριστὰς in the A.V. by 'despiteful' is an archaism rather than a mistranslation for 'insolent': comp. the rendering in Heb. x. 29 ἐνυβρίσας 'done despite unto.'

ἐφευρετὰς κακῶν] i.e. inventors of new forms of vice. Comp. Tac. *Ann.* vi. 1 'ignota antea vocabula reperta sunt'; and the consequences were what the Apostle describes here, see the letter of Tiberius (ch. 6) which commences 'quid scribam vobis, patres conscripti, aut quomodo scribam, aut quid omnino non scribam hoc tempore, di me deaeque peius perdant quam perire me quotidie sentio, si scio'; to which the historian adds the words, 'adeo facinora atque flagitia sua ipsi quoque in supplicium verterant. neque frustra praestantissimus sapientiae firmare solitus est, si recludantur tyrannorum mentes posse aspici laniatus et ictus quando ut corpora verberibus ita saevitia, libidine, malis consultis animus dilaceretur. quippe Tiberium non fortuna, non solitudines protegebant quin tormenta pectoris suasque ipse poenas fateretur.'

γονεῦσιν ἀπειθεῖς] Comp. 1 Tim. i. 9, 2 Tim. iii. 2.

31. **ἀστόργους**] The insertion of ἀσπόνδους after ἀστόργους in the T.R. may have arisen either as a gloss on ἀσυνθέτους, or as a reminiscence of 2 Tim. iii. 3 where ἄσπονδοι follows ἄστοργοι.

32. **οἵτινες κ.τ.λ.**] '*men who knowing well the ordinance of God.*' 'Ordinance,' rather than 'judgment' (A.V.), is the meaning of δικαίωμα here : the former implies a general legal enactment, the latter an individual verdict.

πράσσοντες] '*practise.*' This is the staple of their conduct. A different word ποιοῦσιν is used below, where simple 'doing' is intended to be implied. The same contrast is found in ii. 3. The word θανάτου is best explained here of spiritual death.

οὐ μόνον κ.τ.λ.] Jowett takes this as an anticlimax, and declares that it cannot 'be maintained, as a general proposition, that it is worse to approve than to do evil.' Surely this is a mistake. Many a man from passion or self-interest will do what his conscience does not approve ; but to instigate others to do, to take pleasure in doing, what is sinful, is an aggravation of his state.

συνευδοκοῦσιν] '*sympathize with,*' and so stimulate and encourage by their sympathy. The variants ποιοῦντες, συνευδοκοῦντες found in B, and some manuscripts of the Latin Vulgate, and known to Origen, Isidore of Pelusium and Epiphanius, seem to have been read by Clement of Rome § 35 οὐ μόνον δὲ οἱ πράσσοντες αὐτὰ ἀλλὰ καὶ οἱ συνευδοκοῦντες αὐτοῖς : and the attempts to complete the construction discernible in the insertion of οὐκ ἐνόησαν of D and the οὐκ ἔγνωσαν of G after ἐπιγνόντες above, point in the same direction. But if, as is possible, this was the original reading, it may have been an error of Tertius the amanuensis, in the hurry of writing what was dictated to him. Clement of Rome appears to have taken the words ποιοῦντες, συνευδοκοῦντες to refer to οἱ τὰ τοιαῦτα πράσσοντες κ.τ.λ., but this is surely wrong. Still Clement's testimony to the reading is of the highest importance, as he may have had the Apostle's autograph before him, when he wrote.

CHAPTER II

iii. *State of the Jewish people* (ii. 1—29).

IT is worth while to observe the identity of plan discernible in this chapter and in the last. As in the last section (i. 18—32) St Paul began with a general proposition, and made no direct reference to the Gentiles, this general proposition however involving the condition of the Gentiles as a class; and thence proceeded to the special sins of the Gentiles as a class: so here he starts from a general statement, which implicitly contains a description of the condition of the Jews as a class, though there is no mention of the Jews; and goes on to condemn the Jew through this general statement, though he does not refer directly to him till ver. 17.

Again the universality of the statement is emphasized in each case (i. 18 ἐπὶ πᾶσαν ἀσέβειαν, ii. 1 πᾶς ὁ κρίνων). The Jew, who falls into Gentile profligacy, falls under Gentile condemnation; and the Gentile, who indulges in Jewish pride and self-righteousness, will be punished as if he were a Jew. As a last point of coincidence the two general ordinances are bound together by the repetition of the word ἀναπολόγητος (i. 20, ii. 1). There is no escape either for the one or for the other.

1. ὁ κρίνων] The parable of the Pharisee and Publican is the best commentary on this whole section: compare especially ii. 17—19 with the terms in which the parable is introduced (Luke xviii. 9).

κατακρίνεις] For St Paul's frequent use of compounds of κρίνειν see the note on 1 Cor. ii. 15.

2. ἐστὶν κατὰ ἀλήθειαν] The verb is slightly emphatic, as its position shows. It implies the absolute character of God's judgment. Κατὰ ἀλήθειαν may be illustrated from John vii. 24.

3. σύ] The pronoun is emphatic; 'thinkest thou that thou shalt prove an exception to the general rule?' The Jews held that the judgment was for the Gentiles only, not for the Israelites, the true servants of Messiah. The Apostle's reminder is an echo of the Baptist's language (Matt. iii. 8, 9).

4. ἤ] This is the alternative. 'If you do not trust your own powers of evasion, it follows that you must despise the lavish mercy of God.' Thus vv. 3, 4 set forth the two grounds on which his hearers hoped to go unpunished.

χρηστότητος, ἀνοχῆς, μακροθυμίας] The distinction between χρηστότης, *neutral*, 'a kindly disposition towards one's neighbours' not necessarily taking an active form, and μακροθυμία, *passive*, 'patient endurance under injuries inflicted by others,' is set forth in the note on Gal. v. 22, where the two words work up to the *active* correlative, ἀγαθωσύνη, 'goodness, beneficence' as an energetic principle. There however the terms are applied to human agents; here as applied to God the distinction is somewhat different, χρηστότης implying His 'gracious dealings,' ἀνοχή His 'forbearance,' His 'suspension of judgment,' μακροθυμία His 'long-suffering.' Thus ἀνοχή, which in classical Greek signifies a suspension of arms, 'indutiae,' represents a transient state of things which 'after a certain lapse of time...unless other conditions intervene, will pass away' (Trench *N. T. Syn.* § liii. p. 199). Accordingly in one of the two passages in which it occurs in the N.T. it is connected with the πάρεσις ἁμαρτημάτων (Rom. iii. 25) anterior to the knowledge of the atoning work of Christ.

τὸ χρηστὸν τοῦ Θεοῦ] i.e. 'not knowing that the true purpose of God's goodness is the very reverse of this, intended not to encourage you to sin, but to lead you to repentance.'

5. θησαυρίζεις] '*storest up.*' The idea of θησαυρίζειν is gradual accumulation: 'irae divinae judicia paulatim coacervari, ut tandem universa promantur' Wolf (*Cur. Phil.* iv. 38). The words ἐν ἡμέρᾳ ὀργῆς contain an abridged expression, with the meaning 'so that they will be accumulated upon you in the day of wrath': see the notes on 1 Thess. iii. 13 ἀμέμπτους, where other examples are given, and Phil. iv. 19 ἐν δόξῃ. This appears to be the true sense in James v. 5 also ἐν ἡμέρᾳ σφαγῆς. On this Pauline use of ἡμέρα see the notes on 1 Thess. v. 2, 4.

6. ὃς ἀποδώσει κ.τ.λ.] From the LXX. of Prov. xxiv. 12, a favourite quotation in the N.T., occurring in St Paul here and 2 Tim. iv. 14, in Matt. xvi. 27 and Rev. xxii. 12. Clement of Rome (§ 34) cites it, probably from Rev. l.c., and characteristically combines it with other Old Testament passages. His namesake of Alexandria (*Strom.* iv. 22, p. 625) copies it from the Roman Clement.

κατὰ τὰ ἔργα αὐτοῦ] Explained by the words which follow καθ' ὑπομονὴν ἔργου ἀγαθοῦ. St Paul's doctrine of justification by faith must be qualified and interpreted by such expressions as these.

7. ζωὴν αἰώνιον] sc. ἀποδώσει. This must be the construction, for the accusatives δόξαν, τιμήν, ἀφθαρσίαν cannot be separated from ζητοῦσιν.

8. τοῖς δὲ ἐξ ἐριθείας] Instead of the usual explanation 'those whose starting-point is party-feeling' (comp. iv. 14 οἱ ἐκ νόμου, Gal. iii. 7 οἱ ἐκ πίστεως), it is perhaps better to supply πράσσουσιν 'those who act from party-feeling.' Certainly where the expression occurs again (Phil. i. 17 οἱ ἐξ ἐριθείας), it is not, as some suppose, elliptical, but καταγγέλλουσιν has to be supplied: see the note on ἐξ ἀγάπης there. For ἐριθεία see on Gal. v. 20, Phil. ii. 3. The phrase is especially appropriate to the Judaizing tendencies, where party was set before truth (Phil. i. 17).

ὀργὴ καὶ θυμὸς κ.τ.λ.] The construction of the sentence presents certain difficulties, owing to three main peculiarities of structure. (1) There is a change, the nominatives ὀργὴ κ.τ.λ. occurring where the parallel to ζωὴν αἰώνιον would require accusatives. We must not however remedy this by placing a full stop after ἀδικίᾳ; for, though this would simplify the construction, it would be harsh and not at all after St Paul's manner. (2) The expression ἐπὶ πᾶσαν ψυχήν...Ἕλληνος 'extending to every soul of man' etc. is a sort of afterthought. The first idea of the sentence ἐξ ἐριθείας refers mainly to the Jew; but, as in other cases, the Apostle hastens to make the proposition universal. (3) Lastly, the change of form in the sentence and its extension lead to the addition δόξα δὲ... Ἕλληνι, which finally destroys whatever symmetry remained.

9. θλίψις καὶ στενοχωρία] We gather from 2 Cor. iv. 8 θλιβόμενοι ἀλλ' οὐ στενοχωρούμενοι that στενοχωρία is the stronger word. The terms are perhaps to be distinguished as the temporary and the continuous. More strictly, we may say that the opposite to θλίψις 'compression' is ἄνεσις 'relaxation' (on which word see 2 Thess. i. 7), the opposite to στενοχωρία is πλατυσμὸς or εὐρυχωρία 'enlargement, room to move in.' Here, and in viii. 35, both expressions are derived from Is. viii. 22. On θλίψις and kindred words see the note on 1 Thess. iii. 7 ἀνάγκη καὶ θλίψει.

κατεργαζομένου] 'who worketh out, worketh deliberately.' Below (ver. 10) it is τῷ ἐργαζομένῳ simply.

πρῶτον] As the Jew has priority of privilege, so he has also priority of penalty.

11. οὐ γὰρ] referring to παντὶ τῷ ἐργ. The πρῶτον is overlooked, as being merely incidental and not affecting the ἀπροσωπολημψία of God. On προσωπολημψία see the note on Gal. ii. 6 πρόσωπον λαμβάνειν.

12. ὅσοι γὰρ] 'All alike, for whether under law or not under law, they shall be judged according to their condition.'

13. οὐ γὰρ οἱ ἀκροαταὶ κ.τ.λ.] The sentence is connected with ἐν νόμῳ ἥμαρτον. 'For the mere facts that they are under law, that they are children of Abraham, that Moses is read among them every Sabbath-day (Acts xv. 21), will not rescue them.' Compare James i. 22, 23, 25. For ἀκροαταὶ of hearing without action see the description given by Cleon of the character of the Athenians (Thuc. iii. 38) εἰώθατε θεαταὶ μὲν τῶν λόγων γίγνεσθαι, ἀκροαταὶ δὲ τῶν ἔργων.

νόμου, νόμου] The article is omitted because a general principle is stated. The reference is doubtless to the Mosaic law; but the Apostle divides mankind into two classes—those under law and those not under law.

δικαιωθήσονται] The change of expression from δίκαιοι is perhaps intentional. The one are not *ipso facto* just: the others will be made just.

14. ὅταν γὰρ] The fourth γὰρ in succession. 'The doers of the law, I say; for the principle must be wide enough to admit Gentiles also. They too in a certain sense have a law (νόμος) and so they have a capacity of fulfilling it (of being ποιηταὶ νόμου).'

ἔθνη τὰ μὴ νόμον ἔχοντα] '*Gentiles, classes, that is to say, who have not law.*'

ἑαυτοῖς εἰσὶν νόμος] They have a standard of right and wrong in their own consciences which acts as a law to them. Many parallels have been adduced (by Wetstein and others) from classical authors, e.g. Arist. *Eth. Nic.* iv. 8. (14) ὁ δὴ χαρίεις καὶ ἐλευθέριος οὕτως ἕξει οἷον νόμος ὢν ἑαυτῷ, *Polit.* III. xiii. 14 κατὰ δὲ τῶν τοιούτων οὐκ ἔσει νόμος· αὐτοὶ γάρ εἰσι νόμος, Manilius v. 495 'ipse sibi lex est.' But in all these passages the sense is different. In these it denotes independence, and even (as in the last quoted) self-will. Whereas here the expression implies self-restraint. More to the point is Philo *de Abrah.* § 46 (II. p. 40 ed. Mangey) οὐ γράμμασιν ἀναδιδαχθεὶς ἀλλ' ἀγράφῳ τῇ φύσει σπουδάσας ὑγιαινούσαις καὶ ἀνόσοις ὁρμαῖς ἐπακολουθῆσαι. περὶ δὲ ὧν ὁ Θεὸς ὁμολογεῖ, τί προσῆκεν ἀνθρώπους ἢ βεβαιότατα πιστεύειν; τοιοῦτος ὁ βίος τοῦ πρώτου καὶ ἀρχηγέτου ἐστὶ τοῦ ἔθνους, ὡς μὲν ἔνιοι φήσουσι, νόμιμος· ὡς δὲ ὁ παρ' ἐμοῦ λόγος ἔδειξε, νόμος αὐτὸς ὢν καὶ θεσμὸς ἄγραφος.

15. γραπτὸν ἐν ταῖς καρδίαις αὐτῶν] For the metaphor see Jerem. xxxi. 33, 2 Cor. iii. 3. It is sustained throughout. 'Their heart is their statute-book; their conscience is their witness; their reflexions are their prosecutors or their advocates; God Himself is their Judge.'

ἢ καὶ] '*or, it may happen*'—implying that it is a comparatively rare case. Compare 2 Cor. i. 13 ἃ ἀναγινώσκετε ἢ καὶ ἐπιγινώσκετε, Matt. vii. 10, Luke xviii. 11.

16. ἐν ἡμέρᾳ ὅτε] The process is now going on; but the summing up, the verdict, will take place then. On this brachylogy of ἐν see above on ver. 5 ἐν ἡμέρᾳ ὀργῆς. Of the various readings in this clause ἐν ἡμέρᾳ ὅτε is the best supported, but ἐν ᾗ ἡμέρᾳ perhaps the most probable on internal grounds. Κρίνει however is certainly to be read for κρινεῖ, in accordance with St Paul's usual preference of the present in similar cases for the sake of vividness: see the instances collected on 1 Thess. i. 10 τῆς ἐρχομένης, v. 2 ἔρχεται, 2 Thess. ii. 9 ἐστίν, 1 Cor. v. 13 τοὺς δὲ ἔξω ὁ Θεὸς κρίνει, and comp. Luke xvii. 30 ᾗ ἡμέρᾳ ὁ υἱὸς τοῦ ἀνθρώπου ἀποκαλύπτεται, a good parallel to this passage.

τὸ εὐαγγέλιόν μου] The phrase occurs also ch. xvi. 25, 2 Tim. ii. 8. So τὸ εὐαγγέλιον ἡμῶν 2 Cor. iv. 3, 1 Thess. i. 5, where he associates others with himself. He appeals to the preaching of the Second Advent and the Judgment, the topic of the Epistles to the Thessalonians and of his speech before the Areopagus (Acts xvii.), the characteristic of the first stage of his teaching (see *Biblical Essays*, p. 224 sq.). It is an idle fancy which sees in the phrase an allusion to St Luke's Gospel.

17. ἐπονομάζῃ] '*thou art surnamed*'; as an honourable distinction, with perhaps a notion of its not being their proper name (see vv. 28, 29). The word occurs here only in the New Testament.

τὸ θέλημα] i.e. 'the divine will.' It is used thus absolutely by St Paul here with the definite article, elsewhere (1 Cor. xvi. 12 πάντως οὐκ ἦν θέλημα ἵνα νῦν ἔλθῃ) without it. Examples of both kinds appear frequently in the Ignatian Epistles, *Polyc.* 8 ὡς τὸ θέλημα προστάσσει, *Eph.* 20 ἐάν...θέλημα ᾖ, *Rom.* 1 ἐάνπερ θέλημα ᾖ τοῦ ἀξιωθῆναί με, *Smyrn.* 1 υἱὸν Θεοῦ κατὰ θέλημα καὶ δύναμιν, *ib.* § 11. So too Clem. Alex. *Strom.* vi. 18 (p. 826) θελήματι θέλημα καὶ τῷ ἁγίῳ πνεύματι τὸ ἅγιον πνεῦμα θεωρεῖν ἐθίζοντες. On the other hand, of the devil Heracleon said that he μὴ ἔχειν θέλημα ἀλλ' ἐπιθυμίας, Orig. *in Joann.* xx. § 20 (IV. p. 339). In the passage before us this absolute use is obscured by the proximity of Θεῷ, and in 1 Cor. l. c. θέλημα is almost universally misunderstood as applying to Apollos himself. Compare the absolute use of ἡ ὀργή (1 Thess. ii. 16, Rom. v. 9, xii. 19), τὸ ὄνομα (Phil. ii. 9). These instances 'indicate, as I believe, the true reading in Rom. xv. 32 ἵνα ἐν χαρᾷ ἔλθω πρὸς ὑμᾶς διὰ θελήματος, where various additions appear in the MSS. Θεοῦ in AC, Κυρίου Ἰησοῦ in B, Ἰησοῦ Χριστοῦ in א, Χριστοῦ Ἰησοῦ in DFG, but where θέλημα appears to be used absolutely' (*On a Fresh Revision of the English N. Test.*, 1891, p. 118).

18. δοκιμάζεις τὰ διαφέροντα] Not 'things which are opposed,' as good and bad (so for instance Fritzsche *Rom.* I. p. 129), for it requires no keen moral sense to discriminate between these—but 'things that transcend,' 'ex bonis meliora' in Bengel's words. The phrase occurs also Phil. i. 10.

κατηχούμενος] '*instructed*.' For the word see on Gal. vi. 6.

19. ὁδηγὸν τυφλῶν κ.τ.λ.] The Apostle uses with a latent irony just the terms in which the Jew would describe himself. For ὁδηγὸν τυφλῶν see Wetstein on Matt. xv. 14, for παιδευτὴν ἀφρόνων Prov. xvi. 22, Heb. xii. 9, for νηπίων in this sense, Heb. v. 13.

20. τὴν μόρφωσιν] Compare 2 Tim. iii. 5, where the word occurs again. The μόρφωσις is something different from the μορφή. It is the rough-sketch, the pencilling of the μορφή. Hence it signifies (1) the outline, the framework as it were, like ὑποτύπωσις in St Paul's Epistles; (2) the outline without the substance (2 Tim. l. c.). In μορφή is involved the idea of 'reality,' 'substance.' This may appear incidentally in μόρφωσις, but it is not inherent in the word.

22. ὁ βδελυσσόμενος κ.τ.λ.] Had anything occurred which suggested this contradiction to St Paul? Wetstein refers to Josephus *Ant.* xviii. 3, 5, where it is related that certain Jews appropriated some gifts destined by Fulvia, a proselytess, for the Temple at Jerusalem. This took place in the reign of Tiberius. The incident however does not meet the case here. Obviously St Paul refers to robbing an idol's temple, making gain out of the very things which they professed to abominate. Doubtless some instance had occurred, in which Jews, under pretence of detestation of idolatry, had plundered some heathen temples and gained booty thereby. See Acts xix. 37, a passage which seems to show that such outbreaks were not unusual, arising sometimes perhaps from sincere fanaticism, sometimes from sordid avarice.

Somewhat similarly Josephus, when expounding Jewish law to his Gentile readers, says (*Ant.* iv. 8. 10) βλασφημείτω δὲ μηδεὶς θεοὺς οὓς πόλεις

ἄλλαι νομίζουσι· μὴ συλᾶν ἱερὰ ξενικά, μηδ᾽ ἂν ἐπωνομασμένον ᾖ τινι θεῷ
κειμήλιον λαμβάνειν.   This is a comment on Exod. xxii. 28 θεοὺς οὐ
κακολογήσεις, Deut. vii. 25, 26 τὰ γλυπτὰ τῶν θεῶν αὐτῶν καύσετε πυρί· οὐκ
ἐπιθυμήσεις ἀργύριον οὐδὲ χρυσίον ἀπ᾽ αὐτῶν οὐ λήψῃ σεαυτῷ…ὅτι βδέλυγμα
Κυρίῳ τῷ Θεῷ σου ἐστί, to which latter passage St Paul (like Josephus)
would seem to refer.   Philo is no less explicit (Vita Moys. iii. 26, II.
p. 166) ξοάνων γὰρ καὶ ἀγαλμάτων καὶ τοιουτοτρόπων ἀφιδρυμάτων ἡ οἰκουμένη
μεστὴ γέγονεν, ὧν τῆς βλασφημίας ἀνέχειν ἀναγκαῖον ἵνα μηδεὶς ἐθίζηται τῶν
Μωῦσέως γνωρίμων συνόλως θεοῦ προσρήσεως ἀλογεῖν.   Similarly Origen
(c. Cels. viii. 38) quotes the passage in Exodus already referred to against
Celsus' contention that the Christians are accustomed to boast that they
reviled heathen gods with impunity, and supports his statement by the
general teachings of St Paul (Rom. xii. 14, 1 Cor. vi. 10) in this direction.

23. ἐν νόμῳ καυχᾶσαι] Compare Ecclus. xxxix. 8 ἐν νόμῳ διαθήκης
Κυρίου καυχήσεται.

24. τὸ γὰρ ὄνομα κ.τ.λ.] From the LXX. of Isaiah lii. 5 δι᾽ ὑμᾶς δια-
παντὸς τὸ ὄνομά μου βλασφημεῖται ἐν τοῖς ἔθνεσιν.   In the Hebrew however
there is nothing to correspond either with δι᾽ ὑμᾶς or ἐν τοῖς ἔθνεσιν; and
the sentiments in the original seem to be different from St Paul's application, alluding as it does to the persecution of the Jews in captivity.
This persecution however and this captivity were a punishment for their
sins; thus the additions give correct sense.   The purport of St Paul's
language here is found in Ezek. xxxvi. 20—23, though the expression
there is different.   Compare 1 Tim. vi. 1, Tit. ii. 5, perhaps reminiscences
of the same text; Clement of Rome, § 47 ὥστε καὶ βλασφημίας ἐπιφέρεσθαι
τῷ ὀνόματι Κυρίου διὰ τὴν ὑμετέραν ἀφροσύνην, which is certainly based on
St Paul's words.   It is to be remarked however that here alone of passages
cited by St Paul καθὼς γέγραπται follows, instead of preceding, the quotation.   By this peculiarity and by the introductory γὰρ the Apostle seems
to indicate that he disengages the sentence from its context, and so from
the circumstances of its original application.

25. πράσσῃς] i.e. 'if the law be the standard of your conduct.'   The
phrase is unique.

27. τὸν διὰ γράμματος] Διὰ denotes the circumstances at the time of
the act, 'passing through' which the act takes place.   Compare Rom.
xiv. 20 τῷ διὰ προσκόμματος ἐσθίοντι, 2 Cor. ii. 4 ἔγραψα ὑμῖν διὰ πολλῶν
δακρύων, and perhaps 1 Thess. iv. 14 τοὺς κοιμηθέντας διὰ τοῦ Ἰησοῦ (where
see the note).

28, 29. οὐ γὰρ κ.τ.λ.] For the grammar of the passage it is necessary
to supply Ἰουδαῖος before Ἰουδαῖος (twice), περιτομὴ and ἡ ἀληθῶς περιτομὴ
before the first and second περιτομὴ respectively, and ἐστὶν after περιτομή,
Ἰουδαῖος and καρδίας.

29. οὗ ὁ ἔπαινος] i.e. 'whose proper praise.'   The antecedent is of
course Ἰουδαῖος.   For the idea comp. Gal. vi. 16 τὸν Ἰσραὴλ τοῦ Θεοῦ.

CHAPTER III

iv. *The covenant-privileges of the Jew* (iii. 1—20).

THIS chapter divides itself into three parts: (1) certain objections are stated and answered (vv. 1—8); (2) the position that the Jews also are under sin is established from Holy Scripture (vv. 9—20); (3) as a general conclusion from the results of ch. i. 16—iii. 20, viz. the universal failure of mankind both Jew and Gentile, a universal remedy is necessary, and it is found in Christ (vv. 21—31).

The first of these three sections may be expanded somewhat as follows, as St Paul meets the objections which arise in his mind. *Objection*: 'This view deprives the Jew of his advantages.' *Answer*: 'Not at all: these remain as before. For instance, he is the keeper of the sacred archives.' *Objection*: 'But if some were unfaithful to their trust, their unfaithfulness impugns the good faith of God.' *Answer*: 'No: throughout we must assume that God is true. So far from impugning, it establishes God's good faith. As the Psalmist says, I have sinned that God may be justified.' *Objection*: 'But if so, if it redounds to God's glory, if it does a good work, why should I be punished? How is it just in God to visit me with His wrath?' *Answer*: 'Whatever come, God must be just: for He is the Judge of all the world. The objection in fact amounts to this, that the means justifies the end, a maxim with which I myself have been falsely charged.'

2. πρῶτον μὲν] See i. 8, 1 Cor. xi. 18. Only one privilege is here mentioned. This however was enough for a sample. So the enumeration is stopped that the argument may not be interrupted. The fuller enumeration occurs later, ix. 4.

ἐπιστεύθησαν] *'they were entrusted with.'* The A.V. rendering 'unto them were committed the oracles of God' is ambiguous as regards the construction, which is common in the Pauline Epistles: see the note on 1 Thess. ii. 4 πιστευθῆναι τὸ εὐαγγέλιον.

3. 'For granted that some were unfaithful to their trust, what follows? Not surely that their unfaithfulness destroys, nullifies the faithfulness of God. Away with the thought.'

The sentence is to be connected with the general argument, and so to be attached to πολὺ κατὰ πάντα τρόπον. There is no connexion here between ἐπιστεύθησαν and ἠπίστησαν. The force of the passage appears from the parallel in ix. 6. God's promise stands firm, notwithstanding their infidelity. This promise was only conditional, it applied only to the true Israel. And therefore it is not infringed by the rejection of the faithless.

ἠπίστησαν] i.e. were ἄπιστοι, were untrue to their trust. This meaning seems to be required both by the τὴν πίστιν of the context, and by the parallel, 2 Tim. ii. 13 εἰ ἀπιστοῦμεν, ἐκεῖνος πιστὸς μένει, ἀρνήσασθαι γὰρ ἑαυτὸν οὐ δύναται. The verb ἀπιστεῖν (2 Tim. l. c.) and the substantive ἀπιστία (Wisdom xiv. 25 ἀπιστία ταραχὴ ἐπιορκία—a book constantly in St Paul's mind, see above on i. 20 sq., 30) are capable of the double meaning of ἄπιστος, which is applied not merely to the 'disbeliever' but to the 'unfaithful,' 'untrustworthy' (see Luke xii. 46, Rev. xxi. 8). The substantive is constantly used in this sense in classical writers, e.g. Xen. Anab. iii. 2. 4 ὁρᾶτε τὴν Τισσαφέρνους ἀπιστίαν ὅστις...ἐπὶ τούτοις αὐτὸς ὀμόσας ἡμῖν...αὐτὸς ἐξαπατήσας συνέλαβε τοὺς στρατηγούς ib. ii. 5. 21, and so Philo Leg. ad Caium § 16 (II. p. 562) ἀπιστίαν ὁμοῦ καὶ ἀχαριστίαν πρὸς τὸν τοῦ κόσμου παντὸς εὐεργέτην. See further Galatians p. 154 sq.

μὴ] Dr Jowett's assertion here that 'μὴ is used in the N. T. indifferently in questions intended to have either an affirmative or negative answer' appears to me to arise from a misconception of the Apostle's standpoint.

The fact is that St Paul, as it were, keeps the objection in his own hands. He is not so much arguing with some outward antagonist, as answering difficulties which arise in his own mind. Hence, at the very moment of stating his objection, he negatives it. For mere argumentative purposes it would have run οὐχ ἡ ἀπιστία κ.τ.λ. But the Apostle cannot bear to make even hypothetically and momentarily a statement which involves blasphemy. Therefore he negatives the supposition even while suggesting it. Compare 1 Cor. i. 13. This somewhat injures the clearness of the argument, but it preserves the Apostle's reverence.

4. γινέσθω] 'be found,' i.e. become, relatively to our apprehension. This sense is frequent in the imperative; see the references given in Vaughan, and add Rev. ii. 10 γίνου πιστὸς ἄχρι θανάτου, iii. 2 γίνου γρηγορῶν, 2 Pet. i. 20.

ἐν τῷ κρίνεσθαί σε] 'when Thou pleadest'; certainly not, 'when Thou art judged,' as the A.V. The subject of the verb is God, and the κρίνεσθαι of the LXX. which St Paul reproduces, is the middle voice, used, as in 1 Cor. vi. 6 ἀδελφὸς μετὰ ἀδελφοῦ κρίνεται, of a party in a trial. By a figure common in the Old Testament prophets, perhaps derived originally from Joel iii. 2, God and the sinner are regarded as two parties in a suit (see the references given in Vaughan). At the same time it is highly probable that ἐν τῷ κρίνεσθαί σε here must be regarded as a mistranslation on the part of the LXX., the pronominal suffix being made the object instead of the subject; for in the Hebrew text of Ps. li. 4, as we now have it, the word is בְּשָׁפְטֶךָ, which is κρίνειν, not κρίνεσθαι, and the distinction between the two voices is as clearly observed in the LXX. as in classical Greek. Symmachus translates correctly νικᾶν κρίνοντα, and we need not suppose that the Septuagint translators had a different Hebrew text before them. St Paul, though aware of the mistranslation, would not think it necessary to correct the LXX. in a point which did not affect his argument.

5. **τί ἐροῦμεν**] This expression is used again vi. 1, vii. 7, ix. 14, 30. In all these places the argument seems to have lodged the hearers in some difficult position from which they need extricating. Here the case of David raises the difficulty.

μὴ ἄδικος] The explanation of the μὴ here is the same as in ver. 3.

κατὰ ἄνθρωπον λέγω] 'Pardon me such language, the very use of which needs apology. It is but a foolish, ignorant, human mode of speaking.' On the phrase, which is peculiar to this group of Epistles, see Gal. iii. 15.

6. **ἐπεὶ**] '*since on this supposition*,' and so equivalent to 'otherwise,' 'if it were not so.' The phrase is sometimes strengthened by the addition of ἄρα: see on 1 Cor. vii. 14.

κρίνει] '*otherwise how doth God judge the earth?*' It is perhaps best here (as in ii. 16) to read the present rather than the future (κρινεῖ). The reference is probably to Gen. xviii. 25 ὁ κρίνων πᾶσαν τὴν γῆν οὐ ποιήσεις κρίσιν; rather than to Ps. ix. 8, lxvii. 4, or xcvi. 13. The judgment alluded to is going on day by day. The attempt to restrict the term τὸν κόσμον to the heathen world gains no countenance either from the context or from St Paul's usage elsewhere (see on Eph. ii. 2).

7. **εἰ δὲ**] This, not εἰ γάρ, is the true reading here. It refers back to εἰ δὲ ἡ ἀδικία ἡμῶν κ.τ.λ. (ver. 5), and is in fact the same objection starting up again.

τί ἔτι] The ἔτι is probably argumentative, 'this being the case,' as in Rom. ix. 19, Gal. v. 11.

8. **καὶ μὴ καθὼς**] Some suppose a confused construction here καὶ [τί] μή, καθὼς...φασίν τινες ἡμᾶς λέγειν, ποιήσωμεν κ.τ.λ., the sense being dislocated by the introduction of καθὼς as in 1 Thess. iv. 1, Col. i. 6, where see the notes. It is however simpler to understand γένηται after μή.

τινες] Either the Judaizing antagonists who wished to bring St Paul's doctrine into disrepute as leading to antinomianism, or professed followers who degraded it by their practice (cf. vi. 1 sq., Phil. iii. 18).

ὧν τὸ κρίμα] meaning not 'our revilers,' but all who draw these antinomian inferences. St Paul does not argue against the cavil, but crushes it by an appeal to moral instincts; compare Phil. iii. 19 ὧν τὸ τέλος ἀπώλεια.

9. **τί οὖν; προεχόμεθα;**] Having regard to the usual sense of προεχόμεθα, we shall be led to take τί οὖν προεχόμεθα; together, and

render either 'What privilege do we exhibit?' or 'What excuse do we offer, what defence do we make?' (see below). But this construction is forbidden by the following οὐ πάντως. Προεχόμεθα therefore must be taken alone. The exact meaning of the word here is uncertain. The active προέχειν is not found in the LXX., nor elsewhere in the N. T. In classical usage the middle προέχεσθαι is frequent in the sense of 'to hold out before one as a πρόσχημα.' This πρόσχημα may be either (a) a defence, protection, (2) a pretence, excuse, or (3) a decoration, boast (e.g. Herod. v. 28 where Miletus is described as τῆς Ἰωνίης πρόσχημα). Accordingly some would take it here as a middle, and render 'Have we any protection or shield?' But προέχεσθαι does not appear to be so used absolutely ln the middle. Turning therefore to the passive voice, we might adopt Vaughan's rendering 'Are we preferred?' which would give excellent sense, if there were any instance of this rendering, but I can find none. On the other hand the active προέχειν 'to excel' is found with the accusative of the thing excelled (e.g. Xenoph. *Anab.* iii. 2. 17 ἑνὶ μόνῳ προέχουσιν ἡμᾶς οἱ ἱππεῖς), and the passive προέχεσθαι is used once at least (Chrysippus ap. Plutarch. *Mor.* p. 1038 D οὕτω τοῖς ἀγαθοῖς πᾶσι ταῦτα προσήκει, κατ᾽ οὐδὲν προεχομένοις ὑπὸ τοῦ Διός) in the sense 'to be excelled.' And to this rendering I must adhere, until I find instances of the use which Vaughan adopts.

'What then,' argues the Jew, 'do you mean to tell me that others have the advantage over us?' St Paul's answer is, 'Not at all. We said before that Jews and Gentiles all were under sin. But if we do not give them any advantage over you, neither do we give you any advantage over them. Your Scriptures show that you are not exempted.'

οὐ πάντως] '*not at all.*' As usual the πάντως qualifies the οὐ, not the οὐ the πάντως (see on 1 Cor. v. 10).

προῃτιασάμεθα] '*we before laid to the charge*'; not 'we have before proved,' as the A. V. renders it in its text.

10. καθὼς γέγραπται] Several passages are here strung together. The first of these is taken from Ps. xiv. (xiii.) 1—3, after which in the Prayer Book Version of the Psalms all the rest are added, i.e. τάφος ἀνεῳγμένος...αὐτῶν, though they find no place there in the Hebrew, the Targums, the Chaldee, the Syriac, or the other Greek versions (excluding the LXX.), see Field *Hexapla*, II. p. 105. The verses are omitted in some manuscripts of the LXX. (including A), and are bracketed by the second hand of א, but are found in B. Was then this insertion made in the LXX. from St Paul here, or had St Paul a MS. of the LXX. in which the words occurred together? The former supposition is doubtless the true one. For, first, St Paul does not quote literally in the first part of the quotation, as we shall see; and there is therefore no *a priori* reason that we should expect to find the passage as a whole in any one place in the LXX. Secondly, the absence of the verses in the Hebrew is a strong presumption that they would be absent in the LXX. also. Thirdly, it is

very likely that St Paul's quotation would be inserted in the margin and afterwards in the text of the LXX. of Ps. xiv. (xiii.), on the hypothesis that the words were originally wanting. On the other hand, it is extremely unlikely that, if originally there, they would afterwards have been omitted.

The evidence respecting the text of the LXX. leads to the same result. Origen (in Cramer's *Catena*, p. 18) speaks of St Paul's 'gathering together passages' (ῥητὰ συναγαγεῖν) to show that all were under sin, and refers each severally to its proper place. There is no mention of a text where the passage occurs as a whole. Rufinus however in his translation (Origen, *op.* IV. 504) says 'Illud etiam necessarium ducimus admonendum quod in nonnullis Latinorum ea quae subsequuntur testimonia in tertio decimo psalmo consequentes ex integro posita inveniuntur: in Graecis autem pene omnibus non amplius in tertio decimo psalmo quam usque ad illum versiculum ubi scriptum est ' Non est qui faciat bonum non est usque ad unum.' The mention of the Latin MSS. shows that the earlier part of this sentence was Rufinus' own interpolation : and probably the latter part was also, as there is no trace of it in the fragment in the *Catena*. If however the latter clause were Origen's own, it would show that in his time a very small proportion of the MSS. of the LXX. contained the passage. Eusebius (*in Psalmos*, v. p. 145 *ed.* Migne) does not mention the insertion, but comments on the passage without it. Jerome (*Praef. in Comm. in Isaiam*, lib. xvi. quoted by Field l. c.) in reply to a question raised by Eustochium declares that all the Greek commentators (omnes Graeciae tractatores) mark the passage with an asterisk and pass it over (veru annotant atque praetereunt) as not contained in the Hebrew, though the question of Eustochium clearly implies that the passage was found in the Latin copies ordinarily in use.

οὐκ ἔστιν κ.τ.λ.] The words of Ps. xiv. (xiii.) 1—3 are taken from the LXX., as the exact coincidences of language in the latter part show. I cannot however attribute to a lapse of memory the variation at the commencement which in the Psalm runs as follows, Κύριος ἐκ τοῦ οὐρανοῦ διέκυψεν ἐπὶ τοὺς υἱοὺς τῶν ἀνθρώπων τοῦ ἰδεῖν εἰ ἔστιν συνιὼν ἢ ἐκζητῶν τὸν θεόν, especially as the words occur in the parallel passage also Ps. liii. (lii.) 3, and the rest of the quotation is accurate. I believe therefore that the Apostle gave rather the substance than the words at the beginning, so changing the form, as to adapt it to his context and make a fit introduction. And this is Origen's opinion, as expressed through Rufinus, 'puto dari in hoc apostolicam auctoritatem ut cum scripturae testimoniis utendum fuerit, sensum magis ex ea quam verba capiamus. Hoc enim et in Evangeliis factum frequenter invenies.' For parallel instances see 1 Cor. i. 31, 1 Cor. xv. 45, both introduced by καθὼς γέγραπται.

12. ἠχρειώθησαν] The idea of the original אלח seems to be 'to go bad or sour' like milk (see Gesen. *Thes.* p. 102). The Greek word ἀχρειοῦν occurs twice in the Scholiast to Æschines (p. 10. 3, p. 28. 7).

13. **τάφος ἀνεῳγμένος**] And thus at once a danger and a pollution (comp. Luke xi. 44).

The quotation as far as *ἐδολιοῦσαν* is from Ps. v. 9: then follows Ps. cxl. 3: verse 14 represents Ps. x. 7, and the next three verses Is. lix. 7, 8. Lastly, verse 18 gives us the last half of Ps. xxxv. (xxxvi.) 1, *αὐτοῦ* being changed into *αὐτῶν* to conform to the plurals which precede.

The Jews boasted in the law. They prided themselves that they were children of Abraham. They made a distinction between themselves and the Gentiles. The Gentiles had fallen away from God, were out of the pale of salvation. St Paul shows that their own prophets and teachers had used the strongest possible language about themselves: had thus given the lie direct to their pride and self-sufficiency. Accordingly the condemnation applies equally to them as to the Gentiles.

The Apostle's words however must not be pressed to mean more than he meant by them. Ps. xiv., which contains the strongest condemnation, at the same time speaks of a remnant (ver. 4). And this is St Paul's own language elsewhere (Rom. xi.). He insists on the fact of there being a remnant. Still his main position remains as before. The law in itself did not justify. Else this universal depravity would have been impossible at any epoch.

19. **οἴδαμεν**] 'It is an obvious truth, it needs no argument to show, that the scriptures were addressed to those whom alone they could reach.' The expression *οἴδαμεν* is a favourite one in this Epistle (ii. 2, vii. 14, viii. 22, 28) when used of propositions that commend themselves. It was the tendency of Rabbinical teachers in St Paul's time and afterwards to apply all such passages to the heathen. Hence the Apostle's *οἴδαμεν* as if to preclude this forced reference.

ὁ νόμος] This can only mean one thing. Those who are addressed in the Old Testament, are the people under the Old Testament dispensation, i.e. the Israelites themselves. The Old Testament speaks to Jews, not to Gentiles, and therefore to Jews this severe language applies.

λαλεῖ] '*uttereth.*' The general difference between λαλεῖν and λέγειν is that the former lays stress on the enunciation, the latter on the meaning. Λαλεῖν is loqui, 'to talk'; λέγειν is dicere, 'to speak.' Hence ἡ λαλιά σου 'thy speech' (Matt. xxvi. 73, Mark xiv. 70) implies not the thoughts or the words themselves, but the mode of utterance. When λαλιά is opposed to λόγος, as in John viii. 43 διὰ τί τὴν λαλιὰν τὴν ἐμὴν οὐ γινώσκετε; ὅτι οὐ δύνασθε ἀκούειν τὸν λόγον τὸν ἐμόν, it represents the form, the way of speaking, the language, which was unintelligible to the Jews who had incapacitated themselves from understanding the substance, the underlying truth of the message delivered. Thus λαλεῖν here (comp. Heb. i. 1) has a closer connexion with the hearer than λέγειν, and the distinction between the two verbs is evident when we consider that to interchange them would be intolerable.

ὑπόδικος γένηται] '*may be brought under the cognizance*' of God's tribunal. Ὑπόδικος, though a good classical word, does not occur in the LXX., or elsewhere in the N. T., its place being taken by ἔνοχος.

20. ἐξ ἔργων νόμου κ.τ.λ.] A free citation from Ps. cxliii. (cxlii.) 2, to which St Paul has added ἐξ ἔργων νόμου as his own interpretation justified by what he has said before, ὅσα ὁ νόμος κ.τ.λ. See the note on Gal. ii. 16, where the same passage is quoted and the same comment appears.

διὰ γὰρ νόμου κ.τ.λ.] This idea of law creating and multiplying sin is first thrown out in 1 Cor. xv. 56. There the mention is casual, and has no very obvious relation to the context, though beneath the surface we discern a close connexion. A few months later the thought is worked out in the Epistles to the Galatians and to the Romans (see vii. 7—25). Law is the great educator of the moral conscience. Restraint is necessary in order to develope the conception of duty. This is equally the case with the individual and with the world at large. With the latter, as with the former, there is a period of childhood, of non-age, a period in which external restraints represent the chief instrument of education. The law says, 'Do not, or thou shalt die.' Thus the character of the Law is negative: of the Gospel, positive.

v. *A universal remedy to meet this universal failure* (iii. 21—31).

21. νυνὶ δὲ] '*but now*,' when the world has come of age (comp. Gal. iv. 1 sq.).

δικαιοσύνη Θεοῦ] The idea conveyed in this expression seems to be twofold; first, something inherent in God; secondly, something communicated to us; compare below δίκαιον καὶ δικαιοῦντα (ver. 26). There is thus both the external act, what is done for us, and the inherent change, what is done in us. To describe this second sphere I would use the term 'communication' rather than 'impartation,' because the latter word seems to exclude the need of a moral change in ourselves; whereas in St Paul the idea of this change is very prominent. There is the external act, what has been done for us, our purchase, the atoning sacrifice: Christ died for us. But there must be also the internal change, what is to be done in us: We must have died with Christ. Christ's righteousness becomes our righteousness by our becoming one with Christ, being absorbed in Christ. See *Biblical Essays*, p. 230 sq.

μαρτυρουμένη κ.τ.λ.] In what sense does St Paul mean that this righteousness of God is borne witness to by the law and the prophets? We may answer, By types and special predictions, but here especially by the foreshadowings of the mode and scheme of man's redemption both in the law (e.g. Gen. xv. 6, quoted Rom. iv. 3, Gal. iii. 6) and in the prophets (e.g. Habakk. ii. 4, quoted Rom. i. 17, Gal. iii. 11). It is perhaps to such passages as these, rather than to any direct types or predictions of the Messiah, that the Apostle refers; except so far as these latter bear witness to Him in His character of δικαιοσύνη Θεοῦ.

22. **δικαιοσύνη δὲ**] The δε restricts or defines ; comp. Rom. ix. 30, 1 Cor. ii. 6, iii. 15.

διὰ πίστεως] '*communicated, made available by faith.*'

εἰς πάντας] If καὶ ἐπὶ πάντας of the Textus Receptus be preserved after εἰς πάντας, the prepositions will denote attainment and comprehension respectively, and the whole phrase may be rendered 'reaching unto and extending over all.' But the doubtful words should almost certainly be omitted.

23. **τῆς δόξης τοῦ Θεοῦ**] This glory of God is the revelation of God to the pure and upright of heart through faith, with perhaps the idea of communication also. It is no objection to this view that this glory is evidently something present here (and 2 Cor. iv. 6), and that elsewhere (e.g. Rom. v. 2, Tit. ii. 13) it is spoken of as future. This revelation of God is a present revelation to the faithful; and just as 'the kingdom of heaven' is at once a present and a future kingdom, so there is a present and a future glory of God. The idea conveyed in the words is twofold : (1) the manifestation of God's Person and attributes, the knowledge of God in Himself (John xi. 40, Acts vii. 55) ; (2) the transformation of the faithful into the same image. Thus Meyer is wholly wrong in taking the expression to mean 'the honour which God gives.' Even in John xii. 43, where it is apparently so taken in the A. V., the context (see ver. 41) points to the other meaning. Where the sense which Meyer gives to it is intended, the form is otherwise : John v. 44 τὴν δόξαν τὴν παρὰ τοῦ μόνου Θεοῦ (comp. Rom. ii. 29 ὁ ἔπαινος...ἐκ τοῦ Θεοῦ). Still less can it be explained to mean 'glory in the sight of God,' as others render it.

24. **δικαιούμενοι**] The nominative is grammatically connected with πάντες (ver. 23) ; but logically with πάντας (ver. 22).

ἀπολύτρωσις] On this word see the note on Eph. i. 7. The idea contained here is twofold : (1) a price paid (1 Cor. vi. 20, 1 Tim. ii. 6) ; (2) a deliverance thereby obtained, especially from a bondage or captivity, a deliverance not only from the consequences of sin but from sin itself. For, though the objective element is especially prominent in this passage, as the argument requires, the subjective element must not be ignored.

25. **προέθετο**] '*set before Himself,*' and so 'purposed.' The force of the preposition is not temporal, but local. Comp. Eph. i. 10, with the note.

ἱλαστήριον] '*a propitiatory offering.*' The word is of course an adjective originally, e.g. Joseph. *Ant.* xvi. 17, 1 ἱλαστήριος θάνατος, 4 Macc. xvii. 22 χεῖρας ἱκετηρίους εἰ δὲ βούλει ἱλαστηρίους ἐκτείνας Θεῷ (see Wilkins *Clav.* s. v., Steph. *Thes.* s. v. and Meyer here). This usage of the neuter of adjectives in -ηριος is frequent as applied to victims, e.g. καθαρτήριον, χαριστήριον, διαβατήριον, νικητήριον etc. A good example of the word in this sense is Dion Chrysost. *Or.* xi. p. 355 *ed.* Reiske ἱλαστήριον Ἀχαιὸν τῇ Ἀθηνᾷ τῇ Ἰλιάδι : and this seems to be the meaning here.

On the other hand Vaughan prefers the rendering 'mercy-seat.' The word is used in the LXX. to translate כפרת, i.e. the lid of the ark of the Testimony, translated 'mercy-seat' in the A. V. (see esp. Exod. xxv. 17 sq., xxvi. 34, xxxi. 7). Now the root כפר means (1) in Kal 'to cover,' (2) in Piel (a) 'to forgive' or (b) 'to expiate,' 'appease' (comp. James v. 20, 1 Peter iv. 8 where 'covering' implies 'forgiveness'). Thus the LXX. use of the word ἱλαστήριον is a rendering of this secondary meaning, and is an example of the Alexandrian tone of thought which sees symbolical meanings everywhere, and which derives from homonymes theological lessons. Compare at a later period Philo de prof. 19 (II. p. 561) τῆς δὲ ἵλεω δυνάμεως, τὸ ἐπίθεμα τῆς κιβωτοῦ, καλεῖ δὲ αὐτὸ ἱλαστήριον, Vit. Moys. iii. 8 (II. p. 150) ἧς (τῆς κιβωτοῦ) ἐπίθεμα ὡσανεὶ πῶμα τὸ λεγόμενον ἐν ἱεραῖς βίβλοις ἱλαστήριον...ὅπερ ἔοικεν εἶναι σύμβολον φυσικώτερον μὲν τῆς ἵλεω τοῦ θεοῦ δυνάμεως ἠθικώτερον δὲ διανοίας πάλιν ἵλεω δὲ ἑαυτῇ αὐτῆς. Sometimes כפרת is translated ἱλαστήριον ἐπίθεμα (Exod. xxv. 17, xxxvii. 6), which is a double rendering of the word; but elsewhere ἱλαστήριον only. Thus we can see how the first part of the English word 'mercy-seat' has its origin; but there is nothing either in the Hebrew or its Greek equivalent to represent the idea of a 'seat,' a figure borrowed doubtless from such passages as Lev. xvi. 2, Numb. vii. 89, Ps. lxxx. 1, xcix. 1, Heb. ix. 5, where the symbol of the Divine Presence is spoken of as appearing above the Cherubim which shadowed the mercy-seat. The term 'mercy-seat' came through the 'Gnadenstuhl' of Luther's translation, and the 'seat of grace' of Tyndal and Cranmer. On the other hand Wyclif, followed by the Geneva Bible, adopts the 'propitiatorium' of the Latin versions and translates 'propitiatory,' adding on the first occasion on which it occurs, the note, 'a propitiatory, that is a place of purchasing mercy,' where 'purchase' is used in its old sense of 'pursue after, obtain, acquire.'

The explanation of ἱλαστήριον here in the sense of 'mercy-seat' is as old as Origen (Comm. ad Rom. Lib. III. 8), to whom it gives a handle for much of his favourite mode of exegesis. Our Lord would then be spoken of as the mercy-seat, just as elsewhere (e.g. John i. 14) He is compared to the Shekinah. But there is something abrupt and unsuitable in such imagery here, 'God purposed Him to be a mercy-seat '—abrupt, as the phrase itself shows; unsuitable, because the mercy-seat is, as it were, the source and abode of mercy, not the mediator by whom it is obtained. Moreover, it throws the other imagery of the passage into confusion, e.g. ἐν τῷ αἵματι αὐτοῦ. Different applications of the same illustration indeed are very frequent in St Paul (see on 1 Thess. ii. 7 νήπιοι), but perhaps there is no parallel to a confusion of metaphor like this. Still this last argument must not be pressed too far.

εἰς ἔνδειξιν τῆς δικαιοσύνης αὐτοῦ] Inasmuch as sin required so great a sacrifice. It is better not to go beyond the language of scripture. All the moral difficulties connected with the Atonement arise from pressing the imagery of the Apostolic writers too far. Thus nothing is said here about appeasing divine wrath, nor is it stated to whom the Sacrifice of Christ is paid. The central idea of that Sacrifice is the great work done for us, whereby boasting is excluded.

διὰ τὴν πάρεσιν] '*by reason of the praetermission.*' The A.V. renders this 'for the remission' (as though ἄφεσιν), but in the margin 'or passing over'—the marginal rendering being doubtless due to the Cocceian controversy (though Cocceius himself wrote later), on which see Trench, *N. T. Syn.* § xxxiii. p. 115. But this change is not enough: for the preposition itself must be altered from 'for' into 'owing to, by reason of.'

The distinction between ἄφεσις the revocation of punishment and πάρεσις the suspension of punishment, though denied by Schleusner and others, is borne out by classical usage, Xenoph. *Hipp.* vii. 10 ἁμαρτήματα οὐ χρὴ παριέναι ἀκόλαστα, Joseph. *Ant.* xv. 3. 2 παρῆκε τὴν ἁμαρτίαν, of Herod anxious to punish a certain offence which however for other considerations he passed over, as well as by the writers of the Apocrypha, see Ecclus. xxiii. 2 ἵνα...οὐ μὴ παρῇ τὰ ἁμαρτήματα αὐτῶν ὅπως μὴ πληθύνωσιν αἱ ἄγνοιαί μου, comp. Wisdom xi. 24 παρορᾷς ἁμαρτήματα ἀνθρώπων εἰς μετάνοιαν, a passage which may well have been in the Apostle's mind (see note on i. 20 above). The best commentary on the passage is St Paul's own language in Acts xvii. 30, where the term ὑπεριδὼν expresses the idea exactly (comp. Acts xiv. 16). To substitute ἄφεσιν for πάρεσιν here would entirely destroy the sense. It was because the sins had been passed over and had not been forgiven, that the exhibition of God's righteousness in the Incarnation and Passion of Christ was necessary. Till Christ came, the whole matter was, as it were, kept in abeyance.

ἁμαρτημάτων] Ἁμάρτημα is related to ἁμαρτία as the concrete to the abstract. It is thus an individual offence, a wrong deed done. But on the other hand, whereas ἁμαρτία may be used of an individual sin, ἁμάρτημα never can mean sin regarded as sinfulness.

ἐν τῇ ἀνοχῇ τοῦ Θεοῦ] For ἀνοχή see above on ii. 4. The idea is holding back, forbearance, suspension, thus enforcing the conception of πάρεσις. There is no idea of forgiveness contained in the word: it is a temporary withholding of judgment. 'Indulgentia (i.e. ἀνοχή) eo valet ut in aliorum peccatis conniveas, non ut alicui peccata condones, quod clementiae est,' Fritzsche.

26. πρὸς τὴν ἔνδειξιν] resuming the previous εἰς ἔνδειξιν in a little stronger form; for πρὸς implies more definitely than εἰς the idea of purpose, inasmuch as εἰς only looks to the object, while πρὸς connects the agent with the object. Hence such a use as Rom. viii. 18 πρὸς τὴν μέλλουσαν δόξαν. The insertion of the article here draws attention to the fact that ἔνδειξις has been mentioned already. For εἰς τὸ εἶναι see i. 21; for τὸν ἐκ πίστεως see ii. 8 τοῖς δὲ ἐξ ἐριθείας.

27. ποῦ οὖν ἡ καύχησις;] '*what then has become of the boasting,*' of which he spoke above (ii. 17), and which has been present to his mind throughout. For ποῦ οὖν see on Gal. iv. 15.

ἐξεκλείσθη] The aorist represents the consequences as instantaneous: 'it is excluded *ipso facto.*' See on Gal. v. 4 κατηργήθητε, ἐξεπέσατε.

διὰ νόμου πίστεως] Strictly speaking, it is not a law, but a principle. The Gospel is never called a law in itself 'proprie' (see Gal. v. 23), but only καταχρηστικῶς to distinguish it from another law, and then always with some word appended which deprives νόμος of its power and produces a verbal paradox: as here νόμος πίστεως, viii. 2 ὁ νόμος τοῦ πνεύματος τῆς ζωῆς, James i. 25, ii. 12 νόμος ἐλευθερίας. In these three cases πίστις, πνεῦμα, ἐλευθερία correct and, as it were, contradict νόμος, thus creating an oxymoron. Comp. 1 Cor. ix. 21 ὡς ἄνομος, μὴ ὢν ἄνομος Θεοῦ ἀλλ' ἔννομος Χριστοῦ.

30. εἴπερ κ.τ.λ.] '*seeing that* God is one and immutable, governing all on the same principle, no respecter of persons with one rule for one class, another for another.' In Gal. iii. 20 ὁ δὲ Θεὸς εἷς ἐστιν the meaning, though not quite the same, is yet closely allied to this. On the amount of certainty conveyed in εἴπερ (which is to be read here, not ἐπείπερ) see on 2 Thess. i. 6.

ὃς δικαιώσει] '*and therefore He will justify.*' In other words ὃς δικαιώσει is logically consequent on the oneness of God.

ἐκ πίστεως, διὰ τῆς πίστεως] Many commentators contend that there is no difference of meaning between these two phrases, and that this is one of the many instances where St Paul delights to interchange prepositions for the sake of variety. Other alleged examples of this usage are 2 Cor. iii. 11 διὰ δόξης...ἐν δόξῃ, Eph. i. 7, and Gal. ii. 16, where the same expressions διὰ πίστεως, ἐκ πίστεως occur, as here, in connexion with δικαιοῦν. Prof. Jowett extends this theory, and to illustrate this 'awkwardness of expression' cites Rom. v. 7 ὑπὲρ δικαίου, ὑπὲρ τοῦ ἀγαθοῦ, 'where, as here, different words appear to be used with the same meaning.' I hope to show, when we come to that passage, that to take ἀγαθὸς as equivalent to δίκαιος is virtually to destroy the Apostle's meaning, the whole force of which depends upon the distinction of the terms. To confine ourselves now to the question of prepositions, even if it were true, which it is not, that St Paul elsewhere scatters his prepositions indiscriminately, it is very plain here from the form of the sentence that a distinction was intended, the antithesis emphasizing the change of preposition. The exact nature of this distinction I have endeavoured to point out in the note on Gal. ii. 16. Faith is strictly speaking only the means, not the source, of justification. The one preposition (διὰ) excludes this latter notion, while the other (ἐκ) might imply it. The difference will perhaps best be seen by substituting their opposites οὐ δικαιώσει περιτομὴν ἐκ νόμου, οὐδὲ ἀκροβυστίαν διὰ τοῦ νόμου; when, in the case of the Jews, the falsity of their starting-point, in the case of the Gentiles, the needlessness of a new instrumentality, would be insisted on. The circumcision must not trust to works; the uncircumcision have no occasion to put themselves under the yoke of the law.

The Greek fathers (see Cramer's *Catena*) start from the assumption that there must be a difference of meaning here. Origen says οὐ νομιστέον ὡς ἔτυχε (i.e. at random) ταῖς προθέσεσι (the prepositions) διαφόρως (*l.* ἀδιαφόρως) κεχρῆσθαι, and instances 1 Cor. xi. 12 (ἐκ τοῦ ἀνδρός...διὰ τῆς γυναικός) and other passages, e.g. Rom. xi. 36, 2 Cor. xii. 8, where, as he points out, it is absolutely necessary to preserve the distinction. He interprets the difference here as follows, 'qui ex fide justificantur, initio ex fide sumpto, per adimpletionem bonorum operum consummantur; et qui per fidem justificantur, a bonis operibus exorsi per fidem summam perfectionis accipiunt.'

31.   νόμον οὖν καταργοῦμεν]   Dr Vaughan seems to me to be wrong in his interpretation of this passage, which he takes to mean 'Do we abolish all restraint on moral conduct?' Surely it does not refer to setting men free from a rule of duty; but signifies 'Do we stultify law, do we deny the significance, the value, the effect of law? Was law a mistake from beginning to end?' with a special reference to the Mosaic Law. In other words 'law' here is not equivalent to regulated moral conduct, but to an external system of restraints. The idea is the same as that which is developed on vii. 7 sq. and is not unconnected with our Lord's own words (Matt. v. 17, 18). Here the objection is thrown out, and negatived but not argued. It is reserved in fact for discussion in its proper place (ch. vii.). We have already observed the same treatment of the objection, that St Paul's doctrine denies the privileges of the chosen race (iii. 1, 2). This in like manner is briefly stated, negatived and dismissed, being reserved for a later occasion.

ἱστάνομεν]   On the form of the verb see Winer § xv. p. 106.

CHAPTER IV

vi. *The meaning of the covenant with Abraham* (iv. 1—25).

1. THERE are several points relating to the text of this verse which need elucidation.

(*a*) Are we to read πατέρα or προπάτορα? Undoubtedly the latter. External authority is vastly in its favour: but the correction was made (1) because προπάτωρ is an unusual word, occurring only here in the N.T. or LXX.; (2) on the other hand πατέρα occurs below, vv. 11, 12, and the expression Ἀβραὰμ ὁ πατὴρ ἡμῶν is common elsewhere (Luke i. 73, John viii. 39, 56, Acts vii. 2, James ii. 21).

(*b*) What is to be the position of εὑρηκέναι, if retained? External authority is decidedly in favour of placing the word immediately after ἐροῦμεν, and not after ἡμῶν as in the Textus Receptus. The change is probably due to the fact that the other was in itself the natural order, so long as regard is paid to the meaning which the context requires us to assign to κατὰ σάρκα.

(*c*) But should εὑρηκέναι be retained at all? It is omitted in B 47 Chrysostom. This perhaps is one of those instances in which B almost alone preserves the right reading. Its unsupported authority would not be sufficient to reject the word; but it receives confirmation here (1) from the varying positions of εὑρηκέναι in the other MSS., (2) from the well-known tendency of scribes to supply an elliptical expression (see 1 Cor. iv. 6 φρονεῖν, v. 1 ὀνομάζεται, xi. 24 κλώμενον and other examples given in the *Journal of Philology*, III. p. 85).

Thus εὑρηκέναι must be regarded as at least suspicious. If it is omitted, we shall take the passage thus: 'What then shall we say of our forefather Abraham?' For the same construction after ἐρεῖν we may refer to Plato *Crito* 48 A πάνυ ἡμῖν οὕτω φροντιστέον τί ἐροῦσιν οἱ πολλοὶ ἡμᾶς, Eur. *Alc.* 954 ἐρεῖ δέ μ᾽, ὅστις ἐχθρὸς ὢν κυρεῖ, τάδε and the passages accumulated by Stallbaum on Plato *Apol.* 23 A. A somewhat analogous construction with λέγειν occurs John viii. 54 (ix. 19) ὃν ὑμεῖς λέγετε followed by ὅτι. On the whole, the sense gains by the omission of εὑρηκέναι; the idea being 'Does not the history of our forefather Abraham contradict this view?' For the question is really not what advantage he gained, but in what relation he stood to St Paul's position. If however εὑρηκέναι be retained, the tense expresses, as Dr Vaughan says, the permanence of the result; and κατὰ σάρκα must be taken with τὸν προπάτορα ἡμῶν, whatever position of εὑρηκέναι be adopted. These words ἡμῶν 'of us Jews,' κατὰ σάρκα 'according to the flesh,' are chosen with a view to what comes after. Abraham is not only a father of the Jews, but πάντων τῶν πιστευόντων δι' ἀκροβυστίας (ver. 11), πολλῶν ἐθνῶν (ver. 18); not only κατὰ σάρκα, but τοῖς στοιχοῦσιν τοῖς ἴχνεσιν τῆς...πίστεως (ver. 12), τῷ ἐκ πίστεως Ἀβραάμ (ver. 16).

2. ἔχει καύχημα] '*he has a subject of boast, ground for boasting*'; καύχημα is the matter of καύχησις; comp. 2 Cor. i. 12 ἡ γὰρ καύχησις ἡμῶν αὕτη ἐστὶν κ.τ.λ. with i. 14 ὅτι καύχημα ὑμῶν ἐσμέν; and the passage before us with iii. 27 above.

ἀλλ' οὐ πρὸς Θεόν] This is added to avoid the blasphemy, though it has nothing to do with St Paul's argument: comp. iii. 4, 6. 'Even then let him keep his boasting to himself or to his fellowmen. For "merit lives from man to man, And not from man, O Lord, to Thee."'

3. τί γάρ] Verse 2 having been regarded as parenthetical, it follows that the γάρ of ver. 3 has no reference to οὐ πρὸς Θεόν, but is connected with τί οὖν ἐροῦμεν κ.τ.λ., and introduces the answer to that question. 'What account then are we to give of Abraham our forefather? Why, what does the scripture say?' For the γάρ see εἰ γάρ in iii. 7, where in like manner the γάρ refers, not to what immediately precedes, but to ver. 5.

ἡ γραφή] '*the passage of scripture*.' See the note on Gal. iii. 22. Dr Vaughan takes a different view and instances examples from St John. The usage of St John may admit of a doubt, though personally I think not (see Gal. l. c.); St Paul's practice however is absolute and uniform. On the faith of Abraham see *Galatians*, p. 156.

4. τῷ ἐργαζομένῳ, κ.τ.λ.] The connexion is somewhat as follows. 'Scripture lays stress on Abraham's faith: this language is inconsistent with the idea of wages earned by work done.'

λογίζεται] '*is reckoned*.' Passive, as in ver. 5 (ver. 24 is more doubtful), ix. 8, Ecclus. xl. 19 ὑπὲρ ἀμφότερα γυνὴ ἄμωμος λογίζεται. The first aorist ἐλογίσθην (Xen. *Hell.* vi. 1. 19, Plato *Tim.* § 8, 34 A) and first future λογισθήσομαι (Rom. ii. 26, Niceph. *Rhet.* vii. 22) are always passive according to Veitch. On the other hand, the present is only once (Herod. iii. 95) used by classical writers in the passive sense.

5. μὴ ἐργαζομένῳ πιστεύοντι δέ] i.e. who does not work for wages, does not obtain it by his work, but believes etc. It is by pressing the letter and neglecting the spirit, of such passages as these, that antinomianism in its stronger and in its feebler forms is deduced from St Paul's language. As a matter of fact Abraham did work, he could not help working; but it was his transcendent faith which justified him, the faith out of which all the works arose.

τὸν ἀσεβῆ] A very strong word used again, v. 6, to place the gratuity of the gift in the strongest light. Comp. Barnabas *Epist.* § 5, who says of the Apostles τοὺς ἰδίους ἀποστόλους τοὺς μέλλοντας κηρύσσειν τὸ εὐαγγέλιον αὐτοῦ ἐξελέξατο, ὄντας ὑπὲρ πᾶσαν ἁμαρτίαν ἀνομωτέρους. The parable of the publican and the Pharisee is the best commentary upon St Paul's doctrine of justification by faith; which, like 1 John i. 7 (quoted by Vaughan) when taken in connexion with St John's universal language, implies a subjective process, a change in the person, side by side with the Atoning Sacrifice.

6.   λέγει τὸν μακαρισμὸν] '*pronounces the felicitation.*' For μακαρισμὸς see on Gal. iv. 15. Clement of Rome (§ 50) employs the word with obvious reference to this passage, for he quotes Ps. xxxi. (xxxii.) 1, 2 in the immediate context.

7, 8.   μακάριοι κ.τ.λ.] A quotation from Ps. xxxi. (xxxii.) 1, 2. Here again (see on iii. 10 sq.) St Paul's use of the language of the Psalms shows that he did not mean to exclude the moral element in the reconciliation of the believers to God. The sins indeed are freely forgiven; but a moral change is wrought in the man himself; for the psalmist goes on οὐδέ ἐστιν ἐν τῷ στόματι αὐτοῦ δόλος. Though the idea of the passage quoted is the blessedness of a free pardon, still the latter part of the psalm (esp. vv. 5, 8, 9) was doubtless not absent from St Paul's mind. He does not however quote the whole: he gives the opening words as a reference, trusting to his readers' memories to supply the rest.

8.   οὗ] In the LXX. οὗ is read by א*AB, ᾧ by אᵃ and by the second hand of the early Verona Psalter: but ᾧ was probably the original reading of the LXX. to translate the Hebrew לֹו. In the text of the Epistle the authorities are very much divided: אBDG giving οὗ, the rest ᾧ. In Clement of Rome (§ 50), where the passage is quoted (see the last note but one), A reads οὗ, the Constantinople MS. and the Syriac version ᾧ. It is difficult to say which St Paul wrote. Certainly ᾧ would better suit the order of words: on the other hand, οὗ is more likely to have been altered into ᾧ, and should perhaps on the whole be preferred.

9.   ἐπὶ τὴν περιτομὴν] It is idle here, as elsewhere (see the note on 1 Cor. i. 31), to enquire what particular verb is to be supplied in the ellipse.

11.   σημεῖον ἔλαβεν περιτομῆς] The genitive is better supported than the accusative (περιτομήν); and the absence of the article, urged by Meyer as an argument against περιτομῆς, cannot outweigh the external testimony. But in reality the article here would interfere with the sense, which is 'a sign which consisted in circumcision,' a genitive of apposition, like Col. i. 12 τὴν μερίδα τοῦ κλήρου. The confusion in reading would be helped by the accidental omission of the final σ of περιτομῆς before the initial σ of σφραγῖδα with the result that περιτομὴ would be considered an abbreviation for περιτομήν. The word σημεῖον is used of circumcision in the LXX. of Gen. xvii. 11 εἰς σημεῖον διαθήκης.

σφραγῖδα] 'a seal'; i.e. not a preliminary condition, but a final ratification. So the *Epistle of Barnabas* has (§ 9, 6) ἀλλ' ἐρεῖς· καὶ μὴν περιτέτμηται ὁ λαὸς εἰς σφραγῖδα, connecting the term, as here, with circumcision. Though it may be questioned whether St Paul (2 Cor. i. 22 σφραγισάμενος, comp. Eph. iv. 30) or St John (Rev. ix. 4 τὴν σφραγῖδα τοῦ Θεοῦ ἐπὶ τῶν μετώπων) used the image with any direct reference to baptism, the Christian equivalent to circumcision, it is indisputable that the term was early applied to that rite: Hermas *Sim.* viii. 6 εἰληφότες τὴν σφραγῖδα καὶ τεθλακότες αὐτὴν καὶ μὴ τηρήσαντες ὑγιῆ κ.τ.λ., *Sim.* ix. 16 ὅταν δὲ λάβῃ τὴν σφραγῖδα...ἡ σφραγὶς οὖν τὸ ὕδωρ ἐστὶν κ.τ.λ.; also *Sim.* viii. 2, ix. 17, 31, 2 [Clement] 7 τῶν γὰρ μὴ τηρησάντων, φησίν, τὴν σφραγῖδα compared with § 6 ἐὰν μὴ τηρήσωμεν τὸ βάπτισμα, § 8 τηρήσατε τὴν σφραγῖδα ἄσπιλον, *Clem. Hom.* xvi. 19 τὸ σῶμα σφραγῖδι μεγίστῃ διατετυπωμένον (with the context), *Act. Paul. et Thecl.* 25 μόνον δός μοι τὴν ἐν Χριστῷ σφραγῖδα, Hippol. *Antichr.* 42 (p. 119, Lagarde), Cureton's *Ancient Syriac Documents*, p. 44. Suicer s. v. quotes Clem. Alex. *Quis div. salv.* 39 (p. 957), *Strom.* ii. 3 (p. 434) and later writers.

Indications are not wanting to show that the writer of the Epistle of Barnabas was acquainted with the Epistle to the Romans. Witness this use of σφραγὶς (§ 9) and the phrase τῶν πιστευόντων δι' ἀκροβυστίας (§ 13, 6, see next note), both taken from Rom. iv. 11, κολλώμενοι ἀγαθῷ (§ 20) compared with Rom. xii. 9, and the passage quoted above on Rom. iv. 5, which may have been suggested by Rom. v. 8.

δι' ἀκροβυστίας] The preposition points, not to the instrumentality, but to the condition: uncircumcision was the stage through which they passed into belief. See the note on ii. 27 διὰ γράμματος. The passage in Barnabas § 13 is combined with two Old Testament quotations (Gen. xv. 6, xvii. 5), ἰδοὺ τέθεικά σε, Ἀβραάμ, πατέρα ἐθνῶν τῶν πιστευόντων δι' ἀκροβυστίας τῷ Θεῷ.

12. πατέρα περιτομῆς] To be attached to εἰς τὸ εἶναι αὐτὸν (ver. 11), the intervening clause εἰς τὸ λογισθῆναι κ.τ.λ. being dependent on the preceding εἰς τὸ εἶναι.

The genitive περιτομῆς does not describe Abraham's progeny, as many commentators take it, but his own condition. In other words, the phrase means, not 'a father of a circumcised progeny,' but 'a father belonging to circumcision, himself circumcised.' The meaning is, 'though himself belonging to the circumcision, yet his fatherhood extends beyond the circumcision to all who imitate his faith.' Compare xv. 8, where a similar expression διάκονον περιτομῆς is followed by a similar expansion. The parallel is exact in the two cases, viz. the widening of the circle from the Jewish centre. The prerogative is with the Jew, but otherwise there is equality (Rom. i. 16).

τοῖς οὐκ ἐκ περιτομῆς κ.τ.λ.] Literally 'to those who are, I do not say, of circumcision only, but also to those who walk.' Two different forms of sentence have been confused; as in 1 Cor. xv. 51 πάντες οὐ κοιμηθησόμεθα πάντες δὲ ἀλλαγησόμεθα, where the confusion is between οὐ πάντες κοιμ. πάντες δὲ ἀλλαγ. and πάντες οὐ κοιμ. ἀλλαγ. δέ. Here the two sentences would run (1) τοῖς ἐκ περιτομῆς καὶ τοῖς στοιχοῦσιν, (2) οὐ μόνον τοῖς ἐκ περιτομῆς ἀλλὰ καὶ τοῖς στοιχοῦσιν. A somewhat similar combination is observable in Phil. i. 29. There is no occasion therefore to alter the text either by changing καὶ τοῖς στοιχοῦσιν into καὶ αὐτοῖς στοιχοῦσιν, or by transposing καὶ and τοῖς, as has been proposed.

τοῖς στοιχοῦσιν τοῖς ἴχνεσιν] 'who walk by the steps.' Comp. Gal. vi. 16 ὅσοι τῷ κανόνι τούτῳ στοιχήσουσιν, v. 25 πνεύματι καὶ στοιχῶμεν. The dative with στοιχεῖν, περιπατεῖν etc. marks the line or direction; see the notes on Gal. ll. cc. Hence 'by' is a better rendering here than 'in.'

13. οὐ γὰρ διὰ νόμου] St Paul turns from ἡ περιτομὴ to ὁ νόμος. Circumcision and Law were separate in time and in origin. But from the moment of the institution of the Law they were co-extensive in their operation: for those under the Law were under the Circumcision. The point of the promise not being by law is more lightly touched upon here than the fact of its not being of circumcision. On the other hand in Gal. iii. 7 sq. this converse truth is enlarged upon.

κόσμου] I cannot agree with Dr Vaughan that the absence of the article here (and elsewhere xi. 12, 15, Gal. vi. 14, 1 Cor. iii. 22, 2 Cor. v. 19) with κόσμος 'gives the sense of *such a thing as the world*, so vast, so magnificent.' Like οὐρανός, γῆ, βασιλεὺς etc., κόσμος can be used anarthrous, because it is a quasi-proper name. The same rule applies to numerals (see note on Phil. i. 5, ἀπὸ πρώτης ἡμέρας), because a numeral is sufficiently definite in itself without the addition of the article.

14. The argument, here briefly stated, is elaborated in Gal. iii. 16 sq. Thus the verse must be taken as parenthetical, and verse 15 attached directly to verse 13. 'The law cannot work out the fulfilment of the promise. The effect is just the opposite: it works out as its consequence wrath.'

16. διὰ τοῦτο] i.e. because law, as law, can only result in transgression and punishment. For the idea of κατὰ χάριν 'by way of a favour,' see Eph. ii. 5, 8; for the ellipse after ἵνα, the notes on Gal. ii. 9, 1 Cor. i. 31.

βεβαίαν] '*ratified.*' On the derivation of βέβαιος see Curtius, *Griech. Etym.* pp. 415, 416; for this special meaning compare διαθήκη ἐπὶ νεκροῖς βεβαία (Heb. ix. 17), βεβαίωσις (Phil. i. 7, Heb. vi. 16), βεβαιοῦν (Rom. xv. 8, 1 Cor. i. 6, Heb. ii. 3).

τῷ ἐκ τοῦ νόμου] '*who springs from the law,*' 'who is born, as it were, by the law to Abraham.'

17. πατὴρ πάντων ἡμῶν] We have already arrived at something more than the statement with which the objection started (ver. 1 τὸν προπάτορα ἡμῶν, i.e. 'of us Jews').

ὅτι πατέρα κ.τ.λ.] In the original text (LXX. Gen. xvii. 5 ἔσται τὸ ὄνομά σου Ἀβραὰμ ὅτι κ.τ.λ.) the ὅτι signifies not 'that,' but 'because'; and if we take ὅτι as part of the actual quotation, we must so render it. Here

however, as in iii. 10, viii. 36 and frequently, it probably introduces the
words quoted.

κατέναντι οὗ κ.τ.λ.] I prefer to connect these words with εἰς τὸ εἶναι
βεβαίαν...σπέρματι rather than with what immediately precedes, and to
consider the intervening clause οὐ τῷ ἐκ τοῦ...τέθεικά σε as a parenthesis,
explaining the meaning and substantiating the truth of παντὶ τῷ σπέρματι.
This seems to be the only suitable connexion. Where it is a question of
verification, of confirmation, this reference to the presence of God is
common (2 Cor. iv. 2, Gal. i. 20, 1 Tim. v. 21, vi. 13 etc.).

On the grammatical construction of κατέναντι οὗ see Winer, § xxiv.
pp. 204, 206. I do not however agree with Winer and Meyer in resolving
the sentence into κατέναντι Θεοῦ κατέναντι οὗ ἐπίστευσε, because (1) πιστεύειν
κατέναντί τινος is not a natural phrase, and (2) the passage itself which
St Paul has in mind (Gen. xv. 6) has the dative (ἐπίστευσε τῷ Θεῷ). I
follow Fritzsche in resolving into κατέναντι Θεοῦ ᾧ ἐπίστευσε: comp. for
the dative Matt. xxiv. 38 ἄχρι ἧς ἡμέρας (for ἄχρι τῆς ἡμέρας ᾗ) εἰσῆλθεν Νῶε.
The attraction is made more easy by the fact that the relative precedes
the substantive, as in Matt. l. c., Luke i. 4.

τοῦ ζωοποιοῦντος κ.τ.λ.] This quickening of the dead and evoking
something out of nothing refers *primarily* to Abraham and Sarah (comp.
the phrases σῶμα νενεκρωμένον, τὴν νέκρωσιν τῆς μήτρας Σάρρας, ver. 19) and
the birth of Isaac (τὰ μὴ ὄντα ὡς ὄντα); *secondarily*, to their spiritual
descendants, i.e. the Church and more especially the Gentile Church
(Eph. ii. 1, 5, 10, Col. ii. 12, 13). See also the baptismal formula given
hymn-wise in Eph. v. 14. The Gentile Church rises from the dead with
the risen Christ. In the passages from Ephesians and Colossians, the
resurrection of the Gentile Church is connected with the resurrection of
Christ; and so here, ver. 24. Thus, as at once ζωοποιηθέντες νεκροὶ and
καινὴ κτίσις (comp. Eph. ii. 10 κτισθέντες), Christians can truly be called
τὰ μὴ ὄντα become ὄντα. For the phrase καλοῦντος τὰ μὴ ὄντα κ.τ.λ. as a
description of the creative work of God see 2 [Clement] § 1 ἐκάλεσεν γὰρ
ἡμᾶς οὐκ ὄντας καὶ ἠθέλησεν ἐκ μὴ ὄντος εἶναι ἡμᾶς, Philo *de Creat. Princ.* 7
(II. p. 367) τὰ γὰρ μὴ ὄντα ἐκάλεσεν εἰς τὸ εἶναι, Hermas *Vis.* i. 1. 6 κτίσας
ἐκ τοῦ μὴ ὄντος τὰ ὄντα, *Mand.* i. 2 ποιήσας ἐκ τοῦ μὴ ὄντος εἰς τὸ εἶναι τὰ
πάντα, *Clem. Hom.* iii. 32 τῷ τὰ μὴ ὄντα εἰς τὸ εἶναι συστησαμένῳ.

18. ἐπ' ἐλπίδι] '*on the strength of hope*'; not governed by ἐπίστευσεν,
but independent, as in v. 2: 'contrary to hope he believed under the
condition,' or 'upon the ground, of hope.' The variant ἐφ' ἐλπίδι (read
by CDF) is not sufficiently well supported either here or v. 2 (DF) to find
a place in the text: but it should be read in viii. 20 (אBDF). On similar
aspirated forms see the notes on Phil. ii. 22 ἀφίδω, Gal. ii. 14 οὐχ
Ἰουδαϊκῶς.

οὕτως κ.τ.λ.] Only a part of the quotation (Gen. xv. 5) is given: as
above (ver. 8), his readers would mentally continue it.

19. μὴ ἀσθενήσας κ.τ.λ.] '*without any weakness in his faith he faced*

the facts of.' The removal of the οὐ (of the Textus Receptus) before
κατενόησεν which external evidence demands, brings out the idiomatic
character of the μὴ before ἀσθενήσας and the true significance of κατενόησεν
which is a strong term (e.g. James i. 23, 24 'sees every lineament of his
face in a glass'), 'he clearly perceived,' 'discerned,' and did not flinch
before the fact. Abraham *did* face the fact : see Gen. xvii. 17 where he
is represented as referring to his age, and esp. Heb. xi. 19 λογισάμενος ὅτι
καὶ ἐκ νεκρῶν ἐγείρειν δυνατὸς ὁ Θεός, a passage which may perhaps be
taken to show that the writer of that Epistle was acquainted with the
Epistle to the Romans (see νενεκρωμένον in this verse compared with
Heb. xi. 12).

ἑκατονταετής που] '*about a hundred years old.*' 'The addition of που
qualifies the exactness of the preceding numeral' (Vaughan). The first
promise of a son from whom the chosen race was to spring was made
(Gen. xv. 3 sq.) we cannot say exactly when, but before the birth of
Ishmael which took place when Abraham was eighty-six years old
(Gen. xvi. 16). The second promise of a son Isaac was given when
Abraham was ninety-nine (Gen. xvii. 1), and is associated with the
institution of circumcision (Gen. xvii. 24) ; but Abraham at that time by
a natural exaggeration speaks of himself as a hundred (Gen. xvii. 17 εἰ τῷ
ἑκατονταετεῖ γενήσεται υἱός ;).

20. εἰς δὲ] The connecting particle shows that the true reading must
have been κατενόησεν without the negative : 'he clearly saw, but yet
he did not doubt.'

τῇ ἀπιστίᾳ, τῇ πίστει] For the article comp. 2 Cor. i. 17 τῇ ἐλαφρίᾳ
'the fickleness with which ye charge me.' It is perhaps best to consider
both τῇ ἀπιστίᾳ and τῇ πίστει as instrumental datives.

ἐνεδυναμώθη] A characteristic word of St Paul (Eph. vi. 10, Phil. iv. 13,
1 Tim. i. 12, 2 Tim. ii. 1, iv. 17), peculiar to him and to St Luke
(Acts ix. 22) in the N. T. The simple verb δυναμοῦν is rarer (Col. i. 11,
Heb. xi. 34). Ἐνδυναμοῦσθαι is here used absolutely, as in Acts l. c.:
comp. the absolute use of ἐνεργεῖσθαι (e.g. 2 Cor. iv. 12, Gal. v. 6).

δοὺς δόξαν] The leading idea here is the recognition of God's
almighty power and goodness ; not the feeling of thanksgiving on
Abraham's part.

21. ὃ ἐπήγγελται] '*what He has promised.*' The word for 'to
promise' is necessarily not ἐπαγγέλλειν 'to announce,' but ἐπαγγέλλεσθαι
middle 'to announce on one's part.' Thus ὃ ἐπήγγελται here may be
either 'what has been promised' or 'what He has promised'; for
instances of the perfect and pluperfect passive in a middle signification
are common in the N. T. ; e.g. Acts xiii. 2 προσκέκλημαι, xvi. 10 προσκέ-
κληται, xxv. 12 ἐπικέκλησαι, John ix. 22 συνετέθεινто, 1 Pet. iv. 3 πεπορευ-
μένους. The perfect of ἐπαγγέλλεσθαι occurs in the active sense Heb.
xii. 26 νῦν δὲ ἐπήγγελται λέγων, in the passive sense probably Gal. iii. 19
ᾧ ἐπήγγελται and certainly 2 Macc. iv. 27 τῶν ἐπηγγελμένων τῷ βασιλεῖ

χρημάτων ; comp. Clement of Rome § 35 ὅπως μεταλάβωμεν τῶν ἐπηγγελμένων δωρεῶν.   Here the proximity of δυνατός rather points to the active
sense.   For the N. T. meaning of ἐπαγγέλλεσθαι, ἐπαγγελία implying
always a free proffer, a spontaneous gift on God's part, see the note on
Gal. iii. 14 τὴν ἐπαγγελίαν.

24. λογίζεσθαι] probably passive, as in ver. 4, where see the note.

τοῖς πιστεύουσιν] '*to us, I mean, believers*' etc.   The rendering of the
A. V. 'if we believe' cannot stand.   For the expression here comp.
Eph. i. 19, 1 Thess. ii. 10, 13.   The Resurrection was at that time
especially the cardinal article of the Christian faith (x. 9); I have set
forth some of the practical bearings of the doctrine in the note on
Phil. iii. 10 τὴν δύναμιν κ.τ.λ.

25. ὃς παρεδόθη κ.τ.λ.]   A reference to Is. liii. 12.   There is an opposition between παρεδόθη and ἠγέρθη, as between παραπτώματα and δικαίωσιν.   Christ consented to die because we were dead; He rose to life
that we might be made alive by our acquittal.   In His betrayal and
death we die to sin; in His resurrection we rise to new life.   Thus the
two clauses represent the negative and the positive side of the same
operations.   This is another way of expressing the idea of dying with
Christ which is so common in St Paul (Rom. vi. 5, 6, 10, 11, viii. 10).

CHAPTER V

vii. *The results of this position of righteousness through faith* (v. 1—11).

1. **ἔχωμεν**] If external authority is to be regarded, this (not ἔχομεν) is unquestionably the right reading. In the New Testament generally, as here, it is man who is regarded as at enmity with God, not God at enmity with man. The death of Christ is represented as reconciling man to God, not God to man. I would not say that it would be theologically wrong to speak of God as estranged from us; but the reverse is the usual practice in the New Testament, and the case is exactly represented in the Parable of the Prodigal Son. For God loves us with a father's love, even though we have turned our backs upon Him; just as that father yearned for his son's return.

The force of the phrase is this: 'let us be at peace, let us not continue to fight against God (Acts v. 39 θεομάχοι). Potentially we are justified: let us appropriate our privileges, let us make them actual' (comp. Col. i. 20 sq.). Hence the imperative. For the phrase employed here Wetstein appositely quotes Herodian viii. 7 ἀντὶ πολέμου μὲν εἰρήνην ἔχοντες πρὸς θεούς.

2. **τὴν προσαγωγὴν ἐσχήκαμεν**] '*we have gained our access, entrance.*' Christ is considered no longer as the door, but as the introducer. To realise the force of the metaphor we must recal the formalities with which an Eastern monarch is surrounded. The idea is still further brought out in Eph. ii. 18, and Eph. iii. 12 (where it is strengthened by the phrase τὴν παρρησίαν καὶ προσαγωγήν, 'freedom of speech as well as right of admittance'). See Tholuck and Meyer here, and compare Plutarch *Moral.* p. 522 F.

καυχώμεθα κ.τ.λ.] Καυχώμεθα is best taken as an indicative and connected with ἐσχήκαμεν: ἐπ' ἐλπίδι 'on the strength of the hope' (as in iv. 18), giving the conditions under which we boast. On the expression τῆς δόξης τοῦ Θεοῦ and what it implies, see the note on iii. 23.

3. **οὐ μόνον δὲ ἀλλὰ καὶ**] This ellipse occurs five times in St Paul, in all cases in Epistles of this period (Rom. v. 3, 11, viii. 23, ix. 10, 2 Cor. viii. 19).

καυχώμενοι] The irregularity of the construction recommends this reading. It is more probable that καυχώμενοι should have been changed into καυχώμεθα for grammatical reasons and by mechanical repetition from the preceding verse, than that the indicative should have been changed into the participle to conform with ver. 11. Otherwise the authorities somewhat favour the indicative (καυχώμεθα ℵADFL Chrys. Theodoret, Theophylact, Cyprian; καυχώμενοι BC Origen, Tertull.).

δοκιμήν] The substantive means in the N. T. either (1) 'the process of testing or proving,' 2 Cor. viii. 2; or (2) 'the state or disposition so ascertained, the tested quality,' 'value,' Phil. ii. 22, 2 Cor. ii. 9, ix. 13, xiii. 3, though in all these passages the first meaning might stand. This latter is probably the signification here. This sense approaches very close to τὸ δοκίμιον (James i. 3, 1 Pet. i. 7) and the metaphor of assaying by fire is frequent under other terms also (πύρωσις, πυροῦσθαι, 1 Pet. iv. 12, Rev. iii. 18, Ps. lxvi. 10). Compare the double sense of δοκιμάζειν (see the notes on 1 Thess. ii. 4, v. 21).

5. οὐ καταισχύνει] Very probably St Paul had in his mind Ecclus. ii. 10 τίς ἐνεπίστευσεν Κυρίῳ καὶ κατῃσχύνθη; for in the immediate context occurs ἐν πυρὶ δοκιμάζεται χρυσὸς καὶ ἄνθρωποι δεκτοὶ ἐν καμίνῳ ταπεινώσεως (ver. 5), which illustrates δοκιμὴν above.

ἡ ἀγάπη τοῦ Θεοῦ] Primarily 'God's love towards us,' as the context requires (1 John iv. 10); but this (see Vaughan) 'awakens a response of love in us' (1 John iv. 19) towards Him and towards our fellow-man.

ἐκκέχυται] The word denotes both abundance and diffusion.

6. Two points regarding the text of this verse require consideration.

(1) The ἔτι after ἀσθενῶν must certainly be retained. The preponderance of authority is enormously in its favour. Moreover there was every temptation in a scribe to omit it (see Reiche *Comm. Crit.* p. 38).

(2) The more difficult question remains. At the beginning of the verse are we to read (*a*) ἔτι γὰρ with ℵACD*K, the Syriac (except the Peshito), Marcion, Chrysostom and Theodoret, (*b*) εἰς τί γὰρ with D²FG, Irenæus (Lat.) and the Latin versions, (*c*) εἰ γὰρ (ἔτι) with *h* of the Old Latin, the Codex Fuldensis of the Vulgate, Isidore of Pelusium and Augustine, or (*d*) εἰ γε with B alone? There are also several other variations with but slight support (as εἰ δὲ L Peshito) which may be neglected. The choice seems to lie between the two extremes ἔτι γὰρ and εἰ γε. I should adopt ἔτι γὰρ and consider εἰς τί γὰρ, εἰ γὰρ to have been corrections made to avoid the double ἔτι, and εἰ γε to be a further correction. Possibly however the series of changes began at the other end with εἰ γε as the original reading. In Gal. v. 11 εἰ περιτομὴν ἔτι κηρύσσω τί ἔτι διώκομαι; the first ἔτι is (wrongly) thrown out by the same manuscripts (DFG) which read εἰς τί γὰρ here.

If we read ἔτι γὰρ and so preserve the double ἔτι, the second ἔτι must not be taken in the sense of 'moreover'; but must be explained by the trajection in the first ἔτι (Winer § lxi. p. 692) which gives occasion for the insertion of the word later on to clear the sense. For a repetition of ἔτι in the same member of the sentence comp. Pindar *Nem.* ix. 47 (111) οὐκέτ' ἔστι πόρσω θνατὸν ἔτι σκοπιᾶς ἄλλας ἐφάψασθαι, but it is undoubtedly rare. On the other hand, if εἴ γε be adopted, we may compare Eph. iii. 2 εἴ γε ἠκούσατε: but the construction is not much after St Paul's manner here.

κατὰ καιρόν] *'at the proper time'*: comp. Eph. i. 10, Gal. iv. 4 (with the note), Tit. i. 3. Christ came when the law had fulfilled its work, when the race had attained its majority.

ὑπὲρ ἀσεβῶν] A strong expression (as in iv. 5) to emphasize the greatness of the boon. Such language may have given rise to the extraordinary statement in the Epistle of Barnabas § 5 quoted above (iv. 5), an exaggeration only to be accounted for by passages like these where the Apostles depreciate themselves in order to enhance the grace of God. Failing absolutely to understand St Paul's motive, Celsus wields this saying against the Christians.

7. μόλις γὰρ] 'Died for the impious. This is the strongest proof of His love. For you will scarce find one willing to die for a *just man*; though for the *good* man persons might be found ready to die.'

The more recent commentators generally make the two expressions ὑπὲρ δικαίου and ὑπὲρ τοῦ ἀγαθοῦ as equivalent or nearly so; and consider that ὑπὲρ γὰρ τοῦ ἀγαθοῦ is a justification of the Apostle's use of μόλις 'hardly' in place of οὐ 'not': as if he had meant 'I say *hardly*, for exceptional cases there are.' So Meyer, Jowett, Vaughan (if I understand him aright). Alford is an honourable exception, but he does not quite see the force of the passage.

The fact is that the δίκαιος and the ἀγαθὸς represent two distinct types of character, as the following passages will show.

Clem. Hom. xvii. 5 ὁ δὲ ἐκδικοῦντα καὶ ἀμειβόμενον λέγων Θεὸν δίκαιον αὐτὸν τῇ φύσει συνίστησιν καὶ οὐκ ἀγαθόν...ποτὲ μὲν ἀγαθὸν λέγων, ποτὲ δὲ δίκαιον, οὐδ' οὕτως συμφωνεῖ, xviii. 1 εἰ μὲν οὖν νομοθέτης ἐστίν, δίκαιος τυγχάνει, δίκαιος δὲ ὢν ἀγαθὸς οὐκ ἔστιν...καὶ ὁ Πέτρος ἔφη· πρῶτον ἡμῖν εἰπέ, ἐπὶ ποίαις πράξεσι δοκεῖ σοι ὁ ἀγαθὸς εἶναι, ἐπὶ ποίαις δὲ ὁ δίκαιος... καὶ ὁ Σίμων· σὺ πρῶτον εἰπέ, τί σοι δοκεῖ τὸ ἀγαθὸν ἢ καὶ τὸ δίκαιον. There is much argument between the two on this point, in the course of which (§ 3) St Peter says ὅτι δὲ τὸ δίκαιον ἄλλο ἐστὶν καὶ τὸ ἀγαθὸν ἔτερον καὶ αὐτὸς ὁμολογῶ, ἀλλ' ὅτι τοῦ αὐτοῦ ἐστι τὸ ἀγαθὸν εἶναι καὶ δίκαιον, ἀγνοεῖς, and again § 14 πῶς ἐστι τοῦτο ἀγαθόν, ὃ μὴ δίκαιόν ἐστιν κ.τ.λ. So ii. 13 χωρὶς πάσης ἀντιλογίας ὁ Θεὸς ἀγαθὸς ὢν καὶ δίκαιός ἐστιν, and iv. 13 τῇ φύσει ἀγαθὸν καὶ δίκαιον· ἀγαθὸν μὲν ὡς μεταμελομένοις χαριζόμενον τὰ ἁμαρτήματα, δίκαιον δὲ ὡς ἑκάστῳ μετὰ τὴν μετάνοιαν κατ' ἀξίαν τῶν πεπραγμένων ἐπεξιόντα.

Irenæus i. 27. 1 of Cerdon's teaching of two Gods, καὶ τὸν μὲν δίκαιον τὸν δὲ ἀγαθὸν ὑπάρχειν.

Ptolemæus *Epist. ad Flor.* § 4 (in Epiphan. *Hær.* xxxiii. 7) εἰ ὁ τέλειος

Θεὸς ἀγαθός ἐστι κατὰ τὴν ἑαυτοῦ φύσιν…ἔστι δὲ καὶ ὁ τῆς τοῦ ἀντικειμένου φύσεως κακός τε καὶ πονηρός…τούτων οὖν μέσος καθεστώς, καὶ μήτε ἀγαθὸς ὤν, μήτε μὴν κακός, μηδὲ ἄδικος, ἰδίως τε λεχθείη ἂν δίκαιος. This is exactly what we want. The δίκαιος falls short of the ἀγαθός, but yet he is neither κακὸς nor ἄδικος.

Athenagoras *Legat.* 34 quoted by Wetstein (p. 38 A) οὐ γὰρ ἀπαρκεῖ δίκαιον εἶναι (ἔστι δὲ δικαιοσύνης ἴσα ἴσοις ἀμείβειν), ἀλλ᾽ ἀγαθοῖς καὶ ἀνεξικάκοις εἶναι πρόκειται.

In Clement of Alexandria *Pædag.* i. 8. 62 (p. 135 sq. Potter) there is a whole chapter πρὸς τοὺς ἡγουμένους μὴ εἶναι ἀγαθὸν τὸ δίκαιον. He says (§ 63) τὸ δὲ ἀγαθὸν ᾗ ἀγαθόν ἐστιν, οὐδὲν ἄλλο ποιεῖ ἢ ὅτι ὠφελεῖ (p. 136) with much more to the same effect, καὶ κατὰ Πλάτωνα ὁμολογεῖται ἀγαθὸν εἶναι τὸ δίκαιον (§ 67, p. 138), ὅτι μὲν ἀγαθὸς ὁ Θεὸς καὶ †ἅπαντες† ὁμολογοῦσιν οἱ πάντες· ὅτι δὲ καὶ δίκαιος ὁ αὐτὸς Θεὸς οὔ μοι χρὴ πλειόνων ἔτι λόγων (§ 71, p. 140), and see also the following chapter.

In classical literature one example will suffice, though many could be adduced.

Plato *Resp.* i. p. 350 C ὁ μὲν ἄρα δίκαιος ἡμῖν ἀναπέφανται ὧν ἀγαθός τε καὶ σοφός.

Thus the distinction between δίκαιος and ἀγαθὸς is very much the same as the Aristotelian distinction between the ἀκριβοδίκαιος and the ἐπιεικής (*Eth. Nic.* v. 14), between the man, that is to say, who is scrupulously just, and the man who is prepared to make allowances. Shylock might be δίκαιος, but he was not ἀγαθός. The 'summum jus' may become 'summa injuria.'

And for the matter in hand, there is all the difference in the world between the ἀγαθὸς and the δίκαιος. The ἀγαθὸς, as such, is full of sympathy and consideration for others. The well-being of others is his first concern. He is beneficent and kind. This is the idea of ἀγαθότης. On the other hand the δίκαιος, as such, puts out of sight the feelings of others. He is absolutely without sympathy. Now sympathy elicits sympathy. Consequently the ἀγαθὸς will be met with sympathy: others will be ready to do and to suffer for him in their turn: but the δίκαιος will evoke no such love, no willingness to make sacrifices in return.

Hence St Paul's language here. 'For a *good* man some perchance may have courage to die; for a *just* man you will hardly, if at all, find any one ready to sacrifice his life: yet though we were not only not *good*, were not even *just*, yea, were worse than unjust, worse than sinners (ἁμαρτωλοί), were even ἀσεβεῖς (recklessly and contemptuously set the will of God at defiance), yet Christ died for us.'

τοῦ ἀγαθοῦ] The definite article is added to throw a little more emphasis on the word. Τοῦ ἀγαθοῦ here cannot be neuter, as some take it: for, *first*, the context requires a person; *secondly*, as a matter of fact, people are not so ready to die for a good principle as for a good person, because in the latter case their personal sympathies are excited.

9. οὖν] The οὖν should be retained, its omission in some texts being connected with the manipulation of the reading of the beginning of ver. 6, from a desire to form a suitable apodosis to such readings as εἰ γάρ, εἴ γε. If however εἴ γε be read, εἴ γε...ἀπέθανεν is not the protasis of a new sentence, but is to be connected with what precedes: οὖν therefore must stand in any case.

σωθησόμεθα] "In the language of the New Testament salvation is a thing of the past, a thing of the present, and a thing of the future. St Paul says sometimes 'Ye (or we) were saved' (Rom. viii. 24), or 'Ye have been saved' (Eph. ii. 5, 8), sometimes 'Ye are being saved' (1 Cor. xv. 2), and sometimes 'Ye shall be saved' (Rom. x. 9, 13). It is important to observe this, because we are thus taught that σωτηρία involves a moral condition which must have begun already, though it will receive its final accomplishment hereafter. Godliness, righteousness, is life, is salvation. And it is hardly necessary to say that the divorce of morality and religion must be fostered and encouraged by failing to note this and so laying the whole stress either on the past or on the future— on the first call or on the final change" (*On a Fresh Revision*, 1891, p. 104). The moral condition, not the physical, is the leading idea in σωτηρία, and binds all the meanings together.

ἀπὸ τῆς ὀργῆς] '*from the wrath*' of God: comp. iii. 5, ix. 22, where however ὁ Θεὸς occurs in the context. Compare therefore Rom. xii. 19 δότε τόπον τῇ ὀργῇ, and 1 Thess. i. 10 (with the note), where the word (like τὸ θέλημα, τὸ ὄνομα) is used absolutely.

10. κατηλλάγημεν τῷ Θεῷ] In accordance with the universal language of the New Testament which speaks of mankind as reconciled in Christ to God, not God as reconciled to man. See 2 Cor. v. 18 sq., Col. i. 21. It is true that New Testament writers do use the expression 'the wrath of God' borrowed from the O. T., employing it κατὰ ἄνθρωπον and καταχρηστικῶς; but when they speak at length upon the subject, the hostility is represented not as on the part of God, but of man. And this is the reason why the Apostles never use διαλλάσσειν in this connection, but always καταλλάσσειν; because the former word denotes mutual concession after mutual hostility (Matt. v. 24 and LXX. frequently), an idea absent from καταλλάσσειν. Thus the New Testament is the revelation of the higher truth that God is love.

Prof. Jowett strangely states in his note that 'the comparison of Col. i. 21...shows that ἐχθροὺς may have an active as well as passive meaning.' But surely the common meaning of ἐχθρὸς *is* active, at least from the Attic age onward, and in prose; and it is the universal use in the New Testament.

ἐν τῇ ζωῇ αὐτοῦ] i.e. rising in His resurrection and living in His life.

11. οὐ μόνον δὲ ἀλλὰ] See on ver. 3 above.

νῦν] i.e. under the present dispensation.

viii. *The terms 'life' and 'death' explained* (v. 12—21).

12. **διὰ τοῦτο**] 'This being so—since we have been already reconciled in Christ and look forward to eternal salvation, it comes to pass that as one man brought death into the world, so one man also brought life.'

ὥσπερ] The apodosis should have run, 'so also through one man came righteousness, and through righteousness, life.' Comp. 1 Cor. xv. 22, which contains the germ of this passage, as elsewhere that epistle anticipates this. Thus the apodosis would have expressed the analogy between the First and the Second Adam. But it is lost sight of in a number of dependent clauses, beginning with καὶ οὕτως κ.τ.λ.; and instead of the resemblance, the contrasts of the two come prominently forward in vv. 15 sq. The apodosis disappears; and the sentence is resumed with another protasis in ver. 18, where ἄρα οὖν marks the fact of the resumption.

ἀνθρώπου] The word is more or less emphatic, because the parallel points from the humanity of Adam to the humanity of Christ: see ver. 15.

ὁ θάνατος] Physical death in the first instance and in the Mosaic narrative: but spiritual death as further implied therein; just as in the correlative both physical and spiritual life are included. In the Apostle's mind the two ideas are inseparable.

διῆλθεν ἐφ' ᾧ κ.τ.λ.] Sin passed, as it were, from the one frontier to the other of humanity. The disease was communicated to the whole race, not inasmuch as all were descendants of Adam, but inasmuch as all sinned.

13. **ἄχρι γὰρ κ.τ.λ.**] This is to justify the assertion that all sinned. An objection starts up in the Apostle's mind, 'What about the time before Moses, when there was no law?' and this objection he proceeds to deal with. Yes: sin was there, even when there was no law to make the items appear in black and white.

οὐκ ἐλλογᾶται] *'is not reckoned in the account.'* The sin is there; but it did not take the form of transgression and so is not set down. On the two forms ἐλλογᾶν, ἐλλογεῖν and similar pairs of verbs, see the note on Philemon 18 ἐλλόγα.

14. **ἐβασίλευσεν**] *'reigned,'* dominated, carried all before it; see ver. 21 below.

καὶ ἐπὶ τοὺς μὴ ἁμαρτήσαντας] The omission of μὴ is at least as early as Origen (see Reiche *Comm. Crit.* p. 42); but it is the true reading, (1) as being the better supported, (2) as required by the context, more especially by the καὶ and the πάντες ἥμαρτον. (3) The omission of μὴ if genuine, was more natural than the insertion of μὴ if spurious. It would appear to scribes to be reasonable that Adam's punishment should fall on those only who followed Adam's sin.

The question of the reading being thus decided, it remains to consider what interpretation should be put on the expression ἐπὶ τοὺς μὴ ἁμαρτήσαντας κ.τ.λ. The interpretations which make the penalty of death fall on those who did not actually sin are mainly twofold. The first takes ἐπὶ τῷ ὁμοιώματι closely with ἐβασίλευσεν, explaining the phrase to mean 'by reason of the likeness of the sin'; that is, the likeness only, for, where no law is, there is no direct imputation of sin. But this view is distinctly excluded by the words πάντες ἥμαρτον above. According to St Paul's teaching, all did sin. The other explanation is to disconnect μὴ from ἐπὶ τῷ ὁμοιώματι and by giving a somewhat strained meaning to ἐπὶ τῷ ὁμοιώματι to arrive at the result, 'they did not commit sin, in the sense in which Adam committed sin,' i.e. they were not guilty of actual, but only of imputed sin. The passage however distinctly implies that they did commit actual sin; though it was sin not according to the likeness of Adam's sin. In what way then did their sin differ from his? Calvin replies: 'quia non habebant, ut ille, revelatam certo oraculo Dei voluntatem,' that is, did not sin against an express command, had not transgressed a definite precept, but only the law within (Rom. ii. 14). But this is not quite satisfactory, and a wider application ought probably to be given to the whole passage.

ὅς ἐστιν τύπος] 'Inasmuch as all were involved in the consequences of the sin in the one case, of the righteousness in the other case.' But observe that in both cases the descendants are involved in these consequences by participation and communication, not by imputation.

τοῦ μέλλοντος] Christ is future as regards Adam and Eve and the Jewish world, though not as regards St Paul. The Apostle doubtless has in his mind the Messianic titles ὁ μέλλων, ὁ ἐρχόμενος, on which see *Biblical Essays*, p. 149. Strictly speaking, the life, death and resurrection of Christ are the proper counterpart and counteraction to the sin of Adam, and these are past from the Apostle's standpoint. The fact that Christ μέλλει κρίνειν ζῶντας καὶ νεκροὺς (2 Tim. iv. 1 quoted by Vaughan) has no bearing on the matter in hand, since the grace, the righteousness and the life, which exist already, are alone under consideration. Thus the past tense ἐπερίσσευσεν (not the future) is used in the next verse.

15—17. St Paul has stated the fact of the analogy (ὅς ἐστιν τύπος τοῦ μέλλοντος). He now goes on to speak of the contrasts (vv. 15, 16), and returns to the analogy again (ver. 18 ἄρα οὖν). The contrasts are introduced as a corrective to the impression which might be left by the analogy alone. They are prompted by the overwhelming sense of God's goodness and mercy. These contrasts are two, and are introduced in similar terms (ver. 15 ἀλλ᾽ οὐχ ὡς... going on ver. 15 εἰ γὰρ..., ver. 16 καὶ οὐχ ὡς... going on ver. 17 εἰ γὰρ...). *First*, there is a contrast in character: on the one side τὸ παράπτωμα resulting in θάνατος, on the other τὸ χάρισμα (ἡ χάρις), ἡ δωρεά and all that is implied thereby. *Secondly*, there is a contrast in result: in the one case from the one to the many, in the other from the many to the one.

15. παράπτωμα, χάρισμα] The mere fact that the one is παράπτωμα

and the other χάρισμα, the one an act of rebellion bringing death, the other an act of mercy bringing life, sets the two cases as wide as the poles apart.

τοῦ ἑνός, τοὺς πολλούς] "In Rom. v. 15—19 there is a sustained contrast between '*the* one (ὁ εἷς)' and '*the* many (οἱ πολλοί),' but in the English Version the definite article is systematically omitted: 'If through the offence of one many be dead,' and so throughout the passage, closing with, 'For as by one man's disobedience many were made sinners, so by the obedience of one shall many be made righteous.' In place of any comment of my own, I will quote Bentley's words. Pleading for the correct rendering he says (*Works*, III. p. 224 ed. Dyce), 'By this accurate version some hurtful mistakes about partial redemption and absolute reprobation had been happily prevented. Our English readers had then seen, what several of the fathers saw and testified, that οἱ πολλοί *the many*, in an antithesis to *the one*, are equivalent to πάντες *all* in ver. 12 and comprehend the whole multitude, the entire species of mankind, exclusive only of *the one*.' In other words the benefits of Christ's obedience extend to all men potentially. It is only human self-will which places limits to its operation." *On a Fresh Revision*, 1891, p. 108.

ἀπέθανον] '*died*,' i.e. with Adam's transgression; not 'be dead' (A. V.) which would require τεθνήκασι and would be as untrue to facts as to grammar. In many cases they died and are alive again in Christ (Rev. i. 18 ἐγενόμην νεκρὸς καὶ ἰδοὺ ζῶν εἰμί).

πολλῷ μᾶλλον] Why 'much more'? How comes this *a fortiori* argument? The reason is not expressed, but it underlies all St Paul's theology, as indeed all the N. T. theology; that God is a God of love, that He delighteth not in the death of a sinner, that His will is towards mercy and pardon. Therefore if the effects of sin extended to all, we may be much more sure that the effects of grace will extend to all and this abundantly. There is a similar implication in xi. 15. For πολλῷ μᾶλλον introducing an *a fortiori* argument see above vv. 9, 10, and below ver. 17, 1 Cor. xii. 22, 2 Cor. iii. 9, 11.

ἡ δωρεὰ ἐν χάριτι] '*the boon which consists in a favour*.' The distinction between δωρεά, δῶρον on the one hand and δόσις, δόμα on the other is drawn out by Philo *de Cherub.* 25 (I. p. 154 ed. Mangey) τῶν ὄντων τὰ μὲν χάριτος μέσης ἠξίωται, ἣ καλεῖται δόσις, τὰ δὲ ἀμείνονος ἧς ὄνομα οἰκεῖον δωρεά, *Leg. All.* iii. 70 (I. p. 126) δῶρα δομάτων διαφέρουσι. Τὰ μὲν γὰρ ἔμφασιν μεγέθους τελείων ἀγαθῶν δηλοῦσιν, ἃ τοῖς τελείοις χαρίζεται ὁ θεός, τὰ δὲ εἰς βραχύτατον ἔσταλται ὧν μετέχουσιν οἱ εὐφυεῖς ἀσκηταὶ οἱ προκόπτοντες. The former pair of words therefore represents something much higher and more excellent than the latter. We are thus able to appreciate St James' distinction, which some have deemed meaningless, πᾶσα δόσις ἀγαθὴ καὶ πᾶν δώρημα τέλειον (James i. 17); and we may notice that while δόσις is only called 'good,' the epithet 'perfect' is applied to δώρημα. Consequently as τέλειον is an advance upon ἀγαθή, so is δώρημα upon δόσις. Thus δωρεά is rightly applied by St Paul here and ver. 17 to the gift of righteousness and reconciliation.

τοῦ ἑνὸς ἀνθρώπου] The word ἀνθρώπου is emphatic. It was necessary to introduce the idea of the Second Adam here, just as in 1 Tim. ii. 5 a similar stress is laid on the humanity of Christ to show the necessity that the mediator should be a man. 'Ανθρώπου is therefore added in this second clause, though omitted in the first.

ἐπερίσσευσεν] For the tense compare ἀπέθανον above. The sin of the race was potentially bound up in the sin of Adam: the restoration of the race in the life and death of Christ.

16. καὶ οὐχ κ.τ.λ.] An abridged expression requiring the addition of ὁ θάνατος τῶν πολλῶν after ἁμαρτήσαντος, and οὕτω καὶ before τὸ δώρημα. The starting-point was not one act extending to many; but conversely many acts leading to one. Again the underlying thought is the abundant mercy of God, which counteracts many transgressions by one righteous deed.

ἁμαρτήσαντος] For the form of this first aorist see Lobeck *Phryn.* p. 732. The v. l. ἁμαρτήματος has some support, but not sufficient. Δώρημα is rightly substituted for δωρεὰ of the preceding verse; for there the act of giving was the prominent idea, here the boon granted.

ἐξ ἑνός] probably neuter here, as ἐκ πολλῶν παραπτωμάτων suggests: comp. δι' ἑνὸς δικαιώματος (ver. 18).

δικαίωμα] This word has three senses, all of which are represented in this Epistle; (1) 'an ordinance' (i. 32, ii. 26, viii. 4), its common sense in the New Testament; (2) 'a righteous deed' (v. 18, comp. Rev. xv. 4, xix. 8); (3) 'a sentence, verdict,' here of acquittal. Thus it refers to legislation, to conduct, and to jurisdiction. The second of the meanings given above can be well illustrated from Aristotle: see *Rhet.* i. 13. 1 τὰ ἀδικήματα πάντα καὶ τὰ δικαιώματα (comp. i. 3. 9), *Eth. Nic.* v. 7. (10) καλεῖται δὲ (δικαίωμα) μᾶλλον δικαιοπράγημα τὸ κοινόν· δικαίωμα δὲ τὸ ἐπανόρθωμα τοῦ ἀδικήματος. In this signification therefore, besides its ordinary acceptation of 'a just act' equivalent to δικαιοπράγημα, the word has a special force 'the making right of what is wrong,' and this sense of 'the rectification of an act of injustice' (see Aristotle's *Rhetoric*, ed. Cope and Sandys, I. p. 56) may well come in in the passage v. 18.

17. Observe the accumulation of words, πολλῷ μᾶλλον, τὴν περισσείαν τῆς χάριτος balancing the πολλῷ μᾶλλον, ἡ χάρις, καὶ ἡ δωρεὰ ἐν χάριτι of ver. 15.

τῆς δωρεᾶς τῆς δικαιοσύνης] Though this is the reading of the majority of manuscripts, τῆς δωρεᾶς is omitted by B Origen (in two places), Chrysostom, Irenæus and Augustine, τῆς δικαιοσύνης by C Origen (in one place), while several versions (Vulgate, Peshito and Harklean) smooth the passage down by tbe insertion of καὶ between the two substantives. These phenomena, when tested by internal evidence, render τῆς δωρεᾶς highly suspicious; and suggest that the phrase was originally intended as

a gloss or a substitute for the seemingly awkward expression τῆς δικαιοσύνης, but subsequently crept into the text and was either added to or
displaced the original reading τῆς δικαιοσύνης.

18. ἄρα οὖν] '*well then.*' The contrasts being disposed of, ἄρα οὖν
introduces and sums up the analogy, the resemblance, between the First
and the Second Adam. It is a favourite collocation of particles in
St Paul under similar circumstances (vii. 3, 25, viii. 12, ix. 16, 18, xiv. 12,
19, Gal. vi. 10, Eph. ii. 19, 1 Thess. v. 6, 2 Thess. ii. 15).

ὡς δι' ἑνός] To supply the ellipse we require τὸ κρίμα ἐγένετο, τὸ χάρισμα
ἐγένετο. This elliptical form for the sake of emphasis is not unusual in
the case of two antithetical clauses, e.g. x. 17, Gal. ii. 9, 1 Cor. vi. 13,
Rev. vi. 6, Clement of Rome, 42 ὁ Χριστὸς οὖν ἀπὸ τοῦ Θεοῦ καὶ οἱ ἀπόστολοι
ἀπὸ τοῦ Χριστοῦ.

εἰς δικαίωσιν ζωῆς] '*to justification consisting in life,*' the genitive of
apposition.

19. ὑπακοῆς] On the ὑπακοὴ of Christ comp. Phil. ii. 8, Heb. v. 8.

20. νόμος δὲ] It is not his main subject; but he has been obliged
incidentally to speak of law in order to obviate an objection ; and he
therefore proceeds now to explain the function of law in reference to the
universal sin and the universal redemption.

παρεισῆλθεν] Sin entered in boldly (εἰσῆλθεν), death passed over all
humanity, over all ages (διῆλθεν) ; but law only came in by the way, by a
bye-path (παρεισῆλθεν), had only a temporary application, a partial
dominion. For the metaphor see Gal. ii. 4 παρεισάκτους, παρεισῆλθον.

πλεονάσῃ] Like περισσεύειν, the verb πλεονάζειν has a transitive as
well as an intransitive use (see the note on 1 Thess. iii. 12). Here
πλεονάσῃ is probably intransitive, as being in accordance with St Paul's
general usage, and corresponding more closely to ἐπλεόνασεν of the next
clause.

τὸ παράπτωμα, ἡ ἁμαρτία] The words παράπτωμα and παράβασις (ver. 14)
are closely allied, referring respectively to the consequences on the agent
and to the line transgressed. But both imply a definite rule broken,
a definite line stepped beyond. In other words they presuppose the
existence of a law or rule (νόμος). 'Where there is no law, neither is
there transgression' (Rom. iv. 15).

In this they differ from sin (ἁμαρτία). There will be sin where there is
no law (Rom. v. 13, 14), albeit the sin is not imputed (οὐκ ἐλλογᾶται, see
the note on the passage). Thus, though men sinned before the law was
given, they did not sin 'after the likeness of Adam's transgression
(v. 14 ἐπὶ τῷ ὁμοιώματι τῆς παραβάσεως 'Αδάμ). Hence, though St Paul
declares that law multiplies transgression (as here, see also Gal. iii. 19),
he says on the other hand that it reveals sin (iii. 20 διὰ γὰρ νόμου ἐπίγνωσις
ἁμαρτίας, vii. 7, 13). It does not create, but it evokes sin.

So here: the law came not that the sin might abound, but that the
transgression might abound. The sin did abound all the time (see the

next verse); and the law, making the transgression abound, brought out
this fact patently, forced it upon the conscience. For while transgression
is the violation of some special precept, sin is a violation of an eternal
principle, higher and wider than any code of definite rules.

21. ὑπερεπερίσσευσεν] *'abounded more exceedingly.'* A very strong
word. Πλεονάζειν represents the comparative, 'to increase,' περισσεύειν
the superlative, 'to abound'; see 1 Thess. iii. 12, where they are so
translated in the A. V. But here St Paul is not satisfied with περισσεύειν;
he doubles the superlative (as in 2 Cor. vii. 4). On St Paul's fondness
for cumulative compounds in ὑπέρ, especially in the second chronological
group of his Epistles, see the note on 1 Thess. iii. 10, where examples are
given. Compare also 2 Cor. iv. 17 καθ' ὑπερβολὴν εἰς ὑπερβολήν.

ἐβασίλευσεν, βασιλεύσῃ] *'established its throne, might establish its
throne.'* This is the force of the aorist in both cases: comp. Rev. xi. 17,
xix. 6, and e.g. Herod. ii. 2 ἐπειδὴ δὲ Ψαμμίτιχος βασιλεύσας ἠθέλησε εἰδέναι
οἵτινες γενοίατο πρῶτοι. The sense in ver. 14 is somewhat different: see the
passage.

CHAPTER VI

ix., x. *The influence of our spiritual position upon our conduct* (vi. 1—23).

1. **ἐπιμένωμεν**] The right reading unquestionably (not ἐπιμενοῦμεν); so below, ver. 15 ἁμαρτήσωμεν (not ἁμαρτήσομεν). The conjunctives are stronger than the futures, and represent the indignant rejoinder of some objector, 'Has it come to this that we are obliged to continue in sin? Is nothing left but this?' The antinomian inference, if it hold good at all, must be obligatory, not permissive.

τῇ ἁμαρτίᾳ] Perhaps '*the* sin,' and ἡ χάρις '*the* grace,' referring to v. 20, 21. For ἐπιμένειν τινὶ in the sense of 'to cling to,' see the note on Phil. i. 24.

2. **μὴ γένοιτο**] The thought is abhorrent to the Apostle. The fact is, as he goes on to show, that this is not only a wrong precept, but an actual impossibility. A thing cannot be dead and alive at the same time and from the same point of view. The very conception of the δικαιοσύνη, the χάρις of which he has spoken, is a death to sin—a death ideally complete, but actually more or less imperfect.

οἵτινες ἀπεθάνομεν] '*as men who died*'; either potentially in Christ's death (see vv. 15, 19), or personally when we were baptized. Probably the latter thought is uppermost; compare ver. 3 ὅσοι ἐβαπτίσθημεν.

τῇ ἁμαρτίᾳ] '*to sin*'; the dative of reference, see vi. 10, 11, vii. 4, Gal. ii. 20, 1 Pet. ii. 24.

πῶς] interrogatively with the future introduces an impossibility, as in iii. 6, viii. 32, 1 Cor. xiv. 7, 9, 16 etc. 'The idea is not merely absurd, inconsistent; it is absolutely impossible.'

3. **ἢ ἀγνοεῖτε**] 'Such a supposition betrays the grossest ignorance.' Compare vii. 1, ἢ οὐκ ἐπιγινώσκετε (2 Cor. xiii. 5), and the common Pauline phrase ἢ οὐκ οἴδατε (xi. 2, 1 Cor. vi. 2, 9, 16, 19).

εἰς Χριστὸν Ἰησοῦν] The preposition conveys the notion of incorporation into, both here and in the words below εἰς τὸν θάνατον αὐτοῦ; comp. Gal. iii. 27 ὅσοι εἰς Χριστὸν ἐβαπτίσθητε, Χριστὸν ἐνεδύσασθε, 1 Cor. xii. 13 εἰς ἓν σῶμα, an idea expanded more fully in the expression εἰς τὸ ὄνομα (Matt. xxviii. 19, Acts xix. 5, comp. 1 Cor. i. 13, 15). Similarly in 1 Cor. x. 2 εἰς τὸν Μωυσῆν ἐβαπτίσαντο the reference is to incorporation into the Mosaic covenant. On the other hand in Mark i. 4 εἰς ἄφεσιν ἁμαρτιῶν the meaning of the preposition is different, and signifies the purpose and result of the baptism.

4. συνετάφημεν] As Prof. Jowett rightly observes, the Apostle introduces the phrase 'were buried' instead of 'died' in order to recall the image of baptism, a parallelism which disappears in our present practice of baptism by aspersion. See the idea again more clearly brought out in Col. ii. 12, Eph. v. 14, 1 Cor. x. 2. Perhaps Gal. iii. 27 Χριστὸν ἐνεδύσασθε may be an image taken from another part of the baptismal ceremony, but this is not so certain. In the same way, a lesson drawn elsewhere by the Apostle from the celebration of the Eucharist (1 Cor. x. 16, 17) is impaired by our common practice, which has destroyed the vividness of the image.

εἰς τὸν θάνατον] It is better to connect these words with συνετάφημεν than with διὰ τοῦ βαπτίσματος, as Jowett does.

ἐν καινότητι ζωῆς] 'in a new state, which is life': for before they had been dead (νεκροί). To render, as the A. V., 'in newness of life' would suggest that the old had been in some sense life also. Ignatius *Eph.* 19 Θεοῦ ἀνθρωπίνως φανερουμένου εἰς καινότητα ἀϊδίου ζωῆς is an evident allusion to this passage. Ζωῆς is the genitive of apposition ; comp. i. 23 ἐν ὁμοιώματι εἰκόνος, iv. 11 σημεῖον περιτομῆς, vii. 6 ἐν καινότητι πνεύματος and Winer § lix. p. 666. The idea uppermost in καινότης is 'strangeness,' and therefore a change (comp. 2 Cor. v. 17). See the note on Col. iii. 10, where καινός is distinguished from νέος.

5. τῷ ὁμοιώματι] is to be taken closely with σύμφυτοι 'connate with the likeness' ; for the connexion is at once suggested by the συν-, and is required by the ellipse. The rendering of the A. V. 'planted together in the likeness' is obscure and looks like a compromise. The meaning is, 'If the likeness of His death has been coincident with our birth, has been a part of us from our birth'—the birth here spoken of being of course the ἀναγέννησις, the new birth in Christ by baptism. Τῷ ὁμοιώματι τοῦ θανάτου αὐτοῦ is substituted for τῷ θανάτῳ αὐτοῦ, because it was not Christ's actual, physical death which was spoken of ; but only His death mystically considered, the likeness of His death.

ἀλλὰ καί] For ἀλλὰ in the apodosis after εἰ compare Mark xiv. 29, 2 Cor. iv. 16, xi. 6, xiii. 4, Col. ii. 5 ; in these passages however the apodosis is in opposition to the protasis, 'though' ; 'yet.' Here the force is *a fortiori*, 'if...then certainly': and ἀλλὰ is used to show that there is a distinction in favour of the proposition stated in the apodosis. For ἀλλὰ καὶ comp. Luke xvi. 21, xxiv. 22 'nay more.'

6. τὸ σῶμα τῆς ἁμαρτίας] Prof. Jowett rightly interprets this as 'a continuation of the figure of the old man who is identified with sin and has a body attributed to him.' Dr Vaughan's explanation is hardly

satisfactory, but he justly draws attention to the exact parallel, τὸ σῶμα τῆς σαρκὸς in Col. ii. 11, 12.

7. ὁ ἀποθανών] i.e. the dead in this mystical sense. Death is a release; it liberates from all claims: comp. vii. 1 ἐφ᾽ ὅσον χρόνον ζῇ and Ecclus. xviii. 22 μὴ μείνῃς ἕως θανάτου δικαιωθῆναι, where however the meaning is different.

δεδικαίωται] All claims against him are *ipso facto* cancelled: such is the force of the perfect. Comp. Acts xiii. 39 (where St Paul is the speaker), Ecclus. xxvi. 29 οὐ δικαιωθήσεται κάπηλος ἀπὸ ἁμαρτίας, quoted by Vaughan. This passage throws much light on St Paul's idea of δικαίωσις and δικαιοσύνη, and would repay a deeper study.

10. ὃ γὰρ ἀπέθανεν] '*for the death which He died*'; comp. Gal. ii. 20 ὃ δὲ νῦν ζῶ ἐν σαρκί.

τῇ ἁμαρτίᾳ] i.e. to the temptations and the sufferings inflicted on Him by sin. Christ died to a sinful world, died to a life in which He was every moment bearing the consequences of sin. The dative only so far differs in meaning from the dative τῇ ἁμαρτίᾳ of the next verse, in that He was sinless, we are sinful: but grammatically it is the same.

τῷ Θεῷ] '*unto God*,' and therefore eternally: comp. 2 Cor. xiii. 4.

12. ἐν τῷ θνητῷ ὑμῶν σώματι] Two interpretations are suggested of θνητῷ here. Some take it as though equivalent to νεκρῷ, τεθνηκότι, with reference to νεκροὺς τῇ ἁμαρτίᾳ above (ver. 11). But θνητὸς seems never to have this meaning, not even in Rom. viii. 11, 2 Cor. iv. 11; it always signifies 'subject to death,' never 'dead,' as such. We must therefore give θνητῷ its proper meaning of 'mortal,' and explain the force of the epithet thus: 'If ye are thus living an eternal life to God, why should ye show deference to your bodies which are but mortal, by humouring their passions? The mortal life is not worthy of consideration in comparison with the immortal.'

13. τὰ ὅπλα] '*arms*' (comp. 2 Cor. vi. 7), rather than 'instruments' (A. V.); see the next note.

τῇ ἁμαρτίᾳ] '*for sin*,' i.e. to wage warfare in its service. The rendering of the A. V. 'unto sin' is at least obscure. Sin is regarded as a sovereign (μὴ βασιλευέτω ver. 12), who demands the military service of subjects (εἰς τὸ ὑπακούειν ver. 12), levies their quota of arms (ὅπλα ἀδικίας ver. 13), and gives them their soldier's-pay of death (ὀψώνια ver. 23). For the metaphor comp. 2 Tim. ii. 4 τῷ στρατολογήσαντι.

ἐκ νεκρῶν ζῶντας] '*alive, after being dead*.' A common classical expression, e.g. Demosthenes *de Coron.* 131, p. 270 ἐλεύθερος ἐκ δούλου καὶ πλούσιος ἐκ πτωχοῦ γεγονώς. Dr Vaughan prefers to take the phrase in the usual sense 'from the dead'; but though frequently so found with ἀνάστασις, ἐγείρειν etc., it does not occur with ζῆν. It may be a question whether even Rom. xi. 15 εἰ μὴ ζωὴ ἐκ νεκρῶν ought not to be taken as above. Compare Luke xv. 32 ὁ ἀδελφός σου οὗτος νεκρὸς ἦν καὶ ἔζησεν, which Vaughan quotes on that passage. Here the order ἐκ νεκρῶν ζῶντας, where ἐκ νεκρῶν is emphatic and isolated, seems decisive in favour of the more idiomatic usage.

15. Again, as in vi. 1, the Apostle puts a question. The difference of form has been suggested by what has immediately preceded. The nature of the answer too is somewhat different. In ch. vi. 1 the objector asks, 'Shall we sin more that grace may be more?' St Paul replies, 'The thing is impossible, a contradiction in terms. Sin and grace, life and death, cannot coexist.' Thus the answer starts from the nature of the case. Here the objector asks, 'Are we to sin, because we are not under law, not bound by any definite precepts, but under a higher principle, grace?' The reply is, 'No; because, if you sin, you will become slaves to sin; you will bring on yourselves the penalties of sin.' The answer therefore arises from the effects, the consequences of this course of action.

16. οὐκ οἴδατε] 'Is not this self-evident? You cannot but obey the master to whom you have surrendered yourselves: you become his slaves.' The argument is the same as in Matt. vi. 24.

ἤτοι...ἤ] The only instance of ἤτοι in the New Testament. I should not say with Vaughan that ἤτοι expresses the greater probability of the alternative to which it is prefixed: but rather that it throws greater emphasis upon it. Jelf (Gr. 777. 5) properly says that τοι thus added has the effect of increasing the disjunctive force: comp. Winer § liii. p. 549.

ὑπακοῆς] Here used in a different sense of the true obedience, submission to the will of God. So elsewhere absolutely, v. 19, xvi. 19, 1 Pet. i. 2, 14.

17. ὅτι ἦτε...ὑπηκούσατε δέ] 'One sentence resolved grammatically into two,' is Winer's observation (§ lxvi. p. 785), who instances Matt. xi. 25, Luke xxiv. 18, John iii. 19, vii. 4.

εἰς ὃν κ.τ.λ.] This should be resolved into τύπῳ διδαχῆς εἰς ὃν παρεδόθητε rather than into εἰς τύπον διδαχῆς ὃν παρεδόθητε, which is open to two objections, (1) the harshness of the expression ὃν παρεδόθητε, (2) the improbable construction ὑπακούειν εἰς. For the attraction compare Acts xxi. 16, where ἄγοντες παρ' ᾧ ξενισθῶμεν Μνάσωνί τινι stands for ἄγοντες Μνάσωνά τινα παρ' ᾧ ξενισθῶμεν.

19. ἀνθρώπινον λέγω] The Apostle apologizes for the use of the word δουλεία in connexion with δικαιοσύνη. For the phrase see on Gal. iii. 15 κατὰ ἄνθρωπον λέγω. God's service is not δουλεία but ἐλευθερία (1 Cor. ix. 19, 2 Cor. iii. 17, Gal. v. 13, passages which show that the thought was very prominent in St Paul's mind at this time).

21. οὖν...τότε] The single 'then' of the A. V. does double duty here, as in John xi. 14; and is employed to represent 'then' temporal as well as 'then' argumentative.

τίνα οὖν καρπόν...τὸ γὰρ τέλος] St Paul never uses καρπός of the results of evil-doing, but always substitutes ἔργα: see Gal. v. 19, 22, Eph. v. 9, 11.

Here the γὰρ which follows shows that the expression is equivalent to 'Ye had no fruit.'

23. ὀψώνια] The word ὄψον 'condiment' is defined by a Scholiast on Homer *Iliad* xi. 630 as 'whatever is eaten with bread.' Thus Plutarch says (*Moral.* 99 D) that boys are taught τῇ δεξιᾷ λαμβάνειν τοῦ ὄψου, τῇ δὲ ἀριστερᾷ κρατεῖν τὸν ἄρτον. So Plato carefully distinguishes the two. After mentioning the ἄλφιτα and ἄλευρα, which are to be the staple of the diet in his ideal republic, he continues (*Respubl.* ii. p. 372 C) ἐπελαθόμην ὅτι καὶ ὄψον ἕξουσιν· ἅλας τε δῆλον ὅτι καὶ ἐλάας καὶ τυρὸν καὶ βολβοὺς καὶ λάχανα, specifying various kinds of ὄψον. The word however was used especially of 'fish,' as Symmachus states in Plutarch *Sympos.* iv. 4, p. 667 E πολλῶν ὄντων ὄψων ἐκνενίκηκεν ὁ ἰχθὺς μόνον ἢ μάλιστά γε ὄψον καλεῖσθαι διὰ τὸ πολὺ πάντων ἀρετῇ κρατεῖν. Hence the names φίλοψοι and ὀψοφάγοι (Ælian *V. H.* i. 28) were given to those who preferred this kind of dainty, and fish were called θαλάττης ὄψα, τὰ ἐκ θαλάττης ὄψα (Plutarch *l. c.*), θαλάττια ὄψα (Hippocrates, p. 606. 10), πόντια ὄψα (Euripides *fragm.* apud Athenæum xiv. p. 640 B) and simply ὄψον (Pollux vii. 7, where the word is interchanged with ἰχθύδιον). Diodorus (xi. 57) explains the fact of the assignment of the city Myus to Themistocles (Thuc. i. 138) as ὄψον, from the reason of its situation (ἔχουσαν θάλατταν εὔϊχθυν). So ὀψάριον is used for 'a fish' (John vi. 9; comp. Luke ix. 13, John xxi. 9, 10, 13), and the Latin 'obsonium' also (Juvenal *Sat.* iv. 64). From ὄψον is derived ὀψώνιον 'soldier's-pay,' which is the general, perhaps the universal, use of the word (see however ps.-Aristeas, p. iii. ed. Hody), and is the Greek equivalent of the Latin 'stipendia'; for the word 'obsonia' in Latin (see above) seems never to have acquired this meaning. The derivation of the word explains its use. The soldier's reward for his service was twofold; (1) a ration in kind, which was an allowance of corn (σιτομέτρημα) for making bread, and (2) a small payment in money (ὀψώνιον), by which he might purchase a relish (ὄψον) to be eaten with his bread. Compare Dionys. *A. R.* ix. 36. 5 τό τ' ὀψώνιον τῇ στρατιᾷ καὶ τὸ ἀντὶ τοῦ σίτου συγχωρηθὲν ὑπὸ τοῦ Μαλλίου κατενέγκαντες ἀργύριον (where the rations could not be supplied in kind). A Smyrnean inscription (Boeckh *C. I. G.* 3137) runs as follows, προνοῆσαι τὸν δῆμον ὅπως αὐτοῖς διδῶται ἐκ βασιλικοῦ τά τε μετρήματα καὶ τὰ ὀψώνια, which is explained by a passage in Polybius (vi. 39. 12) ὀψώνιον δ' οἱ μὲν πεζοὶ λαμβάνουσι τῆς ἡμέρας δύο ὀβολούς...σιτομετροῦνται δ' οἱ μὲν πεζοὶ πυρῶν Ἀττικοῦ μεδίμνου δύο μέρη μάλιστά πως. The word occurs in the LXX. (1 Macc. iii. 28, xiv. 32, 1 Esdras iv. 4, 56) always in its technical sense, and in Luke iii. 14, 1 Cor. ix. 7, 2 Cor. xi. 8. From it is derived the Latin 'obsonium'; from ὀψωνεῖν, 'obsono,' 'obsonor,' 'obsonator.' The word occurs in Ignatius' letter to Polycarp in a passage replete with military metaphors (§ 6) ἀρέσκετε ᾧ στρατεύεσθε, ἀφ' οὗ καὶ τὰ ὀψώνια κομίσεσθε. μήτις ὑμῶν δεσέρτωρ εὑρεθῇ· τὸ βάπτισμα ὑμῶν μενέτω ὡς ὅπλα, ἡ πίστις ὡς περικεφαλαία, ἡ ἀγάπη ὡς δόρυ, ἡ ὑπομονὴ ὡς πανοπλία· τὰ δεπόσιτα ὑμῶν τὰ ἔργα ὑμῶν ἵνα τὰ ἄκκεπτα ὑμῶν ἄξια κομίσησθε.

CHAPTER VII

xi. *Our freedom from law illustrated by the analogy of a contract* (vii. 1—6).

1. **ἢ ἀγνοεῖτε**] Connected with οὐ γάρ ἐστε ὑπὸ νόμον (vi. 14). St Paul's thoughts are recalled to this statement, which requires justification, by the expression τὸ χάρισμα just before.

γινώσκουσιν γὰρ νόμον] He is addressing Romans, to whom at all events the conception of law ought not to be unknown.

ὁ νόμος] Here not the Mosaic Law but rather the law generally, St Paul having especially in his mind the law which would be known to his hearers, i.e. the Roman law.

τοῦ ἀνθρώπου] '*the person.*' The phrase has nothing to do with ὁ ἀνήρ 'the husband' in the next verse. Ὁ ἄνθρωπος includes both sexes; and indeed the statement is not confined to the law of marriage. It is a general principle of the law that death cancels engagements.

2. The passage should be compared with 1 Cor. vii. 39, where νόμῳ has been inserted after δέδεται from the verse before us. 'The woman who is subject to a husband' (ὕπανδρος occurs in Polybius and later writers, as well as in the LXX.) 'is bound by law to her living husband' (the rendering of the A. V. 'to her husband as long as he liveth' is misleading); 'but if her husband be dead, she has been *ipso facto* set free from the law of her husband, that is, from the law which gave her husband authority over her and claims upon her.' Κατήργηται ἀπό is equivalent to κατήργηται καὶ ἐκχώρισται ἀπό : comp. Gal. v. 4 κατηργήθητε ἀπὸ Χριστοῦ and ver. 6 below; and for similar phrases, 2 Cor. xi. 3 φθαρῇ ἀπὸ τῆς ἁπλότητος, Col. ii. 20 ἀπεθάνετε ἀπὸ τῶν στοιχείων.

3. **χρηματίσει**] From the primary meaning of χρηματίζειν 'to do business, negociate' spring two secondary uses of the verb, (1) 'to act the part of,' 'to be called' (e.g. Acts xi. 26, Joseph. *B. J.* ii. 18. 7 Ἀντίοχον τὸν Ἐπιφανῆ χρηματίζοντα); (2) 'to give an answer,' 'to deliver an oracle,' and so in the passive 'to be advised' (Matt. ii. 12, 22).

ἐὰν γένηται ἀνδρὶ ἑτέρῳ] '*if she attach herself to another husband.*' The rendering of the A. V. 'man,' both here and later on in this verse, is unfortunate, because ἄνθρωπος is rendered 'man,' ἀνήρ 'husband,' in the context. For this sense of γένηται, γενομένην compare Hosea iii. 4 οὐδὲ μὴ γένῃ ἀνδρὶ ἑτέρῳ.

4. ὥστε] '*therefore*,' to apply this rule in your case.

καὶ ὑμεῖς] The instance produced in ver. 3 is an instance of a release from the authority of the marriage bond by death. So is this. Thus it is a case in point. Beyond this however the similitude cannot be pressed. There the wife was released by the husband's death. Here the wife (i.e. the body of believers) is released by her own death, released from the law, which was her spouse. In the natural marriage relations no strict analogy presented itself to this which was possible in the mystical marriage relations, i.e. that the wife should die, and yet live to marry another.

ὑμεῖς ἐθανατώθητε τῷ νόμῳ] In order that the previous instance might be an exact parallel, we should have ὁ νόμος ἐθανατώθη ὑμῖν (comp. Col. ii. 14, Eph. ii. 15, in which passages the death of the law is more or less connected with the death of the believer to the law, in the Cross of Christ). This however does not accord with St Paul's way of speaking here; for it does not include his idea of the believer dying in Christ, on which he lays so much stress here (vi. 2, 3, 4, 5, 6, 7, 8, 11) and elsewhere. He therefore prefers sacrificing the perfect exactness of the parallel (it was sufficiently exact, as an illustration of the statement ὁ νόμος κυριεύει... ζῇ) for the sake of retaining the image, which had so deep a moral and theological significance to him, and which occupies so prominent a place in the context. Other examples of images doubly applied by St Paul are given in the notes on 1 Thess. ii. 7, v. 4. The phrase καὶ ὑμεῖς implies a large number of Jews or proselytes among the Roman converts.

διὰ τοῦ σώματος τοῦ Χριστοῦ] Compare Col. i. 22, Eph. ii. 16. The idea is: 'Christ's death in His natural body on the Cross'; as in Col. l. c. ἐν τῷ σώματι τῆς σαρκὸς αὐτοῦ διὰ τοῦ θανάτου. The σῶμα here is not the Church of Christ, as the body; this must not be regarded even as an accessory idea (Jowett): for the reference is obviously to a definite act and a definite time, when they passed from the old state to the new, before the body of Christ in this sense could be said to exist.

γενέσθαι ἑτέρῳ] '*be wedded to another*.' The first indications of this image of the Church as the Spouse of Christ occur in 1 Cor. vi. 13 sq., Gal. iv. 26, but both cases represent ideas leading up to this image, rather than the image itself. For the image in all its fulness, see Eph. v. 22—33.

καρποφορήσωμεν] This seems hardly to be a continuation of the same metaphor, 'bear offspring.' Otherwise some more definite word would have been preferred. It is rather in a general sense: see the next verse.

5. ἦμεν ἐν τῇ σαρκί] i.e. under the law. For the law and the Gospel are distinguished as flesh and spirit: the one being a system of external precepts, the other a principle of inward growth. Compare Gal. iii. 3, v. 18, 19 etc., Col. ii. 18, Phil. iii. 3, 4, Heb. vii. 16 νόμον ἐντολῆς σαρκίνης.

τὰ παθήματα κ.τ.λ.] Observe that it is not αἱ ἁμαρτίαι αἱ διὰ τοῦ νόμου.

See the note on v. 20. Jowett gets into much confusion here and else-where, because he does not distinguish 'sin' and 'transgression.'

6. **νυνὶ δέ**] '*as things are,*' under this new dispensation.

κατηργήθημεν] See above, ver. 2.

ἀποθανόντες ἐν ᾧ] The reading of the Textus Receptus ἀποθανόντος has only the very slenderest support; otherwise the inversion of the metaphor would be quite after St Paul's manner: see on 1 Thess. ii. 7. The sentence means that we were liberated by our death (ἀποθανόντες) from the law in which we were held fast. This is the only satisfactory way of taking the passage, which should be punctuated after, not before, ἀποθανόντες, and it makes excellent sense. To explain it, as some do, by supplying τῷ νόμῳ after ἀποθανόντες is very harsh grammatically, because ἀποθανόντες does not suggest the missing dative, as e.g. in Acts xxi. 16 ἄγοντες suggests the missing accusative.

ἐν καινότητι πνεύματος] For the phrase see on vi. 4 above, and for the distinction between πνεῦμα and γράμμα comp. ii. 29.

xii. *The objection 'the law is sin' met* (vii. 7—24).

7. **ἀλλά**] The conjunction here does not qualify ('nevertheless,' 'but still it is true'); it opposes the previous proposition. 'So far from this, it revealed to me the true character, the heinousness, of sin,' as in ver. 13 ἵνα γένηται κ.τ.λ.

οὐκ ἔγνων] '*I did not recognize*'; not as the A. V. 'I had not known,' for (1) this would anticipate the οὐκ ᾔδειν which follows, and (2) an imperfect rather than an aorist would be expected, as e.g. ix. 3 ηὐχόμην. Comp. Winer § xli. p. 352. Ἤιδειν just below is a quasi-imperfect and satisfies this condition.

τήν τε γὰρ ἐπιθυμίαν] The reference is to the tenth commandment (Ex. xx. 17), a single precept being taken as a sufficient example: hence the τε. See above, iii. 2 πρῶτον μὲν ὅτι κ.τ.λ., where again a single example is specified, the rest being tacitly suggested. St Paul however has instinctively chosen the commandment which is the best typical instance for his purpose. The use of τε here is quite conclusive against the view that οὐκ ἐπιθυμήσεις is intended as a general and comprehensive, and not as a special, precept.

οὐκ ᾔδειν] i.e. 'I had not known what lust meant, its sinful nature: with the law it became at once a desire after the forbidden.' Οὐκ ἔγνων 'I did not recognize it,' though it was preexistent: οὐκ ᾔδειν 'I had no acquaintance with it'; it might, or it might not, preexist (here the supposition is that it does not preexist).

8. **νεκρά**] i.e. οὐ καρποφορεῖ. As the apparently lifeless stock of a tree, it gives no signs of activity. This of course is relative to the conscience of the man. Definite prohibition is necessary in order to

produce definite transgression, in whatever form this definite prohibition may be given.

9. ἐγώ] The pronoun represents either humanity at large (Gal. iv. 1 sq.), here personified (comp. 1 Cor. iv. 6); or the individual, so far as from the incapacity of infancy or from external circumstances he could be said to have passed through this earlier stage, when he did not know the law. To St Paul himself the circumstances would apply less than to any man living.

ἔζων] The life here spoken of is not spiritual life, for the awakening of the conscience, the conviction of sin, is a condition of this; but the freedom, the carelessness, which does not paralyse the will, nor trouble the soul. It is the Greek temper, or the temper of a child.

11. ἐξηπάτησέν με] A reference to the temptation of Adam and Eve, when the first divine precept appears. The nature of the deception practised may be ascertained from the narrative in Genesis: where it was at once negative 'Ye shall not surely die,' and positive 'Your eyes shall be opened and ye shall be as gods.' So throughout the ages sin makes a double promise to her victims; first, that no evil consequences will ensue; secondly, that their view of life will be enlarged and that on this increased knowledge will follow increased happiness. The same word ἐξαπατᾶν is used by St Paul in two other passages where he speaks of the temptation of our first parents (2 Cor. xi. 3, 1 Tim. ii. 14).

12. ὁ μὲν νόμος] should have been followed by ἡ δὲ ἁμαρτία; but the digression which ensues upon the introduction of the word ἀγαθή wrecks the sentence. For the interrupted μέν compare Acts i. 1, xxvi. 4, 2 Cor. xii. 12, and Winer § lxiii. p. 720.

ἁγία καὶ δικαία καὶ ἀγαθή] Ἁγία 'holy,' that is to say, having God's sanction, coming from God; δικαία 'righteous,' that it is in itself; ἀγαθή 'beneficent,' this it is intended to be in its effects. On the last two words see the note on v. 7, and comp. 1 Thess. iii. 6 (with the note).

14. σάρκινος] On this word and its distinction from σαρκικός see the note on 1 Cor. iii. 1. Here σαρκικός might stand, but σάρκινος is stronger and more emphatic.

πεπραμένος] 'sold,' and therefore its bond-slave (comp. vi. 16). 'Sin is my task-master, compelling me to do what I would not do of myself.'

15. οὐ γινώσκω] i.e. 'I do it in blind obedience. Sin is so imperious a task-master that he does not allow me time to think what I am doing.' This inference is explained in the next verse, 'This must be so; otherwise I should not be doing what I hate, and omitting to do what I desire.'

16. εἰ δὲ κ.τ.λ.] i.e. 'if at the very time that I do it, my better nature protests against it.'

καλός] Not ἀγαθός (ver. 12), for this would not be in place here.

17. νυνὶ δέ] 'this being so.' 'As we have arrived at this result that by my protest against my own actions I bear testimony to the goodness of the law, then it follows from this' etc. Both νυνὶ δέ and οὐκέτι are

logical rather than temporal: for νῦν in this sense comp. 1 Cor. v. 11, vii. 14, xii. 18, 20; for οὐκέτι Rom. xi. 6, Gal. iii. 18.

ἡ ἐνοικοῦσα ἐν ἐμοί] Xenophon *Cyr.* vi. 1. 41 δύο γάρ, ἔφη, ὦ Κῦρε, σαφῶς ἔχω ψυχάς...οὐ γὰρ δὴ μία γε οὖσα ἅμα ἀγαθή τέ ἐστι καὶ κακή, οὐδ᾽ ἅμα καλῶν τε καὶ αἰσχρῶν ἔργων ἐρᾷ καὶ ταὐτὰ ἅμα βούλεταί τε καὶ οὐ βούλεται, Plato *Phædrus* 14, p. 237 D ἡμῶν ἐν ἑκάστῳ δύο τινέ ἐστον ἰδέα ἄρχοντε καὶ ἄγοντε...ἡ μὲν ἔμφυτος οὖσα ἐπιθυμία ἡδονῶν, ἄλλη δὲ ἐπίκτητος δόξα, ἐφιεμένη τοῦ ἀρίστου κ.τ.λ., *Respubl.* iv. 12, p. 436, iv. 14, p. 439.

18. οἶδα γάρ] 'Sin, I say, is the indweller: for I am conscious by experience that it is not good which thus dwells in me.'

ἐν ἐμοί] '*in me*'; 'When I say *me*, I mean my flesh. For my better self is at war with this indweller.'

τὸ γὰρ θέλειν] The γάρ explains οἶδα above. Τὸ καλόν is to be supplied after θέλειν, a fact not clearly brought out in the A. V.

παράκειται] '*is present, is available*': 'I can summon the will to my aid when I want, but not the performance.'

οὔ] sc. παράκειται; the received text substitutes οὐχ εὑρίσκω, doubtless a grammatical gloss, and lacking in force.

21. τὸν νόμον] here has nothing to do with the Mosaic Law (as Fritzsche II. p. 57 and others take it). It is 'the law of my being.' 'Experience teaches me that this is habitually the case; that the phenomena recur.'

ἐμοί, ἐμοί] i.e. 'my better self, my true personality,' repeated for the sake of emphasis.

22. συνήδομαι γάρ] '*for while I rejoice with*' etc.; in classical Greek the sentence would be introduced with μέν. For συνήδομαι τῷ νόμῳ we may compare such expressions as 1 Cor. xiii. 6 συγχαίρει τῇ ἀληθείᾳ, Phil. i. 27 συναθλοῦντες τῇ πίστει τοῦ εὐαγγελίου, 2 Tim. i. 8 συγκακοπάθησον τῷ εὐαγγελίῳ, 3 Joh. 8 συνεργοὶ τῇ ἀληθείᾳ, where, as here, the preposition governs the case.

νόμῳ] The different senses in which νόμος is used in this passage must be carefully distinguished. First, there is the comprehensive law of my being, which includes the two antagonistic principles (ver. 21 εὑρίσκω τὸν νόμον). Then these two principles are considered and described from an objective and a subjective standpoint. The good principle is called objectively 'the law of God' (ver. 22 τῷ νόμῳ τοῦ Θεοῦ), subjectively 'the law of my mind, of my rational nature' (ver. 23 τῷ νόμῳ τοῦ νοός μου); the wrong principle is termed objectively 'the law of sin' (ver. 23 τῷ νόμῳ τῆς ἁμαρτίας), subjectively 'the law in my limbs' (ver. 23 τῷ ὄντι ἐν τοῖς μέλεσίν μου). 'It is the law of my being that these two opposing laws should be in constant conflict in me.' Ὁ νόμος τοῦ Θεοῦ is used here with a special reference to the Mosaic Law (as in vv. 12, 14, 16), but it is more comprehensive than, and not confined to, this idea.

κατὰ τὸν ἔσω ἄνθρωπον] i.e. 'the hidden man, my very self, my true personality'; comp. 2 Cor. iv. 16, Eph. iii. 16. It denotes that part of

me which holds communication with the divine, which is immortal and
free from the accidents of external circumstances.

23. ἐν τῷ νόμῳ τῆς ἁμαρτίας] This law is the same with ἕτερον νόμον
ἐν τοῖς μέλεσίν μου, so that ἐν ἑαυτῷ might have stood. But the metaphor
is diversely applied. The νόμος is first the victor who takes the captives
(αἰχμαλωτίζοντα), and secondly, the chain which binds them (this is the
force of ἐν, comp. Eph. vi. 20, Philem. 10). For such variations of
metaphor in St Paul see on 1 Thess. ii. 7; and for a similar repetition of
the substantive comp. Acts iii. 16 καὶ τῇ πίστει τοῦ ὀνόματος αὐτοῦ...
ἐστερέωσεν τὸ ὄνομα αὐτοῦ.

24. ἐκ τοῦ σώματος τοῦ θανάτου τούτου] The sense would be simple if
τούτου could be taken with σώματος, but the order of words is against this
connexion. Combining therefore τούτου with θανάτου, we must explain
σῶμα by the preceding phrases ἐν τῇ σαρκὶ (ver. 18), ἐν τοῖς μέλεσίν μου
(ver. 23), of the actual body, regarded as the seat of evil passions, and
thus as an antagonistic power to the law of God. Τοῦ θανάτου τούτου may
mean either 'of this death' which St Paul has described (e.g. ver. 13), or
'of this death everywhere present'; the former interpretation being on
the whole the more probable. The whole phrase then will signify, 'the
body in which this death finds a lodgment.' Though σῶμα is to be
taken literally, θάνατος on the other hand is figurative, implying not
physical, but moral death.

25. χάρις δὲ τῷ Θεῷ κ.τ.λ.] This thanksgiving comes out of place.
But St Paul cannot endure to leave the difficulty unsolved; he cannot
consent to abandon his imaginary self to the depths of this despair.
Thus he gives the solution parenthetically, though at the cost of
interrupting his argument.

ἄρα οὖν] 'to sum up then.'

αὐτὸς ἐγώ] 'I of myself,' i.e. 'I by myself, I left alone, I without Christ.'
The converse appears in Gal. ii. 20 ζῶ δὲ οὐκέτι ἐγώ ζῇ δὲ ἐν ἐμοὶ Χριστός.
Otherwise we must suppose that αὐτὸς ἐγώ refers only to the first clause,
that in fact we have a confusion of two forms, αὐτὸς ἐγὼ δουλεύω νόμῳ
Θεοῦ ἡ δὲ σάρξ κ.τ.λ., and (omitting αὐτὸς ἐγώ) τῷ μὲν νοΐ δουλεύω νόμῳ
Θεοῦ τῇ δὲ σαρκὶ κ.τ.λ.—in other words that τῷ μὲν νοΐ is an epexegesis of
αὐτὸς ἐγώ and that the insertion of the μὲν has changed the form of the
sentence. It is however better to take αὐτὸς here in the sense of 'alone';
and though this interpretation is hardly borne out by the usage of αὐτὸς
ἐγώ in St Paul (e.g. ix. 3, xv. 14, 2 Cor. x. 1, xii. 13), we must remember
that elsewhere the Apostle is speaking of himself personally, not as the
typical man, and therefore the interpretation would not be applicable.

THE EPISTLES OF ST PAUL

III
THE FIRST ROMAN CAPTIVITY

4
EPISTLE TO THE EPHESIANS

CHAPTER I

1. **Παῦλος**] The Apostle abstains from associating any other name with his own, because he is writing a circular letter, from which all personal matters are excluded. No argument therefore can be drawn against the synchronism of the three Epistles from the fact that Timothy is mentioned in the opening of the Epistles to the Colossians and to Philemon, but not here. The only other letter addressed to any church in which St Paul's name stands thus alone is the Epistle to the Romans. For the general parallel between the Epistles to the Romans and Ephesians with respect to motive and destination, see *Biblical Essays*, pp. 388, 395 sq. For the chronological order of the Epistles of the Captivity see *Philippians*, p. 30 sq. and on the circular character of the Ephesian letter, *Biblical Essays*, p. 377 sq.

Χριστοῦ Ἰησοῦ] In all those Epistles which St Paul commences in this way (Rom., 1 Cor., 2 Cor., Phil., Col., 1 Tim., 2 Tim., Tit.), the authorities vary between Χριστοῦ Ἰησοῦ and Ἰησοῦ Χριστοῦ. On the whole it seems probable that the Apostle was uniform in his mode of designation, 'an Apostle' or 'a servant of Christ Jesus.' The variations would then be due to the fact that the other order is much more usual elsewhere, though not in this particular connexion. The amount of authority on either side differs very considerably in the different passages.

διὰ θελήματος κ.τ.λ.] i.e. 'by God's grace, not by individual merit.' The other antithesis which the expression might suggest, 'by God's appointment, not by self-assumed title,' or 'by human authority,' is inappropriate here, as there is no polemical bearing in the context. See the note on Col. i. 1.

τοῖς ἁγίοις] '*to the saints*,' i.e. to the consecrated people of God, the holy race under the new dispensation: see the note on Phil. i. 1. On this form of address, as a chronological mark in St Paul's Epistles, see the note on Col. i. 2.

ἐν Ἐφέσῳ] That copy of the circular letter which was addressed to the Ephesians is here given. See *Biblical Essays*, p. 377 sq.

πιστοῖς] '*faithful*,' i.e. trustworthy, stedfast. The word has here its passive force. The active sense 'believing' would add nothing to the foregoing ἁγίοις. The words πιστοῖς κ.τ.λ. do not limit the persons addressed, but express the charitable assumption that all those into whose hands the letter will fall are true to their allegiance. See the notes on Col. i. 2.

ἐν Χριστῷ] For the expression 'stedfast (πιστὸς) in Christ,' 'in the Lord,' comp. 1 Cor. iv. 17, and see the note on Col. i. 2.

2. χάρις ὑμῖν κ.τ.λ.] See the note on 1 Thess. i. 1.

3. εὐλογητὸς κ.τ.λ.] The Apostle begins as usual with a thanksgiving, which however in this instance takes a more general form, corresponding to the character and destination of the letter, and expands gradually into its main theme. In expression too it differs from St Paul's ordinary type. For the more usual εὐχαριστῶ, εὐχαριστοῦμεν, κ.τ.λ., he substitutes εὐλογητὸς...Ἰησοῦ Χριστοῦ, which form he employs elsewhere only in 2 Corinthians (i. 3). It is copied by St Peter (1 Pet. i. 3), this being the first of several coincidences which St Peter's First Epistle presents to this Epistle of St Paul.

The opening salutation in the letter of Ignatius to the Ephesians shows the influence of St Paul's letter, in the following expressions: τῇ εὐλογημένῃ, πληρώματι, τῇ προωρισμένῃ πρὸ αἰώνων, εἰς δόξαν, ἐκλελεγμένην ἐν θελήματι τοῦ πατρός, ἐν ἀμώμῳ χαρᾷ, and lower down (§ 1) εὐλογητὸς ὁ χαρισάμενος ὑμῖν.

εὐλογητὸς κ.τ.λ.] 'Blessed is the God.' Throughout the New Testament εὐλογητὸς is said only of God, while εὐλογημένος is used of men; e.g. Luke i. 42 εὐλογημένη σὺ ἐν γυναιξίν, but ver. 68 εὐλογητὸς Κύριος ὁ Θεός. Hence in Mark xiv. 61 ὁ εὐλογητὸς is used absolutely as a synonym for 'God' in accordance with Jewish usage, which adopted the formula 'the Holy One, Blessed is He,' to avoid pronouncing the Sacred Name (see Schöttgen on Rom. ix. 5). This limitation of εὐλογητὸς to God is commonly, though not universally, observed in the LXX. also, where for every ten examples in which it is applied to God, it is used once only of men. The exceptions are Gen. xii. 2 (v. l.), Deut. vii. 14, Ruth ii. 20, 1 Sam. xv. 13, xxv. 33. The same distinction appears also in the expressions of Ignatius quoted above, εὐλογημένη, εὐλογητός. In Mart. Polyc. 14 εὐλογητὸς is said of Our Lord. This distinction of usage arises from the distinction of meaning in the two words: for, while εὐλογημένος points to an isolated act or acts, εὐλογητὸς describes the intrinsic character. Comp. Philo de Migr. Abr. 19 (I. p. 453), who, commenting on Gen. xii. 2 (where he reads εὐλογητός, but where A has εὐλογημένος), writes εὐλογητός, οὐ μόνον εὐλογημένος· τὸ μὲν γὰρ ταῖς τῶν πολλῶν δόξαις τε καὶ φήμαις παραριθμεῖται, τὸ δὲ τῷ πρὸς ἀλήθειαν εὐλογητῷ· ὥσπερ γὰρ τὸ ἐπαινετὸν εἶναι τοῦ ἐπαινεῖσθαι διαφέρει κατὰ τὸ κρεῖττον, τὸ μὲν γὰρ τῷ πεφυκέναι τὸ δὲ τῷ νομίζεσθαι λέγεται μόνον, φύσις δὲ ἡ ἀψευδὴς δοκήσεως ὀχυρώτερον, οὕτως καὶ τὸ εὐλογεῖσθαι πρὸς ἀνθρώπων, ὅπερ ἦν, εἰς εὐλογίαν ἄγεσθαι διδασκόμενον τῷ πεφυκέναι εὐλογίας ἄξιον, καὶ ἂν πάντες ἡσυχάζωσι, κρεῖττον, ὅπερ εὐλογητὸν ἐν τοῖς χρησμοῖς ᾄδεται, where the text is apparently corrupt and at all events τὸ εὐλογεῖσθαι should be changed into τοῦ εὐλογεῖσθαι. Hence, where we have εὐλογητός, as here, the sentence should probably be taken as affirmative, not imperative: e.g. contrast Ps. cxviii (cxix). 12 εὐλογητὸς εἶ, Κύριε, with 2 Chron. ix. 8 ἔστω Κύριος ὁ Θεός σου εὐλογημένος and Job i. 21, Ps. cxiii (cxii). 2 εἴη τὸ ὄνομα Κυρίου εὐλογημένον. Winer (*Gramm.* § lxiv. p. 733) quotes such passages as these in favour of supplying εἴη or ἔστω, rather than ἐστὶν here; but for the reason stated they tell against him. It expresses a thanksgiving for an actual fact, not a prayer for a contingent result. In other words God is blessed, as being the absolute and proper object of blessing: Theod. Mops. εὐλογητὸς ἀντὶ τοῦ ἐπαινεῖσθαι καὶ θαυμάζεσθαι ἄξιος (Cramer, *Cat.* p. 104).

ὁ Θεὸς κ.τ.λ.] '*the God and Father of our Lord*' etc.: comp. Rom. xv. 6, 2 Cor. i. 3, xi. 31. From the time of the fathers it has been questioned whether τοῦ Κυρίου is dependent on Θεὸς as well as on πατήρ. The question is entertained by Chrysostom, Jerome, Theodore of Mopsuestia (Cram. *Cat.* p. 104), and others. It is most natural to regard the two substantives as linked together by the vinculum of the common article; and in this passage we are confirmed in preferring this construction by the fact that the first predication is made separately lower down : ver. 17 ὁ Θεὸς τοῦ Κυρίου ἡμῶν κ.τ.λ. The whole phrase will then correspond to another expression, which occurs several times in St Paul, ὁ Θεὸς καὶ πατὴρ ἡμῶν, Gal. i. 4, 1 Thess. i. 3, iii. 11, 13. We are thus reminded of our Lord's words in John xx. 17 'I ascend unto my Father and your Father, and to my God and your God.' On the sense in which the Father can be said to be the God of our Lord Jesus Christ, see below, on ver. 17.

ὁ εὐλογήσας κ.τ.λ.] '*who blessed us*,' i.e. when He called us to Himself in Christ. The point of time contemplated in the tense here is not the conception of the purpose in the Eternal Mind, but the actual fulfilment of that purpose in the call of the believers. This is the force of the following καθώς, '*As* He selected us in His eternal counsels, *so*, when the time came, He called us to the blessings of the Gospel': comp. Rom. viii. 30 οὓς δὲ προώρισεν, τούτους καὶ ἐκάλεσεν. The active εὐλογήσας corresponds to the passive εὐλογητός. It is a case of reciprocation. The dispenser of blessings has a right to receive blessings. So we have conversely, Is. lxv. 16 εὐλογηθήσεται ἐπὶ τῆς γῆς, εὐλογήσουσι γὰρ τὸν Θεὸν ἀληθινόν. There is however this difference in the two cases, that whereas our blessings are confined to words, His extend to deeds. It is not that εὐλογεῖν itself has two distinct meanings; but that with God every word is a *fiat*. Hence, when used of God, or of one who is armed with the authority of God, εὐλογεῖν is not merely 'to speak well of' but 'to do well to.'

ἐν πάσῃ κ.τ.λ.] For the preposition see *Test. xii. Patr.*, Joseph. 18 εὐλογήσει ἐν ἀγαθοῖς εἰς αἰῶνας. Compare such expressions as μετρεῖν ἐν μέτρῳ, ἁλίζειν ἐν ἅλατι, and see Winer, § xlviii. p. 485.

πνευματικῇ] The character of the blessing corresponds to the sphere of the recipient. He is a citizen of heaven, and therefore his privileges are spiritual. The carnal promises of the Old Covenant are exchanged for the spiritual of the New. There is no promise here of material blessings. The Christian has no right to expect such; for this is no part of God's covenant with him.

ἐν τοῖς ἐπουρανίοις] '*in the heavenly places.*' The same expression, τὰ ἐπουράνια, occurs in four other places in this Epistle (i. 20, ii. 6, iii. 10, vi. 12) in this sense, but not elsewhere in the New Testament with quite the same meaning (e.g. John iii. 12, Heb. ix. 23). The words would naturally be connected with εὐλογήσας; and this obvious connexion is doubtless correct. The believer, in the language of this Epistle, has been already seated in heaven with Christ (ii. 6). He is an alien upon earth, but a citizen of God's kingdom (ii. 19). There is his πολίτευμα (Phil. iii. 20). There consequently he enjoys his privileges and receives his blessings. The heaven, of which the Apostle here speaks, is not some *remote locality*, some *future abode*. It is the heaven which lies within and about the true Christian. See especially the notes on Col. i. 13, iii. 1 sq. The promise under the Old Covenant was prosperity, increase, blessing, ἐπὶ τῆς γῆς (e.g. Is. lxv. 16), but under the New it is ἐν τοῖς ἐπουρανίοις.

ἐν Χριστῷ] i.e. 'by virtue of our incorporation in, our union with, Christ.' As God seated us in heaven 'in Christ' (ii. 6), so also He bestowed His blessings upon us there in Him. In the threefold repetition of the same preposition here, we may say roughly that at the first occurrence it is instrumental (ἐν πάσῃ εὐλογίᾳ), at the second local (ἐν τοῖς ἐπουρανίοις), at the third mystical (ἐν Χριστῷ). We are united to God *in* Christ; so united we dwell *in* heavenly places; so dwelling we are blessed *in* all spiritual blessings.

4. καθώς] '*according as.*' The bestowal of blessings was the fulfilment, the realization, of the election in the eternal counsels of God. On this word see the note on Gal. iii. 6.

ἐξελέξατο] '*chose us out for Himself.*' The word involves three ideas: (1) the telling over (λέγειν); (2) the rejection of some and the acceptance of others (ἐκ); (3) the taking to Himself (middle voice). The ἐκλογή here is not election to final salvation, but election to the sonship in Christ and the privileges of the Gospel; see the note on the use of the words in St Paul on Col. iii. 12.

ἐν αὐτῷ] i.e. ἐν Χριστῷ. In God's eternal purpose the believers are contemplated as existing in Christ, as the Head, the Summary, of the race. The ἐκλογή has no separate existence, independently of the ἐκλεκτός (Luke ix. 35, xxiii. 35). The election of Christ involves implicitly the election of the Church.

πρὸ καταβολῆς κ.τ.λ.] i.e. 'from all eternity.' Comp. John xvii. 24, 1 Pet. i. 20. So elsewhere, ἀπὸ καταβολῆς κόσμου (e.g. Heb. iv. 3, ix. 26). Neither phrase occurs in any other passage of St Paul.

ἀγίους κ.τ.λ.] The same two adjectives are combined, v. 27, Col. i. 22. They involve a sacrificial metaphor. The first word ἀγίους denotes the *consecration* of the victim; the second ἀμώμους its *fitness* for this consecration. The meaning of the latter in the Hellenistic dialect is slightly changed from its classical sense. It signifies rather 'without *blemish*' than 'without *blame*.' This more definite sense it owes to the fact that μῶμος is adopted in the LXX. as the rendering of the similarly sounding Hebrew word מום 'a blemish,' just as σκηνή becomes the recognized equivalent of Shechinah (שכינה). Hence ἄμωμος is most commonly used in the LXX. (e.g. Exod. xxix. 1, Lev. i. 3, 10, iii. 1, 6, 9, etc.) to denote victims which are without fault or blemish, as required by the law. So too, Heb. ix. 14 ἑαυτὸν προσήνεγκεν ἄμωμον τῷ Θεῷ, 1 Pet. i. 19 τιμίῳ αἵματι ὡς ἀμνοῦ ἀμώμου καὶ ἀσπίλου Χριστοῦ: comp. Philo *de Profug.* 3 (I. p. 548) τέλεια καὶ ἄμωμα ἱερεῖα αἱ ἀρεταί, *de Cherub.* 25 (I. p. 154) ἄμωμον καὶ κάλλιστον ἱερεῖον οἴσει τῷ Θεῷ, *Quis rer. div. her.* 23 (I. p. 489) ἀσινῆ τε καὶ ἄμωμα τέλειά τ’ αὖ καὶ ὁλόκληρα, etc.; *Test. xii. Patr.* Jos. 19 ἐξ αὐτῆς προῆλθεν ἀμνὸς ἄμωμος.

κατενώπιον αὐτοῦ] '*in the sight of Him*,' i.e. 'of God'; see the note on Col. i. 22. God Himself is thus regarded as the great μωμοσκόπος, who inspects the victims and takes cognizance of the blemishes; comp. Philo *de Agric.* 29 (I. p. 320) τίνας δεῖ καὶ ὅσους ἐπ’ αὐτὸ τοῦτο χειροτονεῖν τὸ ἔργον, οὓς ἔνιοι μωμοσκόπους ὀνομάζουσιν, ἵνα ἄμωμα καὶ ἀσινῆ προσάγηται τῷ βωμῷ τὰ ἱερεῖα, Polyc. *Phil.* 4 γινωσκούσας ὅτι εἰσὶν θυσιαστήριον Θεοῦ, καὶ ὅτι πάντα μωμοσκοπεῖται καὶ λέληθεν αὐτὸν οὐδὲν κ.τ.λ. See also the note on Clem. Rom. 41 μωμοσκοπηθέν.

ἐν ἀγάπῃ] to be taken with the preceding ἀγίους καὶ ἀμώμους: comp. Clem. Rom. 50 ἵνα ἐν ἀγάπῃ εὑρεθῶμεν δίχα προσκλίσεως ἀνθρωπίνης ἄμωμοι. So too Jude 24 ἀμώμους ἐν ἀγαλλιάσει, 2 Pet. iii. 14 ἀμώμητοι...ἐν εἰρήνῃ. The words ἐν ἀγάπῃ stand after the clause to which they belong, as below, iv. 2, 15, 16, v. 2 (perhaps also iii. 18), Col. ii. 2, 1 Thess. v. 13 (comp. 1 Tim. iv. 12, 2 Tim. i. 13). The general usage of St Paul seems therefore to be almost decisive as regards the connexion. Holding this position, love is emphasized as the fulfilment of the law, the totality of Christian duty. Otherwise the words ἐν ἀγάπῃ have been connected either with (1) ἐξελέξατο, which is too far distant, or (2) with προορίσας, in which case the emphasis is hardly explicable. In the two latter connexions the ἀγάπη would be God's love as shown in His predestination or election. The different connexions are discussed by the early patristic commentators.

5. προορίσας] Giving the reason of ἐξελέξατο, '*seeing that He had foreordained us*'; comp. Rom. viii. 29 οὓς προέγνω, καὶ προώρισεν συμμόρφους τῆς εἰκόνος τοῦ υἱοῦ αὐτοῦ, 30 οὓς δὲ προώρισεν, τούτους καὶ ἐκάλεσεν. Here προορίσας is prior to ἐξελέξατο; but prior only in conception, for in the eternal counsels of God, to which both words alike refer, there is no before or after. The word προορίζειν 'to predetermine,' wherever it

occurs in the New Testament, refers to the eternal counsels of God; comp. ver. 11, Acts iv. 28, Rom. viii. 29, 30, 1 Cor. ii. 7; see also Ignat. *Ephes.* inscr. It is not found in the LXX., nor apparently in any writer before St Paul. In Demosth. p. 877 it is a false reading. The substantive προορισμὸς however appears in a work wrongly ascribed to Hippocrates, *Op.* I. p. 79 (ed. Kühn).

υἱοθεσίαν] '*adoption,*' not 'sonship,' which would be υἱότητα. Christ alone, the μονογενής, *is* Son by nature; we *become* sons by adoption and grace. Thus υἱοθεσία never loses its proper meaning: see the note on Gal. iv. 5. The full adoption however can only be then (at the end of the ages) when the bondage of corruption, the bondage of the flesh, is ended and we are called to the liberty of sons. In this sense we look forward to it still, Rom. viii. 23 υἱοθεσίαν ἀπεκδεχόμενοι τὴν ἀπολύτρωσιν τοῦ σώματος ἡμῶν.

διὰ Ἰησοῦ Χριστοῦ] We become sons through incorporation into the Sonship of Christ; see Gal. iii. 26, iv. 6, 7, and especially Heb. ii. 10 sq.

εἰς αὐτὸν] to be connected with υἱοθεσίαν, '*adoption unto Him,*' i.e. to God the Father, '*as His sons.*' As διὰ describes the channel, so εἰς expresses the goal; comp. 1 Cor. viii. 6 εἰς Θεὸς ὁ πατήρ...καὶ ἡμεῖς εἰς αὐτόν· καὶ εἰς Κύριος Ἰησοῦς Χριστός...καὶ ἡμεῖς δι' αὐτοῦ. So John xiv. 6 'No man cometh to the Father but through Me.' For the personal pronoun αὐτόν, used where we should expect the reflexive ἑαυτόν, when referring to the principal subject of the clause, see the note on Col. i. 20. The contracted form of the reflexive pronoun αὑτόν, which some editors would introduce here, has no place in the Greek Testament.

κατὰ τὴν εὐδοκίαν] '*in accordance with the purpose.*' For the various meanings of εὐδοκία see the note on Phil. i. 15. Here it has the sense of 'purpose' rather than of 'benevolence,' so that the whole phrase corresponds to κατὰ τὴν βουλὴν τοῦ θελήματος αὐτοῦ ver. 11. The word εὐδοκία, of which the central idea is 'satisfaction,' will only then mean 'benevolence' when the context points to some person *towards whom* the satisfaction is felt (comp. Matt. iii. 17 ἐν ᾧ εὐδόκησα). Otherwise the satisfaction is felt in the action itself, so that the word is used absolutely, and signifies 'good-pleasure,' in the sense of 'desire,' 'purpose,' 'design.'

6. **εἰς**] The end of redemption, as of all creation and all history, is the praise and glory of God. This same phrase εἰς ἔπαινον (τῆς) δόξης is twice again repeated in the context, vv. 12, 14, as if the Apostle could not too strongly reiterate this truth. As 'thanksgiving' is the crowning duty and privilege of man (see the notes on Col. i. 12, ii. 7, iii. 15, etc.), so 'praise' is the ultimate right of God.

δόξης] i.e. 'the magnificent display,' 'the glorious manifestation.' For this sense of δόξα see the notes on Col. i. 11, 27.

τῆς χάριτος αὐτοῦ] '*His grace,*' i.e. 'His free gift,' 'His unearned and unmerited bounty.' Herein lies the magnificence, the glory, of God's work of redemption, that it has not the character of a contract, but of a largess. The word points to the central conception of St Paul's teaching on redemption; see the note on Col. i. 6. It occupies a very prominent place in this Epistle. The Apostle is not satisfied with once using the expression here, but he repeats it again in the next verse with greater emphasis, 'the *wealth* of His grace.' Even this strong phrase is inadequate to express his whole mind, and, when he recurs to the subject, he employs language stronger still, ii. 7 'the *surpassing* wealth of His grace.' Twice over in the same context he declares parenthetically to his readers that 'by grace they are saved,' ii. 5, 8; three times in the same context, when he is speaking of his own work and mission, he reminds himself that it was an act of God's 'grace bestowed upon him,' iii. 2, 7, 8.

ἧs ἐχαρίτωσεν κ.τ.λ.] '*which He graciously bestowed upon us*,' where ἧs stands by attraction for ἥν, the cognate accusative; comp. iv. 1 τῆs κλήσεωs ἧs ἐκλήθητε, 2 Cor. i. 4 διὰ τῆs παρακλήσεωs ἧs παρακαλούμεθα αὐτοί, where the constructions are precisely similar, and see Winer, § xxiv. p. 203. The various reading ἐν ᾗ has inferior support, and is obviously a scribe's correction of ἧs for the sake of greater clearness.

The word χαριτοῦν signifies 'to bestow grace upon,' 'to endow with grace'; and, as the prominent idea in χάρις may be either (1) the objective bestowal, 'the free gift,' 'the gracious favour,' or (2) the subjective endowment and appropriation, 'gracefulness,' 'well-favoured-ness,' 'attractiveness,' so the verb may have two corresponding meanings. Chrysostom takes the latter sense, interpreting it ἐπεράστους ἐποίησεν, ἐπιχάριτας ἐποίησεν, and he is followed by others. But this meaning would draw us off from the leading idea of the passage, which is the unmerited bounty of God. It is better therefore to adopt the former sense, in which case χαριτοῦν χάριν will be a stronger expression for χαρίζεσθαι χάριν (which occurs e.g. Eurip. and Lycurg. *c. Leocr.* § 100, Isocr. *c. Demon.* § 31), the greater strength being due to the termination which, as in χρυσοῦν, etc., denotes 'to overlay, to cover, with favour.' The word is used elsewhere in both senses: (1) 'to bestow favour on,' 'to be gracious to,' as here; *Test. xii. Patr.*, Jos. 1 ἐν φυλακῇ ἤμην καὶ ὁ σωτὴρ ἐχαρίτωσέ με, and so probably Luke i. 28 χαῖρε, κεχαριτωμένη: (2) 'to endow with graces,' 'to render attractive,' Ps. xvii. 26 (Symm.) μετὰ τοῦ κεχαριτωμένου χαριτωθήσῃ, Ecclus. xviii. 17 (LXX.) ἀνδρὶ κεχαριτωμένῳ, Clem. Alex. *Pæd.* iii. 11 (p. 302) ἀπόστρεψον τὸν ὀφθαλμὸν ἀπὸ γυναικὸς κεχαριτωμένης (a loose quotation of Ecclus. ix. 8, where the word is εὐμόρφου in the text). This second sense naturally prevails in the passive voice, where the bestower of the grace is lost sight of.

ἐν τῷ ἠγαπημένῳ] God, when He gave us His 'Beloved,' gave us all graces with Him; if He withheld not His Son, there is nothing which He will withhold; Rom. viii. 32 πῶς οὐχὶ καὶ σὺν αὐτῷ τὰ πάντα ἡμῖν χαρίσεται; The expression ὁ ἠγαπημένος is unique in the New Testament. See however Ps. xxviii. 6 (LXX.), Is. v. 1.   It occurs in the Apostolic Fathers more than once of our Lord: Ignatius *Smyrn.* inscr. Θεοῦ πατρὸς καὶ τοῦ ἠγαπημένου Ἰησοῦ Χριστοῦ, Clem. Rom. 59 τοῦ ἠγαπημένου παιδὸς αὐτοῦ, τοῦ ἠγαπημένου παιδός σου, and, as here, without a substantive, *Epist. Barnab.* 3 ὃν ἡτοίμασεν ἐν τῷ ἠγαπημένῳ αὐτοῦ, *ib.* 4 ἵνα ταχύνῃ ὁ ἠγαπημένος αὐτοῦ. This title ' Dilectus ' is the common designation of the Messiah in the *Ascensio Isaiae,* e.g. i. 4, 5, 7, 13, iii. 13, 17, 18, iv. 3, 6, etc.

7. **ἔχομεν**] There is a various reading ἔσχομεν here, as in the parallel passage, Col. i. 14. It is more probable however that ἔσχομεν should stand in the text there, than here: see *Colossians*, p. 251.

τὴν ἀπολύτρωσιν] It is a ransom, a redemption, from the captivity to sin. See the note on Col. i. 14, where the metaphor is enforced by the context. So Origen here; Ἀπολύτρωσις ἡ λύτρωσις γίνεται τῶν αἰχμαλώτων καὶ γενομένων ὑπὸ τοῖς πολεμίοις· γεγόναμεν δὲ ὑπὸ τοῖς πολεμίοις, τῷ ἄρχοντι τοῦ αἰῶνος τούτου καὶ ταῖς ὑπ᾽ αὐτὸν πονηραῖς δυνάμεσιν...ἔδωκεν οὖν ὁ Σωτὴρ τὸ ὑπὲρ ἡμῶν λύτρον κ.τ.λ. The ἀπολύτρωσις may be twofold: (1) It may be *initial* and *immediate*, the liberation from the consequences of past sin and the inauguration of a new and independent life, as here; so Rom. iii. 24, 1 Cor. i. 30, Col. i. 14, Heb. ix. 15; or (2) *future* and *final*, the ultimate emancipation from the power of evil in all its forms, as in Luke xxi. 28 ἐγγίζει ἡ ἀπολύτρωσις ὑμῶν, Rom. viii. 23 υἱοθεσίαν ἀπεκδεχόμενοι, τὴν ἀπολύτρωσιν τοῦ σώματος ἡμῶν ; comp. Heb. xi. 35. In this latter sense it is used below, ver. 14, and iv. 30 εἰς ἡμέραν ἀπολυτρώσεως.

διὰ τοῦ αἵματος κ.τ.λ.] This is the ransom-money, the λύτρον (Matt. xx. 28, Mark x. 45), or ἀντίλυτρον (1 Tim. ii. 6), comp. Tit. ii. 14; the price τιμή (1 Cor. vi. 20, vii. 23) for which we were bought. This teaching is not confined to St Paul and the Pauline Epistle to the Hebrews, but is enunciated quite as emphatically by St Peter (1 Pet. i. 18, 19 ἐλυτρώθητε...τιμίῳ αἵματι ὡς ἀμνοῦ ἀμώμου κ.τ.λ.) and St John (Rev. v. 9 ἠγόρασας τῷ Θεῷ ἐν τῷ αἵματί σου: comp. i. 5, vii. 14). So also Clem. Rom. 12 διὰ τοῦ αἵματος τοῦ Κυρίου λύτρωσις ἔσται πᾶσιν τοῖς πιστεύουσιν κ.τ.λ.

τὴν ἄφεσιν κ.τ.λ.] See the note on Col. i. 14.

κατὰ τὸ πλοῦτος κ.τ.λ.] The large ransom paid for our redemption is a measure of the wealth of God's bounty : comp. ii. 7 τὸ ὑπερβάλλον πλοῦτος τῆς χάριτος αὐτοῦ ἐν χρηστότητι κ.τ.λ. (comp. iii. 8), Rom. ii. 4 τοῦ πλούτου τῆς χρηστότητος αὐτοῦ. For the neuter τὸ πλοῦτος, which has the highest support here and which St Paul uses interchangeably with the masculine ὁ πλοῦτος, see the note on Col. i. 27.

τῆς χάριτος] See the note on ver. 5.

8. **ἧς ἐπερίσσευσεν**] '*which He made to abound.*' It is perhaps best to take περισσεύειν transitively, as in 2 Cor. iv. 15, ix. 8, and 1 Thess. iii. 12 (where see the note). Hence the passive περισσεύεσθαι, which is correctly read in Luke xv. 17; comp. 1 Cor. viii. 8 (v. l.). In this case ἧς

will stand for ἦν by attraction: see the note on ver. 6. The construction περισσεύειν τινός however is quite possible; as in Ignat. *Pol.* 2 παντὸς χαρίσματος περισσεύῃς, Luke xv. 17 (v. l.). For περισσεύειν εἰς comp. Rom. v. 15, 2 Cor. i. 5, ix. 8.

ἐν πάσῃ σοφίᾳ κ.τ.λ.] '*in all wisdom and prudence.*' These are the attributes not, as some take it, of God the dispenser, but of the Christians the recipients. This will appear from several considerations. (1) The predication, thus elaborate and definite, would be an unmeaning truism, as applied to God. It differs wholly in character from ἡ πολυποίκιλος σοφία τοῦ Θεοῦ iii. 10, which is quite appropriate. (2) The main idea in the context is the knowledge with which the Christian is endowed, γνωρίσας ἡμῖν τὸ μυστήριον κ.τ.λ. (see the note on these words). (3) The parallel passage, Col. i. 9 ἵνα πληρωθῆτε τὴν ἐπίγνωσιν τοῦ θελήματος αὐτοῦ ἐν πάσῃ σοφίᾳ καὶ συνέσει κ.τ.λ., points very decidedly in this direction. See also Col. iii. 16 ἐν πάσῃ σοφίᾳ. Indeed it is in strict accordance with the general tenour of this and the companion Epistle to the Colossians, in which the higher knowledge of the Christian occupies a conspicuous place; comp. e.g. ver. 17 below, and see *Colossians*, p. 98 sq. with the notes on Col. i. 9, 18, ii. 3, and on Philem. 6.

σοφίᾳ καὶ φρονήσει] '*wisdom and prudence.*' While σοφία is the insight into the true nature of things, φρόνησις is the ability to discern modes of action with a view to their results: while σοφία is theoretical, φρόνησις is practical: comp. Prov. x. 23 ἡ δὲ σοφία ἀνδρὶ τίκτει φρόνησιν. For this distinction see Aristot. *Eth. Nic.* vi. 7 (p. 1141) ἡ σοφία ἐστὶ καὶ ἐπιστήμη καὶ νοῦς τῶν τιμιωτάτων τῇ φύσει...ἡ δὲ φρόνησις περὶ τὰ ἀνθρώπινα καὶ περὶ ὧν ἔστι βουλεύσασθαι (with the whole context), *Eth. Magn.* i. 35 (p. 1197) ἡ μὲν γὰρ σοφία ἐστὶ περὶ τὰ μετ᾽ ἀποδείξεως καὶ ἀεὶ ὡσαύτως ὄντα, ἡ δὲ φρόνησις οὐ περὶ ταῦτα ἀλλὰ περὶ τὰ ἐν μεταβολῇ ὄντα...περὶ δὲ τὰ συμφέροντά ἐστιν ἡ φρόνησις, ἡ δὲ σοφία οὔ, Philo *de Prœm. et Pœn.* 14 (II. p. 421) Σοφία μὲν γὰρ πρὸς θεράπειαν Θεοῦ, φρόνησις δὲ πρὸς ἀνθρωπίνου βίου διοίκησιν, Plut. *Mor.* p. 443 F τὸ μὲν περὶ τὸ ἁπλῶς ἔχοντα μόνον ἐπιστημονικὸν καὶ θεωρητικόν ἐστι, τὸ δὲ ἐν τοῖς πῶς ἔχουσι πρὸς ἡμᾶς βουλευτικὸν καὶ πρακτικόν· ἀρετὴ δὲ τούτου μὲν ἡ φρόνησις, ἐκείνου δὲ ἡ σοφία κ.τ.λ., Cic. *Off.* i. 43 'Princeps omnium virtutum est illa sapientia quam σοφίαν Graeci dicunt; prudentiam enim, quam Graeci φρόνησιν dicunt, aliam quandam intelligimus, quae est rerum expetendarum fugiendarumque scientia: illa autem sapientia, quam principem dixi, rerum est divinarum atque humanarum scientia.' See also the different accounts of the two words in [Plat.] *Defin.* p. 411 D, 414 B. While σοφία was defined by the Stoics to be ἐπιστήμη θείων τε καὶ ἀνθρωπίνων (see the note on Col. i. 9), the common definition of φρόνησις was ἐπιστήμη ἀγαθῶν καὶ κακῶν (Plut. *Mor.* 1066 D, Diog. Laert. vii. 92, Galen, *Op.* v. p. 595 Kühn, Stob. *Ecl.* ii. 6, p. 103, Sext. Empir. p. 720). Thus the serpent in Genesis (iii. 1) and the unjust steward in the parable (Luke xvi. 8) are credited with a high degree of φρόνησις, but they could hardly be called σοφοί. On the other hand God is never designated φρόνιμος in the New Testament, though φρόνησις is sometimes ascribed to Him in the Old (Prov. iii. 19, Jer. x. 12, where it is used in antithetical clauses to balance σοφία). The two words σοφία, φρόνησις (σοφός, φρόνιμος) occur together also 1 Kings iii. 12, iv. 29, Prov. i. 2, viii. 1, Dan. i. 17, ii. 21 (Theod.), 23 (LXX.), besides the instances already quoted. For the relation of σοφία to other words see the notes on Col. i. 9, ii. 3.

9. **γνωρίσας**] '*in that He made known.*' This explains and justifies the strong expression which has preceded, ἐν πάσῃ σοφίᾳ κ.τ.λ. The possession of the whole range of wisdom, theoretical and practical, was involved in the participation in this one mystery. Here is the great storehouse of all truth; comp. Col. ii. 3 εἰς ἐπίγνωσιν τοῦ μυστηρίου τοῦ Θεοῦ, Χριστοῦ, ἐν ᾧ εἰσὶν πάντες οἱ θησαυροὶ τῆς σοφίας καὶ γνώσεως ἀπόκρυφοι, with the note.

τὸ μυστήριον] The subject of this mystery appears from the context. It is Christ as the Great Reconciler, not only of Jew and Gentile, but of heaven and earth. On the signification which this term more especially bears in the Epistles to the Colossians and Ephesians as implying the comprehensiveness, the universality, of the redemption in Christ, see the note on Col. i. 26. See also the same note for the general meaning of the term in St Paul, denoting 'a truth which was once hidden but now is revealed.' This meaning is brought out here by the participle γνωρίσας. For the expression comp. Judith ii. 2 τὸ μυστήριον τῆς βουλῆς αὐτοῦ, where however it is used in a lower sense.

κατὰ τὴν κ.τ.λ.] To be connected not with τὸ μυστήριον, but with γνωρίσας; comp. iii. 9 sq. τοῦ μυστηρίου τοῦ ἀποκεκρυμμένου...ἵνα γνωρισθῇ νῦν...κατὰ πρόθεσιν τῶν αἰώνων κ.τ.λ., Col. i. 26 τὸ μυστήριον τὸ ἀποκεκρυμμένον...νῦν δὲ ἐφανερώθη τοῖς ἁγίοις αὐτοῦ οἷς ἠθέλησεν ὁ Θεὸς γνωρίσαι κ.τ.λ. It is not the mystery itself, so much as the revelation of the mystery after God's long reserve, which fills the Apostle's mind with awe; see also Rom. xvi. 25. For εὐδοκίαν 'purpose, design,' see the note on ver. 5.

προέθετο] '*set before Himself,*' and so '*purposed, planned,*' not 'preordained'; comp. Rom. i. 13, iii. 25. The corresponding substantive πρόθεσις occurs, of God's eternal purpose, just below, ver. 11, also iii. 11, Rom. viii. 28, ix. 11, 2 Tim. i. 9, and of a human purpose, Acts xi. 23, xxvii. 13, 2 Tim. iii. 10. The preposition in this word is not temporal, as in προέγνω, προώρισεν, but local. In the expression ἄρτοι τῆς προθέσεως (Matt. xii. 4) the preposition is obviously local; and all usage points to a local meaning in the connexion in which it occurs here. The verb signifies sometimes 'to propose,' sometimes 'to expose,' but never 'to fix beforehand.' Its meaning is shown by its correspondence in meaning to προκεῖσθαι, e.g. Arist. *Top.* i. 1 (p. 100) ἡ μὲν πρόθεσις τῆς πραγματείας... κατὰ τὴν προκειμένην πραγματείαν.

ἐν αὐτῷ] i.e. 'in Christ'; comp. ver. 4, iii. 11. This first ἐν αὐτῷ is an anticipation of the ἐν τῷ Χριστῷ below, just as the second ἐν αὐτῷ (ver. 10) is a resumption of the same. The reading ἐν αὐτῷ (for ἐν ἑαυτῷ) is quite inadmissible in the Greek Testament (see the note on εἰς αὐτὸν, ver. 5) ; but even if it could stand, it would yield an inferior sense.

10. **εἰς οἰκονομίαν**] '*for* the carrying out of *a dispensation*' ; not 'the dispensation,' for the Apostle contemplates it, as it were, *ab extra*, as a thing hitherto unknown. On the two meanings of οἰκονομία, as (1) the system or method of administration, and (2) the office of an administrator or steward, see the note on Col. i. 25. Here it has the former sense. The same metaphor occurs in various relations elsewhere in the New Testament. God is the great οἰκοδεσπότης in not less than five parables (Matt. xiii. 27 ; Matt. xx. 1, 11 ; Matt. xxi. 33 ; Luke xiii. 25 ; Luke xiv. 21) ; the Church is the household of God (οἶκος [τοῦ] Θεοῦ, 1 Tim. iii. 15, Heb. iii. 2 sq., x. 21, 1 Pet. iv. 17) ; the believers are the members of this household (οἰκεῖοι τοῦ Θεοῦ, Ephes. ii. 19; comp. Gal. vi. 10); the ministers are the stewards or dispensers (οἰκονόμοι, 1 Cor. iv. 1 sq., Tit. i. 7). Accordingly the mode or plan of administering it is called οἰκονομία, *dispensatio*. In the parable of the Unjust Steward (Luke xvi. 1 sq.) the steward seems to be regarded as a freeman ; in Luke xii. 42 sq. however the case is different (ὁ πιστὸς οἰκονόμος, ὁ φρόνιμος, ὃν καταστήσει...μακάριος ὁ δοῦλος ἐκεῖνος κ.τ.λ.), and this is the conception of his position adopted by St Paul in 1 Cor. ix. 17 εἰ γὰρ ἑκὼν τοῦτο πράσσω, μισθὸν ἔχω· εἰ δὲ ἄκων, οἰκονομίαν πεπίστευμαι, 'I am God's slave entrusted with an important office : and a rigorous account will be required of me.' The οἰκονόμοι, 'villici,' 'actores,' 'dispensatores,' of the ancients were generally slaves (Marquardt *Röm. Alt.* V. 1, p. 143, comp. Becker *Charicles* III. p. 23 sq.). The connexion of the different parts of the metaphor is illustrated by Ign. *Ephes.* 6 πάντα ὃν πέμπει ὁ οἰκοδεσπότης εἰς ἰδίαν οἰκονομίαν.

But not only is the way paved for this application of the word in other applications of the metaphor by our Lord and His Apostles. The extended use of οἰκονομία in classical writers was also a further preparation. It had been commonly applied to the administration, more especially the financial administration, of a state, regarded as a great οἰκία (Aristot. *Pol.* iii. 14, p. 1285 ὥσπερ ἡ οἰκονομικὴ βασιλεία τις οἰκίας ἐστιν, οὕτως ἡ βασιλεία πόλεως καὶ ἔθνους ἑνὸς ἢ πλειόνων οἰκονομία), to say nothing of other more remote uses (e.g. of military government, Polyb. vi. 12. 5 ; of the arrangement of topics in a speech or a poem or any other literary production, Dion. Hal. *de Isocr.* 4, Quintil. *Inst.* iii. 3, Aristot. *Poet.* 13 ; of the adjustment of the parts in a building, Vitruv. i. 2 ; of the diffusion of nourishment through the human body, Aretæus, p. 305, ed. Kühn ; and of administration or of distribution generally). The βασιλεία τῶν οὐρανῶν had also its own οἰκονομία, its system or plan of administration by which its goods—its gifts and graces—were administered and dispensed. The central feature of this system was the Incarnation and Passion of the Son. Viewed objectively, and with regard to the Giver, this was a dispensation of *grace* : viewed subjectively, and with regard to the recipient, it was a dispensation of *faith* (1 Tim. i. 4 οἰκονομίαν Θεοῦ τὴν ἐν πίστει). The 'Word made flesh' was the pivot of the world's history, the key to the Divine administration of the universe. This was 'the *dispensation* of the mystery which had been hidden from the beginning' (iii. 9). Hence the fathers, starting from this application in St Paul, employ the word with a more and more direct and exclusive reference to the *Incarnation* and its attending consequences, till at length it becomes a technical term of patristic theology with this meaning ; Ignat. *Ephes.* 18 ἐκυοφορήθη ὑπὸ Μαρίας κατ᾽ οἰκονομίαν [Θεοῦ], comp. § 20 ἧς ἠρξάμην οἰκονομίας εἰς τὸν καινὸν ἄνθρωπον Ἰησοῦν Χριστόν ; Justin *Dial.* 45 γεννηθῆναι σαρκοποιηθεὶς ὑπέμεινεν ἵνα διὰ τῆς οἰκονομίας κ.τ.λ., 120 κατὰ τὴν οἰκονομίαν τὴν διὰ τῆς παρθένου (comp. c. 67, 103) ; Athenag. *Suppl.* 21 κἂν σάρκα Θεὸς κατὰ θείαν οἰκονομίαν λάβῃ ; Iren. i. 6. 1 ἀπὸ δὲ τῆς οἰκονομίας περιτεθεῖσθαι σῶμα ; *ib.* i. 10. 3 τὴν...οἰκονομίαν τοῦ Θεοῦ τὴν ἐπὶ τῇ ἀνθρωπότητι γενομένην (comp. i. 7. 2, i. 14. 6, i. 15. 3) ; Origen *c. Cels.* ii. 9 ἐν γὰρ μάλιστα μετὰ τὴν οἰκονομίαν γεγένηται...ἡ ψυχὴ καὶ τὸ σῶμα Ἰησοῦ, *ib.* ii. 26 τίς γὰρ ἂν...ὀνειδίσαι ἐδύνατο ἡμῖν ἐπὶ τῷ τὸν Ἰησοῦν τοιαῦτα παρὰ τῇ οἰκονομίᾳ λελαληκέναι ; *ib.* ii.65 λαμπροτέρα γὰρ τὴν οἰκονομίαν τελέσαντος ἡ θειότης ἦν αὐτοῦ ; Clem. Alex. *Strom.* ii. 5 (p. 439) Ἰσαάκ... τύπον ἐσόμενον ἡμῖν οἰκονομίας σωτηρίου. So at a later date Theodoret can say, *Dial.* ii. (IV. p. 93) τὴν ἐνανθρώπησιν τοῦ Θεοῦ Λόγου καλοῦμεν οἰκονομίαν.

Hence we often find ἡ οἰκονομία used absolutely for 'the Incarnation.' Accordingly ἡ οἰκονομία is opposed to ἡ θεότης, when the human nature of Christ is contrasted with the Divine ; e.g. Chrysost. *ad* 1 *Cor. Hom.* xxxix. (X. p. 368) ἄλλως, ὅταν περὶ τῆς θεότητος διαλέγηται μόνης, φθέγγεται, καὶ ἑτέρως, ὅταν εἰς τὸν τῆς οἰκονομίας ἐμπέσῃ λόγον. So also this same writer *ad Matt. Hom.* i. (VII. p. 6) says of the first three Evangelists in contradistinction to St John that ἡ σπουδὴ γέγονεν τῷ τῆς οἰκονομίας ἐνδιατρῖψαι λόγῳ καὶ τὰ τῆς θεότητος ἐκινδύνευεν ἀποσιωπᾶσθαι δόγματα. Similarly elsewhere θεολογία and οἰκονομία are opposed, as the two main divisions of theology in its wider sense, the former relating to the divine nature in itself, the latter to the incarnation and work of Christ, the dispensation in time; e.g. Greg. Naz. *Orat.* xxxviii. 8 (I. p. 668) ὅτι μὴ θεολογία τὸ προκείμενον ἡμῖν ἀλλ᾽ οἰκονομία. See Suicer, *Thes.* s.vv. θεολογία and οἰκονομία for examples. In this connexion the word is almost universally used by the fathers, where it occurs in a technical sense; and of this usage we have the germ in this passage of St Paul. During the Monarchian and Patripassian controversies however it was for a short time invested with a wholly different meaning, which had no connexion with its use in St Paul. As μοναρχία was used to express the absolute unity of the Godhead, so οἰκονομία designated the relations of the Divine Persons in the Godhead ; e.g. Tertull. *adv. Prax.* 2 'nihilominus custodiatur οἰκονομίας sacramentum, quae unitatem in trinitatem disponit,' *ib.* 8 'Ita trinitas per consertos et connexos gradus a patre decurrens et

EPISTLE TO THE EPHESIANS.   321

monarchiae nihil obstrepit et οἰκονομίας statum protegit,' Hipp. *c. Noet.* 8
ὅσον μὲν κατὰ τὴν δύναμιν εἶς ἐστι θεός, ὅσον δὲ κατὰ τὴν οἰκονομίαν τριχῆς ἡ
ἐπίδειξις; comp. Tatian *ad Græc.* 5. On this point see especially Gass,
Das patristische Wort οἰκονομία in *Zeitschr. f. Wiss. Theol.* XVII. p. 478 sq.
(1874). This application however was momentary and exceptional; and
does not disturb the main current of usage which runs continuously in
the channel cut for it by St Paul.

τοῦ πληρώματος] *'which belongs to,* which was brought about in, *the
fulness'* etc. For the genitive expressing the time comp. Jude 6 εἰς
κρίσιν μεγάλης ἡμέρας: comp. Plat. *Leg.* i. p. 633 C χειμώνων ἀνυποδησίαι
καὶ ἀστρωσίαι (with Stallbaum's note). The absolute genitive of time,
which is so common, e.g. νυκτός, ἡμέρας, etc., is only an extension to
sentences of its rarer connexion with individual substantives which we
have here. On the meaning of πλήρωμα as 'the full complement,' 'the
complete tale,' see the detailed note on *Colossians,* p. 257 sq. On the
sense in which the time of the Advent could be regarded as the πλήρωμα
τῶν καιρῶν (or τοῦ χρόνου) see the note on Gal. iv. 4.

τῶν καιρῶν] *'of the seasons,'* not τοῦ χρόνου as in Gal. iv. 4; comp.
Mark i. 15 πεπλήρωται ὁ καιρὸς καὶ ἤγγικεν ἡ βασιλεία τοῦ Θεοῦ. Each
season had its proper manifestation; till at length, when all the seasons
had run out, the crowning dispensation itself was revealed. The summing
up (ἀνακεφαλαίωσις) was impossible, until the πλήρωμα of the seasons had
arrived. The idea involved in τῶν καιρῶν, as distinguished from τοῦ
χρόνου, is substantially the same as in Heb. i. 1 πολυμερῶς καὶ πολυτρόπως
πάλαι ὁ Θεὸς λαλήσας...ἐπ᾿ ἐσχάτου τῶν ἡμερῶν τούτων ἐλάλησεν ἡμῖν ἐν
υἱῷ. For the meaning of καιρός, as superadding to χρόνος the idea of
adaptation or *propriety,* see the note on 1 Thess. v. 1.

The words which follow show that in this expression, τὸ πλήρωμα τῶν
καιρῶν, no separation is made between the first and second Advent. The
Incarnation is regarded as the beginning of the end. The dispensation,
contemplated as a *unity,* is contrasted with the several seasons which
preceded. This mode of speaking accords with the language of the
Apostles generally; the Gospel belongs to the end of the ages; it is the
closing scene of the world's history: comp. e.g. Acts ii. 17, 1 Cor. x. 11,
Heb. i. 2, 1 Pet. i. 20, 1 Joh. ii. 18, Jude 18. The ἀνακεφαλαίωσις began
when the Word was made flesh, though the completion is still delayed.

ἀνακεφαλαιώσασθαι] *'so as to gather up in one.'* The infinitive introduces the consequence: see notes on Col. i. 10, iv. 3, 6. In this compound,
while the preposition (ἀνὰ) refers to the prior dispersion of the elements,
the substantive (κεφάλαιον) describes the ultimate aggregation in one.
Thus the whole compound involves the idea of *unity* effected out of
diversity. It differs from συγκεφαλαιοῦσθαι (the two words occur
together in Iren. v. 29. 2) only in the emphasis which is thus thrown on
the several parts before the union is effected. The preposition has the
same force as in ἀναγινώσκειν, ἀνακρίνειν, ἀνακυκᾶν, ἀναλογίζεσθαι,

ἀναμανθάνειν, ἀναμετρεῖν, ἀναπεμπάζειν, ἀνασκοπεῖν, ἀναστρέφεσθαι, etc., or in the distributive ἀνὰ μέρος, ἀνὰ δύο, etc., and implies the process of *going over* the separate elements for the purpose of uniting them. Others attribute to it the idea of *restoration, reunion*; and Tertullian insists strongly on this point; *de Monog.* 5 'adeo in Christo omnia revocantur ad initium,' *ib.* 11 'affirmat omnia ad initium recolligi in Christo,' *adv. Marc.* v. 17 'recapitulare, id est, ad initium redigere vel ab initio recensere, etc.' So interpreted, it was a serviceable weapon against the dualism of Marcion, who maintained a direct opposition between the work of the Demiurge and the work of Christ. He had a right to press this idea in the corresponding word ἀποκαταλλάσσειν of the parallel passage, Col. i. 20, 21 (see the note there); but the sense of the preposition ἀνὰ here seems to be quite different. The verb ἀνακεφαλαιοῦσθαι has the following senses: (1) 'to sum up,' 'to recapitulate'; Aristot. *Fragm.* 123 (p. 1499) ἀνακεφαλαιώσασθαι πρὸς ἀνάμνησιν: comp. Quint. *Inst.* vi. 1. 1 'Rerum repetitio et congregatio, quae Graece dicitur ἀνακεφαλαίωσις, a quibusdam Latinorum *enumeratio*, et memoriam judicis reficit et totam simul causam ponit ante oculos, etc.'; (2) 'To comprise,' Rom. xiii. 9 εἴ τις ἑτέρα ἐντολή, ἐν τῷ λόγῳ τούτῳ ἀνακεφαλαιοῦται; (3) 'To exhibit in a compendious form,' and so 'to reproduce,' *Protev. Jac.* 13 μήτι εἰς ἐμὲ ἀνεκεφαλαιώθη ἡ ἱστορία Ἀδάμ; But in none of its senses does it involve the idea of bringing back to a former state. Τί ἐστιν, writes Chrysostom, ἀνακεφαλαιώσασθαι; Συνάψαι. The word cannot however contain any immediate reference to the headship of Christ, as this father goes on to suggest, since it is derived from κεφάλαιον, and not directly from κεφαλή. Thus the expression implies the entire harmony of the universe, which shall no longer contain alien and discordant elements, but of which all the parts shall find their centre and bond of union in Christ. Sin and death, sorrow and failure and suffering, shall cease. There shall be a new heaven and a new earth. Ps.-Hippol. *c. Beron.* 2 (p. 59 Lagarde), evidently referring to this passage, speaks of τὸ μυστήριον τῆς αὐτοῦ σωματώσεως, ἧς ἔργον ἡ τῶν ὅλων ἐστὶν εἰς αὐτὸν ἀνακεφαλαίωσις. There is also an obvious reference to it in a fragment of Justin Martyr's *Treatise against Marcion*, quoted by Irenæus (iv. 6. 2) 'Quoniam ab uno Deo, qui et hunc mundum fecit et nos plasmavit et omnia continet et administrat, unigenitus Filius venit ad nos, suum plasma *in semetipsum recapitulans* etc.' The earlier fathers lay great stress on this idea, that the ἀνακεφαλαίωσις is effected by the Divine Word taking upon Himself the nature of His own creature; comp. e.g. Iren. iii. 21. 10 sq. Thus creation returns, as it were, unto Him from whom it issued forth. He is not only the δι' οὗ, but also the εἰς ὅν; see the note on Col. i. 16, where other similar expressions in St Paul are given.

By this same term, ἀνακεφαλαίωσις, and with an obvious allusion to St Paul's language, Irenæus describes the work of the Antichrist, who shall concentrate and summarize in himself all the elements of evil, all

the idolatry and all the wickedness, which have been since the beginning:
v. 29. 2.

14. ἀρραβὼν] '*an earnest,*' as in 2 Cor. i. 22, v. 5 τὸν ἀρραβῶνα τοῦ
πνεύματος, where the word is used in the same connexion; comp. Polyc.
Phil. 8, *Act. Thom.* 51. It is a genuine Shemitic word עֵרָבוֹן (derived from
עָרַב 'to entwine,' and so 'to pledge'), and occurs in the Hebrew of
Gen. xxxviii. 17, 18, 20, where it is transliterated, rather than translated,
ἀρραβών, in the LXX. We might have imagined therefore that its use
was derived from the Hebrew through the LXX. But it occurs at an
earlier date in classical authors, e.g. Isæus *de Cir. her.* 23, Aristotle
Pol. i. 11 (p. 1259), Antiphanes *Fragm. Com.* III. p. 66 (Meineke),
Menander, *ib.* IV. p. 268, 283; and we must therefore suppose that
the Greeks derived it from the Phœnicians, as the great trading and
seafaring people of antiquity (comp. Ezek. xxvii. 13). Though (so far as
I can discover from the latest authorities) there is no trace of the word in
extant Phœnician remains, yet the close alliance of this language with
the Hebrew renders its Phœnician source highly probable. The relations between the Hebrews and the Greeks at an early age were too
slight to suggest that the Greeks borrowed it from the Hebrews. Greece
was chiefly known to the Hebrews as the great slave market, where
the Phœnician traders sold their sons and daughters (Joel iii. 6, Is. lxvi.
19, Zech. ix. 13). The word was also introduced early into Latin
(whether through the Greeks or through the Carthaginians, it is impossible to say), and occurs several times in Plautus. In earlier Latin
there was a tendency to clip it at the beginning (Plaut. *Truc.* iii. 2. 20
A. 'Perii, *rabonem*! quam esse dicam hanc beluam? Quin tu *arrabonem*
dicis?' S. '*Ar* facio lucri'); whereas in the fashionable dialect of a
later age it was systematically clipped at the end (A. Gell. xvii. 2 'Nunc
arrabo in sordidis verbis haberi coeptus ac multo videtur sordidius *arra*,
quamquam *arra* quoque veteres saepe dixerint et compluriens Laberius').
In this latter form it appears in the law books; and so it has passed into
the modern Romanic languages, *arra, arrhes*. The former mutilation
may be compared with *bus* for *omnibus*; the later with *mob, photo*, etc.
The word is also found in the Egyptian ⲁⲣⲏⲃ.

It must be observed that the expression is not ἐνέχυρον 'a pledge,' but
ἀρραβών 'an earnest.' In other words the thing given is related to the
thing assured—the present to the hereafter—as a part to the whole.
It is the same in kind. So Varro *de L. L.* iv. p. 41 'Arrabo sic dicta, ut
reliquum reddatur. Hoc verbum a Graeco ἀρραβών reliquum ex eo
quod debitum reliquit'; comp. Clem. Alex. *Ecl. Proph.* 12, p. 992
οὔτε γὰρ πᾶν κεκομίσμεθα οὔτε παντὸς ὑστεροῦμεν, ἀλλ' οἷον ἀρραβῶνα
...προσειλήφαμεν, Tertull. *de Resurr. Carn.* 53 'non arrabonem, sed
plenitudinem'; see Pearson *On the Creed*, p. 615, note (ed. Chevallier).
The patristic commentators on the passages in St Paul insist strongly on
this force of ἀρραβών, and St Jerome more especially on this passage

complains that it is obliterated in the rendering of the Latin Version, though he himself has left 'pignus' in his own revision in all the three passages where the word occurs. Of the Latin fathers Tertullian gives 'arrabo' (*Resurr. Carn.* 51, *adv. Hermog.* 34, *adv. Marc.* v. 12); and Vigilius Thapsensis 'arra' (*de Trin.* xii.). The others give 'pignus,' in quoting the passages of St Paul. In Iren. v. 8. 1, though the translator gives 'pignus,' the meaning of Irenæus himself is clear; 'Quod et pignus dixit Apostolus (hoc est *pars* ejus honoris, qui a Deo nobis promissus est) in Epistola quae ad Ephesios est.' Thus the expression ὁ ἀρραβὼν τοῦ πνεύματος includes the idea, which is elsewhere expressed by ἡ ἀπαρχὴ τοῦ πνεύματος (Rom. viii. 23), the *first-fruits* of a harvest to be reaped hereafter. The actual spiritual life of the Christian is the same in kind as his future glorified life; the kingdom of heaven is a present kingdom; the believer is already seated on the right hand of God: comp. the note on Col. i. 13, ii. 13, iii. 1—4, and see below, ii. 6. Nevertheless the present gift of the Spirit is only a *small fraction* of the future endowment. This idea also would be suggested by the usual relation between the earnest-money and the full payment; comp. Theophrast. in Stob. *Floril.* xliv. 22 (II. p. 168, Meineke) πολλαπλασία ἡ τιμὴ τοῦ ἀρραβῶνος.

But the metaphor suggests, and doubtless was intended to suggest, another idea. The recipient of the earnest-money not only secures to himself the fulfilment of the compact from the giver, but he *pledges himself* to accomplish his side of the contract. By the very act of accepting the part payment, he has bound himself over to a certain reciprocation. The gift of the Spirit is not only a *privilege*, but also an *obligation*. This idea of an obligation is enforced in the context here, and in 2 Cor. i. 22, by the mention of the *sealing*; and in the latter passage it is still further emphasized by the reference to the *security* (ὁ βεβαιῶν ἡμᾶς...εἰς Χριστόν). The same idea appears again in iv. 30 μὴ λυπεῖτε τὸ πνεῦμα...ἐν ᾧ ἐσφραγίσθητε κ.τ.λ. The Spirit has, as it were, a lien upon us.

INDEX OF GREEK WORDS

INDEX OF SUBJECTS

Thornapple Commentaries

Alexander, Joseph Addison
The Gospel According to Mark
The Gospel According to Matthew

Bernard, J. H.
The Pastoral Epistles

Henderson, Ebenezer
The Twelve Minor Prophets

Hodge, Charles
A Commentary on the Epistle to the Ephesians
An Exposition of the First Epistle to the Corinthians
An Exposition of the Second Epistle to the Corinthians

Lightfoot, J. B.
Notes on Epistles of St. Paul

Maier, Walter A.
The Book of Nahum

McNeile, Alan Hugh
The Gospel According to St. Matthew

Plummer, Alfred
The Epistles of St. John

Shedd, William G. T.
Commentary on Romans

Westcott, Brooke Foss
The Gospel According to St. John

Baker Book House, Box 6287, Grand Rapids, Michigan 49506